# PIRELLI

TECHNOLOGY
AND PASSION
1872–2017

# PIRELLI

## TECHNOLOGY AND PASSION

## 1872–2017

Carlo
Bellavite
Pellegrini

Third Millennium
Publishing

To Enrico Parazzini

First published in Great Britain in 2017 by
Third Millennium Publishing, an imprint of
PROFILE BOOKS LTD
3 Holford Yard
Bevin Way
London WC1X 9HD
*www.profilebooks.com*

The first version of this work was originally published in Italian in 2015 by
Società editrice il Mulino with the title *Pirelli: Innovazione e passione 1872–2015.*
© 2015 by Pirelli & C. S.p.A., Milano and Società editrice il Mulino, Bologna

Copyright © Pirelli & C. S.p.A and Third Millennium Publishing, 2017

Typeset in Minion by MacGuru Ltd

Printed and bound in Great Britain by
Clays, Bungay, Suffolk

ISBN 978 1 78125 877 4

# Contents

## IN-DEPTH ANALYSIS

## APPENDIX: OWNERSHIP STRUCTURES

## TIMELINE

## DOCUMENTARY SOURCES AND BIBLIOGRAPHY

## *Index of names*

# Acknowledgements

After having completed this research project, I would like to mention and thank a number of people. Firstly, my heartfelt and sincere thanks go to Marco Tronchetti Provera, who as President of the Pirelli Foundation, promoted this project and made it possible. Next I would like to thank and to remember Carlo Azeglio Ciampi, who allowed me to consult his private diaries and publish those parts I thought interesting and relevant to the history of Pirelli. In addition, I would like to express my personal thanks to Enrico Parazzini, who supported me in this project. Moreover I am sincerely grateful to Maria Grazia Peraro, who constantly and continuously supported my efforts aimed at the publication of this book.

I would also like to thank Alberto Pirelli, Maurizio Abet, Enrico Albizzati, Serafino Balduzzi, Mario Batista, Filippo Bettini, Maurizio Boiocchi, Maurizio Bonzi, Gustavo Bracco, Giorgio Bruno, Giuseppe Cattaneo, Antonio Calabrò, Francesco Chiappetta, Paolo Dal Pino, Paolo Ferrari, Luciano Gobbi, Andrea Imperiali, Valeria Leone, Franco Livini, Giuliano Menassi, Riccardo Perissich, Giovanni Pomati, Maurizio Sala, Francesco Tanzi, Uberto Thun, Nicola Verdicchio, Gerardo Braggiotti, Carlo Buora, Federico Imbert, Andrea Kerbaker, Piergaetano Marchetti and Giuseppe Morchio, whose testimonies were an important element in the reconstruction of historical events. Regarding this, I would also like to thank Arrigo Andreoni, Antonio Campo Dall'Orto, Marco Dubini, Giovanni Ferrario, Vittorio Giaroli, Maureen Kline, Gavino Manca, Paolo Maria Noseda (who translated the original version of the book into English), Stefano Pileri, Giorgio Rossi Cairo, Paolo Rubini, Giuseppe Sala (who in the meantime was appointed mayor of Milan) and Nino Tronchetti Provera.

A further thanks also goes to the many people who collaborate with the Pirelli Foundation, and in particular to Chiara Guizzi and Martina De Petris, who assisted me in the complex task of sourcing documents, and also to Donatella Panazza and Laura Lana, who both helped me in different ways. I am also grateful to Luigi Campiglio, Enrico Parazzini and Maurizio Dallocchio, who had the patience to read the numerous drafts and helped me improve the text with their suggestions and observations. I also thank Laura Pellegrini, Rocco Cifone and Valentina Cipolla, who assisted me in the correction and revision of the text.

My last thoughts are for my daughters Benedetta Rachele and Beatrice Carlotta and for my wife Francesca to whom this book is dedicated, who have always supported and shared my new cultural, humanistic and professional ventures, encouraging me to face the challenges of the global scenario.

# Foreword

When Dr Tronchetti Provera asked to meet me in the spring of 2010, I was finishing a draft of the economic and financial history of the credit institution that, rising from the ashes of Banco Ambrosiano, was to become Intesa San Paolo. I had introduced that work on Banco Ambrosiano to Dr Tronchetti Provera through Enrico Parazzini, who I had met some time before at the Catholic University, where I explained to him my research methods. The initial idea for this project arose from that conversation. My meeting with Dr Tronchetti Provera took place on the first floor of the dark, elegant, majestic company headquarters that dominate the corner of Viale Piero e Alberto Pirelli and Via Bicocca degli Arcimboldi. It was May and the backdrop for the meeting was the contrast between the overcast sky – hesitant between sun and rain – the half-light of the delicate colours of the meeting room, and the deep green of the hanging garden just visible from the corridor.

The conversation immediately took on the pleasant turn of an open and intellectually stimulating debate with someone practiced in knowing how to listen and pay attention to the other, while discreetly studying his reactions. We analysed the sometimes anomalous role of a large industrial group in a nation like Italy, as well as the many difficulties to overcome in order 'to do business' and 'to have the ambition to be industrialists'. His calm tone, and the brilliant and convincing pace of his discourse, impressed me. He also described the characteristics of the role of the manager with a personal, clear and authoritative manner as 'enthusiasm, vision and great effort', thus underpinning the importance of a stable ownership structure for both companies and banks. He reviewed in general the virtues of stability as an unavoidable condition for good governance, not only for single businesses, but for the system as a whole. Evoking the figure of Jacques Delors, he mentioned how at times stability was considered negative rather than positive. In the following years, much of what he said at our meeting would form part of the political and economic agenda not only of Italy, but of the principal European Union states.

I fully shared his serene yet cuttingly lucid analysis. In the mid-1990s, in preparation for my doctoral thesis on economic policy, I had devoted my research on the relationship between stability and efficiency in financial systems, emphasising the importance of stability in a world that, at the time, was hurriedly sacrificing this very principle in its anxious quest for efficiency. As he went on with his talk, Dr Tronchetti Provera pointed out (not without a touch of bitterness) that the destiny of large companies in our country seemed to be the object of an inexplicable desire for voluntary annihilation – a spasmodic and irrational quest for negativity that went beyond every reasonable barrier, and in his words, was a *'cupio dissolvi'* (a yearning for self-destruction).

For a moment, the evocative power of these images left me hesitant. My memory fumbled, by thoughts oscillating between two different suggestions: Qohelet's famous opening phrase, 'a breath and then nothing', and the final oration-confession of the Prince of Salina in *The Leopard*, when the Sabaudian government offers him the office of Senator of the Kingdom. Still, we immediately recognised that the most fitting comparison seemed to be to a nation that, at the very end of the Renaissance, had lost political power and was favouring other nations by neglecting its economic dynamism and cultural centrality and favouring the characteristics of a sterile Mannerism from which real life had long since been drained. All this appears even more serious if one remembers that throughout our nation's history, well-motivated men have always known how to offer ingenious proposals in every field of human expression. The history of Pirelli is a perfect example of this!

At the end of our meeting, Dr Tronchetti Provera told me he appreciated my research and desired that rigorous analytical research be carried out on Pirelli's history, with particular attention to the events of the last 20 years. He also offered to entrust this task to me, if I were interested. He thought it was an advantage that I was a scholar of corporate finance and not an historian, that I belonged to the complementary academic and professional worlds, and finally – at least up to that moment – I came from outside the world of Pirelli. We agreed that I would have access to the materials in the Pirelli Foundation archives, so that I could decide how to proceed. At this point, I was certain that my previous research on the history of a large bank would now be capped by a thorough and all-round analysis of a major Italian company.

As I walked through the long open corridor, I saw the stupendous 15th-century Bicocca degli Arcimboldi residence, and it was then that I realised this first meeting had aroused my curiosity about the style of the Pirelli Group, which continually placed classical and modern elements side by side. These elements appear skilfully combined in this large company firmly rooted in the industrial history of our nation, but which renews its entrepreneurial challenge every day by launching itself with acumen and determination into the future. One also perceives this same style in the Company's headquarters in the Bicocca premises, and in the faces of the people I later had the pleasure of getting to know. This is precisely the distinctive character that Pirelli has developed in its almost 145 years of history. My intuition was confirmed some time later, when I met Leopoldo Pirelli's son Alberto. During our conversation, the descendant of this great family, whose features bear a strong resemblance to his father's, passionately made a point on how the Pirelli family and management had indeed developed a management method for the Company which was not restricted to scientific and technological knowledge. This mission could be defined as one of absolute responsibility towards all stakeholders, regardless of any form of profit or privilege. All this involves not only developing specific attention to corporate social responsibility over time, but also creating a corporate brand with an impeccable reputation and the ability to actively participate in the needs and aspirations of the local communities in which the Company operates, from Italy to South America and from the Middle East to the Far East.

In the following days, I contacted Antonio Calabrò, Director of the Pirelli Foundation, to examine the materials held in the Pirelli archives. The headquarters of the Pirelli Foundation is in a rose-coloured villa in the Bicocca district, one of the few buildings that survived the radical reorganisation of the Pirelli Group's facilities in the mid-1990s. In the large consultation room with windows overlooking many of the buildings that currently form the Bicocca headquarters, I was to find further evidence for the intuition I alluded to above. The first confirmation lay in the atmosphere to be found in that building: the walls of the Foundation foyer elegantly decorated with phrases in diverse typefaces in a material similar to rubber, commemorating various landmark events in the life of the Company, such as the launch of various historical products including the Cord tyres and the famous Cinturato. It was a testimony to the people who, with their unfailing effort, laid the foundations of the Company. The charisma of the founder, Giovanni Battista Pirelli (1848–1932), was palpable, as was the collective commitment of the Pirelli family, the choices made by its later generations, and the sacrifices of all of those who – often over generations – have worked for the Group.

In the room opposite this meeting room on the first floor, this mosaic skilfully continued with a display of the key characteristics of the Pirelli Group and personal mementos of landmark figures from Pirelli family such as Piero (1881–1956), Alberto (1882–1971) and Leopoldo Pirelli (1925–2007), and notable workers who have formed part of the Group from its very beginning. Interspersed between these mementos are splendid drawings and sketches, which, with their diverse styles from over a century, constitute a true masterclass in publicity of the Group's products, just as the founder had sagaciously foreseen from the very beginning. What I felt and what had struck me following from my very first visits to Bicocca was noticeably reinforced as soon as I was able to start examining the archive materials. Its abundance of highly interesting contents and its perfect organisation gave access both to the history of the Company and to the personal story of the Pirelli family.

The documents dated from the incorporation of Pirelli & Co, a limited partnership, on 28 January 1872. In the heavy black volumes, catalogued with light-coloured and often faded labels, the company records and minutes of the various companies created following that date was clear evidence of the distinctive features of the Group's history from its foundation, and which are manifest in its continuity to the present day. Similar evidence could be inferred from the contents of the much more elegant light-coloured folders containing varied collections of formal and informal miscellanea about the history of the Group; budget reports, Board and shareholders' minutes, public and private documents tracing the constituent characteristics of the Group, all highlighting organically those aspects fundamental for the success and prosperity of any business initiative. Often the documents confirmed the importance of constant attention to the dynamics of overall productivity; the necessity to explore new projects and products, aware that these could be profitable investments; the need to monitor prices of raw material daily and to forecast trends to optimise working capital and stock; the importance of issues regarding research and development. What also emerged was the central role attributed to finance, starting from the constant identification of the optimal financial structure applicable to various and changing scenarios and consequently, the ownership structure and corporate governance which were already factors of great importance in that period. Another hallmark feature of Pirelli in that period was the focus on industrial relations, and the dignity of workers and their material and moral necessities from a Ricardian perspective.

Already in the initial phase of the Group's history, many concepts underlying the choices instrumental in its growth and development were defined. These ranged from the necessity to pursue an international dimension, to the division of production into business units with precise demarcations of business activities, costs and responsibilities. There was also a focus on real estate as a fundamental requirement of the Company to reformulate the dislocation of its production as the Group was operative in urban areas under never-ending expansion. Moreover, in periods of administrative, economic and financial reorganisation it became evident that precise timing for these activities was of utmost importance, especially in an increasingly globalised world, and with the growing importance of new media such as newspapers and advertising. This process continued until the end of the 19th century with the arrival and advancement of electricity, and through into the early 20th century with telephony and other associated technologies. This last segment represented a high-priority industrial opportunity for one of the world leaders in the production of cables.

I felt like an archaeologist who, while digging in an urban site that is still alive and vital, is able to clearly interpret from his research the expansion over the course of time of an entire and complex entity. The documents in my hands offered an increasingly clear testimony of the history of one of the greatest Italian industrial groups. What emerged was consistent with its history and faithfully outlined the recent past and the present, and even sketched out possible future developments. During my research, I was struck by the close connection between what was repeatedly confirmed year after year by both the Pirelli corporate bodies and its top management, and institutional debate on the issues of economics, industry, finance and society in Italy and in Europe during the years of the financial crisis. The significance of this correspondence and its timing also added another interesting opportunity to my project, a reflection on Italy's industrial history which could give some inspirational insight for the future. It seemed I might be able to contribute to renewing the important testimony of the institutional and civil commitment which has permeated the entire history of Pirelli, a company not only concerned with its own development and its capacity to create wealth, but which is also closely interwoven with Italy itself.

I was experiencing something unexpected. Whether this was due to my background, or to my academic and professional contacts with democratic Catholicism in its various expressions, I was accustomed to a scenario in which common good was a well-entrenched concept. Now I found myself before liberal tradition to which I was less accustomed, and in which I noted that these same concepts had been deeply rooted for a much longer time. More than a century of liberal tradition in one of its highest and most well-conceived forms was standing in front of me. It is for these reasons that this research would contribute further significance to my previous works; it had meaning for Pirelli, but also for the nation.

It was the moment to meet Dr Tronchetti Provera again. It was almost summer. I told him I would have to examine the Pirelli Group from its very origins to make the consistency of purpose implicit in its history emerge in its entirety. I also made clear that the result would be a narrative and a necessarily asymmetric analysis focused on identifying the genetic characteristics of the Company over the long term in order to then focus analytically on the events that followed the 1992 turnaround. True to style, Dr Tronchetti Provera listened carefully and – as I made my case – he provided valid and concrete examples of how the elements I had identified were indeed the founding values of Pirelli. Neither did it escape his attention how such issues would progressively become more relevant over time. We soon came to an agreement about every aspect[1] of the work, including scheduling regular discussions and the possibility of meeting with other key players in Pirelli's recent history.[2]

I thought it necessary to include this foreword as a genesis of my contacts with Dr Tronchetti Provera and the motivations behind this research project so the reader will have a clear idea from the outset about the aims and perspectives of this project, and how it was planned and implemented. The Italian edition of the book was published in June 2015 and presented in Milan on 30 June. Just a few days later, Dr Tronchetti Provera and I decided that the book should be translated into English and published by a British publishing house. Over the last two years I have been working to prepare the English edition of the book, encompassing the

---

1   We also formally decided that the research would take into consideration only the history of the Company and not that of the Pirelli family, except in passing and when it assisted the needs of analysis and narration.

2   Discussions with Maurizio Abet, Enrico Albizzati, Mario Batista, Filippo Bettini, Maurizio Boiocchi, Maurizio Bonzi, Gustavo Bracco, Giorgio Bruno, Antonio Calabrò, Giuseppe Cattaneo, Francesco Chiappetta, Paolo Ferrari, Andrea Imperiali, Valeria Leone, Giuliano Messani, Gavino Manca, Enrico Parazzini, Alberto Pirelli, Giovanni Pomati, Maurizio Sala, Francesco Tanzi, Uberto Thun and Nicola Verdicchio and outside the Company with Gerardo Braggiotti, Carlo Buora, Antonio Campo Dall'Orto, Marco Dubini, Giovanni Ferrario, Vittorio Giaroli, Luciano Gobbi, Federico Imbert, Andrea Kerbaker, Piergaetano Marchetti, Giuseppe Morchio, Riccardo Perissich, Stefano Pileri, Paolo Rubini, Giorgio Rossi Cairo and Giuseppe Sala.

merger between Pirelli and Chemchina. Because of the above-mentioned reasons, the English edition of the book progressively became different from the Italian one and more suitable for an international audience. The work is organised into various sections.[3] The first analyses the Group's affairs over the first 120 years of its history. The aim of this first section, which also includes an analytical and detailed overview, is to bring the economic, managerial and financial elements driving the history of the Group to the forefront in the narrative history. This first and introductory section allows a clear understanding of the second section, which analytically examines the affairs of the Group from the end of the 1980s to 2016, covering the reorganisation of Pirelli following the Continental deal, the investments made in innovative technologies during the 1990s, the involvement in the telecommunications sector with the purchase of Telecom Italia, up to the more recent focus on core businesses after the abandonment of the telephony, and the redefinition of the proprietary and control structure of the Group.

---

3   The material in the book is composed of the text, the graphs, the chronology, the bibliography of source documentation and the appendices. The text, which can be read separately, has numerous cross-references to a chronology that allows the interested reader to delve into specific elements present in that text. In turn, all the references in the chronology are illustrated in the bibliography, both as documentary sources and as bibliographical entries.

PART I

———

# ORIGINS AND DEVELOPMENT

———

# CHAPTER 1

# The First Steps of a Great Company

When Pirelli & C., a limited partnership, was established on 28 January 1872, its founder, the engineer Giovanni Battista Pirelli, was only 23 years old. Though young, he led a very intense life,[1] combining rigorous dedication to his studies with fervent participation in the events of the nation; indeed, at a very young age he was involved in Garibaldi's 1866 and 1867 campaigns. Unlike other young men of his generation imprisoned in the myth of the Risorgimento, which in those years was celebrating its epilogue, Giovanni Battista realised very soon that the natural continuation of his involvement in the life of his country was no longer at the battlefront, but in a commitment to the emerging industrial development of the country. The founder contemplated what he could do for his country to help it grow and prosper over the years. It was in this perspective that, with the support of Giuseppe Colombo – his professor at the Milan Polytechnic – that he won the 300,000 lira Kramer prize soon after his graduation. The prize allowed him to spend the last part of 1870 and most of the following year in Switzerland, France and Germany, where he met with many important industrial advances of

---

1 Giovanni Battista Pirelli was born on 27 December 1848 in Varenna, a village on the Lecco branch of Lake Como. He came from a 'modest but not poor family' (Pirelli 1946). His father Santino was a baker, while his mother, Rosa Riva, came from a family of housepainters (Tranfaglia 2010). After attending a technical school in Varenna, in 1862 he went on to the Regio Istituto Tecnico Inferiore (the Royal Technical Lower School) in Milan and in 1865 enrolled in the Faculty of Mathematics at the University of Pavia. At 17, he became a volunteer for Garibaldi and participated in the Third War for Independence, being involved in the military operations in Trentino. Among the not-so-glorious aspects of that campaign were the troops led by Giuseppe Garibaldi who won the victory on the field at Bezzecca, while the regular army was defeated at Custoza and the Navy at Lissa. The war ended with the annexation of the Veneto to the Kingdom of Italy, thanks only to the brilliant victory of the Prussian allies over the Hapsburg Empire at Sadowa. In 1867, at 18, Giovanni Battista Pirelli took part in Garibaldi's unfortunate venture to Rome that ended at Mentana because of Napoleon III's opposition. He then returned to his studies at the Milan Polytechnic, where he received his degree in Mechanical Engineering in September 1870.

the period (Tranfaglia 2010). Giovanni Battista Pirelli happened to be travelling through Europe at a time of great political and military turbulence. He witnessed some of these epochal events first hand, as transpires from his rather discreet and modest memoirs from that period. According to his son Alberto (1946), Giovanni Battista had developed an interest in the innovative rubber industry[2] even before departing for his period of study abroad, perhaps inspired partly by his mentor, Giuseppe Colombo. Indeed, during his travels abroad, he paid a great deal of attention to this new and fast-growing industry. Pirelli & C. was founded with capital of 215,000 lira some months after his return to Italy. As Pirelli writes, the purpose of the Company was 'the transformation by means of chemical and mechanical processes of a vegetable product, known as caoutchouc, or Indian rubber, into objects which are widely used and known in business as caoutchouc or elastic rubber articles'. The initiative was a start-up created with venture capital for a new product, thus a high-risk project, but with a good probability of giving a valid return with a positive net present value.

The ownership structure of the Company was composed of a certain number of equity underwriters, who took on a risk return profile very similar to that of today's venture capitalists. These underwriters entrusted the management of the Company[3] solely to Giovanni Battista Pirelli.

As was customary in those times, both abroad (Dunlavy 1998) and in Italy (Bellavite Pellegrini 2001, 2003), the Company By-laws provided neither a clause 'of a plutocratic character', such as one share–one vote, nor a clause with a cooperative and democratic character, based on the principle of one head–one vote. A mixed provision in the Statutory was adopted providing for voting rights, which decreased gradually as the number of shares held by a single partner increased. At that time, gradualism in voting rights was greatly appreciated for various reasons.

---

2   The birth of the rubber industry is conventionally set in 1884 with the discovery of the vulcanisation process, combining sulphur with rubber at a high temperature. According to Alberto Pirelli (1946), his father's attention to the rubber industry found its origins in a news story of the time. In fact, Pirelli wrote, 'At the time, the Royal ship 'L'Affondatore' was sunk between Ancona and Falconara, and rubber hoses for the pumps that could facilitate the raising of the hull were not to be found in Italy. This created an emotional uproar in the nation (the hoses were supplied at the time by France) and the episode impressed on the young graduate's mind was one of the signals that he intuitively collected about the importance that several applications of rubber might have'.

3   This refers to the position of sole administrator in a joint partnership.

## TABLE 1.1. LIST OF SHAREHOLDERS

| Shareholder | Shares (lira) |
| --- | --- |
| Davide Sforni | 55,000 |
| Antonio Bosoni | 5,000 |
| Lorenzo Prinetti | 5,000 |
| Dott. Giovan Battista Pensa (proxy for Teresa Kramer) | 5,000 |
| Dott. Onorato Zucchi | 20,000 |
| Conte Sanseverino Alfonso | 10,000 |
| Giovan Battista Pirelli | 5,000 |
| Abramo Vita Sforni | 5,000 |
| Marchese Visconti Ermes | 10,000 |
| Comm. Cantoni Eugenio | 10,000 |
| Comm. Brioschi Francesco | 10,000 |
| G. Buttafava | 5,000 |
| Duca Raimondo Visconti di Modrone | 5,000 |
| Avv. Calogna Achille | 5,000 |
| Dott. Garavaglio Alfonso | 5,000 |
| Emilio Broglio | 5,000 |
| Cremonesi prof. Secondo | 5,000 |
| Cingia dott. cav. Luigi | 5,000 |
| Varese cav. Angelo | 5,000 |
| Colombo cav. Giuseppe | 5,000 |
| Antonio Lombardo | 5,000 |
| Nobile ing. Porro/Parro Ercole | 5,000 |
| Nobile Carlo Castiglioni | 5,000 |
| Sig. Speroni G. | 5,000 |
| Avv. Brioschi | 10,000 |

*Source: G.B. Pirelli & C. (limited partnership), Act of Incorporation in plain copy, 28 January 1872 (n. 1097). Act prepared by Dott. Stefano Allocchio, notary resident in Milan. The initial share capital was 215,000 lira.*

Firstly, on both sides of the Atlantic there was a strong prejudice against one share-one vote ownership structures, deemed excessively plutocratic. Moreover, scaled voting rights achieved two other objectives considered positive by the economic and financial communities of the time. On the one hand, it stabilised control by effectively removing the Company's vulnerability to a takeover. Changes or decisions could be made without generating the well-known problems linked to the creation and management of consent and to the coordination of collective choices that drive cooperative entities. On the other hand, a system of checks and balances was created that adequately balanced the interests of those who only invested with equity and of those who, besides investing in equity, also contributed with specific managerial skills.

In line with this approach, the Company would always attribute great importance to a stable ownership structure, considered a necessary means to allow the management to focus on developing innovative long-term investment projects. Similarly, the financial structure of the Company was also a direct expression of the ownership structure, since the financing of the start-up was through the partners' progressive endowment of equity. Production began in June 1873 in the Sevesetto factory near Milan.[4] As expected for a start-up project, things were not easy at first.[5] During the spring of 1874, Pirelli explained to the partners the reasons behind the financial losses in the first months of activity during the second part of the previous year, and requested the raising of equity[6] to make up for these losses. Giovanni Battista demonstrated confidence in the rapidly improving economic situation and in the Company's growing capacity to create value, also fortified by a flattering comment made by the Board of Auditors, a group of far-sighted, benevolent and protective deities who were convinced by his skill and determination.

One particular initial difficulty to face was the choice of management, a critical element for any start-up. Since this was a completely new sector for Italy, an

---

4   The location of the first factory was near Milan Central Railway Station.

5   Giovanni Battista Pirelli wrote in 1874: 'The workforce is disorderly, part of the capital is lost and part of the clientele alienated'.

6   Pending the seasoned equity offering, on 19 June 1874 the Company received a 100,000 lira short-term subsidy from the Banca Popolare di Milano. Pirelli intended to extinguish the debt 'by means of gradual payments that the annual profits of the company would not hinder me from making'. In reality, the debt was reimbursed much more quickly, as soon as the capital increase operations were successfully implemented.

objective difficulty did exist[7] in trying to identify the appropriate managerial skills for launching production. Pirelli believed he could recognise the necessary technical expertise for the rubber sector in Antoine-Aimè Goulard, a manufacturer from the Seine valley first met in Paris 'around the end of August 1871'.[8] Goulard turned out to be an unfortunate choice, and Pirelli did not hesitate in getting rid of the incompetent Frenchman. Indeed, from its very outset, the Company attributed great importance to the influence of management in the development of a large company, and consequently dedicated much time and energy in training an excellent managerial team,[9] also formulating optimal policies for their appropriate remuneration and incentivisation. Indeed in time Pirelli became one of the leading management schools in Italy. Combining his natural entrepreneurial abilities with

---

7   Regarding this, Alberto Pirelli (1946) wrote: 'Ing. Pirelli tried to get himself hired as a worker in some foreign factories, but didn't succeed.' To this end, wrote Pirelli in a letter, 'I tried everything; I even had special backing, but I encountered categorical refusals and the utmost suspicion wherever I went'. During a trip through Europe in the early 18th century, the Tsar, Peter the Great, also worked for some time in a naval shipyard in Amsterdam in order to steal the secrets of sailing ship construction from the Dutch workers.

8   Goulard's willingness to move to Italy derived from the fact that he had been deprived 'of his factory during the two sieges of Paris'. When Giovanni Battista Pirelli met Goulard in August 1871, he found himself in Paris at one of the most dramatic moments in French history. The capital was besieged by the Prussians in the winter of 1870–1871 and had suffered terrible destruction during the insurrection of the Commune (March–May 1871), crushed with difficulty by the regular government with its seat at Versailles. From these particulars, another characteristic of the Company's history emerges: the extreme wariness to mention events of major and minor importance not connected directly or closely to the life of the Company.

9   Among these, Alberto Pirelli (1946) recalls 'Emilio Calcagni, who entered the Company in 1873, just after he turned 20. He had never studied at an Upper Technical Institute, but under the Founder's guidance, he was able to provide assistance with the work in the field of producing technical articles made of rubber. He was among the top executives of the Company for a good 48 years, after which he became a member of the Board of Directors; Francesco Piazza was for 33 years the Technical Director of the other rubber production areas and of insulated electrical conductors; the engineer Leopoldo Emanueli who [was] also involved in that area and, in particular, with underwater cable production and the laying of cables in Italy and abroad; the accountant Carlo Fratino who rose to the post of Administrative Director and who was with us for 41 years.' Lastly, Alberto Pirelli (1946) remembered a lesser-known character, the senior cashier, Lorenzo Ramelli, whom he cited as an example of his great dedication to work. Pirelli wrote, 'Lorenzo Ramelli, the senior-cashier, beat the seniority record with 53 years of service; precise and scrupulous, he willingly came to the office even on Sunday; one day he asked for two hours off ... to get married'.

his growing experience in the economic and political worlds, from the very start of his activities, Giovanni Battista focused his energies on devising new products and innovative projects, thus giving the Company access to the many potentialities of the fast-growing rubber industry.[10]

Firstly, it was clear that the capacity to optimise the various production factors intelligently and innovatively favoured not only the generation of an impressive method of production, but gave unexpected successes. An example of this was a contract to produce telegraph batteries for the Army's Engineering Division, which Giovanni Battista won with an original solution of his own. Secondly, in a country at the dawn of industrialisation, it was obvious that the State would be one of the main clients. Free from any sense of inferiority when faced with foreign competitors present on the market for longer, the Company immediately competed in public tenders. Despite being an expression of newly developing private capitalism, Pirelli immediately proved to be skilled in dialoguing with the public and political sectors. This dialogue *inter pares* was to become a constant characteristic of the Company throughout its history. In this perspective, the positioning of Pirelli and his shareholders within the current of liberal politics and economic liberism facilitated contact with the public authorities, in an era in which ideological fences produced prejudicial barriers that were almost insurmountable.

Even though competition was exclusively foreign during the Company's first years of activity, quite soon the Pirelli Company[11] was to face its most serious threat: a competitor not only Italian, but also Milan-based. The entire story is told in a memorandum written by Giovanni Battista Pirelli. After selling his business in France to his partners in 1873 and undertaking not to engage in other activities in transalpine countries, the French technician François Casassa[12] arrived

---

10 In the mid-1870s, Pirelli produced transmission belts, all-rubber tubes or with canvas, tubes with metal spirals, valves, rings and gaskets, various cords, mats, objects in ebonite and waterproof fabrics.

11 In order not to overly complicate the text, the Company will be referred to simply as Pirelli, without giving in detail its exact name and type of company each time it is mentioned. The evolution of the company type and all the extraordinary operations relating to it will be explained in detail as the book continues.

12 In the above-cited memo, Pirelli described Casassa's personal and entrepreneurial history for his shareholders. One learns that Casassa was of Savoyard origin and that he began in 1842 as a simple worker. Over the next 30 years, he built a remarkably large company and accumulated a considerable personal fortune. The tone of the writing, the way Casassa's

in Italy towards the end of 1876, with the aim of setting up a factory in Milan. Pirelli, who had met Casassa in Paris in 1871, was forced to view the prospect of his undertaking in Italy as a serious threat for the future of the Pirelli company. Without wasting any time, Pirelli proposed a different possible scenario to the French industrialist: a merger between the two companies. This solution transformed what could have been a formidable competitor into an ally; it opened up the possibility of using his undoubted managerial skills, his long-standing contacts, and commercial relations. Thus, in a shareholders' meeting the following resolution was approved: the winding up of Pirelli & C. and the foundation of a new limited partnership company, 'Giovanni Battista Pirelli, François Casassa & Co.', in which Pirelli would be co-director with Casassa. Pirelli's good luck and his ability to turn the situation to his own advantage brought an expert manager to the new Company, and this was to have a major impact on the development of sales, especially in foreign markets.

The significant growth in turnover of the new company in the late 1870s was sustained with gradual increases of equity that financed both the working capital and also new investments without continually needing to resort to borrowing from banks. After increasing the share capital from 200,000 to 350,000 lira in a shareholders' meeting on 18 May 1873, a further proposal was made to increase equity from 350,000 to 550,000 lira some years later at a Shareholders' General Meeting on 15 January 1877. As seen in Table 1.1, the leading Pirelli shareholder was Francesco Casassa with 23.64% of the equity, the second was Davide Sforni with 16.36%, while Giovanni Battista Pirelli held 4.91% of the equity.

Pirelli was well aware of the need to continue to identify new possibilities of investment in innovative projects that would be financed with increases in capital, and continued to mould the Company as part of a vital, dynamic process.

Besides consolidating the production of elastic rubber, in the early 1880s Pirelli began to produce cables, wires and insulated electrical cables to occupy a leading position in the newly developing sectors[13] of electricity, telegraphy and telephony,

---

life is narrated, his origins and the results he achieved remind one to some extent of the description of the life of Jean Valjean in *Les Misérables*.

13  Pirelli's involvement in the affairs of Edison, one of the principal Italian electricity companies, was quite close from the beginning. Edison was founded in Milan in July 1882 by Giuseppe Colombo, a professor at the Polytechnic, Giovanni Battista Pirelli's teacher and a member of the Pirelli Board of Auditors. Pirelli himself would become a member of the

industrial sectors which were soon to become important during the Second Industrial Revolution. To consolidate the Company's technical and economic success, Pirelli also invested in the communications sector which then took on a fundamental role in the Company's activities in the new decade. The Company participated successfully in the Italian Exhibition held in Milan in 1881, as well as the International Exhibition of Electricity in Vienna (1884, February). In addition, in that same period the Company acquired a stake in the newspaper *Il Pungolo*, believing that this could be functional in disseminating economic and industrial culture in Italy.

A few years later, some important changes were needed to accommodate the rapid evolution of the Company's activities. On 15 May 1883, Pirelli & C., a limited shares partnership in which Pirelli remained the sole director, [14] was incorporated with an endowment of 2 million lira. [15] The new company took over the assets and liabilities from Giovanni Battista Pirelli e François Casassa & Co., a limited partnership put into liquidation. The choice of a limited shares partnership in which Pirelli remained the sole director was twofold; firstly, the increased dimension of the Company, and secondly, emerging scenarios concerning the economic systems of the Company and the country which Pirelli was able to identify more clearly in

---

Edison Board of Directors in 1889. Castronovo (1980) writes: 'The Company [Edison] had installed a 400 kW plant in the old Santa Radegonda theatre, a stone's throw from Piazza del Duomo, and the year after it began to equip the central areas of the city with a permanent street lighting system'. A memorandum presenting Pirelli (February 1884) declared: 'An important example of this production (electrical cables) is that it was used in most of the network distributing electric lighting to illuminate the Scala Theatre at the end of 1883'.

14 The change in the form of the Company brought into question the previous agreements made between Pirelli and his partners on payment and incentives for the managing director. All this gave rise to an overall review of the director's payment package (Tranfaglia 2010). When the new company was constituted, Giovanni Battista Pirelli had 364 shares out of the total 4,000 and 13 votes, or 9.1% of the capital. Still we have seen that a direct proportionality did not exist between holding shares of the capital and voting rights. At the meeting for the approval of the 1883 annual financial statement, the first of the new company, 38 partners were present, representing 3,046 shares, equal to 76% of the stock and 191 votes. At the moment of the constitution of the new company, the main shareholder was François Casassa, with 503 shares and 17 votes, or 12.57% of the capital. Casassa died shortly afterwards, in 1886.

15 This capital was the result of the increase over time in the current value of the Company's economic capital. In fact, Giovanni Battista Pirelli declared: 'This Company founded with just over L200,000 saw its capital increase more than fivefold in only 8 years' (Pirelli & C/ BIL 1883).

the mid-1880s. In the 1884 annual report Pirelli described a period of consolidation of existing investments, especially those in the field of elastic thread and submarine cables. Regarding the latter, for some time Pirelli had been involved in negotiations with the government to obtain the concession of a contract for 'laying submarine cables to connect our islands to the continental telegraph network, along with the related maintenance'. This was an important business deal which would guarantee Pirelli not only major public contracts, but also allowed the Company valuable know-how in the cables sector that could be applied to different types of networks to be inserted into cables.[16] Following the increase in the number of workers in the Sevesetto factory (reaching 1,000 in 1888) and the progressive, rapid changes in Italy's political and social climate, in the mid-1880s, the Company developed a constant, non-paternalistic behaviour towards its employees, with the institution of a relief fund and a welfare policy for its personnel.

The prospects for new business in submarine cables, implemented in the spring of 1886, obliged the Company to adopt a more complex organisational and managerial structure. The new production required the setting up of a production plant by the sea and a vessel with specific characteristics necessary for laying underwater cables. A factory site was located in San Bartolomeo near La Spezia, which was a strategic location, since a vessel with the required characteristics – the *Città di Milano* – was also based in the La Spezia military port. It was to remain under the protection of the Italian Royal Navy, which would also see to its maintenance and all provisions required for the task. This contract was enormously important, not just for the Company, which had taken on an important technical and financial challenge, but also for the programme of infrastructures promoted by the *Sinistra storica*, the 'Labour Party' at that time, at the helm of united Italy. Pirelli would lay[17] and provide the maintenance for 13 submarine cables between the islands and the continent and between Apulia and Albania for a period of 20 years. Shortly

---

16  Confalonieri estimates that from 1884 to 1885 about 40% of the total Pirelli production was made up of supplies for the government, while exports only came to 4%.

17  Alberto Pirelli (1946) described the work of laying cables as follows: 'Laying a cable on the sea bed, even as deep as 5,000 or 6,000 metres, extending it uninterruptedly for thousands of kilometres, grappling it up when it breaks during the laying and bringing it back up to the surface from the deep, buoying it in stormy seas, and then picking it up again and continuing the job; organising naval expeditions that will be at sea for months, even taking on board live animals to ensure food, those are a few chapters of that adventure story about industry and the sea.'

afterwards, the Company was also commissioned to construct and maintain the telegraph cables between Italy and the colonies in Abyssinia.[18] In a short time, cables were laid connecting Apulia to the Tremiti Islands, Mazara del Vallo with Pantelleria, the Egadi Islands with the continent and with each other, the continent with Sardinia, and Livorno (also known as Leghorn) with the islands of Gorgona and Giglio. The successful outcome of these operations and its echo led the Spanish government to entrust Pirelli with the laying and maintenance of a submarine cable between the Balearic Islands and the Iberian Peninsula. This was probably the Company's first contact with Spain, which would host the Company's first foreign factory at the beginning of the 20th century. In September 1892, only a few years after undertaking this new activity, the Company had laid 1,190km of cables in Italy, 616km in the Red Sea and 726km in the Spanish seas. It was a demanding programme which was to increase over time. To finance these investments, after having undertaken increase of capital almost every two years, in 1887–1888 the Company resorted for the first time to the placement of a bond issue, which was possible thanks to the good reputation it had acquired.

The new challenges arising in the dynamic and competitive sectors in which the Company operated aroused further thoughts about its financial structure, organisation and corporate governance. Regarding the need to hire a commercial and administrative manager, Pirelli expressed some pioneering views and comments on the subject of corporate governance at the shareholders' meeting, defining the Company as 'an intricate collection of delicate organs' which had to maintain 'that order, that energy and that unity of direction which today are the foundations for continued fortune in the field of industry and commerce'. Indeed, Pirelli recognised sound corporate governance as one of the key factors for the continued development and success of a company in a competitive scenario.

In these first decades in the life of the Company Giovanni Battista Pirelli demonstrated that he was an innovator, and thus an entrepreneur in the true Schumpeterian sense of the term, capable of finding promising investment projects wherever they happened to be. From this perspective an orderly and well-reasoned process of business diversification with respect to its core activities may be seen as one of the stable and long-lasting elements that characterise the history of Pirelli.

---

18 The increasing size of the Company and its involvement in public contracts was probably due to Umberto I's visit to the Pirelli factories on 25 May 1890.

The following years represented a frantic period in the history of the nation and a less than brilliant period in the history of the Company. The Sinistra storica's growing difficulties led to Transformism, i.e. a continuously changing government coalition, resulting in the financial crisis of the early 1890s which also brought with it a number of disasters in the banking sector.

The overall economic scenario began to improve towards the mid-1890s, triggering the previously mentioned extraordinary moment of growth, the Second Industrial Revolution. Faithful to its vocation as an innovative company, Pirelli dedicated itself to implementing new products. It began production of lead-insulated submarine cables for electricity networks, a rapidly expanding segment due to the growing demand for lighting in urban centres. The cable segment continued to provide new investment projects due to the ongoing development of various types of networks using cables as carriers. In the space of a few years, in addition to the production of electricity cables which brought brilliant financial results for the Company in 1898 and 1899, Giovanni Battista Pirelli branched out into producing cables 'with several pairs of insulated conductors with air circulation' that were needed for large underground telephone network systems. He had indeed sensed a growing demand in the sector, already present in the United States, and which was now making its appearance in Europe.[19]

The innovative nature of the Company meant that it had to constantly scout for new segments in the world markets. For this reason, both the founder and his descendants would dedicate a great deal of time and energy to study and business trips, during which they visited the factories of rival companies[20] in Europe and the United States, and in other parts of the world such as South America and the Far East, which were the principal producers of natural rubber at the time.

---

19  In his report to the shareholders' meeting on 26 March 1899, Giovanni Battista Pirelli explained the dynamics of the new sector of telephone cables, commented on the new investments and the launch in Italy of the new production, and reported that he had 'obtained, at the same time as the start-up of the telephone company "Alta Italia", a very good order for cables for the Milan network'.

20  These visits, that might surprise the reader because they ran the risk of indirectly benefiting its competitors, were commented on by Alberto Pirelli as follows: 'Everyone, including the Americans, has sections they are jealous about, including mixture specifications and costs; but in general, the dominant concept, and rightly so, is that a company's success depends on the combination of a whole set of factors, including organisational capacity and production efficiency in particular, and that an exchange of technical visits could not be a dangerously decisive element, but instead may be of benefit to the interested parties and to the industry's general progress.'

TABLE 1.2. LIST OF UNDERWRITERS OF CAPITAL FOR
PIRELLI & C. AND THE AMOUNT UNDERWRITTEN

| Year | Turnover | Δ (percent) |
|------|----------|-------------|
| 1873 | 132,336.48 | |
| 1875 | 390,770.57 | +195 |
| 1879 | 719,958.48 | +84 |
| 1881 | 1,031,880.63 | +43 |
| 1883 | 1,751,838.11 | +70 |
| 1885 | 2,494,885.46 | +42 |
| 1888 | 3,767,499.87 | +51 |
| 1890 | 4,257,525.31 | +13 |

Source: Our elaboration from Pirelli & C. balance sheets

A social issue arose connected in the 1890s in Italy due to the growing number of workers in the industrial sector and their needs concerning salary, health assistance and disease prevention, none of which had existed in the agricultural economy that had prevailed only 20 years earlier. These legitimate requests were underlined by the increasing importance of the Socialist Movement in that historically confused era, marked by a liberal, but hardly forward-looking, political class favourable to an authoritarian turn of events that was the forerunner to the institutional crisis which was to mark the end of the century. The bloody Milan riots in May 1898, along with the failures of the authoritarian di Rudinì and Pelloux governments, paved the way for a reform policy promoted in the early years of the 20th century by Prime Minister Giovanni Giolitti. These issues became particularly important for Pirelli, which had registered a considerable increase in employees. When commenting on the 1891 annual financial statement, Pirelli had emphasised his concerns about 'the attempts at disturbances that foreign elements were trying to provoke among our workforce'. Some years later, the Milan factory was involved in the events of the May 1898 riots. Some episodes that marked those bloody days had their genesis in the areas directly in front of the Pirelli factory (Tranfaglia 2010).

At the end of the 19th century a nucleus of labour policy and industrial relations was forged that would characterise Pirelli for a considerable part of the following century. The assumptions were simple, linear and consistent, but could not be waived by any of the stakeholders. The oft-repeated major premise of company policy stipulates that interference of a political nature regarding events unconnected to the Company and the Group is strictly forbidden. For a company that operates in national and international markets as a competitor and not as a monopoly, the contest regarded only its competitors, not the various stakeholders of the Company itself, to whom the Company dedicated a great deal of attention. Consequently, high productivity, technical progress and innovation were identified as the long-term drivers which, by creating value, allowed the Company to cover all costs both for its productive factors and, in particular, for human resources in all its various expressions. Indeed, long before the public sector did so, the Company promoted and completely financed a welfare policy, beginning with the creation of a mutual fund for aid and social security[21] for its employees.

Many of these commitments derived from the founder's own thoughts. With a liberal background, and despite his past support of Garibaldi and lack of sympathy for the socialist movement (whose leaders respected him), Giovanni Battista Pirelli was in no way a reactionary. He viewed with suspicion the end-of-century authoritarian stance of the governments and had fought against it (Tranfaglia 2010), but above all, as an entrepreneur, he proved to be skilled in dealing with concrete problems in a manner that was intellectually free of ideological prejudices and substantially immune to paternalistic traits. He was well aware of the need to keep politics outside the company gates and maintain a civil and constructive dialogue regarding the Company's ability to generate revenue for all its stakeholders.

At the turn of the century, among the many innovations of that extraordinary moment of economic growth, 'tyres for automobiles'[22] became particularly

---

21  In the agreement between the Company and the Workers' Commission for improvements in treatment and miscellaneous provisions following the presentation of the Workers' Memorial of May 1902, we read: 'Keep in mind (response by the workers' organisation to its members) that to obtain one's rights it is absolutely necessary to know how to perform one's own duties. Therefore, demonstrate for this point that you achieved and felt that breath of new civilization that the new century has brought us: uphold your reasoned views not with violence nor abuse, but by being civil and dutiful and without undermining your self-dignity.'

22  The first inkling of a cohesive reflection about the world of 'tyres for automobiles' contained in the managing director's report to the shareholders was seen in the 1904 report to the annual financial statement (12 March 1905). However, a letter dated 21 September 1900 does exist that reports Giovanni Battista Pirelli's impressions after a visit to Fiat in the previous

important for Pirelli's future. The invention of the internal combustion engine and the emergence of the new and fast-growing car industry – celebrated by the Futurists as the key to modernity – spurred the Pirelli Company to plan and produce a new product: the natural evolution from tyres for velocipedes and bicycles. When the Company began to produce its first car tyres, it already had almost 30 years of experience in the rubber sector. Despite this head start, the set-up and manufacture of car and heavy lorry tyres proved to be an unexpectedly difficult technical[23] and commercial challenge. One finds clear evidence of the critical issues encountered in this new production in the prudent, almost circumspect words of Giovanni Battista Pirelli, and also in the somewhat disheartened words of his son Alberto, who recognised that 'the business unit of tyres for cars is demanding a long and costly start-up, but I believe it is now close to coming out of this initial phase'. It is reasonable to hypothesise that by 1904–1905 Pirelli had still only implemented a minimum production of automobile tyres. There is further testimony to these difficulties in a memorandum written in English by Alberto Pirelli for a visit to New York in February 1909. He summarised for his American audience the great difficulties the Company had encountered in automobile tyre production, concluding in very clear terms that 'the difficulties that arise in the details of the manufacture of automobile tyres are far beyond any expectations'.

In addition to the production difficulties created by the constant evolution in vehicles in terms of speed, acceleration and weight, there were also commercial difficulties. The limited national consumer demand for automobile tyres only identified the product with certain foreign brands, which were supported by intense advertising.

---

year, from which one can deduce that on that date Pirelli was already active in the sector, at least on an experimental level. Alberto Pirelli (1946) wrote: 'We began manufacturing tyres for velocipedes in 1890. A Pirelli patent relates to the use in cloth bicycle tyres of a rather loosely woven fabric that had the sole purpose of keeping the material together. This principle was retrieved and applied in general for car tyres very much later.' He does not specify the precise moment they started producing 'tyres for automobiles', but refers in general to the reports to the annual financial statement in the early years of the 20th century.

23  Alberto Pirelli (1946) wrote: 'In the still primitive evolution of motoring, tyres continued to be an Achilles heel. And, alas, there were countless problems at the beginning due to the malfunctioning of those heels, creases in the fabric, blowouts of the frame, cracking, rapid wear and tear, tread detachments and early ageing. Getting half-way through a trip in a car without one or more blow-outs was a real miracle.' He added, 'Tyre production for lorries and more particularly for heavy-load lorries, encountered even greater obstacles compared to tyres for cars.'

For this reason, Pirelli found a market that was hostile solely because it was an Italian company. A possible combination with Fiat which, after the 1907 crisis (Castronovo 2005), had taken the position as the leading Italian car producer, could perhaps have alleviated these difficulties, but relations with the Turin-based company were not smooth from the beginning. The Pirelli Company faced up to these difficulties through a coordinated implementation of various technical, organisational and commercial actions. The Company quickly became aware of the need to combine methodical research for technical excellence with an innovative and diversified communication that went beyond simple consolidated declarations of the success the Company had met with at international exhibitions from the Far East to Egypt, and the Universal Exhibition in Milan in 1906. This new form of advertising was facilitated by the gratifying successes obtained by racing cars using Pirelli tyres in the early years of the 20th century.[24] The files of the Pirelli Historical Archives contain numerous posters for the first car races. These sketches are impressive and their celebration of the achievements in this new industry is highly evocative. Some are authentic works of art; they often portray female figures wearing a peplos, resembling a delicately drawn Artemis, others, a Minerva with firmer features, or even young women of the belle époque celebrating victory by handing laurel wreaths to the winning drivers. The ability of the Company to represent and communicate its products and increase sales became the advertising tradition that Pirelli would cultivate with great care over the course of time, turning it into a unique marketing instrument. The advertising campaigns from the early 20th century present the entire range of Pirelli products in a classical style aimed at juxtaposing the beauty of nature with the works of man. Indeed we can consider what we know today as the Pirelli Calendar as having these same roots. At times, there were also advertisements whose perception and description of reality is subtly ironic.[25] The long P of Pirelli also goes back to that period. In 1958, Vittorio Sereni wrote in the Pirelli magazine: 'The idea of the capital letter stretching out

---

24 Futurism also celebrated the automobile as the image of modernity and the seductive vision of the future. In the Pirelli Foundation Archives, there is a copy of a splendid advertisement, dated 1914, in which a stylised car with fiery red contours and dominated by the Pirelli tyre logo is launched towards the future (see cover image).

25 For example, in an advertisement promoting the characteristics of Cord tyres, against the background of the English countryside, a fox runs nimbly on the tyre in its escape from a pack of hunting dogs.

horizontally to create a roof over the other letters in the name was born in New York one day way back in 1908.'[26]

The beginning of the new century also coincided with the establishment of the first factory outside Italy, in Villanueva y Geltrù in Spain, about 50km south of Barcelona. The new Spanish factory went into operation towards the end of 1902, producing electricity cables and wiring. Construction of the new plant, financed through an increase in capital from 5.5 to 6 million lira was due to a change in Spain's customs policy which required the production of all materials on Spanish soil in order to continue making profits from such sales. Although the weight of the foreign sector on Pirelli's total turnover had grown significantly over time, up until then Pirelli had not established any factories abroad.

Pirelli's first contacts with Spain dated back to 1888, when it began laying submarine telegraph cables to the Balearic Islands, and since then it had built up an efficient network of company agents. This presence in Spain was an innovative choice and provided momentum for the Company's progressive internationalisation. From the turn of the century to the major reorganisation in 1920–1921, this process was gradual, without any direct setting up of subsidiaries or associated production companies abroad. There were three phases in internationalisation of the Company. First, Pirelli proceeded to set up foreign sales branches, also established in the form of companies in key cities such as in London, Brussels and Paris. Then it proceeded to establish other production plants abroad, in particular in Southampton in England.[27] Finally, the company policy of foreign expansion branched out through the acquisition of stakes in other companies, for example the Sociedad Italo-Argentina de Electricidad, which provided utilities in Buenos

---

26 Sereni specifies that 'It was an idea of the moment, springing from a request by a Pirelli representative already in New York. The commercial and advertising jungle was already thickening in those parts and a name that was not exactly unknown, but certainly still young needed to stand out with its own proper sign in order not to be submerged. "How about this?" the visitor newly arrived from Italy asked. And he sketched a P with a very unusual shape. "Yes, that could work," the other replied after a first look. "Yes, that's just right." Satisfied, he looked at it again and mentally saw a poster with that P triumphant against the background of a sky.'

27 The Southampton factory produced cables and electricity conductors. Pirelli and the General Electric Company of London underwrote its capital in equal parts, though the responsibility in the technical field was reserved to the Italian company. It was an undoubted success and good for the company image. A successful Italian company had established a plant in what was, at the time, the most industrialised nation in the world.

TABLE 1.3. PERCENTAGES OF PIRELLI & C. FOREIGN
SALES ON THE TOTAL (1885–1910, IN LIRA)

| Year | Foreign sales | Total sales | Percentage weight |
|------|---------------|-------------|-------------------|
| 1885 | 93,665.15 | 2,494,885.46 | 3.76% |
| 1888 | 227,121.59 | 3,767,499.87 | 6.03% |
| 1890 | 768,621.13 | 4,257,525.31 | 18.05% |
| 1892 | 930,989.29 | 4,190,471.39 | 22.22% |
| 1895 | 2,209,000.00 | 7,096,826.53 | 31.13% |
| 1897 | 3,179,000.00 | 9,865,555.08 | 32.22% |
| 1900 | 4,360,000.00 | 13,489,120.20 | 32.32% |
| 1902 | 3,443,500.00 | 12,209,544.90 | 28.20% |
| 1904 | 3,138,000.00 | 13,309,543.48 | 23,58% |
| 1906 | 4,558,000.00 | 19,101,774.38 | 23.86% |
| 1908 | 4,263,700.00 | 18,662,310.89 | 22.85% |
| 1910 | 7,216,900.00 | 22,956,059.03 | 31.44% |

*Source: Our elaboration from Pirelli & C. annual financial statements*

Aires. The acquisition of this stake in Argentina[28] was Pirelli's first involvement in South America. Moreover, the financial requirements for developing energy companies in South America led to the establishment in June 1913 of the Columbus Société Anonyme d'Enterprise Electrique, with its headquarters in Switzerland. This was Pirelli's first shareholding in a foreign finance company, and was an

---

28  The presence of Pirelli in Argentina was very significant throughout the 20th century, and remains so. During the inauguration of the optical fibre factory in 1987, the then-President Raul Alfonsín declared: 'We are at a company which trusts our country. A company which has been based in Argentina for three quarters of a century and which over time has walked along its path, accompanying the situations experienced by the country. It trusts Argentina, it is Argentinian; at least to a great extent we feel it is ours.' Similarly, in March 1998 the then-Argentinian President Carlos Menem said that 'To talk of Pirelli is to talk of a part of Argentina's history, especially in the field of industry and production, and also to some extent, sport. I have memories of my infancy and childhood, because my father's company sold these tyres along with others, but Pirelli was one of the most popular of that time and this.'

invaluable experience which served as a forerunner for the establishment of the Compagnie Internationale Pirelli in Brussels in 1920, of the Volta company in Zurich in 1929, and culminating in the incorporation of Pirelli Holding in Basel in 1937, which was the parent company of the entire foreign operations of the Group. The reasons for the Company's internationalisation were rooted in the increasingly global nature of the products on the market, the continual search for economies of scale and the favourable economic and political climate that characterised the period between the turn of the century and the outbreak of the First World War.

The continual growth of the Company led to an important innovation in its corporate governance. From 1 January 1905, Piero and Alberto Pirelli – Giovanni Battista's two sons – flanked their father as co-directors in the company admin-istration. For the first time, the one-man company administration became a three-man directorship, the first expression of a Board of Directors. At that time, Piero and Alberto, born in 1881 and 1882 respectively, were 24 and 23 years old.[29] The two young men had already been active in the Company's operations for about a year. Aware of his sons' natural inclinations, Giovanni Battista assigned them different briefs. His idea was successful and over the course of time this was consolidated with Piero dealing with the organisational, production and administrative aspects of the Company, while Alberto dealt more with national and international relations. Over the years, this choice lead to Alberto taking on important public and institutional roles. As early as 1904, before he became part of the co-direction of the Company, Alberto had demonstrated his diplomatic skills on a long trip with meetings in various destinations from the United States to Brazil. In fact, rising sales made it increasingly important to monitor the prices of raw materials in their place of origin. For that reason, after a couple of fruitless attempts made by some of the company managers, Giovanni Battista decided to

---

29  Tranfaglia (2010) briefly reconstructed the personal stories of the two brothers. Both went to the Parini senior high school for classical studies in Milan and successively enrolled in the Faculty of Law at the University of Genoa, graduating in 1903 and 1904 respectively. Tranfaglia wrote: 'Along with the professional preparation for their future work, the Milanese entrepreneur made sure that from their infancy his two sons learned to read, write and speak the principal Western languages (English, French and German) and that after graduating from law school, they took some specialist courses at the Polytechnic and the Bocconi University in Milan to master notional knowledge about economies, mechanics and cost-accounting.' Giovanni Battista had been on the Bocconi Board of Directors since 1902, the year it was founded. This contributed to establishing a long-lasting and still-current relationship between the Pirelli Company and the Bocconi.

send Alberto[30] to explore the rather chaotic evolution of the world's largest market for natural rubber, Brazil.[31] Alberto described his long trip from August to December 1904, including a spell spent in North America, in letters sent to his father[32] from Manaus. They are extremely interesting due to his portrayal of trends in rubber prices, but even more so because of his attentive and precise description of life in Brazil at the time. The vivacious and intense tone of the descriptions were similar to excerpts of novels by the great Brazilian writer Jorge Amado (1912–2001) in which he immortalises Brazil and its people, a fascinating melting pot of races, cultures and traditions. Alberto's account of the feverish negotiations for supplies of raw materials, of solemn promises made and simultaneously broken, and about the conflicts among the various key players in the market, provide a dramatic description of the characteristics of a market based on unbridled capitalism. In his reflections about betrayed trust that leaves 'a sad legacy: discontent and disagreements, reciprocal accusations of broken promises and dishonesty', the young Alberto seems to confirm that intuition that would accompany him throughout his life, namely that rules and social capital are the essence of a well-functioning

---

30  Alberto Pirelli (1946) recalls the beginning of this trip in the following way: 'A first experiment and then a second one of direct buying in the Amazon in the midst of Italian emissaries had negative results. When I was in the United States in the summer of 1904, my father sent a telegram inviting me to go to the Amazon to set right the mishaps of the second attempt and to study the market. That was a gift for me at the age of 22.' In a letter he sent to New York, along with his instructions, he wrote: 'You will not view with displeasure the opportunity for a bold and lengthy mission, worthy of a young man who wants to get ahead. Have a good trip.'

31  Towards the end of the 19th century, Brazil's Amazon region registered an important increase in the demand for rubber. Around 1890 demand rocketed, reaching a peak in 1912, when the proceeds connected to rubber represented 40% of the entire sum of Brazilian exports. The opera house in Manaus, inaugurated in 1896 and celebrated in the film *Fitzcarraldo*, originated from the wealth that came to the entire region, thanks to the boom in rubber production. The introduction of rubber production in South East Asia seems to have had a curious origin. In 1876, a load of rubber seeds was smuggled from the Amazon to England and ended up in the Royal Botanical Gardens at Kew in London. From there the seeds were sent to the British Colonies in South East Asia, where huge rubber plantations were created. Considerable quantities of the product were put on the market at the beginning of the 20th century. Rubber production in South East Asia contributed to the end of Brazilian rubber's golden age.

32  Tranfaglia (2010) dedicated a few pages to Alberto Pirelli's trip in 1904. In New Jersey, Alberto met the scientist Thomas Alva Edison, who 'was kind enough to take a few minutes to show a young Italian of 22 his first tests with the electric phonograph'.

market and an important bulwark to avoid the disintegration of the society on which the market is founded.

Halfway through the first decade of the 20th century, Pirelli was a company that had achieved success in all the sectors it had decided to enter, but it also needed to make major investments in new plants because the existing facilities had reached their production capacity limit. This problem had worsened over time, even though the Company had already resorted to a system of aggregating areas and buildings adjoining the plants. Available space was progressively diminishing also because the city was expanding eastward towards the site where the original headquarters of the Company was located. For these reasons, a decision was taken to move the entire production of the Milan factory to an outlying area,[33] Bicocca, located between what were then the municipalities of Greco Milanese and Niguarda. This area had excellent characteristics for establishing a factory, and at the same time, was an interesting option for further aggregations of land and buildings if production increased significantly in the following years. The area in question was in the north-eastern outskirts of Milan where Greco railway station would be built. Thus, it would be an extremely useful logistics centre for transporting materials and finished products. The new Bicocca plant began operating in 1909 and until almost the end of the 20th century was one of the Group's most important production sites in Italy and the world. Above all, it increasingly took on the identity of the company headquarters. The progressive urbanisation of the areas where the production plants were originally established raised the prospect of requalifying disused areas and their subsequent use.[34] The size of the new plants and the specificity of the area meant that further infrastructures would soon be needed. For the first time, the involvement of the Company in various aspects of the real estate sector clearly took form.

---

33  Confalonieri (1980) describes the moving of the Pirelli plants within a larger project to create an industrial zone in the north-eastern part of Milan: 'It was about initiating the creation, in the outskirts of Milan, of an industrial quarter where some important industrial companies would be transferred, such as the Breda Company and the Pirelli Company [that were at the time located] practically in the city centre.'

34  Regarding this, Confalonieri (1980) cites the minutes of the Central Committee of the Banca Commerciale Italiana of 15 December 1906: 'The companies interested in moving their plants, which will allow them to rid themselves of the currently occupied areas at a rather considerable profit, sought the aid of bankers and local capitalists to ensure the purchase, at very favourable conditions, of a vast property situated between Sesto San Giovanni and Greco Milanese in a particularly favourable position for the construction of industrial plants which would have a direct connection with the railway.'

The planning and construction of the new premises coincided with two important deadlines: firstly, the prolonging of the Company's date of termination, which was extended[35] for another 20 years until 1927, and secondly, the renewal of the contracts for the laying and maintenance of submarine cables in the Mediterranean and the Red Sea, which were due to expire in June 1908. These were also renewed for another 20 years. In 1912 the Company was commissioned to construct and lay two submarine cables to connect the cities of Tripoli and Benghazi in the Sirte area of Libya with Sicily – in all, 1,350km. In the same period, on 4 April 1909, the Company received another important recognition when Giovanni Battista Pirelli was appointed Senator of the Kingdom of Italy.

In the years preceding the war, exports increased significantly, especially to the Central European countries, which made the reorganisation of logistics more complicated when war broke out in 1914. Alberto Pirelli gave a precise explanation to the shareholders of the connection between the choice of investments projects and financial decisions. The young co-director explained how investment projects arose from the Company's active participation in the discovery and implementation of new production technologies for the Company's traditional business. Financing of working capital was either provided internally or by borrowing from banks; still, it was necessary later to rationalise the financial structure in order not to compromise its equilibrium in the long term.

At the beginning of August 1914, war broke out in Europe. In a certain way it was as if the pendulum of European history had swung back to 1870, when Prussia had defeated and humiliated France. After a long period of peace – most unusual for Europe – the still-unresolved France–Germany dispute was rekindled on the Rhine. Pirelli was very soon involved in the cataclysm that was shaking Europe and that would permanently undermine its political and economic power, as well as its prestige and moral authority at an international level.

It was the first time that the Company, established at the beginning of a long period of peace, had had to face the numerous uncertainties of a conflict that from the outset was different from previous ones. In the industrialised and standardised world, war had also taken on new, unknown forms. The conflict posed various

---

35 The problem of the Company's date of termination is not merely a matter of form in this case. It is closely connected to the clauses about profit sharing and severance pay for the directors in the event of the Company winding up. Thus, renewal of the termination date meant an explicit declaration of the Pirelli family's extended involvement in the Company.

questions which had no simple answers. For the first time in Pirelli's history, at the shareholders' meeting to approve the 1914 annual financial statement, the directors' reports gave ample space to an event that was apparently external to the life of the Company. If one analyses these reports carefully, however, the directors dealt with the conflict to the extent that it was important for company affairs, not betraying the long-consolidated company policy. Even before Italy entered the war, Pirelli had to face significant logistical and commercial problems. Europe was cut in two by the rapid turn of events that August. Although the ports of access for raw materials remained accessible, the export situation was more complex. For Pirelli this meant the loss of exports to Central European countries and rendered operation in its commercial branches in warring countries very difficult, if not impossible. Above all, the cessation of exports to the Austro-Hungarian Empire was a harsh blow, as these had rocketed in the years leading up to the war.

In this regard, the Company adopted a very rigorous policy. It decided to suspend the supply of materials to the Central Powers at the start of hostilities, well before Italy entered the war by becoming part of the Triple Entente. This intransigent policy allowed the Company to remain unharmed by criticism from those who considered it guilty of having supplied sensitive materials to enemy forces, and at the same time qualified it to be entrusted by the Italian government to undertake production for the massive war effort. It is striking how during the war company management was so forward-looking in cultivating, one might even say a little cynically, certain conditions such as commercial channels, clientele and export flows that would allow it to return rapidly to its international dimension once hostilities ended.

This ability of the Pirelli management to imagine the world after the war arose from two considerations: first, the awareness that the ending of hostilities would be more complex to manage than the years of the conflict, which were rather desensitised by the abundance of orders; second, a clear perception that 'the war will make situations that seemed to have been overcome rise again with an aftermath of all kinds of new problems to disturb the souls of those belonging by inclination and schooling to the Liberalist school of thought'.[36] In writing these lines, Alberto Pirelli realised very well that the powers unchained and the tensions aroused by

---

36  Letter to Luigi Einaudi dated 12 January 1916, from Alberto Pirelli's Private Archives, cited by Tranfaglia (2010) on page 61.

the conflict would have a long-lasting impact, well beyond the conclusion of the war, and would sweep away an established order to give space to a future with, at the very least, uncertain contours. In the meantime, the European war posed a series of serious logistical and organisational problems that ranged from sourcing raw materials to the growing number of white-collar and blue-collar employees called into military service,[37] as well as the difficulty of communicating with the foreign branches in various European countries.

In any case, Italy's entry into the war meant an immediate and significant increase in orders for Pirelli: sales increased fourfold between 1914 and 1918.[38] Pirelli had an important role in supplying electricity cables for various uses, as well as tyres for the Italian and Allied armies. Montenegro (1985) writes that

> during the war Pirelli's Italian factories managed to satisfy something like 80% of the Italian Army's requirement for electricity cables for field telegraphs and telephones. They also met the needs of the French Army in large measure, besides covering a conspicuous part of the demand for tyres, semi tyres and full rubber tyres for military vehicles, bicycles and airplanes, and guaranteeing the supply of an extremely varied number of technical items for the army, navy and air force.

For some years, the Company was completely absorbed in the events regarding the war. Significantly, Giovanni Battista Pirelli wrote a letter to General Alfredo Dall'Olio (20 February 1916), Plenipotentiary for the Italian Army procurement, underlining 'his readiness to produce war materials'. In 1916, to deal with these requirements, the Company approved the construction of a factory in Vercurago, near Lecco, and the purchase of lands adjoining the Bicocca factory.

This willingness and dedication was highlighted by the speed with which the submarine cables connecting the continent to Sardinia were repaired in late autumn of 1918, after a breakdown that interrupted communications with the island. During the campaigns at sea for submarine cable maintenance which was

---

37  On 31 December 1917, the Company had about 11,000 employees, of which 2,000 were in military service.

38  Turnover went from 47.5 million in 1914 to 64 million in 1915, then 90 million in 1916, 165 million in 1917 and 190 million in 1918.

TABLE 1.4. PERCENTAGE BREAKDOWNS FOR PIRELLI &
C. EXPORTS BASED ON TOTAL EXPORTS (1892–1910)

| Countries | 1892 | 1894 | 1896 | 1898 | 1900 | 1902 | 1904 | 1906 | 1908 | 1910 |
|---|---|---|---|---|---|---|---|---|---|---|
| Spain and Portugal | 35% | 32% | 25% | 33% | 44% | 30% | 12% | 8% | 4% | 2% |
| England | 20% | 21% | 25% | 21% | 15% | 24% | 30% | 26% | 30% | 34% |
| Austria & Hungary | 10% | 10% | 9% | 5% | 3% | 4% | 5% | 9% | 4% | 3% |
| America | 15% | 10% | 9% | 12% | 14% | 13% | 22% | 19% | 27% | 28% |
| Belgium, Holland & Germany | – | 11% | 14% | 14% | 11% | 10% | 12% | 18% | 12% | 13% |
| France | 8% | 3% | 7% | 7% | 5% | 7% | 8% | 9% | 4% | 5% |
| Switzerland | 2% | 3% | 2% | 3% | 1% | 3% | 4% | 3% | 2% | – |
| Russia, Eastern nations & others | 10% | 9% | 10% | 5% | 7% | 8% | 7% | 8% | 17% | 15% |
| Total | 100% | 100% | 100% | 100% | 100% | 100% | 100% | 100% | 100% | 100% |

*Source: Our elaborations of Pirelli & C. annual financial statements*

part of the agreement with the government, on 16 June 1919, the steamer *Città di Milano* sank near Filicudi in the Aeolian archipelago. Its sad fate marked the end of an era. Another vessel with similar characteristics, previously owned by the defeated Imperial German Navy, soon replaced the lost vessel and the horizon of Pirelli's activities continued to progressively expand until it encompassed the entire Mediterranean and then the Atlantic Ocean with the laying of cables for South America.

As the directors had foreseen, the end of the war was a critical moment for the Company. All the unresolved or even supposedly resolved contradictions that the war had aroused now created a necessarily more fragile situation within the Company. The enormous production of war materials ceased almost immediately and the Company was soon in a precarious financial condition. The dizzying increase in sales due to orders for the war effort had generated an increasingly considerable volume of working capital and, above all, bank debts.[39] Moreover, many European governments were intending to levy taxes on war profits.

There were two ways in which to remodel the financial structure and reduce the bank debt. The first was to continue increasing turnover, exploring new investment projects with healthy margins, without asking anything from shareholders. The second and very different stance was to tackle the problem head on with successive seasoned equity offerings, and place the development of new investment projects in the background. The directors did not hesitate in choosing the second route. With an ironclad logic, any possible new investments were postponed until the financial structure had been reorganised.

Asking shareholders to invest additional equity in the confused scenario of 1919–1920, in which the desirability of share investments in Italy was, at the least, uncertain, as Giovanni Battista himself states in the budget meetings of 1918 and 1919, was not something to be taken for granted. It meant that in nearly 50 years of life Pirelli had acquired a reputation of utter respect within the market, and this allowed it to emerge from a seriously difficult situation substantially unharmed. In the brief span of two years, the Company progressively increased its capital, bringing it first to 60 million and then to 120 million lira.

Though the financial situation was dealt with brilliantly and resolved, the Company in the period labelled 'the two red years' had a very hard time finding a modus vivendi in its increasingly complex industrial relations. On 10 September 1920, workers occupied the Pirelli factory for two weeks. The day before, during the Extraordinary Shareholders' Meeting convened for a seasoned equity offering, Giovanni Battista Pirelli had pointed out that the Company had remained relatively unharmed in respect to politically slanted trade union demands. Faithful to the policy lines he had drawn *ab origine*, the Lombard industrialist argued that politics should stay outside the factory gates and that salary demands should be negotiated between the stakeholders, but within the Company. Pirelli had always been characterised by its focus on the welfare programme that it had recently

---

39 As Giovanni Battista Pirelli infers, the Company was in a precarious financial position, characterised by an ownership structure unbalanced by bank debts. These had been incurred to pay suppliers, since the main creditor, the government, had payment times exceeding the normal commercial practices. This tardiness in payment by public administration seems deeply rooted in Italian national history.

developed, together with a further project to build housing for its employees. This is why the occupation of the factory, even in the context of an incandescent political climate loaded with rancorous demands, was difficult for the management to comprehend. Even though it was not a defeat, it certainly rang alarm bells about a future fraught with uncertainties.

Although for half a century the Company had opposed an ideological approach to industrial relations and had analysed its scope of action, prospects and obligations with a certain intellectual honesty, now oppressive anti-capitalist ideology and rhetoric was sweeping all of that away. Still, in reacting to these upheavals, the management avoided giving in to reactionary temptations. Its aim was to identify the best measures to benefit all the stakeholders, without slipping into that less complicated, and thus rather tempting, authoritarian style which was ultimately sterile, but which was one of the most common choices made by the Italian industrial class in the following years.

# CHAPTER 2

# Between the Two World Wars

The early part of the 1920s was an important moment for the reorganisation of the Company and its production. The scenario in the years immediately following the First World War – to which the Company was able to respond energetically – also reinforced the conviction that major management restructuring of the Company was required to diversify the risk in the Group's operative and financial activities.[1] Indeed, the dramatic experience of the war and the uncertainty of the post-war years posed serious economic and political repercussions, not only for Italy, but for Europe as a whole. Once the management confirmed the solidity of the Company's financial structure, a general reorganisation plan was put into motion.

In that period, the Group's activities were divided into three different sectors. The first was the production of the Group's four Italian plants which were part of Pirelli & C., a limited partnership.[2] The second was the Company's shareholdings in a vast number of Italian manufacturing companies – including the Makò cotton mill in Cordenons, and Società Anonima Tessuti Industriali in Saronno – mainly operative in the textile weaving and public road transport sectors.[3]

---

1  Anelli, Bolchini, Bonvini and Montenegro (1985) wrote: 'The development strategy of the company focuses principally around three axes: 1) to reinforce its international presence; 2) to create an operative organisation to provide all the company's financial requirements and to carry out those operations necessary for it to continue its strategy of expansion; 3) to decrease the dependence on foreign sourcing of raw materials.' This choice of strategy was confirmed in the Directors' report to the general shareholders' meeting which deliberated that all sources of income from Pirelli & C. be conferred to the Società Italiana Pirelli.

2  These regarded the plants in Milan, founded in 1872, La Spezia (1886), Bicocca (1908) and Vercurago (1916).

3  The Group's shareholdings in the textile sector were justified by the need to produce the internal framework for the tyres, whereas the shareholdings in public road transport was strategic in publicising and promoting tyres through the capillary network of activities pertinent to the automobile sector, from garages to public transport.

The third regarded its foreign operations which the Company had started when opening its plant in Villanueva y Geltrù (Spain) in 1902. In the 20 years that followed, Pirelli not only created a network of foreign sales outlets but also constructed some factories outside Italy.[4] Construction commenced in 1917 for the last of these – Pirelli S.A. Platense, in Buenos Aires – which was to produce industrial electrical cables. Soon after the First World War, Pirelli acquired two plantations in the Far East, the first in Ulu Tiram in the Malay Peninsula near Singapore, which was sold in 1928, and the second in Boenisari Lendra, on the island of Java. The aim behind the acquisition of these plantations was to guarantee a regular source of raw materials at stable prices. Although Pirelli & C. held shareholdings in its foreign companies, they each operated autonomously under their own management.

These reorganisation activities also included the incorporation of a joint stock company named Società Italiana Pirelli, to which Pirelli & C. was to transfer its Italian factories and other financial assets pertaining to their activities, a seasoned equity offering from 1 to 100 million lira. Technically, this deal had to be underwritten entirely by Pirelli & C. against the contribution of the previously mentioned assets. This operation meant that the ownership structure of Società Italiana Pirelli would have been the same as the joint stock company. The newly constituted company was to manage the industrial activities of the Group, whereas the Limited Partnership was to oversee the Group's general strategy, management and coordination, with a particular focus on the financial activities of the Group and the provision of different sources of funding, typical of a holding company. The same reorganisation strategy was carried out for the Group's foreign activities. In 1920, Compagnie Internationale Pirelli was incorporated in Brussels; its entire share capital was owned by the Italian limited partnership which, by means of a similar model, was also entrusted with the management of the Group's foreign business.

In this way, the Limited Partnership held control of Società Italiana Pirelli in Italy and Compagnie Internationale Pirelli abroad; the latter – as a subholding – controlled the Group's foreign companies. Pirelli & C. still held shareholding in those Italian companies which were not directly involved in the production of cables and tyres and which were later defined as 'diversified activities'.

---

4   This is also explained further in the first chapter.

TABLE 2.1. SHAREHOLDINGS IN COMPAGNIE
INTERNATIONALE PIRELLI ON 31 DECEMBER 1921

| Investee company | Country |
| --- | --- |
| Pirelli Limited | United Kingdom |
| Comercial Pirelli | Spain |
| Pirelli Platense | Argentina |
| Société Belge Pirelli | Belgium |
| Caucciù Pirelli | Romania |
| Produits Pirelli | Switzerland |
| Société Française | France |
| Società Egiziana Prodotti Pirelli | Egypt |

*Source: CIP annual financial statement, 31 December 1921*

This reorganisation brought about numerous innovations in the Company. Firstly, Pirelli & C. ceased to be the focal point for the entrepreneurial activity of the Group; this role was taken on by Società Italiana Pirelli. In the Limited Partnership the managerial activities were carried out by Giovanni Battista Pirelli from 1872 to 1904,[5] and later jointly with his sons Piero and Alberto, whereas Società Italiana Pirelli was governed by a Board of Directors which met for the first time on 29 November 1920. The Board included three directors of the Limited Partnership, representing the Pirelli family, and three other managers who had worked with the Company for many years and who were in charge of the technical and production sectors: Emilio Calcagni, Fabio Palandri and Giuseppe Venosta.[6] Similarly, the

---

5   For a brief period – from 1877 to 1884 – the management role was shared with François Casassa.

6   Alberto Pirelli (1946) described Venosta as follows: 'He entered our company in 1906 at the age of 26 with a technical role in that field (pneumatics) and he rapidly climbed the rungs of the company to be entrusted with the entire production of rubber-based goods and later, with the management for the sale of the same.' Carlo Fratino – long-time manager of the administration sector of the Company – Guido Valerio, and the Marquis Roberto Visconti di S. Vito were called on to serve on the Board of Auditors.

Board of Directors of Compagnie Internationale was formed by three managers and two external members, Alfred Orban and Eduard Wiener.

The termination of the company reorganisation coincided with a favourable period of economic growth in the mid-1920s; the tyre and electrical cables sectors benefited most and showed significant growth in this period. Indeed, the decision taken during the war of maintaining the current commercial channels in view of the end of hostilities proved to be a winning choice. The Company also participated in the incorporation of Società Italiana Reti Telefoniche Interurbane, together with another two companies, one Italian and one foreign.[7] This participation was the Group's first contact with the telephone communication sector. This interest in the telephone sector was a logical consequence of the Company's business in the production of electrical cables, but was to abruptly terminate during 1925, when Società Italiana Pirelli participated in Società Generale Italiana Telefoni, which was to be granted a government concession for the national urban telephone network. The Italian government, however, divided up this concession into five areas, and as a consequence Pirelli decided not to participate directly in the public bid. The involvement of Pirelli in the electrical and telephone sectors was aimed at maximising the benefit from tenders deriving from the rapidly expanding cable and networks markets.

The year 1922 marked the 50th anniversary of the incorporation of the Company, the same year in which the Fascist Party took power. It was a well-known fact that the liberal classes that had governed the country since its unification had proved ineffective in the difficult post-war period. Liberal governments had shown many shortfalls in most European states; in reality, they were not able to manage the numerous contradictions that the war had generated. The effect was manifest in various ways, from nationalist sentiments shared equally by the victors and the defeated, legitimate requests of survivors in stark contrast to those of Socialists backed up not only by the Soviet experience, but by the greater social and political awareness of public opinion, seen both in the factories and later, at the battlefront. In Italy, the Liberal State, and above all, its governing classes, imploded when unable to give reliable answers to the social and institutional mayhem of the years

---

7   This was the joint stock company Vittorio Tedeschi, which was controlled by the Banca Commerciale and the International Western Electric Co. As Pirelli already had historical links with the Credito Italiano bank, it may be deduced that the shareholding was structured in agreement with the two large banking groups of that period.

immediately following the conflict. This gave way to an authoritarian, anti-Liberal and more Nationalist solution in the form of the Fascist Party. Despite the great events which were shaking the country, Pirelli remained faithful to its tradition. There is no trace of this political upheaval – not even a chance mention – in the Company's official and informal documents which, to the contrary, often refer to new projects and the national and international successes of the Pirelli products on the market.

One can consider the Company's approach to the new regime as mainly that of 'wait and see'. In its early years, the Fascist period represented a rapid and easy solution for Italian industrialists to resolve the problems that had set in after 1918. A little more far-sightedness, however, showed that this could be no more than a temporary solution. If anything, one could see a certain scepticism in Giovanni Battista Pirelli's trust in authoritarian solutions, as consistently shown in the course of his long life; his son Alberto's analysis of the situation was more complex and detailed.[8] The most probable explanation was that, on the one hand he looked on the Fascist regime with the due suspicion of his class, but at the same time, he agreed with some of the social and economic ideologies of the emerging regime. Alberto found himself having to live through crucial years in which he had to decide between his activities at a national and international level in favour of his country, and other political issues which unavoidably favoured the party in power at that moment. This was a fine line to draw because there was a fundamental difference between supporting the political ideals of a liberal state and those of an authoritarian state.[9] During the 1920s these latent contradictions were of minor importance, but were to take on much greater significance towards the end of the 1930s.

The Company benefited from the prevailing economic growth which was a global phenomenon in the period between 1921 and 1922; it innovated its products

---

8   Piero covered a more internal role in the Company and, in the initial period, had less contact with the political milieu. Alberto (Tranfaglia 2010) stated the following in his notes of 13 January 1923, written just two months before the March on Rome: 'I accompanied the Prime Minister [Mussolini] to London, also because I had to turn down various positions that he had offered me and I couldn't but dedicate some days to the meetings in London.'

9   The figure of Alberto Pirelli is quite similar to some other famous civil servants, such as Raffaele Mattioli and Alberto Beneduce, who never sided with Fascism. Nevertheless, these persons were never key shareholders in the public companies that they managed; they only covered management roles. Alberto Pirelli carried out his role as civil servant to the full as minister plenipotentiary in the negotiations for the war reimbursements.

with the launch of the Cord and Superflex lines of tyres and continued production of various types of electrical cables. Among these activities, the production of high-tension cables for the distribution of electricity in urban areas was particularly important, as was the installation of electrical plants in private homes.[10] This last activity tended to follow a cyclic growth, much in line with the ups and downs of the construction sector. Between 1922 and 1925 the increase in both turnover and the range of activities required major reorganisation and thus, an overhaul of the Company's financial and corporate structure was carried out between 1925 and 1927.

Società Italiana Pirelli promoted a seasoned equity offering from 120 to 150 million lira through the issue of 300,000 shares, of which 120,000 were one share–one vote.[11] The possibility of issuing multiple voting shares was to create a separation between ownership and control, thus permitting the controlling Limited Partnership Pirelli & C. to consolidate its control[12] on the operative company, thus minimising the resources destined for this investment.

TABLE 2.2. TYPOLOGY OF SHARES OF
PIRELLI & C. AS OF 30 APRIL 1929

| Typology of shares | Number of shares | Nominal value (in lira) |
| --- | --- | --- |
| Type A shares | 335,012 | 167,506,000 |
| Type B shares | 45,682 | 22,841,000 |

*Source: Pirelli & C., minutes of the Board of Directors meeting, 13 May 1929*

---

10 The company documents contain much reference to the successes obtained in the difficult sector of high-tension cables, two in the United States (one in Chicago and another in New York) and a third in Latin America in Lima, which earned the Company a world record in the sector.

11 While the Category A single-voting shares were the same as those already in circulation, the Category B multiple-voting shares were new, conferring to the holder the right to five votes per share.

12 There was a total of 563,422 votes available, of which multiple voting shares were 228,410, accounting for approximately 40% of the total.

During the following spring the roles and duties of Pirelli & C. were redefined as the previously assigned institutional roles were considered as being excessive. The decision was taken to liquidate that portion of assets considered excessive in favour of the Società Italiana Pirelli, assigning these to the shareholders of Pirelli & C. in lieu. In this way, the role of Pirelli & C. was focused more on the management of its property in the Milan urban area and in the controlling shares of Società Italiana Pirelli. The latter received those shares which had previously been held by the Limited Partnership of the Italian companies engaged in diverse activities, the controlling share packet of Compagnie Internationale Pirelli, and the land and premises not located in the Milan urban area. Società Italiana Pirelli also increased its equity by 5 million lira against the new endowment which it received. A few years later, the Group once again changed its corporate organisation. The justification for this was that on the one hand, the role of the Limited Company had become marginal, while Società Italiana Pirelli – which had received new and very important resources – was to take over the management and control of the Group's foreign operations.[13] The preparatory undersigning of the multiple-voting shares issued by Società Italiana Pirelli and subsequently underwritten by the limited company had the effect of safeguarding the control of the pre-existing owners of the Group.

All of these operations were preliminary steps which were necessary before reorganising the Group's financial structure. During 1926, debts with banks had once again reached significant levels, both due to the working capital and for investments. For this reason, the Board of Directors of the Società Italiana Pirelli undertook to issue bonds in dollars on the US stock market, which was in rapid expansion in that period and was showing great interest in European companies. The Company contacted the investment bank JP Morgan in New York to follow this deal.

In that same period, other important Italian companies, among which Fiat, also approached the US market by issuing bonds for their companies. In the Roaring Twenties, the Wall Street stock market had an unprecedented growth which had contributed to rendering this type of investment opportunity popular with small investors. For large Italian companies, the US capital market had already surpassed

---

13  This solution had undoubtable advantages. As was seen later, the technical consulting services for the Group's foreign subsidiaries were carried out by Società Italiana Pirelli.

that of the United Kingdom in importance for this type of financial operation. The Company furthermore was an excellent borrower and with an excellent 'rating' given its diversity of activities and its widespread geographical presence, which tended to minimise any risk for creditors. Pirelli issued a $4 million convertible bond[14] in equity of Società Italiana Pirelli at a rate of 7% for a 25-year period with an estimated repayment price of 105. This did not jeopardise the control of the Company, which remained firmly in the hands of Pirelli & C., which in turn held the entire type B shares through the Limited Partnership.

The entire operation was an undoubted success for the Italian group, culminating in the Company being listed on the Wall Street stock market, the first Italian company ever to do so.[15] At the start of the US quotation operation, the Company was also listed in the Milan Stock Exchange, only a few years after this had been deliberated by the Board of Directors on 3 July 1926. It was surprising that the Company had not yet been listed, having been operative for more than 50 years, and with its diverse and fragmented shareholding. Furthermore, despite being in private hands, the Company was watchful of its financial structure and its capital market activities. Considering that no specific information regarding this emerges from the official or unofficial documents of the Group,[16] a possible justification could be that previously the Company did not require public financing to raise funds on the market, being fully provided by its incumbent shareholders. The reason that pushed the Company to enter the public market during the 1920s was the growing number of shareholders which required greater liquidity, and thus the most viable option was to approach the stock market and public funding. Following approval of the Annual Financial Statement in 1926, external members were invited to be part of the Pirelli Board of Directors: Alberto Lodolo, Carlo Feltrinelli, leading representatives of the electricity industry concentrated in the newly

---

14  The Società Italiana Pirelli Board of Directors' report of 4 April 1927 documented that the Pierpont Morgan Bank insisted that the bonds be issued as convertible bonds, 'warning that if this was not conceded then there would have been a spread of at least four points in the price of the granting of the loan'.

15  Following a proposal by the National City Bank, on the 13 May 1929 the Board of Directors of Società Italiana Pirelli deliberated to list the shares on the Amsterdam Stock Exchange.

16  There is only a fleeting mention of this operation in the Directors' report to the company accounts of 1889, in which the management stated that they did not retain the Company to be ready for such a step.

formed company La Centrale, and Gerolamo Serina, the Company's long-serving notary and mind behind the 1926 corporate restructuring.

At the end of the 1920s Società Italiana Pirelli focused on acquiring greater participation and involvement in the telephony industry in Italy, particularly in the Centre-South regions, to generate greater business for the electrical cable sector.[17] The involvement of Pirelli in the emerging telephone industry was to take on an even more important role, both for Società Italiana Pirelli and for Compagnie Internationale Pirelli. Regarding the latter, in 1929, the Board of Directors of the controlling company took the decision to incorporate a company in Switzerland to be assigned the Group's international shareholdings in the electrical and telephone sectors. This proposal, however, in part questioned the existence of the Holding Company, constituted in Belgium less than 10 years previously. The justification for this change in its telephone and electrical activities was the greater importance of the Swiss financial market compared to Belgium, regarding both potential business opportunities and the availability of fresh capital.[18] Almost immediately following this decision the company Volta was founded on 26 October 1929 in Zurich, to which the Società Italiana Pirelli conferred some of its shareholdings in the sector.

In the second part of the 1920s, the Company's foreign operations, under the coordination of Compagnie Internationale Pirelli, also showed constant growth. As well as consolidating its sales network in Barcelona through the company Comercial S.A., the Group also constructed a factory in Spain for the production of tyres, in Manresa, Catalonia. In 1929, the factory in Burton-on-Trent in the north of England also started production.[19] Thus, the Group consolidated its presence in

---

17 Similarly the Company promoted a capillary diffusion of its tyres through an commercial agreement with constructors of original equipment, participation in companies operative in public road transport and in a wide range of automobile competitions. Montenegro (1985) wrote: 'The Milanese company has been able to construct, to the same level or even better, than other competitors; it has a dense network of dealers covering all areas from large cities to the smallest country villages; their warehouses continually request new supplies and it also has continual contact with an army of agents in numerous sales outlets in Italy and abroad.'

18 Indeed, in June 1913 Pirelli participated in the founding of the financial company Columbus, with registered offices in Switzerland, which had the mission to sustain the growth of the electrical utilities sector in South America.

19 In a pleasant way Alberto Pirelli (1946) illustrates this project as follows: 'Burton-on-Trent is a town in the industrial North of England and is known as the centre of the largest

the United Kingdom, not only in the electrical cable sector but also in the pneumatic tyre sector.[20] In this same period, the Group was also focused on reinforcing its presence in the South American market, a continent which was to play an ever-more important role in the Company's growth. In Argentina, where the Group had already been present since 1917 with the incorporation of Società Platense, it opened another factory in Buenos Aires for the production of electrical cables and other rubber-based products. Finally, the Group founded the company Pirelli S.A. Companhia Industrial Brasileira in San Paolo in 1930, initially to produce electrical conductors but which was later converted for many other of the Group's product lines.

In the 1920s, the Group also started to pay attention to the real estate sector. There were two problems to face; the first and less urgent regarded the future use of land owned by the Company in the built-up area of Milan and which were still controlled by Pirelli & C. following the company restructuring of 1926. The second and more pressing one was the need for housing for the workers of the Bicocca plant, and more generally, social housing for the Group's employees. Società Italiana Pirelli found itself involved in a project which was headed by some of its employees; they formed a cooperative for the construction of housing units. For a series of reasons, partly due to the complicated scenario of that period and partly to inexperience, the construction company found itself in difficulty. Pirelli had to intervene to prevent the cooperative from going bankrupt, and with it, the demise of the remarkable project that it had underwritten.

In October 1929, the Wall Street Stock Exchange – which until then had shown long periods of euphoria – collapsed. During the course of the next two years,

---

producers of beer in England, which drinkers refer to as Burton water'. Some photographs of the inauguration of the plant are found in the Pirelli historical archives. In one of these, a long procession of automobiles enter through the gates of the plant, while another shows the elegant profile of Edward VIII, then Prince of Wales, who spoke at the inauguration ceremony and who listens attentively to the technical explanations of Piero Pirelli on the functioning of one of the machines.

20 Pirelli had already built two factories for the production of cables in the UK, the first in Southampton in 1913 and the second in the nearby town of Eastleigh in 1927; this was a cooperation between Pirelli and the General Electric Co. through the joint venture Pirelli-General Cable Works which had been founded some time previously. Alberto Pirelli (1946) acknowledged the technological excellence that had been achieved in these factories as follows: 'They have produced more high tension, fluid filled cables in a single year than Milan has produced in a lifetime.'

the gross domestic product of the major industrial countries showed a decline of approximately 20%. In the early 1930s no effective strategy was identified to respond to the emerging economic crisis which was triggering severe political and civil repercussions; the introduction of stringent fiscal and economic policies rendered impossible even the most tentative of recoveries. In this context, totalitarian states seemed to better respond to those current queries. This phenomenon represented a profound criticism to the free market economy of before, which seemed to have failed.

The Great Depression eventually reached Italy, although at a much later date. It should be noted that during the start of the crisis the Directors' report stated that 'the action of the national government has contributed to reduce the effect of the general depression which is worse elsewhere'. This partially valid statement, verbalised in the Directors' report of a private industrial company, can be construed as a manifest and unexpected tribute to the economic policy adopted by the central government. Indeed, Pirelli did not require any public support; in its 70 years of activity it had always avoided any form of comment or praise regarding such matters. This stance regarded not only the relations between the Company and the regime in power, but also between the Pirelli family and the regime. Another scenario also emerged: during the 1930s, the Company in general showed a certain degree of warming to the Fascist regime, which seemed to contradict – albeit partially – one of the foundations that Giovanni Battista Pirelli had placed at the base of a successful industrial policy. It was in this period – on 20 October 1932 – that the Company's founder died. If on the one hand his death had no direct effect on the management, having already left the Company in the hands of his sons Piero and Alberto for some years, on the other hand his death saw the demise of one of the most important Italian industrialists, a multifaceted person with wide, varied interests, as summed up in Emilio Calcagni's statement in the Board of Directors' meeting.

Despite government propaganda, as the 1930s progressed the minutes of the Board and the shareholders' meetings of the various companies of the Group, both in Italy and abroad, seemed to contain more and more information regarding the global economic crisis.[21] The Company was almost unscathed by one of the most

---

21  On 21 March 1934 the following was recorded: 'The almost absence of orders in the urban telephone cables sector continues as well as for the distribution of electrical power in relation

serious crises to hit Italy between 1932 and 1935, thanks to the diversification of its activities and to its far-sighted, competent management. Indeed, since the company restructuring at the beginning of the 1920s, the Group's activities could be divided into three different segments: cables, tyres and other diversified activities. In 1931, while the rubber sector showed disappointing performance due to the increased cost of raw materials, the cable segment showed a notable growth in the urban and interurban telephone cables sector, 'through our subsidiary company SIRTI which was awarded government tenders', while poor performance was shown by the diversified activities. In the following financial year, when both the tyre and telephone cable sectors stagnated, the Company identified an interesting business segment: the production of cables for the electrification of the national railway lines, which was an emerging and fast-growing business. During the following financial year, the pneumatic sector – in which the Company had carried out significant technical improvements – seemed to improve, whereas the cable production sector continued to stagnate.

Towards the mid-1930s the international context became even more difficult, presenting prospects fraught with anguish and incertitude for Europe and the entire planet. The continued crisis was a tough trial for the governments in power, which were unable to implement effective policies to combat the ever-worsening situation. Queues outside soup kitchens were a common sight, in both Europe and the United States.

From November 1935 sanctions imposed on Italy due to its hostilities in Ethiopia blocked the exportation of Pirelli products to most European countries with the exception of Switzerland and Austria, as well as to most extra-European countries with the exception of Argentina and Brazil. This new scenario seemed to be a rerun of what had happened during the summer of 1914 following the breakout of hostilities; Europe split between warring factions, causing a revolution in the productive and logistic structure of the Pirelli group of companies. As in 1914, again just over two decades later the Company was not unprepared for these adverse conditions. The sanctions applied against Italy did not have any particular negative effect on the Milan-based company, which had already built up a diversified

---

to the regrouping policy operated by the companies operative in these sectors', while on 20 March 1939 the Board of Directors of Pirelli was informed that the Spanish factory in 'Villanueva had been blown up and burnt to the ground on the retreat of the 'Reds', despite the opposition of the workers and their families'.

international base. The rapid deterioration of the international situation, which promised very uncertain consequences, also posed a potential threat to the future of the foreign companies under the control of Società Italiana Pirelli. The Italian nationality of the controlling company could have represented an insurmountable problem for the future. The Belgian Holding was at the helm of a diversified international group spread over different countries which, in the case of conflict, could have found themselves on opposing fronts. Furthermore, the location of the Holding Company also posed other problems regarding the fate of Belgium in the eventuality of a new conflict. What had happened in the summer of 1914, with the German military campaign encroaching on neutral Belgium and blocked at the Marne by French armed forces, was still fresh in people's memories. For this reason, two possible solutions were studied and soon adopted. The first consisted in lessening the Italian character of Compagnie Internationale Pirelli, by the incorporation of a new ownership structure in which Società Italiana Pirelli held only 30% of the shareholding of the Belgian company directly, and making it more difficult to identify the majority shareholders for the remaining part.[22] The second consisted in the progressive liquidation of Compagnie Internationale Pirelli and the constitution of a new holding company in Switzerland with an endowment of equity of 12 million Swiss Francs to manage the Group's foreign activities. Compagnie Internationale Pirelli transferred to this new company – Pirelli Holding S.A. of Basel – the shareholdings that it held in the various companies in foreign countries.[23] Later, Pirelli Holding S.A. was merged with Volta, also incorporated

---

22  In restructuring the ownership of the holding of the foreign subsidiaries, Montenegro (1985) attributes importance to 'finding in the various countries where Pirelli operated and in particular, in those countries with strong financial markets, "friendly" groups with the financial wherewithal and willing to be associated in the management of an ever-growing economic empire'. Regarding this last point of view, the writer also agrees regarding the need for Pirelli to find new interlocutors in Switzerland, while the need to find local investors willing to participate in the companies operating in various counties is a characteristic for a later date.

23  This consists in the participation in the following companies: 1) Pirelli General Cable Works, Southampton; 2) Pirelli Limited, London; 3) Pirelli S.A. Platense, Buenos Aires; 4) Sociedad Immobiliare Italo-Argentina; 5) Pirelli Far East; 6) Motor Columbus. In 1936 CIP took over a company in Belgium which became Pirelli SACIC. Regarding this, Alberto Pirelli (1946) wrote: 'This is a company worth earmarking even as an example – another example is the tyre factory in Manresa and another example can be found in Italy – of companies which were on the verge of bankruptcy and which, after being taken over by Pirelli, and assisted with technical and commercial experience, following restructuring and modernisation, not only have they picked up their activity, but they have given excellent results'.

in Switzerland in 1929. The collocation of the Holding Company of the Group's foreign interests in Switzerland met two requirements which were becoming ever more pressing: the need to access a larger capital market and to take advantage of Switzerland's neutrality in the case of war.

During the second half of the 1930s, the link between Pirelli and the regime became progressively closer, which from a certain point of view, was inevitable. Indeed, Pirelli was also involved in military contracts for the war in Ethiopia, but progressively it was to become a close interlocutor of the regime in the climate of political and economic autocracy which reigned. Perhaps more than any other similar organisation, Pirelli was able to continue its research to propose new products for the market. This was particularly important for the rubber sector, a vital market segment, as the country was dependent on foreign supplies of the raw material. The Company promoted research into the production of synthetic rubber which would have allowed complete autonomy in this important commodity both for civil and military purposes.[24] To this aim, the government backed SAIGS (Società Italiana per la Gomma Sintetica), a joint venture between Pirelli and IRI (Institute for Industrial Reconstruction) for the production of synthetic rubber which would have been of utmost importance, even in the post-war period. The issue of self-dependence featured frequently in the Company's minutes and Board of Directors' reports over the next few years as the world slipped inexorably towards the outbreak of the Second World War. The Company's main focus was on production, which was to involve three areas: substituting natural rubber with synthetic rubber, the use of rayon instead of cotton, and the introduction of aluminium instead of copper. At intervals, the company documents strayed from the aseptic neutrality which had been their distinguishing trait to a more triumphal and celebratory note, as if losing their more contrary tone to become more of an encomium of the regime's economic policy. In the latter part of the 1930s, Pirelli found itself not only having to face economic sanctions imposed on Italy, but was also caught up in the Spanish Civil War. Catalonia, the historical location of the Company's Spanish plant, had remained solidly in Republican hands since the early period of the conflict. Little news of the Spanish conflict reached Italy, and in any case it was filtered by the propaganda machine of Franco's regime. Official

---

24 The Board of Directors' minutes give much information on how Nazi Germany dedicated much energy into researching the production of synthetic rubber.

documentation from that period show that the Pirelli plants in Spain did not suffer any damage during the years of the Civil War, partly because the area where the plant was located was far from the Republican front. The production plant was in reality commandeered – albeit unofficially – with the aim of upholding the Republican war effort. In the final part of the Civil War, just before the occupation of Barcelona by Franco's troops, the factory in Villanueva y Geltrù was burned to the ground by the retreating Republican army.[25]

In August 1939, and for the second time in only 25 years, Europe was plunged into a global conflict which was to upturn its political and economic equilibria. Once again, the spark was caused by the unresolved contrast between Germany and the Western democracies of France and Great Britain. Indeed, this was the third conflagration to break out on the banks of the Rhine since 1870. Following Germany's crushing invasion of Poland, France and the United Kingdom declared war on 3 September 1939. As in 1914, Italy did not enter the conflict immediately; it was Germany's impressive and lightning victory over France that later convinced the Fascist regime to enter the conflict, on 10 June 1940.

The rapid succession of events once again presented new challenges for the Group, which found itself not unprepared. These challenges were now represented by the Italian nationality of the shareholders of the Holding Company which controlled its foreign interests. To combat this, a far-sighted strategy had been adopted to rapidly dilute the relationship between two companies and at the same time to transfer the registered offices of the Holding to Switzerland, liquidating what remained of the Brussels-based company.

Although the Italian activities of the Group were conditioned by the scenario in Italy at that time, the continuation of the Group's foreign activities were also of vital importance. The clear-sightedness shown by the managers of the Group regarding its future was to constitute the basis for the Company's continuity in the post-conflict period. This was a very realistic approach, born from a lucid evaluation of the destiny of war. It is reasonable to imagine that Alberto Pirelli was

---

25  It is interesting to underline that this destruction came about notwithstanding the fervent opposition of the workers of the plant who, despite their Republican tendencies, considered absurd that the production plant be destroyed, putting their livelihood at risk. In the following years, the Company made requests to the Francoist government at various times to be able to take advantage of contributions to rebuild the plant, but no agreement was ever made.

well-versed in the Anglo-Saxon habits and customs prevailing on both sides of the Atlantic; he well understood the immense economic, financial and military possibilities of the United Kingdom and even more importantly of the United States, if the latter was to enter the war. All of this, however, passed unnoticed by the Rome–Berlin Axis. Not by chance Alberto Pirelli dedicated much effort in creating direct contact with the British authorities in the early years of the conflict, aimed at formalising the exclusion of the Swiss Holding from the blacklist of companies of hostile countries.

This objective was achieved without too much difficulty from the UK authorities, which accepted the principle of a negligible portion of Italian capital in the Pirelli Holding, but matters were not as easy with the US authorities. Following the Armistice of Cassibile on 8 September 1943, when the conflict was drawing to an end, the American authorities formally requested to be informed regarding the percentage of the equity of the Swiss Holding held by Italian nationals. Indeed, the Americans had already placed the Group's foreign companies on a blacklist, as they considered them as being controlled by a company belonging to a hostile foreign nation. In 1944, close negotiations were held in the attempt to sign a further agreement with both Allied governments. In order to be removed from the blacklist, Pirelli Holding made a series of important concessions to the UK and the US governments. These also consisted in allocating to a blocked deposit all those shares held by Italian nationals, the concession of the right of vote to the Allied governments and the removal of the Pirelli family members from the Board of Directors[26] of the Swiss company. This agreement was however to have a limited duration, as the end of the conflict and the victory of the Allied nations were near, but it was to take on greater importance once hostilities ceased. During the entire period of war, Pirelli Holding received continual information on the affairs of its subsidiary companies in all parts of the globe, apart from the plantations in the Far East, which had been taken over during the advance of the Japanese troops in Asia. In reality, the various subsidiary companies continued their activities with discrete results, even without any coordination from the Swiss Holding which was impossible due to the ongoing conflict. Good management practice had been

---

26 In that date, the Board of Directors of Pirelli Holding was formed by five persons: Alberto Pirelli – President and Chief Executive Officer, Piero Pirelli – Chief Executive Officer, Alfred Sarasin – Vice President, and Carl Abegg and Oscar Dollfuss – Directors. Of these five members of the Board of Directors, three were Swiss citizens.

TABLE 2.3. SHAREHOLDINGS OF SOCIETÀ
ITALIANA PIRELLI IN 1940

| Companies controlled by the Group |
| --- |
| Fabbrica Riunite Industrie Gomma di Torino |
| Società Anonima Cotonifici Riuniti |
| Società Anonima Prodotti Sala ed Affini (SAPSA) |
| Società del linoleum |
| Fabbrica Italiana Conduttori Elettrici di Napoli (FICE) |
| Pirelli Revere |
| Società Anonima Edilizia Mirabello |
| Società Italiana Reti Telefoniche Interurbane (SIRTI) |
| Società Anonima Filati Lucidi Davide Riboldi |
| Società Esercizi Automobilistici |
| Gruppo Gomma Sintetico |
| Società Partecipazioni e Finanziamenti Industriali |
| Società Italiana Conduttori Elettrici di Livorno (SICE) |

*Source: Minutes of the Board of Directors' meeting,
Società Italiana Pirelli, 4 March 1940*

instilled in the Group, not only in the Holding Company, but also in its subsidiaries worldwide, and these results were even more significant if one considers that technical assistance and consulting for the foreign subsidiaries had previously been delivered by the Italian head company. This ceased with the start of the war and commenced again only in 1946 at the end of the hostilities.

The issues that affected the Group in Italy, however, were different and of a much more serious nature. In the early years of the war, a decisive change was made in the future strategy and priorities of the Company, which seemed almost to fold upon itself as it faced numerous and continual emergencies in its attempt not to fall foul of the ongoing events. Paradoxically, phenomena such as industrial relations and more in general corporate welfare, which had previously been repressed by the economic policies of the totalitarian regime, made a comeback. Indeed, these were to become pressing issues on the political and economic agendas of the early years following the end of the conflict. The difference between this period and the period following the First World War was that the economic issues which had emerged from this period of conflict did not seem to cause any worry for the company managers. This most likely indicates that there had been a total and definitive separation between Pirelli and the Fascist regime. It is clear that Alberto Pirelli – the institutional expression of the Company – nourished various perplexities regarding the regime's ideology, but these were to become more concrete only after the start of the hostilities.

During the second part of the conflict, Pirelli was actively engaged in guaranteeing the continuity of its production and management as well as maintaining acceptable working conditions and levels of safety for its employees. In autumn 1942, the joint Anglo-American airborne forces started to bomb Italian cities, with Milan suffering a devastating bombardment on 24 October 1942. Later that year, the Company suffered more and more damage from Allied bombing, as Italian factories were prime targets. To face up to this new aspect of the hostilities, the Company decided to relocate its administrative activities to various sites, thus vacating its premises near Milan Central Station. Similarly, its logistics operations were also relocated to various other warehouses. In March 1943, the Pirelli employees also participated in the wave of strikes in protest against the regime and the conflict. This was the first workers' demonstration for 20 years and was a tough blow for the already shaky dictatorship. The situation then deteriorated following the armistice of 8 September 1943. The peninsula was divided between the Allied Forces which advanced from the South to engage the Axis Powers which held the North. This situation isolated the Company's Italian plants, which were forced to continue operating autonomously until liberation.

In the period between autumn 1943 and liberation, the level of production in Italy never ceased, but fell progressively, and despite the difficulties of the period a certain level was always maintained. It was as if industrial production and economic issues took second place in that dramatic moment in Italy's history. Soon after the armistice, the German military authorities seized control of the production in the Bicocca plant. This had the effect of creating a united front; everyone involved with the Company – the family, the managers, the staff and, most importantly, the workers – took up a decisive and inflexible stance against the Nazi-Fascist barbarity. This was manifested in a continual and systematic series of sabotage operations within the plant against the German and Fascist troops, and outside by supporting the Italian resistance which was supplied with money and materials.[27] The company archives contain a short memorandum which summarises clearly (16 June 1945) how this collaboration with the Resistance forces took place.

As in 1918 – albeit with an international scenario that seemed even more complex – again in 1945 the end of hostilities left many issues to be resolved regarding the future. The redoubtable Soviet Army had invaded all of Eastern Europe and the last battles on Italian soil had coincided with a bloody civil war that had brought the entire country to its knees. In the summer of 1945, public opinion gave a severe and not entirely unjustified verdict[28] against the entire category of industrialists whom they considered to be guilty of conniving with the Fascist regime. This regarded Pirelli as well as most of the other large Italian groups. On 7 May 1945 the Company was placed under receivership,[29] first under the control of Giuseppe Rossari, later to become Chief Executive Officer of the Group's cables company, and then Cesare Merzagora,[30] who later was to become the secretary to the Board of Directors.

No comprehensive documentation is available regarding that tumultuous period, although details are found in Alberto Pirelli's personal archive. In a memorandum sent to the Justice Commissioner of the National Liberation Committee (CLN) of the Lombardy Region and sent also in copy to Cesare Merzagora, Avvocato Becca stated that the Pirelli family owned approximately 27% of Pirelli & C., which in turn controlled 15% of Pirelli SpA. It was due to these shareholdings and

---

27  To this regard, Tranfaglia (2010) wrote: 'Alberto Pirelli, as his brother Piero, in the last twenty months of the war, supplied beyond any doubt financial aid to the Partisan organisations to which also Giovanni Pirelli was associated, having been engaged in combat in the Valle d'Aosta, in the attempt to escape from the Nazi request for goods and workforce, as has already happened in all North Italy.'

28  This was also translated into the Legislative Decree No. 472 of 4 August 1945, which established the termination of office of directors of private companies with a turnover greater than 1 million lira. The penalty for those who had held government positions during the Fascist regime was possible imprisonment.

29  We must also remember that the Republic of Salò, in a completely different context, also promulgated a provision for the nationalisation of Pirelli in January 1945. The minutes of the Board of Directors of 22 February shows a list of the companies and organisations which were subject to nationalisation, divided by group of productive activity.

30  Cesare Merzagora resigned as Director of Pirelli for the first time when he was appointed Minister for Foreign Trade.

## TABLE 2.4. SHAREHOLDINGS OF PIRELLI SpA IN 1945

| Group of production companies | Shareholding |
| --- | --- |
| Group: Tyres and Similar | Superga, Fabbriche riunite industria Gomma Torino |
| | Linoleum Salpa, Società per azioni |
| | Pirelli Revere |
| | Saga, Società applicazioni gomma antivibranti |
| Group: Synthetic Rubber | Saigs, Società anonima Italiana gomma sintetica |
| | Istituto per lo studio della gomma sintetica |
| Group: Conductors | Fongaro e C. Electrical Conductors |
| | Società italiana conduttori elettrici |
| Group: Textiles | Cantiere di Tolmezzo |
| | Filati Lucidi |
| Group: Automobiles | Società Lombarda servizi autostradali |
| | Società autostradale Friulana |
| Group: Real Estate | Gruppo Edilizia Mirabello |

*Source: Pirelli, minutes of the Board of Directors, 22 February 1945*

also for their personal capacities that the Pirelli brothers held positions in the companies pertaining to the Group. It was also stated that 'there is no evidence that Alberto Pirelli has held any significant role during the past regime up to the date of July 25, 1943. In the period after September 8 of the same year, he did not participate in the so-called Social Republic, but he also operated clandestinely to help the resistance and the liberation forces in various forms'. All of these actions led to the removal of the receivership, and the Company was returned to its rightful owners.

There is a report written by Merzagora on 7 May 1946, at the end of his period as receiver,[31] which summarised his activities which were focused on the continued

---

31 Tranfaglia (2010) reconstructed the personal affairs of Alberto Pirelli over the period

production and on improving the unstable financial situation. Probably during the period of receivership the important relations that Alberto Pirelli had cultivated with the Allies in the second part of the conflict played an important role in the decisions which were made following the end of the conflict. In that same period, Alberto Pirelli published the book *La Pirelli: vita di un'azienda industriale* (*Pirelli: Life of a Corporation*). This was a very interesting publication, containing a wealth of information on the history of the Company, supported by many personal recollections which turned out to be a welcome and useful digression by evoking some moments of the Company's corporate history.

The aim of this publication was closely connected to the urgency of that moment, the need to assert the role of the Company and of the Pirelli family to the new government and the Democratic state that was growing from the ashes of Fascism. Not accidentally the volume gave an analytical study of the activities of the Group until the end of the 1920s which then progressively were diluted into general or anecdotal reconstructions covering the next 15 years; although the text may only have touched on or even omitted specific details, it did not contain false or imprecise information on the dangerous liaisons that the Company had held with Fascism in the second part of the 1930s.

At the same time, the country was leaving Fascism and the tragedy of wartime behind, and on 2 June 1946 Italy became a Republic. Just a short time previously, the Pirelli Company had been handed back to its owners, but with a legacy fraught with complex challenges to be faced. The Group's financial structure had to be reorganised and additional resources were to be found before restarting production, and carrying out repairs and maintenance on the war-damaged machinery. At first, this was achieved by increasing the seasoned equity offering of the Limited Partnership which supplied liquidity to underwrite the pro-quota equity in the industrial company. In 1947, Pirelli significantly increased its equity, also by drawing on its reserve funds, from 2.2 billion, to 3.3 and later to 4.95 billion lira. This was an important manoeuvre which ended in 1948 when the Company

---

1945–1946. Alberto Pirelli was removed from his position as Chief Executive Officer of the Company in July 1945 and was subjected to a purge trial. In October 1945 Pirelli presented an official petition against the still ongoing trial which was accepted on 30 April 1946. This acceptance was a prelude to the return of Alberto Pirelli as Chief Executive Officer of the Company. Also Merzagora gave his essentially positive evaluation of the moderation on which the purge process was implemented for the class of industrialists.

deliberated a new increase in its equity of 7 billion, of which 5 billion lira was financed with the issue of new consideration shares and the remaining 2 billion lira from the restatement gain calculated on shares already issued.

The second step was equally urgent: to start up production and to source raw materials which were in short supply. This aspect was quickly resolved during the summer of 1946, due to supplies received from the Allied authorities (UNRRA), which in the following year was implemented more organically through the European Recovery Program, better known as the Marshall Plan. The logistics organisation imposed in wartime to allow the Company to survive the bombardments was also reorganised. The most pressing challenge, however, was to re-establish relations with the workforce. At the end of the war and with the fall of the dictatorship, any form of industrial relations had moved far into the backwaters. The Company managers were already aware of this phenomenon in the final years of the war and started to dedicate resources to a policy of corporate welfare. Immediately after the end of the war, the two Pirelli brothers constituted a Foundation bearing their names with the mission of improving economic conditions for company employees; a significant number of shares derived from the earnings of the Limited Partnership established many years previously were destined for this initiative. The Directors' report to the Annual Financial Statement of 30 September 1946[32] contained indications regarding the strategy that the Company was to adopt in the coming years. The key issue regarded industrial relations and, above all, the fear that the workforce could have been motivated by ideology in negotiating their rights and wages. In line with the Company's long-standing industrial relations policy, it was firmly stated that the workers' wages were to be pegged to the rate of production. In the company report, however, something else was also stated: a request for common intents and objectives to be shared between all stakeholders in the Company. This request was neither untoward nor out of place; it underlined once again the same principle that Giovanni Battista Pirelli had sustained on founding the Company.

In 1946 production started to increase, both in the cables and diversified activities sectors, while the tyre sector continued to suffer repercussions from

---

32 Also including the period of receivership, the financial year started in January 1945, and closed on 30 September 1946. The general part was stated in its entirety in the Directors' report to the company accounts of 30 September 1946, as this represented a programmed manifesto of what were to be the Company's objectives for the coming years.

the widespread black market which continued to operate openly. In 1947 the Company celebrated the 75th anniversary of its incorporation. This was a very important year, representing the relaunch of the Company's activities following the war, thanks also to the adhesion of the Marshall Plan,[33] from which Pirelli received credit to the sum of $4 million for the purchase of raw materials. Regular contacts and technical consulting services started again with the Group's foreign subsidiaries. The most serious problem faced by the foreign subsidiaries was how the dividends deriving from their activities could be paid to Pirelli Holding in Basel. This was a long-term and complex problem to resolve which was indirectly attributable to the architecture of the new international financial system, the celebrated Gold Exchange Standard signed in Bretton Woods in 1944. This scenario placed the survival of the foreign group at risk as unable to receive those dividends accrued by its subsidiaries. In Argentina, there were even rumours that Platense was to be nationalised, and to contrast this possible scenario, all activities of Platense were conferred to a new company, Industrie Pirelli, whose equity was later distributed among local investors. This strategy of involving local financers in the shareholdings of the foreign subsidiaries in relation to the real economic and financial scenarios of each country became progressively more common when dealing with the Group's foreign subsidiaries. This was to prove an excellent method of involving local oligarchies and was an important political strategy to counteract any possible ideological manoeuvres, favouring nationalisation of Pirelli assets or popular uprisings against foreign capital.

Towards the end of the 1940s, the most pressing problems of the post-war period seemed to have been more or less overcome. The victory of the Christian Democrats over the left-wing parties on 18 April 1948 unquestionably consolidated the Democratic and Western values of the newborn Italian Republic. There were two important issues in that period; firstly, the Company seemed to be entirely absent from any political arena, even at its top management level. Secondly, until the end of the 1940s, Pirelli had not launched any new product lines apart from its continuing research activities in the production of synthetic rubber which were carried out with IRI and Montecatini in the industrial plant in Ferrara. Towards the end of the 1940s, the Italian group's activities seemed to be more and more

---

33 Tranfaglia (2010) wrote that 'Alberto Pirelli participated in those years in high-level meetings on the implementation of the Marshall Plan in Europe and in particular, in Italy'.

concentrated into three business units: cables, pneumatic tyres and diversified activities. In line with these business units, three key Chief Executive Officers – Luigi Rossari for cables, Franco Brambilla for tyres and Emanuele Dubini for diversified activities – were co-opted to the Board of Directors and appointed Chief Executive Officers of their respective divisions, further consolidating the new structure. Moreover, in 1947, a bond loan for 4 billion lira expiring in 1966 and with a 5% face value interest rate was issued, and later, subscribers of this bond were offered the option of converting them into another bond issued in 1948 and expiring in 1973 and a 6% face value interest rate. The placement of this bond was carried out by the newly founded Mediobanca.[34]

---

34 Mediobanca was founded on 10 April 1946 as a special financial institution controlled by three national banks.

# CHAPTER 3

# From the End of World War II
# to the 1970s

At the beginning of the 1950s, the Italian economy grew rapidly. The need to start reconstruction after the war, and the more serene climate that prevailed at that time both in Italy and Europe following the incertitude and difficulties of the immediate post-war period were ideal for Pirelli to relaunch production of its traditional cables and pneumatic tyres.

In the early 1950s, the cable division benefited greatly from the revival of construction and the high demand for cables from the telecommunications sector. The situation for the tyre sector showed a similar trend, with impending mass motorisation promising excellent prospects for tyre producers. Although the period was undoubtedly favourable, the Company did not commit the error of considering its business returns as rent, but took advantage of the circumstances to invest in significant innovations, the construction of production plants, and real estate. The Company had achieved international excellence for its submarine isolated cables and high-tension, fluid-filled cables, while it began[1] launching new models in the tyre sector, of which the 'Cinturato' tyre was particularly successful, and Pirelli decided to build a new plant near Turin for the production of these tyres. The Company also continued its research into the production of synthetic rubber, a legacy of Italy's period of autarchy, but which had remained more an idea than an actual project, mainly due to the high costs involved. It was clear that

---

1    Pirelli also participated in the incorporation of the Autobianchi car company, together with Fiat and Edoardo Bianchi, a move which formed part of its strategy of participating in the setting up of companies with the potential of becoming good future customers. It does not seem plausible, as Scalfari and Turani (1974) suggest, that Pirelli's investment in Autobianchi was something of a challenge to Fiat.

synthetic rubber was the way of the future,[2] a challenge Pirelli was well prepared for, having already set up the company Società per la Gomma Sintetica together with the IRI and Montecatini. In order to meet these demands, both the Limited Partnership Pirelli & C. and Pirelli SpA would begin a programme of increasing their equity within the next few years and would also undergo major changes in their real estate assets. The Limited Partnership transferred its various properties to the real estate company Immobiliare Bligny, entirely controlled by Pirelli SpA, in exchange for shares in major Italian industrial companies. The same period[3] marked the beginning of the definitive restructuring of the area in front of Milan central railway station, and the construction of the 'Pirelli Skyscraper', to become the Group's management and administrative headquarters. The aim of this project was to group in a single site the offices previously located across various sites due to the war. Contemporaneously, the transfer of major share packages from the Operative Company to the Limited Partnership further confirmed the management role that Pirelli & C. had taken on.

During the early 1950s, the Directors' reports to the company financial statements reveal an increasing degree of macroeconomic analysis of the Italian situation, and at times even of the European scenario. The reports provide a thorough and methodical analysis, serving not only as a management report on the running of an industrial company, but also as what could almost be considered a series of conclusions regarding the overall performance of the economic and financial scenarios. Regarding Italy, these reports reiterate the need for close correlation between company productivity and growth of salaries. In an economy closed to the movement of capital, and with fixed exchange rates focused on exports – as the Italian system was at that time – this strategy proved to be effective, rigorous, simple and far-sighted. What is striking is the insistence with which this concept has been reiterated over time. During the 1950s, Italy saw no significant increase in inflation, and rises in wages were linked to the growth of the real economy. Indeed, in that period Confindustria, the General Confederation of Italian Industry, had adopted an immovable stance towards industrial relations which was in stark

---

2   It was probably for this reason that Pirelli made the costly decision to sell to a Dutch group the Southeast Asian rubber plantations it had owned since the early 1920s.

3   It was no coincidence that during the same Board meeting which decided this transfer, the Board was informed of the project to build new premises in Piazza Duca d'Aosta, opposite the Centrale railway station.

contrast with Pirelli's historically more open approach, and therefore the Company took a backseat role in the life of Confindustria. It is reasonable to assume that the company managers understood that the market had once again become competitive, and with the prospect of becoming ever more so. The scenario was ideal, but there was still a 'bottleneck' which prevented real economic growth. Thus, having decided to maintain a lower profile, both in the activities of Confindustria and more importantly in the political forum, the Directors' reports progressively took on the character of a programmed political economic manifesto.

Following the initial difficulties of the post-war period, Pirelli Holding deliberated on an important programme for its foreign operations involving the incorporation and acquisition of new companies and the reorganisation and expansion of those subsidiaries already part of the Group. The 50th anniversary of Pirelli's presence in Spain in 1952 was marked by various events. The Spanish plants were expanded, a qualified minority participation was acquired in a Canadian cable company, and an important programme was implemented to refurbish the historical UK-based production plant in Burton-on-Trent. A company was also incorporated in Mexico for the production of cables with the American group Anaconda Wire and Cables. To finance these operations, Pirelli Holding addressed the Swiss financial market and issued a series of bonds to raise the necessary equity, while the larger overseas industrial companies, such as Pirelli Brasileira, proved capable of independently issuing corporate bonds on the US market.

By the mid-1950s even Pirelli's foreign group had taken on a precise connotation; indeed, it had built up sufficient experience in the industrial sector to identify the various historical and institutional factors which characterised the capitalist economies in which it operated. The Group had developed consolidated relations in two main areas, Europe and Latin America,[4] making it possible to identify the general features and characteristics of the investments made in those countries up until then. As regards Europe, the investments made in Spain (the Group's first factory outside Italy) performed well overall, as did the production and trading activities in the United Kingdom, the second European country where the Group had set up production facilities, and which would prove to be a sound investment. The same, however, could not be said for France, even less so for Belgium, which both provided meagre returns on investment for Pirelli. In Latin America, the Group had been present in

---

4   Pirelli was marginally present in North America, and markedly so in Canada in the cable sector.

Brazil since the 1930s with its own production plant, but its first contacts with that country went back even further, to the early years of the century, and had proved to be profitable. In Argentina however, where Pirelli began operating in 1917, the results were not so positive. Notwithstanding the political, economic and social turmoil that both Latin American countries underwent during the 1900s, Pirelli realised that it was significantly more difficult to do business in Argentina than in Brazil.

On 26 March 1954, Alberto Pirelli's son Leopoldo – born on 27 August 1925 in Velate Varesino not far from Milan – was appointed as director of the Company, making him the third generation of the Pirelli family to work for the Group. When Leopoldo joined the Pirelli SpA Board of Directors he was 28 years old[5] and had already worked in the Company for some years after graduating in Engineering from Milan Polytechnic; he was following the same path that Giovanni Battista has traced for his sons Piero and Alberto. Piero Pirelli passed away unexpectedly on 7 August 1956, and this opened the door of the limited liability company Pirelli & C. to this young member of the family who would later be appointed Chief Executive Officer.[6] Following the death of Piero, who had been Chairman of Pirelli since 1932 (the year of the death of his father Giovanni Battista), the post of Chairman was taken on by Piero's brother Alberto, and the young Leopoldo became Deputy Chairman of the Company. Not long afterwards, in the spring of 1959, Alberto Pirelli suffered a stroke which left him partly paralysed on his right side. Despite remaining in his role as Chairman,[7] this severe impediment hastened the conferment of operational and managerial tasks to Leopoldo.

---

5   Alberto Pirelli and Ludovica Zambeletti had four children: Ninì, the eldest, was born in 1916; the second, Elena – born in 1917 – was the wife of Franco Brambilla, Chief Executive Officer of the Group's tyre sector; the third, Giovanni, was born on 3 August 1918; and then Leopoldo. Giovanni Pirelli chose a different lifestyle, opting for the humanities instead of economic disciplines. Tranfaglia (2010) wrote: 'In 1948, the eldest child left Milan and the Company for the Istituto Storico Croce in Naples where he followed lessons by its director, the historian Federico Chabod.' The not always easy relations between the father and son were described in the book *Legami e conflitti: Lettere 1931–1965* by Elena Pirelli Brambilla, published by Archinto.

6   Following the death of Giovanni Battista in 1932, and until the death of Piero in 1956, the two general parners of Pirelli & C. were the brothers Alberto and Piero. On the death of Piero, Leopoldo stepped in to take his place. Only later, in 1961, with the appointment of Egidio Gavazzi as partner, were there three directors of the limited liability company.

7   Leopoldo Pirelli became Chairman of Pirelli on 3 March 1965, while Alberto remained honorary Chairman until his death on 19 October 1971.

This change in company management came just before the intense period of economic growth in the late 1950s and early 1960s, which would come to be known as the economic boom, a period of exceptional growth for all the business units into which the Company had been organised. The cable segment, in its various components, benefitted 'in relation both to the increase in the production of electricity, and to the growth of the telephone sector'. The tyre sector rode the historic wave of mass motorisation, while the intense growth in demand carried the residual segment of diversified activities along with it.

The Group was not caught unprepared in the face of the favourable investment opportunities offered by the dynamic and effervescent market of the time. Ever-faithful to its traditions, the Company had continued to invest in research and to launch new products onto the market, such as the new BS3 tyre, presented at the Turin Auto Show. On 5 April 1960, the Group's general meetings were held 'in the brand-new complex called the Pirelli Centre'. This was the official inauguration of the famous Pirelli Tower, the only one in the Lombardy metropolis and which became the symbol for the now global Group, and also a familiar landmark for the city of Milan. For anyone leaving Milan Central Station – an imposing monument built by the Fascist regime in a desire to express its splendour – the Pirelli Tower, an elongated form which evokes the form of a sailing boat, is seen to the right. There could not be a more pitiless juxtaposition: the Central Station shows no vertical dynamism whatsoever; indeed, it seems to project itself towards the ground, whereas the Pirelli Tower is tall, *erectum ad sidera*.[8] Designed by Giò Ponti with the collaboration of Pierluigi Nervi, it was a truly avant-garde project for those years.

Various equity operations were effected to finance these investments, which served to further strengthen the financial structures of the various companies within the Group. Pirelli & C. effected an initial increase in equity from 2.64 to 4.95 billion lira by increasing the nominal value of its shares, and the from 4.95 to

---

8   The Tower project had undergone a long period of gestation. It had been presented to the building commission of the Milan City Council on 2 February 1955, but the definitive agreement between the municipality and Pirelli was only finalised on 27 August 1958 – with the definitive terms regarding the handing-over of the area and the implementation of the plan. Regarding the finished project, Walter McQuade in *Architectural Forum* (1961) writes: 'This is a building which would honour any city in the world, especially vertical New York. It is a building which has plenty to teach those who still consciously practice architecture. It is a building that most architects would have been proud to have designed, one of those legacies that mankind can leave behind itself.'

TABLE 3.1. EVOLUTION OF THE NET PROFIT FOR THE
YEAR AND TURNOVER OF PIRELLI SPA (1948–1958)

| | Net profit | Turnover | | |
|---|---|---|---|---|
| | for the year | Gross revenue from industrial & trading activities | Dividends, interest & miscellaneous income | Total turnover |
| 1948 | 1,108,212,791 | 3,891,677,136 | 476,171,477 | 4,367,848,613 |
| 1950 | 1,834,004,968 | 3,656,855,748 | 847,709,024 | 4,504,564,772 |
| 1952 | 2,487,555,189 | 7,175,603,535 | 1,326,902,049 | 8,502,505,584 |
| 1954 | 3,318,960,821 | 9,196,681,575 | 2,217,390,683 | 11,414,072,258 |
| 1956 | 3,477,488,546 | 9,322,508,361 | 2,416,814,073 | 11,739,322,434 |
| 1958 | 3,570,658,961 | 9,679,693,433 | 3,231,587,426 | 12,911,280,859 |

*Source: Our calculations from the Pirelli SpA Annual Financial Statements*

6 billion lira with the issue of new shares which were underwritten by the Group's directors and shareholders.

Société Internationale Pirelli, meanwhile, effected an increase in equity from 27 to 36 million Swiss francs, taking advantage of the positive performance of the Swiss financial market. The increase of equity of Société Internationale was used to finance the construction of tyre production plants in Greece and Turkey, two countries where the Group was not yet operative, both of which seemed to offer promising investment opportunities. Initially, a production plant was constructed in Patras in Greece as there was no local producer of any significance. Turkey also represented an ideal opportunity to enter a country with optimal growth prospects, and thus a further production plant was built in Izmit on the Aegean coast,[9] in collaboration with local investors.[10] The Company's ability to involve the

---

9   It was a plant which is still active, used by Pirelli since 2010 to supply tyres to Formula One racing.

10  Aside from Israel, constantly exposed to the threat of war, Turkey was the country which

local economic and financial communities would prove decisive in the following decade, in which multinationals were to suffer strong ideological accusations of exploitation in many emerging countries.

Despite the Group's resolute growth strategy on the various continents and on the outer fringes of Europe, at the end of the 1950s, the most interesting prospects for the Group were in Europe. The Treaty of Rome, signed in 1957, represented the first step in a long and complex process of European integration. Some form of pan-European union was considered the best solution to combat the risk of a new war in Europe,[11] and its creation so soon after the Second World War lent further weight to the project. The idea of a form of economic integration between various European countries was a new perspective for that time, one which was prophetic in certain ways. It meant establishing permanent peace on the banks of the Rhine, where the Graeco-Roman and the Germanic people – two great civilisations of Europe – met and clashed in ancient times, and where two world wars had broken out in the 20th century. The Kantian prophecy of 'perpetual peace' finally seemed to be taking shape on European soil.[12]

In this context of change and innovation, tracing the contours of the future corporate Europe proved to be no easy task. The management of Pirelli set to work on this monumental undertaking, soon realising that the process of European integration would create a series of risks, but also opportunities. The element of risk arose from the greater competition between the various producers, due to the removal of the remaining customs barriers protecting its domestic products. Pirelli had no particular fears in this regard: its almost 100 years of history as a multinational group had been a constant quest to provide the maximum overall efficiency of its various productive factors, whether technical, economic,

---

provided the best guarantees to foreign investors wishing to invest in the Middle East, thanks to the widespread operations to secularise the State and modernisation of the institutions following the dissolution of the Ottoman Empire, under the leadership of Mustafa Kemal (1880–1938), widely known as Ataturk.

11  In an interview on 11 December 2009, Carlo Azeglio Ciampi, the former President of Italy, reminded me that the setting up of the single currency had been motivated by reasons which were both economic and political in nature, the latter being a way of averting war in Europe. He told me he considered it fundamental that the euro should be created by his generation, which still had a 'living historical memory' of past conflict as it had seen the Second World War devastate Europe.

12  In 1795 Immanuel Kant (1724–1804) wrote a prophetic essay called 'Perpetual Peace'.

commercial or logistic. Its survival over the long term showed that this shrewd combination of factors had generated good results. The potential opportunities offered by integration, however, were more difficult to define, ranging from the creation of a much larger market of consumers, to the possibility of accessing a financial market which was much larger than the individual national markets.[13] Pirelli management was aware of all these factors; its reports, however, give much greater emphasis to the potential opportunities than the understandable risks associated with the unknown nature of the challenge that lay ahead. The introduction of the new European economic area also required greater coordination between Pirelli SpA and Société Internationale Pirelli, one which went beyond the consolidated division of roles of the former as the Holding Company of the Group's activities in Italy, and that of the latter, which coordinated all its overseas activities. It was also for these reasons that the Company decided to undergo a complex process of reorganisation involving a significant increase in equity as well as the reallocation of various share packages, to be transferred to Pirelli SpA by Société Internationale Pirelli. The latter would transfer a series of shares representing approximately 40% of the total of its activities in exchange for 8 million shares in Pirelli SpA. In this way, the overseas holding company would become one of the Italian group's biggest shareholders, with a capital share of more than 10% and strengthening its control of Pirelli SpA.

The assets consisted of shares in various European and non-European companies, the most significant from four countries in particular: Spain, United Kingdom, Brazil and Argentina. This contribution was one element in a larger operation involving the Group's equity aimed at reorganising its financial structure in the following manner; Pirelli would issue a bond for the sum of 20 billion lira, to be placed on the market with a coupon rate of 5.5%, expiring in 1980, an operation to be carried out by Mediobanca, thus increasing its equity from 30 to 68 billion lira. This considerable increase in equity was to be effectuated partly using capital reserves, for a sum of approximately 15 billion lira, while the remaining part to be financed by the issue of new shares would be offered first to the Company shareholders for a net total equal to the 8 billion lira previously assigned to Société Internationale.

---

13 It was no coincidence that the Company requested listing of the share on the main stock markets of Paris, Frankfurt and Amsterdam, with the aim of reserving the shares deriving from a future capital increase for its foreign investors.

In the early 1960s, when the economic climate continued to be favourable, these significant increases of the Company's equity contributed to financing the complete restructuring of the Company's production facilities in Italy, including the tyre plants in Settimo Torinese, Figline Valdarno, Rovereto and Pizzighettone, and the Arco Felice[14] cable factory near Naples. Société Internationale Pirelli also launched a significant investment programme which involved building production plants in Greece and Turkey, in Tarragona in Spain, as well as a new cable factory in Brazil in the state of Rio Grande do Sul and expanding its high-tension cable production plant in Eastleigh, UK.

Pirelli SpA also acquired a West German tyre production company, Veith Gummiwerke of Sandbach, near Frankfurt-am-Main, with about 7% of the market share of the German tyre market and a turnover of approximately a quarter of Pirelli's tyre business unit. This was the first time that Pirelli had acquired a medium-large company with consolidated market experience instead of setting up a new company. This event also marked the Group's first foray into the German market with a production company acquired by Pirelli SpA and not by Société Internationale Pirelli. This decision was in line with the Company's new policy, adopted following its reorganisation in 1962; as the Federal Republic of Germany was part of the European Common Market, it was necessary for this stake to be held by the Milan-based parent company. While the years of great economic expansion were coming to a close, many unresolved issues tempered by the tumultuous years of growth began to emerge once more in the management reports, and above all in the Company's financial statements. Towards the end of 1963, the rapid economic growth registered in the previous years began to slow significantly. In a more stationary economic climate, the rate of growth of salaries began to outstrip productivity which, in the 1964 financial year, sent the Company's financial statements slightly into the red, for the first time in history.[15] Taking on the

---

14  The 1955 edition of the Rivista Pirelli magazine gives a brief description of the Arco Felice plant: 'The plant, currently nearing completion, stands on the beautiful bay of Arco Felice, covering an area of 75,000 square metres, which once belonged to the Armstrong shipbuilders. The Company was faced with the two-fold problem of developing its cable production in general, and of rationally locating the production of its underwater cables, previously divided between Bicocca of Milan, for construction of the cores, and La Spezia for the insulation.'

15  The loss amounted to 74 million lira, excluding the first six months of 1873, in which a negative economic result was registered due to the fact it was the start-up of a company which was highly innovative for its time.

## Table 3.2. Shares transferred from Société Internationale Pirelli to Pirelli SpA on 19 June 1962

| Company name |
| --- |
| Comercial Pirelli S.A., Barcelona |
| Compañía de Inversiones, Barcelona |
| Productos Pirelli S.A., Barcelona |
| Pirelli Limited, London |
| Pirelli General Cable Works, London |
| Industrias Pirelli S.A., Buenos Aires |
| Pirelli S.A. Platense, Buenos Aires |
| Pirelli S.A. Companhia Industrial, Sao Paulo |
| Pirelli Cables Conduits (Canada) |
| Condumex Anaconda Pirelli (Mexico) |
| Pirelli Hellas, Athens |
| Turk Pirelli, Istanbul |

| Geographical areas | Indicative current value of the shares transferred per geographic area (millions of Swiss francs) |
| --- | --- |
| Spain | 58–60 |
| Great Britain | 86–88 |
| Argentina | 49–50 |
| Brazil | 71–72 |
| Canada | 8 |
| Mexico | 8 |
| Greece | 8 |
| Turkey | 10 |
| Total | Approximately 300 |

*Source: Minutes of the Pirelli SpA Board of Directors' meeting held on 19 June 1962*

role of Company Chairman previously held by his father Alberto[16] on 3 March 1965, Leopoldo Pirelli had an arduous task ahead of him. Apart from the losses registered in the 1964 financial year, it was the general industrial scenario in Italy that represented a more worrying prospect for the Group. In the mid-1960s, the prospects of doing business in Italy were very uncertain for any company. This was not only due to the economic and political scenarios, but also the institutional context. Indeed, the private sector faced the prospect of public intervention in the country's economy, a concern heightened by the State's decision to nationalise the electric utilities companies in 1962.

These apparent contradictions in the economy had roots far in the past, and had never been resolved definitely. In the 1930s, the aim of public intervention in the economy was to protect Italy's unstable industrial and financial systems from the violent effects of the recession, a strategy similar to that adopted by the United States in later years following the 2007–2009 financial crisis. The beginning of the Second World War and the end of the Fascist regime had not resolved the dilemma regarding how such an intervention should be implemented, and for how long. Even the right-wing governments that successively came to power had chosen to maintain this ambiguous stance which affected the industrial sector above all, since the public nature of the Italian financial system at that time remained unquestioned. These events had somehow moved into the background, partly due to the spectacular performance of the Italian economy in the 1950s and early 1960s. The change in economic circumstances brought the issue of the relationship between public and private enterprise back to the forefront of the economic and institutional debate. The lack of economic growth and a major plan for public investment in infrastructure put private investment at risk. Furthermore, the space left for the private sector risked becoming excessively limited, squeezed as these enterprises were between the need to balance the books – especially regarding labour costs – and finding new investment opportunities when their most feared competitor

---

16 On 2 April 1965, date of the first general meeting presided over by Leopoldo, the Board of the Company consisted of the following members: Alberto Pirelli, Honorary Chairman; Leopoldo Pirelli, Chairman; Angelo Costa, Deputy Chairman; managing directors Franco Brambilla, Emanuele Dubini and Luigi Rossari; and directors Mario Braschi, Luigi Bruno, Giovanni Falck, Giovanni Fummi, Albert Nussbaumer, Luigi Orlando, Eugenio Radice Fossati and Prospero Trissino da Lodi. The Board of Statutory Auditors was made up of Guido Rossi as Chairman and Enrico Biamonti and Angelo Corridori as standing statutory auditors.

had become the State. There was also another danger, which was even subtler and more difficult to combat. Until then, Pirelli's growth strategy had been based on the Company's ability to obtain supplies by acquiring shares in potential client companies. This manner of procuring business had pushed into the background any question regarding economy of scale or any other related synergies, including the quest for dialogue with the political sector, or at least in Italy. Continuing this strategy would now prove more difficult, if not impossible, as most customers in the cable sector were state-controlled companies, and thus demand was dependent on the investment decisions of these enterprises.

The directors of Pirelli were well aware of this situation, as seen by the lengthy discussion in the 1964 budget report. The position expressed is clear: the State has an important role to play, one of regulating and implementing credible monetary and fiscal policies which are 'not fragmentary or contradictory', but which must not invade the sphere of private economic activity. For this reason, the report deals with the most important points regarding this issue, asking that 'the merits of private enterprise be recognised', but above all that 'the rights of capital should be recognised; it is absurd to think that the economy can develop without adequate remuneration'.[17] Although this last statement may seem paradoxical, it is one which is ahead of its time, providing a snapshot of the spirit which would characterise the years to come. Indeed what worried the business world was the spreading of a certain mentality throughout the social, political and economic sectors of Italy, one ideologically opposed to entrepreneurial activity, even before entering in conflict with the concept of capital. Faithful to its history and values, the Company chose the path of mediating between the demands of the various stakeholders and those of its workers, against a political backdrop which proved to be increasingly opposed – if not downright hostile – to the reasoning of industry and its investors.

The nationalisation of the electric utilities companies, as mentioned previously, also affected Pirelli as it involved transferring industrial assets to the State in exchange for compensation to the value of 1,500 billion lira, to be paid over a period of 12 years. Many of these companies therefore found themselves deprived

---

17  The long interview given by Leopoldo Pirelli to Piero Ottone and published in *Corriere della Sera* on 27 January 1966 describes the key elements of the Company and how it intended to deal with the ever-more complex issue of company information, probably intended as a kind of disclosure of the functioning of a large company, for a public audience which knew little about what this involved.

of their core businesses which had been transferred to the State, but with large sums of liquidity. Nevertheless, the endowment of liquidity that the former electric utilities companies would receive as compensation from the State, and the fact they were mainly publicly held companies,[18] made them interesting prospects for companies for investment. In this context, Pirelli & C. Limited Liability Partnership decided on a merger through acquisition of three former utilities companies: the hydroelectric company Alto Chiese, the electrical company Verbanese and the Alta Toscana hydroelectric company, with compensation credits of just over 8 billion lira, and an increase in equity from 12 to 20 billion lira at the same time, to meet the rights of the merged companies' shareholders.

In the same period, Pirelli was faced with a major technological challenge in the tyre sector, due to the launch of the new 'radial tyre'[19] by French company Michelin, which soon became the market standard. The Company was forced to follow suit, requiring it to overcome numerous technical difficulties, which were only solved in the 1970s with the launch of its P7 and P3 series. The previous 'Cinturato' tyre introduced in the 1950s, whose innovative advertising campaigns were created by the Dutchman Bob Noorda, had represented a technological turning point, and it was this model which had accompanied the process of mass motorisation in Italy.

In the late 1970s, the Group's growth dynamic was asymmetrical: while growth and investment abroad continued, both in South America and in those eastern European countries with planned economies, especially Romania and the USSR – countries which at that time represented the new business frontier – the situation in Italy for the Milan-based company was far from easy. While its economic activity continued in a reasonably satisfactory manner, thanks to its consolidated diversification, industrial relations became increasingly explosive. In the late

---

18  Despite the unavailability of analytical data regarding the Company's ownership structure, it is known that its body of shareholders was somewhat fragmented during the 1960s. For this reason, a reinforcement of the Company assets and liabilities via a merger by acquisition had as a crucial element the nature of the body of shareholders of the incorporated company, which necessarily had to be a public company so as not to jeopardise the balance of different interests and the managerial role.

19  To describe this tyre, Manca (2005) writes: 'It was a new type of tyre, whose casing was built on steel wires, substituting the overlapping plies of traditional tyres. The part under the tread was made from rayon body cords, running at right angles to the centre of the tyre, giving a tyre with fewer layers of body cords on the sidewall, allowing the tyre to flex more.'

1960s, the growth rate of salaries exceeded that of productivity; for many political and ideological reasons, neither industry nor the political parties were willing or able to correct this drift, which jeopardised the economic equilibrium of corporate Italy up to the early 1980s. The results of this situation were rates of inflation and of increase in public debt significantly higher than those of other major European countries which were grappling with similar problems.

The years 1968 and 1969 were characterised by violent outbreaks of unrest. What had been predicted as far back as the early 1950s – perhaps as an act of propitiation – was beginning to materialise. In the minutes of the Board of Directors' meeting of 29 November 1968, the detailed description of these episodes – strikes, picketing and suspension of production – has all the traits of a neorealist film. One comment in particular is especially striking: 'The protests, which began over a problem related to piece-work, has swelled into something much bigger and more violent, giving the distinct impression that our company is nothing more than a pawn in a larger game, whose boundaries we are unable to see.' The object being negotiated – or rather, debated – was no longer the issue of payment for work, but the very nature and economic and social meanings attributed to the concept of what a corporation represented,[20] meaning that the strikes formed part of a much broader political struggle. Despite Giovanni Battista Pirelli's moral legacy of leaving politics outside the factory gates, as the Company prepared to enter its second century it found itself in a situation completely different to what had been imagined by its founder all those years ago. Further evidence of this comes from the description of an act of sabotage involving tyres from its associated Greek and Spanish subsidiaries, scattered in retaliation all over the plant, 'in the most unlikely places', as a 'serious act of provocation', although the author of the minutes does not explain the reasons why the arrival of railway wagons filled with Greek- and Spanish-produced tyres should provoke such a reaction. The doubt remains as to whether this arrival had been interpreted as an act of strikebreaking by the distant Greek and Spanish plants; the act may also have been intended to punish the Company for its 'intrinsic conspiracy' with the right-wing regimes[21] governing these countries in 1969.

---

20  It is worthwhile remembering that some of the cells of the future Red Brigades originated in the Company's Bicocca production plant.

21  Manca (2005) describes it as 'the 'wild night of September 1969'. The entire episode is described as follows: 'The operation was interpreted as a provocation by the protesting

In this situation, Pirelli maintained a stance that was both responsible and resolute. While rejecting those requests it deemed unacceptable, it did also agree to some other requests put forward, leading to the signing of an agreement on 21 December 1968. Despite the fact that the stipulation of this agreement led to a significant increase in costs for Pirelli, the protests continued throughout 1969, a year which ended with an unwillingness on the Company's part to agree to further wage rises, since 'agreeing to such demands would seriously compromise its competitiveness, with clear prejudice to the interests of the company and its workers'. Once again, the historic stance adopted by Giovanni Battista Pirelli in his time was reiterated, a pioneering version of the stakeholders vision, according to which any conflict should not be between the various stakeholders in the Company, but between the Company and its competitors on the global market. To this regard, it is useful to underline the statement contained in the SIP (Société Internationale Pirelli) 1968/1969 budget report which draws attention to the high quality of the Group's products, 'one which – as the Group prepares to enter its second century – continues to safe guard and to strengthen the production carrying the name of Pirelli'. A comment which attests to a proud and stubborn recognition of belonging to a long and glorious tradition of industrial culture, one which would be severely put to the test over the course of the 1970s.

---

workers, who reacted by unloading the tyres and using them to barricade the doors of the factory. The night which followed was one of violence and devastation: around thirty vehicles were overturned and smashed, office windows were broken, plants ripped up, various production departments damaged and the canteen devastated.'

# CHAPTER 4

# The Quest for Size Efficiency

The 1960s had drawn to a close in a vortex of increasing contradictions which jeopardised the prospects of the Company, not only in terms of growth, but also for its very survival. Although competition was increasing on an international level, the best of the Group's managerial and economic resources were being taken up with the complex issue of industrial relations. The difficult economic circumstances characterising the late 1960s had caught the Group at a time of transition to a new generation, which was also the prelude to a change in its management structure and governance. Leopoldo Pirelli was aware of the difficulty with which the Company had reacted to Michelin's innovative radial tyre which was characterised by slowness and uncertainty.[1] The effects of this delay had affected Pirelli's income statement, having reduced its market share in the 'original equipment' and 'spare parts' business sectors in favour of its French competitor. Leopoldo Pirelli believed that the source of this delay and growing inefficiencies lay in the insufficient size of the Company's tyre business unit, which did not allow for appreciable cost synergies or the availability of sufficient critical mass to allow investment in research and development with regard to turnover.

There was an element of truth in this diagnosis, which could be extended to

---

1    Manca (2005) describes the attitude of the managers of Pirelli's tyre business unit, led by Franco Brambilla – Elena Pirelli's husband and Leopoldo's brother-in-law – who were required to respond to the innovative skills of their French competitor. Manca writes: 'Brambilla trusted the Company's engineers greatly, because the Group had always shown great efficiency and reliability. Pirelli was also notorious for its emphasis on product quality, having won various international awards in addition to the numerous patents and licences filed by the Company each year, proof of an undeniable aptitude for innovation. And so, faced with this difficult challenge, after his initial reaction of incredulity and irritation, Brambilla and his staff responded with optimism and will, setting themselves targets that would soon prove to be beyond their reach. It was certainly not easy to determine how to manage the recovery, or gauge how long it would take, and the entire process was a roller coaster of euphoria and depression.'

much of the history of the Company's tyre segment, from the start of its operations to the beginning of the 20th century. Until then, however, performance in this segment had been good, even in times of intense competition, such as during the early years of marketing a new product, and in the period following the Second World War. While the size factor was undoubtedly an important issue for the tyre sector, it is reasonable to assume that excessive importance had been attributed to this, as often happened in those years, in real managerial situations and academic studies alike. The cause of the delay and inefficiencies observed by Leopoldo Pirelli lay mainly in the economic and political problems of the country. Although the Company could do little about these external factors, it was not completely helpless. Indeed this was probably the motivation behind Leopoldo Pirelli's decision to chair the Confindustria commission, tasked with reforming and innovating the statute of the trade association.[2] Leopoldo continued his father Alberto's tradition of civic engagement, albeit using different means and approaches. A second and serious source of problems in the Company lay in the progressive weakening of its management structure, at a very time when difficulties external to the Company were increasing.

In light of the above, the Company strategy during Leopoldo Pirelli's period as Chairman was focused on research and development of opportunities to integrate various tyre producers in Europe. There were three possible contenders: Michelin, Continental and Dunlop. The French company was much larger than Pirelli, and any integration with Michelin would mean an acquisition of Pirelli. The German company Continental was similar in size to Pirelli, but posed problems of geographical overlap and of corporate governance, issues which would prove highly problematic in the case of an international union. Thus the Chairman of Pirelli set up negotiations with the British company Dunlop to discuss the possibility of a merger.[3] In February 1970 the Pirelli Board of Directors examined

---

2   In addition to Leopoldo Pirelli, the 'Pirelli Commission' was composed of Gianni Agnelli, Giuseppe Bordogna, Renato Buoncristiani, Furio Cicogna, Roberto Olivetti, Giuseppe Pellicanò, Enrico Salza and Giuseppe Vallarino Gancia. Leopoldo Pirelli viewed it as an important commitment, in keeping with Pirelli's tradition of civic engagement in the communities where his activities were based, and in Italy first and foremost.

3   During their interviews with the author, both Marco Tronchetti Provera and Alberto Pirelli stressed the excellent personal relationship that developed between Leopoldo Pirelli and Reay Geddes, chairman of Dunlop.

'the proposed integration between the Pirelli Group, Société Internationale Pirelli and the Dunlop Group'. Dunlop was slightly larger than Pirelli, in terms of both turnover and number of employees and plants, but not in terms of profitability.[4] The intended project was ambitious, involving the integration of the two groups' industrial activities, which were complementary in product range[5] and geographical location. Pirelli was present in Europe and Latin America, while Dunlop covered what was once the British Empire and more recently the Commonwealth, with facilities in Asia, Africa, North America and Oceania. The Group resulting from the merging of Dunlop with Pirelli would occupy third place on the world tyre market. As this operation was a merger of equals, an aggregation formula was chosen with a strategic plan taking into account the needs of each business unit in the entire Group, but without requiring that the three controlling companies merge, but could continue to operate as separate financial holdings. For this reason, a formula was established whereby 'each of the two groups took substantial ownership stakes of between 40% and 49% in the current and future associated industrial companies of the other', thus each of the two groups would constitute a qualified minority shareholder in the other's industrial companies. The diverse participation of the minority partner was motivated by the different geographical locations of the various companies; the 49% minority shareholding format was applied to British, Italian or Common Market countries, whereas the 40% minority shareholding format was applied to extra-European countries.[6] This complex corporate architecture also required that the three parent companies return their respective shareholdings in the event that the agreement was dissolved. Responsibility for the new group, which would take the name of Union Dunlop/Pirelli (or simply

---

4   At the time of the 1969 end of year financial statement, Pirelli had a minor total turnover of 670 billion lira, 82 factories and 76,000 employees, 42,000 of which were in Italy, while Dunlop had a turnover of 730 billion lira, with 102 plants and 102,000 employees.

5   Dunlop had focused its production in the tyre and diversified products segment, but was not involved in the cables market.

6   In reality, Société Internationale Pirelli also played an important role in the redistribution of the shareholdings in the non-European companies. In particular, in the event that it was the Pirelli Group which surrendered the minority share while continuing to hold 60%, the majority share would be divided between the 40% held by Pirelli SpA and the 20% held by SIP. If the Pirelli Group took on the minority share of 40%, this would be divided equally between Pirelli and SIP.

Union), would lie with a central steering committee[7] led by the Chairmen of the two groups, Leopoldo Pirelli and Reay Geddes,[8] and a total of eight managing directors, four from each group.

The decision not to proceed with a cross-border merger which would have rendered the entire operation easier, but probably politically impracticable, required a complex and preparatory reorganisation of the Company. All shares in the Group's Italian industrial controlled and associated companies were concentrated in a company called Industrie Pirelli,[9] 49% of which was then transferred to Dunlop. These preliminary operations were required to finalise the agreement with Dunlop, signed in London 'at four o'clock in the morning of Tuesday 10 November [1970] following another day of intense negotiations'.[10] The signing of the agreement with Dunlop was an excellent outcome with interesting prospects, but replete with unknown elements easy to identify, but difficult to quantify. While

---

7   Manca (2005) offers a good description of the complicated organisational formula adopted in the Union: 'The formula adopted for the Union was based on a series of committees with equal powers and extremely clear terms of reference, consisting of three tasks: to study the coordination of the two groups' strategies, to collect information relating to the topics under discussion and to pass this to the boards of directors of the two companies, so that the appropriate decisions could be made. Various other committees (two sectorial, the others functional) with equal powers revolved around the central committee, with the generic names Tyrco (Tyre Committee); Cipco (Consumer and Industrial Products Committee); Finco (Finance Committee); Planco (Planning Committee); Perco (Personal Committee) and others. The meetings of the central committee took place in London and Milan in alternation; they began in the late morning to allow guests to arrive from various countries, and ended in the late afternoon, with a working breakfast in the middle.'

8   Manca (2005) provides the following description of Reay Geddes: 'Tall, handsome, authoritative, with a spirit younger than his years, he loved Italy. He loved to say of himself, with typically British modesty that he had "no particular managerial, financial or scientific qualifications, but simply the innate gift of being able to recognise a person's qualities at first sight". Educated at Eton and Cambridge, a Midland Bank official, he joined Dunlop before the outbreak of the Second World War and climbed through its managerial ranks, culminating in him leading various inquiry commissions and being honoured as Baronet.'

9   Pirelli would have transferred its industrial shareholdings to Industrie Pirelli. The latter would effect an equity increase in favour of Pirelli in respect of the transferred shareholdings. The Dunlop Group would do the same; the transferee and transferor companies would be called Dunlop Holding and Dunlop respectively.

10  The creation of the Union also led to the closing of Pirelli's financial year being moved from 31 December to 30 April, because of timing of the presentation of the British companies' accounting sheets. For this reason, the Union's first financial year had the unusual duration of 16 months, from 1 January 1971 to 30 April 1972.

the chosen arrangement had made it possible to conclude negotiations and had led to the setting up of an international group – somewhat revolutionary according to those years – many of the major industrial management issues had remained unresolved or were momentarily shelved. More specifically, the structure of the merger risked relegating benefits arising from cost synergies of an industrial nature to the sidelines, while rendering those linked to potentially interesting and mutually beneficial research and development activities, though over time Dunlop would reveal itself to be technologically underdeveloped and less inclined toward innovation than Pirelli.

Certain issues remained unresolved, primarily associated with financing the new development and the settlement by the parent companies of any debts accrued by subsidiaries of the new group. One important issue, not properly examined in the planning phase, was the intrinsic difference between the Anglosphere approach to financing adopted by Dunlop and the more Italian or European model used by Pirelli. It could be said that the entire Union was characterised by a significant degree of risk with regard to the different regulation standards and requirements.

This all became clear during the groups' first shared financial year, which coincided with the death of Alberto Pirelli on 19 October 1971.[11] The life of the Pirelli founder's second son had spanned an era of extraordinary economic, cultural and scientific growth in which Pirelli had actively and consciously participated – becoming a leading Italian business and a major multinational company[12] – and

---

11  On 20 October, the Italian daily financial newspaper *Il Sole 24 Ore* paid tribute to Alberto Pirelli in an article by Gavino Manca: 'Always attentive, despite his age and many commitments, to the evolution of ideas throughout the world, Alberto Pirelli read Snow's essay on "two cultures" – humanist and technocratic – more than ten years ago. Following a number of astute comments – some of which were critical – he observed that, as an industrialist, he considered himself to have a certain humanist mentality; but perhaps the inverse was more true of him, borne out by the vivid, typically humanist conscience, of subordination of the Economic to the Political, and the Political to the Moral. The truth is that Alberto Pirelli's personality, like all truly complete personalities, resists any attempt at classification, a process which is naturally limiting.'

12  Public opinion in the 1970s grew progressively more hostile to industry and to capitalism. In this climate, multinational companies – often deemed guilty (and at times justifiably so) of engineering the indiscriminate exploitation of Third World countries by the West – became the object of much criticism and protest. The contents of the SIP financial statement for the 1970–1971 financial year make for interesting reading (5 October 1971). In light of the negative public opinion in Europe towards multinational companies, the Swiss holding company of the Group's foreign operations stresses how Pirelli has for some time been using local capital

ended on the eve of one of the most difficult periods experienced by the Company, due to celebrate its centenary the following year. In 1971, Industrie Pirelli – the company to which the Pirelli Group's industrial activities had been transferred – recorded an extremely negative economic performance in Italy, registering losses of over 100 billion lira. These negative outcomes were due to the climate of continued turbulence, both within and outside the Company, which began at the end of the 1960s and would define the decade to come. While the companies in Italy in which Pirelli was majority shareholder found themselves in difficulty, the companies in which Dunlop was reference shareholder in the United Kingdom performed satisfactorily in Europe and very well in the rest of the world.

The losses recorded by Industrie Pirelli[13] required both careful analysis and rapid decision-making – measures not usually easy to reconcile – compelling the two parent companies to take a stance regarding the recapitalisation of the Italian company. Notwithstanding the obvious requirements to compensate for pro rata losses so as not to alter the existing ownership structure, the agreement by way of which the Union had been set up did not include specific measures for a similar event. As far as Dunlop was concerned, however, the decision revolved around the issue of whether or not to include the shareholding in Industrie Pirelli in the con-solidated financial statement. Indeed, the British company was required to draw up a consolidated balance sheet which would reveal the significant losses suffered by Industrie Pirelli in Italy, resulting in negative repercussions for the stock market listing and for the overall financial structure of the British holding company. It did however have the option of not consolidating the Industrie Pirelli shareholding in the Dunlop Holding balance sheet. This option involved certain technical difficul-ties, which could be overcome by representing the financial instruments relating to Dunlop Holding's stake in Industrie Pirelli as shares with limited voting rights and privilege with regard to the repayment of capital, and only those held by Pirelli

---

in investment projects implemented in the various countries around the world (4 June 1973; 24 October 1973). It was a shrewd and mindful policy that had been fostered by the Group – in theory if not in practice – since it opened its first overseas factories in Europe and further afield. The policy was a way of promoting the Pirelli brand; it also allowed the Company to create 'a favourable atmosphere, conducive to obtaining satisfactory economic performance' in the countries where it operated (23 October 1974).

13  According to the agreements made, 51% of Industrie Pirelli was held by Pirelli SpA, and 49% by Dunlop.

as ordinary shares with full voting rights. The greater problem was how to implement this strategy. The approach chosen enabled Dunlop Holding to represent the various shares within the Union in different forms, and thus there was no need to consolidate the participation in Industrie Pirelli nor to settle the losses accrued. This decision put the future of the Union in jeopardy. Indeed, not recapitalising would cause a dilution of Dunlop Holding's shares in Industrie Pirelli, particularly if the Italian company suffered further losses in the following years, as proved to be the case. The dilution of its shareholding represented a progressive lack of interest by Dunlop Holding in the Union's Italian activities. Furthermore, if such a principle were applied to other companies in the Union registering losses, the respective ownership stakes of the parent companies would undergo significant variation, jeopardising the overall architecture of the cross-border agreement.[14]

The continuing significant losses suffered by Industrie Pirelli also had the adverse effect of causing a great deal of energy and effort to be channelled into the implementation of an effective management strategy, aimed at achieving satisfactory economic results for the Company. This diversion of resources, however, meant that the finalisation of the Union activities – in 1971, still a rough draft – was put aside. The Companies soon realised that the future of the Union depended largely on their ability to make the Italian company profitable once more. Indeed, the Union was performing satisfactorily outside and discretely within Europe; the weak links in the chain were the two countries of origin: the United Kingdom and Italy. In the early 1970s, however, while results recorded by Dunlop in the United Kingdom were modest, but still satisfactory, those of Industrie Pirelli were extremely negative,[15] penalising the overall profitability of the Union as a whole. In this difficult context, Pirelli set about developing a five-year restructuring programme for Industrie Pirelli for the period 1973–1977. As well as identifying any

---

14  Manca (2005) recalls that after this decision 'the work of the coordination committees slowed down considerably, starting with the central committee but most apparent with regard to the planning committee, which effectively closed down, if not officially then at least in terms of its activity'.

15  In light of Industrie Pirelli's profoundly negative performance, caused mainly by the difficult economic climate in Italy and therefore by external factors, its prospects for growth were linked to its capacity for research and development. Dunlop's situation in the United Kingdom was a different matter. Its modest performance represented the 'swan song' of a company with outdated facilities, products and technology, and that would be overwhelmed by an irreversible crisis just a few years later.

TABLE 4.1. THE FINANCIAL RESULTS OF
INDUSTRIE PIRELLI (1968–1980, IN LIRA)

| Years | Profit for the financial year |
|---|---|
| 1968 | 7,638,689,497 |
| 1970 | 701,198,341 |
| 1972 [a] | 3,720,832,060 |
| 1974 | −2,600,000,000 |
| 1976 | 0 |
| 1978 [b] | 2,807,820,566 |
| 1980 | 3,961,795,779 |

*[a]From 1972 onwards, financial statements up to 30 April.*
*[b]From 1978 onwards, financial statements up to 31 December.*
*Source: Our calculations based on the minutes of the SGMs*
*and Industrie Pirelli financial statement records*

'critical issues', the plan involved an analysis of the activities which were 'currently making a loss but which should remain part of the Group', as well as research into new investment projects which could also absorb labour force from activities experiencing structural decline. It was a judicious plan, but not aggressive enough to tackle the grave situation. In particular, the plan did not place enough emphasis on creating a credible financial framework for the implementation of the management and governance actions required to survive the recession. Not long after the situation worsened even further, thwarting the efficacy of the newly developed plan.

The difficult economic situation soon enveloped the whole of Europe. In 1974, the Pirelli Group's companies in Europe suffered severe losses, forcing the Italian parent company to formulate a further, more incisive business plan over the course of the following year, which placed an emphasis on the restructuring of Industrie Pirelli as a fundamental step towards the recovery of the entire Group. By this time it was clear that such a process was crucial to the survival of the Union. Differently from the initial plan developed in 1973, the new five-year plan prepared between 1975 and 1976 was more complex, but also much more systematic and exhaustive. This new plan was devised to tackle a continually worsening situation, one which required constant and careful reassessment and update of the business plan and data, which were often obsolete due to the rapid and dramatic progression of events. The plan concerned the overall financial equilibrium of the Group, which was significantly worse than in the two previous years. This downturn jeopardised the relaunch and restructuring of the Group in Italy, and risked compromising the equilibrium of the Holding Company due to the enormous losses suffered by the subsidiary and the burden of obligations undertaken by the parent company in favour of Industrie Pirelli. The minutes of the Board Shareholders' General Meeting and SGMs of the various companies of the Group – bound in large, austerely covered books – reveal the sense of tragedy of that time. These losses registered during the mid-1970s represented one of the most dramatic moments in the entire history of the Company, and was considered to be a battle against time.

This time, however, the plan was implemented in a thorough and orderly manner, beginning with an estimate of the Group's financial requirements over a period long enough to be credible notwithstanding the evident urgency of the moment, and with the understanding that the tyre sector would have taken a positive trend in the mid-term. It was a monumental commitment; the resources necessary to relaunch the tyre sector over the following five years were estimated at 270 billion lira, two thirds for investments and the remaining third to finance working capital. Finance was raised through the divestment of activities, by sourcing internal resources, and by accessing external resources on the capital market through the financial institution headed by Enrico Cuccia which had taken the shaky Bicocca company in hand. The months between mid-1975 and the autumn of 1976 proved dramatic; during the Board meeting of 20 February 1976 Leopoldo Pirelli posed a question which, until a short time before, would have seemed entirely rhetorical: 'There are two alternatives: either we believe that Industrie Pirelli can achieve a state of economic equilibrium in a relatively short period of time, or we believe that an equilibrium cannot be achieved in a space of time that does not irreparably damage the fate of the Holding Company, in which case all support[16] should cease.'

The concrete proof that this was not a rhetorical statement was to be found in a working hypothesis which was illustrated during the same Board meeting

---

16  Leopoldo Pirelli was referring here to the support provided by the Holding Company to Industrie Pirelli.

suggesting that the tyre division be separated from Industrie Pirelli and divided into two distinct companies: one dedicated to research and the other to the tyre sector. Regarding the latter, Leopoldo Pirelli proposed to identify an industrial partner which could take on a 50% shareholding in the operating company, or alternatively, the total divestment of this business unit. Pirelli was very close to a scenario which it had never faced in its entire history, that of divesting its tyre production activity.

Despite the dramatic nature of the period, several key points remained clear. Firstly, that the Company would continue to support research in innovative projects ranging from the new radial tyre model – later launched as the P3 model – to fibre optics aimed at increasing the transmission capacity of telephone lines, for which initial experiments were carried out in 1977. Secondly, that Pirelli was moving towards selling off part of its investments in its diversified activities sector, some of which had been in structural crisis for some time. The initial divestitures in this sector were the prelude to a focus on a number of core businesses. Although Pirelli was shutting down some activities to finance the tyre business unit, other activities were shut down because the Company realised that the diversified activities unit would never have generated a sufficiently viable economy of scale. Furthermore, it would have been difficult to attract sufficient management expertise to this business unit due to its highly diversified range of products. Lastly, Mediobanca, which watched over the entire financial restructuring and re-launch of the Group, proposed a further possible method of sourcing financial resources from the capital market to reinforce the finances of the parent company. This involved issuing convertible bonds into ordinary or privileged shares in some of the Group's high-performing foreign subsidiaries which were considered as good investment opportunities, such as Pirelli Brasileira.[17]

While the Group's attention in the mid-1970s was focused almost exclusively on Industrie Pirelli and the Italian scenario, Société Internationale Pirelli and the European and extra-European companies of the Union continued to show a positive economic performance. Overseas, the Group concentrated on focusing its

---

17 These were essentially indirect convertible bonds, not into the equity of the issuing company, but into the equity of another company of the Group. Pirelli Brasileira had also grown to a considerable size. At the beginning of 1981, Pirelli Brasileira was the 11th-largest private Brazilian company after five oil producers, four car manufacturers and a consumer goods company.

activities through various targeted acquisitions, such as those in the cable sector in the United States and Australia, the incorporation of new companies, and construction of tyre production plants in countries where the Group was not present, such as Nigeria and Algeria.[18]

Documentation from that period regarding Société Internationale Pirelli gives an overall picture of the global events of the era, perhaps one of the few studies of an Italian multinational. The large red binders containing the Société Internationale Pirelli company documentation are divided into dossiers containing the minutes and appendices from the individual Board meetings and Shareholders' General Meetings. All of the documentation is written in French given that English was used for the first time in the 1980s, and then mainly in appendices containing quantitative elements such as business plans or presentations of interim accounting reports.[19] In some instances the managing director provided a country-specific or geographic analysis in the form of a presentation to the Board, and these discussions were often preceded by a brief description of the social and political conditions of the countries in question. These descriptions, often in the form of brief comments or even rough draft, regarded situations which would otherwise have required long and profound analyses of the trials and tribulation of those years.

On 19 May 1976, while examining the situation in Argentina, the Board of Société Internationale was informed that 'the programme of the new government[20] is very ambitious. The climate is spoiled by a large degree of corruption.' Also in relation to Argentina, the minutes from 18 May 1979 refer to 'the liberal orientation

---

18  It is interesting to note the perceptions regarding the development of potentially emerging countries at the end of the 1970s. Algeria and Nigeria were both reasonable investment choices. Algeria was a fast-growing country in the Maghreb, having overcome political tensions following its separation from France, while Nigeria's oil resources seemed to promise a rapid level of economic development, not replicated in its civil society or democratic institutions.

19  Despite the various locations of the Société Internationale Pirelli's Board meetings, generally held in Basel or Lugano, one has the impression that the required language was French (due to established tradition dating back to a time when the registered office of Société Internationale was in Brussels), chosen over English, which played a very subordinate role.

20  This refers to the military junta led by General Videla, who overthrew the ruling democratic government with a coup on 24 March 1976. With regard to Argentina, see also the appraisal of the new government at the Board meeting on 16 May 1977.

of the government in power since the fall of Peronism in 1976, adopts its policies to the arising circumstances'. On 9 February 1981, meanwhile, a positive opinion is expressed with regard to the situation in Turkey, a country where 'following the installation of the military government[21] in Ankara last September, the country is enjoying a situation of civil peace essential for its economy, while the policy of monetary austerity has managed to stop the breakneck pace of inflation'.

In the light of these tumultuous historical events which appeared ever more frequently in the minutes of Société Internationale, the company approach is consistent with Giovanni Battista Pirelli's legacy: a neutral stance regarding political or social tensions such as the case of Argentina or open to innovation as Turkey was considered in those years. When possible, the Group aimed to safeguard those elements which would have allowed it to continue its activity in a climate of growth and prosperity.[22]

At the end of 1976, the Group's economic situation in Italy began to show signs of improvement. This scenario continued for the entire following year; taking advantage of the favourable climate, the Company effected a further seasoned equity offering of approximately 50 billion lira aimed at reinforcing the financial structure of Industrie Pirelli, and relaunching the project of integration with the Union. The terrible crisis that had gripped Industrie Pirelli in the 1970s had raised serious concerns as to the development of the ambitious Union project. As already noted, the companies controlled by Dunlop had showed modest performance in the United Kingdom in the 1970s, whereas performance was satisfactory in the rest of the world. When the first signs of crisis emerged, not long after the agreement was signed, both groups had essentially retreated back to their own corners. As such, the Union stumbled through the mid-1970s, without any particular benefit or harm to either of the contracting parties. Towards the end of the decade, it became clear that Industrie Pirelli was nearing recovery and this meant that the process of development and further integration of the three

---

21  This refers to the military coup which took place in Turkey in September 1980. In the specific case of Turkey, deriving directly from the political and cultural legacy of Ataturk, the army guaranteed the secular nature of the Republic.

22  Interesting in this regard is a comment made concerning Brazil (29 October 1976), describing the situation in the country as 'a clash between the government, which seeks to promote foreign investment, and the military with its nationalist policies that opposes such investment'.

companies controlled by the Union could be completed. During the constantly evolving and 'tormented 1970s', Leopoldo Pirelli had sensed – or perhaps merely hoped – that relaunching the integration project of the Union would present further opportunities for both groups. It was a project pursued with obstinacy by the chairman of Pirelli: he had been convinced for some time that the Pirelli tyre business was not large enough in terms of size, a belief that had led to the agreement with the Union. In line with this belief, he then attempted to launch the idea of a European tyre company,[23] to which the two groups would be required to transfer their European business units. The British group's response to this new proposal was cursory and of general disinterest. Specifically, Dunlop believed that the proposal had two major limitations: the first was a certain apprehension of losing control or not having a significant shareholding in the equity of the new company; the second was that the British group would have to have underwrite the risk pertaining to the Italian operations. Indeed, these were the same issues that had already led Dunlop in 1972 to progressively lose confidence in the Union. After receiving the British group's objections once again, Pirelli also started to lose faith in the project, and consequently in the future of the Union.

It was the performance of the market that brought the definitive break-up of the Union. At the end of the 1970s, Dunlop was overtaken by a profound crisis, similar to that which had caused so many problems for Industrie Pirelli in Italy almost 10 years before. Unlike the historically resourceful Pirelli, which had managed to get back on its feet despite many difficulties, Dunlop paid a high and bitter price; an outdated company, weak in terms of innovation and research, it was unable to survive the serious crisis that swept through the United Kingdom at the beginning of the new Conservative era. In mid-1977, Dunlop was forced to recapitalise to consolidate its weakened financial structure. Pirelli expressed its willingness to recapitalise the British company if Dunlop restored the original ownership structure of Industrie Pirelli. The Italian group was focused on achieving economic stability, whether through further capital increases or painful decisions such as the divestiture of real estate of historical significance for the Company and indeed, it was close to achieving this goal. At the beginning of 1978, it decided to sell the Pirelli Tower, which housed the Company's

---

23 The idea of a European tyre company would become feasible for the Pirelli Group at the end of the 1980s, with the establishment of Pirelli Tyre Holding.

registered office, to the Lombardy Regional Authority for the sum of 43 billion lira. Designed as its corporate landmark, Pirelli had occupied the Tower for just short of 20 years. Beyond the symbolic value of the building – still referred to today as the 'Pirelli Tower' or 'Pirellone' – its sale was not a defeat or capitulation, but indicated a clear understanding of the fact that such an operation could help put an end to the Company's difficulties. Despite this move, 1978 and 1979 brought fewer rewards than expected, partly thwarting the important sacrifice made by the Company.

At the beginning of 1979, the Company implemented yet another financial restructuring of Industrie Pirelli in two steps. The first was a seasoned equity offering of 55 billion lira, of which 40 billion to be underwritten by a banking consortium, and 15 billion by Pirelli SpA. The second was the consolidation of a short-term bank debt for the sum of 100 billion lira at a subsidised interest rate. These two measures allowed the Group to deal with yet another weakening of the economy, and to enter into the 1980s with a steadier footing. The Company proceeded to sell off parts of its tyre business unit, and did likewise with cables the following year.

At the end of the 1970s, the Group continued to expand abroad through a number of acquisitions in the cable sector. In particular, the Group acquired Trefimetaux, the cable division of the French multinational Pechiney, which took on the name of Treficable Pirelli France, an acquisition which marked the entry of the Pirelli Group into the French cable market.

The beginning of the 1980s saw the end of the Company's partnership with Dunlop. This prospect had been in the pipeline for some time, as it had become clear that the Union was more restrictive than beneficial, having failed to achieve any of its original objectives. It is reasonable to assume that the discouraging news regarding Dunlop's ownership structure from Campbell Fraser[24] – Reay Geddes's successor as chairman of Dunlop – and a Société Internationale board

---

24 Manca (2005) provides the following description of Campbell Fraser: 'A graduate of the University of Glasgow, he was employed by the Economist Intelligence Unit, the renowned London-based research and analysis centre, before becoming public relations officer for Dunlop, and then director of the New Zealand associated company and radio and television commentator on industrial and economic issues. He did not have the air of a chairman. His manner was somewhat brusque and informal; intelligent and determined, he participated in the launch of the Union with great conviction, but began to distance himself more and more as the problems and disputes increased.'

member, unexpectedly hastened the dissolution. Fraser alerted Pirelli to an intense and growing interest by investors in the Far East in the Dunlop Group's shares on the capital market. There was also reason to believe that at least 20% of the Group's capital was already in the hands of these investors. Even with a widely spread shareholding, control of the company was still in the hands of its management, but the even remote prospect of a substantial change in the ownership of Dunlop was the last straw, and which led to the end of the partnership. The entire history of the Union is masterfully summarised in the 1980 accounting balance sheet report, among the important events that occurred after the end of the financial year. Dunlop's unwillingness to recapitalise Industrie Pirelli in the wake of its losses resulted in Dunlop's stake in the Group's main Italian company being reduced to a modest 19% compared to the initial 49%. The same fate would probably have befallen Pirelli, hence its unwillingness to finance Dunlop's losses, which had proved to be both significant and long-lasting. This mutual unwillingness put an end to the Union, a move which was regarded positively by the press and the market.

Although the end of the partnership was viewed favourably by the market, it was a negative outcome for Pirelli, particularly given that the entire affair had absorbed Company resources for a decade. From a technical point of view, the dissolution of the Union as stipulated in the initial agreement was fairly simple. In 1981, the two companies returned their minority shares in the respective groups. Some years later, during an official ceremony at the College of Engineering in Milan on 3 October 1986, Leopoldo Pirelli pronounced what came to be known as the 'ten rules of the good entrepreneur', and dedicated the eighth rule to a historical evaluation of the Union. On this subject the chairman of Pirelli declared, with playful and subtle irony, that:

It seemed like the ideal union, but sadly, despite the respect and friendship between Pirelli and Dunlop, the marriage failed, or better, was never consummated. And this occurred for a variety of reasons; crises for Pirelli in Italy in the 1970s, followed by crises for Dunlop in Britain, the impossibility of reconciling the differences between Latin and Anglosphere mentalities. Perhaps even a little bad luck. In any case, it failed and ended in divorce. It was a hugely negative experience for Pirelli (and also for Dunlop), for which I feel entirely responsible, but if I could return to 1969 and 1970, I would marry Dunlop again. I do not regret the decision made at that time,

although I would try to consummate the marriage on the wedding night
or even, perhaps – like the youth of today – even earlier.[25]

Following the end of the Union, Pirelli carried out two equity increases
between the end of 1980 and the beginning of 1981, which aimed to establish
credible industrial prospects for the incipient 1980s in the relatively short period
spanning 1980 and 1982.

Despite being a stand-alone entity, the challenge of coordinating the ownership, organisation and management of Société Internationale Pirelli abroad and
Industrie Pirelli in Italy still remained. Regarding Italy, it was decided to demerge
the cable sector into a company directly and entirely owned by Industrie Pirelli,
as previously done with the tyre sector. These two operations which distributed
the activities of the tyre and cable sectors between two specific companies made
the entire deal more credible in the eyes of the financial market. Pirelli first issued
bonds convertible into ordinary or savings shares for a total of 50 billion lira, and
contemporaneously issued savings shares for a further 50 billion lira, then carried
out a further seasoned equity offering of just under 30 billion lira.

Reorganising relations with Société Internationale Pirelli and the international
structure of the Group would prove more complex. Since its incorporation, the
Pirelli family had always had the role of reference shareholder in the Pirelli & C.
Limited Liability Partnership, with a modest overall shareholding.[26]

Pirelli had been a very 'one of a kind' company, in which the Pirelli family
held both a managerial role and the status of reference – but not controlling –
shareholder. Cases such as this were fairly frequent in the capitalist economies of
the 19th and early 20th centuries, a key factor being that it was not compulsory to

---

25  From *Il Sole 24 Ore* on 4 October 1986.

26  Disclosure of the ownership structures of limited liability companies, including those listed
on the stock market, is relatively recent, both in Italy and in many other industrialised
countries. It was introduced in Italy with the establishment of the Italian Securities and
Exchange Commission (Commissione Nazionale per le Società e la Borsa, CONSOB) with
law 216 of 7 June 1974. Full information on the participation in of the 10 largest shareholders
in SGMs, and the percentage of share ownership by the same, is contained in the minutes
of the SGMs of the two Italian companies, Pirelli & C. and Pirelli SpA, from 1977–1978
onwards, although the provision of data including more precise and accurate details
regarding ownership percentages begins with the meeting of 24 March 1981 for Pirelli & C.
and 16 July 1982 for Pirelli SpA. Due to the nature of this research, it has been decided to list
the ownership structures of the main companies of the Group in the Appendix.

make voting rights directly proportional to the number of shares held. In Pirelli's specific case, the family continued to play an important role for two reasons. In legal terms, the directors of a limited liability partnership cannot be replaced. For a long time, the Pirelli family had held all directorship positions in the Limited Liability Partnership, over which it had exercised firm control. The managerial performance of the various members of the family had proved to have been excellent over time. Analysis of the ownership structure of the two main companies of the Group – Pirelli & C. and Pirelli SpA – at the beginning of the 1980s reveals their shareholding arrangements, as shown in Tables 4.2 and 4.3.

On 24 March 1981,[27] the leading shareholder in Pirelli & C. was Mediobanca,[28] with a shareholding of 11.08%, followed by a Gim, a company belonging to the Orlando Group,[29] with a 10% shareholding; the third shareholder in order of importance was Sai, with 7.85%. At the beginning of the 1980s, Mediobanca and the Orlando Group held just under 30% of the shares with voting rights in Pirelli & C.[30] There were other minor shareholders, but at that date, none of the first 10 shareholders were directly linked to the Pirelli family.[31] It was a dispersed ownership structure, involving a group of controlling shareholders, in which the Pirelli family played no primary role.

The situation regarding the ownership structures of the two holding companies in Italy and abroad – Pirelli SpA and Société Internationale Pirelli – was more complex. Both were limited companies with dispersed ownership structures, due both to the various seasoned equity increases carried out and to issue bonds convertible into shares of the two companies; this posed a certain risk for both companies in the absence of a limited partnership formula nor a voting trust.

---

27 See Appendix 1.

28 The Group led by Mediobanca also included Sade Finanziaria, with a shareholding of 4.03%.

29 The Orlando Group historically held a shareholding in the Pirelli company, due in part to the acquaintanceship of the two families. Smi was also involved in this group, with a second shareholding of 4%.

30 As of this date no shareholders' agreement existed between the Pirelli & C. shareholders.

31 This does not mean that the Pirelli family did not have a shareholding in the capital of Pirelli & C. on that date; the calculation is based on pioneering data collection methods. The first clear reference to Fin.P. (the Pirelli family financial holding in the capital of Pirelli & C.) dates back to 26 April 1983, a date on which the Company owned a shareholding of 3.16% in the capital of the Limited Liability Partnership. The other main shareholders in Pirelli & C. on that date are those previously listed, with the addition of Cam, the predecessor of Camfin, with a shareholding of 2.10%.

Overall, the stakes of the reference shareholders, Pirelli & C., Société Internationale Pirelli and the Pirelli family in Pirelli SpA was 21.15% and reached just over 25% if Mediobanca was included. In turn, Pirelli & C. with an 18% stake was the reference shareholder in Société Internationale Pirelli. This was a rather fragile structure which risked further weakening with the dissolution of the Union which, due to its dimensions, acted as a deterrent to any unwelcome attention, and because of the further capital operations needed to restore the Group's competitive edge.

To resolve these problems, a decision was made to restructure the Group both in Italy and abroad, a solution that arose from a specific consideration. It seemed that the current industrial and management set-up of the Group, with two parent companies, one in Milan and one in Basel,[32] had become inefficient and needed revision. During Leopoldo Pirelli's presentation of the elements underpinning this new restructuring programme to the Pirelli SpA Board of Directors, he stressed the need for both parent companies to 'be equally involved in operational management' and therefore in 'coordinating the operational management of the operating companies themselves'. In reply to this problem, two solutions were identified, one regarding the management and the other the ownership of shares which would have guaranteed equal involvement by both parent companies in the operations of the Group, and which would also have favoured greater coordination between the two companies. Indeed, both companies were to hold equal shareholdings in each of the operative companies and, more importantly, were to hold equal shareholdings in a new company, Pirelli Société Générale (PSG), which was to be incorporated. This new company would have the mandate 'to manage the shareholdings in all subsidiaries with the aim of achieving the internal industrial and financial vocation of each'. In brief, this was a management company with the role of aligning the objectives of both parent companies, and of coordinating the industrial and management vocation of each efficiently. The operational headquarters of the management company would be divided between Milan and Basel, where Société Internationale Pirelli was based. To achieve this, however, there was

---

32  Manca (2005) makes the following observation on the choice of Basel: 'What surprised me was [the] decision to locate the registered office of the new company in Basel, in a building occupied partially (but to a large extent) by the Société Internationale Pirelli staff. The phrase *Da Basilea si manovra meglio* [Basel makes for easier manoeuvrability], used by one newspaper in its headline on the story, was a great stretch of the truth, given that much of the production and management activities, both in terms of its staff and facilities, were still based in Milan.'

TABLE 4.2. OWNERSHIP STRUCTURE OF
PIRELLI & C. ON 24 MARCH 1981[a]

| Shareholders | Percentage owned on capital with voting rights |
| --- | --- |
| Mediobanca | 11.08 |
| Gim | 10.00 |
| Sai | 7.85 |
| Sade Finanziaria | 4.03 |
| Smi | 4.00 |
| Bank Oppenheimer | 2.50 |
| Bastogi | 2.16 |
| Rominvest | 0.95 |
| Sifi | 0.94 |
| Generali | 0.56 |

[a]*From an overall total of 18,506,666 ordinary shares.*
*Source: Our calculations based on the minutes of the general meetings of Pirelli & C.*

TABLE 4.3. OWNERSHIP STRUCTURE OF
PIRELLI SpA ON 16 JULY 1982

| Shareholders | Percentage owned on capital with voting rights |
| --- | --- |
| Pirelli & C. | 9.25 |
| Société Internationale Pirelli | 8.10 |
| Mediobanca | 4.84 |
| Smi | 4.04 |
| Spafid (fiduciary) – Pirelli family | 3.80 |

*Source: Our calculations based on minutes of the Pirelli SpA SGMs*

a need to solve the problem regarding the control of the two parent companies. This was eventually resolved by transferring Société Internationale Pirelli's former shareholding in Pirelli SpA (of approximately 7%) to Pirelli & C. In this way, Pirelli & C. would be the reference shareholder in both parent companies, with a stake of approximately 18%. In the absence of a shareholders' agreement, it was a modest stake for a reference shareholder.

To implement the preliminaries regarding the equality of the direct or indirect shareholdings of the parent companies in the various operative companies which was the basis for this plan, the shareholdings of many of the subsidiary companies also had to be restructured,[33] involving the transfer of substantial share packages. Specifically, the limited liability company became a shareholder

---

33 The relative shareholdings of Pirelli SpA and Société Internationale Pirelli in the main European and non-European operating companies were outlined as follows during the Board meeting of 15 April 1982:

*Percentage shareholdings of Pirelli SpA and Société Internationale Pirelli in the companies of the Group by geographical area*

| Company | Percentage of shares held by Pirelli SpA | Percentage of shares held by Société Internationale Pirelli |
|---|---|---|
| Industrie Pirelli | 76.9 | – |
| Pirelli France, Sacic (Belgium), Veith (Germany) | 99 | – |
| United Kingdom (tyres) | 61.8 | 38.2 |
| Argentina | 32.4 | 52.2 |
| Brazil | 29.5 | 55.8 |
| France (cables) | – | 81.6 |
| Mexico (cables) | 7.8 | 12.2 |
| Spain | 39.7 | 59.4 |
| Turkey | 20.4 | 30.6 |
| United Kingdom (cables) | 42.6 | 57.4 |
| Australia (cables) | 6.8 | 43.2 |
| Canada (cables) | 28.6 | 71.4 |
| Greece | 25.7 | 54.1 |
| Peru | 15.0 | 31.4 |
| United States | 20.0 | 80.0 |

in the cable company in France and increased its shareholdings in Australia, the United States and Brazil, while Société Internationale Pirelli became involved in the operating companies in Italy and Germany. This was a complex organisational scenario, but it had not been easy to find a common and convincing solution. On the one hand, there was no doubt that the dimensions of the stakes that Pirelli & C. held in the two holding companies of the Italian and foreign companies was an issue to consider, but on the other hand there should have been no doubt regarding its control. Indeed, the management and strategy of the entire Group was intended to be entrusted entirely to the Milan-based limited liability partnership, independent from the direct or indirect stakes that this held in the two parent companies. However it is difficult to interpret the abstract yet reasonable preoccupation of Leopoldo Pirelli regarding the alignment of the incentives of the two parent companies. While the need to coordinate their actions seemed much more apparent, the decision to establish a management company did not seem particularly appropriate as a solution. Due to how the operation was structured, there was a risk that a misalignment in the incentives of the two parent companies could impact directly on Pirelli Société Générale. One of the merits of the new structure was to restore clearer policymaking and coordination powers to Pirelli & C. Overall, this restructuring did not produce any particular advantages to the Group and was a transitory solution which lasted for some years, until a new and more comprehensive reorganisation of the Group was implemented in 1988.

In the mid-1980s there was a clear improvement in the general economy which was seen not only in the industrialised countries but also in some previously marginal economies, headed by Southeast Asia, which showed intense growth rates. This economic expansion was accompanied by a slew of neoliberal economic doctrines which had emerged in the United States in the 1970s and spread throughout the world. Italy too recorded a reasonable rate of economic growth, and performed well on the financial markets. The country also showed a change in perspective regarding entrepreneurial activity from the previously ideological approach which had characterised the previous decade and which had put its very survival in jeopardy. In the historical and political climate of the early 1980s, 'doing business' once more was seen as a difficult, but worthy cause, as well as a shared value. By the mid-1980s, the Pirelli Group had overcome the difficulties of the previous decade, thanks also to a series of successful innovations which were well-received by the market. At the start of 1983 the continued success of the pneumatic tyres models P4, P6 and P8 constituted the first concrete response to the intense innovation and research activities and in the race against time with Michelin. In the cable sector in the same period, Pirelli dedicated a great deal of attention to fibre optics. The Company had realised that telecommunication cable technology was evolving towards fibre optics and directed its energies towards this sector. A decision was made to coordinate a single research centre for the development of fibre optics, as research activities were already ongoing within the Group in Italy, United Kingdom, United States and Brazil. Furthermore, a policy was implemented to acquire companies already established in the sector, particularly in the United Kingdom and United States. Indeed, these two countries in particular[34] seemed to offer the best prospects for fibre optic cables which were requested in ever-growing quantities due to the growth of the information technology sector and data transmission in those years.

The situation involving the tyre sector, which had become reasonably profitable again following the events of the 1970s, was more complex. Pirelli had for some time been harbouring feelings of inferiority towards the two major international players – the US company Goodyear and French Michelin – which were much larger than the Italian company and had built up an unreachable market share over time. Ever since its partnership with Dunlop – which, in the meantime, had sold most of its activities to the Japanese company Sumitomo – the Pirelli Group's ambition, and that of its chairman, had been to pursue a policy of growth by external means, which would allow the Italian group to achieve third or fourth position globally, similar or slightly smaller in dimension to Firestone. Indeed, Leopoldo Pirelli's diagnosis of the tyre market had not changed over time, nor had his strategy. In his view it was necessary to initiate a major process of growth by external means, via a large-scale merger or acquisition, which would allow the Pirelli Group to make that small, effective step in terms of research and product range, for it to successfully compete on the global market. This profound conviction held by Leopoldo Pirelli is remembered by some as an 'obsession with size', which must be interpreted within its correct historical context in which such concepts were popular among many economists and corporate analysts of the time. This desire to seek greater growth through acquisitions without paying sufficient attention to the real net cost of the integration process would take the Company near the brink in the second half of the 1980s.

---

34 In 1985 (4 March 1985) Pirelli acquired 60% of the British company Focom and 10% of the American company David Systems, both active in the optoelectronics sector.

# CHAPTER 5

# The End of an Era

In the mid-1980s, the ownership structure of the Pirelli Group underwent some major changes. In 1984, a shareholders' agreement was reached regarding the capital of Pirelli SpA, which included Pirelli & C. with approximately 16% of the capital, and other long-standing Pirelli shareholders such as Mediobanca, Smi and Sai.[1] Overall, this agreement regarded approximately 30% of the Pirelli SpA capital. The most important new development, however, was in the ownership structure of Pirelli & C.; the Shareholders' General Meeting of 26 April 1983[2] registered the entry into the Company of Cam[3] SpA, which would change its name to Camfin SpA during the following financial year. The chairman of the company was Silvio Tronchetti Provera,[4] head of the family of the same name. Camfin was

---

1   The other shareholders that had taken part in the agreement were Fidis, Ras, Assicurazioni Generali, Montedison, Falck and Gemina.

2   On this date, Cam owned 2.10% of the capital of Pirelli & C., which rose to 2.52% at the SGM of 19 April of the following year, at which point the company had already changed its name to Camfin.

3   The name Cam stands for Consorzio Approvvigionamenti Metallurgici e Meccanici (consortium for metalworking and mechanical supplies). Spagna (2005) briefly describes the company's history as follows: 'Established in 1915, Cam started life as a consortium of iron and steel and metallurgical companies, to manage the purchases of raw materials for its members, including the Falck Group. At the end of the 1930s, Cam's business model also included liquid fuels, an astute business choice with great potential for growth. During the 1950s, the consortium was renamed Consumatori Combustibili e Ghise SpA.'

4   Silvio Tronchetti Provera, father of Raffaele Bruno, Roberto and Marco, was born in July 1911. He never knew his father – a career official in the Royal Army – who died in the Libya Campaign in the spring of the same year. At the beginning of the 20th century, the Tronchetti Provera family was one of Italy's biggest wine producers. Silvio Tronchetti Provera attended high school at a Swiss college, and after finishing school, he returned to Italy to take care of what was left of the family's estate, which had suffered at the hands of incapable or perhaps dishonest administrators who had poorly advised his mother. Marco

the Holding Company for a group of industrial companies, operative mainly in the energy, oil and raw materials sectors. At the beginning of the 1980s, the Camfin Group[5] had consolidated turnover of approximately 200 billion lira, excellent profitability and significant cash flow, so much so that the Camfin shareholders decided to apply to list the company on the capital market in 1986.[6]

By invitation of Leopoldo Pirelli, the Tronchetti Provera family decided to invest the large sums of liquidity generated by the Camfin Group in the capital of the Pirelli & C. Limited Partnership and to become part of the Pirelli Group,

Tronchetti Provera remembers his grandmother as 'a very sweet woman, but not cut out for business'. After successfully putting his family's business affairs to right, Silvio Tronchetti graduated in Economics at Bocconi, and left for Abyssinia in 1935 as an army officer in the Edolo regiment, the same in which his father had previously served. Following the end of hostilities in East Africa, Silvio Tronchetti Provera joined the Falck Group in 1937. For the young manager and industrialist, the world of Falck would become a point of reference for his entire life. Spagna (2005) describes Silvio Tronchetti Provera's involvement in Cam: 'In the 1950s, Silvio Tronchetti Provera, still manager of Falck, took on the role of managing director of Cam. Towards the mid-1960s, when he decided to leave the Group, he received shares in Cam as a severance package, and became shareholder and chairman. Silvio Tronchetti Provera's business choice proved excellent in the early 1970s when, as a result of the oil crisis, oil prices reached an unprecedented high. Dealing in the import and sales of oil products, Cam enjoyed ever-greater success. At this point, Silvio Tronchetti Provera decided to focus Cam's activities exclusively in the energy sector, before acquiring control of the company in the early 1980s.'

5   The Camfin shareholders included the Falck family, with whom the Tronchetti Provera family had a long-standing relationship, and which had a stake of approximately 30%.

6   Cam Finanziaria SpA was created in the 1980s, changing its name to Camfin at the meeting to approve the financial statements on 30 September 1984. Camfin's financial year ran from 1 October to 30 September of the following year, until 1990 when the closing of the fiscal year was moved to 31 December. The Camfin Board of Directors first considered the idea of listing the stock on 12 July 1985, with formal resolution by the Board on 22 November of the same year. It was the SGM of 30 January 1986 (convened to approve the financial statement closed on 30 September 1985) which resolved to initiate the listing procedure. At the time of the resolution, the Tronchetti Provera family, through the financial company GPI (Gestioni Partecipazioni Industriali) held 52.8% of the share capital of Camfin; the Falck family, meanwhile, through shares of 25.04% and 9.01% held by Acciaierie e Ferriere Lombarde (Lombardy steel and iron works) and Acciaierie di Bolzano (Bolzano steel works) respectively, was the second shareholder, with a total percentage of 34.05%. The listing procedure took place through a capital increase of 18 billion lira, to be set on the market through a consortium guided by the financial institution Euromobiliare. The holding company controlled three wholly owned subsidiaries: Cam Energia e Calore, which dealt in the trade of oil products and systems; Cam Prodotti, which dealt in raw materials for the iron and steel industry, and Partner Data, responsible for managing all the Group's information activities.

not only because it was considered an excellent investment, but because they believed that over its long history Pirelli had demonstrated values and industrial approaches that Camfin shared. In particular, the two families were united by the wise and consistent juxtaposition of the dual roles of major shareholder and family lineage with managerial inclinations. In this sense, Leopoldo Pirelli had found in Marco Tronchetti Provera[7] someone who had his sights set on a major family-run enterprise.[8] Thus, the Tronchetti Provera family not only invested in the capital of the Limited Liability Partnership, but also added to its resources with the injection of a young, capable and innovative management team.

The Tronchetti Provera family's decision to invest its Camfin profits in Pirelli & C. had the effect of significantly increasing its stake in the Limited Liability Partnership, becoming its fourth-largest shareholder[9] in just a few years, after Mediobanca, Gim and Gemina, but before Fin.P., the company through which

---

7   Marco Tronchetti Provera was born in Milan on 18 January 1948. After graduating in Economics from Bocconi, he carried out a period of work experience at the Peninsular and Oriental Steam Navigation Company (P&O) in London, a major international transport and logistics company, whose managing director was a friend of the Tronchetti Provera family. With regard to this experience, Spagna (2005) writes: 'In almost two hundred years of history, P&O had become a major multinational group operating throughout the value chain of maritime transport and associated logistics, with a hundred ports in eighteen countries. In 1971, P&O was experiencing a revolution in the way it conducted maritime transport, and in its logistics management. The cargo ships in which loose goods were transported were being progressively substituted with container ships. The goods were put directly into the container by the customer and sorted directly before the intermodal terminal and then in the port terminal.' In an interview with the author, Marco Tronchetti Provera remembers that it was this experience that taught him the importance of building intermodal terminals not only in ports, but most of all 'close to where the goods actually are – at the production plants themselves'. It was this awareness that led him to set up his first direct enterprise in the form of the Sogemar company, which managed an intermodal terminal near Rho station, on the western outskirts of Milan. Later, towards the end of 1986, Marco Tronchetti Provera sold Sogemar to the Contship Group, belonging to Angelo Ravano, and invested the resulting liquidity in Camfin shares.

8   Marco Tronchetti Provera remembers having convinced his father to invest the liquidity from Camfin in Pirelli following a suggestion from his father-in-law, Leopoldo Pirelli (Marco having married Cecilia Pirelli, Leopoldo's daughter). Leopoldo's request 'to bring the families together' was well received by Marco and his family, in light of the difficulties successfully overcome by Marco's father Silvio, who – little older than a teenager – had had to work hard to protect and rebuild what remained of his family's estate.

9   More precisely, Camfin's shareholding increased from 2.99% (as recorded during the SGM of 29 March 1985) to 3.08% (in that case in the portfolio of Cam Energia e Calore) on 29 April 1987 (22 March 1988), reaching 5.00% on 28 April 1988 and 5.61% on 20 April 1989.

the Pirelli family held its stake in the Limited Partnership.[10] The growth of Camfin's presence as a shareholder of Pirelli & C. was confirmed by the nomination of Marco Tronchetti Provera as general partner of Pirelli & C.[11]

In 1985, various major operations concerning the Group were carried out, both in Italy and abroad. In Italy, a merger took place between Pirelli & C. and Caboto-Milano Centrale. Caboto was an insurance broker which became 'the leading company providing this service in Italy' in 1984, and which had merged with Milano Centrale the previous year. The merger between the two companies increased Pirelli's range of activities to include insurance broking and real estate. The purpose of the merger was probably not solely industrial, but was also intended to strengthen the share ownership; indeed, for some time already, the Pirelli & C. shareholders had requested that the highly fractional ownership structure be consolidated and that the corporate governance system be entirely reviewed. Thus, one could say that the underlying justification for Camfin's entry into the Pirelli & C. capital was the need to involve a friendly group in its formal and substantive governance. Similar considerations were true for the merger with Caboto-Milano Centrale, specifically the desire to involve certain shareholders of the brokerage firm in the ownership structure of the Limited Partnership, including Find of the Rocca Group, and Acquedotto De Ferrari Galliera of Genoa.

The apprehension regarding the weakness of the Pirelli & C. ownership structure was due in part to the unexpected and hugely successful buyout of BI-Invest by Montedison, which had affected the market, but even more so to the presence of various industrial groups, not historically linked to Pirelli, in the share ownership of the Limited Liability Partnership. In particular, at the SGM of 29 March 1985, it was noted that Cir of Carlo De Benedetti held 2.8% of Pirelli & C. Towards the end of the summer, as the dates set for the merger with Caboto-Milano Centrale drew near, market rumours began to circulate – and were quickly picked up by the press – crediting the Carlo De Benedetti Group as the holder of a growing share in Pirelli & C. The reasons for this increased presence of the De Benedetti Group in

---

10  On that date he was the sixth-largest shareholder, with 5.13% of the capital.

11  The concomitant entry of Marco Tronchetti Provera, Alberto Pirelli and Luigi Orlando into the Board of Directors of Pirelli & C. brought the number of managing partners to six, including Leopoldo Pirelli, Egidio Gavazzi and Vincenzo Sozzani, who had taken the place of Emanuele Dubini a short time previously. For the first time since its constitution, the Board of the Limited Partnership had more than three members.

Pirelli are not known. The good personal relationships[12] between Leopoldo Pirelli and Carlo De Benedetti rule out the possibility of a 'buyout' attempt, because the Limited Liability Partnership was protected by its legal status. It is probable that De Benedetti considered Pirelli & C. to be a good investment, and perhaps also saw the possibility of playing a key role in the affairs of the Limited Liability Partnership.

All of this contributed to accelerating the completion of a shareholders' agreement, which was already on the drawing board and which was signed on 5 May 1986. Thirteen shareholders took part, holding a total of 54.77% of the capital with voting rights in the Limited Partnership.

Compared to several months previously, the Group headed by Carlo De Benedetti had reduced its holding in the capital of Pirelli & C., generating a significant capital gain. De Benedetti offered Orlando and Pirelli the option of buying out part of the shares he had acquired; part of these shares were bought by the Tronchetti Provera family. Representing the major shareholders in the agreement in the Executive Committee were Enrico Cuccia for Mediobanca, Marco Tronchetti Provera for Camfin, Ambrogio Puri for Fin.P. and Luigi Orlando for Gim.

While the issue of corporate governance played a fundamental role for Pirelli in the mid-1980s, following a period of stagnation the Group finally witnessed a newly invigorated phase of industrial activity. In the tyre sector, Pirelli acquired the German company Metzeler Kautschuk, placed on the market by Bayer, which had decided not to invest further resources in the reorganisation of the company, and deemed the tyre division to be a marginal business unit. Metzeler was a well-known brand in Germany, and a major motorcycle tyre producer, having ceased its production of car tyres several years before. This acquisition would permit Pirelli to double its European market share to 44% for motorcycle tyres. The German company also carried out research into new materials, and had a consolidated distribution network for car parts in Europe, Brazil and more recently the United States. While Pirelli continued to pursue its size-related strategy in the tyre sector, further demonstrated in its acquisition of a 10% share in Ceat, in the cable sector it continued to invest in fibre optics.[13] Société Internationale acquired 20% of Carlo

---

12 The following clarification was made in a statement in *Il Sole 24 Ore* on 30 August 1985: 'No operation of this kind [takeover bid] is currently underway, nor is such an initiative conceivable given the personal relationship between Mr De Benedetti and Mr Leopoldo Pirelli.'

13 *Il Sole 24 Ore* on 14 January 1986 comments: 'Pirelli knew it was only the beginning of a

TABLE 5.1. COMPOSITION OF THE PIRELLI & C.
SHAREHOLDERS AGREEMENT (5 MAY 1986)

| Shareholder in the agreement | Percentage possessed |
|---|---|
| Mediobanca | 7.94 |
| Gim | 7.57 |
| Sai[a] | 5.52 |
| Fin.P. (Pirelli family) | 5.27 |
| Camfin | 5.03 |
| Sabaudia[b] | 5.03 |
| Other shareholders signatory to the agreement:[c] | |
| Acquedotto De Ferrari | 3.26 |
| Fimedit Fiduciaria | 0.91 |
| Find | 4.12 |
| Gemina | 2.60 |
| Smi | 2.76 |
| Il Gallione | 1.92 |
| Sade Finanziaria | n/a |

[a]*The aforementioned article in* Il Sole 24 Ore *on 30 August 1985 refers to an action of rounding the shares in the capital of Pirelli & C. by various main shareholders, including Sai*

[b]*Sabaudia was the name of the company in which the Cir Group had concentrated its shareholding in Pirelli C.*

[c]*Some of these shareholders, in particular Acquedotto De Ferrari Galliera, Fimedit, Find and Il Gallione, were ex-shareholders of Caboto, which had recently merged with Pirelli & C. (29 April 1986)*

*Source: Our calculations based on extracts of Pirelli & C. shareholders' agreement*

challenge in which, in all probability, most of the fortunes of the Group would be wagered on the cutting-edge technologies of the 1990s. Over the last four years, Pirelli had built up a veritable multinational network of alliances, acquisitions and system groups, including control of Focom (advanced optoelectronic components) in Great Britain; a shareholding in Velec (broadband cabling for towns and cities) in France; investment in David (fourth generation private branch exchanges) in the United States, and the diversification in Solari and the start-up of Boselli Systems in an equal joint venture with IBM Italy in its home country.'

Gavazzi Holding[14] (a Swiss manufacturer of instruments for technology, measurement and control) via an exchange of shares and the incorporation of Celikord, a new company that produced metal wires for the Turkish tyre market for which 49% of the capital would be held by local investors. All of these investments required new resources, acquired through various means: a considerable seasoned equity offering of approximately 140 billion lira, the divestiture of various marginal activities, and the issue of convertible bonds into shares of the two parent companies and other companies attractive to possible investors.

At the end of 1986, Pirelli also undertook an ambitious programme to redevelop the Bicocca area, following the progressive dismantling of the last tyre production units which were to be moved elsewhere, such as to the new plants in Settimo Torinese and Bollate, whereas the technical department and research laboratories would remain in the historical site. It is important to remember that resizing the Bicocca site had begun as far back as the mid-1970s, but this latest phase was a major step for the Company. Pirelli had been operating in Bicocca since 1908, and the Group had come to be associated with the area; indeed Bicocca and Pirelli were almost synonyms and used interchangeably by the general public. This was not the first time that the Company had redeveloped industrial areas due to the progressive expansion of the urban area of Milan, but previous relocations had never caused the Company to lose its geographical and symbolic points of reference. In the period between the wars, Pirelli had progressively dismantled the area near the Milan Central Station where its first production facilities had stood, and where the Pirelli Tower was built after World War II. Similar projects also followed in other areas of the city. This complex restructuring of the entire Bicocca industrial area – the historical heart of Pirelli's activities – was a far-reaching project which included the building of the 'Milan-Bicocca Technology Centre', which not only involved Pirelli but the entire city of Milan through its universities, industry and research institutes.

In September 1985, Leopoldo Pirelli set the project in motion with a press conference in the 15th-century Villa degli Arcimboldi, confirming the nature of the plan as an 'Integrated Technology Centre'. The method chosen by Pirelli to restructure the Bicocca area involved applying experience acquired abroad to the Italian

---

14 The Carlo Gavazzi Holding held the entire equity of the Italian company Carlo Gavazzi SpA, which had two sites in Italy and several companies overseas. These included a holding in Reactor Control, an American company operating in the nuclear energy sector.

context: it was a highly innovative operation that was also of great benefit to the local community. The project not only represented an early example of modern territorial marketing, it also focused on the creation of a veritable 'old town centre in the suburbs'. This bold metaphor used in the Bicocca project presentation was a fitting description of the multitude of uses that the project intended to bring to the area. The combination of new meeting places, shopping centres, places of culture, business premises and infrastructural interchanges represent the 'dense mosaic' of the old city on a large scale.

The years 1985 and 1986 were very rewarding for the Pirelli Group, thanks to the excellent performance of its stock, aided also by a period of euphoria on the stifled Italian capital market. In November 1986, following the approval of the financial statement up to 30 June of that same year,[15] the Pirelli Group's positive performance was unanimously praised by the press. From the columns of the newspaper *Il Sole 24 Ore* the attentive observer Emilio Moar gave a lucid and realistic appraisal of the difficulties experienced by the Group and how they had been overcome:

Within the Group there are still situations to resolve and margins to recover, but compared to years past, recovery has undoubtedly taken place, and a consistent one at that. The Company is gradually reaping the fruits of the vast restructuring operations undertaken in its production and sales departments, operations requiring a great deal of effort in organisational and commercial terms. The Pirelli Group has successfully modernised, and has emerged, invigorated, from a market situation that posed serious problems which the Group addressed drawing on its own strength.

The market was clear on the strategy for the cable sector, but was less convinced by the plans for the tyre sector and even less so for the diversified activities. It is likely that the now stable economic management issues, and the discrete success achieved through the recent acquisitions, had reinforced the long-standing belief of Leopoldo Pirelli and the management team to achieve strategic growth in the tyre sector through external product lines, precisely the same strategy adopted

---

15  Pirelli approved the financial statement on 30 June. The Company would make the financial year coincide with the calendar year starting on 31 December 1989, after a financial year of just six months that had run from 1 July to 31 December 1989.

with Dunlop in the past. The aim behind the latest acquisitions, such as Metzeler in Germany, was to absorb competitors and technology, and consolidate the Group's presence, both geographically and in range of products. Pirelli had not yet entered the United States, but establishing its presence in this market was an intermediate step in a much broader strategy.

Indeed, the detailed analysis carried out by Leopoldo Pirelli revealed that economies of scale of being a larger enterprise would permit the Company to launch a global challenge to the major international players, who were much larger than Pirelli. The global tyre market, however, had been an oligopoly for some time, and it would not be easy – even in abstract terms – to hypothesise a successful integration with one of the other large producers. While on the one hand there was growing integration and consolidation among manufacturers in the sector, this trend, as filtered by the trade press, was deceptive; indeed, it was increasingly depicted as a categorical imperative and the failure to expand was equated to exclusion from the market. For the Pirelli chairman, this challenge was a matter of personal conviction, and at the end of the 1980s, as the uncertain horizons of globalisation began to become clearer, he concluded that the field of action for a possible integration should not be limited to Europe – as had been the agreement with Dunlop in 1970 – but should involve the global market, if the opportunity arose.

At the end of 1986 during the Pirelli and Société Internationale Pirelli Board meetings, the Chief Executive Officer of the Group Filiberto Pittini gave a long and detailed analysis of the tyre market, Pirelli's positioning, and its prospects. From the minutes, it was evident that the Company had established contacts with its main competitors some time previously, with a view to resolving the issue of Pirelli's insufficient size. Showing great clear-sightedness, the situation was described as being 'too big to limit itself to market niches, too small to compete satisfactorily with the first big producers'.[16] These contacts did not bring positive results for Pirelli, however, with the exception of 'a technical-scientific collaboration with Bridgestone which, while satisfactory in practice, did not provide the desired solution'. In a highly dynamic market, the Group was too dependent on the Italian and

---

16  It is understandable how this feeling of incompleteness could become frustrating for the management of the Group. Marco Tronchetti Provera remembers being struck by a flier in the office of one of the Group's managers, describing Pirelli's mission as that of being an 'intelligent follower' of the major world producers.

Brazilian markets, while it was absent in important areas such as the United States and France. Additionally, the competitive advantages that had been gained over time in the medium-high-end product range were quickly being eroded. Indeed, there was an objective disparity between its strong commitment to technological research and development and the effective results obtained. For these reasons, the future global role which was envisaged for Pirelli was one which could be 'achieved only through a merger or acquisition operation on a significant scale which will enable the company to operate in conditions more similar to those of our more qualified and aggressive competitors'. Thus, the inauspicious die was cast.

Pirelli considered the possibility of acquiring General Tyre, but was forced to reconsider given that the US company already had technical agreements with Continental, which proceeded to acquire the former company shortly thereafter. At this point, Pirelli turned its attention to the possibility of acquiring 80% of the capital of another American tyre company, Armtek Armstrong Tire. This company was the tyre division of Armtek, a diversified products company in the rubber field, with registered office in New Haven, Connecticut. It had a turnover of approximately $400 million, 2,700 employees and three production plants in California, Iowa and Tennessee, representing a very marginal share of the American market of 2–3%. It was a low-profile operation, aimed as it would seem exclusively at giving Pirelli a production base in the United States. This 'bridgehead' on American soil would not be able to undergo significant expansion without considerable investments. Having evaluated the situation, Pirelli decided not to proceed, also because there was another prospect on the horizon, the possibility of an integration with the American tyre giant Firestone, which although appealing, was extremely demanding.

The first leaks regarding ongoing negotiations between Pirelli and Firestone appeared in the press just before the middle of February 1988. As with General Tyre previously, the negotiations were complicated from the very outset; on this occasion there was a concomitant interest of the Japanese company Bridgestone in Firestone. By 16 February 1988, however, Bridgestone had already reached an agreement with Firestone to set up a joint venture in which Firestone would have contributed its tyre division; this agreement envisaged that 75% of capital in the new company would be held by Bridgestone for a total value of $1.25 billion, while Firestone would have remained the minority shareholder with a 25% stake. Despite this unfavourable arrangement, on 5 March 1988 the Pirelli Board of Directors decided – partly in consideration of the two previous experiences – to launch a bid for at least two thirds of the capital of Firestone at $58 per share,[17] for the sum of $1.93 billion. At the time when Pirelli made this offer, Firestone had a turnover of $3,860 million (of which tyres made up approximately 70%), net profits of $145 million, and 23 production plants in 10 countries across four continents, including North America, South America, Europe and Oceania.

Firestone was slightly larger than Pirelli's tyre business unit, and this merger would have made Pirelli the third-largest tyre producer in the world after Goodyear and Michelin. More than one member of the Board expressed legitimate doubts as to the soundness of such a large-scale operation. The Chief Executive Officer De Giorgi, however, who had replaced Filiberto Pittini, gave a detailed outline of the measures Pirelli would take in the event that the public offer was successful. An agreement had in fact been made with Michelin, whereby the French company would take over Firestone's activities in Brazil from Pirelli at a cost of $650 million, and which were of little interest to Pirelli given its long-standing and widespread presence in the country. The French company would also take over the US Master Care sales and assistance network, and 50% of Firestone's synthetic rubber and diversified products activities in the United States, for a total of $150 million. By selling assets for approximately $800 million, Pirelli intended to reduce the total cost of the operation. Michelin's interest in this operation was essentially motivated by its desire to stop the expansion of the Japanese group, and to strengthen its own presence in the United States. For Pirelli, the positive outcome of the operation depended on three factors: raising at least two-thirds of the capital of Firestone, eliminating the poison pills, and the desire of Firestone's shareholders not to enter into an agreement with Bridgestone.

For a number of days, the impression of the market was that the Pirelli offer would be successful, despite the Firestone stock immediately exceeding the Pirelli offer price. The Japanese company Bridgestone had indeed lingered over their decision, giving the impression of uncertainty. It was during those days that Leopoldo Pirelli outlined the reasons for Pirelli's interest in the operation to the press. He recognised that the tyre market 'was by now a global market, to be tackled with a global strategy', which required production facilities in the various geographical areas, and centralised management of financial, technological and

---

17  At the beginning of March, the Firestone share was quoted at approximately $45 on Wall Street. Pirelli's offer therefore involved a premium of approximately 27%.

organisational resources. There were three main reasons behind this changing scenario: 'the broadening and globalisation of the markets; the need to dedicate large investments to automated processes that require large production volumes and therefore specialisation; and the need to dedicate considerable sums to research and development'.[18]

The interview ended with a question regarding the possibility of a counteroffer by Bridgestone, to which Leopoldo Pirelli replied laconically: 'We already consider the price to be very interesting.'

During the frenetic week in mid-March 1988 following its initial indecision, the attitude of the Firestone management regarding the Pirelli offer seemed rather confused. Indeed Firestone began to consider Pirelli's proposal with greater interest, also because the market considered any valuation of Firestone stock in excess of Pirelli's offer to be unrealistic. It is not known whether Firestone's behaviour was sincere, or simply a way of forcing Bridgestone to bid higher. On 19 March, the Japanese company raised its bid, offering $80 per share, thus valuing Firestone at $2.6 billion. In the light of this latest offer, Pirelli decided to withdraw from the negotiation and, in keeping with its previous statements, informed the market: 'that it had learned that Bridgestone had presented a counteroffer, in agreement with the management of Firestone, of $80 per share against its own offer of $58. Pirelli had always said that its offer would remain within the bounds of its business interests: the amount offered by Bridgestone is not in keeping with such a policy.'

The failure of the tender offer for Firestone moved Pirelli to renew its interest in Armstrong Tires, which it acquired for $190 million. This was an ill-fated acquisition, as the company was suffering structural losses, had no specific brand, and

---

18  In a long interview with *Il Sole 24 Ore* on 9 March 1988, a few passages of which are provided here, Leopoldo Pirelli expressed his point of view as follows: 'Today Pirelli represents 7% of the world market, a figure which rises to 12% in Europe and 35% in Italy. This would not be a bad situation if the first two tyre producers Goodyear and Michelin were not approximately two and a half times our size. This means that in order to have the same incidence of research and development costs on turnover, if Goodyear and Michelin spend 250, Pirelli can spend just 100, despite having to ensure its competitive presence on the same huge range of products. It is clear, therefore, that there is an issue of size. As far as our offer is concerned, I want to make it clear that we are not raiders; we are industrialists presenting an interesting and advantageous offer to the shareholders of Firestone, as part of a precise industrial strategy. As far as the operative Group is concerned, we believe that a highly competitive 5 billion dollar business has many options open to it on the financial markets to finance the acquisition.'

was subject to social security liabilities and labour costs which were twice those of its competitors.

In the spring of 1988, the Pirelli Group carried out a complete restructuring of the Company, just a few years after the previous one following the dissolution of the Union with Dunlop. The company architecture established in 1982, which involved control being shared equally between the two parent companies – Pirelli and Société Internationale Pirelli – over the management company Pirelli Société Générale, was already showing some signs of weakness. Created to align the potentially divergent objectives of the two parent companies, the Basel company had been able to do very little about the divergent strategic visions of the two reference shareholders with regard to the management of the operating companies. Paradoxically, the presence of the management company also made the development and implementation of strategic policies by the two parent companies more complex and less effective. From a management perspective, Pirelli Société Générale had not achieved any of the tasks that it had been assigned. Its location in Switzerland made it more difficult for it to operate, in light of the anticipated creation of a European Single Market which would not include the Swiss Confederation. Secondly, the period following the 1982 reorganisation had seen the emergence of a greater sensitivity towards issues of control and corporate governance, which had led to the signing of shareholders' agreements both in Pirelli SpA and in the Limited Liability Partnership. Pirelli & C.'s shareholding in the capital of the two parent companies (approximately 18%) was too modest to allow it to act firmly and authoritatively as the reference shareholder for the entire Group. The restructuring plan for the Group was conceived and proposed by Marco Tronchetti Provera, Board member of the Limited Liability Partnership since June 1986. In November 1988, thanks also to the success of his reorganisation process, Tronchetti Provera became Chief Executive Officer of Société Internationale Pirelli. He considered the 1982 restructuring operation to be overly complicated and inefficient, particularly in terms of the presence and role of Pirelli Société Générale.[19] His idea was to adopt a more cohesive chain of control, involving more significant stakes in the various

19 I explained my confusion regarding the reasons for the establishment of Pirelli Société Générale in 1982 to Dr Tronchetti Provera. He replied by saying he had had the same doubts at the time, and only managed to formulate various theories. Giorgio Rossi Cairo too, in an interview with this author, expressed a similar opinion to Tronchetti Provera, referring to the choice of basing the office in Basel as 'difficult to understand'.

companies in the Group. In his opinion, the reasons for a possible divergence of the objectives of the two parent companies was not immediately comprehensible, and as such, he sought to rectify this situation as soon as possible.[20] He also deemed it necessary to introduce the drafting of consolidated financial statements,[21] *quam celerrime*, something that the Group did not have and which penalised it in terms of disclosure on the capital market. The managing directors of the Group's companies were not overly enthusiastic regarding the proposals, but in the end they accepted.

The restructuring plan involved concentrating the ownership and management of all of the Group's operating companies under Pirelli & C. Thus, Société Internationale Pirelli would transfer all of its holdings in operating companies to Pirelli & C., with the exclusion of certain holdings in the tyre sector. In return, Pirelli & C. would carry out an equity increase in Société Internationale Pirelli, to reach a shareholding of 35–40%. Société Internationale Pirelli's shareholding in Pirelli SpA would then be increased by a further 10%, as Pirelli & C. would transfer its direct holding in Pirelli SpA to the Swiss company. Similarly, Société Internationale Pirelli would have been able to carry out a pro-rata equity increase in Pirelli & C., because of the transfer of the shareholdings received by the Limited Liability Partnership. In this way, Pirelli & C. would hold approximately 35–40% of the Swiss company.

---

20 The following is one possibility: Pirelli & C. and Société Internationale Pirelli represented different types of parties; the former represented managers, the latter the various branches of the Pirelli family. This brought with it the need to align the aims and incentives of the two companies, in order to achieve a stable, long-term compromise between stakeholders and shareholders. The dividends policy adopted by the two parent companies towards Pirelli & C. allowed this result to be achieved for a long time. This dividends policy, to which the company minutes (of Société Internationale Pirelli especially) dedicate a great deal of attention, may also have been a way of managing consensus between the various shareholders of the Limited Liability Partnership.

21 There was another atypical aspect that had caught the attention of Marco Tronchetti Provera: the difference in dividends paid to Pirelli & C. by the two parent companies, given the same risk. It is a known fact that two businesses with the same performance and risk need to have the same value, unless there are reasons linked to regulation, market collapse or the existence of private benefits, according to the literature on agency costs (Jensen and Meckling 1976; Jensen 1986). This difference was probably due to the systematic payment of script dividends by the Brazilian, British and Argentinian subsidiaries to Pirelli Société Générale. Partial confirmation of this can be found in the explanation of this procedure by Vittorelli to the Société Internationale Pirelli Board of Directors.

The Group's chain of control took on a strongly united appearance, with a precise division of tasks according to which Pirelli SpA would act as holding company for the operating companies, while the Swiss company would take on the role of financial coordination, thus also taking advantage of its geographical location. In this way, the 'diarchy'[22] between the Italian parent company and its overseas counterpart (first Belgian, then Swiss), which had lasted almost throughout the entire 20th century, would be phased out. The press, understanding the purposes of the operation, reacted mostly positively.

The project also involved the transfer of all shares in tyre-operating companies not yet transferred to Pirelli, including those in Armstrong, to a holding company with registered office in an EU country. The capital of this company – Pirelli Tyre Holding with registered office in Amsterdam[23] – was initially divided between two companies, with approximately 80% held by Pirelli SpA, and the remaining 20% by Société Internationale Pirelli, with the aim of listing it on the Dutch capital market. The final step consisted of establishing the Pirelli Gestion Financière (Pi. ge.fi.), led by Marco Tronchetti Provera, with the aim of obtaining resources on the financial markets, optimising liquidity and managing investments for the Group.

The reorganisation of the Group continued in relation to the specific project involving Pirelli Tyre Holding, to which all of the Group's tyre sector companies had been transferred by the end of 1988. This project was finished by spring of 1989 and the company resulting from the various transfers had a turnover of 4,100 billion lira, with 29 plants operating in 9 different countries, and a sales network presence in 60 countries. In June 1989, approximately 20% of the Company's equity was put on the Dutch market, for which Pirelli hoped to earn approximately 350 billion lira. At the same time as these reorganisation operations involving the Group's tyre companies, Pirelli launched a series of new tyre models on to the

---

22  It was a structure which had remained unchanged since the first major company reorganisation in 1921–1922. This 'diarchy' – sometimes real, sometimes apparent – had been skilfully used in certain specific cases (for example during the Second World War) to diminish the Italian group's ownership of the Basel company, thus excluding it from the blacklist of companies from enemy countries.

23  The choice of Amsterdam was made based on the importance of Holland on the international market in terms of disclosure and the quality of its regulation. However, it was a stock market in progressive decline. The weight of the capitalisation of the Dutch financial market on the total capitalisation of the Eurozone financial markets decreased from 18.37% in 1996 to 9.13% in 2006 (Bellavite Pellegrini 2008).

market: the P2000, P4000, P700-Z models for cars, and the TH25 and TH15 for industrial vehicles. The year 1989 proved to be a successful one for Pirelli. The Company was once again involved in Formula One racing, its new products were well received by the market, and the reorganisation of the year before began to bear fruit. The drafting of the consolidated financial statement was also invaluable in forecasting various scenarios and facilitating financial disclosure, providing the market with a clearer picture of the Group's assets and liabilities. The press placed particular emphasis on the positive managerial results obtained, but also on the considerable size achieved by the Pirelli Group (with a consolidated turnover of 10,000 billion lira[24]), and on its position as one of the few Italian multinationals in the global market.

The Group did not let the favourable moment slip by, and at the end of 1989, it carried out an equity increase in Pirelli SpA and issued convertible bonds or warrants into the shares of its overseas subsidiaries, which might have been of interest to investors. Société Internationale Pirelli – now with Marco Tronchetti Provera as Chief Executive Officer – also implemented an equity increase to support the similar operation carried out by Pirelli SpA. The Swiss Company's operation was similar to Pirelli's, combining an equity increase (which would have had the effect of slightly diluting the shareholding in Pirelli SpA, reducing it from 48% to 45.1%) with the issue of a warrant eventually convertible into Pirelli equity underwritten by 'friendly groups'. At the end of the year, the Pirelli Group incorporated a number of Italian wholly owned operating companies, the most important of which was Industrie Pirelli. The company created during the initial phase of the Dunlop operation had functioned as a container for the Group's industrial activities in Italy. Almost a decade after the dissolution of the Union, and following the wide-ranging reorganisation process carried out the year before, it no longer made sense to maintain a holding company solely for the Italian industrial activities, as this would be in direct contrast with the recently completed reorganisation process. This merger brought the brand owned by Industrie Pirelli back under

---

24 The tyre segment contributed to this result with a turnover of approximately 4,000 billion lira, generated by the activity of the 31 plants in 10 countries with a total of 31,270 employees. The turnover of the cable sector was slightly higher, at 4,320 billion lira, with 71 plants in 12 countries and 19,674 employees. Finally, the diversified activities segment had a turnover of 1,500 billion lira, with 43 plants in 13 countries. The companies of this latter segment included famous brands such as Superga, K-Way and Pirelli Bedding.

FIG. 5.1. DIAGRAM OF THE PIRELLI GROUP CHAIN OF CONTROL IN 1988[a]

[a]*Controlled by Jody Vender with 2.5% of the shares, Sopaf joined the shareholders' agreement on
20 March 1989, taking the percentage ownership to 60.1%.
Source: Our calculations based on official documentation provided by Pirelli & C.*

Pirelli's control, and restored both the land occupied by the Bicocca plant and
the shareholdings in the diversified activities sector – which the Group had been
planning to sell – as assets of the Holding Company.[25]

By the beginning of 1990, the hard work of the previous few years was beginning to pay off. The reorganisation process had contributed to restoring the
Group's competitive edge, and minimised the transactional costs generated by the
previous organisational structure. The reorganisation process had also enabled the
introduction of consolidated financial statements, a beneficial instrument in terms
of disclosure and communication with the market. These elements had improved
the market's opinion of the Group by highlighting the considerable size and global
calibre that had been achieved. These strengths, however, were offset by various
weaknesses, both of a transitory and a structural nature. A new shareholder had
become involved in Société Internationale Pirelli, whose majority shareholder
was Pirelli & C. Indeed, the Swiss BZ Bank had bought up a considerable block[26]

---

25  Following the heavy losses of the 1970s and early 1980s, Industrie Pirelli was also useful to
the Group from a fiscal point of view, with the possibility of obtaining merger deficits able to
compensate the Group's prospective profits.

26  *Il Sole 24 Ore* on 14 February 1990 writes: 'According to accredited sources, the Swiss bank
has acquired a package of shares in SIP, for itself and on behalf of clients, in the region of
20%.' This estimate is reliable. There is an indirect confirmation of this in the minutes of a

of shares in Société Internationale Pirelli but this shareholding would not affect the control of the Company. The initiative was led by the Swiss financier Martin Ebner – managing director of BZ Bank – and some of his clients. A second cause of concern was the progressive weakening of the management team, a slow process which dated back to the 1970s, and which was potentially problematic given that the Company needed to deal with new challenges that were appearing on the horizon.[27]

Major events in Europe in the previous years were opening up more dynamic investment opportunities in the new markets of the Eastern European countries, opportunities that would have been unthinkable just a few years previously. Standing on the threshold of the 1990s, the atmosphere in Europe was one of hope. The repercussions of the events of 1989 were not easy to foresee; the barriers and Iron Curtain that had divided Europe for decades had been swept away so rapidly that many still were unable to fully comprehend the reality of this new scenario. It was as if Europe – small and divided for years – had suddenly become bigger and, more importantly, free. The implosion of the totalitarian regimes in the Eastern European countries had restored the geography of Europe to its pre-1914 situation, leading people to hope that the terrible 'short 20th century' of totalitarianism (Hobsbawm 1994) had finally ended. What had happened in the East had posed a series of challenging questions to the West regarding the very idea of Europe. The demolition of the cement walls and barbed wire fences that had separated the East from the West would contribute to raising questions regarding even the most subtle barriers separating the various nations of Western Europe. The signing of the Maastricht Treaty and the end of the Common Market in 1992 were two important elements in the process of European integration. It was in this period that the fundamental role played by Europe in the everyday lives of its citizens and in its economy became ever clearer. Capitalism seemed to have won on all fronts; it was not clear, however, which form of capitalism.

---

Board meeting, according to which BZ Bank intends to participate in the Pirelli SGM 'with a symbolic share of 10%'.

27 The appraisals of the quality of Pirelli's management in the 1980s are almost unanimous, and point to the fact that the Company's great managerial tradition had been growing progressively weaker, having failed to stay abreast of the sudden change in the times, or to grasp the first signals of the globalisation which would completely overturn the Company's established habits in terms of management.

All of these elements represented challenges for Pirelli. Throughout the nearly 120 years of its history, the Company had always operated in a context of international competition, regarding new developments introduced by the evolution of national and European institutions as opportunities to further develop its own business.

In the summer of 1990, Leopoldo Pirelli celebrated his 65th birthday and 25 uninterrupted years as Chairman of the Group, having accompanied it through the most difficult years of its long history. He had kept the Group together during the 1970s and had reorganised it in the decade that followed. He had contributed to creating one of the first Italian industrial groups that was attentive to and conscious of the various local situations in which it operated, and he had done so in a context charged with social conflict and open protest against the role of businesses and business people throughout the world. In this sense, Leopoldo had carried on the legacy of his lineage, bringing it into line with the times. He had always dedicated more attention to the tyre sector than to other of the Company's business units, probably due to personal interest and involvement. In this respect, he had one regret: that of not having been able to oversee the increase in size which would have enabled the Company to become one of the leading global tyre producers. Indeed, all previous attempts to achieve that goal had not brought about the intended results. It is reasonable to assume that Leopoldo Pirelli was hopeful and optimistic for the future, confident in the continuity of the family-run company. This optimism was founded on the involvement of the fourth generation of the family, represented by his son Alberto and his son-in-law Marco Tronchetti Provera, who first became part of the Group following the invitation extended to the Tronchetti Provera family by Leopoldo Pirelli years earlier. Leopoldo hoped to bring his own time with the Company to a close with a high-profile operation, which would be his legacy to the Group. Despite continuing his consolidated analysis of the tyre market, Leopoldo had not forgotten past events, in particular the Dunlop affair, and had reflected on the corporate governance strategies to adopt in the event of a new merger operation. The Pirelli Chairman's intentions were announced during the SGM to approve the 1989 budget: 'In terms of the tyre segment, the majority of the market is covered by six groups; the first three are just over double the size of the second three, and we belong to this latter group. Strategically speaking, we should probably aim to join the first Group, but we can certainly survive for a long time as we are.'

As had occurred 20 years previously with Dunlop, the possible contenders for a merger in this case were cross-border options, and could theoretically include Michelin, Goodyear, Firestone-Bridgestone, Continental and some of the new Japanese companies that were successful at that time, such as Sumitomo, Yokohama and Toyo; however, most of these solutions were impractical for various reasons.

A merger with Michelin or Goodyear would have meant the acquisition of Pirelli by the French or US company, as was the case for Firestone-Bridgestone. A merger with the Japanese companies would not resolve Pirelli's size issue, and made little geographical or logistic sense. The only remaining contender was Continental, and it was on this company that Pirelli focused its attention.

The German company was slightly larger than Pirelli, and given the Group's aim of becoming the world's fourth-largest tyre producer, was the ideal choice from a size perspective. A merger between Pirelli and Continental would create a 13% share of the world tyre market. The geographical presence of the two groups complemented each other well: Pirelli was market leader in Italy and Latin America, while Continental led the market in Germany and Austria, and boasted a stronger US presence than Pirelli. The merger would also have allowed Pirelli to amortise its considerable investments made in automation. During the Board meeting of 14 September 1990, Leopoldo Pirelli outlined the possibility of a potential merger with Continental. In contrast to what had occurred with Dunlop, the entire operation would be based on the premise that 'any merger would be dependent on a defined majority share ownership and a single management strategy and policy line'. This did not mean that the Italian company necessarily had to be in charge, but the need to form a clear and cohesive majority was essential.

The Dunlop lesson had been learned. Continental, however, was not the right company to which to apply these propositions, for two reasons: first because of the institutional context of the German market, and also because of the specific nature of the company itself. The German capital market is the best-known example of a credit-oriented system, and in this sense, the institutional framework in which Pirelli operated with regard to Continental was certainly more consistent for the Italian company than the Anglosphere context had been. German company law, however, includes a series of regulations which make any integration between two companies – even if both German – extremely difficult, unless supported by a large body of stakeholders and constituencies. This consensus was all the more important if the operation was a cross-border merger. A central attribute of the corporate governance system of large German companies is its two-tier board,

TABLE 5.2. MARKET SHARES OF THE MAIN
PLAYERS IN THE TYRE SECTOR (1990)

| Company | Market share held (%) |
| --- | --- |
| Michelin | 21 |
| Bridgestone | 18 |
| Goodyear | 16 |
| Continental | 7 |
| Pirelli | 6 |
| Sumitomo/Dunlop | 6 |

*Source: Our calculations based on minutes of SGMs and
official documentation provided by Pirelli & C.*

which governs the responsibilities of the different company bodies, dividing them between the supervisory board and management board. The former is composed of representatives of shareholders and certain categories of stakeholders, including labour institutions and banks. As some of the competences of the SGM are delegated to the supervisory board, the consensus of this committee must be either obtained or removed to implement any form of integration with a German company. There was a further problem in the specific case of Continental: a clause in the articles of association limiting share possession, whereby no single shareholder could hold more than 5% of the company's capital. To carry out the merger with Continental, this clause would have to be abrogated. All of this required a qualified majority of shareholders.

Pirelli had considered all of these problems, and deemed the entire operation to be subordinated to the elimination of the clause limiting share possession, and to obtaining all necessary authorisations from the German and European regulatory authorities. The Italian company had also established a group of German and Italian shareholders which held over 50% of the capital of Continental, and which supported Pirelli's initiative. The plan developed by the Italian company[28] involved the acquisition of all activities of Pirelli Tyre Holding by Continental.

To finance this operation, Continental would need to effect a seasoned equity offering 'in the region of 50–66% of its entire existing capital. Once this increase had been made, Pirelli Tyre Holding would have the majority of votes in the control Group', having underwritten the deal in its entirety. Following a series of rumours and leaks, the first precise information appeared in the national press on 18 September 1990, but was received with reservation as there was no mention as to how the operation would be carried out. The German company's response to the proposal was highly ambiguous, releasing a statement in which it revealed having received a proposal for the acquisition of the activities of Pirelli Tyre Holding. This essentially related to the first part of the operation, but Continental failed to mention the second part: the shift of control of the company into the hands of the Italian group. What clearly emerged from the outset was that the management of Continental – and in particular the chairman of the management board Horst Urban – was opposed to the merger. Less clear-cut was the position of Continental's major German shareholders, including Deutsche Bank, represented by chairman of the supervisory board, Ulrich Weiss. These shareholders were initially in favour of the merger, on the condition that it took the form of a merger of equals, a condition for which Pirelli harboured serious concerns in light of its previous experiences.

Around 20 September, an outside observer would have deemed the chances of a merger between Pirelli and Continental to be reasonably favourable. The situation degenerated rapidly and unexpectedly on 24 September, however, when the chairman of Continental's management board, Urban, wrote a severe letter, vigorously lambasting Pirelli's proposal. The minutes of the Pirelli Board meeting from 25 September carry the original text of Urban's letter in full; its lecturing tone was reminiscent of that of a severe editor rejecting a research article sent to an important international journal and emphasising its shortcomings. In particular,

---

28  It was Merrill Lynch that offered a significant share of Continental's capital to Pirelli. The investment bank had previously offered the same share to Michelin, with whom the Italian company had considered a joint venture. Mediobanca did not act in the initial phase of the operation, but was subsequently involved in conceiving a way of dividing the entire Continental share block among different shareholders, in order to get around the restriction in the articles of association limiting the possession of capital to 5% of the shares with full voting rights.

Urban complains of the attitude shown by Pirelli's management at the meeting on the previous 19 September in Frankfurt, during which the Italian company refused to withdraw the initial project, as requested by Continental. The managers of Pirelli had also publicised the negotiations in a manner not in keeping with the style of these agreements. Finally, Urban complained of the unwillingness on the part of the Italians to reveal both the ownership structure of Pirelli and the nature of the agreements with the group of Continental shareholders who had backed the Italian proposal. Leaving aside Urban's tone, there was an element of truth to his accusations regarding the way in which the negotiations had been conducted, and the need for greater disclosure regarding the Continental shareholders who supported Pirelli. Urban's stance – albeit expressed polemically – did not differ greatly from that of Weiss,[29] which was expressed in a more conciliatory manner.

In short, the deal had come to a standstill. Unable to convene an immediate Shareholders' General Meeting to eliminate the clause in the articles of association that hampered the operation, following the request made by Weiss and Urban, Pirelli attempted to set up negotiations with Continental. Following a break lasting the entire month of October, rather lukewarm talks resumed at the beginning of November, starting with a more definite counteroffer from Continental. The German company, however, had another request: that Pirelli undertake not to buy or sell shares in Continental and not to convene an Extraordinary Shareholders' Meeting, whether for the purposes of removing the clauses, or for the purposes of 'any other resolution associated with a merger with Pirelli'. It meant asking Pirelli to adopt a stance of absolute inertia, an unfeasible option for any bidder company in a merger operation, as it essentially constituted the passivity rule in reverse! Another proposal that emerged from the talks was that of forming two groups of shareholders: the first associated with Pirelli and its supporters and the second consisting of German shareholders, 'linked by a pool agreement'. As stressed by Leopoldo Pirelli, it was a solution very different to that imagined by Pirelli, one which neither permitted complete control of Continental, nor consolidated its holding in the company. For these reasons, Pirelli decided to refuse Continental's requests and to convene an Extraordinary Shareholders' Meeting for

---

29 After his initial support of the idea of a merger with Pirelli, Weiss was thrown by the unexpected opposition from Urban and the management of Continental. The German press, too, presented Weiss's ambiguous behaviour and that of Deutsche Bank, the shareholder he represented, in a bad light.

the elimination of the restrictions posed by the articles of association. A SGM was convened for 13 March 1991 by request of a German shareholder, Alberto Vicari of Wiesbaden, who was not a supporter of Pirelli, but who objected to Urban's behaviour and wanted clarification regarding Continental's prospects.

The last few months of 1990 and the first few of the new year were spent in a sterile *drôle de guerre* which, if not helpful to Continental, was certainly damaging to Pirelli. In January 1991, Continental's management interrupted the negotiations with Pirelli once more, having concluded that the synergies identified by Pirelli were excessive and that the German company could develop a stand-alone strategy that would benefit its own shareholders. Also contributing to this change in direction was the convocation of the aforementioned SGM, which would permit the shareholders to express their opinion on the future of Continental. The views of the major German shareholders not hostile to Pirelli were changing. Through its representative Ulrich Weiss, Deutsche Bank[30] expressed a negative opinion on the merger, blaming Pirelli for non-compliance with Continental's requests regarding the freezing of shares; soon after, other German shareholders of Continental followed suit. For Pirelli, it was a completely different scenario from the premises on which the operation had been conceived. The German attitude was mixed; on the one hand, there was haughty hostility towards Pirelli from Continental's management, led by Urban, the chairman of its management board; on the other, German public opinion was divided into two contrasting sentiments, the first a subtle, but thinly veiled nationalism in the form of an aprioristic disapproval of an Italian company, and the second a mixture of embarrassment and unease due to the clear change in direction taken by Deutsche Bank. It was like 8 September all over again, but this time with the roles reversed. Although Continental was

---

30 There is indirect confirmation of these events in the diaries of Carlo Azeglio Ciampi, who on 14 February 1991 writes: '11.30am Pirelli. He is coming to discuss his problems following the failure of the Pirelli-Continental operation. The conduct of Deutsche Bank, which has changed position (first in favour, then against) is critical. He is asking me to report the matter to Poehl, at least so as to limit the outcry resulting from the conflict; Pirelli is prepared to close the affair with a compromise (a loss for him)'. Following this meeting, Ciampi notes a telephone call with Poehl on 28 February 1991: 'Regarding the Pirelli-Continental issue, I urge that the dispute between the two parties be tempered; Poehl replies that in relation to my reference to the Bank for International Settlements (BIS), he has already taken care of this with Deutsche Bank (Kopper). He believes that the resistance to the merger comes from the car industry; the behaviour of Deutsche Bank is in any case critical.'

the only feasible partner for a merger, the German company was not without its problems, all potentially hazardous to the success of the integration, particularly for Pirelli. The economic situation was worsening in Europe, and tyre producers, including Continental, were beginning to suffer losses. Even if the deal were successful, Pirelli would be faced with the twofold task of shouldering the costs of the operation and restructuring the German company.

In the meantime, the 13 March SGM was drawing near, and there were two sets of issues to discuss. The first regarded raising the required majority to 75% of shares to abolish the voting limit of 5% for the divestiture of important sectors of Continental's activity, and for the withdrawal of the supervisory board. The second block of topics was devoted to examining the abolition of the limit of 5% on share possession, and to the mandate to the advisory board to examine the integration of Pirelli Tyre Holding with Continental. Due to the way the agenda was organised, the SGM would highlight the effective presence of Pirelli and its supporters in the ownership structure of Continental, and the effective opinion of the Continental shareholders regarding the idea of a merger with Pirelli. The response was clear and was in favour of Pirelli. The first three points were rejected with 65.97% of votes against, while the fourth was approved. The fifth, from which Pirelli had decided to abstain, was rejected.[31] Pirelli emerged as the winner of the head-to-head of 13 March, although there was the distinct possibility that the resolutions would be contested by certain shareholders, as indeed happened. Given the results of the general meeting, the heads of Continental were forced to recommence negotiations with Pirelli.

When the negotiations started up again in May 1991, the situation was no different to that at the end of the previous September following Continental's rejection of Pirelli's initial proposal. There did, however, seem to be one important difference; in a surprise turn of events, the supervisory board of Continental had removed its chairman, Horst Urban (the harshest opponent of the merger with Pirelli up to that point), replacing him with von Gruenberg. Although the opinions of the new chairman did not differ from those of Urban, negotiations were resumed. Pirelli proposed the creation of a holding company that would control

---

31 This decision to abstain may at first glance seem puzzling. The point had been proposed by the aforementioned Alberto Vicari, and Pirelli's abstention stood to mean that the business plan formulated by the Italian company was one possible method of integration, but not the only one.

the entire capital of Continental and of Pirelli Tyre Holding. Shareholders in this holding company would be Pirelli, Société Internationale Pirelli and the Continental shareholders, as well as various minorities from two major Japanese companies, Yokohama and Toyo. For a brief moment, it appeared as though the operation might succeed.[32] Despite the promising change at the head of the Continental advisory board, the ultimate outcome was disappointing. Having realised the level of interest in the project proposed by Pirelli, the heads of Continental had decided to find a way to achieve the merger with Pirelli, but were ultimately unwilling to give up control of the company arising from a merger with the Italians and their allies. This prompted the suggestion of a 'light' form of integration with Pirelli in the form of a 'collaboration' of sorts, as they were defined in the minutes of Pirelli's Board meeting.

This solution was light years away from what the Pirelli Group had intended, also because it implicitly evoked the failure of the operation with Dunlop. Nevertheless, Pirelli kept an open mind, and did not veto the confused proposals presented by Continental's management. Although Pirelli's actions may seem inconsistent, they were driven by two valid motivations. Firstly, in June 1991, an important change had taken place in Pirelli SpA's top rungs, with Giovanni Battista De Giorgi and Ludovico Grandi being replaced by Piero Sierra and Marco Tronchetti Provera. While Sierra came from Brazil and was extraneous to the deal, Marco Tronchetti Provera – member of the Pirelli Board of Directors from its beginning – had always been critical not only of the validity of the merger, but also of its chances of success. Indeed, Tronchetti Provera agreed with some of the views held by Urban, despite the somewhat brusque manner in which these were expressed; he was also aware of the serious problems afflicting Continental. For this reason, the new Chief Executive Officer of Pirelli clearly interpreted the ambiguous positions of Deutsche Bank and Weiss as an attempt to find the right solution for Continental, while maintaining control over the company. Tronchetti

---

32  *Il Sole 24 Ore* on 11 July 1991 carries a positive comment from Leopoldo Pirelli regarding the change in chairman of the advisory board of Continental: 'The climate has changed since the former chairman left, and obviously I am referring here to Urban. And today we find ourselves in a constructive climate, with great willingness on the part of both parties to find a solution which suits both groups.' This impression held by Leopoldo Pirelli was substantiated by the first declarations of the newly elected von Gruenberg, who responded as follows to a journalist's question on the probability of a merger: 'Why not, if the merger is in Continental's interests.'

Provera's aim was to reach a clear and definitive solution in the shortest time possible to avoid any destabilising effects that long, drawn-out negotiations might have on the Pirelli Group. Concerned about the future, he began preparing to relaunch the Group following what he presumed would be the failure of negotiations with Continental.

So while Continental continued to move slowly, Pirelli was keen to arrive at some kind of conclusion. Those who had invested in the shares of Continental to support Pirelli's project were clamouring to know the result of the operation, which had been dragging on for almost a year. The summer passed without any further developments, and when work began again in the autumn, Continental presented Pirelli with its proposal, dashing any hopes of integration. After further checks, the new chairman of the supervisory board, Hubertus von Gruenberg, assured Pirelli that 'the management of Continental, which still shares the views expressed by Horst Urban, would consider any solution which puts Pirelli in a position of control to be a defeat'. Instead, Continental proposed a 'collaboration', which had the limitation of leaving Pirelli and Continental 'in autonomous and competitive positions on the markets, with differentiated and potentially divergent interests, at least as regards those not unified by the formation of business units'. The analysis by the Pirelli Board of Directors laconically concluded that 'it could lead to future difficulties in terms of relations between the two groups'. The ghost of Dunlop continued to make its presence felt. Both time and patience were rapidly running out for Pirelli's management. Nevertheless, the Company agreed to explore the hypothesis of a 'collaboration', under two binding conditions. The first was the formation of a stable core group of shareholders who would express the same views on policymaking, coordination and control of the Group; the second required a willingness on the part of German institutional investors to take on the block of approximately 25–30% of votes that Pirelli's allies had invested in Continental.

Part of this package was to remain with the German shareholders, and part would be transferred to the Japanese companies Yokohama and Toyo, interested in becoming shareholders of the new company. It was the same request made previously, this time with the additional request to the German company to help resolve the most urgent problem: taking on the shareholdings of the 'friendly investors' who had supported the project. The prospect of an effective integration with Continental continued to fade, and Pirelli, no longer believing in any possible positive outcome, began to face the prospect of a challenging and uncertain future.

TABLE 5.3. SHARES HELD BY PIRELLI'S 'ALLIES'
IN THE CAPITAL OF CONTINENTAL

| Pirelli's allied shareholders | Percentage of ownership in Continental |
| --- | --- |
| Italmobiliare | 3.1 |
| Finistahl (Falck Group) | 1.0 |
| Inverbar (Rocca Group) | 5.0 |
| Mediobanca | 5.0 |
| Sal Oppenheimer | 1.5 |

*Source: Our calculations based on minutes of Pirelli & C. SGMs*

Negotiations came to a close at the end of November and Leopoldo Pirelli informed the Board that continuing negotiations with Continental while exploring the possibility of 'collaboration' had demonstrated that any resulting synergies would be insignificant, should the two companies remain independent. This was the theory that Pirelli had held for over a year. Moreover, no solution had been found for the shares belonging to the groups that had supported Pirelli. The Italian company had therefore decided to stop pursuing any attempts at collaboration or other forms of integration with Continental. The frustration of having to shelve the long and fruitless negotiations with Continental, combined with the uncertainties regarding the future, cast a shadow over the Italian group. According to the minutes of the Pirelli Board meeting marking the end of the negotiations with Continental, not a moment was spent reflecting on the past, despite the fact that Pirelli continued to hold a significant number of shares in Continental. Following the brief report which confirms the close of talks with Continental, the agenda was dedicated entirely to the future and to the first measures to be taken to safeguard the Company, which was about to enter the darkest period of its long history, and its assets. The date 30 November 1991 was an important one for Pirelli, marking the end of an era, and a sudden leap into the future.

PART II

---

# THE REBIRTH

---

# CHAPTER 6

# The Turnaround

While the failure of the Continental merger negotiations on the one hand represented a setback for the Company, on the other it liberated Pirelli from a project that was proving to show a number of drawbacks. Towards the end of 1991 it could be clearly seen that the Group's economic and financial equilibrium had been jeopardised, and that the previous year's events had put an end to the strategy desired by Leopoldo Pirelli. What should have been the final stage in an industrial victory lap had in actual fact been a setback that put the very survival of the Group at risk. Additionally, this had occurred at a time in which the international economic situation showed signs of decline, and in Italy the critical economic condition was also exacerbated by an increasingly difficult political climate.

It seemed inevitable that the Group would have to undergo restructuring, but in that final quarter of 1991, not everyone was sure to what degree. This reorganisation process was not triggered exclusively by the Continental saga, but had deeper roots. The Continental deal had certainly exacerbated a sense of exclusion and inferiority that had progressively undermined the equilibrium and determination of the Group's management team.

The origins of Pirelli's difficulties, however, predated the Continental deal, which had simply contributed to bringing matters to a head. For far too long, the Group's attention had been focused to a worrying extent on tyres, and it had almost exclusively sought size-related advantages. During the long period in which Leopoldo Pirelli led the group, multiple almost dogged attempts had been made to achieve significant growth through external means, with a view to achieving leadership in the global tyre manufacturer ranking, and each of these attempts had failed. This previously mentioned 'obsession with size' had meant that systematic research on global productivity – necessary for the growth of any business – was relegated to the background. This lack of efficiency had manifold consequences; from the early 1970s the quality of Pirelli's management – one of the Company's strong points – had begun to decline. Although the Company continued to carry out research and to innovate, it was less able to create products that were more competitive than those of its rivals. Similarly, its ability to identify and make use of technological innovations that offered good investment projects had been reduced. The Group needed to define its objectives and to rapidly create greater levels of coordination between its foreign and Italian divisions.

The scenario was clear to Marco Tronchetti Provera, who had taken on the difficult task of following on from Leopoldo Pirelli. Tronchetti Provera understood that the Group's restructuring process would take place in very unfavourable conditions; at the end of 1991 Europe was suffering from an unstable and confused economic and institutional climate.

Tronchetti Provera saw two sides of this complex situation: it represented a huge challenge, but an even greater opportunity; he believed that in the New Europe, market competitiveness would no longer depend on the size of a company, but rather on its capacity to create value, and therefore on its dynamics of productivity. As such, the major upheavals taking place in Europe and Italy did not worry him; he saw them as an opportunity for growth, provided that Pirelli was in a position to respond to them quickly. Whereas rumours in the media focused on potential allies for Pirelli in the tyre sector, in the wake of the failed merger with Continental, Tronchetti Provera was increasingly convinced that the Company did not need to grow in terms of size, rather it needed to recover its productivity and economic margins. He did not believe that tyres could be merely considered as a commodity; the new CEO was not simply interested in the size of the Pirelli Group, but rather in its capacity to create value for its shareholders. There was a need to reclassify the product, to target it towards high-end vehicles and at the same time move from original equipment to the replacement parts market that offered higher margins. There were still two important issues to be addressed: whether Pirelli had the ability to innovate its product[1] rapidly, and how long it would take to achieve this. In both cases the answers were positive.

The reorganisation process that took place between late 1991 and late 1994 has gone down in history as a quintessential turnaround.[2] Mediobanca was involved

---

1  In this regard, Tronchetti Provera told this author in an interview: 'Fortunately, the product was there, but it needed to be organised.'

2  The Pirelli turnaround can be adopted as an academic case study, as it contains all of the key elements necessary for an operation of this kind, from economic, financial, institutional and management perspectives.

in a dual capacity as shareholder and stakeholder in the entire process, and supervised the methods and timing involved. Company documents from that period give the reader the striking impression that the reorganisation process was both titanic and prodigious, indeed, the scale of the operation was impressive, taking place simultaneously on several fronts, which were closely connected and interdependent from an economic, financial, organisational and – above all – temporal perspective. The turnaround process constituted both a departure from the old status quo to the creation of a new one, a process which required a stable financial framework embracing all business sectors, from those being decommissioned to those which were involved in new investment projects, and also to the ongoing incentivisation of personnel. As in the mosaics that adorn the apses of the Byzantine churches in Ravenna, and the Norman churches in Sicily, each tile in this huge work was judiciously placed to create harmony. Two elements, however, stand out as exceptional: the ability to choose the right timing, and the quality of the managerial team.

In the context of continuous and uncertain evolution, Marco Tronchetti Provera and the other Pirelli managers demonstrated their ability to seize the moment. The turnaround of the Company was made achievable by the cohesion and motivation of the management team coordinating the events.

Absolute priority was given to the restructuring of Pirelli, and therefore, the fate of the Company's interest in Continental was temporarily set aside, with the exception of those aspects linked to the financial implications of Pirelli's obligations. As with any restructuring or expansion project, the Company's financial structure was examined to hypothesise a framework of medium-to-long-term interventions that would allow Pirelli to successfully undertake the complete restructuring process and its subsequent relaunch. Mediobanca proposed Carlo Buora[3] as a suitable candidate to support Tronchetti Provera, and he joined Pirelli in autumn 1991 as the Finance Director. Tronchetti Provera and Buora were assisted by Enrico Parazzini,[4] who joined the Group in May 1992 to take on the role

---

3   Carlo Buora was born in Milan in 1946 and graduated with a degree in Economics from Bocconi University in 1971. He had performed a managerial role with the Merloni Group, with Snia Viscosa and with the Benetton Group, which he left to join Gucci before moving to Pirelli.

4   Enrico Parazzini was born in Milan in 1944. He also graduated with a degree in Economics from Bocconi University in 1968, and previously worked as a manager in the Honeywell Bull Group.

of Planning and Control Manager. Tronchetti Provera, Buora and Parazzini were the top tier of the managerial team that supervised the financial, planning and control aspects of the entire Group. The impact of a new Planning and Management Control process, implemented by Enrico Parazzini (who had already worked for 20 years with an Anglo-Saxon approach with the US multinationals Honeywell and General Electric), involved innovative methods and measures, and proved crucial as it provided the Group with a state-of-the-art system with which to face the challenges that would inevitably emerge in the new century.

Pirelli's financial structure had been significantly weakened, both from losses from ordinary management of around 100 billion lira, other significant costs, fees, compensation and depreciation associated with the Continental deal, calculated at approximately 350 billion lira,[5] and finally through the allocation of significant funds for depreciation and restructuring costs, equivalent to a further 220 billion lira. The total loss amounted to approximately 670 billion lira.

At the end of 1991, the Group's total debt stood at approximately 3,204 billion lira, while its net worth was 2,314 billion lira, with an estimated current value of approximately 3,500 billion lira. A comprehensive financial plan was presented to enable the relaunch of the Group.[6] The first step consisted of an equity increase of

---

5   The overall amount of 350 billion lira was calculated as follows: approximately 30 billion lira for the devaluation of the 5% of Continental held by Pirelli Tyre Holding, 150 billion lira in compensation to investor friends who had bought shares in Continental and 170 billion lira in miscellaneous costs. This quantification of economic losses also had to take account of the 65 billion lira for the purchase of 5% of Continental by Pirelli Tyre Holding and a further 150 billion lira to purchase option rights from the new investors (the cost of the option right on 32% of Continental held by Mediobanca). Overall, the estimate in terms of cash flow was 565 billion lira.

6   The relaunch was not subordinate to the restructuring process; instead the two aspects moved at the same pace. A great deal of attention was placed from the outset on monitoring investments and on selecting investment projects presented by foreign subsidiaries. Whereas previously the parent company announced the allocation of capital dedicated to investments for the current year, the procedure changed in May 1992 and subsidiaries were asked to present a business plan for approval by the central administration. Enrico Parazzini, head of Planning and Control for the Group, confirmed to me in an interview that the change in the process produced benefits in terms of making management accountable and improving the selection of investment projects. It is interesting to note that prior to this change, the Pirelli management was more than familiar with the techniques of drafting a business plan and capital budgeting to determine the actual net value of projects, but did not apply these techniques because the centralised capital allocation system meant this process was unnecessary.

approximately 500 billion lira over an extremely short period, while the second consisted of a large-scale decommissioning programme, particularly in the diversified activities sector and the Bicocca properties aimed at raising an estimated 1,000 billion lira over the next 18 months. Finally, Mediobanca,[7] which had played a key role in the operation, provided the Company with two separate credit lines for 750 billion lira each, one for five years through a pool of credit institutions, and the other for three years, through another pool of banks led by Credito Italiano.

This initial step was necessary to create financial stability, within which to implement a credible corporate restructuring plan in an increasingly complex economic scenario. The plan led to an important initial decision: to proceed with the decommissioning of the diversified activities unit,[8] an idea that had been in the pipeline for some time. As far back as the 1970s, at times shares had been sold to cover losses. Now the Group needed to generate revenue as quickly as possible and the divestment of the diversified activities sector allowed it to focus on its two remaining business units. Strictly speaking, diversified activities was neither small nor unprofitable as a sector – it had a turnover of approximately 1,500 billion lira with a respectable profit margin – but it did not allow for significant improvements in productivity, nor did it have the potential for specific investments or provide suitable managerial skills, given the wide range of products in question. The divestment of this sector signalled the end of an era. Over the course of the following year – precisely 1992, during which Pirelli celebrated 120 years in business – the Company relinquished a sector that, like the cable sector, had always been part of its journey.

The new year began with Extraordinary Shareholders' Meetings to approve an

---

7   The care that Mediobanca took in monitoring the Pirelli situation derived not only from the historical and well-established ties between Mediobanca and Pirelli, but also from the fact that the former was heavily exposed in the Continental saga. To this end, Ciampi wrote in his diary on 3 December 1991: '4pm Cingano. It relates above all to the Pirelli-Continental saga. Mediobanca believes that there is a chance that Pirelli can recover; this explains the important financial commitment made a few days ago.'

8   Parazzini (1999) writes: 'The new strategic vision translated into a decision to focus company activity on the two areas of core business, cables and tyres, in relation to which it is believed that the Group possesses specific and distinct skills that will enable it to compete stably and successfully. The diversified products sector is therefore to be decommissioned, with the joint effect of generating monetary flows, which can lower indebtedness, and reducing the scale of the competitive front and, therefore, the need for investment to support growth. Important property sales were made at the same time.'

equity increase. Leopoldo Pirelli's speech was dedicated to explaining particular details of the Continental deal,[9] while Marco Tronchetti Provera outlined the aims of the equity increase and the guidelines for the relaunch of the Company. The Pirelli Chairman spoke at the meeting about the 'cost of compensation' to investors totalling 136 billion lira that related to 'conditional promises made to certain parties who had decided to invest in Continental with the expectation that the value of shares would increase following the merger'. He added that this promise had an expiry date of the end of 1991, by which time, 'if an agreement had not been reached on the merger of Pirelli and Continental's tyre businesses, the Pirelli Group would compensate them for any damages suffered through the investment'. Pirelli had also purchased a call option from Mediobanca, at a strike price of DM60 per share, for two years, extendible to five, on 32% of Continental's shares.

At the meeting, Tronchetti Provera outlined the fundamental details of the Pirelli restructuring plan, and also referred to certain operational aspects. Regarding the tyre sector, it was crucial to recover productivity quickly despite the unfavourable conditions. Tronchetti Provera was willing to accept a reduction in turnover, provided that this meant positive profit margins. In his opinion, Pirelli was performing below its production capacity, and therefore could shut down certain factories, such as the Greek plant in Patras, while maintaining the same production capacity. This viewpoint regarded Europe as a single market 'served by factories located in five different countries that can be coordinated to serve as a widely spread, but united, source of production'. Furthermore, as previously mentioned, the Chairman intended to target the Company's products towards high-end vehicles, and shift its presence from the original equipment market to the higher-value replacement parts market. The cable market also needed to recover efficiency, although with two distinct considerations. Whereas tyres continued to absorb liquidity in their day-to-day management, cables continued to generate it. Furthermore, Pirelli was the world's second-largest manufacturer of cables,

---

9  Over the course of the meeting Leopoldo Pirelli stated that he had not wished to involve the Italian government in the situation, as it related to negotiations between two private companies, although he assured the audience that he had kept the Ministry of Industry informed at all times (21 February 1992). This comment is consistent with the history of the Company generally, which had aimed to keep politics at arm's length. It cannot however be denied that, given the size of the companies and the nature of the cross-border operation, political involvement was inevitable. Continental did not hesitate to involve all possible institutional figures from the Lower Saxony government.

TABLE 6.1. SOME FUNDAMENTAL DATA RELATING
TO THE PIRELLI GROUP IN THE 1992–1994 PERIOD
(SUMMARY DATA IN MILLIONS OF EUR)

|  | 1992 | 1993 | 1994 |
|---|---|---|---|
| Operating result | (92) | (7) | 53 |
| Net profit | (96) | 40 | 45 |
| Pirelli & C.'s share of net profit | (96) | 41 | 46 |
| Equity | 1,552 | 1,640 | 1,798 |
| Net liabilities (assets) | 1,359 | 1,088 | 778 |
| Gearing ratio[a] | 0.88 | 0.66 | 0.43 |

[a]*Ratio between equity and net financial position.*
*Source: Our calculations based on official Pirelli & C. documents*

a position which still conferred a competitive advantage on the Company, albeit a market lead that was somewhat in decline. The cable sector was on the brink of important innovations, both in terms of technologies and of the structure of the market.[10] A massive innovation was underway in the form of the transition from copper to fibre optic cables. The biggest changes, however, came from the impending process of privatisation of the utilities sector, both nationally and across Europe, particularly in the electronics and telecommunications sectors. The prices of various types of cables, and the amount of investment that would take place in years to come, would therefore be determined by the methods and timescales used in the privatisation process. One of Pirelli's methods for achieving consolidated sales in the cable sector had been to invest – as a significant, but always minority shareholder – in companies, organisations and consortia operating in the different

---

10  Vittorio Giaroli recalled how, at the beginning of the turnaround, the cable sector 'more closely resembled a confederation of organisations across different countries than the business unit of a multinational company'. Furthermore, Pirelli's long-standing presence in the various countries was established thanks to the cable sector, which continued to enjoy a strong cultural identity at the expense of a less cumbersome business unit coordination structure.

industries in which electrical, telecommunications and, in particular, telephone cables were used. This business method had become progressively less viable due to the ongoing presence of the public sector. Nevertheless, in a scenario of privatisation, Pirelli would have to reassess its role. Tronchetti Provera's response to those who asked what lay ahead for the Group consisted of a message of hope that revolved around Pirelli's employees: 'Our recovery forecasts are based on the belief that our management team has tackled the challenge of increasing the efficiency of the sector with determination, an awareness of the problems, and coherent aims. In this country, suitably motivated people respond in ways that are unparalleled in the rest of the world.'

As the seasoned equity offering received approval from the market, the Group took its first steps in the restructuring process: on 14 February 1992 Marco Tronchetti Provera became Executive Vice Chairman of Pirelli,[11] as well as retaining the role of Chief Executive Officer.[12] This appointment was promoted by Mediobanca. At 44 years of age, the '*dottore*', as he became known thereafter, found himself at the helm of the ship sailing through the heart of a storm. He was still relatively unknown to the public at large, which began to take notice of him in those early months of 1992. Having sketched out the guidelines of the business plan, Tronchetti Provera and his managerial team began to implement the individual elements of the turnaround process, starting with the personnel. The majority of the managers involved in the restructuring process came from outside the Company. They were figures who had been successful in their professional lives

---

11 Vincenzo Sozzani took on the role of managing director of the Société Internationale Pirelli in place of Tronchetti Provera. An executive committee was also established, consisting of Leopoldo Pirelli, Marco Tronchetti Provera, Piero Sierra, Filiberto Pittini, Alberto Pirelli, Vincenzo Sozzani and Alfred Sarasin.

12 Mediobanca, who supervised the first steps of the turnaround, would have looked favourably upon Marco Tronchetti Provera directly taking on the role of Chairman of the Group. It was Tronchetti Provera himself who objected to a solution of this kind and asked Leopoldo Pirelli to remain as Chairman of the Group. Pirelli's press release, following the Board meeting on 14 February 1992, stated that 'Leopoldo Pirelli and Filiberto Pittini believed that the moment had arrived to suggest to the Board that the executive responsibilities be transferred to those who would be managing the company in future years.' On 12 March 1992 Ciampi made a note in his diary of something Leopoldo Pirelli had confided to him: 'Mr Pirelli wants me to be aware of Mediobanca's behaviour towards him. Having convinced him not to resign last autumn, following the failure of the Continental deal, they then forced him to step down in February.'

and had joined Pirelli because they wanted to be part of the Group's restructuring project. Tronchetti Provera soon became aware of the various production and managerial systems in operation around the world[13] and, within only a year, had replaced approximately 80% of the management team and asked others to take 'a step back'.[14] In many cases this was not a matter of lack of confidence or of fault finding, as it was clear that the Group had been managed by honest people; these decisions were related to the desire, and above all, the need: 'for there to be no links with the past, in order to be able to consider the situation in a detached manner'. As stated previously, Buora and Parazzini were placed in charge of Finance, Planning and Control, with Giuseppe Bencini and Giuseppe Morchio in charge of tyres and cables, respectively.

To increase productivity, priority was given to information systems, which was entrusted to Arrigo Andreoni.[15] Over the course of the summer of 1993, the IT department adopted a new version of SAP, primarily for the tyre sector. This

---

13  Speaking at the Meeting dell'Amicizia in Rimini in 2004, Tronchetti Provera recalled this moment as follows: 'First of all, I travelled to fifteen countries across the world over the course of a short few weeks to hold face-to-face meetings with the heads of the various Pirelli units. I knew I would have to replace many of them, and I did so together with Mr Carlo Buora, but I tried to explain to each of them why the change was necessary. Some who had held important senior management positions up until that point did not accept the restructuring measures, but others did, and continued to contribute to the new direction we were taking, with that spirit of involvement, that company loyalty, that has always been one of Pirelli's most entrenched values.'

14  It is important to recognise and remember the human and professional value of those who participated, in the absolute majority of cases in a collaborative and non-conflictive way. Enrico Parazzini recalled: 'While, on the one hand, those who joined brought with them an injection of external professionalism that was necessary at the time of the turnaround, on the other we must not forget the value of those who took a step back. They were good people.' Similarly, Carlo Buora, in an interview with this author, recalled that 'the company recognised the soundness of the management, but didn't consider it to be entirely suitable to its needs. In any case, it was decided to optimise it for other functions, and the management accepted.' Both men see this important willingness by management to act in the interests of the Company as a distinctive feature of Pirelli. Giorgio Rossi Cairo focused, on the other hand, on Tronchetti Provera's notable ability to involve those who came from the outside: 'He knew how to foster growth in those who joined from the outside in an orderly and rational way. He knew to place a lot of emphasis on performance, but at the same time to provide a lot of incentive.'

15  Arrigo Andreoni, with a degree in chemical engineering from Milan Polytechnic, joined Pirelli on 1 April 1993. He had gained much experience in the field of IT systems with the Montedison Group.

decision arose from the firm conviction of Tronchetti Provera and Buora, not-withstanding the doubts expressed by Giuseppe Bencini, managing director of the tyre sector. Between autumn 1993 and the end of 1994, the Group's tyre sales and production units across the world began to adopt SAP. This system received unequivocal and significant acknowledgement at the Pirelli executive convention at the end of 1994, when Tronchetti Provera declared: 'Unlike our competitors, we have the means to compete on a global scale. It is called SAP.' The complete standardisation of IT systems implemented by Andreoni during, and following, the turnaround gave greater stability and facilitated the organisation and coordi-nation of the Group's activity, which was invaluable in the early years of the new millennium and again following the crisis in 2008. Invaluable contribution was given by Accenture – then still Andersen Consulting – in the implementation of the SAP information system and business process re-engineering in the Group's Italian and international activities. This task was undertaken by Diego Visconti, Gianfranco Casati, Silvio Mani, and later, by Fabio Benasso, who joined the project in 1993 to continue for the entire second part of the 1990s.

A third important element was implementing the concept of what were known as professional families, placing the highest levels of excellence at the core of the Group. Such experts would be in a position to foster a high-level technical skills profile throughout the world. This would also help in breaking the chains of per-sonal relationships, and redirect them into more institutional channels. And finally, the consultants involved in defining the strategic approaches took on a more significant role during the turnaround; in practice, they became assistants to the project management; they included Giorgio Rossi Cairo[16] and Vittorio Giaroli of Value Partners. Unlike other leading consultancy companies that apply a single organisational plan to multiple and distinct company circumstances, Value Part-ners was able to tailor its consultancy to address the Group's specific situation.

The Company was able to negotiate the fine line dividing restructuring from development. Condumex, a Mexican cable company, was sold to the local 'Grupo

---

16  During the delays in the Continental deal, Rossi Cairo briefly expressed his doubts about Pirelli's management system to Tronchetti Provera. The meeting only lasted a very short time because Tronchetti Provera responded: 'You are absolutely right, but everything has frozen completely and at the moment I can't do anything.' Vittorio Giaroli reminded the author that in that period, Marco Tronchetti Provera asked Value Partners to design a highly effective system, capable of monitoring the ability to implement management decisions.

TABLE 6.2. TURNOVER AND FUNDAMENTAL
DATA RELATING TO PIRELLI CAVI IN THE
1994–1996 PERIOD (DATA IN BILLIONS OF
LIRA – HISTORICAL EXCHANGE RATES)

|  | 1994 | 1995 | 1996 |
| --- | --- | --- | --- |
| Financial situation data | | | |
| Turnover | 4,831 | 5,532 | 5,123 |
| Net profit | 169 | 170 | 217 |
| EBITDA | 473 | 615 | 628 |
| Statement of assets data | | | |
| Net fixed assets | 1,632 | 1,629 | 1,620 |
| Operating capital | 726 | 823 | 593 |
| Net invested capital | 2,358 | 2,452 | 2,213 |
| Equity | 1,329 | 1,418 | 1,391 |
| Net financial position | 730 | 733 | 513 |

*Source: Our calculations based on minutes of meetings
and Pirelli & C. financial statement records*

Carso' with a significant profit, and Pirelli Bedding was sold through Pirelli France, signalling the start of the decommissioning process of the diversified activities. The pursuit of the primary aim of recovering productivity resulted in the closure of several factories, including Villafranca Tirrena, a Sicilian motorcycle tyre manu-facturer, and Tivoli, which produced tyres for agriculture. Although it was no longer competitive as it had been subject to structural losses for a number of years, the closure of the Sicilian factory gave rise to a protracted trade union dispute.

Between the end of 1991 and spring of 1992, the overall number of Group employees was reduced by 5,000 units, equivalent to 12% of the total, which created tension with the Italian trade unions. Indeed, unlike other industries where the structure of the market or its regulations allowed for advantages from location (albeit increasingly marginal), fierce competition had put a stop to such protective measures. Positive and sustained aggregate factor productivity had thus become fundamental in all industrial activities and, at least in Italy, labour was a factor that weighed heavily on overall costs. Pirelli's stance was not wantonly or ideologically hostile to its workers or their representatives;[17] it did, however, seek to communicate the following: 'a strong signal needed to be sent in Italy, and to the Group, that things had changed'.[18]

At the Société Internationale Pirelli Board meeting, Tronchetti Provera summarised certain aspects of the Group's turnaround plan, and focused in particular on 'a new organisational structure' that encompassed both the company framework and the product distribution channels. Regarding the first point, Parazzini (1999) writes: 'A strong policy of centralisation of authority was adopted, represented by a reduction in the number of managers at operating units and in the reorganisation of corporate activities which would be given the role of defining the Group's overall strategies and guidelines.'

Concerning the product distribution channels, Pirelli launched second and third brands in Europe, aimed primarily at the lower end of the market with a higher price elasticity of demand. Meanwhile, through its US subsidiary Pirelli Armstrong, Pirelli had entered into an agreement with Sears & Roebuck, the main sales channel on the US market.

Against a backdrop of the initial success brought about by the turnaround, the Continental saga still remained unresolved. At a meeting on 21 January 1992, Leopoldo Pirelli clarified the details of the operation and of the Group's commitment to pay compensation to its friendly investors. Tronchetti Provera had adopted a clear stance in relation to Continental: to leave it temporarily to one side and regard it as a financial investment in relation to which they should 'protect its worth, including recovering the costs incurred'. This approach derived from two considerations. First, the absolute priority of the Group was to proceed with the turnaround; among other reasons, this was also important to prove that Pirelli tyres had a future independent of its recent past with Continental, and this was the

---

17 The agreements surrounding the closure of the Villafranca Tirrena factory adequately safeguarded the workers. This issue was the subject of one of the first meetings held between Tronchetti Provera and the governor of the Banca d'Italia, Ciampi, who wrote in his diary on 19 June 1992 that he 'met with Tronchetti Provera. An introductory visit. He has recently taken over the running of Pirelli. He spoke to me of the company's circumstances, of the need to close certain factories, unfortunately in the South.'

18 From an interview conducted by this author with Tronchetti Provera.

only way to justify the huge investments made. There was also the risk of drawing time and energy away from the restructuring process, and continuing to invest in projects which had since been abandoned. Second, having upheld its commitments to the supporting investors, Pirelli proceeded to mark down the shares held by Pirelli Tyre Holding in Continental. Pirelli had also purchased an option from Mediobanca on 32% of Continental's equity. The Company was also awaiting the outcome of the ongoing appeal at the Court of Hannover, lodged against the resolutions of the meeting of 13 March 1991, and hoped that Continental would soon become profitable again. As it lacked any means of enforcement, however, Pirelli's strategy was to bide its time while the events took their course.

On 19 May 1992, the Court of Hannover upheld Continental's case, thus rescinding the shareholders' resolution to abolish the 5% shareholding ceiling. Although Pirelli was no longer interested in the abolition of that clause in order to take control of Continental, it lodged a court appeal against the decision to maintain the value of its investment. Indeed it was clear that the abolition of the clause limiting shareholding would contribute to an increase in Continental's capitalisation. The dispute with Continental now became increasingly complex. Another meeting, convened on 3 July 1992, recorded the rejection of the resolution to abolish the 5% shareholding ceiling, denying voting rights to the 38.4% of Continental that belonged directly or indirectly to Pirelli, objecting to the existence of a 'joint pact', in conflict with the 5% clause.[19] Pirelli's reaction was immediate. The Company, having responded that 'Pirelli and Mediobanca have proven that there is no other agreement between them, nor between them and the other shareholders in Continental' deemed this approach 'arbitrary and unjustified'.

Although Tronchetti Provera followed the news from Lower Saxony closely, both he and the shareholders supporting him continued implementing the recovery programme with determination. In July 1992, the vehicle parts unit was sold (mainly represented, in terms of non-tyre parts, by Metzeler and other small companies in Spain and the United Kingdom) to the British company BTR for approximately 240 billion lira, and in January 1993 the decommissioning

---

19 It should be remembered that Pirelli had a purchase option on 32% of the capital of Continental, but it did not hold these shares. It is unclear whether the term 'joint pact' meant 'concerted action'.

plan continued with significant transactions. The majority of the Bicocca areas belonging to the Technology Pole were sold for an overall total of approximately 190 billion lira. The major sports shoe brands Superga and K-Way were sold to a company belonging to the Sopaf Group, for 103 billion lira, generating a profit of approximately 70 billion lira. Although they failed to capitalise fully on the value of the businesses being sold, these transactions were concluded relatively quickly.

The economic, political and, above all, institutional climate made it difficult to determine the macroeconomic climate in which the Group's turnaround would take place. At the end of the summer of 1992,[20] however, certain significant factors had begun to emerge. Any noticeable improvements in the various sectors did not relate to the conditions in the market, but were attributable exclusively to the increase in global efficiency and factory productivity. Pirelli could only rely on its own strengths; it was clear that, while cables continued to generate revenue – albeit on an increasingly smaller scale – the ongoing process of relaunching the tyre sector was still not generating profits. There was a need to generate positive margins in the tyre sector before cable sector margins decreased further. Towards the end of the year, some optimistic signs began to emerge. The Group's overall debt reduced significantly, thanks partly to the divestment operations which had generated revenue with buyers taking on part of the debt, which fell from 3,204 billion lira at the end of 1991 to 2,632 billion lira at the end of 1992, while net worth grew from 2,314 to 3,005 billion lira. Employee numbers were reduced from 51,572 units in 1991 to 45,726 in 1992. A number of factories had been closed without impacting negatively on the overall turnover, which increased marginally from 8,145 billion lira in 1991 to 8,252 billion lira in 1992.

Nevertheless, the Group's market prospects for 1993 remained negative, and it was obvious that it had to shift into high gear. Over the course of these months,

20  In his diary on 16 September 1992, Carlo Azeglio Ciampi wrote: 'Increase in rates. I am taking my time; from the Reuters table it seems that the UK rate increase had no effect on the value of sterling. It seems useless and psychologically counterproductive to increase our rates.' Moreover a referendum in France in September 1992 on participation in the Maastricht Treaty passed by a hair's breadth, thanks to the authoritative support of then-President François Mitterrand. A similar referendum, on the other hand, resulted in Denmark's rejection of the Maastricht Treaty. In his diary on 20 September 1992, while in Washington, Ciampi wrote that Lamont, the governor of the Bank of England, had declared: 'In the United Kingdom, the European Exchange Rate Mechanism is officially dead.' This statement helps us to better understand the events of the previous week.

Tronchetti Provera became increasingly aware of the importance of keeping the market informed of the situation at Pirelli because 'we want the innovation to reflect an equally innovative productive system'.

At the beginning of 1993, the dispute with Continental drew to a close. Consistent with its previous statements, even in the wake of the turbulent events of the previous summer, Pirelli reiterated clearly that it was willing to consider selling both its shareholding in Continental and the 32% option, if an interesting offer were made. Obviously, this depended on Continental's profitability. Furthermore, the currency crisis had caused negotiations between Pirelli and Continental to accelerate sharply. The September 1992 crisis saw the withdrawal of the lira from the European monetary system while the Deutschmark remained firmly in place. This seemingly negative situation, however, had a positive side as the devaluation of the lira against the Deutschmark had created unprecedented margins.

TABLE 6.3 ROI, NOPAT, EVA AND WACC OF THE
PIRELLI GROUP IN THE 1992–1995 PERIOD

| Indicators | 1992 | 1993 | 1994 | 1995 |
| --- | --- | --- | --- | --- |
| ROI[a] | 4.1% | 5.1% | 6.9% | 10.3% |
| NOPAT[b] (Lit./billions) | 217 | 259 | 339 | 475 |
| EVA[c] (Lit./billions) | (631) | (572) | (446) | (253) |
| WACC[d] | 12.5% | 12.5% | 12.5% | 11.8% |

[a]*Return on Investment.*
[b]*Net Operating Profit after Taxes.*
[c]*Economic Value Added.*
[d]*Weighted Average Cost of Capital.*
*Source: Our calculations based on official documentation*
*supplied by Pirelli and financial statement records*

Pirelli gave Deutsche Bank and Mediobanca a mandate to seek a suitable offer for its shareholding in Continental. At the beginning of April the Continental saga – which had been dragging on since September 1990 – concluded with a healthy profit for Pirelli.[21] Pirelli had sold its 5% ownership and all of the Continental shares that were covered by the Mediobanca option, at a unit price of DM250 per share. Overall, the operation generated DM733 million, of which DM153 million for the 5% stake in Continental and DM580 million for the shares covered by the Mediobanca option. The buyer was the Government of Lower Saxony and an associated group of companies. This was an important step forward for Pirelli. The Continental saga, which had placed Pirelli near collapse, and drained huge amounts of energy and resources from the Company, was finally definitively over. The Group could now continue moving along its chosen path with greater determination.

Over the course of 1993, various projects launched at the beginning of 1992 also began to show results. That year, the new P200 Chrono and P5000 Vizzola tyre models were introduced for the replacement market. Despite no longer being involved in Formula One, Pirelli tyres had performed well in major international car and motorcycle competitions. As a company that had participated in car racing since the early 20th century, Pirelli benefited greatly from this channel of communication. The challenge inherent in sporting competitions demonstrated the exceptional technical quality of the Italian product, and thus a number of well-known cinema and sports personalities were brought on board to help deliver this message. In 1993, American actress Sharon Stone, a sex symbol of the time, was chosen for the campaign, while in 1994 it was the African-American athlete from Alabama, Carl Lewis. The powerful image of Lewis on the starting blocks ready for a sprint and wearing red high heels instead of running spikes, drew on his victories in the 100 metres at the Olympics in Los Angeles in 1984 and Seoul in 1988. The general public appreciated these advertisements, which increasingly served to earn Pirelli a name as an energetic, seductive company, combining reassuringly classic images with more engaging modern ones, and helped the Company regain credibility among its stakeholders.

During the meeting to approve the 1992 financial statements, Marco Tronchetti Provera provided an overview of the current state of the restructuring process. Within a context that was still critical, the Company's renewed capacity to improve efficiency through constant growth in productivity had proved to be the key factor. A reduction had taken place both in the number of factories (from 102 to 90) and

---

21  It is worth remembering that the book value for Continental in Pirelli's financial statements was DM207 per share.

the number of employees (approximately 6,000 employees fewer). Furthermore, changes of a more structural nature had also been introduced, such as the Total Production Manufacturing method, an innovative methodology based on continuous improvement in quality and productivity, obtained through the direct involvement of personnel. More generally, thanks also to the work of the team of consultants from McKinsey and Value Partners, the Company focused on a value-based managerial philosophy which did not, however, fully embrace the increasingly dominant shareholders' vision. If, on the surface, these decisions appeared to follow a trend that was particularly popular in the 1990s – on account of their ability to respond to the rapidly changing times in a concrete and determined way – in reality they had much deeper roots, which were born far back in the Company's history. The absolute focus on matters of efficiency and productivity, the continuous monitoring of the financial structure, the capacity for communication and the attempt to find solutions to corporate governance that were compatible with the Company's strategies were elements identified as the required premises to meet and satisfy the legitimate expectations of the shareholders and all categories of stakeholders. In Pirelli's case, this managerial philosophy was not a new concept imported from across the Atlantic, but rather a legacy of its founder, Giovanni Battista Pirelli. The Group continued, throughout the tumultuous period of the turnaround, to place huge importance on the then-emergent issue of sustainable growth, including also ethics and the environment 'which had traditionally been a matter of real importance for the Group'. Tronchetti Provera and the new management represented continuity for Pirelli's founding values, modernising them while retaining their original tenets. It became increasingly clear during this period that Pirelli was experiencing a true revival. The great industrial enterprise, founded in the late 19th century, was to continue its journey with foundations in keeping with that period, but which still embodied the same pioneering spirit and values as before, and with renewed enthusiasm.

Just as the founder had worked to expand the Group internationally into Continental Europe prior to 1914, and into South America over the course of the 1920s, at the beginning of the 1990s the new management team explored new frontiers, including Eastern Europe but also China and Southeast Asia, which were becoming key markets to develop. The first modest improvements in the tyre sector, in the second half of 1993, coincided with the onset of a somewhat anticipated crisis in the cable industry. The cause of this was of a technological nature, associated with the progressive replacement of copper cables with fibre optics, but was also exacerbated by privatisation in the utilities sector. Despite having dedicated most of its efforts to revitalising the tyre sector, Pirelli was not taken by surprise the changing cable sector, although the production structure was still excessively fragmented. The Group continued its research into fibre optics, and received significant orders for submarine cables with a high proportion of fibre optics. This marked the Group's renewed commitment to an activity that had its first steps in the 19th century. Nevertheless, in the second half of 1993, the market experienced a rapid decline in demand for cables, particularly telecommunications cables. From a company perspective, this decline – particularly evident in France and the United States – was combined with a significant fall in prices in the United States due to a reduction in the cost of fibre optic cables. It was a worrying situation; fibre optics should have represented an important technological innovation, but instead was likely to become a commodity. Pirelli was walking on the edge of a razor, believing that market conditions – which had been extremely negative up until that point – would improve in 1994. This unstable scenario was evident in Tronchetti Provera's speech to the Société Internationale Pirelli Board on 13 December 1993, during which he gave a statement on the progress of the Group, declaring: 'The performance in the cable sector is still positive, but in decline, whereas in tyres it is still negative, but improving.'

In order to address the cable crisis, Pirelli could implement two strategies: one was to continue working to restore productivity and efficiency to offer the client 'a combined cable, installation and accessories package'. The other was to play an active role in the privatisation process which also meant greater interaction with institutions. At the end of 1993, Tronchetti Provera examined the possibility of Pirelli participating in the process of privatisation of utilities, which was still under examination. Aside from negotiations that had taken place with various national governments for commissions in the submarine cable sector, Pirelli had already dealt with utilities sector managers in the early 1900s for the supply of electrical and telecommunications cables. Indeed, Pirelli had proved successful in becoming a shareholder in such companies, albeit without taking control, following a strategy of supporting its interests and receiving commissions from those companies in which it was a shareholder. Stakes in these companies also brought other advantages, ranging from research and development benefits to the creation of interlocking directorships and opportunities to monitor the dynamics of individual markets directly. The nationalisation of many electrical and telecommunications utilities made this strategy less viable, and thus Pirelli found itself in a position of negotiating as a supplier of goods and services with the shareholders and management of these now public companies. For the Pirelli Group, the prospect of privatisation of the sector brought with it risks and opportunities. The risks lay in terms of defining investments and establishing rates, and in the effective skills of the Company's management, since they had not engaged in the market in this way for some time; the opportunities lay in the potential of participating as a player in the energy and telecommunications markets which, in those years, were moving away from the monopolistic model. There were reciprocal interests at stake. Pirelli found the situation interesting, and so did the telecommunications companies; having Pirelli as a shareholder could constitute a competitive advantage, particularly in terms of information. In light of these considerations, Tronchetti Provera decided to monitor the process to privatise Stet, which at that time held an Italian monopoly on telephone systems. Pirelli's Operations Vice Chairman sensed an impending significant development in the telecommunications sector.[22]

At the end of 1993 Carlo Azeglio Ciampi was Prime Minister, having been appointed on 28 April of the same year by President Scalfaro to form a technocratic-institutional government. Of the many critical issues faced by Ciampi's government in its single year in office, the economic situation was the most worrying. Ciampi had inherited a public debt of approximately 110% of the gross domestic product (GDP), and an annual budget deficit that well exceeded the 3% limit of GDP set out under the Maastricht Treaty for countries that were soon to adopt the euro. Already in 1992, the Amato government was engaged in scaling back public involvement in the economy and promoting privatisation,[23] which had become more urgent following the financial crisis of September 1992. Nevertheless, it was Ciampi's government that instigated a seismic shift in the Italian capitalist system. Ciampi was well aware that competitive structures and a capable management team would facilitate an increase in the capital value of privatised companies over

---

22 This entrepreneurial intuition, which was further confirmed by Tronchetti Provera's participation in the G7 conference in Brussels in February 1995, gave rise to investments in fibre optics and systems management, which preceded those in telecommunications.

23 The Minister for State Investments in the Amato government, Giuseppe Guarino, presented Decree Law no. 333 to the Council of Ministers on 11 July 1992. The law provided for the transformation of IRI, Eni, Enel and INA into joint stock companies, and created two superholding companies for the shares. This project was abandoned, however, and it was agreed that the companies would be governed directly by the Treasury Minister.

time. Nevertheless, the Prime Minister was equally committed to stable control, by virtue of which long-term and non-financial industrial investors would be able to pursue policies aimed at maximising the value of companies, without any onset of opportunistic behaviour or free riding.

Regarding the privatisation of Stet, in order to establish a core of industrial investors that could bring about stability in control, Tronchetti Provera brought the French company Alcatel, and a group of Italian investors, on board in the project.[24] The memo 'Telecom Italia. An opportunity and an ambitious challenge' presented by Pirelli to the president of IRI (the holding company which controlled Stet) on 9 June 1993 reads:

The telecommunications industry is undergoing a process of global concentration. The future of the sector appears to be increasingly dominated by a small number of national producers who will be able to compete on a global scale. It is within this competitive context that the privatisation of Stet and its subsidiaries is taking place in Italy. There is a risk that this will occur through the pure and simple sale of individual parts to the highest bidder: the probable consequence of this approach would be the progressive deindustrialisation of Italy in relation to these important technologies and services, and the consequent progressive loss of know-how.

In light of the above, the analysis drafted by the management of Pirelli stated that:

Italy cannot recover the advantage gained against the competition by pursuing 'me too' strategies or autocratic strategies: what is needed, instead, are global-based strategies that bring together various specialists capable of deriving mutual benefit from potential synergies, which cannot yet be described in detail but which are clearly identifiable in terms of the convergence of technologies and the globalisation of the client base. Italy's barycentric role in this could be achieved not only thanks to the number and prestige of the Italian players and their potential allies, but

---

24 Tronchetti Provera involved Enrico Cuccia and Vincenzo Maranghi in the project, and they viewed it positively.

also through programmes of investment in research, made possible by the strategic weight of the Italian market.

This plan was drawn up by Pirelli in collaboration with Mediobanca. The Pirelli-Alcatel project was presented both to the Minister for Industry, Paolo Savona, and to the Treasury Minister, Piero Barucci. Given the strategic significance of the project for the two nations involved, Tronchetti Provera also informed Carlo Azeglio Ciampi and Eduard Balladur, the then-Prime Minister of France, of the plan, receiving full support from both. At this point Tronchetti Provera met with Romano Prodi who, as Chairman of IRI, was the shareholder of reference in Stet. Initially, it seemed that the project had met with interest and approval, but shortly afterwards Tronchetti Provera received a phone call from Savona warning him that he had 'sensed a strange atmosphere'. This phone call was followed by an article by Prodi in *Corriere della Sera*, in which the chairman of IRI explained the reasons why he was against the project.[25] Tronchetti Provera responded a number of times, providing his perspective and, at the Société Internationale Pirelli Board meeting, emphasised that 'it was never our intention to take control of Stet, but rather our efforts are directed towards creating a solid company that can play a competitive role in the telecommunications system'. At the Shareholders' General Meeting he also declared that: 'Pirelli's interest in Stet is of a purely industrial, and not financial, nature, in the sense that it is in the Group's interest to strengthen its ties with the main global operators in the telecommunications field, as occurred in the United States, in order to serve as a technological partner'. In *Corriere della Sera* on 27 November 1993, Tronchetti Provera wrote: 'The observations made by Professor Romano Prodi in yesterday's edition of *Corriere della Sera* did not relate to the industrial logic of the Pirelli project, of which the IRI Chairman approved,

---

25  On 20 November 1993 in *Corriere della Sera*, Prodi wrote: 'Stet is not intended for a select number of large investors but (forgive my rhetoric) for the Italian people and to a lesser extent for foreigners. No European country has ever allowed foreign operators to take the helm in the telecommunications industry.' And further: 'how would the French government react if Stet, in agreement with Michelin, requested permission to form the core of France Telecom?' Prodi then provided three guidelines for the privatisation of Stet: a) 'no' to a combination of manufacturing and service companies; b) a search for global alliances that would bring together European, American and Asian partners in order to face truly global competition; c) agreements with shareholders operating not only in the area of telephony, but also in the areas of all other new services associated with the transmission of data and images and all of the new interactive connections.

and to which he suggested only minor modifications when it was presented to him last June. I am not aware of the reasons for his change in attitude.'

Carlo Callieri, Vice Chairman of Confindustria, expressed a similar position in *Corriere della Sera* on 27 November 1993:

I feel the need to clarify that the development of telecommunications is essential in the competitive context that is emerging, as a factor of integration within the increasingly well-defined and internally flexible business system. This factor of integration takes on the same significance for competitive purposes as the traditional factors of production. It seems to me, therefore, that it is unacceptable for the Chairman of IRI, the majority shareholder in Stet, the monopolist in the Italian telecommunications market, to speak so peremptorily on the matter: while his reasons may be valid, his methods most certainly are not. The government, as shareholder of last resort in the interests of the country and its production system, is the only authority entitled to make decisions, after having consulted with IRI and Stet, but also with those with a legitimate interest in the Italian production system. That a matter of this significance for the competitive future of the country could be decided upon without a complete and transparent investigation by the government is wholly unacceptable.

Aside from the tone used by the Chairman of IRI, paradoxically, the analysis of the telecommunications market provided by Prodi was not very different from that given by Tronchetti Provera. What was different was the method used to arrive at the results. A more detailed analysis, however, suggested that even this difference was more apparent than actual. So what did the Chairman of IRI really object to? It is possible that Prodi had doubts regarding the ownership structure proposed by Pirelli-Alcatel, not so much due to the nationality of the industrial shareholders, but rather to the involvement of the Italian banks as shareholders. It is reasonable to assume that Prodi sensed that Mediobanca had a rather overbearing presence in the project in general. Although Tronchetti Provera had undoubtedly received advice from Cuccia, the project was industrial, rather than financial, and as such it was led by Pirelli, just as some years later when Pirelli took on the role of reference shareholder in Telecom Italia. In any case, this episode contributed to creating tension in the dealings between Prodi and Tronchetti Provera.

The close of 1993 coincided with the end of the second year of the turnaround.

Overall performance was very positive, despite the loss recorded again in the consolidated income statement due to extraordinary costs of the restructuring process. Debt had fallen from 2,633 billion lira at the end of 1992 to 2,128 billion lira at the end of 1993, while net worth had increased from 3,005 lira to 3,180 billion lira. Within a period of two years, Pirelli more than halved its gearing ratio, bringing it down from 1.38 to 0.67, while employee numbers decreased to 42,132 units from 45,276 the previous year. Although turnover had apparently increased from 8,252 billion lira to 9,210 billion lira, in reality this was due to exchange rate depreciation during that period.

The period between 1993 and 1994 marked the end of the most rigorous phase of the reorganisation process. At the beginning of 1994, the Pirelli Group re-entered the capital market by issuing a convertible bond into Pirelli shares, for an indicative value of approximately 1,000 billion lira. In the Shareholders' General Meeting the Board also asked to be conferred a mandate to proceed, if necessary over the following five years, to increase equity by up to 500 billion lira and to issue convertible bonds of up to 1,000 billion lira.

While Italian institutional and political events moved towards the so-called Second Republic, with the centre-right coalition led by Silvio Berlusconi winning the political elections on 27 and 28 March 1994, the Italian economy entered a phase of growth and significant innovation, supported by the devaluation of the lira and great industrial transformation. Over the course of 1994, Tronchetti Provera and the managerial team decided that the scenario was ideal to continue its expansion in China and the Far East, while continuing to support research and development in fibre optics and telecommunications and to develop innovative products in the tyre sector.

Issuing convertible bonds, however, gave rise to the problem of control, perhaps not in the short term, but for the future. The direct reference shareholder, Société Internationale Pirelli, did not intend to underwrite its own equity increase quota 'from the moment the operation surpasses the financial dimensions of the company'. This position did not mean, however, that the parent company did not believe in the validity of the restructuring plan. This decision was consistent with the need to maintain the financial equilibrium of the Swiss company, without further reinforcing it and the parent company, Pirelli & C. Nevertheless, the decision not to underwrite resulted in the significant reduction of the shareholding held by Société Internationale Pirelli in the Italian company which would have been reduced from 49% to 37% in the event of full subscription of the convertible bonds.[26] The dilution of the shareholding did not jeopardise the control of the Company, but it did highlight the need for further consolidation of the financial and ownership structure of the parent companies post-restructuring. While at that time it was simpler for the market to invest directly in Pirelli SpA, in the future, when the recovery process was complete, investors would also look favourably upon the companies upstream of Pirelli in the chain of control, as they would hold significant shares in a completely recovered company. As such, the Société Internationale Pirelli Board, having considered the possibility of selling part of the business, thus generating revenue to reinvest in Pirelli shares, decided to increase the capital, despite the potential risk deriving from the presence among the shareholders of BZ Bank and the investors it represented. The Swiss company, however, had received a commitment from Pirelli & C. to fully subscribe any shares not taken up.

In the summer of 1994, the restructuring process was almost complete. Another positive factor was the successful outcome, on 15 July 1994, of the difficult trade union negotiations with the Pirelli Armstrong Tires employees, which put an end to a contract that had been excessively detrimental to Pirelli. Readers will recall that the tyre division of Armtek – later known as Pirelli Armstrong Tires – had been purchased by Pirelli in the wake of the unsuccessful public bid to purchase Firestone. Having previously been considered and then rejected, the decision to proceed with Armtek was made in the aftermath of the unsuccessful agreement with Firestone. It was a largely ill-fated purchase because of the company's modest market share and as it was subject to structural losses, but primarily because of the massive labour and benefits costs that continued for three years after its acquisition in July 1991. The lamentable performance of Pirelli Armstrong Tires, and the excessive costs associated with its workforce and employee benefits, posed a threat to the Pirelli tyre division, making it impossible to achieve a satisfactory economic performance in that business unit unless the dispute was resolved. The successful negotiations with the embittered American unions to draw up a new work contract for the employees of Pirelli Armstrong Tires, therefore, could be regarded as the removal of a significant structural obstacle preventing the tyre division from becoming profitable once again.

---

26  The majority shareholding of 37% was further reinforced by a 5% share held directly by Pirelli & C. in Pirelli SpA. Overall, the direct and indirect shareholding of the parent companies in Pirelli SpA was 42%.

At the end of 1994, many pre-established objectives had been met, despite the negative market climate. During those same difficult years, other tyre and cable producers had also implemented important restructuring processes. In the second half of 1994 the macroeconomic scenario also showed significant signs of improvement, harbinger of the recovery that would characterise the rest of the 1990s. Prerequisites for extraordinary growth began to emerge from the United States and in the fast-growing information and communication technology sector. It was reasonable to predict that there would soon be unprecedented demand for information transmission cables. Indeed, it was no coincidence that in that same period the cable sector had overcome its most critical phase and, although margins were falling, demand had recovered satisfactorily, particularly in the areas where it had previously suffered the most, specifically France and the United States. The scenario in the tyre sector also seemed to be improving; the Company had completed its product reclassification process, including innovations in relation to its 'time to market', which was reduced from three years prior to the restructuring process to six months in the subsequent period. The decision taken previously to target the high end of the market proved highly successful.

By the end of 1994, it could be said that the turnaround was complete. A total of 28 factories had been closed, of which 21 in the cable sector and 7 in the tyre sector. Employee numbers had dropped from 51,572 three years earlier to 38,185 units. Similarly, the number of companies in the Group had decreased considerably, from 261 in 1991 to approximately 200. This had been one of the most comprehensive restructuring processes ever to have taken place in Italy, and it relaunched the Group toward new horizons. This extraordinary example of teamwork gave rise to elements that constituted both company history and a path toward the future. The turnaround was based on a foundation of restructuring and planning, from which it never strayed.

Pirelli's turnaround represented a remarkable process of industrial reorganisation from all perspectives, not just financial. Proof of this lay in the careful attention paid to the managerial, technological, logistical, organisational and planning and control aspects which constituted the bricks necessary to 'build a business'. From this perspective, the legacy inherited by Tronchetti Provera and his managerial team was industrial in nature. The Company had also built upon its history in the planning phase, and had proved itself capable of continuing to perform research and development with determination, even in moments of uncertainty. All these decisions had borne fruit over time. Pirelli's – and the

Group's – financial, ownership and corporate governance structures were also revised as part of the turnaround, elements which are increasingly important in the life of a large company.

Just as 30 November 1991 had signalled the end of the negotiations with Continental and the beginning of the restructuring process, so the end of the turn-around and the relaunch of Pirelli onto the global markets were closely linked. In order to plan for the future, however, it was important to ensure the stability of its ownership structures. For Pirelli & C., the shareholders' agreement had provided proof of cohesion, and at the same time had benefited from significant managerial results. In 1994, Camfin, represented by Tronchetti Provera, was the fifth leading shareholder of Pirelli & C.[27] In a manner consistent with its status in law, man-agement had been performed by the partnership up until that point, without too much emphasis being placed on the slight disparities that existed in terms of the percentages owned by individual shareholders. The signing of the shareholders' agreement did not introduce any major changes to this well-established tradition. Nevertheless, on 27 October 1994 Camfin purchased a 2.89% share of Pirelli & C. from Sopaf, to add to the share held by the Camfin Group, equivalent to 4.96%. In so doing, Camfin became the leading share holder in Pirelli & C., holding the most significant percentage of all shareholders, equal to 7.85% of the capital of Pirelli & C.

This purchase took on a certain symbolic value, and can legitimately be regarded as the final act of the turnaround. The reasons that drove Camfin to become the leading shareholder of Pirelli & C. are threefold. On the one hand Camfin needed to sufficiently maximise the value of the investment previously made, which had not generated much satisfaction thus far. The end of the turn-around would make shareholdings in companies upstream of Pirelli desirable. Furthermore, the fact that Camfin became the leading shareholder of Pirelli & C. at that time had a particular significance. This role was only reached at the end of the restructuring process. Regardless of the financial value of the investment, and given the legal structure of the Limited Partnership, this purchase allowed the managerial skills of those who had successfully performed the restructur-ing process to be demonstrated in a position at the forefront of the field. It was

---

27  On 20 June 1994 Camfin was the fifth leading shareholder in Pirelli & C., with 4.96%, after Mediobanca with 7.51%, Gim with 6.68%, Gemina with 5.31% and Sai with 4.98%.

FIG. 6.1. THE OWNERSHIP STRUCTURE OF CAMFIN SpA IN THE PERIOD
1986–94

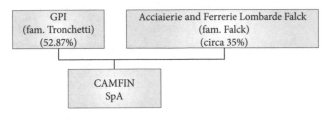

18 September 1986 (after valuation)

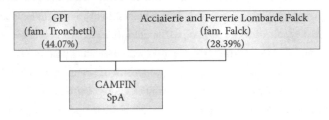

29 April 1994

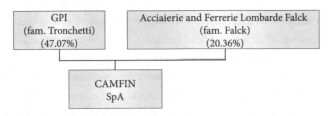

*Source: Our elaborations based on official documentation supplied by Pirelli & C.*

now necessary to establish a unit of company command and coordination that did not emerge either in opposition to the Pirelli family or in conflict with the shareholders' agreement, but as a natural and logical progression of the same. In this way Camfin assumed a position of command among the shareholders in the partnership, in preparation for new challenges. For this reason Tronchetti Provera dedicated the beginning of the following year, 1995, to stabilising the company chain of control upstream of Pirelli, in Camfin itself. Finally, the increased significance of Camfin shares in Pirelli relegated Mediobanca's role in the Bicocca company's capital to second position.

# CHAPTER 7

# Growth

While the end of 1994 marked the conclusion of Pirelli's turnaround process, with reports of a consolidated net profit and positive performance, including the tyre sector, the second half of the 1990s should have launched the Company towards wider horizons. The definitive resolution of the remaining critical issues in the tyre and cable sectors would create a path of stability and sustainable growth, with a focus on new investment opportunities on the markets. The main difficulty in the tyre sector was the United States; despite significant improvements in 1994 following the resolution of the previously mentioned trade union disputes, Pirelli Armstrong Tires was still far from being profitable. With the intention of definitively resolving the long-standing matter of the subsidiary, at the end of 1994 the Pirelli Board appointed Giovanni Ferrario as the CEO of the US company. Over the course of the following two years, Ferrario succeeded in relaunching the still convalescent American company, implementing a strategy that to some extent contradicted what had been done in the past. The new CEO closed the factory in Nashville, Tennessee – the scene of continuous and unyielding trade union disputes[1] – moving all manufacturing activities to the factory in Hanford, California. Secondly, Ferrario revolutionised the Company's distribution network which, in the United States, had revolved primarily around the Sears & Roebuck brand. This brand no longer generated profit margins for the Company, and so the decision was made to focus on the Pirelli brand which, up until that period, had only had a modest presence in the United States. As such,

---

1  Strong tensions were evident in relations with the workers and unions at the Nashville factory. Giovanni Ferrario recalls that on his first visit to the factory, he saw a worker who was supposed to be supervising the mixtures sitting on an armchair made from tyre scraps. He stabbed an arm of the chair with a knife, a move that was clearly intended to instil fear. The challenge was made more difficult by the overall climate in which the recovery took place. Indeed, it seemed clear that there was a desire to create conditions that would result in the definitive expulsion of Pirelli from the United States.

the decision was made not to focus on local manufacturing, but rather to import high-end models directly from Europe – and Germany in particular – to sell in the United States. As part of this same reorganisation process, Pirelli's distribution chain was also reassessed, and was progressively uncoupled from local tyre dealer networks. Despite some initial uncertainty, this resolute action proved successful, giving the Pirelli brand increasing recognition in the United States, particularly in the high-end market.

The situation was different, however, in the cable sector, which had also been significantly affected by the turnaround, despite having maintained a positive return. As the second leading global manufacturer in the cable sector, Pirelli had significant market power. In that period, cables presented an attractive growth opportunity for the Company as there were significant margins for improved productivity but, unlike in the tyre sector, geographical expansion was also an option,[2] particularly in Eastern Europe and the Far East. Furthermore, cables provided the Group with the opportunity to enter more innovative sectors such as photonics, which were growing rapidly, and fibre optics linked to the early phases of the Internet. This had been a recurrent factor throughout Pirelli's history. Due to their very nature as conductors, cables had always represented an opportunity for Pirelli to become involved in innovative businesses, from submarine connections to energy, telephones and finally telecommunications. Furthermore, cable manufacturing plants usually preceded those for tyres, and thus the scenario was promising for Pirelli. Tronchetti Provera did not overlook the fact that the current revolution in telecommunications, information systems and fibre optics meant an excellent business opportunity for the Company,[3] if it was capable of taking advan-

---

2   In January 1995, for example, Pirelli entered into a joint venture in the Malaysian telecommunications cable sector, subscribing for 30% of the capital in a company in collaboration with a local group. The opportunity to engage in a joint venture in China was identified in spring 1996 (18 April 1996) and implemented in summer 1996 (26 September 1996), representing Pirelli's first industrial involvement in China.

3   The protagonists of the last 25 years of Pirelli's history unanimously acknowledge Marco Tronchetti Provera's ability 'to always pay careful attention to the development of technologies and know when to seize opportunities' (from an interview with Carlo Buora). In reference to Tronchetti Provera, Spagna (2005) writes: 'I try to predict technological leaps. I have often been successful, across various fields. In the transport industry, I understood that containers were the future; with regard to tyres, previously considered a standard component of a vehicle, I saw that there was still a lot of technology which could be developed. That is how high performance tyres were born, and then intelligent

tage of any momentary gaps in technology and manufacturing. The privatisation of telecommunications companies in those years represented a further interesting opportunity for Pirelli, provided that the Company managed to take on an industrial role in the process. For these reasons, Pirelli decided to invest significantly in fibre optics and photonics.

To proceed successfully along this path, greater stability had to be brought to the ownership structure, and in particular to identify one of the shareholders among those who had signed the Pirelli & C. shareholders' agreement to take on the role primus inter pares as Cam Energia e Calore had become Pirelli's leading shareholder with a stake of 7.85%.

The increased weight of shares controlled by the Pirelli and Tronchetti Provera families would also reshape the influence of Mediobanca on Pirelli. It was decided, therefore, to integrate Cam Energia e Calore and Fin.P., the two companies through which the Tronchetti Provera and Pirelli families respectively held their shares in Pirelli & C. In the spring of 1995 Cam Energia e Calore resolved to transfer its Pirelli & C. shareholding to Fin.P., increasing the shareholding of Fin.P. in Pirelli & C. from 4.63% to 12.45%, while Cam Energia e Calore effectively remained a shareholder in Pirelli & C. through its shareholding in Fin.P. Following the conclusion of the deal, the two families held a substantial share of the capital with voting rights in Pirelli & C., significantly larger than that of Mediobanca. The dynamics of power between the two families, however, had changed. Following the transfer of the Pirelli & C. shares and the subsequent capital increase, Cam Energia e Calore had become the leading shareholder in Fin.P., with a percentage of capital with voting rights of 63.64%.

At almost the same time, an important change took place in the ownership structure of the company upstream from Camfin. As mentioned previously, Gestioni Partecipazioni Industriali (GPI) – Camfin's controlling shareholder, controlled by the Tronchetti Provera family – had maintained its shareholding in Camfin slightly below 50% in the years subsequent to its listing on the stock exchange. Following the previous operation, GPI began to increase its shareholding in Camfin to over 70% two years later.

---

tyres that communicate with the vehicle, and "run flat" tyres that never deflate. In the telecommunications industry, on the other hand, the technological leap was evident, and today it is becoming a reality.'

TABLE 7.1. PARTIES TO THE PIRELLI & C.
SHAREHOLDERS' AGREEMENT OF 27 MAY 1996

| Shareholder in the shareholders' agreement | Percentage ownership |
|---|---|
| Fin.P. SpA | 12.45 |
| Mediobanca SpA | 8.96 |
| Gemina Participations Sa (L) | 5.98 |
| Sai SpA | 5.67 |
| Assicurazioni Generali SpA | 4.9 |
| Ras SpA | 3.0 |
| Sade Finanziaria SpA | 2.86 |
| Cir SpA | 2.0 |
| Gim SpA | 1.0 |
| Lucchini Siderurgica SpA | 1.0 |
| SMI SpA | 1.0 |

*Source: Our calculations based on extracts from the shareholders' agreement Pirelli & C.*

There were two main reasons behind GPI's significantly increased shareholding in Camfin, both of which were connected to Marco Tronchetti Provera's role in those years. On the one hand, the success achieved by the restructuring process combined with the significant personal effort explain the increase in shareholding while, on the other, Tronchetti Provera became increasingly active among the GPI shareholders and, together with Jody Vender's Sopaf, purchased the shares held by his brother Roberto in GPI. Once the GPI reorganisation process was completed, Tronchetti Provera held 60% of the capital, and Sopaf became the second leading shareholder, with a percentage slightly over 30%.

The definitive end of the restructuring period did not bring less attention to the factors that had brought success to the Company: both products and the market continued to be monitored, as was the quality of management and the vital planning and finance sectors. The idea was to promote 'constant restructuring and innovation, which needs to be supplemented with growth programmes and the development of new technologies, new products and new markets'. Although the market was once again anticipating the announcement of a deal, the Company's modus operandi did not vary significantly from that of the previous years, except that greater emphasis was paid to the concept of development. Regarding this Tronchetti Provera declared:

> Rapid market development means that innovation has to take place, even during restructuring, in order to regain competitiveness, and this is something that the Group has managed to achieve. Innovation means looking at the market and at your competitors, and imagining what the market will require tomorrow, and consequently placing yourself in a leadership position, something which is key for a global company such as ours. And so in the tyre sector, where we are still global manufacturers, we need to focus on the high end of the market. The advances in the cable sector will be in telecommunications with photonics and in the energy sector with superconductors.

This was a necessary step given the rapidly changing scenario and with the possibility that the Company's traditional businesses could suddenly become obsolete. This was a serious challenge for the tyre sector, where the potential increase in productivity was rather minor. Accordingly, the Company continued to abide by the decision, which was proving successful, to standardise the tyre sector IT systems by introducing SAP, and to plan tyre production systems that enabled a higher degree of flexibility in production, also as a response to price dumping policies applied by new Japanese producers, and to take advantage of more advanced technologies which were helpful for producing small batches.

In the cable sector – which had potential for greater increases in productivity – the technological frontier was represented by photonics, involving replacing electrical impulses with light, which had possible applications in the telecommunications sector. This prospect allowed Pirelli to enter an innovative sector, and benefit from its research activities in new technologies with a wide variety of applications. The Company invested in 'the development of equipment to enable the best possible use of fibre optics', but also explored far-reaching business horizons. The G7 conference in Brussels in February 1995 – attended by the US Vice President Al Gore – marked the launch of the information superhighways and the birth of the Internet. This proved to be an historical event; 20 ministers and 45 business

TABLE 7.2. GPI's SHAREHOLDING IN CAMFIN SPA
BETWEEN 28 APRIL 1995 AND 28 MARCH 1997

| Date | Percentage shareholding |
|------|------------------------|
| 28 April 1995 | 47.07 |
| 30 April 1996 | 53.63 |
| 15 July 1996 | 65.76 |
| 28 March 1997 | 70.68 |

*Source: Camfin meetings, minutes of 28 April 1995, 30*
*April 1996, 15 July 1996 and 28 March 1997*

people participated in the G7 meeting, with Marco Tronchetti Provera[4] one of the four Italian entrepreneurs invited. The experience provided Pirelli with insight into the potential of the fibre optics market, and also laid down the foundations for later projects leading to deals with Cisco and Corning, and subsequent investment in telecommunications.

In the second half of 1995, the Bicocca Project was definitively set in motion by adding to the Technological Centre presented by Leopoldo Pirelli almost 10 years earlier, a residential area to be developed by Milano Centrale, a company controlled by Pirelli & C., which had become part of the Group in 1985 through the merger between Pirelli & C. and Caboto. At the shareholders' meeting to approve the 1995 Pirelli Annual Financial Statement, Leopoldo Pirelli publicly announced his decision to resign as Chairman of the Company, a role he had held since taking over from his father Alberto in 1965. The resignation was expected, as it had been announced privately during the Board meeting to convene the shareholders' meeting in question. Indeed, at the beginning of the restructuring process, Pirelli had already expressed his intention to relinquish his leadership in favour of the Executive

---

4 Tronchetti Provera emphasised in his speech that 'the Pirelli Group fully agrees with the objective of creating a worldwide integrated Telecommunication system, open to competition and based on common standards ensuring its interoperability. The European industry thus must get prepared to operate in a more dynamic and increasingly competitive market'.

Deputy Chairman, Tronchetti Provera. In expressing his willingness to lead Pirelli & C. for a final term and to remain Deputy Chairman of Société Internationale Pirelli, Pirelli[5] stated that he hoped Tronchetti Provera would be appointed as Chairman of the Company, and that his son, Alberto, would take over the position of Deputy Chairman.

The election of Tronchetti Provera as Chairman coincided with a new phase in the political life of the country. The centre-right coalition that had won the March 1994 political elections soon went into crisis, and at the beginning of 1995 was replaced by a mixed coalition with members from the previous majority and opposition parties to support a technocratic government led by Lamberto Dini. The new government had a simple mandate: to monitor the problematic public finance situation, to promote pension reforms and to call early political elections. These elections took place in April 1996, and were won by a centre-left coalition, with the support of non-reformist left-wing parties. Led by Romano Prodi, the new government had the task of leading Italy into the single currency in compliance with the Maastricht criteria.

This task was shared by most political parties in Parliament at that time, and was of vital importance for the future of Italy's industrial and manufacturing activities. To achieve this objective, however, the policy of privatising companies whose controlling interests remained in public hands had to continue. The new government's Minister for the Economy was Carlo Azeglio Ciampi who, as Prime Minister between 1993 and 1994, had set the privatisation process in motion and who was one of the staunchest supporters of privatisation.[6]

The emerging scenario was of great interest to Pirelli. It was indeed obvious that Pirelli might be interested in benefiting from the potential industrial value of privatising public telecommunications companies. The Company was less

---

5    Among the many expressions of respect received by Leopoldo Pirelli, perhaps the most significant was made by Sergio Cofferati, the general secretary of CGIL (Italian Left-Wing Trade Union), who began his trade union activity at Pirelli. Having acknowledged that Leopoldo Pirelli had contributed to making Pirelli an advanced model within the industrial relations system of the 1970s, Cofferati paid an unexpected tribute to Pirelli: 'Engaging in a handover, even when it is not forced by statutory requirements or company crises, is a confirmation of the style of the man.'

6    In his diary on 17 December 1999, Ciampi wrote: 'I did it because there was a need to send certain messages, particularly in relation to credibility; the privatisations were an initiative to gain trust and credibility.'

interested, however, in direct financial involvement, as this would reduce its potential to finance growth in its traditional areas of activity.

At the end of 1996 and into the beginning of 1997, the Company was unsure of how to proceed, given that the conditions for privatisation were unclear, especially those regarding Telecom. More generally, Pirelli's industrial involvement in the process of privatising telecommunications companies would necessarily involve dialogue and interaction with the political world. The Company's relationship with politics was as adverse as it had ever been at any point throughout its history. Faced with the dilemma of whether or not to participate in the privatisation process under the specified terms, a potential third option emerged: to consider operations that were not so closely linked to the political world, but were involved in the development of innovative businesses. In fact, the decision not to participate in the large-scale privatisation operations reinforced Pirelli's understanding that a healthy acceleration in its research and development activities of new technologies in the information system and fibre optics sectors would give the Company a significant role in the increasingly animated world of telecommunications.

For these reasons, the Company decided to opt out of the Telecom Italia privatisation process, sensing that there was little room for a purely industrial involvement, as had been the case with Alcatel. It maintained a certain interest in the privatisation of Sirti, however, which was taking place in the spring of 1997. Pirelli had been involved in the incorporation of Sirti and still held a 3.07% shareholding in the company through Pirelli Cavi e Sistemi.

Pirelli had signed a shareholders' agreement relating to 52% of the capital with Stet, the leading shareholder in Sirti with 48.93%, which also contained a pre-emption clause in the event of sale of the controlling share. There seemed to be no hidden risks associated with the methods of purchasing those shares as the company was involved in a business activity which was connected, downstream, with the activities of Pirelli Cavi e Sistemi. On 28 November 1997, the Pirelli Board resolved to purchase 87% of the capital in Sirti for a total of 1,355 billion lira. Pirelli's offer was in two parts: it would first purchase 39% of the capital from Telecom, which undertook to maintain a stake in Sirti for a further five years with a residual shareholding of 10%, and it would place a public purchase offer on the market for the remaining 48%. At the end of 1998, however, while due diligence checks were under way on the company's accounts, Telecom Italia, Sirti's main client, decided not to proceed with the Socrates Project, which

TABLE 7.3. MARKET CAPITALISATION AND
MARKET CAPITALISATION/GDP RATIO IN
ITALY IN THE 1990–2000 PERIOD

| Years | Overall market capitalisation in Italy (€ thousands) | Capitalisation/GDP in Italy (percentage share) |
|-------|------------------------------------------------------|------------------------------------------------|
| 1990  | 66,752,000                                           | 9.52                                           |
| 1991  | 68,449,000                                           | 8.94                                           |
| 1992  | 71,032,000                                           | 8.82                                           |
| 1993  | 102,630,000                                          | 12.37                                          |
| 1994  | 119,779,000                                          | 13.65                                          |
| 1995  | 150,064,000                                          | 15.84                                          |
| 1996  | 172,075,000                                          | 17.14                                          |
| 1997  | 295,542,000                                          | 28.18                                          |
| 1998  | 475,793,000                                          | 43.59                                          |
| 1999  | 691,590,000                                          | 61.36                                          |
| 2000  | 762,520,000                                          | 64.02                                          |

*Source: Our calculations based on Thomson Financial Datastream, Istat*

involved setting up a cable network between Italy's main cities.[7] This decision had a significant impact on Pirelli's evaluation of the company completed only two months earlier. After another two months of negotiations, Pirelli and Telecom Italia decided not to proceed with the agreement in relation to Sirti. It is reasonable to assume that this unpleasant experience reinforced the belief of Pirelli's top management that the best option was to continue developing in-house skills in

---

7   The Socrates Project was created in 1993–1994 following an idea by Ernesto Pascale, who observed that Italy was the only developed country with absolutely no cable television network. The Socrates Project would have provided an opportunity to reach approximately 10 million people over the course of 10 years, with an estimated overall investment of approximately €6 billion. The shelving of the Socrates Project had lasting repercussions on the methods of developing broadband in Italy via DSL.

innovative technologies, and focus less on the prospect of becoming a telecommunication network provider.

During the beginning of 1997 it became increasingly likely that Italy would become part of the single European currency from the outset. This was partly due to the high level of international credibility of certain ministers in office, and in particular, Carlo Azeglio Ciampi. This prospect risked rendering Société Internationale Pirelli redundant. Following the 1988 reorganisation process, the Swiss holding company held the direct controlling interest in Pirelli SpA, owning between 45% and 51% of its shares. The introduction of a single currency not shared by the Swiss Confederation would render the controlling interest of the Swiss company in Pirelli obsolete. Furthermore, a new regulation was introduced in Switzerland at the end of 1997 which made it a concrete possibility that Pirelli & C. would have to purchase the voting rights on the remaining shares covered by the shareholders' agreement in the event that it exceeded 50% of the capital with voting rights of SIP.

Before proceeding with this planned restructuring process, Tronchetti Provera deemed it necessary to complete other rearrangements in order to reinforce his family's hold on the companies upstream of Fin.P., which was the leading shareholder in Pirelli & C. As a first step, GPI purchased the remaining 12.6% shareholding held by the Falck Group in Camfin, through Acciaierie e Ferriere Lombarde, gaining a 65.76% shareholding in Camfin. This paved the way for a potential merger between Fin.P. and Camfin to shorten the chain of control between the Tronchetti Provera family and Pirelli & C. As part of this arrangement, it is noted that the Pirelli family had taken over the 13% shareholding that Sopaf held in GPI, the parent company of Camfin, and consequently also of Fin.P.

At the end of 1997, GPI's shareholding in Camfin increased to 70.68%, while at the same time CMC, controlled by Massimo Moratti, obtained a 4.92% shareholding in Camfin. The scheduled reorganisation programme underwent a sudden acceleration, not only because of the impending date of 1 May 1998, when the single currency was to be introduced, but also because the BZ Group, a shareholder controlled by Swiss financier Martin Ebner, had continued to increase its shareholding in the capital of Société Internationale Pirelli. Following a vain attempt to take over SIP, and having sold its stake in Siemens, the BZ Group's participation in Société Internationale Pirelli's capital, which dated back to 1990, had evolved over the years into a non-hostile presence. This was in part because, following the 1988 rearrangement, Pirelli & C. held a percentage of shares in the Swiss company that approached an absolute majority in voting rights. Furthermore, Ebner presented himself as a passive investor, who had more than once expressed his esteem for the Pirelli management team and positive opinion of the Group's industrial prospects.[8]

The two contemporaneous developments, the pending introduction of the euro, and the increased interest by BZ Group in Pirelli, inspired Tronchetti Provera to pursue two goals simultaneously: to shorten the chain of control and to involve the BZ Group as shareholders in Pirelli, but under some specific limitations. The idea was to proceed with a merger by incorporating Société Internationale Pirelli – whose role had become increasingly marginal – with Pirelli SpA. This deal would result in a significant dilution of the shares held by Pirelli & C. in the new company to be created from the merger. Tronchetti Provera hoped to involve Ebner in the deal to partially address this situation. Indeed, given the Swiss financier's real interest, the opportunity of detaining a significant shareholding in the operating company, rather than in a Swiss holding company, was most interesting. Ebner and his clients were also interested in holding Pirelli's shares which were easier to liquidate on the market than those of Société Internationale Pirelli. The first step in this proposed integration plan presented by Tronchetti Provera to the Pirelli Board involved SIP purchasing the participation certificates held by the BZ Group, and the conversion of these into ordinary shares. The second step involved Pirelli & C. – through its wholly controlled subsidiary Pirelli & C. Luxembourg – presenting a public purchase offer for all SIP shares in circulation, at a pre-fixed price of 350 Swiss francs per share.

Through the intervention of Pirelli & C. Luxembourg, Pirelli & C.'s stake increased from 44.8% to 62.4% to then fall to 59% following the conversion of the participation certificates between the end of 1997 and March 1998. Société Internationale Pirelli's shareholding in Pirelli Partecipazioni also decreased from 100% to 91.96% following the sale of the 4.92% stake held by Pirelli & C. and the 3.12% stake held by the BZ Group.

Following the conclusion of the public purchase offer, SIP would be removed from the Swiss list and the merger by incorporation of Pirelli SpA would proceed.[9]

---

8   Various sources have expressed a more or less positive opinion of Martin Ebner, who always behaved 'within the boundaries of good taste and decency'. It should also be remembered that, while Ebner was kept 'at arm's length' by the Swiss financial establishment, Pirelli and Mediobanca carried out normal business interactions with him.

9   In reality, in order make the deal possible, the SIP company headquarters was transferred from Switzerland to a country within the European Union where the headquarters of Pirelli

At the end of the whole process, Pirelli & C. and the BZ Group would possess a stake of not less than 30.01% and 10% respectively of the capital with voting rights in Pirelli SpA. The plan to involve the BZ Group required the Swiss bank to exercise its voting rights according to the indications by Tronchetti Provera as managing partner of Pirelli & C. This agreement was met with a certain amount of doubt as some believed that Ebner should follow instruction from Pirelli & C. and not one of its managing partners. To address this matter, and above all to ensure that the Company benefit from Ebner's esteem for Tronchetti Provera, it was proposed that Tronchetti Provera distance himself from the Pirelli Group before implementing the agreement with Ebner. The agreement also included two option rights: the first related to the BZ Group's right to sell its 5% share to Pirelli & C. in two 2.5% portions, and the second was a purchase option in favour of Pirelli & C. relating to a second 5% bundle of shares. Both of these rights would expire on 13 March 2003.

While, on the one hand, the deal would generate a substantial profit for the Swiss financier, on the other it drew a large and essentially non-hostile block of shares[10] to help stabilise the control structure of Pirelli SpA. Ebner subsequently made a friendly purchase of a share of the capital of Pirelli & C., bringing his share-holding in the Limited Liability Partnership to 6.38% in the year 2000.

According to the 1996 financial statements, the Group's performance for that year was excellent; consolidated net profits grew by 43% to 436 billion lira, despite a slight decrease in turnover. This positive trend continued during 1997, a year in which the Group set its future objectives in motion. In the tyre sector, the Company not only continued to implement policies launched during the restructuring process by focusing on replacement parts and high-end tyres, it also focused on certain products that offered potentially significant growth rates.

---

Partecipazioni was to be transferred. Immediately after the merger, the headquarters was transferred to Italy.

10　The deal, a first major example of a cross-border merger, was overseen exclusively by Mediobanca, as it was a financial rather than an industrial deal. Mediobanca had some doubts when arranging the transaction, as it did not look favourably on what it considered to be an unmerited benefit in favour of the BZ Group. Mediobanca's Chief Executive Officer, Vincenzo Maranghi, in particular did not look kindly on the fact that Ebner held shares in Pirelli & C., but at the same time wished to preserve the status quo in the company architecture. These doubts caused moments of tension between Marco Tronchetti Provera and Vincenzo Maranghi, which were overcome thanks to the intervention of Mediobanca's Chairman, Enrico Cuccia. An authoritative source reported that the elderly banker commented at the time, referring to the dispute, that: 'There is no spiritual chemistry between you.'

Pirelli concentrated on truck tyres in South America and particularly in Brazil, where it invested approximately 300 billion lira to renovate the Gravatai factory, which had produced motorcycle, farm machinery, truck and bus tyres since the mid-1970s. Developments also took place in the motorcycle tyre division; Pirelli had not been very successful in this segment of the tyre sector in the past, which had largely been entrusted to the German subsidiary Metzeler. To overcome these limitations, the new Dragon series of tyres was launched under the Pirelli brand, and these proved to be a success for less traditional motorcycles. In 1996 Pirelli had its car tyres approved once again for BMW, Mercedes and Porsche, and for the first time also Audi, thanks to the determined effort of Maurizio Boiocchi, who was appointed head of the research and development unit in Germany. Indeed, the innovative decision to appoint an Italian to lead the research and development activities in Germany proved to be a success.

The greatest growth opportunities, however, were in the cable sector. These opportunities were primarily geographical, relating to markets in the Far East, where Pirelli was awarded significant orders for the construction of a submarine cable system between the islands of Java and Bali. Despite the difficulties experienced in the early 1990s, the demand for traditional cables was on the increase once again. The field of photonics, in particular, in that period offered technology gaps which gave rise to positive net present value investments. In mid-1997, Pirelli was one of the few companies operating in this field, and had a significant technological advantage over its competitors. It was on the basis of this competitive advantage that Pirelli built its strategies for the future.

TABLE 7.4. ROI, NOPAT, EVA AND WACC FOR THE PIRELLI GROUP IN THE 1996–1998 PERIOD

| Parameters | 1996 | 1997 | 1998 |
|---|---|---|---|
| ROI | 11.3% | 12.2% | 12.7% |
| NOPAT (Lit./billions) | 604 | 582 | 549 |
| EVA (Lit./billions) | 12 | 24 | 30 |
| WACC | 10% | 9% | 8.3% |

Source: Our calculations based on official documentation supplied by Pirelli & C.

FIG. 7.1. PIRELLI & C. CHAIN OF CONTROL ON 22 MAY 1998, PRIOR TO THE
REORGANISATION PROCESS

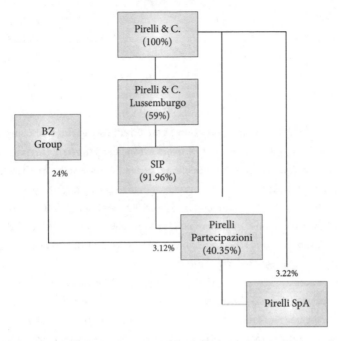

*Source: Our calculations based on minutes of shareholders' general meeting (22 May 1998)*

# CHAPTER 8

# New Horizons

In mid-1998, as the reorganisation of the Pirelli Group chain of control was under way, Marco Tronchetti Provera felt the need to strengthen the shareholding of Fin.P. in Pirelli & C. The capital of Fin.P. was held by the Tronchetti Provera and Pirelli families and this company had become the shareholder of reference in the Pirelli & C. shareholders' agreement, having continued to increase its stake in the Company. In June 1998, following the merger by incorporation of Fin.P. and Camfin and before the exchange of shares, Camfin also became part of the Pirelli & C. shareholders' agreement.[1]

The ownership structure[2] of Camfin changed significantly following the merger with Fin.P. as GPI's shareholding dropped from 70.78% to 51.47%, and a number of former Fin.P. shareholders became involved in the company, including Giuseppe Gazzoni Frascara and Carlo Acutis, with respective shareholdings of 9.33% and 9.30%.

In the years following the restructuring process, Camfin significantly increased its shareholding in Pirelli & C., thus reinforcing its role as reference shareholder in the shareholders' agreement.

In the same period, Mediobanca adopted a different strategy regarding its participation in the shareholders' agreement. In 1999 Mediobanca decided to offer a portion of its shares in Pirelli & C. to the other members of the shareholders'

---

1  The technical aspect of the transaction involved Camfin increasing its equity by transferring the 29,579,878 shares of the subsidiary Fin.P. held by third parties. In this way Camfin would have full ownership of Fin.P. The third-party shareholders, in exchange for the transfer, would receive approximately 12 million Camfin shares.

2  The members of the Pirelli family decided to sell the Fin.P. shares before the Camfin transfer, and to use the liquidity obtained from that transfer to purchase a 13% shareholding in GPI, Camfin's parent company put up for sale by Sopaf.

TABLE 8.1. COMPOSITION OF THE PIRELLI & C.
SHAREHOLDERS' AGREEMENT (24 SEPTEMBER 1998)

| Member of the shareholders' agreement | Percentage ownership |
|---|---|
| Camfin SpA | 13.41 |
| Mediobanca SpA | 11.69 |
| Partecipazioni Industriali SpA holding company | 5.91 |
| Sai SpA | 5.61 |
| Ras SpA | 5.31 |
| Assicurazioni Generali SpA | 4.85 |
| Edizioni Holding SpA | 4.00 |
| Cir SpA | 2.00 |
| Smi SpA | 1.98 |
| Lucchini Siderurgica SpA | 1.03 |

*Source: Our calculations based on extracts from the
Pirelli & C. shareholders' agreement*

agreement on a pre-emptive basis. At the same time, Camfin expressed a willingness to purchase any shares offered for sale by Mediobanca that were not purchased pro rata by other members of the Pirelli & C. shareholders' agreement. In the second half of 1998, Edizione Holding, the Benetton family holding company, became a shareholder of Pirelli & C., with an investment of approximately 100 billion lira and a 4% shareholding.

In the summer of 1998, Pirelli purchased the cable and energy division of Siemens, thus becoming the leading global manufacturer in the sector. This purchased division had a turnover of approximately 1,700 billion lira, 6,200 employees and 15 factories across various European countries, as well as Turkey, South Africa and China. This was an important purchase, bringing about a significant increase in size in Pirelli Cavi e Sistemi, and facilitating Pirelli's geographical expansion in the global cable market. The purchase also included the Siemens research and development division in the power cable industry, an investment giving Pirelli the potential to achieve absolute leadership in the sector. To this end, Pirelli made two further significant purchases in 1999 and 2000, as well as a number of other smaller ones.[3] First, it bought out the power cable business units of the British group BICC General, which had a turnover of approximately €700 million, 3,500 employees and 11 factories across various countries,[4] but mainly concentrated in the United Kingdom and Italy, representing 80% of the overall turnover. Specifically, this transaction strengthened Pirelli's presence in the submarine cable market, as BICC was a technological leader in this sector in the United Kingdom. Secondly, Pirelli purchased the energy division of NKF,[5] which specialised in cables for utilities. Through these purchases, Pirelli doubled its turnover in cables in just three years, bringing it to approximately €3.4 billion and thus consolidating its market leadership position.

Regarding the tyre sector, Pirelli purchased a majority stake in the Egyptian company Alexandria Tyre Company, but most importantly it also signed an agreement with US company Cooper Tire, the eighth-largest tyre manufacturer in the world. Cooper Tire provided Pirelli with access to its vast sales network in the United States, and in return Pirelli made its consolidated experience and long-standing presence in South America available to its partner. This agreement – which did not involve an exchange of equity – was an important alliance in the tyre sector, rather similar to the technological agreement with Michelin.[6] Just under 10 years after the failed merger with Continental, the strategy adopted in the 1990s to prioritise creating value for shareholders over the size of the company had been successful. The other major innovation in the tyre sector was the adoption of the Modular Integrated Robotised System (MIRS) to integrate production

---

3   In 1999, through the Australian subsidiary Pirelli Cables Australia, Pirelli purchased the cables and energy division of Metal Manufacturers. The purchased company had a turnover of approximately €180 million, and its core business involved manufacturing low- and medium-voltage cables for the construction sector. Pirelli also purchased from Sirti a further 50% shareholding in the Italian company FOS (Fibre-Optic South) for 72.5 billion lira (13 September 1999), as well as the remaining 50% of Pirelli Cable Indonesia.

4   There were factories in Zimbabwe, Angola, Mozambique, Malaysia, China and Singapore.

5   This purchase took place in the wider context of the merger between two Dutch companies, Draka and NKF. The agreement involved the transfer of the two NKF factories to Pirelli, one in Delft in Holland and the other in Pikkala in Finland.

6   Pirelli and Michelin signed an agreement for the development of PAX System, a tyre that would solve the problem of punctures.

TABLE 8.2. CAMFIN SpA's PERCENTAGE STAKE IN PIRELLI
& C. BETWEEN 22 MAY 1998 AND 10 MAY 2001

| Date | Percentage shareholding |
|------|------------------------|
| 22 May 1998 | 12.45 |
| 25 May 1999 | 16.48 |
| 11 May 2000 | 25.64 |
| 10 May 2001 | 29.62 |

*Source: Pirelli & C., minutes of the meetings of 22 May
1998, 25 May 1999, 11 May 2000 and 10 May 2001*

and sales, which was launched during the year 2000. The work of Renato Caretta, head of research and development, was vital in the early stages of the development of MIRS. Subsequently, Maurizio Boiocchi, who had previously led the research undertaken in Germany – an important market for the automotive industry – accelerated the pace of innovation, enabling Pirelli to successfully develop its premium strategy. MIRS enabled the Company to develop and manufacture both high and very high end tyres in small quantities, with a very fast development time, thus facilitating a truly innovative logistics and customer service system.[7]

In early 1999, the Pirelli & C. Board of Directors' three-year term expired, and Leopoldo Pirelli reiterated his intention not to serve for another term,[8] as announced three years previously. There were various reasons, including age, which led Pirelli to take this decision. During his final shareholders' meeting as managing partner with Pirelli & C., he eloquently declared that 'an elderly person can keep track of [innovations], though it takes great effort to do so, but only a

---

7   The Next MIRS production system, the second and innovative generation of the initial MIRS system, was installed in the Settimo Torinese factory which was completely restructured in 2009.

8   Vincenzo Sozzani, a general partner since 1984, also decided not to serve another term. They were replaced in their roles as partners by the managing director for finance, Carlo Buora, and Carlo Alessandro Puri Negri, who had contributed to the development of the real estate sector of Pirelli & C.

young person can ride the waves they set off'. He also stated that he was pleased to leave the Group in the capable hands of Marco Tronchetti Provera and his own son Alberto, who had complementary personalities and skills. Consequently, Tronchetti Provera was appointed Chairman of the Limited Liability Partnership and Alberto Pirelli was appointed Deputy Chairman. It was the first time since its foundation that Pirelli & C. had a Chairman that did not bear the Pirelli surname, although that Chairman was still part of the family.

While continuing to perform its traditional role as holding company and reference shareholder for the Group over the course of the preceding years, Pirelli & C. had also updated its business activities. It had progressively distanced itself from financial activities, since its relatively small size made it difficult to operate in such markets, whereas it increased its involvement in real estate. It started operating in the real estate sector following the merger with Caboto in the mid-1980s, and then successfully pursued these activities through its subsidiary, Milano Centrale. On a number of occasions the Group had been required to redevelop large industrial areas, and sometimes to find new uses for these spaces. This practice became increasingly common between the 1980s and 1990s, when Pirelli started the Bicocca Project which involved redeveloping the Group's historical industrial zone as large industrial complexes in north-east Milan were no longer required.

Scattered as they were throughout the Company's history, these experiences had never coalesced into a unified industrial project, as they were considered to lie outside Pirelli's traditional business activities. While various types of real estate activities had never been part of the Company's business activities, two factors emerged over time which contributed to change this perspective. Firstly, after a long period of stagnation, the real estate sector underwent significant growth from the mid-1990s, particularly in the Lombardy area. Moreover, in that period, the market's perception of the real estate sector changed radically. Indeed, the sector began to take on a more complex form combining industrial factors such as construction with other factors linked to service, development and more general managerial activities, including the integrated management of technical, economic and financial aspects associated with large residential and commercial building complexes under construction or already built.

The radically changing scenario in real estate made this sector more interesting to the Pirelli Group, as it provided the ideal opportunity to put its managerial know-how to use. These reflections led Pirelli & C. to resume its activities through its subsidiary, Milano Centrale, with a particular focus on the property sector. It submitted a non-hostile tender offer on the entire capital of Unim, a real estate company founded from the divestment of the property-related activities of the Istituto Nazionale di Assicurazioni. The offer was successful, with Pirelli gaining control of 89.088% of the company's capital.[9] Similarly, in collaboration with Benetton Group and the Caltagirone and Vianini Group, Pirelli participated in the 'Grandi Stazioni' project by the Italian State railways (Ferrovie dello Stato), which focused on the redevelopment and integrated management of 13 large railway station complexes in major Italian cities, and in conjunction with other Italian and foreign institutional investors, purchased 50% of the company Risanamento Napoli.

The Company quickly adopted the Preda Code of Conduct for listed companies, which had been drawn up in the context of an ever-increasing emphasis on corporate governance. Indeed, the ownership structure of the company that controlled the Group represented an appropriate balance between a public company and a company with a core group of shareholders. The Pirelli family had never been the reference shareholder, never having held a percentage of capital with voting rights in excess of 15%, but had taken on the role of guiding shareholder in the Group. Furthermore, the Pirelli family had always shown a strong managerial vocation, which had enabled them to combine the role of shareholder with that of front-line manager for more than a century. For these reasons, the Company had always been acutely aware of issues of corporate governance, long before such matters took on their current significance. The latter half of the 1990s was a moment of rapid growth in capital markets around the world. The reasons behind this sometimes turbulent growth, defined by Alan Greenspan – the then-President of the Federal Reserve Board – as 'irrational exuberance', lay mainly in the exceptional positive response of the capital markets towards the major technological innovations of those years, and in particular towards the Internet.

On both sides of the Atlantic ocean there was a sense of unlimited trust in the virtues of market capitalism which had succeeded in defeating its ideological

---

9   The total indicative value of the transaction was approximately 4,300 billion lira, of which 3,550 billion lira was controlled by institutional investors and 750 billion lira directly by Milano Centrale. Following the withdrawal of Unim from the list, the deal involved a series of spin-offs of Unim's properties, on the basis of their future placement on the property market. Approximately 1,700 billion lira in property was to be immediately transferred to Iniziativa Edilizia, a company in which Milano Centrale held a 25% shareholding and Morgan Stanley property funds held a 75% shareholding.

opponent. The triumph of capitalism had also returned a previously divided Europe to a situation which resembled that of the period prior to 1914. Once more, the Old Continent seemed capable of taking on a key role in the global economic and political scenario. The advent of the euro had indeed created a single capital market, leading to greater economic integration among European nations, something which had been unimaginable until very recently. It almost seemed that new technologies might be capable of rendering traditional manufacturing methods obsolete, and thus establish a golden rule for uninterrupted economic growth. For a time it seemed that economic crises, and the associated ordeals of unemployment and poverty, were destined to become mere relics of the past.

In a climate of such great optimism, the telecommunications sector without doubt represented a fundamental crossroads, particularly given its close association with the new technologies. The process of liberalising the telecommunications sector, in both the United States and the European Union, contributed to this perspective. On the other side of the Atlantic, the 1996 Telecommunications Act (the first intervention by Congress in the telecommunications sector since the 1934 Communications Act) had two objectives: 'the promotion of competition in all markets, and the breaking down of legal barriers that posed an obstacle to the convergence of telecommunications and TV: mobile and fixed, local and long distance' (Cambini, Ravazzi and Valletti 2003). In a European Union context, the 1993 European Council Resolution set 1 January 1998 as the date for total liberalisation of voice telephony. Indeed, the process of liberalisation of the telecommunications sector and promoting competition was derived from a clear political desire to formulate prices more in line with costs, thus promoting the interests of the consumer. The United Kingdom was an exception in this context, as liberalisation had begun with the 1981 Telecommunications Act, which approved the establishment of British Telecom as a separate entity to the Post Office. Subsequently, in 1984, 51% of British Telecom was offered on the market, and a simultaneous decision was made to establish a legal duopoly between the incumbent and the newly established company, Mercury, for a period of seven years until 1991.

Given its long-standing involvement in the cable sector, Pirelli naturally found itself at the centre of the developing business opportunities, and was not caught unprepared. The Company had been involved in the fibre optics sector since the mid-1980s through FOS, in a joint venture with Sirti, a subsidiary of Telecom Italia. Furthermore, it had continued to engage in research and monitoring activities, and had kept an eye on innovations in the market, even during the years of the turnaround, and had entered into research agreements with major Italian and European university institutes. Soon the Company found itself in a leading position in the photonics research[10] sector, 'an area in which the convergence with electronics and network software is key'. Pirelli had gone on to explore related fields of research, and had found itself engaged in terrestrial optical systems, drawing on its skills in fibre optics to develop optical components.

There was, however, an important difference in terms of areas of competence that was very clear to the company heads. Indeed there was an important difference between Pirelli taking on the role of optical technology supplier for large integrated systems manufacturers of the period and it becoming a manufacturer and supplier of those systems. The role of manufacturer was reserved for companies that could not only use their skills in the fibre optics field, but also in the electronics and network management fields, or in software, two sectors in which Pirelli had no specific skills. It is no coincidence that the main manufacturers of integrated systems were the leading electronics companies of the period. There were two difficult barriers to overcome. First, the supply of these integrated systems required knowledge of electronics and software that did not fall within the scope of the Company's traditional business areas. Second, the other integrated systems suppliers – Pirelli's potential competitors in that market – were significantly larger than Pirelli. For these reasons, despite being well positioned the field of terrestrial optical systems, it was difficult for Pirelli to successfully transform itself into an integrated systems supplier. The sector consisted of two distinct businesses, featuring complementary elements which Pirelli diligently explored to identify how it could enter and establish itself in the market.

The research plan which had led the Company to engage in terrestrial optical systems suggested that this technology was of much greater value to an integrated systems manufacturer than to a 'single platform' manufacturer, as Pirelli was at the time. Furthermore, it seemed clear that an alliance with a manufacturer of this kind would not only offer excellent placement opportunities within the terrestrial optical systems field, but would provide the Company with new growth prospects in certain niche markets, particularly in the optical components field in which

---

10 In the early 1990s the Pirelli Group was sufficiently organised to ensure that its research activities were suitably protected by patents. Previously, a researcher from the Group had mistakenly published important research findings in a scientific journal, without considering whether these were patent protected.

Pirelli had a very good footing. This analysis proved correct, and it was the market that made the first move by knocking on Pirelli's door. In the summer of 1999, John Chambers, CEO of Cisco – one of the leading manufacturers of integrated systems at the time – approached Pirelli through Merrill Lynch to investigate the possibility of an alliance in line with the terms outlined above.

This was an extremely appealing prospect for Pirelli. On the one hand, it could put its know-how in terrestrial optical systems to the best possible use, while on the other, it could continue to serve as an optical components producer and supplier to Cisco in the photonics market. Indeed, the American company was an ideal partner for Pirelli, as it had successfully developed a strategy focused more on the assembly and creation of integrated systems than on the manufacture of single components, a strategy that complemented that of Pirelli. In December 1999, the two companies reached a far-reaching agreement which was founded on three significant points.

First, Pirelli would transfer its terrestrial optical systems activities to Cisco for an indicative value of approximately $2.15 billion. It was a significant amount, but in line with the valuations of the period. Given that Cisco – in accordance with the aforementioned strategy – did not intend to purchase Pirelli's optical components business, the agreement also included the incorporation of a joint venture named OTUSA (Optical Technologies USA), to carry out research and development of optical components and submarine optical systems in which Cisco would invest approximately $25 million for a 10% shareholding. Finally, the American company secured itself a constant supply of these components from Pirelli, for approximately $20 million in the first year and $30 million in the second. As an important corollary to this last point, Pirelli undertook not to transfer shares or assets relating to the components business to any company operating in the same sector for a period of two years following the signing of the contract.[11] This agreement allowed Pirelli to form a strategic alliance with one of the most important companies in the market, while enabling it to continue to play a role in both the basic optical technological sector and in research and development of fibre optics, considered viable businesses for the future. The signing of this agreement created many waves on the market; indeed Tronchetti Provera commented on the agreement with

---

11 The following companies were mentioned in the agreement: Marconi, Fujitsu, Nortel, Lucent, Alcatel, Ciena, Corvis, Juniper Networks, Ericsson and Siemens.

Cisco as follows: 'There are many competitors operating in the terrestrial optical systems field, and the optical and electronic areas require greater integration, but we have neither the electronic technology nor the software. Pirelli will invest the $2.5 billion in further development of the technologies that we already do possess.'

Over the course of several months, the agreement with Cisco brought about new and entirely unforeseen developments. Indeed the alliance provided Pirelli with an opportunity to develop in the optical components field, and the joint venture with Cisco represented an excellent opening to penetrate the American market. Towards the end of February 2000, Pirelli began considering the idea of submitting an initial public offering for OTUSA on Nasdaq, which was continuing to rise inexorably.

Pirelli chose Merrill Lynch as advisor in this process and placed other equally appropriate solutions for OTUSA's future on the back burner. The procedure for listing on the Nasdaq market placed great emphasis on the managerial team and on the identification of interested investors. Pirelli began this procedure in March 2000 when the market showed its first signs of a slowdown which, in retrospect, was a prelude to a rapid decline and the bursting of the stock price bubble for new technologies. This new scenario created uncertainty regarding the unquestionably reasonable price set by the Company for the initial public offering for OTUSA.[12] Nevertheless, Pirelli decided not to change its plans, and continued along its chosen path, which soon proved rather more arduous than expected.

Regarding possible investors, in mid-March 2000 Pirelli approached Summit Partners – the major US venture capital company and experts in the optical sector – and started negotiations regarding a possible participation of Summit Partners in the planned initial public offering for OTUSA. These negotiations ran aground in July 2000 due to the requests by the venture capital fund which Pirelli considered excessive.[13] The quest to find local managers to support the Pirelli

---

12  Pirelli's expectations in relation to the valuation of the economic capital of OTUSA at the time of the initial public offering were in the region of €300 million. These expectations were fully in line with a reasonable valuation of the capital compared with the estimates arising from the investigation into the transfer of patents from Pirelli Cavi e Sistemi and Optical Technologies Italy to OTUSA.

13  Summit Partners had requested more rights and guarantees than those granted to Cisco, including the assurance that the placement price would be double the subscription price, meaning they requested a guaranteed return of 200%.

management team proved no more successful. None of the managerial contacts pursued by Pirelli culminated in an agreement, and so it was decided to entrust the coordination of the business in the United States to Kevin Riddett, CEO of Pirelli Cables USA. Faced with these discouraging results, it seemed logical and reasonable that the top management of the Group would assume managerial responsibility for OTUSA, bringing their skills and reputation to this organisation in the crucial period of the initial public offering and making OTUSA potentially more appealing to the market. Pirelli top management received advice on this matter from their US advisors, and as such Pirelli's involvement was based on a business rather than managerial involvement, by giving the Group's top managers a purchase option on a shareholding in the company. And so in the spring of the year 2000 and in the context of a wider reassessment of the Group's remuneration policy, a formal process was started to assign shareholdings of 6%, 4% and 2.5% of the OTUSA capital to Tronchetti Provera, Morchio and Buora respectively. This assignment was, however, subject to the fulfilment of the company reorganisation process which Pirelli had decided to implement along with the OTUSA initial public offering.

In May 2000 Pirelli set an extraordinary transaction in motion, intended to provide the American company with the intellectual property associated with the component sector. First, Pirelli Cavi e Sistemi transferred the company unit in question to Optical Technologies Italia which, in turn, transferred it to its Dutch associated company Optical The Netherlands. Both expert valuations regarding the transfers came to very similar values, approximately €180 million. Patents were also transferred to OTUSA for an indicative value of €47 million. In the month of June, Pirelli successfully completed these extraordinary transactions.

At this time, Pirelli was contacted out of the blue by the investment bank JP Morgan. The American company Corning – with which Pirelli had an established business relationship in the fibre optics field – had expressed interest in the patents held by OTUSA. The idea of a 'twin-track' approach, as previously theorised by Giuseppe Morchio, was taking form. In effect, these licenses were of great significance to Corning's strategic development plans; while their interest in the patents[14]

---

14　With regard to the patents, it is worth recalling the involvement of Piergiovanni Giannesi, who oversaw, among other things, the arrangement of the securities transferred to Cisco and Corning, and who in the 1990s strengthened the role and effectiveness of Pirelli's patents office.

was reasonable, this unexpected expression of interest created uncertainty in Pirelli's top management. Indeed, there were no formal obstacles arising from the previous agreement with Cisco to prevent Pirelli from entering into negotiations with Corning, and Corning was not one of the companies listed in the agreement with Cisco. Nevertheless, in the days following this initial expression of interest, certain rumours began to circulate on the market regarding a possible merger between Corning and Nortel. Such operation would have prevented any possible agreement between Pirelli and Corning, as Nortel was one of the companies to which Pirelli had undertaken not to transfer assets in its agreement with Cisco. As the events unfolded, this prospect rapidly vanished, driving Corning to redouble its efforts to explore a possible agreement with Pirelli for the purchase of OTUSA. Corning was also determined to pursue this strategy because of the numerous purchase and integration transactions that were taking place among its main competitors in the sector, and as certain operators in the telecommunications sector had decided to keep their optical activities independent, in order to also supply competitor parties on the market.

In a meeting in Milan, the Corning CEO John Loose personally expressed an interest in OTUSA to the Pirelli top management. At that point, Tronchetti Provera explained to Loose that Pirelli had begun the process of listing OTUSA on Nasdaq, and would only consider offers that were extremely persuasive. When asked to indicate the region of Corning's potential offer, Loose responded that it 'would be in excess of $2 billion'. This amount was at least seven times greater than Pirelli's expectations for OTUSA on Nasdaq. This statement stunned Tronchetti Provera and his colleagues at the meeting.[15] Following the formal initiation of talks, in early August Corning submitted an indicative initial offer of approximately $2.5 billion. At this point the Pirelli top managers decided to force the issue, having realised the importance of OTUSA to Corning, as the former possessed patents that would allow the US company to compete with its main rivals. Opting to take a calculated risk, Pirelli told Corning that it was expecting an offer of no

---

15  Tronchetti Provera recalled that on that occasion it was difficult for those present to contain their sudden excitement. Morchio and Buora tried to catch Tronchetti Provera's eye continuously throughout the meeting, and he in turn couldn't believe that Loose's proposal was genuine. Nevertheless, the top management of Pirelli, astonished by the amount, which was unimaginable, asked their Merrill Lynch advisors whether an estimate of this kind could have economic value, and were assured by the experts in the American business banking sector, who were well aware of Corning's development plans, that it could.

less than $4 billion. In that period Corning's market capitalisation amounted to approximately $80 billion, and as such, the requested amount fell well within the bounds of reason for Corning, given the strategic importance of the patents. This request was taken into consideration by the heads of Corning, and negotiations were opened on the basis of this new figure. Leading the negotiations for the Italian company was Luciano Gobbi, who kept the Company's top management in Europe informed from New York. In order to be able to meet Pirelli's higher request, the US company wanted to pay the agreed amount in Corning shares. Given the volatility of equity prices and the clear downward trend of the market, Corning's offer was not acceptable to Pirelli. Faced with a final request from the Italian company to pay in cash, it seemed that the negotiations would fall apart.[16] After a few days of deadlock, Corning expressed an interest in reopening the negotiations and, on 1 September 2000, drew up an indicative valuation of OTUSA of between $4.5 and 5 billion. Negotiations were concluded in September, and approved by the Pirelli Board on 26 September 2000. The agreement involved the transfer of 90% of the capital of OTUSA to Corning for a sale price of $3.51 billion in cash, compared to an overall valuation of the economic capital of the company of $3.9 billion, and a further ancillary contract that involved the transfer by Pirelli Cavi e Sistemi to Corning of other patents for approximately €100 million. The agreement with Corning caused a true stir in the market. It was not the price in absolute terms that was particularly surprising, but rather the market multiples involved in the transaction.

The scale of the transaction brought to the fore a factor that had previously been overlooked in the context of the agreement with Corning, specifically the existence of three stock options in favour of some of Pirelli's top management. Even in the context of the numerous bonuses received by the management team due to the incredible success of the agreement, these three stock options were very significant – estimated at approximately $456 million before tax[17] – given the entity

---

16  Luciano Gobbi recalled to this author that he had extended his stay in New York following the stalling of the negotiations, as he suspected they would resume.

17  The exercise of the three stock options resulted in a different tax rate for the three beneficiaries, as was recalled in Pirelli's Board of Directors report of 21 March 2001. Indeed while Morchio and Buora, employed by Pirelli through employment contracts, had a tax rate liability of 12.5% on the overall amount, Tronchetti Provera had a full tax rate of 46.25% on the amount received.

of the transaction. The amount in question had far exceeded all expectations.[18] Nevertheless, as stock options had been assigned to members of Pirelli's top management and were related to the capital of a subsidiary, and given the significant amount involved, this scenario caused a certain commotion on the market and in the media. Pirelli was reprimanded by CONSOB for not having informed the market of the existence of the stock options. The Company responded that they had not thought that 'the effects of a resolution made by the governing bodies of the company in question would be capable of influencing the valuations of the company's economic, asset and financial values and consequently the investment decisions of the market operators'. In reality, the entire situation seemed to have been caused by a series of random circumstances rather than a deliberate or premeditated decision. Indeed, it may be useful to summarise the deal with Corning that was overseen by Luigi Guatri, chairman of Pirelli's Board of Statutory Auditors and Rector Emeritus of Bocconi University. The assignment of the stock options on the capital of the subsidiary to members of Pirelli's top management was not only legitimate, it was also prudent, given the climate of the US market in which the initial public offering was to be submitted. In reality, it was Pirelli's local advisors that 'had insisted that the incentivisation plans involve managers who were known and well-regarded on an international scale'.[19] With this advice, it had seemed obvious to involve the Group's front-line managers in the operation. Furthermore, another factor favouring this assignment was that no suitable managerial figures in the US market willing to offer their professional services for the OTUSA listing had been identified.

The option strike price had been fixed at 12 times the company's turnover, the same factor applied just a few months previously in the Cisco transaction. An independent valuation by the venture capital group Summit Partners in relation to the presumed current value of OTUSA's economic capital at the time of listing also confirmed this figure, which also corresponded with independent valuations carried out by Pirelli, estimating the potential value of the company at approximately $250 million. Having transferred the component parts unit of the

---

18  In this regard, Professor Luigi Guatri, chairman of Pirelli's Board of Statutory Auditors, stated to *Il Sole 24 Ore* on 14 October 2000: 'I am entirely at peace, I would challenge anyone to attribute a greater value to those shares than that which was assigned, specifically 12 times the turnover.'

19  Extract taken from an interview with Luigi Guatri on 14 October 2000 in *Il Sole 24 Ore*.

company and the previously mentioned Pirelli Cavi e Sistemi patents to OTUSA, it was not by chance that the board of Optical The Netherlands – OTUSA's direct parent company – also resolved to formally issue options, as Pirelli had previously done.[20] This decision was taken on 11 July 2000, a date previous to Corning's expression of interest. The overall situation developed unexpectedly following Corning's offer, most probably calculated in consideration that Corning needed OTUSA's patents.

Faced with the unexpected size of the stock options, Pirelli's top managers discussed the best approach to take. They considered the possibility of not exercising the stock options, but this solution was deemed not to be viable for two reasons. First, the three beneficiaries of the stock options harboured mutually incompatible attitudes and opinions which were entirely legitimate, but which could have broken up the Company's management team if they were to emerge. Second, opting not to exercise the stock options could have been erroneously interpreted by the market as the scenario that had arisen was subject to formal or substantial errors that could have invalidated the stock options. As this was absolutely not the case, the decision to exercise the stock options was taken.

The extraordinary growth of the financial markets over the course of the latter half of the 1990s had inspired much interest among the public, and had focused an unprecedented degree of attention on corporate issues in Italy. This growing level of involvement not only gave rise to greater awareness of financial and corporate matters among the public, it also led to a more positive public opinion towards the world of economics and finance. This was a significant change from previous years, and in particular the 1970s, which had been characterised by a mixed sentiment of distrust and suspicion towards all economic institutions. Nevertheless, the seemingly endless growth in the markets led to the emergence of a new form of corporate-centred gossip, unimaginable just a few years previously, except regarding the private lives of leading industrialists and bankers. In this market climate, the signing of the agreement with Corning and the stock options affair were received by the public with much curiosity and a hunger for details, immortalising this event and transforming it beyond all logical reason into a symbol of

---

20 The Pirelli remuneration committee that passed a resolution on the stock options met on 20 March 2000 and was made up of Tronchetti Provera in his role as Company Chairman, and Luigi Orlando and Ennio Presutti, both independent directors, as provided for by the Code of Conduct for listed companies. Tronchetti Provera abstained.

roaring capitalism. This detailed summary of the Corning agreement excludes any possibility of formal allegations against the deal.

Nevertheless, the entire situation raises certain questions that go beyond the specifics of the case. Indeed, despite its long managerial tradition, Pirelli was not used to high levels of incentivisation, except on an incidental basis. Now, the signing of the agreement with Corning gave rise to significant recognition for a few individuals, not only among top management but also for 34 co-workers who had participated in the negotiations. This created a significant division between those who, because of their assigned roles or for purely random reasons, were excluded from the incentivisation process. Disappointment and an understandable sense of regret might have led, in the medium term, to destabilisation and to the erosion of the Company's management, potentially creating a protracted period of dispute regarding the definition of roles and compensation. This did not occur, however, thus demonstrating once again that Pirelli's managerial team was very solid, resting on a well-consolidated foundation of professional and personal integrity.

Aside from the significance of managerial actions regarding company performance, the Corning case gave rise to a further element of meta-economic reflection, specifically the presence of forces that the classical Greeks and Romans in broad terms referred to as fortune. When facing fortune, it is difficult to determine what sort of approach one should adopt. It did not seem appropriate to adopt a contrite attitude to atone one's sins, neither did it seem correct to address the situation with elation and short-sightedness, confident that the events in question had been successfully resolved. Tronchetti Provera believed that the proceeds of the stock option should be subject to the highest possible tax rate applicable to him. He also chose to donate a portion of these proceeds, and of the bonuses received in the year 2000, to the Silvio Tronchetti Provera Foundation, which conducted scientific research and had been established in memory of his father, who had passed away in 1996.

The successful signing of the agreement with Corning created a massive inflow of liquidity for the Company, which gave rise to a modest appreciation of all the securities of the Group's subsidiaries. Initially the top management of the Company declared that they would invest this liquidity in developing the Company's core business. It proved possible, however, to simultaneously combine investments in the Company's core business with a number of significant external acquisitions. Soon, the market not only began to scrutinise Pirelli's investment

TABLE 8.3. ROI, NOPAT, EVA AND WACC OF THE
PIRELLI GROUP IN THE PERIOD 1999–2000

| Parameters | 1999 | 2000 |
|---|---|---|
| ROI (%) | 8.6 | 11.4 |
| NOPAT (€ million) | 266 | 275 |
| EVA (€ million) | 0.4 | 0.4 |
| WACC | 7 | 7.8 |

*Source: Our calculations from official documents provided by Pirelli*

projects, but also placed a degree of pressure on the Company to carry out external growth operations. In the spring of 2001, this expectation of the market exerted influence on the Company's management. Since the market did not regard the investment projects announced by Pirelli in its traditional business sectors as being exhaustive, the market could begin to suspect that the Company could run short of investment projects if it were to delay any longer. As such, in the spring of 2001 Pirelli began to examine a number of dossiers submitted by certain investment banks. Among these was the opportunity to purchase the fibre optics department of Lucent Technologies, incorporated in 1996 as an AT&T spin-off, and which the US company had decided to dispose of after a very significant loss in the first quarter of that year. This interest, however, did not progress into negotiations or an offer, as the valuation of $4 billion for the fibre optics branch of Lucent Technologies was deemed 'unrealistic' by Pirelli. Furthermore, the worsening financial and management crisis involving Lucent Technologies, and the proposed idea of a merger between the latter and Alcatel, which never became reality, lessened Pirelli's interest in the US company. The serious crisis which gripped Lucent Technologies, derived in part from poor strategies, was a clear symptom of the more profound problem ahead for technology stocks which had entirely unpredictable parameters. In that same period, Pirelli received an invitation to reinvest its returns from the Corning deal in RCS, Rizzoli-Corriere della Sera, the leading Italian newspaper and media group. This potential created a stir among certain of the RCS shareholders, who feared the potential involvement of Pirelli as a major shareholder in RCS. This prospect, however, was never given serious consideration by Pirelli's shareholders, who saw an investment in RCS as too closely linked with the political sphere.

It seemed clear, however, that Pirelli's new investments and projects should, yet again, involve 'changing tack': combining new paths with Pirelli's already established areas.

# PART III

# IN the WORLD of TELECOMMUNICATIONS

# CHAPTER 9

# The Acquisition of the Telecom Italia Group

Although following the conclusion of the deal with Corning, Pirelli had declared its intention to reinvest the enormous amount of liquidity obtained from its core businesses, it was already clear in early 2001 that the Company was considering other potential projects. The market was putting increasing pressure on Pirelli to make new acquisitions.

Not only did investment banks, attracted by the Company's liquidity, submit several dossiers including one concerning the acquisition of Lucent's fibre optic branch, but also some Italian industrial and financial groups turned an interested gaze towards the financial resources and the management skills shown by the Company. Various rumours were heard on the market, from the aforementioned potential shareholding of the Company in the Rizzoli-Corriere della Sera Group, to Pirelli's interest in Fiat's then uncertain fortunes.

Among various events stirring the Italian corporate sector in spring 2001, it was clear that Telecom Italia had an increasingly uncertain mission which was undermining its shareholders' confidence in the company's top management. Less than two years after the historic hostile takeover bid that Olivetti had launched on the recently privatised Telecom Italia, the new shareholders and the management team that they appointed seemed to have lost their vision and drive.

## 9.1 Pirelli's expertise in telecommunications: the Telecom Italia objective

Throughout its history, Pirelli had fostered a natural interest in telecommunications. Through the cable sector, the Company had always directly or indirectly controlled the evolution of the world of telecommunications in Italy since its inception.[1] This market had in fact represented one of the main customers

---

1   According to Brezzi (2004): 'the history of Italian telecommunications until 1964 can be

for its cable business unit. For this reason, the company had garnered significant technical skills in the telecommunications sector. The same interest that had been expressed by Pirelli in 1994 in the privatisation of Stet should be interpreted in this sense. Pirelli's interest in the telecommunications sector seemed to

---

divided into six periods. The first period (1881–1903) involves government monopoly and privatisation. The second period (1903–1925) is characterised by joint (inter-city) public management and (single-city-based) private management. The third period (1925–1964) covers the regional monopoly of the five private operators, which gradually merged to form the Stet group.' As in other industrial events, in telecommunications Italy also seemed to be a latecomer. In 1904, the density of subscribers per 100 inhabitants was 0.07, significantly lower than that of France (0.31) and Germany (0.90), without mentioning the Nordic countries, which registered values well in excess of one unit. At the beginning of the third period, for the first time, Pirelli's history crossed paths with that of telephone services. Mucchetti (2003) also reminds us of Pirelli's presence in telecommunications following the incorporation of Teti, one of the five service providers, in 1924. In 1925, pursuant to Royal Decree Law no. 339 of 8 February 1923, the government granted public sector bodies, companies and individuals 'the exercise of all or part of the right to set up or operate telephone lines for both public and private use'. The law also provided for the obligation by providers to pay in 20 annual instalments for the systems that they had acquired and carry out a plan over the two subsequent five-year periods for the reorganisation and development of the systems. The national territory was divided into five areas and the licences were entrusted respectively to Stipel (for Piedmont and Lombardy), Telve (for the Triveneto area), Timo (for Emilia-Romagna, Marche, Umbria, Abruzzo and Molise), Teti, which reported to La Centrale (for Liguria, Tuscany, Lazio and Sardinia), and the last licence was attributed to Set, which was owned by Setemer of the Swedish industrial group Ericsson (for Campania, Puglia, Basilicata, Calabria and Sicily). The individual service providers undertook to pay a licence fee to the state based on their gross revenue that amounted to 5% for Stipel, 4.5% for Teti and 4% for Telve, Timo and Set. The licence fee was based on the economic and social characteristics of the different areas. The companies also undertook to develop the systems in light of the technological innovations of the time, while the granting of any tariff increases was the responsibility of the government. The subsequent events in Italian telecommunications intersected with the crisis of the 1930s. As early as 1927, SIP had acquired the majority equity stake in Telve and Timo, but it had subsequently fallen into difficulty at the onset of the crisis. A few years later, Banca Commerciale Italiana, which had in the meantime come into possession of the majority of SIP's capital, moved this holding to Società Finanziaria ed Industriale Italiana, known as Sofindit. The latter represented the vehicle with which, in the autumn of 1933, Banca Commerciale Italiana ('Comit') sold most of the troubled shareholdings held by Comit itself to IRI (Istituto per la Ricostruzione Industriale, or Institute of Industrial Reconstruction). Almost simultaneously, on 21 October 1933, IRI incorporated Società Torinese Esercizi Telefonici (Stet), which decentralised the holding functions of three licence holders (Stipel, Telve and Timo), whose majority holding was held by Stet. Only in the post-Second World War period, in November 1957, did IRI acquire, through Stet, the majority equity stakes of Teti and Set. This controlling role taken on by the State, through IRI, in the capital of all five licence holders allowed for the total reorganisation of the sector, which was launched in 1964.

coincide with the growing expectations of some of the shareholders of reference of Olivetti, Telecom Italia's parent company, who considered that its investment in telecommunications, which dated back only two years, was already over. In this regard, in an interview for *Corriere della Sera* on 2 August 2001, Tronchetti Provera stated that 'The market perceived it as a spur-of-the-moment deal, but that is not the case. While it is true that the negotiations were very swift, our keen interest dates back over a number of months. Pirelli has been monitoring Telecom Italia for years, ever since the Stet bid. We were and are far from unprepared.'

In the spring of 2001, the control chain of the Telecom Italia Group continued to maintain the structure derived from the 1999 takeover. Technically, the public bid had been launched by Tecnost, a listed company that had merged with Olivetti in 2000 and which at that time was controlled by the latter. Olivetti's ownership structure, however, remained unchanged; its main shareholder, with an approximately 23% shareholding, was the Luxembourg-based company Bell. This company had been the vehicle with which Olivetti's CEO, Roberto Colaninno, and the financier Emilio Gnutti – the promoters of the Telecom Italia takeover – had aroused the interest of a wide range of investors. They had first provided the financial wherewithal to acquire a major stake in Olivetti, and later to prepare for the hostile takeover bid on Telecom Italia. In particular, the Bell shareholders reporting to Gnutti – mostly industrialists from the Brescia area who were represented by Gnutti himself – concentrated their investments in Hopa, a financial company which had become Bell's principal shareholder. Indeed, the greatest concerns of Hopa's shareholders regarded the continuation of their commitment in Telecom Italia. The value of the investments that they had made in Hopa and Bell depended on the performance of Olivetti shares which, in the spring of 2001, was rather disappointing. Furthermore, in the scenario of that period, Bell's asset balance was becoming increasingly fragile.

The possibility of Pirelli becoming involved was a potential exit strategy, particularly given that the perspectives of Colaninno and Gnutti were becoming increasingly divergent. While the former held significant power in the running of the Group, despite a relatively modest investment, Gnutti felt differently. Indeed, Colaninno felt a growing need for a stable ownership structure that could help to carry out long-term investments, while Gnutti – under pressure from the different shareholders he represented – considered it reasonable to secure the investment in the short term. The mutual trust that had characterised these two driving forces behind the Telecom Italia takeover was being eroded.

Federico Imbert, a Naples-born corporate banker with Chase Manhattan in Italy and advisor to Gnutti, with whom he had participated in the Telecom Italia deal in 1999, noted the increasingly palpable discomfort of the shareholders and persuaded them to entrust him with the task of helping to find a buyer. He believed that Pirelli possessed all the necessary characteristics of an industrial enterprise capable of managing the increasingly complex strategic development of one of Europe's largest telecommunications companies.

### 9.2 Technology and competition: the changing telecommunications market

The two years ending in the summer of 2001 was a crucial moment for the telecommunications companies that had taken full advantage of the euphoria generated by the Internet; indeed they now cast aside – at least temporarily – the important development policies they had followed during the 1990s. However, the burst of the dot-com bubble and the impeding global economic crisis of 2001 once again forced the telecommunications company to face difficult investment choices in a new scenario characterised by greater liberalisation and privatisation.

In this new context, Imbert believed that Pirelli's financial means and management skills were truly excellent; however, his opinion regarding the incumbent operators was unforgiving. Indeed, he no longer recognised in them a strategic vision, an industrial project or even the management skills to operate in an increasingly complex market. While the prospect of a possible sale met with growing interest from Gnutti and the group of shareholders from Brescia, there was increasing opposition from Colaninno. For these reasons, one can assume that the latter had tried to strengthen the shareholding structure of Olivetti's parent companies without taking into account the core group of the Brescian shareholders.

This scenario led Imbert to forge a relationship with Buora, and subsequently with Tronchetti Provera himself. While in principle the reasons that may have led Pirelli to manifest its interest in the Telecom Italia Group were justified and wholly acceptable, the implementation of a project of such a scope involved several levels of complexity. In terms of size, Telecom Italia Group's multiples were far greater than Pirelli's, especially regarding the level of debt, which was approximately 20 times that of Pirelli,[2] and derived from the takeover bid and the two-year period 1999–2001. However, it was not the Telecom Italia dimension factor that held the

---

2　This calculation does not take into account Olivetti's debt.

attention of Tronchetti Provera and his team, fully aware that their management skills were sufficient to meet the challenge, but rather the need to verify that the acquisition represented an investment with a positive net present value. Pirelli's potential investment in Telecom Italia had to be based on the certainty of developing a solid industrial project.

Tronchetti Provera carefully weighed the costs and benefits of the project from a business perspective, and came to the conclusion that it was interesting for two reasons. First, it had been demonstrated[3] that the Telecom Italia Group could produce significant cash flows. Tronchetti Provera realised that in a short time telecommunications companies would take on very different characteristics from those previously shown by 'telephone companies'. This insight was not immediately obvious; indeed the Telecom Italia Group showed a major technological gap compared to similar companies in other countries, notably in its limited broadband infrastructure which was soon to support the transmission of data and information for a variety of media. The Chairman's presentation of the annual report on operations and on the programme of the Italian Communications Regulatory Authority (Autorità per le Garanzie nelle Comunicazioni) on 20 July 2006 confirms this analysis, acknowledging the immeasurable work carried out by the Telecom Italia Group in the subsequent years: 'In terms of broadband deployment, we ranked last. At present, despite having started at the bottom, Italy is growing with a rate of increase (187% in two years) which is significantly higher than that of the EU-15: today, the number of lines stands at a total of seven million, making Italy the fourth-ranked European country in this regard.'

Italy was penalised by a significant delay in the development of broadband, a system which enables the transmission of large quantities of information. This delay was due partly to the almost total absence of cable television in Italy. Indeed, one of the factors that influenced broadband development was the percentage of cable television subscribers present in various countries around the year 2000. Where this type of connection was available, such as in the United States, Canada or in the Netherlands, broadband development was achieved through cable. Where there was only a minimal presence of cable television, the broadband system was instead developed through the disaggregation of local landline telephone infrastructures

---

3   Tronchetti Provera recalled that 'Buora had arranged a cash flow analysis of the Telecom Italia Group, from which it appeared that the cash flows were good'.

(local loop unbundling,[4] as in the case of Italy, the United Kingdom, Switzerland and Germany, using the DSL – Digital Subscriber Line).[5] In this general scenario, the interruption of the Socrates Project played a fundamental role in limiting the diffusion of broadband via cable in Italy.[6]

Broadband was to represent for the Telecom Italia Group what cables had historically represented for Pirelli; it would allow the transmission of a large mass of information, thus constituting a bridge to the future. The type and nature of this information and its related content would be a business area to be developed from zero. Indeed, Pirelli's Chairman foresaw a rapid evolution in the telecommunications sector, characterised by a growing osmosis between various forms of communication, from landline and mobile phones to television and the Internet, once suitable telecommunications infrastructures were in place.

For these reasons, telecommunications companies were required to possess additional professional skills related to areas such as media and content, or to enter into large-scale mergers with companies operating in complementary sectors. These considerations drove Tronchetti Provera to proceed with the proposed

---

4   The economic theory on telecommunications has brought to light the way the aggregation of the local infrastructure for landline telecommunications constitutes an important element for the development of competition. Historically, the copper pair connection between end user and local distribution exchange – the so-called local loop – was considered as a natural monopoly that did not allow for competition in the sector. Granting market entrants the use of these access lines without any significant investment in the local area thus favours competition in the networks (Schwartz 2000). There are two different positions regarding this issue. On the one hand, new operators push for a high level of disaggregation of the network, arguing that in this way innovation is encouraged by combining new technologies with the components of the existing network. On the other hand, the incumbent operators oppose this position, arguing that excessive disaggregation may also increase transaction costs for the competitors and create problems of incompatibility of the competitors' interfaces with the incumbent operators' infrastructure. From this perspective, the role of pricing takes on great importance. Rates that are too low in fact constitute a disincentive to invest in the local network, while rates that are too high push new entrants to bypass the existing network and create new networks, thus stimulating competition between infrastructures.

5   DSL and ADSL use the traditional twisted copper pair as a support, but are able to provide advanced services, allowing the transport of asymmetric flows with a speed of up to 8 Mbit to the customer and up to 1 Mbit from the customer to the network.

6   There is a third mode of broadband development via the disaggregation of the local infrastructure with the creation of alternative FTTH (fibre to the home) networks. This last mode has particularly been deployed in some countries such as Sweden, Denmark, Norway, Finland and outside Europe in Japan and South Korea.

acquisition of Telecom Italia Group. However, the primary role that the Telecom Italia Group was taking on in the national economic context, and the events of recent years, meant that institutional controls had become indispensable before any potential acquisition could take place.

In the spring of 2001, the general elections ended with a clear victory for the centre-right, bringing Silvio Berlusconi back to government. This victory was easily foreseeable after the split that had characterised the centre-left coalition following Romano Prodi's removal from the role of Prime Minister in October 1998. As opposed to what had happened two years previously during the period of the takeover bid on Telecom Italia, this time the political sector was keeping a close eye on events. Now the institutions clearly perceived the gradual weakening of the Telecom Italia project headed by Colaninno and Gnutti, and there were still many doubts regarding the future of the group. For these reasons, the checks run by Tronchetti Provera with various institutions elicited positive responses regarding Pirelli's possible involvement in Telecom Italia. Pirelli's top management, however, was well aware of the specificity of the sector in which the Telecom Italia Group operated, where national and international regulatory aspects were of paramount importance, and inevitably, inseparable from politics.[7] This was an important aspect as, up until that moment, Pirelli had no previous experience in operating in a closely regulated market. This did not mean that the Company was unfamiliar with the public sector with its long-standing history as a supplier of electrical cables for telecommunications and submarines, involving close liaisons with

---

7  There is a further anecdotal testimony of these sentiments. In an unpublished mimeographed document entitled 'Telecom Italia 2001–2006: the diary of a manager', Enrico Parazzini, who subsequently became Telecom Italia's Chief Financial Officer, quotes an interesting conversation that took place on 28 May 2001, between Tronchetti Provera, Buora, Braggiotti and Parazzini himself, as a result of a conference call with New York during the negotiations with Lucent. After the conference call, the conversation took on a relaxed tone, and Tronchetti Provera seemed to be having fun and teasing his interlocutors about the available options: 'Marco Tronchetti Provera seemed very determined [about Lucent] and let it transpire that he would be happy to move the barycentre of the Group to the United States, emphasising the aspects of strong competitiveness in that market and the independence that such a choice would open in expressing our potential as individuals and as a company as a whole. Carlo Buora, who emphasised the risks for the company in the United States and the management effort required, and Gerardo Braggiotti, in his capacity as advisor, seemed to be more cautious.' Jokingly, Tronchetti Provera added, addressing Buora: 'Of course there are those who would prefer to live off the cash we have, or go to Rome … with less risk and competition than in the United States, but with many more constraints'.

public sector agencies and the governments of many countries. Being subject to strict regulatory constraints, however, was an entirely new situation for the Pirelli Group. Although this factor was not underestimated by the management and main shareholders, the prevailing idea was that the ongoing privatisation of the telecommunications company would involve the adoption of strict market parameters for a company previously under public authority control. There was some truth in this assessment, but nevertheless it proved difficult to identify a precise perimeter for the scope of action of a company such as Telecom Italia, which was subject to formal regulation and deep-rooted practices which were far from easy to reform.

### 9.3  The Telecom Italia deal

On 28 July 2001, at an emergency meeting of the Board of Pirelli SpA, Tronchetti Provera announced that negotiations were ongoing with the Luxembourg company Bell SA and with other parties to take over 1,700,000,000 Olivetti SpA ordinary shares, totalling approximately 23% of the share capital of the latter.[8] The negotiations took shape over the following two days. The unit purchase price of the shares was €4.175 per Olivetti share corresponding to an implicit purchase price of Telecom Italia of €15.90 per share[9] with a total outlay of approximately €7 billion, compared to a current listing at the time of approximately €2.30 per Olivetti share. A company under Italian law called Olimpia was used for the acquisition of the shares; Olimpia's capital was divided between Pirelli SpA, with a shareholding of 60%, and Edizione Holding together with other Italian investors held the remaining 40%.[10] Pirelli and Edizione Holding contributed a further 265,302,200 ordinary

---

8   Purchasers undertook to also buy 68,409,125 '2001–2002 Olivetti ordinary warrants' for a unit price of €1.0875. There were around 1,700,000,000 Olivetti shares comprising 1,552,662,120 shares transferred from Bell and 147,337,880 shares that Pirelli was to transfer to Olimpia, which had in turn purchased from Bell and others (28 March 2002).

9   If we consider the share price of Telecom Italia, the premium is reduced to 36% compared with the average January–July price, which was €11.68 per share. We should also remember that the price of a Telecom Italia share, normalised after the merger between Olivetti and Telecom, corresponded to €4.73 per share. Moreover, the consensus as at 27 July 2001, on Telecom Italia's price by some of the principal market brokers was as follows: Credit Suisse 13.99, Intermonte 11.40, Deutsche Bank 15.50 and SSSb 14.50. The average price was therefore €13.85 per share, which represented a 28.81% premium compared with the market price of €10.75 per share.

10  Initially, Edizione Holding's shareholding was to be 40%, but this share was judged too large by the controlling shareholders of the Benetton Group. The involvement of Intesa BCI and

Olivetti shares[11] to the new company, thus increasing the share in Olivetti held by Olimpia to 27%. In this operation, Pirelli's total financial commitment was to be approximately €4.5 billion, about half of which derived from existing liquidity and the remaining part from debt, to be completely written off by a specific divestment programme. In this regard, Pirelli's Chairman announced that the Pirelli Group would dispose its truck tyre and power cable activities in order to maximise the resources it could contribute to its telecommunications activities. This operation was approved unanimously in the following Board meeting.[12]

To supplement the explanation provided by Tronchetti Provera at the Pirelli Board of Directors' meeting (28 July 2001), an authoritative opinion prepared by Lazard was produced confirming that Telecom Italia held an enviable position in the Italian market. This aspect was the necessary prerequisite for profitable further developments outside its country of origin. In relation to the price, which incorporated a premium over the current listing of the shares of approximately 71%, Lazard maintained that 'Large operators are generally appreciated by the market, which tends to allocate valuation parameters that are relatively higher for the leaders than their competitors.' Nevertheless, this was a significant premium, even for Italy, where the financial literature highlights high premiums in this kind of transaction. We must also remember that the structure of the transaction did not grant Olimpia absolute control over Olivetti, although it was the reference shareholder with a stake just below the 30% threshold, beyond which the obligation for a mandatory takeover bid would be triggered. Although substantial, the price paid cannot be deemed unreasonable. The price did indeed reflect a multiple of the value of the company compared to the EBITDA of 8.15 compared to a European industry average of 8.24 in August 2001.

Furthermore, in the space of the few hours on 30 July that separated the

---

Unicredito Italiano, both with a 10% share, was required to overcome these reasons, which became apparent only shortly before the acquisition.

11  Pirelli and Edizione Holding would contribute, respectively, 130,980,000 and 134,322,250 Olivetti shares. This further contribution lowered the average weighted cost of Olimpia's stake in Olivetti to €3.95 per share.

12  In the minutes of the Pirelli SpA Board meeting of 27 September 2001, Carlo De Benedetti declares that he 'shares completely the strategic choice behind the Telecom operation, since it meant entering into a very important sector from the point of view of profitability', while Luigi Orlando 'hopes that perhaps finally the general public may correctly interpret the intention and strategies of the industrial plan'.

conclusion of the negotiations and the signing of the formal agreements, Bell's shareholders received an informal expression of interest by another large European operator in the telecommunications sector.[13]

Apart from the logical progression of the various events, it is reasonable to consider that the deal was hastened at the end of July for two reasons: from the sellers' point of view, it was well known that they urgently needed to sell their stakes, while it is plausible that the buyer decided to push negotiations given that other European telecommunications sector operators were interested in Telecom Italia, and the shareholders led by Colaninno were considering other possible options. In essence, the acceleration of the entire deal left Colaninno with no credible alternative but to sell Bell SA's shareholding in Olivetti. The deal for the control of the telecommunications group had taken place with the capital of a Luxembourg company which controlled less than 30% of Olivetti shares. For this reason, the obligation for a takeover bid had not taken effect on Olivetti, nor had a 'domino effect' takeover bid on Telecom Italia or its publicly listed subsidiaries.[14] If, on the one hand, this circumstance penalised Olivetti's minority shareholders, on the other hand, it was justified by previous events in the telecommunications group's chain of control.

The terms of the deal were rather complex and needed to be ironed out over the following months, given that the entire deal also appeared to be conditional on obtaining the required authorisations from the competent authorities. By that date, the sellers had undertaken to ensure that some members of the Boards of Directors

---

13  Federico Imbert told the author that prior to signing the agreement with Olimpia he had received a telephone call from Telefónica's Chief Financial Officer. On behalf of the Spanish company, the CFO offered up to €5 for each Olivetti share. Imbert informed Gnutti, who did not take this proposal into consideration as he had already made commitments with Olimpia. The possible control premium that the Spanish company was willing to pay was far greater than that paid by Pirelli. A confirmation of the presence of an offer by Telefónica is found on 13 August 2001 in *Business Week*, which stated: 'Spain's Telefónica bombarded Colaninno's investors on cell phones with a higher offer'.

14  We must also remember that the relative value of a possible 'domino effect' takeover bid also on Telecom Italia's subsidiaries would have resulted in a commitment of at least $100 billion of liquidity, since it was no longer possible to even use the debt, after the transaction carried out by Colaninno in 1999. It was an extremely large amount for any investor. As Tronchetti Provera declared to the *Herald Tribune* on 3 August 2001: 'no bank would have financed a full scale takeover bid for Telecom Italia at a cost of $100 billion and so there was no other way to do the transaction'. This concept was often quoted by the foreign press.

TABLE. 9.1. EV/EBITDA MULTIPLE OF THE MAIN
EUROPEAN TELECOMMUNICATIONS COMPANIES IN 2001

| European telecommunications companies | EV/EBITDA[a] |
|---|---|
| Deutsche Telekom | 10.3 |
| Swisscom | 10.2 |
| France Telecom | 9.3 |
| KPN | 8.6 |
| Telecom Italia | 7.6 |
| Portugal Telecom | 7.6 |
| Telefónica | 7.3 |
| Telia | 12.5 |
| OTE | 5.7 |
| TDC | 8.4 |
| Telekom Austria | 5.7 |
| Telenor | 6.3 |

*[a]This is the EV/EBITDA ratio, e.g. the value of the company (including third-party sources of capital for debt) compared to income before taxes, depreciations and devaluations, i.e. a measure similar to the gross operating margin
Source: Schroeder Salomon Analysis,Telecommunication Service, 10 August 2001*

of Olivetti and Telecom Italia would resign, which they did on 27 September 2001. At Pirelli's Board meeting of 10 September 2001, Tronchetti Provera outlined the entire agreement. In contrast to what had been established (28 July 2001), it was decided that Olimpia's capital would initially be held 80% by Pirelli and 20% by Edizione Holding, with the understanding that Pirelli could sell to one or more parties up to 20% of Olimpia's capital. All these resolutions were made on the day before the attack on the Twin Towers in New York. The initial phase of Olimpia's commitment in Telecom Italia proved to be an uphill climb. The corporate governance elements agreed between Pirelli and Edizione Holding were closely modelled on Olimpia's ownership structure, with a Board of 10 directors, one-fifth appointed by Edizione Holding. The same principle applied to Olivetti and its listed subsidiaries, in which Edizione Holding was to appoint the Vice Chairman. The shareholders' agreements would last for three years. Olimpia's Extraordinary Shareholders' General Meeting would decide with the favourable vote of 81% of the share capital, and the Board resolutions concerning relevant matters would be taken with the favourable vote of at least one of the two directors appointed by Edizione Holding. In the event of a possible deadlock at Olimpia or on the Boards of Olivetti and its listed subsidiaries, the agreements provided for a put and call option – a put by Edizione Holding, and call by Pirelli – under conditions that were not disadvantageous. For Olimpia, the entire operation involved a total outlay of €7.8 billion, €5.2 billion of which was equity from the industrial partners, who would also provide an additional €800 million as a non-interest-bearing loan. The remaining amount of €1.8 billion in five years was to be provided by a consortium of banks. Pirelli was to provide 60% of the equity, equal to €3.12 billion and 80% of the non-interest-bearing loan equal to €640 million. Thus, for a total contribution of €3.74 billion, Pirelli had liquidity of €1.6 billion and credit lines for €4.7 billion. Pirelli's level of debt at the end of the deal was back in line with the ratio prior to the deals with Cisco and Corning.

Confirming the industrial nature of Pirelli's commitment in Telecom Italia, in August 2001 Pirelli's management examined a dossier significantly entitled Operation Don Quixote, outlining a plan for the possible merger with Telefónica. The document examined the characteristics of the two groups, their ownership structures,[15] as well as the development prospects of the two merged companies. To date, the Operation Don Quixote dossier has not been made public. This is a document of 20 pages, dated 24 August 2001, drawn up by Value Partners, Pirelli's long-term strategic advisor. The dossier reviews the main strategic and economic indicators of Telecom Italia and Don Quixote, which, with a rudimentary knowledge of Spanish literature and a rapid consultation of the document, is understood to be simply a code name for Telefónica. It is interesting to note that, in analysing the salient elements of the Telefónica business, the document sets out some of Telecom Italia's development policies of subsequent years, such as the exclusive focus on control stakes in all foreign investments. The document also takes into consideration a

---

15 Telefonica's ownership structure had an 88% free float, a stake of 6.8% by BBVA, of 3% by La Caixa, and of 1% each by the Spanish and Portuguese governments.

summarised comparison between the two companies and highlights the fact that the fundamentals of the two companies were very similar, with a slight predominance for Telecom Italia both in terms of revenue and in EBITDA. By contrast, Telefónica was slightly less indebted and its capitalisation was somewhat greater. The analysis of the different areas of turnover compared between Telefónica and Telecom Italia highlights a prevalence of Telecom Italia both in domestic wireline and data, and in the mobile sector, with 46% and 28% respectively compared to 35% and 24%, while Telefónica prevailed in international wireline and data with 33% compared to Telecom Italia's 13%. Furthermore, Telecom Italia's revenues totalled €32 billion compared with Telefónica's €31 billion, and similarly Telecom Italia's EBITDA was €14.3 billion, compared with Telefónica's, which was €12.5 billion. Telecom Italia's debt was €26 billion, compared with the €25.3 billion debt of Telefónica, which was capitalised almost €70 billion, compared with Telecom Italia's €66.5 billion. A possible merger between the two companies would have given rise to the world's largest landline and Internet-access operator, as well as the largest European operator in terms of consolidated revenues and the second-largest in terms of capitalisation, after Vodafone. More specifically, the new company would have been the largest telecommunications operator in Europe and in South America both in terms of turnover and profitability. Regardless that this project ultimately did not go through, it is interesting to highlight two aspects: one was the fact that the prospect of a merger with Telefónica had solid roots in Telecom Italia's history, while the other was that the industrial development policies of subsequent years can already be found in this document.

At the beginning of September 2001, two alarming factors emerged. First, the original version of the project involved two industrial shareholders in Olimpia, but was modified by the reduced initial commitment of Edizione Holding. This altered scenario required the involvement of other institutional investors, Intesa BCI and Unicredito Italiano, not by chance the leading Italian banks at that time. These two banks entered Olimpia's ownership structure (14 September 2001) with a 10% share each and with the right to appoint one member on the Board of Directors of Olivetti and in all its listed subsidiaries. The two banks also negotiated options to exit Olimpia's capital in the event of a deadlock at the shareholders' meeting of the latter or in the Board of Directors' meeting at Olivetti and Telecom Italia, or in the event of expiry of the three-year agreement or a change in control at Olimpia or Pirelli. These conditions were not dissimilar to those agreed by Edizione Holding and Pirelli, demonstrating that the entrepreneurial risk of the entire project was borne only by Pirelli, which had nevertheless established joint control over Olimpia with Edizione Holding.

The second reason for concern stemmed from the difficult market situation, as the deadline of 27 September approached, when the European Commission was to announce its verdict on the entire deal.

The steady fall of Olivetti's share price risked jeopardising the guarantee granted by Olimpia to the financing banks in exchange for opening the credit line for €1.8 billion. For this reason, it became increasingly likely that the Olimpia shareholders would have to pay the difference. These fears materialised and took on gigantic proportions on 11 September, when the attack on the Twin Towers sowed panic in the world's financial markets. The severity of the episode and its exceptional nature risked invalidating the entire deal. It was no longer concerned solely with the destiny of the individual shareholders, but the ownership stability of one of the leading companies in the country in terms of capitalisation. Nonetheless, the situation's peculiar conditions offered some hope that had not existed until that moment. On Natalino Irti's advice, Olimpia believed that there were grounds to renegotiate the contract signed on 30 July, as it had subsequently become overpriced. This perspective could have brought about two results: that of making the commitment less burdensome, but also that of involving the sellers themselves or at least a part of them in the stabilisation of the financial structure of Olimpia regarding its commitments with the banks. Following intense negotiations, an agreement was reached.

On 19 September 2001, a new version of the 30 July agreement was signed. Olimpia and the majority of Bell shareholders agreed that on 27 September Olimpia would purchase 552,000,000 Olivetti shares from Bell at the price of €4.175 per share, while by 12 October, Olimpia would proceed with the purchase of the remaining 1,000,662,120 shares, as well as 68,409,125 Olivetti warrants, at €4.175 for the shares and at €1.0875 for the warrants. At the time of the second deadline, the Bell shareholders undertook to sign a debenture loan issued by Olimpia for €1,032,920,000 with a duration of six years at a fixed rate of 1.5% payable as a term lump sum, i.e. in zero-coupon form. Repayment of the underwritten loan would be in the form of assignment of approximately 263 million Olivetti shares to the Bell shareholders. Furthermore, the agreement provided for the Monte dei Paschi Group to supply funding of approximately €500–750 million, while the Banca Antonveneta Group was to provide a further €260 million. Both banks were Hopa shareholders and had a direct interest in the successful conclusion of the negotiation.

FIG. 9.1. TREND IN THE PRICE OF TELECOM ITALIA AND PIRELLI
SECURITIES FROM 1 JULY 2001 TO 31 OCTOBER 2001: COMPARISON WITH
THE MIB30 INDEX, 1 JULY 2001 (BASE DATE = 100)

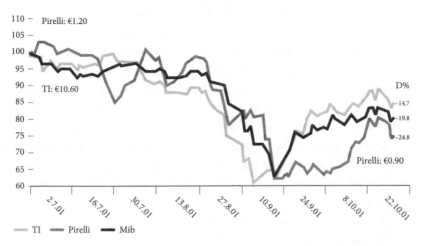

If, on the one hand, the terms of the agreement highlighted a negotiated solution to overcome this moment of difficulty, it nonetheless seemed rather unusual to record a further involvement of a part of the sellers, even as stakeholders. In this regard, we should keep in mind that Emilio Gnutti favoured this new involvement alongside Olimpia, as he respected the ability of Pirelli's management and believed that the industrial project that the new shareholding structure was looking to develop was attractive. It is interesting to note that Gnutti's involvement was based on a shared business plan that until recently had been absent. The deal was closed with no further difficulty. To implement the planned transactions, Olimpia made two capital increases for a total of €1,562,596,250 in order to settle the second part of the transaction that had taken place on 5 October. In this way, it was possible to convene the Shareholders' General Meeting of Olivetti on 13 October 2001, for the election of the new Board, which would remain in office for the three-year period 2001–2003. The new Olivetti Board was made up of 16 directors, including Marco Tronchetti Provera as Vice Chairman and CEO, and Enrico Bondi and Carlo Buora as CEOs, while Gilberto Benetton was the other Deputy Chairman and Antonio Tesone was Chairman. The shareholders' meeting of Telecom Italia chose Marco Tronchetti Provera as Chairman, Gilberto Benetton as Deputy Chairman and Enrico Bondi and Carlo Buora as CEOs.

The entire operation was completed with the election of the new Boards of

Olivetti and Telecom Italia, which marked the emergence of new perspectives for Pirelli and Telecom Italia. Tronchetti Provera had already discussed what it meant for Pirelli to acquire this stake during the Board meeting of 28 July 2001. On that occasion, he had underlined that Telecom Italia's new priority commitment in the telecommunications field entailed a new focus of the Pirelli Group's activities on some specific activities with high added value aimed at the high end of the tyre industry, but a gradual disengagement, with an expected income of at least €2 billion, 'for the remaining traditional activities of the Group, which nevertheless generated a high cash flow and with significant market positions, such as the truck tyre and energy business units'. This was, in part, a new perspective for the Group. It must be pointed out that until then, innovative investment projects had been created within the Group's existing activities, and not from external acquisitions, even if these were made in market segments that the Group had long been familiar with and in which, from the mid-1990s, it had renewed its commitment. Soon, Pirelli's involvement in the Telecom Italia Group became predominant, even if Pirelli's traditional activities were never put aside.[16]

On 27 September 2001, the European Commission approved the entire operation. In conjunction with this authorisation, the first part of the deal was completed, and the Boards of Olivetti and Telecom Italia, as previously agreed, had co-opted the top management of Pirelli and Edizione Holding, and consented to the guidelines of the industrial and strategic plan that Tronchetti Provera had

---

16 To understand the sentiments motivating Pirelli's management in those days, it is interesting to read what Parazzini wrote in an unpublished mimeographed document: 'On the morning of July 29th, I received a telephone call from Carlo Buora: "Do you fancy going to Rome?" he asked me. "To do what?" I replied, knowing full well that he would have been pleased if I, having already guessed what he meant, replied simply that I did. But I was pleased to see that, on an occasion like that, he would offer up some of the words with which he was so parsimonious; and offer them up he did. "Now we have to take charge of the company and we need to do this at once. Actually, we need to think of who to send to Telecom (Italia). It cannot be done from Milan: we need to go to Rome; you should be the Chief Financial Officer."' Parazzini continues: 'Once the personal and family aspects had been handled, I began to ponder the commitment that was expected of me; Telecom Italia in the world was about five times the size of Pirelli in terms of turnover; its debt, consolidated with Olivetti's debt, was equal to more than forty times that of Pirelli [Pirelli's debt at that time was indeed around €1 billion]. Basically, it was scary. A huge workload was expected not only of me, but also of the aforementioned management team that was to be established in the following weeks, as soon as we could understand how to integrate ourselves into the situation that we would find.'

announced to the financial community. This plan outlined specific management perspectives and spelled out some focal points, which were also reiterated in the letter that the new Chairman of Telecom Italia addressed to the shareholders containing comments on the 2001 budget. These were the same management cornerstones given when he had taken on the responsibility for leading the Pirelli Group, i.e. 'the principle of value creation in seeking to take advantage of all the opportunities for business and technological development',[17] the implementation of consolidating actions for a strong recovery of efficiency and profitability, as well as the adoption of a policy of strict control of costs and investment (7 May 2002). The industrial plan involved the development of segments with high growth potential, such as access to broadband services, Internet access and an integrated commercial approach by the larger companies. As regards the restructuring of the portfolio, priority was given to investments that could allow for a controlling role. However, new international acquisitions in the wireline sector were ruled out. In mobile telecommunications, the company wanted to increase its revenue per customer through value-added services, and to become the main GSM operator in Latin America. From a financial point of view, the Group wished to increase its structural efficiency and financial flexibility, starting by strengthening Olivetti's balance sheet. This meant placing particular attention on the financial position of Olivetti, whose debt rating had suffered substantial deterioration over the preceding 18 months. Indeed, Moody's dropped its rating from A3 with a stable outlook in February 2000 to BAA2 with a negative outlook in 2001. A similar rating was issued by S&P, which lowered it from BBB+ in December 1999 to BBB in December 2001. Telecom Italia, as from March 2001, had also received a BAA1 rating from Moody's and BBB+ from S&P.

The new ownership structure that had taken control of the Group in the summer of 2001 was faced with a complex situation which demanded resolute action. Olimpia seemed to possess everything that had been lacking in previous years. From this point of view, the new structure was well organised to bring the expectations of the shareholders into line with the protection of the stakeholders and the implementation of an appropriate form of corporate governance.

---

17  Press release of the Board of Telecom Italia of 27 September 2001. The Strategic Guidelines presented on the same date state that 'the creation of value should have taken place through a) the company culture and customer service; b) a long-term commitment; c) the management's track record.'

The completeness and transparency of the information in the annual financial statements of Telecom Italia, from 2001 onwards, represented an ideal example of good corporate governance. The cause of the above success was also in part due to Pirelli's history, which had always been deeply rooted in corporate culture and which represented an additional factor in the difficult task of moving the Telecom Italia Group closer to the values of the competitive market. Telecom Italia's critical issues[18] were viewed as a challenge. Perhaps Pirelli underestimated the pervasiveness and ramifications of the political connections that were inherent to such a company as well as a lack of awareness on the part of the political class of what a modern telecommunications company could mean for the country. Nonetheless, there was a significant difference between the chain of control of Bell, based on Luxembourg companies, and that organised by the new Olimpia shareholders. While the former was essentially organised on consolidated debt, the latter's chain of control – although longer and opened out from Pirelli's parent companies to include Telecom Italia and Tim – was not only based on a large mass of liquidity, but was also based on Camfin, a publicly traded company listed on the Milan stock exchange since 1986.

---

18  It is interesting to note, in this regard, what Parazzini writes in the aforementioned unpublished mimeographed document, commenting on the acquisition of Telecom Italia with Claudio De Conto on the evening of 27 July 2001: 'How much does Telecom Italia cost?' asked Parazzini. 'A little over 4 euros per [Olivetti] share,' answered De Conto. 'This is not cheap, but it seems to be in line with the evaluations of the sector, if higher than the market. It won't be impossible to create some value on it; although it won't be easy. It will take years of hard work; there should be many areas for improvement and development.'

Annex 9.1. Chain of control of the Telecom Italia Group after the takeover bid by Tecnost-Olivetti

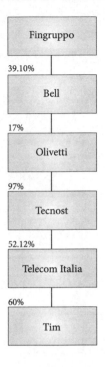

## ANNEX 9.2. THE PIRELLI GROUP'S CHAIN OF CONTROL AFTER THE INCORPORATION OF OLIMPIA

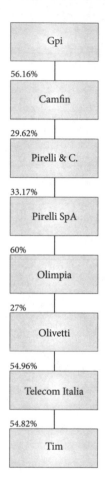

# CHAPTER 10

# The Restructuring of the Telecom Italia Group and the Pirelli Group

The process of acquisition of Olimpia's stake in Olivetti lasted just over two months, from 28 July to 5 October 2001. During this period, only Enrico Bondi's co-optation to the Telecom Italia Board and the powers that he held allowed Pirelli's management to monitor – albeit from the outside – the actual situation of the company and form an opinion regarding what initial steps needed to be taken. Alongside Tronchetti Provera and Buora, the first Pirelli managers to run Telecom Italia from its Rome headquarters included Francesco Chiappetta[1] for legal matters, Enrico Parazzini for financial matters, and later Gustavo Bracco for human resources.[2] By the end of September when Pirelli's top managers were appointed to the Olivetti and Telecom Italia Boards, the new management set out in the footsteps of Pirelli's consolidated management tradition.

Tronchetti Provera spoke for the first time about the objectives set for Telecom Italia at the Pirelli Board meeting (19 September 2001), identifying three specific business areas: land-wireline telecommunications, mobile telecommunications and the Internet. This was the first statement concerning the business plan, which was announced to the market one week later on 27 September 2001. Tronchetti Provera's opening statement on Telecom Italia's business plan bore a certain resemblance to the initial steps taken in Pirelli's turnaround. Prior to setting

---

1   Francesco Chiappetta, born in Rome in 1960, moved from Assonime, where he had been the deputy managing director for the period 1994–2001. Previously, he had covered various roles at CONSOB.

2   Gustavo Bracco had joined Pirelli on 1 December 2000, from Fiat. His move to Telecom Italia took place on 1 October 2001. He remained with Telecom Italia until the 2008 SGM. It is important to mention here that the information given by Chiappetta, Parazzini and Bracco (to each the author is most grateful) was invaluable for the reconstruction of the events recounted in this volume. Similarly, the author would also like to thank Maurizio Abet for the valuable contribution to the research for this publication.

precise corporate objectives – deferred until completion of a more detailed plan presented to the market on 14 February 2002 – Tronchetti Provera reiterated to the financial community the basic principle of value creation. The key issues focused on customer care and strict discipline regarding costs and investments that the new management was to put into practice at once. It was a clear message that stressed the purely industrial nature of the new management, and how value was to be created for shareholders through long-term commitment. In the new business plan, broadband development held strategic importance and hence the network played a fundamental role in Telecom Italia's future development. In this new context, traditional services would lose value, due to a decrease in demand and therefore Telecom Italia required an industrial and strategic outlook consistent with these changes.

## 10.1 Safety measures for Telecom Italia

Immediately afterwards, the newly appointed Chairman of Telecom Italia and Executive Vice Chairman of Olivetti reviewed the Group's debt situation, with specific reference to Olivetti. Indeed, before implementing any new investments or divestments, it was necessary to secure the Group's financial structure, start-ing with Olivetti, which was saddled with the most debt. For this reason and acting on the mandates granted by previous Extraordinary Shareholders' General Meetings, Olivetti's new Board of Directors carried out an equity increase of up to a maximum of €4,079,803,958. Olimpia subscribed to 50% of this increase, thus obtaining a 28.73% stake in Olivetti.[3] The obvious goal of this deal was to strengthen Olivetti's financial structure. However, it did not manage to tackle the underlying structural weakness, which would be solved only with the merger with Telecom Italia, which could not be foreseen at that time. It should be noted, however, that in the initial meetings with the financial community, Pirelli's man-agement declared that 'Olivetti's debt and Telecom Italia's debt were to be managed

---

3   After the capital increase, the weighted average cost of the Olivetti shares, held by Olimpia, had fallen to €3.34 per share. It was further anticipated that the conversion of the debenture loan by Bell would decrease the book value to €3.13 and subsequently to €2.78 per share (17 December 2001). If we consider the average book value after the capital increase, we obtain an individual average cost of Telecom shares equal to €12.73 per share, which in turn corresponds to a price of €3.78 per share, if normalised after the merger between Telecom and Olivetti.

as a unified whole'. At the end of 2001, the rating agency S&P raised Olivetti's outlook from negative to positive, marking the first tangible result in reducing the company's inherited debt.

As well as consolidating the company's finances to give greater financial stability to the Group and meet the covenants with the banks, Tronchetti Provera's remarks at the press conference can be interpreted as a formal commitment by Olimpia towards Telecom:

Jointly with our partners, we have invested significant financial resources in the Group, firmly believing that our commitment to its industrial management can make a decisive contribution to the strengthening of a strategic sector for the country. We are finalising the arrangement of significant further funding to ensure that the Group has fresh financial means, even in the unstable situation of the financial markets in the wake of the tragic events of the last few weeks. Our top management team has extensive experience and great international standing. We have clear plans on how and where we need to direct the Group's activities. We have the utmost motivation to achieve the ambitious objectives that we set for ourselves, in the interest of our shareholders, customers and employees. The stakes are high, but we believe that, realistically, we possess the skills and means required to succeed. We are asking our shareholders for their patience and trust regarding our commitment to present a Group that will be strengthened in all its areas within the next 24 months. At the end of the year, we will present the detailed plans that the top management team is preparing, in order to allow the market to fully grasp the scope of our activities to strengthen the Group.

Essentially, Tronchetti Provera maintained that a period of approximately two years was necessary to complete the restructuring process of Telecom Italia and to see the first results from the new management.

In the meantime, an initial difficulty emerged. CONSOB, the Italian authority monitoring the financial market, maintained that Pirelli alone exercised control over Olimpia, while the latter had de facto control over Olivetti. For these reasons, CONSOB asked Pirelli to prepare consolidated financial statements with Olimpia. Pirelli was opposed to this interpretation, which it deemed as being unfounded (27 September 2001). The argument put forward by Pirelli concerned the issue that the company, while holding 60% of Olimpia's equity, did not exercise autonomous control, since the shareholders' agreements signed with Edizione Holding included a clause for a qualified shareholder majority in Olimpia with 81% of the equity with full voting rights. Had Pirelli been forced to consolidate Olimpia, the result would have been an acknowledgement in the accounting records of consolidation of the debt held by both Olimpia and Olivetti, which was controlled de facto by Olimpia, at least in the view of CONSOB.

According to this scenario, Pirelli's capital ratios would have significantly worsened, jeopardising not only the existing covenants with the banks, but the whole structure of the Group's debt, given the limit imposed by the Bank of Italy on individual banking groups not to exceed 25% of the regulatory capital for each assigned group. At the beginning of November, CONSOB declared that it considered that 'Olivetti is controlled de facto by Olimpia, which is in turn subject to control by Pirelli'. On 6 December, Pirelli made an appeal against CONSOB's request in relation to both points. CONSOB's response came on 8 January 2002 with the rejection of Pirelli's appeal and a reiteration of its position. Pirelli immediately presented a new appeal to the Lazio Regional Administrative Court (which is in charge of national second degree of administrative justice), also bearing in mind that the deadline for drafting the 2001 financial statements was approaching. On 25 February 2002, the latter upheld Pirelli's appeal and hence that there was joint control of Olimpia by Pirelli and Edizione Holding. This ruling allowed the Group to draw up the first financial statements under the new management.

During the Telecom Italia SGM of 7 November 2001, as a result of which the new Board of Directors representing the new shareholders took up office as a whole, approval was granted for the transfer of the head office from Turin to Milan. This decision was forged in the wider context of the reorganisation and concentration of the Group's corporate activities, which were to be transferred from Rome to Milan. This choice was made as the new management sought to strengthen the corporate aspects of the company, which hitherto had been neglected more than other functions. Over a few months, between 2001 and 2002, some new committees were established, including the management committee, dedicated to monitoring the evolution of the Group's strategic development guidelines on a monthly basis, and the international steering committee, whose purpose was to define guidelines for the management of the Telecom Italia Group's foreign stakes. An investment committee and a procurement committee were also set up in order to coordinate the Group's purchasing processes effectively.

TABLE 10.1. OLIMPIA'S STATEMENT OF ASSETS
AND LIABILITIES AS AT 27 SEPTEMBER 2001

| Assets | Millions of euros | Liabilities & Equity | Millions of euros |
|---|---|---|---|
| Stake in Olivetti | 8,246 | Equity | 5,183 |
| Loan to Olivetti | 491 | Debts | 3,620 |
| Current assets | 66 | | |
| Total assets | 8,803 | Total liabilities | 8,803 |

*Source: Our calculations from the financial statements and SGM minutes*

Basing the corporate activities in Milan had strong business motivations and, despite all the guarantees for protection of employment and for the development of the different local territories where the company was located, it symbolised a break with the past, a step which immediately attracted the attention of the world of politics, leading to a perhaps undesirable media interest. A major own-share buyback programme was approved, aimed at propping up the share price. In response to questions by small shareholders, during the same meeting Tronchetti Provera offered further clarification on the new management team's programmes. In particular, the newly elected Chairman of the company (7 November 2001) returned to the issue of wireline telecommunications, stating that the new management would strengthen the domestic role of the company, which was a prerequisite for any growth abroad. While, on the one hand, competition could create benefits for the consumer, at the same time it was important not to forget the necessity to carry out infrastructure investment to upgrade the network, which would inevitably generate debate with the Regulatory Authority. The Chairman of Telecom Italia was well aware that the sector was structured differently in the United States as telecommunications companies at that time were being concentrated around a small number of operators.[4] It was a very different scenario in Europe, which had

---

4   Cambini, Ravazzi and Valletti (2003) write: 'The US experience can teach us important lessons. Firstly, it is more appropriate to leave it to technology to verify whether or not

seen the breakdown of a large number of telecommunications companies in the 1990s.

Tronchetti Provera reiterated that he believed that the process of modernisation of Telecom Italia was a major project to support the country's growth and develop its competitiveness.

The debt, which was approximately 43.4 billion lira on 30 September 2001, continued to be the top priority.[5] The debt exposure had been structured in its entirety, from the time of the takeover bid, through the use of short-term bank loans. This debt management mode was useful for the deal, but completely inappropriate for a company of Telecom Italia's size, as well as by then being obsolete on the market. Over the following two years no substantial innovations were made regarding management of the debt and only at the end of 2001, the Board of Telecom Italia approved a programme for the overall rescheduling of financial debt, through the issuance of corporate bonds with different timescale profiles.[6] The average duration of the debt was thus extended, making it more compatible with the risk-return profile of the total assets and with greater flexibility. During the Board meeting of 28 November 2001, the company defined an important two-year divestiture plan for non-strategic assets for an indicative value of €6 billion, the time frame indicated as necessary for the reorganisation of the Group. The stakes in the former satellite consortia (Eutelstat, Intelstat, Immerstat and New Skies Satellites) were sold for approximately €550 million to a newly formed company whose majority was held by a closed-end fund owned by Lehman Brothers; the stake that Finsiel held in Lottomatica for an equivalent value of €212 million was granted to the takeover bid launched by De Agostini. The most significant divestment was the sale

---

natural monopolies exist, rather than imposing a desired market structure by means of administrative decisions. From this point of view, the breaking up of AT&T can be considered with hindsight as completely useless. A second observation connected to the first is that the optimal size of companies in the telecommunications sector is very large. The number of Regional Bell Operating Companies has dropped from seven to four in a huge market.'

5   This amount also takes into consideration the put option in favour of JP Morgan on Seat.

6   The issuance of €2.5 billion, which took place at the end of January 2002, was a success. The *Wall Street Journal Europe* quoted some highly positive comments made by financial analysts: 'We like Telecom Italia bonds given the company's commitment to reduce its debt levels and the progress made so far in debt reduction. Its credit ratings are solid compared with for example Deutsche Telekom and France Telecom.'

of the 26.89% stake in Auna, a Spanish telecommunications operator, to Endesa, Unión Fenosa and Santander Central Hispanico for $1.85 billion. This stake was of a financial nature and did not allow Telecom Italia to have a presence in the industrial management of the company. Just a few months after taking up office, this sale provided clear evidence of the industrial nature of Olimpia's investment in Telecom Italia.

The annual financial statements at 31 December 2001 closed with a loss of €2.068 billion, following the application of asset adjustments and allocations for nonrecurring costs for €4.613 billion. The adjustments for almost €3.4 billion concerned mainly the goodwill payments for the stakes held in the telephone companies in South America and Central Europe. At the end of the 2001 financial year, Telecom Italia capitalised just over €62 billion, had almost 110,000 employees and a net financial debt of almost €22 billion,[7] having grown by approximately €4 billion from the previous year end.[8]

The initial results of the debt restructuring began to be felt. Compared to the previous end-of-year accounts in 2000, Telecom Italia's share of debt with a maturity exceeding one year had increased from 31% to 64% and its total consolidated revenues were almost €31 billion, showing an increase from the previous year.

The revenue breakdown clearly highlighted how over 80% was from wireline and mobile telecommunications, sectors that were beginning to show a decline in their cash flow production. Although other activities were still mere options for the future, they also represented good investment projects. The debt needed to be reduced as quickly as possible, before the cash flow from the declining traditional activities decreased significantly, while waiting for the new investments to start generating their own cash flows, given that the Group was planning to invest €15 billion over the subsequent three years. As early as 2001, Telecom Italia had made

---

7   This is the consolidated debt of the Telecom Italia Group, which does not include the debt held by Olivetti. Overall, at the end of the 2001 financial year, the total debt of the Olivetti-Telecom Italia Group was about €41.4 billion including the put option on the capital of Seat in favour of JP Morgan. Within one quarter, the total debt of the Group was reduced by €2 billion.

8   Please note that Telecom Italia's debt had gone from €8.1 billion at 31 December 1999, to €17.2 billion at 31 December 2000, reaching €22.6 billion as at 30 September 2001, including the €3 billion of the put option in favour of JP Morgan. During the same period, the debt on Olivetti shifted from €19.2 billion on 31 December 1999, to €18.5 billion on 31 December 2000, to €17.8 billion on 30 September 2001.

investments for just over €11 billion, almost €7 billion of which was of strictly industrial. Nevertheless, it was necessary to accelerate the divestiture operation: in the early months of the following year, Telecom Italia sold its stake of 19.61% in Bouygues Decaux Telecom to the French operator Bouygues SA, which already controlled 55% of Bouygues Telecom, for €750 million.

However, Telecom Italia was facing a situation that Pirelli had already experienced at the time of the turnaround, that is, the need to complete the restructuring, cancel the debt and invest in innovative sectors, before the margins from its cash generating activities were notably reduced. Telecom Italia showed similar characteristics, but of different dimensions. In light of this analysis, the 2002–2004 plan progressively took shape from autumn of 2001, and was approved on 14 February 2002. It prioritised safeguarding Telecom Italia's leadership position in wireline and mobile telecommunications in Italy, which was considered a prerequisite for future internationalisation. This strategy focused on those countries where the company could have the control of operational activities by using the expertise accumulated in its core business. For mobile telecommunications, the plan focused on some South American countries, Eastern Europe, Greece and Turkey, as well as the continuation of divestitures in non-strategic, non-controlling stakes, and in marginal business segments. The plan emphasised the recovery of efficiency in the various support functions, from procurement and IT to the corporate area, and on the systematic identification and exploitation of growth segments in both the domestic and international markets. As a result, the development of the Internet became particularly interesting, especially in the domestic market, using the broadband system that would significantly increase its reach to households and businesses (7 May 2002), and through methods for accessing the network. In this way, the country would start to bridge the gap that separated it from its competitor countries. The business plan[9] set out to achieve other ambitious goals, some of

---

9   The plan was well received by the market and the financial press. The *Wall Street Journal* of 15 February 2002 quoted the favourable impressions of certain analysts: 'The fact that the new management has moved so quickly to carry out its asset disposal plans gained great credibility in the market. And this means that the management also has credibility as far as the targets are concerned.' The Italian press, using a different tone, also emphasised similar aspects. In particular, *Milano Finanza* on 15 February 2002 wrote: 'The main difference between Roberto Colaninno and Marco Tronchetti Provera is their different approach to the management of the Group: Shortly after the aggressive takeover bid, Colaninno addressed the financial problems vehemently, while Tronchetti Provera has given great importance

TABLE 10.2. OWNERSHIP STRUCTURE OF
TELECOM ITALIA SpA AS AT 31 DECEMBER
2001 AND AT 31 DECEMBER 2002

| 31 December 2001 | | 31 December 2002 | |
|---|---|---|---|
| Shareholder | Ownership percentage of equity | Shareholder | Ownership percentage of equity |
| Olivetti | 54.96 | Olivetti | 54.94 |
| Ministry of the Economy and Finance | 3.46 | – | – |
| Italian institutional investors | 10 | Italian institutional investors | 10.55 |
| Foreign institutional investors | 22.82 | Foreign institutional investors | 22.42 |
| Small shareholders | 8.76 | Small shareholders | 8.63 |

*Source: Our calculations from the SGM minutes of Telecom Italia SpA*

TABLE 10.3. REVENUE BREAKDOWN OF TELECOM ITALIA
SpA BY BUSINESS AREAS AS AT 31 DECEMBER 2001

| Business areas | Contribution percentage share |
|---|---|
| Landline telephone services | 50.6 |
| Mobile telephone services | 30 |
| Internet and Media | 5.7 |
| International Operations | 5.5 |
| IT Services | 5.9 |
| Telecom Italia Lab and satellite services | 2.3 |
| Total | 100 |

*Source: SGM minutes, approval of financial statements from 31 December 2001*

which were on a one-off basis, while others were more long-standing. The former included streamlining the Group's structure by reducing the number of companies from 700 to 350, to generate cash flow of at least €25 billion in the period 2002–2004 and to carry out further investments for €16 billion, all of which were achieved. Among the latter goals, the company aimed to focus on the provision of integrated services and applications in certain high-potential customer segments such as the public administration sector, and to consolidate its leadership role in South America, on a par with Telefónica.

The 2001 financial statements showed another critical issue that had not been identified at the time of the purchase: the financial statements of Seat Pagine Gialle featured a put option in favour of JP Morgan at a strike price of €4.20 per share. JP Morgan's involvement stemmed from its role as the investment bank for commitments made by Telecom Italia in favour of the Luxembourg company Huit II. This commitment came to the fore only in the autumn of 2001, leading to the renegotiation of the agreement with the American bank by reducing the strike price of the put option to €3.40 per share and proceeding to the allocation of €569 million by Telecom Italia to pay for the first part of the transaction (7 May 2002), referring the conclusion of the deal to the original maturity date of 2005.[10]

During the second half of 2001 and the early months of 2002, the Pirelli Group registered the substantial resilience of the tyre sector and an increasingly marked decline in the cable sector. As regards tyres, the Company decided to focus its 2002–2005 three-year plan on the growth strategy in the high end segment in which it had increasingly positioned itself as one of the major market players. At

---

to the industrial aspects.' The new management's attention to the industrial aspects is also underlined in *Affari e Finanza* on 18 February 2002: 'In the presentation of the business plan for the next three years, Marco Tronchetti Provera has repeatedly emphasised that he is an industrialist. We might ask: why is Tronchetti Provera going to such lengths to emphasise this? And we could also ask: an industrialist as opposed to what or who? Probably as opposed to a "financier", or maybe, even worse, to a "(corporate) raider" or even only to a "majority shareholder". This was not the only "anti-financial" signal intended as an expression of the desire to go his own way, without being too influenced by stock market prices and the often schizophrenic trends of so-called "market sentiment". He reminded analysts and large investors that often the sector indexes on which they base their work are too heterogeneous, and the telecommunications sector index brings together very different businesses.'

10 However, it is important to remember that the Company carried out a devaluation of the stake in Seat respectively for €600 million in 2001 and €3.3 billion in 2002.

that time, however, it was the real estate activity developed by Pirelli & C. Real Estate that provided the greatest contribution to value creation among the Pirelli Group's activities. The Pirelli & C. Board minutes immediately reveal the growing importance of the real estate sector, demonstrating a change in the work dynamics. Following an introduction by the Chairman, and by Giovanni Ferrario,[11] who illustrated the performance of the cable and tyre sectors, Carlo Alessandro Puri Negri continued with observations concerning the evolution and prospects of the real estate activity.

Pirelli & C. Real Estate, whose listing was being prepared, was a company entirely controlled by the Limited Partnership Pirelli & C., which 'operated both in (residential and commercial) real estate asset management providing strategic management service, and with stakes with qualified minorities in the equity of the initiatives undertaken, and in specialist services for the same initiatives and for third party customers'. The real estate company had progressively completed and extended the skills that Pirelli had acquired in the field of property redevelopment of disused industrial areas. Despite the division between the two corporate aspects and their respective roles, there was still potential for synergy between Pirelli and the Telecom Italia Group. One of these areas was research by means of agreements between the Pirelli Labs and the Telecom Italia labs (7 May 2002), given that the former had developed expertise in the fibre optics sector and the latter in electronics. The 2002–2004 business plan provided for increased investment for research in collaboration with university departments, especially in the development of broadband services and network access, as well as for the mobile and wireless systems.

Real estate was another area of potential synergy. It is important to remember, however, that most of Telecom Italia's properties had been sold prior to Pirelli's management. For this reason, the Pirelli Board approved a complex project called Tiglio I, to which a second project, Tiglio II, was added, aimed at the integration between the real estate activities of the Pirelli and Olivetti-Telecom Italia groups to maximise the benefit from these. The project provided for the transfer of all the assets to a newly created company with its simultaneous indebtedness, the subsequent contribution of the assets to a real estate fund, and lastly the sale of the shares in the fund on the market. This was the same model used up to then

---

11  Giovanni Ferrario had been appointed CEO of Pirelli on 5 November 2001.

by Pirelli & C. Real Estate, even if in this instance it had a broader scope. This model entailed the transfer of real estate assets to a real estate fund that generally referred to Morgan Stanley (28 March 2002), in which Pirelli's real estate company remained a minority shareholder, usually with a 25% stake, and occasionally holding up to 49% of the shares.

The Tiglio I and Tiglio II deals enabled Telecom Italia to pay off the real estate assets and, through the debt mechanism, advance the collection and invest the relevant share in the subsequent capital gains arising from the placements. These sale and lease back operations involved a 12.6% return on Telecom Italia's investments for 2002 and 13.9% for 2003, higher than the cost of the leases, which can be estimated as being between 6.8% and 8.40%.[12] It was a consolidated operating procedure for almost all industrial and service groups around the world, such as France Telecom, British Telecom, Deutsche Telekom, KPN, Swisscom and Telenor.

Pirelli & C. Real Estate also entered into similar agreements with Camfin Group companies with the aim of creating synergies (13 May 2002). It was an aggressive business method, based on significant debt ratios, which were nevertheless in line with those of the sector as it underwent significant growth in those years. The business opportunities also included the management of the facility activities conducted by Telecom Italia and Olivetti, with the aim of transferring them to one or more vehicles. In May 2002 (13 May 2002), the procedure for the listing of Pirelli & C. Real Estate was formalised, with 40% of its equity as the object of a global bid that took place in the month of June and yielded approximately €400 million to the parent company Pirelli & C. In May, the Pirelli Board reviewed the 2002–2004 development plan, well aware of the considerable investment that had been made in the Olivetti-Telecom Group. From Pirelli's point of view, all this implied the

---

12 The explanatory report of the deal as a whole, attached to the minutes of the Pirelli SpA Board of Directors' meeting of 27 March 2002, reads: 'A comparison between the cost of the leases, expressed as a percentage of the transfer value of the property (the yield) and the average cost of capital (WACC equal to 10%) shows a positive difference of 3.2% on administrative property and 1.40% on industrial property. A further comparison of the average yield of the expected capital of Telecom Italia in 2002 and 2003 (ROI target of Telecom Italia SpA of 12.6% for 2002 and 13.9% for 2003) and the yield on the industrial property shows a gain of 4% and 5.3% respectively. Similar considerations also apply to Seat, the only other company that will directly use a significant portion of the real estate properties involved in the transaction. The yield on the Seat real estate is 8.65%. The comparison with the weighted average capital cost of Seat (WACC of 9%) shows a positive difference of 0.35%.'

prospect of possible divestitures to support the health of Olimpia's balance sheet. However, it was a theoretical scenario at that time, since the 2002–2004 three-year plan did not envisage any divestiture projects by Pirelli. Also in this case, the event had certain similarities with the past. Just as the Camfin Group had supported its growing investment in Pirelli & C. through a series of divestments, so could the investment in telecommunications potentially require reconsideration of Pirelli's priorities and range of activities. The Olivetti-Telecom Italia deal was also one of the most discussed issues raised by Pirelli's small shareholders during the meeting to approve the 2001 financial statements. Tronchetti Provera summarised the stages of the deal to the shareholders, stressing how the liquidity used by Pirelli had been generated from transactions with Corning and Cisco. He also reminded the shareholders who were weary of Olivetti-Telecom's debt burden that provisions were being made to reduce this to €9 billion during 2002 (13 May 2002), but while making it clear to Pirelli shareholders that Telecom Italia was in need of cultural restructuring:

> The intention is to apply Pirelli's industrial culture to Telecom Italia, which is a different company that has been through different owners, and has a corporate culture originating in the public sector, with consequent merits and flaws. Our commitment is to demonstrate that the new management is pursuing an industrial philosophy aimed at exploiting existing strengths, including in terms of culture, and new resources already at work within Telecom itself.

The second half of 2002 was a relatively quiet period with Pirelli showing a promising trend in the tyre sector, but with an 'unprecedented crisis in the telecommunications cables sector' that risked jeopardising its economic balance, while Telecom Italia stuck closely to the agreed business plan and showed interim results that were more than satisfying. The divestiture plan also proceeded smoothly and was well-received by the market. In an interview with *Il Sole 24 Ore* on 28 June 2002, Enrico Bondi – one of Telecom Italia's two CEOs – stated that the company had already completed two-thirds of the total divestures envisaged in the business plan. Moreover, the Group's CEO recalled:

> There is a point that I would like to emphasise. Telecom Italia, like all companies, entered into the dizzy race for acquisitions. But it is also the

company that left it first: when we arrived a year ago, we realised that we had to change direction. Our strategy is to get out of all the minority stakes we hold abroad where we cannot exercise our function as an industrial group.

In June, the 25% stake in Mobilkom Austria was sold to Telekom Austria for €716 million, and in August of that same year, Telespazio was sold to Finmeccanica for €245 million, while the last disinvestment of the year was the 29% stake in Telekom Serbia, which was sold for €195 million. These sales contributed to an improved evaluation by the rating agencies, which changed from steady to positive, although their opinion remained unchanged. It should be noted that the first foreign acquisition of a certain significance was made in 2002, namely a further 17.45% of the Greek operator Stet Hellas for €108 million in addition to the 63.95% stake already held, thus raising the total holding to 81.40%. This acquisition marked a change of course from before, as holding this majority stake permitted the industrial management of the equity stake, albeit within a logic of international diversification.

After the attacks of 11 September, equity market prices dropped significantly and persistently, a global trend that had little to do with the activities of individual companies. While on the one hand it was clear that the market did not reflect the economic multiples of cable and telecommunications companies, and hence those of Pirelli or the Olivetti-Telecom Group, this persistent decline in prices jeopardised the now enlarged Group as a whole. At the end of 2002, Olivetti's share price dropped below the €1 mark, approaching the threshold that meant the repayment of Olimpia's guarantees towards the banks at the end of the coming April. This scenario was to have a serious impact on the Group as a whole, exposing Olimpia's shareholders to risk and a likely worse rating of the debt of various companies of the Group. A clear signal was needed for the market which took the form of shortening the chain of control to create value for the shareholders. However, this process was not feasible in the limited time available, and so the most immediate alternative was to rapidly strengthen Olimpia's financial structure. The quickest route meant involving the Bell shareholders who, after 11 September 2001, were open to renegotiating the terms of the agreement made that previous July. Indeed, Gnutti was not averse to a new involvement in telecommunications, and therefore looked favourably on the possibility of becoming a shareholder of Olimpia. It was a complex deal that was concluded as follows: first, Olimpia returned the €1.032

billion bond underwritten by Hopa and issued the previous year. The debenture loan was not repaid in cash, but through the transfer by Olimpia of 100 million ordinary shares and 164 million Olivetti convertible bonds to Hopa. The company Holy – entirely owned by Hopa – was subsequently merged by incorporation with Olimpia, with the provision that Holy would have net assets of not less than €960 million and be debt free. Hopa and Holinvest, another subsidiary of Hopa, also held 4.64% of Olivetti's ordinary share capital and convertible bonds for a potential 7.21% stake. These two companies moved to their subsidiary company Holy, 100 million Olivetti ordinary shares and 164 million convertible bonds deriving from the repayment of the loan by Olimpia, as well as €99 million in cash and a block of 19.99% of Holinvest shares. As a result of its merger with Holy, Olimpia increased its net assets by at least €960 million and reduced its debts by €476 million, registering a significant profit improving its financial structure. Moreover, as a result of these operations, Hopa joined Olimpia's ownership structure with a 16% stake. Concurrently, the stakes of Pirelli and Edizione Holding were reduced respectively to 50.4% and 16.8%, while those of the two banks were reduced to 8.4% each. There was also another aspect to be taken into consideration; since Holy held 19.99% of Holinvest, as a result of the merger by incorporation, Olimpia became the owner of this direct stake in Holinvest, while the remaining part of Holinvest's equity was owned by Hopa. The reason for this complex corporate deal arose from the fact that the percentage stake of Olimpia in Olivetti would otherwise constantly and significantly exceed the threshold of 30%, triggering a mandatory takeover bid. This way, Olimpia was not required to consolidate the stake in Holinvest as it remained below this threshold. Relationships between Olimpia and Hopa were governed by an independent shareholders' agreement, separate from that with the Olimpia shareholders. Olimpia also obtained a pre-emption right on further shares held by Holinvest. At the end of 2002, the Treasury sold its entire residual stake of 3.5% with voting rights and 0.7% of the savings capital for a total of €1.434 billion. Despite this sale, however, the Treasury still had the option to exercise its golden share.

In the meantime, the operating companies of the Telecom Italia Group were about to prepare the financial statements at 31 December 2002. The consolidated financial statements of the Telecom Italia Group showed a positive situation. Despite the fact that the Group's turnover had decreased slightly from the previous year, the company still showed profits of just over €4 billion and debts of approximately €18 billion, i.e. about €4 billion less than the previous year. The revenue breakdown had not substantially changed with wireline and mobile tele-communications continuing to constitute just over 80% of the Group's turnover, while the Internet, media and the two information technology segments accounted for the remaining part for the Group and for the market. Compared to the previous year end, Telecom Italia's market capitalisation had decreased significantly, regis-tering a 19% fall due to adverse stock market conditions.

From an industrial point of view, the financial statements of the preceding year had been positive. The company wasted no time in implementing its plans, obtaining significant results in cost savings, in the rationalisation of the Group and in the related divestitures, with the reduction of the existing debt. These divestitures had generated resources for €5.8 billion, while the number of com-panies had dropped to 416, including the 30 new acquisitions. Staff numbers had also been cut by 7.5%, half of these in the wireline telecommunications sector. This not only was a clear implementation of the 2002–2004 three-year plan res-olutions, but had also taken place well ahead of schedule. Furthermore, during the early months of 2003, the 28.57% stake in the Brazilian company Globo.com was sold to Tim Brasil for €15 million. As from 1 January 2003, Telecom Italia Sparkle was incorporated, entirely controlled by Telecom Italia, to which the parent company had transferred the Wholesale International division (24 May 2003), in order to develop the international businesses independently. Moreover, the stake in Seat Pagine Gialle was devalued to €0.668 per share.

The company had also paid specific attention to the issues of product and service innovation, customer satisfaction and more in general to improve the dis-closure process and utmost attention to all stakeholders (24 May 2003). However, this intense programme did not seem to convince the market, which continued to penalise the shares of the entire Telecom Group. If, on the one hand, it was a difficult market phase following the collapse of the technology bubble, the serious terrorist attacks of the previous year and the wars that followed, on the other hand, the long chain of control was perceived as an increasing hindrance to value creation for shareholders.

## 10.2 Shortening the chain of control

From his arrival into the world of telecommunications, Tronchetti Provera had been determined to shorten the chain of control as soon as the markets allowed (7 May 2003) to enable greater valuation of telecommunications shares by the market. After the Telecom Italia deal, the organisational structure was now characterised by three companies with holding functions, i.e. Pirelli & C., Olimpia and Olivetti, with the latter two companies owning almost the same assets.

The conclusion of the deal with Hopa at the end of 2002 had strengthened Olimpia's control over Olivetti and made it possible to shorten the chain of control through Telecom Italia's merger by incorporation with Olivetti. This integration, however, implied a significant dilution of Olimpia's stake in the new post-merger Telecom. Despite never having exceeded the 30% ownership limit in Olivetti (24 May 2003), the Hopa transaction had theoretically given Olimpia the power to significantly increase its stake in the new Telecom, since Hopa held a significant number of Olivetti shares not held by Olimpia. In theory, the percentage of Olimpia's stake in the telecommunications group would decrease by approximately 28.5% to a value between 13% and 15% (24 May 2003). Despite Tronchetti Provera's reiteration that 'control' over the companies did not depend solely on the number of shares owned, the presence of a reference shareholder with a small percentage of shares could nevertheless have potentially negative repercussions on the stability of the company's ownership structure. After the restructuring of a few years earlier, the most important asset held by Olivetti had become its stake in Telecom Italia. As Olivetti no longer had a precise industrial mission, it was clear that the two companies were potentially complementary, given that following the Tecnost merger three years previously, the debt arising from the takeover bid was placed entirely with Olivetti. A merger by incorporation between Telecom Italia and Olivetti would allow the Group's liquid assets to be managed jointly with its debt in the company resulting from the merger. This meant putting the entire debt mass on the same level as the still-large cash flows generated by Telecom Italia and just above those created by Tim. It is no coincidence that the entire deal was called Safe Harbour, as it indeed represented a safe harbour for the Group's creditors.

However, certain difficulties still needed to be overcome. First of all, Telecom Italia's merger by incorporation with Olivetti and the simultaneous change of the company name and business purpose involved the possibility of withdrawal for Olivetti's minority shareholders in accordance with Italian law. Such protection, however, threatened to create an unequal treatment towards the Telecom Italia small shareholders who received as part of a share exchange the shares of a heavily indebted company without any autonomous cash flow. While protection by means of withdrawal was a legal requirement for Olivetti shareholders, the fears of the Telecom Italia minority shareholders needed to be dispelled through the solidity of the share exchange ratio. There was also one final aspect to consider, i.e. the treatment to be granted to the shareholders of Telecom Italia without voting rights. A possible conversion of savings shares into ordinary shares would not have gone down well with the market, and a voluntary takeover bid for all shares without voting rights in circulation would have resulted in an excessive financial burden for the company. The Group's top management considered this deal very important to continue to build a positive relationship with the market after the stormy clashes that had marked the previous management.

Meetings of the Boards of Directors of both companies took place on 11 March 2003 to approve the Extraordinary Shareholders' Meetings for the merger, to be held on 24 May. A share exchange ratio of, respectively, seven Olivetti shares for every Telecom share, for both ordinary shares and for those without voting rights, was approved, while the right of withdrawal was granted in favour of the Olivetti shareholders (6 May 2004). A voluntary and partial takeover bid was also approved on a percentage defined somewhere between 16% and 19% of the ordinary and savings share equity of Telecom Italia, subject to the completion of the corporate merger procedure. Although this measure was intended to provide further protection for Telecom Italia shareholders as no right of withdrawal could be applied, the market's reaction was initially negative, penalising both ordinary shares prices and those without voting rights of Telecom Italia. The deal was submitted to the financial community in London on 13 March and received a hostile reception. Institutional investors failed to be impressed by the fact that in the presentation of the 2002 results and the outlook for the company, which had taken place in Milan in the previous month, on 14 February 2003, the project as a whole had not been mentioned.

What did not convince the institutional investors, particularly the hedge funds, seemed to be the share exchange ratio,[13] which could be inferred clearly

---

13 The Belgian consulting company Deminor, which claimed to represent 8% of the Olivetti capital, evaluated the share exchange ratio as nine Olivetti shares for each Telecom Italia share. On 4 April 2003, *Il Sole 24 Ore* quoted Telecom Italia's response: 'These are observations to which Telecom Italia and Olivetti have already given, repeatedly, long and comprehensive answers in recent times. The share exchange is based on a long historical series of market data, which "balances out", also considering Telecom as the sum of its parts and as a result giving a value to Olivetti, as many analysts have done, not taking the ad hoc data from one day as a reference.' It should also be noted that the independent advisors Reconta, Deloitte and the one appointed by the Court of Ivrea declared that the share exchange ratio of seven Olivetti shares for each Telecom Italia share was fair. *L'Unità* on 24 April 2003 reported that, according to Reconta's valuation: 'in the valuations for mergers,

TABLE 10.4. DIVESTITURES OF NON-STRATEGIC 'ASSETS'
OF TELECOM ITALIA SPA 2001–2003 (DATA IN € BILLION)

| Divestitures | 2001 | 2002 | 2003 |
|---|---|---|---|
| Satellite Consortia | 0.5 | | |
| Bouygues | | 0.8 | |
| Mobilkom Austria | | 0.8 | |
| Lottomatica | | 0.4 | |
| 9 Telecom | | (0.6) | |
| Auna | | 2 | |
| Telespazio | | 0.2 | |
| Sogei | | 0.2 | |
| Teleaustria | | 0.6 | |
| Real Estate | | 0.8 | |
| Others | | 0.1 | |
| Seat | | | 3.7 |
| Real Estate | | | 0.4 |
| Others | | | 0.2 |
| Total | 0.5 | 5.3 | 4.3 |

*Source: Our reclassification from Telecom Italia's financial statements*

from the stability achieved by the ratio between the equity prices[14] of the two companies over a rather long timescale (7 May 2003), as well as from the consensus of

---

the ultimate purpose is not so much the determination of absolute values of the company's economic capital, but the identification of comparable values when determining the share exchange'.

14  On 19 March 2003, *Il Sole 24 Ore* wrote: 'Tronchetti reiterated that the deal had become urgent because Telecom, although having better results than its "comparables", was consistently penalised by the market indeed because of the cumbersome structure of the chain of control. The share exchange of seven Olivetti shares for one Telecom share is the exact result of what has been expressed by the stability in the share price trend of the two companies, both in the last year and over the last three months.'

many analysts, whose average observations showed a share-exchange ratio of 6.58 with a median of 6.74. The company took steps to provide a detailed explanation of the project to the market. In a presentation that took place in New York on 12 May 2003, the project received a less hostile reception also because, at this second meeting, more emphasis was placed on certain ingredients of corporate governance that were perceived as favourable by institutional investors. In particular, of the 15 members of the Board of Directors, eight would be independent, three of whom would represent minority shareholders, just as two members of the Board of Statutory Auditors would likewise represent minority shareholders. Similarly, the committee for internal audit and corporate governance was to be made up entirely of independent directors. These views were shared by ISS (Institutional Shareholder Services), an independent US corporate governance company that issued a positive evaluation of the entire deal.

From the largest shareholder's point of view, the launch of the voluntary public takeover bid also aimed at offsetting the possible impact of the right of withdrawal by Olivetti shareholders, the consequences of which were still unknown. The dilution of Olimpia's stake in the company following the merger did indeed depend on the percentage of Olivetti shareholders who would exercise the right of withdrawal. Should this figure be insignificant, the dilution effect would be maximum. Regardless of the financial aspects of the entire deal, analysed by the incorporating company Olivetti, the voluntary takeover bid could also have had the aim, after the merger, of helping ensure that Olimpia's stake – the extent of which would derive from the combined effect of the exercised right of withdrawal and the voluntary takeover bid – would not be excessively diluted. In the final days before the SGMs, the Liverpool fund[15] filed an urgent appeal with the Court of Milan, applying for a freeze on the voting rights of Olimpia and Olivetti prior to the extraordinary general meetings. This appeal was rejected.

Both meetings of 24 May 2003 approved the entire project. For Telecom, the project was approved by a 92.73% majority of the capital represented at the meeting, equal to 63.55% of the total capital. The remaining 3.96% capital was opposed, while 3.29% abstained. The approval of the merger project by the SGM allowed the launching of the voluntary takeover bid, which took place in July 2003. This ended

---

15  A source revealed to the author that evidence emerged during the hearing demonstrating that the Liverpool fund held only a few Olivetti shares.

positively. Respectively, 9.73% and 11.83% of Telecom ordinary and without voting rights equity participated in the bid (31 July 2003).[16] The merger deed was signed on 4 August 2003. The capital shareholding held by Olimpia in the company formed by the merger had fallen to 11.85% of the ordinary share capital. A dilution of such an extent clearly outlined the problem of the hold which the new reference shareholder had on the new Telecom. If, on the one hand, a shorter chain of corporate control had exposed Olimpia to dilutions that weakened its control, on the other hand, it is important to remember that these measures were taken to add value to Telecom Italia. Olimpia began working towards this goal in the months following the deal. As early as October (11 November 2003), Olimpia purchased 2.6% of the Telecom Italia ordinary shares, thus bringing its capital shareholding to 14.16% of the equity.

Approximately two years after its entry into the world of telecommunications, the merger between Olivetti and Telecom Italia showed significant results which were achieved ahead of schedule. The merger between the two companies definitively stabilised the debt situation and allowed the market to fully exploit the ongoing business plan. From the reference shareholder's point of view, this was also a courageous deal because it made the company competitive again, and because it also envisaged a temporary increase in debt to finance the voluntary takeover bid and the right of withdrawal (24 May 2003). Table 10.5 shows the overall dynamic of the Group's indebtedness at the end of the first two years.

The debt had increased less than anticipated, due to the limited extent of the right of withdrawal and the low percentage of participation in the takeover bid; indeed, Olimpia's hold over the operating company had weakened. There was clearly a necessity to stabilise the ownership structure and there were increasing difficulties in representing the relevant premium paid two years earlier to Bell shareholders in accounting terms. When the merger deed between the two companies had been completed on 4 August 2003, the merger between Pirelli & C. and Pirelli SpA was also finalised.

The purpose of this deal was similar to that described previously, i.e. to shorten

---

16  The withdrawal and the voluntary public takeover cost €5.285 billion in total and provided the first interruption, however smaller than expected, of the process for the systematic reduction of the Group's debt. The value of the withdrawal was established at €0.9984 for the Olivetti shares and, respectively, at €8.010 and €4.820 for the ordinary and the savings shares of Telecom Italia.

the corporate chain in the Pirelli Group. From the time when Pirelli had concluded the purchase of the stake in Olivetti through Olimpia, the market had treated the shares of both companies harshly, including Pirelli SpA's shares which lost approximately 75% of their value. This drop in share prices was only partially reflected in the fundamentals of the Group. Nevertheless, these had suffered also due to the difficult market environment and the heavy crisis that had involved the entire cable sector from the second half of 2001. In 2002, Pirelli SpA's year-end financial statements had closed with a loss due to the significant decrease in turnover in the cable sector. These disappointing results were evened out by the positive performance in the tyre sector, where continuous investments and the progressive repositioning toward the high end were showing their effects. The company drivers for the years to come were taking shape. The focus on high-end products – later called prestige and premium products – was pursued with determination, and brought in important approvals from the most successful car manufacturers in those years (11 March 2003). The increasingly narrowing and specific high-end market niche with considerable profit margins, such as the winter segment, followed not only a Schumpeterian component of product creation, but also the famous Say's Law, whereby supply creates its own demand.

The first half of 2003 did not contribute any new elements to this scenario. While growth in the tyre sector continued, uncertain prospects were registered for cables, especially telecommunications cables (31 July 2003; 11 November 2003). Again in this case, the market expressed a negative opinion of the role of Pirelli & C. which, following the listing of Pirelli & C. Real Estate and the shareholding in Olimpia by Pirelli SpA, had taken on the appearance of a holding company. Also in this case, a shorter chain of control, through a merger by incorporation of Pirelli SpA in Pirelli & C., would produce positive effects on the value of the shares. It was therefore necessary to convert Pirelli & C. from a limited liability partnership joint stock company into a public limited company (11 March 2003). It was an epochal event in the history of the Group: the limited liability partnership joint stock company Pirelli & C. had been operating seamlessly on the market since 1883. For these reasons, after this transformation, the Company took on the name of Pirelli & C. SpA, juxtaposing the old name of the limited liability partnership joint stock company with that of the new public limited company. Also in this case, the transformation involved the possible attribution of the right of withdrawal for the shareholders of the Limited Liability Partnership, since Pirelli & C. was to change its business purpose. Approval was granted for an equity increase by Pirelli & C. for a maximum amount of €1.014 billion offered as an option to shareholders with combined warrants in case of subscription, by 30 June 2006, of further shares for €254 million. After the equity increase and transformation into a public limited company, Pirelli & C. Luxembourg and Pirelli SpA were incorporated into Pirelli & C. SpA. At the time of the Board of Directors' resolution on the merger, Pirelli & C. was controlled by a shareholders' agreement that grouped together 56.48% of the equity.

In turn, Pirelli & C. controlled 41.7% of Pirelli SpA, whose second shareholder was Landesbank Baden-Wurttemberg with 5.55% of the capital. This deal would bring a real benefit to the shortening of the chain of control also through the merger by incorporation of Pirelli & C. Luxembourg, wholly controlled by the Limited Liability Partnership, which held 27.5% of Pirelli SpA. The merger involved a dilution of the effect of the shareholders' agreement which, even in the case of full subscription of the capital increase, would hold approximately 38% of the new company Pirelli & C. SpA.[17] In turn, Camfin was the largest shareholder of Pirelli & C. with a 29.9% stake, 20.34% of which had been granted to the shareholders' agreement. To continue exercising its reference role, but mainly because it was confident in the reorganisation of the Group, Camfin subscribed in full to the pro quota portion of the equity increase of Pirelli & C. In turn, Camfin had also approved an equity increase of approximately €160 million and another €40 million in warrants, to procure the resources required for the pro quota subscription of the equity increase of Pirelli & C. The SGM of 7 May 2003 approved the merger between the two companies. Also in this case, the effective ownership structure of the company derived from the merger was the outcome not only of share exchanges, but also of the percentage of withdrawal by the shareholders of the Limited Liability Partnership, notification of which had not yet been given at the time of the SGM resolution. Unlike what had happened in Olivetti, approximately 19% of the ordinary share of Pirelli & C. exercised the right of withdrawal. This percentage was higher than expected and had the effect of mitigating the dilution effect of the shareholders' agreement over the equity of Pirelli & C., which thus amounted to 42%.

The new corporate structure also allowed the entire Group to define improved corporate governance in order to make it even more attractive in the eyes of international investors. However, we must not forget that Pirelli had always given great

---

17 In turn, Pirelli & C. SpA would hold 61.2% of Pirelli & C. Real Estate, 50.4% of Olimpia. Furthermore, it had complete control over Pirelli Cavi e Sistemi Energia, Pirelli Cavi e Sistemi Telecom and Pirelli Tyre Holding.

importance to corporate governance, which was a constituent element of its history. Not by chance, the Company had adopted a self-governance code since its issuance, as well as approving regulations for transactions with related parties much earlier than the rest of the market competitors. Entry into the world of telecommunications and the need for absolute attention in dealings with all stakeholders had further accelerated this sensitivity within the Group, which had been driven by Francesco Chiappetta who, in the light of his previous professional experience, attributed great importance to issues of corporate governance. The importance of these aspects was also emphasised by the difficult relationship with the market that the Company had experienced in the spring of that year. The adjustment of the chain of control that took place in 2003 allowed the introduction in the following year – following the approval of the financial statements and implementation of new rules in line with Company Law reform – of some further innovations, such as the introduction of a code of ethics, and the presence of minority shareholders in the corporate bodies through the adoption of the list vote.

The market reacted with interest, but without much enthusiasm, to the completion of the two mergers. However, in the summer of 2003, there was a feeling that the international economic situation showed signs of improvement, and that the burden of uncertainty permeating the economic context in the first two years of Telecom Italia's management would soon vanish. There was some truth in this perception. Similarly to the market, the company also found itself at a turning point. It had taken two years to turn its back on the past and had created the conditions for virtuous growth. At the beginning of August 2003, the Telecom Italia Group finally settled one of the burdens from its past, selling to a consortium of investors (6 May 2004) a 61.5% stake of the company resulting from the demerger of Seat Pagine Gialle at a price of €3.033 billion. That sale was linked to changes in the legislation, which made advertising possible even at the regional level, thus making this sale interesting for Telecom Italia. Before making this divestiture, Seat Pagine Gialle had made a partial demerger of its own directories and directory assistance activities, for the benefit of a new company that took the name of Seat Pagine Gialle, while the demerged company – named Telecom Italia Media – would deal with the provision of Internet access and media services and had 'the objective of accelerating the process for the convergence of telephone, Internet and content'.[18]

---

18 From the slides entitled 'Telecom Italia from 1998 to the Present Day' presented in the Board

TABLE 10.5. DYNAMICS OF DEBT OF OLIVETTI/
TELECOM ITALIA GROUP DURING THE PERIOD
2001–2003 (DATA IN € BILLION)

| Entries | September 2001 | 2001 | 2002 | 2003 |
|---|---|---|---|---|
| Initial debt | 43.4[a] | | | |
| Disposals | (0.5) | | | |
| Net cash flow | (1.5) | | | |
| Final debt | | 41.4 | | |
| Disposals | | | (5.3) | |
| Net cash flow | | | (0.3) | |
| Final debt | | | 35.8 | |
| Withdrawal and voluntary bid service | | | | 5.3 |
| Disposals | | | | (4.3) |
| Net cash flow | | | | (3.5) |
| Final debt | | | | 33.3 |

*[a]Including €3 billion for the put option of JP Morgan*
*Source: Our reclassification from Telecom Italia's financial statements*

This reorganisation was intended to focus the Group's commitment on the media segment. In this way, two autonomous companies were established, with the first dedicated to sales. At the end of 2002, Telecom Italia Media and the new Seat Pagine Gialle had pro forma consolidated turnovers of €577 million and €1.445 billion respectively. The sale of the controlling stake in the new Seat Pagine Gialle also helped to close the put option issue in favour of JP Morgan, of which the

---

meeting of Pirelli & C. SpA of 26 January 2006. This kind of scenario would inevitably also have an impact on the television sector.

TABLE 10.6. OWNERSHIP STRUCTURE
OF PIRELLI & C. AT 7 MAY 2003

| Shareholder | Percentage owned on share capital with voting rights |
|---|---|
| Camfin | 29.9 |
| Serfis | 9.59 |
| Generali | 6.18 |
| Hpi | 5.94 |
| Premafin | 5.66 |
| Mediobanca | 5.32 |
| Edizione Holding | 5.28 |
| Allianz | 5.11 |

*Source: Our calculations from official documentation provided by Pirelli & C.*

new team was aware after the completion of the 2001 deal. The sale of the portion of the new Seat had simultaneously enabled the settlement of the commitment with JP Morgan more than two years ahead of the expected deadline of December 2005, and the deconsolidation of €3.681 million in net debts (10 May 2004). Almost concurrently with the sale of Seat Pagine Gialle, Telecom Italia made a significant second acquisition abroad. The company e.Biscom paid €250 million to purchase the entire capital of Hansenet Telekommunikation, a broadband operator that operated in the Hamburg area, equipped with network infrastructure, and which was the second operator of its kind after Deutsche Telekom. The purpose of this deal was to expand the range of its broadband services in selected European cities with high development potential, to demonstrate to the market its ability to manage sophisticated broadband systems in other European cities by taking advantage of already consolidated activity in the sector. In essence, it was a pilot experiment to verify broadband feasibility in offering commercial content with high added value, such as movies, music, games and other services. Hansenet could become the model for the exploitation of the entire network in years to come, as well as the prototype for a new presence abroad by the telecommunications

TABLE 10.7. WRITE-DOWNS ON THE CONSOLIDATED
FINANCIAL STATEMENTS OF TELECOM ITALIA SPA
IN THE PERIOD 2001–2003 (DATA IN € MILLION)

| Entry | 2001 | 2002 | 2003 |
|---|---|---|---|
| International fixed assets | (2136) | | 195 |
| 9 Telecom | (892) | | |
| Telekom Austria | (225) | | |
| Solpart Brazil | (151) | | |
| Bolivia | (192) | | |
| Med 1 | (55) | | |
| Chile | (35) | | (195) |
| Globo.com | (586) | | |
| International moveable assets | (547) | | |
| Maxitel | (293) | (90) | |
| Bitel | (127) | | |
| TIM do Brasil | (127) | | |
| Lan | | | (235) |
| Internet and Media | (416) | | |
| Satellite Ti Lab | (291) | | |
| Argentina | (406) | | |
| Stream | (248) | | |
| Put Seat | (569) | (3286) | |
| Turkey | | (2341) | |
| Digitel | | (75) | (191) |
| Maxitel | | (90) | |
| Netco Redes | | (96) | |
| GW Blu | | (103) | |
| Seat/TI Media | | (286) | (348) |
| Epiclink | | | (57) |
| Other | | (135) | (162) |
| Olivetti Group | (383) | (111) | |
| Total | (4996) | (6523) | (1188) |

*Source: Our reclassification from Telecom Italia's financial statement*

229

group. Telecom Italia was potentially becoming less of a telephone company and more of a worldwide telecommunications company, with an ever-growing capacity for content transmission. Indeed, this was the eve of major technological innovations, which took place during the subsequent two years and would profoundly change the world of telecommunications. Such transformations, which also became increasingly evident thanks to the development of new applications for the Internet, had already been advocated by the Telecom Italia management since the summer of 2001, albeit as part of the reorganisation process.

In August 2003, following processes for shortening the chain of control, the restructuring phase of the telecommunications group could be considered completed, having fulfilled the goals ahead of schedule that it had set out to achieve. As shown in Table 10.7, during the two year period 2001–2002, this reorganisation had also entailed write-downs for €11.519 billion, plus an additional €1.188 billion during 2003, bringing the total for the three-year period to €12.707 billion. The years to come were supposed to be dedicated to the implementation of the strategies set out by the new management, which indeed started with the industrial opportunity of broadband development in wireline and mobile telephone services, Internet, and video and data transmission, i.e. in what is known as quadruple play.

ANNEX 10.1. CHAIN OF CONTROL OF THE TELECOM ITALIA GROUP AT THE
TIME OF THE MERGER BETWEEN OLIVETTI AND TELECOM ITALIA
(4 AUGUST 2003)

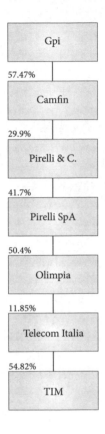

ANNEX 10.2. CHAIN OF CONTROL OF THE PIRELLI/TELECOM GROUP AFTER THE OLIVETTI AND TELECOM MERGERS AND BETWEEN PIRELLI & C. AND PIRELLI SPA (4 AUGUST 2003)

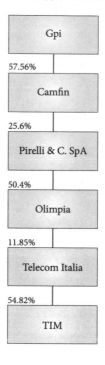

ANNEX 10.3. ORGANISATIONAL CHART OF THE PIRELLI GROUP AFTER THE
MERGER BETWEEN PIRELLI & C. AND PIRELLI SpA

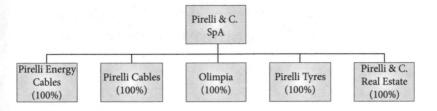

# CHAPTER 11

# An International Player in the Telecommunications Sector

The mergers had allowed the various goals to be achieved. The shortening of the entire group's chain of control had laid the foundations for an increased valuation on the market, and the process for Telecom Italia's reorganisation could be considered complete. This result was achieved ahead of the schedule established on completion of the acquisition. The necessity to strengthen Olimpia's stake in Telecom following its dilution to 11.5% in the wake of the merger between Olivetti and Telecom, however, still remained. For this reason, in October 2003 (11 November 2003), Olimpia placed a convertible bond in Telecom shares with maturity in 2010 to JP Morgan, and received 2.6% of Telecom Italia's capital in return, thus increasing its total stake to 14.16%.[1] Subsequently, in November (11 November 2003), Olimpia approved a €700 million equity increase intended for a new purchase of Telecom Italia shares, which increased its stake to 17.01%.

By strengthening its stake in Telecom, the Olimpia shareholders showed their confidence in the company's prospects. It is interesting to note that maintaining an adequate percentage of equity with voting rights that could allow Olimpia to exercise the role of reference shareholder for the telephone group implied, for the Olimpia shareholders, having to undergo continuous increases in equity. Against these injections of equity, Olimpia received a flow of significant dividends from the Telecom Group, necessary to service the existing debt; it did not, however, distribute these dividends to its shareholders in the period between its incorporation and spring 2007.

Telecom Italia's 2003 year-end results were excellent. In the Chairman's letter

---

1 We must bear in mind that, in addition to Olimpia's direct stake in Telecom, Holinvest held a further 3.7% of Telecom Italia's capital. Holinvest's majority shareholder was Hopa, in turn a shareholder in Olimpia, while the minority shareholder was Olimpia itself. Hopa had no management role in Olimpia, nor in Telecom.

accompanying the financial statements (6 May 2004), Tronchetti Provera highlighted the results obtained in terms of a significant debt reduction, divestitures of non-strategic assets and adjustment of the values of equity investments and start-ups featured in the portfolio for approximately €12 billion. These were significant results obtained by the successfully reorganised company, characterised by good profitability compared to its competitors, and ready to become an international player in the telecommunications field. It was, however, a natural development.

The effective work for rate liberalisation carried out in Italy in those years had significantly eroded the ability to generate cash flow in its characteristic business, also because the Group continued to derive approximately 80% of its revenues in Italy (6 May 2004). The Group's total revenues had remained stable at nearly €31 billion, and the sector breakdown in the different business areas had likewise not changed significantly when compared to 2001. The real challenge was broadband development and the technological integration between wireline, mobile, Internet and television, as well as the development of its Brazilian activities. In Brazil, just as in Italy, the goal was integration between wireline and mobile services. Strategically, the merger between wireline and mobile was seen as the true key to value creation and the first step towards this required activation of TIM's license. As described in greater detail below, the subsequent step involving the integration of TIM and Brasil Telecom was apparently approved by Daniel Dantas, Brasil Telecom's shareholder of reference, but was actually thwarted because Dantas and his shareholders were pursuing different objectives.

This contribution continued to enjoy significant predominance in the wireline and mobile sectors, while other business areas undoubtedly capable of generating value, such as Group and market information technology, needed more time to fully realise their potential. Only the effort to control costs, exercised from the start, had enabled constant and significant profitability, which was inevitably destined to decrease both for country-specific reasons, and due to the worldwide dynamics in the telecommunications industry. As during Pirelli's turnaround between 1992 and 1994, the insightful combination of ordinary management cash flows and divestitures of non-core assets had helped the Company to recover. Thus, at that stage, although in the different context of a renewed race against time, the large debt burden saddling the Group had been reduced significantly before the cash flow from ordinary operations could deteriorate more markedly. Furthermore, it was clear that 'the golden age' of the telecommunications sector at the end of the 1990s, was now a mere memory. During the third year of Olimpia's

## FIG. 11.1. OWNERSHIP STRUCTURE OF TELECOM ITALIA AS OF 31 DECEMBER 2003[a]

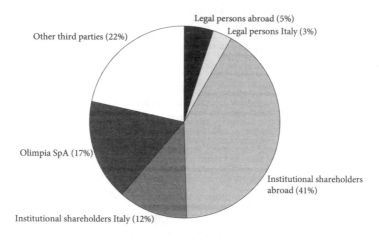

*[a]The composition of the shareholders' list of Telecom Italia SpA reported by CONSOB on 31 December 2003 was as follows, both with regard to the percentages held on ordinary share capital, and on the voting capital: Caisse des Depots et Consignations (1.39%), Banca D'Italia (2.3%), Market (77%), Olimpia Spa (17%), Brandes Investment Partners LLC (2.02%).*
*Source: Official documentation of shareholders' list, CONSOB (composition of shareholders' list)*

## FIG. 11.2. OWNERSHIP STRUCTURE OF TELECOM ITALIA AS OF 31 DECEMBER 2004[a]

*[a]The composition of the shareholders' list of Telecom Italia SpA reported by CONSOB on December 31st, 2003, was as follows, both with regard to the percentages held on ordinary share capital, and on the voting capital: Hopa Spa (3.367%), Banca d'Italia (2.25%), Assicurazioni Generali Spa (2.004%), Market (71.732%), Olimpia Spa (17%), Brandes Investment Partners LLC (3.618%).*
*Source: Official documentation of shareholders' list, CONSOB (composition of shareholders' list)*

commitment to the Telecom Italia Group, the international telecommunications context remained uncertain and its dynamics were reflected detrimentally in the stock prices of telecommunications companies.

Between the end of 2003 and the start of 2004, there was still an interesting and broad portfolio of real options that Telecom could implement, which provided real openings to become an international player. After the reorganisation of the previous years, these openings had become real possibilities and were based primarily on more targeted geographic diversification, in Brazil for Latin America, and in Greece and Turkey for Europe. Regarding Brazil – a country that Pirelli knew well – young, dynamic and with great potential for development, the increasing role that the company was exercising in the mobile phone sector constituted added value compared to other competitors. Furthermore, the revenues resulting from the conspicuous investments in broadband services, a segment in which Telecom had expanded beyond its national borders to achieve significant results in France and Germany, made it possible – through the integration of wireline, mobile and Internet into an actual multimedia network – to offer innovative services such as the transmission of videos, images, movies and other high-added value media other than the human voice. Unlike Pirelli's restructuring, where options gravitated around products such as cables and tyres, with which the Company had been familiar for over a century, in this case the time frame to exercise the option was somewhat uncertain, and depended on the evolution of applications and technical protocols that were not easy to predict in terms of methods or timescale.

The market did not seem to fully realise this. At the beginning of 2004, it seemed that the Telecom Group still needed to take one more step towards making the Group's structure more efficient in terms of value creation. The missing link was the merger between Telecom Italia and TIM, that would allow the Group to definitively rationalise the technological development of the platforms and rationally manage both corporate activities and the cash still generated by the company's operations in the mobile phone sector. From a financial point of view, the previous year's merger had brought cash flow generated by wireline telephone services to the same level of the outstanding debt. The cash flow produced by mobile phone services, however, remained at a lower level on the corporate chain, as TIM was controlled by Telecom. Not by chance the market seemed to imagine, or perhaps even yearn for a possible integration between Telecom and TIM, as it was potentially interesting for investors. Moreover, the merger would allow Telecom not to distribute the dividends paid by TIM to other minority shareholders.

## 11.1 The merger between Telecom and TIM

At the beginning of 2004, however, this operation was not feasible. Integration represented the final convergence between wireline and mobile phone services and this solution – which was very attractive from a technological point of view – at that moment was not yet feasible. Tronchetti Provera (21 January 2005; 7 April 2005) explained that in the first part of 2004, the merger between Telecom Italia and TIM could not be implemented for technological reasons as the major technology suppliers had not yet processed platforms and protocols to make a viable technological integration model and thus a feasible industrial solution. Only towards mid-2004 did the situation change radically, providing an opportunity for innovative perspectives that up to that point had remained on the sidelines of possible mainstream technologies.[2] Until then, mobile network operators had favoured radio-relay systems, as they enabled them to avoid paying lease network circuits. Integration between a mobile service and a wireline provider created the possibility of abandoning radio-relays and using wireline networks. Basing connections exclusively on wireline networks would have been an important result of the integration between wireline and mobile services.

Despite the fact that integration between wireline and mobile technology had been very much debated in previous years, Siemens was the first technology supplier to attempt to take this path (21 January 2005). This new technological perspective was also interesting for Telecom Italia, as it had made conspicuous investments in broadband services, a sector that had grown exponentially in Italy in 2004 for the number of users. The convergence of wireline and mobile services, together with the increase in broadband usage, accelerated the transformation of Telecom Italia into a worldwide player in telecommunications, which was why the new ownership group had invested in the company. The main synergies between wireline and mobile networks concerned the placement of mobile radio sites in those spaces dedicated to wireline phone systems, the use of backhauling lines with wireline network carriers,[3] the unification of the data networking backbone

---

2    As regards this integration, in 2008, during an interview with *Il Sole 24 Ore* on 5 June 2008, Franco Bernabè, Telecom's managing director, declared: 'The wireline mobile integration that we are conducting was begun by him [Marco Tronchetti Provera] with the Telecom-TIM merger. The integration process was interrupted after Marco Tronchetti Provera's departure, and has now started again'.

3    A backhauling connection is a connection linking radio base stations, i.e. mobile network

both at a regional aggregation level and at a national core level,[4] and the adoption of a single control and service platform. Consequently, Telecom Italia had spent money investing in radio-relays, which could have been avoided by using the existing network. Furthermore, backhauling connections began to use fibre optics, so much so that Vodafone – the leading worldwide mobile network operator – had gradually started a campaign for the acquisition of companies focused on wireline network services. In this way, the same interconnection nodes in IP technology are used to exchange traffic with networks of other operators,[5] the same operational support systems (OSS) can be used for fault management, configuration management and data collection,[6] and for customer relations and billing, thus unifying the processes of planning, engineering and operation of wireline and mobile networks.[7]

Indeed, the long-awaited change was emerging, and with it, a technological

---

access with the station controllers. In the case of two separate businesses, the mobile telephone company is driven to give preference to the radio-relay carrier to connect the radio base station to the station controller, and hence to the core network.

4   The total amount of data managed by networks concerns the almost absolute majority of data that relates to the wireline network. In fact, of approximately 44 million terabytes, only 1 million relates to the mobile network. However, the growth rates of wireline and mobile services are 23% and 66% per year respectively. It is obvious that the integration between the backbone data of the wireline network and mobile network can constitute an advantage for those who adopt this strategy.

5   The system that enables the management of telephone signalling over Internet Protocol networks is IMS (IP Multimedia Subsystem), and this can be a single platform for both networks. There are few integrated operators to date, but all operators are moving in that direction by speeding up plans for a convergent approach to service platforms. In this respect, two separate companies could not converge, as the IMS platform is guided by marketing timescales.

6   The information technology expenditure for telecommunications operators is very important (between 35% and 40% of the total investment). Large systems can be broken down into the following areas: enterprise resource management, customer relationship management billing, network and services data base, network management and data centre infrastructure. With the exception of the billing platform, which has special features for mobile services, in all other cases the integration of such platforms offers a strong advantage on the market, including in terms of efficiency of investment and cost. In the case of two different companies, integration is by no means feasible.

7   A single company can integrate its processes and people, even if some skills are necessarily dedicated, as for example those relating to access networks, radio for mobile and copper and fibre optics for wireline services. The remaining part of the network segments can be engineered and managed with integrated cores. In fact, it is possible to manage the two networks with little more than what is traditionally required by a single network.

discontinuity that could help the Italian group achieve a competitive advantage over its competitors, as it had foreseen this market trend in advance. The most advanced platform suppliers, such as Cisco, Nokia or Ericsson and the new arrival Huawei, were finally able to provide converging platforms that – according to Telecom's Chief Technological Officer, Stefano Pileri – were technologically valid. In order to implement these synergies, however, the wireline network company had to be integrated with the mobile network company.

For these reasons, at the end of 2004 (7 December 2004; 21 January 2005), Telecom Italia's Board convened an extraordinary meeting to authorise the merger by incorporation of TIM with Telecom Italia,[8] which was a brave decision indeed. Firstly, it grasped the opportunity for technological change almost as soon as it emerged, taking all difficulties of an operation of such scope into account, including numerous technical, logistical and organisational issues. Indeed, this process required a profound reorganisation of the Group in a short space of time, integrating into a single company the entire business model of the commercial and marketing structures, and of those relating to network administration, control and development, as well as information technology. The duties of approximately 14,000 Group employees were to change. The merger between Telecom and TIM also involved a difficult amalgamation between two companies with different cultures and corporate identities. Indeed, while Telecom Italia had been a public company since the start, on the other hand, TIM – established in the mid-1990s – had immediately adopted a market-oriented approach. Furthermore,

---

8    Again in *Il Sole 24 Ore* of 22 January 2005, Tronchetti Provera reiterated that 'The operation was "spurred" by the acceleration of technological innovation in recent months, as part of a trend that is becoming well-established in the sector.' The largest investment banks expressed a very positive opinion on the entire operation. An equity research publication by Morgan Stanley of 8 December 2004 stated: 'TI-TIM: cheap stocks, strong catalysts-Stay overweight'. Similarly, *Il Sole 24 Ore* of 7 December 2004 quoted a positive opinion by Merrill Lynch, according to which: 'There is also a strategic logic. The merger between Telecom Italia and TIM, that officially sets sail today, is destined to become an operation with important industrial implications.' The market also gave an immediate very favourable response to the entire operation. In 9 December 2004, *Corriere della Sera* wrote: 'It has surpassed every expectation. In the aftermath of the announcement of the Telecom-TIM merger, the response of the stock exchange did not leave many doubts. At the end of the day, the verdict on the maxi reorganisation was more than positive: Telecom has gained 3% (2.97% savings shares), TIM 5.8% (5.28% savings shares), Pirelli & C. SpA 4.1% and Camfin 4.3%. A sign that the operation presented to the market as "market friendly" is a step in the right direction.'

The arrival in Paris of Itala gommata Pirelli,
winner of the Beijing–Paris rally, 1907.
*(Press M. Branger)*

A group of graduates from Milan Polytechnic, 1870.
Giovanni Battista Pirelli stands in the middle.

Domenico Bonanimi and Umberto Ubaldi, 'The organisation of the Pirelli Group on its 50th Anniversary', 1922.

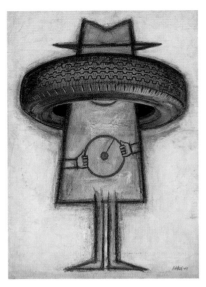

Bob Noorda, advertising poster for
Cinturato Pirelli, 1959.

Riccardo Manzi, rough sketch for
Cinturato Pirelli, 1961.

An inside view of the Pirelli factory in Germany, 2008.

*(Carlo Furgeri Gilbert)*

The packaging process at the factory in Slatina, 2008.

*Carlo Furgeri Gilbert*

The Italian President Napolitano (in grey) and Marco Tronchetti
Provera (right) at the factory in Settimo Torinese, 19 March 2011.

The 'Spina', designed by Renzo Piano, at the new plant in Settimo Torinese, 2014.
*(Enrico Cano)*

The cooling tower in the Pirelli headquarters during a Motorsport event, 2013.
*(Davide Scotti)*

The corner at Sainte Devote in Monaco during the Formula 1 Grand Prix.
*(Mark Machin/Alamy)*

Pedro de La Rosa taking part in the Pirelli Private Test, Abu Dhabi, 2011.
*(Luca Grilli)*

the merger also meant considerable advantages for corporate governance given that it made management actions more effective, eliminating overlapping at the corporate level. The potential operational efficiency was indeed significant, and it was possible to manage the two networks with slightly more resources (in terms of expertise and quality) than those traditionally employed by a single network.

From an industrial point of view, synergies for approximately €1.5 billion were estimated in the three-year period 2005–2007 from the possibility of using common platforms, while the corporate synergies between the two companies had already been achieved. These savings were achieved entirely for the benefit of both former Telecom shareholders and TIM shareholders, now owners of a single stock following the merger. From this perspective, the network was considered necessarily important as a strategic asset. From a financial point of view, the operation was going to be expensive. TIM's evaluation was consistent, in the different fairness opinions requested, estimated at approximately €48 billion, in line with the multiples of that period. At the end of 2004, the company capitalised approximately €46 billion.

TABLE 11.1. MOBILE PHONE MARKET MULTIPLES
(TELECOM ITALIA SPA, TIM AND THEIR
'PEERS') AS OF 31 DECEMBER 2004

| Company | ev/ebidta | P/E | FCF Yield (%) | Div Yield (%) |
|---|---|---|---|---|
| Telecom Italia SpA | 5.8 | 13.4 | 8 | 5 |
| Telefónica | 7.0 | 19.2 | 7 | 4 |
| Deutsche Telekom | 4.9 | 9.6 | 10 | 3 |
| France Telecom | 5.3 | 10.5 | 10 | 2 |
| British Telecom | 4.2 | 10.6 | 9 | 6 |
| TIM | 6.8 | 16.4 | 6.4 | 6.1 |
| Vodafone | 6.0 | 13.7 | 8.4 | 2.0 |

Source: Credit Suisse First Boston, Goldman Sachs, Deutsche Bank, Centrosim, Lehman Brothers, Mediobanca, Unicredit, RasBank, Chevreux, Abn Amro

Following approval by the Board meetings of Telecom and TIM of 7 December 2004, the merger finally took place a little over a year after the merger between Olivetti and Telecom. This latest merger, however, would interrupt the ongoing efforts towards debt containment and reduction, which had fallen to €29.5 billion at the end of 2004, in an economic scenario that appeared uncertain at best.

Telecom Italia held a 54.82% stake of TIM's capital and so to guarantee the success of the operation, Telecom Italia decided to launch a preventive voluntary public offer on two-thirds of the free float and on TIM's savings shares. Extending the public offer to savings shares was necessary to enable the reference shareholder to achieve an adequate stake in the equity of the no voting rights shares, thus creating the basis for approval of the merger resolution. Only after completing these two preventive voluntary public offers could the merger by incorporation of the two companies be implemented. In essence, the preventive voluntary public offer was not required by law. However, the significance of this offer on TIM's ordinary and without voting rights free float was similar to that of a right of withdrawal in favour of TIM shareholders, if the merger were rejected. Unlike the merger between Olivetti and Telecom, which met with strong opposition, this new integration was immediately welcomed by the market. Not only did the entire Group benefit from substantial rises, including the shares of Pirelli Group companies involved in equity increases to support the merger, but it was also considered an act of exemplary advanced corporate governance, and received the respect of the market. From the time of Olimpia's debut as reference shareholder, Telecom Italia had adopted the corporate governance models required by the Code of Self-governance with the introduction of some specific regulations for transactions with related parties, and providing for a majority of independent directors on the Board.[9] This attention to corporate governance was also confirmed by the thorough and detailed information regarding the benefits for its stakeholders, which were included in the year-end financial statements of those years.[10] This

---

9  These directions were adopted without any specific regulatory requirement, at least in Italy.

10  In this respect, the specialised press also emphasised how the telecommunications company had supplemented the financial statements with the sustainability section. This section introduced and analysed, according to 314 indicators divided into 57 macro areas, the degree of satisfaction of the eight types of selected stakeholders, i.e., customers, suppliers, competitors, state and institutions, environment and communities, employees and shareholders.

improvement in corporate governance – again, under the guidance of Francesco Chiappetta – was not unnoticed by Assogestioni which, through its representative, declared its 'keen appreciation of this commitment and the company's sensitivity towards corporate governance, as well as the protection of minorities, welcoming the degree of completeness of the information contained in the report on corporate governance'.

This operation was devised in a market-friendly manner, which most likely contributed to its positive reception. The public offer was launched, on 3 January 2005, at a price of €5.60 per share for both ordinary shares – i.e. with a premium of approximately 20% on current listings – and without voting rights shares, and ended on 21 January, with the tender of 31.2% of TIM's ordinary share capital, but only 6.4% of the no voting rights equity (7 April 2005). The two-third proportion was thus exceeded for ordinary shares, but not for no voting rights shares. In this way, Telecom now held 84.8% of TIM's ordinary share capital. Overall, the entire operation cost €13.804 billion, €11.3 billion of which was funded by a series of credit lines granted by a number of banks, whereas the remaining part was funded by liquid assets owned by Telecom itself. Regarding the debt, often referred to as unsustainable, the *Financial Times* of 26 February 2005 wrote: 'Net debt will be of €44 billion after the TIM merger. But, given a market value of €52 billion and a stable operating performance, it is manageable.'

Shortly afterwards, on 23 January 2005, the Boards of Telecom and TIM, having noted that the voluntary public offer had achieved two-thirds of the required threshold, at least for ordinary shares, respectively approved a share-exchange of 1.73 Telecom shares for each TIM share for ordinary shares, and 2.3 for without voting rights shares (7 April 2005). The shareholders' meeting of 12 April 2005 approved TIM's merger by incorporation with Telecom (see Annex 11.1), and thus the restructuring of the entire corporate chain was considered completed. From the spring of 2005 onwards, Telecom Italia could be considered a true player in the telecommunications sector, capable of developing innovative business prospects and of building possible strategic alliances with both Telecom operators and content providers. The far-sighted vision of what had been forecast by Olimpia shareholders in the summer of 2001 now seemed to become a reality. As in the case of previous mergers, again Olimpia's control on Telecom required consolidation.

Towards this aim, Olimpia carried out a new equity increase of approximately €2 billion, intended for the purchase of Telecom Italia shares, so as not to excessively dilute its shareholding in the company (7 December 2004). This commitment was also aimed at stabilising Olimpia's situation, and to conserve its rating, something that was of great importance for Pirelli. Two of the banks that were Olimpia's shareholders – Intesa and Unicredito – immediately declared that they were not willing to subscribe the equity increase for their respective stakes. Hopa, however, had no objection while Edizione Holding, despite having firmly consented to the deal, was first hesitant but later declared itself in favour. In January 2005 (25 February 2005), this operation was completed, with Pirelli having subscribed not only its shares, but also those of the two banks, thus increasing its stake from 50.4% to 57.66%, the stake held by the two banks was reduced from 8.4% to 4.77% and Edizione Holding and Hopa maintained their stakes respectively at 16.80% and 16%. Overall, Pirelli's outlay was €1,008 million for its portion and €366 million for the exercise of the rights transferred by the two banks.

The successful conclusion of this equity increase enabled Olimpia to buy Telecom Italia shares so that despite the dilution effect of the merger it maintained 18% of equity with voting rights, allowing it to serve as a reference shareholder and maintain the strategic value of its stake.

There were also two further commitments to be met: the expiry date of the agreement between Olimpia and Hopa, and of that with Intesa and Unicredito, expiring respectively in May and October 2006. If the first affected the entire Olimpia group, the second concerned Pirelli alone. Pirelli granted the two banks an opt-out option, that took into account various scenarios, including the possible non-renewal of the agreement. To comply with its portion of Olimpia's equity increase, Pirelli had, in turn, engaged in a similar operation for approximately €1 billion. As Pirelli's reference shareholder, Camfin thus approved an equity increase to support that of Pirelli. Seizing the opportunity offered by RCS Mediagroup's decision to divest its stake in Pirelli shareholding, Camfin exercised its pre-emptive right reserved to participants in the shareholders' agreement and strengthened its stake in Pirelli's shareholding to 26.90%. It was clear, however, that not only Pirelli, but also Camfin, was ready to embark on an asset swap – by which means the Pirelli Group had entered the telecommunications sector four years previously – in a more comprehensive manner. By not taking this step, the increasing commitment in telecommunications would be untenable, not so much financially, but because the Group's management needed to focus on certain business sections that had greater added value.

This meant that both Camfin and Pirelli had to redefine their priorities. There is no doubt that in the years of the Pirelli Group's commitment to Telecom, the management's greatest focus was on telecommunications. This does not mean that Pirelli's business had been abandoned or neglected, but it was considered as a potential subject for an asset swap. At the start of 2004, Pirelli was reaching the end of the three-year industrial plan; the tyre sector continued to grow satisfactorily both in terms of profitability and market share. In this context, the strategic decision to target the high-end market achieved increasingly outstanding results. The situation in the cables sector – the Group's other long-standing business area – was radically different; between 2001 and 2002, the sector had experienced another of its recurrent and perhaps most acute crises that continued throughout 2003.

By contrast, the Company continued to draw satisfactory results from the real estate sector and its specific growth model. Moreover, Pirelli had continued to devote attention to innovation, from technological issues through the work of Pirelli Labs, to those of a corporate nature by attributing increasing importance to corporate social responsibility, and taking the lead in such issues within the Telecom Italia Group. This was the scenario in which Pirelli's 2004–2006 business plan was drafted, based essentially on the premise of an asset swap. Indeed, the Company's prospects and business plan rested on the implementation of this concept. Neither of the extreme and opposite solutions was actually feasible. Although it was difficult to keep the Group intact, it was also difficult to envisage that the proposal of an asset swap plan would succeed in making Pirelli the direct reference shareholder of the telecommunications group, unless in the case of a merger with Olimpia.[11] However, as the hypothesis of a merger between Olimpia and Pirelli was not on the agenda, Pirelli continued to operate as an industrial company with diversified interests.

The 2004–2006 business plan was born from a series of necessary compromises, and thus maintained a certain discretion in its implementation. Although the cornerstones of Pirelli's managerial action had been reinstated, concurrently innovative solutions were also envisaged to enable the Company to pursue its commitment in the telecommunications sector.[12] It was not an easy task, and in spring

---

11  To those who mentioned a possibility of this kind to him, Tronchetti Provera replied: 'There is no forecast for a merger between Olimpia and Pirelli', and that it was a 'decision to be taken by all Olimpia shareholders, not just by Pirelli'.

12  Likewise Camfin, which had invested in fuels and in new environmental technologies, was faced with a similar choice. In the case of Camfin, however, the choice took on even more drastic dimensions, given that the need to support its role as Pirelli's reference shareholder

2004 its contents were still not yet clear, particularly given that the timing of the merger with TIM was not foreseeable. However, in the summer of 2004, Pirelli & C. SpA, exploiting a favourable spell in the real estate market, sold 8.37% of Pirelli & C. Real Estate to institutional investors for €90 million. In this way, the percentage held by Pirelli & C. in the real estate company dropped to 52.77%. The 2006 deadlines, however, still required significant additional resources. The acceleration of the prospect of a merger between Telecom and TIM soon brought Pirelli's top management face to face with the need to implement the proposed asset swap.

As it was not possible to depend significantly on debt, there were three feasible scenarios relating to the possible sale of one of the three company businesses: tyres, cables or real estate. The sale of tyres was never given serious consideration, both due to the positive performance of the business units and because for the market it represented the very soul of the Company. Moreover, the tyre sector has a technological, and hence innovative, component that far exceeds that of cables. Indeed, in those years important innovations were taking place in the tyre sector, particularly regarding materials, which were giving increasingly advanced performance results. The ever-constant monitoring of high-end products made the Milan-based company's capacity for technological innovation crucial, given that a combination of mechanical and electronic elements was characteristic of the most successful cars, and influenced their performance greatly. The technological and organisational evolution of the tyre sector could be perceived as having a great influence on the choices made by the Company.

## 11.2  The sale of Pirelli Cavi [Cables]

Of the other two businesses, cables – which had recorded disappointing performances in recent years – was the Company's first, having started in 1872, although this was less associated with the Group in the collective consciousness of the market. Real estate and its recent development, meanwhile, represented a new sector for the Group, and indeed the first sales plan to be examined was for the real estate sector and not cables which had benefited from the period of great euphoria derived from the capital market. Although the hypothetical value of the equity shareholding in Pirelli & C. Real Estate was only enough to partially address

---

risked transforming the company into a holding company and not into the leader of an industrial group, as it had been up to that moment.

Pirelli's likely needs, this possibility was analysed in depth, but soon it became clear that there were no buyers for real estate.[13] It is reasonable to believe that, even then, some had reservations regarding the real estate business model adopted by Pirelli, which entailed primarily the ownership of minority stakes and high levels of debt, typical of the sector in those years. For these reasons, the asset swap option became non-negotiable. During the Board meeting of 11 November 2004, for the first time, an assessment was made of the possibility of selling the cables sector, which in 2004 had produced a turnover of €3,208 million, generating a net profit of approximately €110 million, and which had a total of 52 plants and 12,000 employees. Some initial estimates of the sale price of the sector estimated its value at approximately €1.1–1.3 billion, in line with Pirelli's forecast commitments.

It was the end of an era. The decision to sell the cables business may have been influenced by the disappointing performance of previous years and the uncertainty of the future, as well as the inability to sell the real estate sector. In any case, the prospect of selling the cables sector renewed and relaunched Pirelli's commitment to telecommunications. Furthermore, at the time of purchasing the Olivetti shares in 2001, selling the cables sector had already been suggested. The task of selecting possible investors interested in the cables business was initiated and a competitive bidding process took place, leading to 10 non-binding bids by private equity funds, from a total of 32 parties invited to present expressions of interest. From this initial list, a smaller group of investors interested in the acquisition was identified; from these, Pirelli started exclusive negotiations with Goldman Sachs Capital Partners, a subsidiary of the American investment bank in the private equity sector. An agreement was reached with the US fund, which identified the company's value at approximately €1.3 billion. The agreement also included a €135 million loan to the buyer, as well as the potential to benefit from future growth. Also in this case the operation was approved with a unanimous vote by the Board. The prospects attributed by the new ownership group to Pirelli's cables business unit centred around continuity with the past, so much so that the new shareholder immediately communicated its full confidence in the company's management to the market.

If the sale of cables represented a crucial stage in Pirelli's life between 2004 and

---

13 Tronchetti Provera reminded the author of his attempt to sell the real estate sector and not the cables sector, and of the fact that he did not succeed in his aim due to the lack of buyers.

2005, other important new developments characterised its shareholding structure and its prospects for development. Pirelli continued to be supported by a shareholders' agreement, which held approximately 43% of the equity, within which Camfin was the reference shareholder with approximately 20%. Aside from Mediobanca, which had historical ties with Pirelli, no other banks had ever joined the agreement, whereas leading Italian insurance companies were part of it. Towards the end of 2004 (7 December 2004), an innovative event took place. Camfin sold a total share of 1.9% of Pirelli's capital to Intesa and Capitalia, allowing them to join the shareholders' agreement. Both banks agreed on a share of 1.51% of Pirelli's equity, which increased slightly over the following years. It is reasonable to believe that Intesa's involvement arose not only from the role that it held in Olimpia, but also because it was the leading intermediary in Italy. Capitalia's stake consisted of a non-significant cross-shareholding, given that Pirelli also held 1.9% of Capitalia through its Luxembourg subsidiary Pirelli Finance.

Concurrently, at the highest levels of the chain of control, GPI undertook to admit the two banks, with a total 6.5% holding, into Camfin's capital, in addition to Mediobanca and Assicurazioni Generali, which had already joined Pirelli's shareholders' agreement. In this way, the share held by GPI in Camfin dropped from 57.56% to 50.13%. The involvement of the banks in Camfin was a method to lighten the burden of the forthcoming equity increase and meant that the industrial choices made at lower levels of the chain were shared, also in consideration of the role that Mediobanca and Assicurazioni Generali were gradually assuming in Telecom.

During the same period, Pirelli, together with other shareholders of the RCS syndicate, participated in the purchase of shares put on sale by Gemina (Romiti family), progressively increasing its capital shareholding (Bellavite Pellegrini 2013). This stake, which reached 4.81% of RCS Mediagroup's equity, as agreed with the other shareholders at the time of the distribution of Gemina's shares, was included in the shareholders' agreement established by the major shareholders of the publishing company.

Meanwhile, the 2004 year-end financial statements of the Telecom Group were positive overall. Debt had fallen to €29.5 billion and, for the first time since 2001, the absolute value of the cash flow intended for the reduction of the debt arising from ordinary management was higher than that arising from the divestitures of assets. These were mainly linked to the sale of the remaining 14.8% of Telekom Austria for approximately €780 million and the sale of the entire capital of Digitel, the Venezuelan telecommunications operator, for €450 million. For the first time, the majority shareholding of a telephone operator controlled by the Telecom Italia Group had been sold. With these sales, the reorganisation of the inherited shareholdings of other telephone operators had been completed. In 2004, devaluations also had less bearing than in earlier years, amounting to approximately €720 million, as shown in Table 11.2.

TABLE 11.2. DEVALUATIONS ON THE CONSOLIDATED
FINANCIAL STATEMENTS OF TELECOM ITALIA IN 2004

| Entry | 2004 |
| --- | --- |
| International fixed assets | |
| Entel Chile and Etecsa | 195 |
| International moveable assets | |
| Maxitel, Bitel, TIM do Brasil | 7 |
| Finsiel | 27 |
| Lan | 56 |
| Med Riorganisation | 158 |
| Internet and Media assets | 282 |
| Olivetti Group | – |
| Total | 724 |

*Source: Our reclassification from the financial statements of the Telecom Italia Group*

Furthermore, the year-end financial statements showed an increase in the company's capitalisation to slightly over €44 billion, following the favourable market trend, and a 1.3% increase in revenues, which reached €31.237 billion and a net profit of €2.135 billion. The breakdown of revenues still recorded a significant increase in mobile phone services, and a positive positioning of wireline phone services. However, the essence of the Group's very nature had changed over the years; the Telecom wireline network had become an infrastructure capable of offering a modern service both to retail customers and to the Group's competitors.

The telephone, computer and Internet sectors were combined with a return by Olivetti to the status of independent industrial business in the field of printers, under the direction of Giovanni Ferrario, former Pirelli CEO. In terms of the structure of business units other than wireline and mobile units, Telecom Italia Media became particularly interesting between 2004 and 2005. The company was established in August 2003, following the demerger of Seat Pagine Gialle, subsequently sold to a group of investment funds (6 May 2004). In the next two years, under the direction of Enrico Parazzini as managing director, Telecom Italia Media implemented a complex reorganisation of its own assets, which transformed 15 companies across six different sectors into four companies in the media sector. Antonio Campo Dall'Orto played a fundamental role in the renewal of La7 network and the repositioning, replacing in February 2007 Enrico Parazzini who maintained the position of Chief Financial Officer of the Telecom Group and since that date was also the Chairman of Telecom Italia Media. It should be remembered that the Telecom Italia Group made its first investment in the media sector in 2000, under its previous management when it acquired Tele Montecarlo from the Cecchi Gori Group, with the probable intention of turning it into an information medium to counterbalance the major private commercial networks.[14] In keeping with the Chairman's position, according to which Telecom was neither right- nor left-wing, the new shareholding structure had no political interest or leanings. It decided, nevertheless, not only to retain this investment but also to relaunch it, believing that if properly managed it could create value. For these reasons, in the space of just a few years, the television network La7 increased its audience share significantly, moving from about 1.3% to about 3.3%, with an investment of approximately €400 million, concentrated in the digital terrestrial sector, comparable with the industry average of the period. In that period, investing in the digital terrestrial sector was the only path possible to change the audience and market shares to reach a break-even, something obtainable with a share close to 10% of the audience, after which a greater audience share created greater profitability. During the period between August 2003 and the end of 2007, the company increased its capitalisation from 782 to 900 million.

Following the completion of the merger with TIM, the complex corporate

---

14 Antonio Campo Dall'Orto imagined a 'manifesto of intent' for the television network, centred around the versatile values of the 'word', often impoverished to the point of debasement by commercial television. It was an innovative and somewhat daring challenge for a commercial television channel also, in view of the high intellectual involvement that viewers had to devote to its programmes. This intuition, however, was successful.

'patchwork' of the Group seemed to have found its equilibrium in terms of structure. The merger between Telecom and TIM, however, had increased its debt to approximately €46.7 billion, but this was reduced to €39.8 billion at the end of 2005. Nevertheless, prompt action was needed to continue to reduce the debt, including through continuing with the policy of divestitures which had slowed down in 2004, but which was now urgent. A new strategy needed to be found; many of the divestitures of the period 2001–2004 had been made to provide greater clarity in a scenario of inconsistent and unprofitable shareholdings, a situation that was finally overcome at the end of 2004. The prospect of a further and significant debt reduction – again, within a limited time frame given the declining margins of the sector – required new ideas regarding the future of the Group. These revolved around two complementary aspects, i.e. the need to sell the majority shareholdings and, at the same time, the existence of a strict constraint on possible acquisitions to render the Group's geographical articulation more complete, due to the significant increased indebtedness. All of this raised further questions regarding the geographical and sector location of the assets to be sold. Above all, however, it revealed the need for the entire range of industrial options involved in the merger process between TIM and Telecom to be profitable in the shortest possible time. However, the freedom of choice of possible strategies was limited, as many resources had been used in the merger with TIM and thus, between the summers of 2005 and 2006, Telecom Italia's strategies centred on these lines of development.

At the beginning of 2005, Telecom commenced the sale of the majority shareholdings of operators in wireline and mobile phone services, as well as other assets. The 54.76% majority shareholding held by Entel Chile – the country's second operator – was sold to Almendral Holding, which was owned by a group of local investors, for €934 million. During the summer, the entire capital of TIM Peru was sold to Sercotel, a subsidiary of the Mexican company America Movil, for €329 million. Telecom and its subsidiaries also carried out divestitures in the information technology sector. Telecom sold both Finsiel, an IT company specialised in public administration software, for €165 million to Cos of Alberto Tripi, and Buffetti, whose core business involved IT programmes for businesses and professional firms for €77 million, and purchased 95% of Liberty Surf from Tiscali's French subsidiary for €266 million. Finally, towards the end of the year, real estate properties were also sold for €633 million. A summary of the dynamics of the divestitures and of debt in the two-year period between 2004 and 2005 may be

251

useful to the reader. With regard to debt, the dynamics of the 2004–2005 two-year period is shown in Table 11.3.

Similarly, the Telecom Group reviewed its geographical priorities. In the summer of 2005, as part of a consortium with the Saudi operator Oger Telecom the Group won the tender for the purchase of 55% of Turk Telekom, the national wireline operator in Turkey. This acquisition consolidated the Italian group's presence in Turkey, given that Telecom was already present in the mobile sector, owning 40% of Avea.[15] In Turkey, the crisis inherited from the previous management of Is TIM, whose license was worth 1 billion and had not yet been activated, was settled by the merger with Aycell, from which Avea was established. Aycell was the public company, and through this operation, the foundations were laid for a possible integration with Turk Telecom.

The most important challenge for the Group's development, however, was to be played out in Brazil. We have seen that Olimpia's ownership group immediately devoted great attention to the South American country as this represented an important strategic option. In Brazil, there was a real possibility of achieving additional profits, designed specifically to add value to the Group which could make it more attractive than its competitors. Already in 2003, Telecom had rationalised the shareholdings in the mobile sector through a series of licenses acquired between 1998 and 2001, thus becoming the second telephone operator in the country. The wireline sector, however, was in the hands of three different operators resulting from the privatisation and demerger of the former monopolist Telebras. One of them was Brasil Telecom, in which Telecom Italia had a significant minority share[16]

---

15  On 19 February 2004, the merger was completed between Is TIM, 49% of which was owned by TIM International and 51% by Is Bank, and Aycell, GSM operator entirely owned by the Turkish state wireline telephone operator, Turk Telekom. TIM International held 40% of the share capital in the new company Avea, born from the merger, while the remaining 60% was owned respectively by Turk Telecom for 40%, and the Is Bank group for the remaining 20%.

16  The minority stake held by Telecom Italia was not directly in Brasil Telecom, but in Solpart, which in turn held 51% of the voting rights in Brasil Telecom Participaçoes, which held 99% of the voting rights in Brasil Telecom. The remaining 62% of Solpart was held by another company, Techold Participaçoes. The latter was therefore in essence the party that controlled Brasil Telecom. Techold Participaçoes was indirectly controlled through Opportunity Zain and Invitel, by two funds constituted respectively by Citigroup and two Brazilian pension funds. Both Citigroup and the pension funds had entrusted the administration of these funds to Opportunity, and in particular to its founder: the controversial financier Daniel Dantas, who therefore – through this complex corporate structure – managed Brasil Telecom.

with associated shareholders' rights, enabling it to participate in its governance and control. Relationships with Brasil Telecom and its management team had never been easy. Even before the merger between Telecom Italia and TIM, the idea had arisen to take control of the Brazilian wireline telephone company, potentially then merging it with TIM Brasil. In the spring of 2005, following the resolution of a lengthy dispute[17] between the two shareholders of Brasil Telecom, this hypothesis seemed to become a reality.

Under Brazilian regulations, those who hold a stake of over 20% of the voting rights are considered to be 'subsidiary parties', and as such cannot operate in the same territorial areas. As Telecom Italia's rights of control were automatically reinstated, the acquisition of the mobile license by Brasil Telecom constituted an illicit overlapping between this and those licenses acquired years previously in TIM Brazil.

In response to Telecom Italia's request for the recognition of its reinstatement in the control group of Brasil Telecom, in January 2004, Anatel – the Brazilian regulatory authority – while recognising Telecom's right to be reinstated in relation to the voting rights, responded negatively to Telecom's request, confirming the anomalous situation and requesting that the parties enter an agreement within 18 months to resolve the overlapping of the mobile licenses.

This decision, in essence, placed Telecom Italia in Dantas's hands – if it failed to reach an agreement, it risked penalties that would jeopardise its large-scale investments in TIM Brasil. It had long been clear that the transaction would not be easy in terms of planning and execution. Indeed, in March 2005, Dantas, who in 2003

---

17  The privatisation rules required that any party who, like Telecom Italia, took part in the control of a privatised wireline telephone company, in this case Brasil Telecom, could not activate the mobile license until the same operator had achieved some specific objectives relating to the universalisation of wireline phone services (the so-called 'metas'). Brasil Telecom was managed by the financier Daniel Dantas who, despite the relevant benefits that would arise for Brasil Telecom, did not speed up this process. An agreement was reached whereby Dantas temporarily took over approximately half of the capital shareholding owned by Telecom Italia in order for the latter to exit the voting capital, to overcome the regulatory repayments preventing it from launching mobile phone services (Telecom nevertheless maintained 38% of Solpart's economic capital). The agreement entailed the automatic recovery of its original voting rights once the regulatory repayments were met (i.e. on 1 January 2004) or the 'metas' were fulfilled by Brasil Telecom, whichever occurred first. A few months later, despite the commitments undertaken simultaneously, Dantas decided to have Brasil Telecom participate in a new tender for the allocation of a smaller mobile network license, which the company won at the price of $150 million.

TABLE 11.3. DIVESTITURES OF ASSETS OF THE
TELECOM ITALIA GROUP DURING THE PERIOD
2004–2005 (DATA IN MILLIONS OF EUROS)

| Divestitures | 2004 | 2005 |
|---|---|---|
| Telekom Austria | 800 | |
| Sky | 100 | |
| Mirror | 100 | |
| Tiglio | 100 | |
| Other assets[a] | 100 | |
| Entel Chile | | 1,100 |
| TIM Ellas | | 1,300 |
| TIM Peru | | 400 |
| Real Estate | | 700 |
| Other assets[b] | | |
| Total | 1,200 | 3,500 |

[a]*They relate to the following divestitures: W Euskatel, CIPI. Ebegg, Cirsa, Netco
Redes, Euskatel, CIPI*
[b]*C-Mobil, Elettra, Finsiel, Bolivia*
*Source: Our reclassification from the financial statements of the Telecom Group*

had already been removed from the management of the Brazilian Pension Funds, saw the termination of the fiduciary agreement that bound him to Citigroup, justified by a long list of oversights and omissions in managing its investments. Nevertheless, the impending expiry of the 18-month period imposed by Anatel led to the opening of negotiations with Brasil Telecom and Opportunity, which still controlled it, concluding with an agreement that put an end to the long dispute between the parties and enabled the reinstatement of Telecom Italia's control rights in Brasil Telecom and the resolution of the overlapping of licenses through the integration of the mobile phone services offered by Brasil Telecom and TIM Brasil. This agreement also opened the door for a further agreement with the other Brasil Telecom shareholders, mainly Citigroup and the Pension Funds, in order to achieve complete wireline/mobile integration between TIM Brasil and Brasil Telecom, which would create value for both companies and all of their shareholders. By contrast, Citigroup – believing that it could miss out on the possibility of maximising its investment in Brasil Telecom following the agreement reached between Telecom and Dantas – initially challenged the agreements at every opportunity and blocked their execution. Indeed, this also impeded the successful integration between the mobile phone activities of Brasil Telecom and TIM Brasil, designed to resolve the overlapping of licenses within the time frame required by Anatel.

Subsequently, however, Citigroup started discussions with Telecom and consequently, Telecom Italia's management drew up a detailed plan, in case the decision was made to proceed. The current values of the two companies, Brasil Telecom Participaçoes and Brasil Telecom, were estimated at a little over €4 billion and approximately €3.565 billion, respectively. This complex action plan, however, did not go beyond the draft phase; at the end of September 2005, Telecom decided not to participate in Solpart's capital. Indeed, in light of Citigroup's demands, the entire operation was not logical from a financial perspective. With great realism, the Telecom Italia Group's management surrendered to the evidence and accepted that the operation with Brasil Telecom was not feasible due to the unacceptable demands made by Citigroup. In light of other important results obtained in previous months, this decision went unnoticed. In order to preserve the value of its shareholding in Brasil Telecom, and with the 18-month deadline – which had been extended for a further 18 months – about to expire, Telecom Italia decided to transfer its shares in Solpart to a trust.

In this way, Telecom Italia would legitimately rid itself of the indirect equity shareholding in Brasil Telecom and the associated governance rights, thus independently resolving the issue of the overlapping mobile licenses arising from its simultaneous control over Brasil Telecom and TIM Brasil, thereby avoiding any penalties imposed by Anatel.

The Telecom Group's 2005 financial statements showed positive trends in the Group's major business areas. Even the possibility of integrating various existing technologies into an Internet-based single data and information system was increasingly credible, and became the Group's business focus on 'value-added services, the key variable to counteracting the decline in traditional voice traffic'. All of these issues counterbalanced the prospect that in years to come, 'the Italian telecommunications market [would develop] along a growth trajectory less pronounced than in the past, aligning itself with the pace in Europe'.

TABLE 11.4. DYNAMICS OF DEBT OF THE
TELECOM ITALIA GROUP DURING THE PERIOD
2003–2005 (DATA IN MILLIONS OF EUROS)

| Entries | 31 December 2003 | 2004 | 2005 |
|---|---|---|---|
| Initial debt | 33.3 | | |
| Takeover bids and other purchases of TIM shares | | | 13.8 |
| Other financial investments | | | 1.1 |
| Industrial investments | | | 5.2 |
| Dividends paid | | | 2.3 |
| Capital repayments | | | 0.1 |
| Sale of stakes and other divestitures | | | (3.8) |
| Conversion of the C.B. 2001/2010 and capital increases for exercise of options | | | (1.8) |
| Flow generated by operational activities, net of other requirements | | | (9.9) |
| Final debt | 33.3 | 32.9 | 39.9 |

*Source: Our reclassification from Telecom Italia's financial statements*

The revenues of the Telecom Italia Group had decreased slightly to a little under €30 billion and the net profit had been recorded at €3.216 billion, while debt – as mentioned previously – increased to €39.858 billion, up from the previous year's €32.862 billion. By the end of 2005 the task of reducing the debt, which had peaked at €46.7 billion following the merger with TIM, was beginning to show its effect. The revenue structure of individual business units had not changed; the general stability of revenue from wireline phone services continued, and larger growth was recorded in the mobile sector. All other business sectors had a modest influence on the overall revenue, and particularly in relation to the wireline and mobile sectors, though their dynamics were different. Although the financial year had closed with a positive result, the start of 2006 would bring with it new challenges. The Telecom Board had approved the 2006–2008 business plan that included approximately €14 billion for investments, and a forecast debt at the end of 2007 similar to that prior to the merger with TIM, i.e. €33.5 billion. The plan also placed specific emphasis on broadband technology in the wireline sector, which was estimated to increase revenue by approximately 1%, and which relied on the growth of the activities in the mobile sector in Brazil. In the short term, however, the stability of Olimpia's shareholding had to be addressed, as this could have significant influence on the ownership and management equilibrium within the Telecom Group.

Since the start of its renewed involvement in the telecommunications group in September 2001, Hopa had played a marginal role. Indeed, Hopa had initially signed a loan, issued by Olimpia, for €1,032,920,000 at a rate of 1.5% for six years with a zero coupon. Following the renegotiation of the bond, in December of the following year, Hopa had become an Olimpia shareholder. Furthermore, in the aftermath of the agreements resulting from its entry into Olimpia's capital, Hopa continued to hold 80.01% of the shareholding of Holinvest, a company that, in turn, controlled a substantial Telecom shareholding. Holinvest's minority shareholder was Olimpia itself. Despite the fact that Hopa was the third largest Olimpia shareholder, with a holding not unlike that of Edizione Holding, consistent with the agreement made at the end of 2002 (19 December 2002), it had never had an active role in the corporate governance of Olimpia or Telecom, but rather had performed the role of financial investor. The agreement that governed relations between Olimpia and Hopa was indeed different from that in force among Olimpia shareholders, and, in order to safeguard the investment that Hopa shareholders had made in Olimpia, it provided for specific protection in their favour.

Indeed, it was established that, in the event of a disagreement on certain matters such as a proposal to call an Extraordinary Shareholders' Meeting or the non-renewal of the agreement, Hopa would be entitled to bring about the demerger of Olimpia, receiving its proportional share of assets and liabilities. Similarly, the agreement also provided for the potential demerger of Holinvest, establishing that these operations could also be adjusted by cash settlement. In that event, Pirelli and Edizione Holding would buy back the Olimpia shares held by Hopa, and Hopa would act similarly by repurchasing the Holinvest shares that would be attributed, pro rata, to Pirelli. Furthermore, the requirements of the agreement meant to protect Hopa also extended to cases of disagreement on additional issues, such as the choice of investments, purchases and funding. Except for the provision on a deadlock in the SGM or the non-renewal of the agreement, the other guarantees were far more extensive than those typically in place to protect shareholders not directly involved in management, even if they hold significant amounts of shares. While not participating directly in management, Hopa had a kind of veto power that, in essence, required a good relationship, if not an underlying agreement, with Olimpia shareholders.

The above-mentioned relationship began in a positive manner, up to the point when, in the summer of 2005, new facts emerged. This period in Italy was characterised by a very lively capital market arising from both founded and alleged rumours regarding possible operations for the acquisition of banks. While these events do not fall within the scope of this book, it should be remembered that Hopa's Chairman, Emilio Gnutti, had some involvement under civil and criminal law, which led to the deterioration of the relationship of mutual esteem and trust with the other Olimpia shareholders. Concurrently, the deadline of the agreement between Olimpia and Hopa shareholders, set for 8 May 2006, was approaching. The end of the agreement, if it were not to be renewed, in fact constituted one of the scenarios involving Olimpia's demerger and the concurrent payment of compensation in favour of Hopa for a total of €208 million.

The hypothesis of the non-renewal of the agreement carried challenging consequences for Olimpia: from the significant compensation to be paid to Hopa to the possible involvement of cash settlements for the shareholdings, but above all, in the event of Olimpia's demerger, the relative allocation to Hopa of a 2.8% stake in Telecom. To this stake, Hopa could add the 3.7% of Telecom Italia shares held in Holinvest, also subjected to demerger. The potential of the non-renewal of the agreement would result in a significant reduction of Olimpia's stake in Telecom and, through the demerger mechanism, the emergence of an autonomous and significant shareholder in Telecom, unless a choice was made to utilise payment regulations for these relationships. It should be pointed out that the company's equity had featured the direct presence of some of Olimpia's shareholders, such as Pirelli and Benetton, that had acquired a share of 1.36% and 0.52% of the equity, but also other parties, including Assicurazioni Generali and Mediobanca. If the stakes taken by the Olimpia shareholders in Telecom were intended to strengthen that of the Holding Company from the outside, the presence of some protagonists from the Italian financial market nevertheless suggested the establishment of a shareholders' agreement between some of the major shareholders of the telecommunications group.

However, it was not only Olimpia's ownership structure that was evolving. The events of the previous summer had weakened Hopa's Chairman, Emilio Gnutti, and he had decided to resign as Company Chairman. The end of Gnutti's involvement in Hopa triggered divergent perspectives and contradictions within the shareholding of the company founded by him, as a number of banks had taken on an increasing role in its management. The termination of the agreements with Olimpia meant a potential loss of equity of approximately €1 billion for Hopa. Despite the presence of such a rapidly evolving situation, Olimpia nevertheless outlined its strategy. The prospect of renewing the agreement with Hopa, which was certainly interesting, nevertheless presented some limitations. First, there was the reputational factor that led Olimpia to hope for a clear change in Hopa's governance in favour 'of the institutional shareholders', i.e. the banks (26 January 2006). Some of these had also participated, as bond holders, in loans made in favour of Olimpia on the occasion of the two agreements with Hopa (19 September 2001, 19 September 2002, 19 December 2002). Secondly, Olimpia's inclination was to limit the potential of Hopa's intervention in management (26 January 2006). Although there was no preliminary condition for an absolute closure against Hopa, Olimpia gave formal notice on the agreement in compliance with the requirement for three months' notice, i.e. 8 February 2006.

What followed was a complex deal that saw the intervention of Bruno Ermolli for Olimpia and Roberto Poli for Hopa. Both parties immediately realised that there was no space for a renewal of the agreement, also because the positions within Hopa's shareholding group were in turn subject to a complex structure. As such, negotiations were initiated on how to demerge the two companies and particularly in relation to the potential cash settlement terms. Faced with a potential capital loss of €1 billion, Hopa shareholders tried to set the price on the date most favourable to them, trying to obtain full compensation, which, however, Olimpia shareholders wanted to reduce. An agreement was reached in the following terms: Pirelli and Edizione Holding bought back 16% of Olimpia's capital owned by Hopa, and likewise, Hopa repurchased the portion of Holinvest held by Olimpia (11 May 2006). Both transactions were fully paid up in cash. Overall, the outlay for Olimpia was €497 million, of which, in light also of the compensation previously agreed and then renegotiated, €86 million were received. Concurrently, Olimpia's right of first refusal was also established at 65% of the 492.7 million Telecom Holinvest shares, while the remaining 35% could be sold freely on the market. Hopa and Holinvest undertook not to proceed to purchase additional Telecom shares without the prior agreement of Olimpia, which granted Holinvest the possibility of restoring its stake in Telecom up to a share of 3.68% of the ordinary capital (27 July 2006). In this way, Pirelli ended up with a stake of 70.46% in Olimpia, while Edizione Holding's stake rose to 20%. The two shareholder banks saw their overall shares diluted from 20% to 9.54%.

In the same period, Intesa and Unicredit notified Olimpia and Pirelli that they wanted to exercise the option to sell their Telecom capital shares at the end of the designated period, i.e. 4 October 2006 (11 May 2006).[18] The two banks' decision had been in the air for quite some time, at least since the previous year when both had opted not to participate in the increase of Olimpia's capital, which had become necessary to support the integration between Telecom and TIM. The banks, after five years of participation in Olimpia's capital, felt that they had exhausted their institutional representational role for any industrial shareholders joining Olimpia's industrial project.[19] It cannot be excluded that the changed political and institutional context spurred the two banks to disengage from a context that was becoming increasingly complex for the telecommunications group. Consistent with their role, both banks had requested and obtained an option to sell their stake in Olimpia with expiry on 4 October 2006, five years from their entry. Since the autumn of 2006, Olimpia's ownership structure was to be characterised by only two shareholders, Pirelli and Edizione Holding, unless some other industrial party, of adequate standing, were to express an interest in sharing the outlook and strategies of the telecommunications group.

---

18  *Il Corriere della Sera* of 28 January 2006 quoted the following remarks made by the Intesa Chairman, Giovanni Bazoli: 'In 2001, we decided to accompany the Pirelli Group in the Telecom Italia operation, and today marks the natural end of our participation in Olimpia.' However, Bazoli also added that: 'the collaboration with the company led by Tronchetti Provera is destined to continue, although in a different form'.

19  Intesa and Unicredit joined Olimpia's capital in September 2001, in partial replacement of Edizione Holding, whose potential 40% initial investment in Olimpia's equity had to be decreased to 20%.

TABLE 11.5. SOME FUNDAMENTALS OF THE TELECOM ITALIA GROUP FROM 2001 TO 2006[a]

| (in billions of euros) | ITA GAAPto | | | IAS/IFRS | | |
|---|---|---|---|---|---|---|
| | 2001 | 2002 | 2003 | 2004 | 2005 | 2006 |
| Revenues | 32 | 31.4 | 30.9 | 28.3 | 29.9 | 31.3 |
| EBITDA | 13.7 | 14 | 14.3 | 12.9 | 12.5 | 12.8 |
| EBITDA Margin (%) | 42.7% | 44.6% | 46.3% | 45.5% | 41.8% | 41.1% |
| EBIT | 5.1 | 6.1 | 6.8 | 7.6 | 7.5 | 7.4 |
| EBIT Margin (%) | 16% | 19.3% | 22% | 26.9% | 25.1% | 23.8% |
| Net result | (3.1) | (0.8) | 1.2 | 1.8 | 3.2 | 3 |
| Capex (%) | 22.6% | 15.6% | 15.9% | 17.7% | 17.3% | 16.4% |
| Operating Free Cash Flow (%) | 18.8% | 27.6% | 29.9% | 30.5% | 27.2% | 22.3% |
| Net financial position (NFP) | 38.4 | 33.4 | 33.3 | 32.9 | 39.9 | 37.3 |
| Market capitalisation | 62,219 | 50,362 | 34,308 | 44,067 | 45,210 | 42,219 |

[a]Table 11.5 illustrates the trend of the main economic and financial indicators of the Telecom Italia Group between 2001 and 2006: the turnover remained substantially stable at around €30 billion, offsetting the decrease in revenues due to the decline of the wireline phone sector and the effect of the rate reduction introduced by the regulatory Authority, with the growth of mobile phone services not only by voice, but above all for data and images; the gross operating margin had been eroded due to the effect of the reduction in prices, while performance had grown, as had net profit which, having reached its peak for the decade in 2005, stabilised at €3 billion. The commitment to invest was robust, with the highest turnover percentage compared to the European 'peers' of the time, as well as the operational cash flow. In this context, debt was reduced from €43 billion at the end of September 2001 when the new management took control, to 373 billion at the end of 2006, absorbing approximately €20 billion used in the two takeover bids connected with the Olivetti/Telecom mergers in 2003 and TIM/Telecom in 2005. The financial market's response to these results was positive, as is clear from the trend in stock market capitalisation that, in the period following the Olivetti/Telecom merger, grew by 23% from €34.3 billion in 2003 to 42.2 in 2005.

ANNEX 11.1. CHAIN OF CONTROL OF THE TELECOM ITALIA GROUP
FOLLOWING THE MERGER BETWEEN TELECOM ITALIA AND TIM (12 APRIL

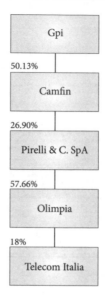

ANNEX 11.2: OLIMPIA OWNERSHIP
STRUCTURE AS OF 27 JULY 2006

| Shareholder | Percentage owned of share capital with voting rights |
|---|---|
| Pirelli & C. SpA | 70.46 |
| Edizione Holding | 20 |
| Intesa | 4.77 |
| Unicredit | 4.77 |

ANNEX 11.3: CHAIN OF CONTROL OF BRASIL TELECOM IN THE SPRING OF 2005

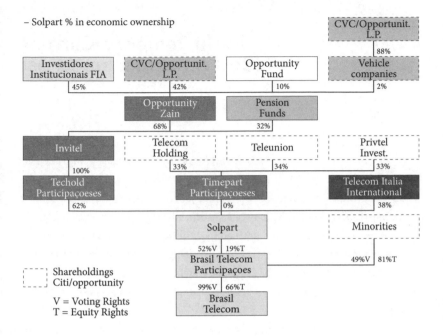

– Solpart % in economic ownership

# CHAPTER 12

# Mala Tempora Currunt
# (Bad times are upon us)

At the start of 2006 – when the mosaic-like telephone group seemed to have established its industrial and financial set-up – paradoxically, Olimpia's ownership structure was showing signs of rapid weakening. Up until that time, the shareholders had not been satisfied by the stock's performance, but this was part of a generally modest trend in the telecommunications sector across Europe. If the average annual price of Telecom Italia's ordinary shares had suffered a significant reduction from €3.89 to €2.28, equal to 41.38%, in the period between 2001 and 2006, the other major operators had also recorded a significant fall in equity market prices.

As seen in Table 12.1, over the period under consideration, France Telecom and Deutsche Telekom recorded negative performances of approximately 55.72 % and 43.08 %, respectively. If we take into account the slightly different time frames, then these performances are significantly different, as shown in Table 12.2.

In the period between 1 October 2001 and 11 September 2006, Telecom Italia's performance was in line with British Telecom's, with Spain's Telefónica the only company with a higher index rating. Turnover figures are shown in Table 12.3. It should be considered that the Group's turnover had not yet reached its full potential, particularly in light of the huge investments made.

Over the time period in question, the company had maintained an average investment percentage compared to its turnover which exceeded that of its main European competitors. This performance, however, was not reflected in growth in size, since the Italian group had been falling behind by its main competitors, mainly due to its programme of disinvestments.

While in 2001 the Telecom Italia Group's turnover was not significantly different from that of Telefónica, and was higher than Vodafone's at the end of the period, not only was Telefónica's turnover twice that of the Italian company, but Vodafone also showed a slightly higher turnover. It seems reasonable to assume

TABLE 12.1. AVERAGE PRICES OF THE ORDINARY SHARES OF THE MAJOR TELECOMMUNICATIONS COMPANIES IN EUROPE 2001–2007 (IN EUROS)

| | 2001 | 2002 | 2003 | 2004 | 2005 | 2006 | 2007 | Performance 2001– 2007 (%) |
|---|---|---|---|---|---|---|---|---|
| Telecom Italia | 3.89 | 2.51 | 2.19 | 2.60 | 2.68 | 2.28 | 2.16 | -44.47 |
| France Telecom | 49.94 | 18.21 | 20.55 | 21.30 | 22.21 | 18.32 | 22.11 | -55.72 |
| Deutsche Telekom | 24.02 | 13.09 | 12.65 | 14.92 | 15.29 | 13.03 | 13.67 | -43.08 |
| Telefonica | 13.91 | 9.65 | 9.53 | 12.04 | 13.26 | 13.51 | 18.31 | 31.63 |
| British Telecom | 346.49 | 228.73 | 183.99 | 185.69 | 213.62 | 242.11 | 309.7 | -10.61 |
| Vodafone | 179.94 | 113.68 | 121.78 | 133.13 | 140.19 | 123.63 | 159.62 | -11.29 |

*The table also includes 2007, which is analysed in this chapter. British Telecom's and Vodafone's listings are in hundredths of pounds sterling.*

*Source: Our calculations based on official documentation provided by Pirelli*

TABLE 12.2. PERFORMANCE OF THE MAIN TELECOMMUNICATIONS COMPANIES IN EUROPE FROM 2001–2006

| Time period | Telecom Italia | Vodafone | Telefonica | France Telecom | Deutsche Telekom | British Telecom | DJ Stoxx TLC |
|---|---|---|---|---|---|---|---|
| 28 July 2001–11 September 2006 | −29.4% | −20.8% | 7.6% | −60.2% | −54% | −31% | −21.2% |
| 1 October 2001–30 June 2005 | 5.7% | −7.5% | 23.7% | −13.1% | −7.3% | −14.8% | −1.5% |
| 1 October 2001–11 September 2006 | −7.6% | −21.9% | 20.4% | −38.1% | −29.9% | −6.1% | −5.5% |

*Source: Reuters, historical series normalised by dividends*

TABLE 12.3. ANNUAL PERCENTAGE OF INVESTMENT
IN RELATION TO THE TURNOVER OF THE MAIN
EUROPEAN TELEPHONE COMPANIES (2001–2007[a])

|  | Telecom Italia | Telefónica | France Telecom | Deutsche Telekom | British Telecom | Vodafone |
|---|---|---|---|---|---|---|
| 2001 | 22.7 | 27.1 | 18.8 | 22.5 | 15.1 | 19.2 |
| 2002 | 15.9 | 13.3 | 16.0 | 14.2 | 13.1 | 17.4 |
| 2003 | 15.9 | 13.1 | 11.0 | 10.8 | 14.4 | 13.0 |
| 2004 | 17.1 | 12.4 | 10.9 | 10.6 | 16.2 | 14.3 |
| 2005 | 17.3 | 14.1 | 12.3 | 15.6 | 16.1 | 13.6 |
| 2006 | 16.4 | 15.1 | 13.0 | 18.1 | 16.1 | 13.5 |
| 2007 | 17.6 | 14.2 | 13.2 | 12.8 | 16.1 | 14.3 |
| Media | 17.5 | 15.6 | 13.6 | 14.9 | 15.3 | 15.1 |

[a]*2007 was also considered in relation to investments.*
*Source: Our calculations based on official documentation provided by Pirelli*

TABLE 12.4. ANNUAL TURNOVER OF THE
MAIN EUROPEAN TELEPHONE COMPANIES
(2001–2007[a], IN MILLIONS OF EUROS)

|  | Telecom Italia | Telefónica | France Telecom | Deutsche Telekom | British Telecom | Vodafone |
|---|---|---|---|---|---|---|
| 2001 | 30,818 | 31,053 | 43,026 | 48,309 | 20,559 | 22,845 |
| 2002 | 30,400 | 28,411 | 46,630 | 53,689 | 18,727 | 30,375 |
| 2003 | 30,850 | 28,400 | 46,121 | 55,838 | 18,519 | 33,559 |
| 2004 | 31,237 | 30,322 | 47,157 | 57,880 | 18,623 | 34,133 |
| 2005 | 29,919 | 37,882 | 49,038 | 59,604 | 19,514 | 29,350 |
| 2006 | 31,275 | 52,901 | 51,702 | 61,347 | 20,223 | 31,104 |
| 2007 | 31,290 | 56,441 | 52,959 | 62,516 | 20,704 | 35,478 |

[a]*2007 was also considered in relation to turnover. The dynamics of turnover, however, does not necessarily take into account the variation of the Group's scope, mainly due to the disinvestments carried out.*
*Source: Our calculations based on official documentation provided by Pirelli*

that such a gradual delay in terms of size was in part due to constraints imposed by the national regulatory authorities. Italy was an anomalous market due to a mobile network operator, Wind, that was owned by a state-controlled company (Enel), and unlike other European countries, it had three mobile network operators of significant importance.

## 12.1 Telecom Italia's new prospects

However, during the spring of 2006, Telecom Italia finally had all the prerequisites in place to implement all its previously set goals. Telecom was the only European telecommunications company with a wireline/mobile platform which could offer important savings, and which would be capitalised in a subsequent stage. For these reasons, Telecom's competitors grew increasingly angry with the Italian Authority, because Telecom's competitiveness was constantly growing. Interesting and completely neutral evidence of this positive assessment of the telephone group's management strategy may be found in the annual report on the activities carried out and on work programmes presented in Rome, on 20 July 2006, by Corrado Calabrò, the Chairman of the Italian Communications Authority. In his report, Calabrò acknowledged how, in the period between 1998 and 2005, 'the final prices of telephone services decreased by 15% compared to an average 17% increase in the general index of consumer prices and a 15% growth in the prices of public utility services as a whole'. To cope with this decrease in prices, the Telecom Italia Group had managed, between 2002 and 2005, to increase its productivity by 25%, obtaining a significantly higher result than that of its European competitors. This result was remarkable, as the incumbent Italian monopoly had been significantly eroded. Indeed, approximately 1.6 million lines were transferred from the incumbent operator to its competitors, 'with the lowest access rate in Europe, which is set to decrease again next year'. The Chairman of the Authority also recalled that broadband in Italy had recorded growth in those years that was greater than the average growth in other European countries. In relation to this, Calabrò wrote:

> We rank in first place when it comes to the distribution of third generation mobile phone services (UMTS), with 10 million activated lines. Italy is the first country to launch commercially 'on the go' TV broadcasting with DVB-H technology; we rank among the first positions for television via computer (IPTV). Internet users in Italy have exceeded 28 million. In relation to broadband deployment, we used to rank at the bottom. At present,

although we started on the back foot, Italy is growing at an increase rate (187% in two years) significantly higher than the European rate, which is fifteen: today, the number of lines stands at a total of seven million, making Italy the fourth country in Europe. Broadband is not a complementary service, one of many technologies: it is one of the main drivers of a country's progress, an engine that promotes the development of the national production system.

These findings are confirmed by the Annual Implementation Report on the Electronic Communications Sector in the EU published by the European Commission. In the five-year period between 2002 and 2007, broadband networks recorded a 250% increase for Deutsche Telekom, 683% for Telefónica, 904% for France Telecom and 1,252% for Telecom Italia, which was second only to British Telecom, which recorded a 1,837% increase. If, by contrast, we take the following three years into consideration, the results change dramatically. Between 2007 and 2009, Telecom Italia recorded a mere 12% increase compared to 24% for Telefonica's, 32% for both France Telecom and Deutsche Telekom, and 38% for British Telecom.

In the meantime, the Italian political and institutional context was also changing rapidly. At the time of the Olimpia's acquisition of Bell's stake in Olivetti, in July 2001, Silvio Berlusconi, who had followed the telephone group's vicissitudes with distracted indifference, had been Prime Minister for just a few months. Five years later, in the spring of 2006, the widespread feeling in the country was of a growing dissatisfaction with the government, believed to be guilty of not having been able to capitalise on the favourable economic situation and loosen some of the unresolved economic and social tensions, first and foremost, that of public debt. In the April 2006 general elections, the centre-left coalition led by Romano Prodi was more successful in interpreting this widespread dissatisfaction and won the elections, albeit by a narrow majority. As such, the country now had an interlocutor who was attentive to the country's industrial policies.

While Telecom was preparing to implement its new projects, the Pirelli Group was dealing with the decrease of its business scope, following the sale of the cables division. In its new development programmes, Pirelli had identified – in addition to tyres and real estate – a renewed interest in 'second generation' photonics products through its start-up company Broadband Solutions and similarly so in the environment sector, through Pirelli & C. Ambiente Holding, established in early

2005, and which grouped together and managed the environment-related activities of both Pirelli and Camfin.

At the beginning of 2006 (14 February 2006), Pirelli started to examine a reorganisation project for its tyre business, focusing on the possible listing of Pirelli Tyres, followed by the sale of a significant minority stake in the same company. The aim of the project was to exploit the favourable situation of the market value for the tyre sector, and strengthen the equity structure of Pirelli & C. SpA with the proceeds from the sale. The Company benefited from high multiples, thanks to the positive trend in the sector, but the project took quite some time to be implemented. A new company called Pirelli Pneumatici was incorporated, with the intention of being listed, and was placed at the top of the chain of companies that produced tyres. In June 2006, the entire reorganisation project for the new listing was complete, including an agreement between the two companies, which regulated the use of the Pirelli Tyre trademark until 2015. An offer of approximately 35% of the company's equity was established against the possible scenario of an overall appreciation of the economic capital of Pirelli tyres in the range of €1.9 to 2.3 billion.

The timing of the operation proved ill-fated; on the eve of the listing in the latter part of June, the market took a turn for the worse. This was also due to the profit warnings issued at that time by Bridgestone and Goodyear, while Michelin had preceded its competitors by launching profit warnings a few weeks earlier. In this new context, the prerequisites for the initial public offering were not ideal. The project was not entirely shelved, however and Pirelli evaluated the prospect of a private placement of Pirelli Tyre, which immediately caught the attention of some financial investors. In July, Pirelli perfected this alternative path by placing 39% of Pirelli Tyre with some investors for an equivalent value of €740 million, with a call option for seller and buyers to be exercised within four and a half years. For the banks, this meant the possibility of placing approximately 25% of the company's equity on the market, while Pirelli had the option of repurchasing this portion once the company was no longer in its initial public offering phase. It was a second-best solution that nevertheless placed the company's equity in the lower part of the estimate made two months before.

This latest step towards defining Pirelli's scope and strategies now allowed the Group's management to focus its attention exclusively on Telecom. The national telecommunications regulatory framework was in a period of rapid evolution. Faced with a clear, established tendency towards a rapid reduction in rates and a decrease in demand for regulated services, Telecom experienced a setback in the launch of 'Unico', the first wireline-mobile convergent telephone. Unico was to be a mobile phone that could automatically use the wireline network at home or in the office, while it would function as a normal mobile phone outside. It was estimated that Unico could sell approximately one million units over the next two years and would be the first project to be implemented following the merger between Telecom and TIM. Furthermore, a possible agreement with one of the major international players in the media content would also give the project a head start. The Unico project, however, was blocked by the Telecommunications Authority in June 2006, having previously suspended other innovative offers for high-speed Internet, including the offer of services using broadband technologies at 8MB, instead of the existing 2.5MB system. The new technologies would have permitted the creation of appropriate platforms for the transmission of content via mobile phones and had received a positive reception from the Italian financial market.

For Telecom, this was a significant setback, not only because of the delays that failure to implement the new products would cause to the Group's economic equilibrium, but also in terms of the fulfilment of the wider project that the telecommunications group had envisaged long before the merger between Telecom and TIM. Indeed, the above-mentioned report by the Chairman of the Authority, who nevertheless expressed appreciation for what Telecom Italia had done over the years, features a passage that reveals the opinion of the sector's regulatory authority and suggests scenarios that have little to do with the Group's prospects for development:

In light of the profound changes in the market that has taken place in recent years as a result of technological innovation, with the advent of new generation networks and the integration between wireline network and mobile network, it is necessary to adjust this discipline to adapt it to the new situation, thus ensuring full and effective equality of treatment to all market operators. To this end, in the context of the activities carried out by Telecom Italia, we need to take a step forward on the path of the separation between regulated and non-regulated services, acting in relation to governance and independent checks. International experience has shown that this path is most effective when the operator itself takes on binding commitments. I am asking Telecom Italia to express its willingness in this regard.

This request for 'willingness', however, sounded ambiguous, as it referred to regulatory aspects that were outside of the powers of individual national authorities, and governed instead by European regulations. In any case, the Authority introduced a new and potentially disruptive issue for the future of the Group, relating to ownership and governance of the network, with specific distinction between 'regulated' and 'non-regulated services'. This reflection threatened the 'cutting-edge' industrial project that had received widespread approval. In contrast with what could possibly occur in other regulated sectors such as electricity or gas, in the case of telecommunications, the network assumed the nature of an integrated platform servicing different kinds of media content that constituted the very business of the telecommunications company.[1] The debate on the division of the network was not applicable in other countries, precisely because of the peculiarity and sophistication of the characteristics of the telecommunication network. Moreover, the network conveyed, in an organic manner, accurate and painstaking knowledge of consumer characteristics and preferences, not available to general content providers in those years, before the advent of providers such as Google and Facebook. The prospect of new regulations regarding ownership and governance of the network risked undermining the prospect for innovative business that the Company wished to develop, and constituted a potential 'invasion of the pitch' in an already complex European regulatory framework. The Regulatory Authority was concerned with promoting a context of competitiveness and consumer protection, particularly regarding regulated services. It failed, however, to fully realise that the scenario had changed completely over the previous years and that the monopolistic management of the 'telephone company' was already a thing of the past.

## 12.2 Marco Tronchetti Provera's industrial project

Despite these warning signs that contributed to arousing legitimate concern,

---

1 More specifically, it can be said that the Group's project aimed to obtain, through use of the most innovative mobile phones, what a few years later would be achieved by Apple with the iPhone and the iPad. It is worth mentioning that a few years earlier, in 2000, during the speculative bubble connected to the new technologies, the merger took place between America Online and Time Warner, i.e. between an Internet provider and a content provider. In more recent times, the *Financial Times* of 12 June 2012 reported that 'Apple has struck a new alliance with Facebook to integrate the social network into its iPhone, iPad and Mac operating system'.

Telecom's management implemented its programme. If the future of the Group lay in a single platform for wireline and mobile that could transmit both the human voice via Internet and content based on other types of support, it was content that was missing from the overall plan. As it was not a media company, the telecommunications company had not developed content, and thus its natural collaborators were media sector operators. The prospect of a commercial agreement with a major media company was indeed interesting for the Telecom Group, which could transmit its content via broadband. There were two possibilities in this regard: to employ either a national or an international operator. The Telecom Group chose the second option without hesitation, as the first was not feasible for political more than financial reasons. Indeed, in Italy Mediaset would have been the natural counterpart, but an agreement with Mediaset was objectively difficult due to the outstanding political connections present among Mediaset shareholders. This, however, did not mean that Mediaset was not interested in a possible agreement with Telecom.

Internationally, the company News Corporation was the most well-known operator in the media sector, its major shareholder being the Australian tycoon, Rupert Murdoch. In light of these statements, the Authority would therefore look favourably and with interest on a possible collaboration between Pirelli-Telecom and News Corporation, which would not be subject to all of the limitations inherent in a potential collaboration with Mediaset.

However, it was News Corporation that made contact with Telecom, and not vice versa. Links with News Corporation existed from the time of the merger between Stream and Tele Plus. Moreover, in September 2004, Telecom Italia had sold 19.9% of Sky Italia to News Corporation. It was therefore natural to start negotiations with Rupert Murdoch's company. News Corporation had an interest in seeking an agreement with Telecom, both to reduce its dependence on the costly and limited use of satellite, and because the telecommunications company came equipped with a vast and diversified reference market within Italy, with the potential to involve sector operators in Europe and South America. Although the Italian group had stated from the outset that the ongoing talks with the publishing group were primarily aimed at exploring possible agreements 'regarding content', the market believed that there was also the possibility of a share exchange between Telecom and News Corporation, through the possible transfer by the latter of the Italian subsidiary Sky to Telecom. It was a situation that captured the interest of the market, which hoped for the involvement of the media company in Olimpia's shareholding or directly in Telecom. The market also approved the strategy undertaken by Telecom Italia to seek an agreement with one of the major content providers, as it considered the future of the two sectors to lie precisely in 'on-demand videos' and 'quadruple play', through content broadcast via broadband, and therefore different to what was offered via satellite by Sky or via digital terrestrial television by Mediaset.[2]

During the summer, the negotiations continued intensively, without however reaching a conclusion. In order to accelerate the ongoing negotiations, on 7 September 2006, Tronchetti Provera and Murdoch met on the latter's sailing yacht,[3] but no agreement was made.[4] Their meeting, with the aim of finalising the preliminary work completed over previous months in preparation for the integration between media and telecommunications that was both parties objective, turned out to be merely casual. The prospect for the transformation of the company into a point of convergence between Telecom and the media company halted abruptly.

Judging from the content of the requests made by Murdoch to Tronchetti Provera, an objective and sudden change in perspective could be observed after many months of constructive negotiations which had come close to completion. Indeed, if not entirely attributable to the breakdown of negotiations, this was instrumental in the significant slowdown which set in. The Italian political world had shown a certain coldness towards the prospect of an agreement between Olimpia and News Corporation, something which Murdoch took duly into account in carrying out the assessments that led to his strong doubt regarding

---

2   In 2013, British Telecom launched its own independent television channel, called British Telecom Sport, which quickly became the main competitor of BSkyb (British Sky broadcasting) in the field of sporting events offered to pay-TV viewers.

3   This meeting, perhaps because of its unusual location, has always aroused curiosity. Press reports of the period indicate that Murdoch's sailboat, 56 metres in length and called Rosehearty, was moored in Greek waters near the island of Zakynthos, once owned by the Serenissima Republic of Venice and known as the place where the poet Ugo Foscolo was born in 1778. The meeting was also attended by Carlo Buora and Riccardo Ruggiero, the two managing directors of Telecom Italia, and the French-Tunisian financier Tarak Ben Ammar.

4   Tronchetti Provera recalled that the meeting only lasted a few minutes. Murdoch began by asking, as a condition for continuing the negotiations, whether he could obtain the majority of Olimpia's capital, which meant becoming Telecom's reference shareholder. Pirelli's Chairman stated that not only was this possibility not open to negotiations, but that it was not even feasible, as had been pointed out repeatedly, and as Murdoch himself very well knew. Buora also remembered the meeting with Murdoch in a similar manner, recalling that he had the clear impression that the Australian tycoon would gladly have avoided the meeting, and that the terms of Murdoch's request had been tailor-made to obtain a refusal.

any further involvement in Italy. The events of the days immediately preceding the meeting had strengthened his position regarding this assessment. On 2 September 2006, Tronchetti Provera met Romano Prodi – Prime Minister since spring of that year – in Cernobbio, during the annual Ambrosetti symposium.[5] It is reasonable to assume that, on this occasion, Telecom's Chairman updated the head of government on the progress of the negotiations with News Corporation.[6] Although the tone of the conversation is not known, there is sufficient clarity regarding the topics discussed. Telecom's Chairman asked Prodi to be granted a certain amount of flexibility in corporate decisions, in light of the combination that he was negotiating with Murdoch.[7] It is difficult to imagine what other issues were discussed

---

5   The yearly meeting promoted by the Ambrosetti network took place on the terrace of the room where the Prime Minister was staying. The meeting was also attended by Riccardo Perissich, in charge of institutional relations for Telecom, and Prodi's advisor, De Giovanni.

6   According to Palazzo Chigi's documentation, Tronchetti Provera had already met Romano Prodi once before in this regard, on 19 July. On that occasion 'Tronchetti Provera illustrated to Prodi the project for a strategic agreement with Rupert Murdoch. The project's aim was for Murdoch to enter Telecom Italia, with the transfer of Sky, with which the Murdoch Group was to obtain Telecom shares. From an industrial point of view, the agreement was based on the synergies that could be achieved between Telecom's network activities and the multimedia content covered by the activities of the Murdoch Group.' The press release by the Prime Minister's Office is in partial contradiction with Telecom's press release of 5 September 2006, which stated: 'In relation to the continuing rumours regarding the possibility of agreements relating to share exchanges with the publishing group News Corporation, at the request of CONSOB, Telecom Italia reiterates what has already been notified on 3 August 2006. In confirming that there are ongoing talks and negotiations with the above publishing group regarding the provision of content in the field of media, we emphasise once again, in particular, that at present there is no understanding or agreement with reference to possible share exchanges.' Il Sole 24 Ore's interpretation of Palazzo Chigi's official statement is as follows: 'Reading between the lines, it appears that the deal with Murdoch was beginning to show signs of strain. The existence of tax problems is confirmed, which were, however, resolved by Telecom's tax advisors. Tronchetti also reveals that alternative options were being considered – General Electric and Time Warner – which strengthened Telecom's position. On this occasion, the sale of Brasil Telecom was also raised, with estimated proceeds of 7–9 billion.' For the purposes of better understanding the facts, it is important to note the use of the expression 'that at present there is no understanding' in Telecom's press release to CONSOB. In actual fact, there were no agreements of a binding in nature, the disclosure of which, through a statement to the market, was mandatory. The press release was part of an attempt to maintain proper communication with the market in that period.

7   This evidence is also confirmed by the press release by the Prime Minister's Office of 13 September, which stated: 'On this occasion, Mr Tronchetti updated Prime Minister Prodi on the progress of the negotiations with the Murdoch Group. In this regard, Mr Tronchetti – having stated that the tax problems that had arisen in the meantime for the

during their conversation given that on 2 September they were not known or foreseeable, as they depended on the continuation of the negotiations with News Corporation, which, as we have seen, were not successful.[8]

## 12.3 In the maelstrom of politics

At this confused juncture, an unexpected event took place. On 6 September and thus on the eve of the meeting with Murdoch, Telecom's top management received 'a document prepared by an "anonymous investment bank" and sent by the Prime Minister's Secretariat to Marco Tronchetti Provera'. This document,[9]

counterparty had been resolved, also thanks to the assistance provided by Telecom Italia's tax advisors – informed Mr Prodi that Telecom Italia had adopted a stronger position in terms of negotiations, give that: 1) Telecom Italia had strategic options which provided alternatives to the Murdoch Group, represented by Time Warner and General Electric respectively. Mr Tronchetti had informed Murdoch of these alternatives; 2) Telecom Italia could have strengthened itself financially and in terms of capital through the divestiture of its subsidiary Brasil Telecom, from which it could have obtained financial resources of €7–9 billion. Finally, Mr Tronchetti informed the Prime Minister, Mr Prodi, of his forthcoming meeting with Murdoch a few weeks later.'

8   There is indirect evidence of this in the documentation of the 'Cielo Rosso [Red Sky]' Plan, dated 5 September 2006, which in fact only features some of the hypotheses, of an open-ended nature, to be reviewed during the meeting with Murdoch that was to take place two days later.

9   *Il Sole 24 Ore* of 14 September 2006 outlines the document in the following terms: '28 pages in total, full of graphs, numbers and projections, offering two anti-takeover bid options to Marco Tronchetti Provera: a) Internal Breakdown (developing an internal division for the network with a board made up by a majority of external members); b) Spin-off and subsequent listing with a substantial (controlling) shareholding of the Cassa Depositi e Prestiti [State owned financial institution]'. The analysis begins with a snapshot of the Telecom Italia Group's financial structure, and makes two basic observations: 'a) Telecom has a level of profitability higher than that of its international competitors, but it presents a high level outstanding debt', while 'the domestic telecommunications market is characterised by very limited prospects for growth. In response to this situation, it is appropriate to evaluate the possibility of an extraordinary operation on the wireline infrastructure.' In this regard, it is interesting to note that an article published on *Corriere della Sera* of 8 August 2006 states the following: 'The solution that could perhaps make the operation (i.e., an agreement between Telecom Italia and News Corporation) palatable for the government, also in relation to the market, would be to unbundle the telephone network and resell it to the Loan and Deposit Fund.' Moreover, an article that appeared in *Il Messaggero* of 8 September 2006 comments: 'Last weekend, the head of the government supposedly went further. "TIM must remain in Telecom's portfolio". This is how the Prime Minister supposedly ruled out the speculations circulating on the market regarding the possible sale of the mobile division. Which would represent be a radical change in Telecom's

entitled 'Spin-off of the Telecom Italia network: Industrial approach and economic-financial considerations', first reviewed Telecom's positioning in relation to its comparables, highlighting that the company presents a higher than average profit capacity, but also 'a high debt exposure'. It also pointed out that, in the context of lower prospects for growth of the market for wireline and mobile telecommunications on a national level, there was a need to implement 'new guidelines for development, in particular through the expansion of international activities' and to continue in its pursuit of new technologies. These new guidelines were to allow 'the continuing negative trend of Telecom Italia shares in the last two years'[10] to be tackled, and to reduce the possibility of takeover bids by financial investors, including foreign investors. The prospect that the plan develops 'in response to this scenario is to evaluate an extraordinary operation relating to the wireline network infrastructure', to which a potential Enterprise Value estimate of approximately €25–30 billion is attributed. The plan regards the wireline network infrastructure as 'a basic asset for the recovery of the competitiveness of the country system', and for the company on the basis of a significant reduction in debt. The plan identifies two methods for carrying out this operation: the internal breakdown method adopted by British Telecom, or that of a spin-off of the wireline network and its subsequent listing overseen by Terna. As can be deduced from reading the Rovati Plan on pages 14 and 22, the document seemed implicitly to lean more towards the second solution, which could be achieved through the involvement of the Loan and Deposit Fund in the capital of the company that would manage the wireline

---

strategy. TIM cannot be touched, and neither can the network. And Olimpia must retain an Italian majority.' In response to this article, on the same day, 8 September, Palazzo Chigi issued the following statement: 'The information featured today in *Il Messaggero* concerning the hypothetical "halt" imposed by the Prime Minister on the sale of TIM, must be strongly denied, with appropriate emphasis. The imaginative interpretations of journalists who attribute intrusive ultimatums to the government on the industrial choices and policies of Italian and international companies are directly opposed to the methods of an executive that considers the protection of autonomy and the projects of major Italian companies to be important.'

10 This assertion is based on an incomplete and approximate analysis. Despite the fact that the document on page 8 states that the Telecom stock does not appear to be undervalued in terms of the comparables, with a 13.5 price/earnings ratio against British Telecom's 10.4, France Telecom's 9.5, Deutsche Telekom's 10.7 and Telefonica's 12.8, no indication is given that the stock's performance is in fact better than that of the comparables. In relation to this, see Table 12.1.

network following the spin-off of the network itself. From Telecom's point of view, this prospect would allow the attainment of:

a)  a gross capital gain of 16–21 billion (with a potential tax effect of 5–7 billion);

b)  an extraordinary cash flow of approximately €10–11 billion net of the tax effect, which is accompanied by a reduction in debt of approximately 17–20 billion (in the event of total allocation of the liquidity to the net financial position).

Moreover, the document did not overlook the circumstance that the entire plan had been drawn up against the will and without the involvement of the telecommunications company, and proposed some possible measures aimed to 'convince Telecom Italia to accept the possibility of a spin-off, other than a correct assessment of the value of the wireline network'; such measures included the possibility of operating freely on the market in terms of the development of commercial offers and 'greater certainty in the setting of rates'.[11]

Notwithstanding the discretionary assessment of the scenarios referred to in the document, which has come to be known as the Rovati Plan (named after its author, Angelo Rovati, an economic advisor to the Prime Minister's Office), it was difficult to believe that it had not received even tacit approval from Palazzo Chigi. It was not to be.[12] As Rovati himself declared in the following days, the plan had been prepared by himself personally, while Romano Prodi had been kept in the dark.[13] This turbulent

---

11  A further point is quoted on page 19 of the document: 'Ensuring governance rules so as to protect the industrial interests of Telecom Italia and to support a role/image of reference shareholder including in the infrastructural component of the telecommunications market'.

12  Pages 15 and 17 of the document, however, feature the logo of the Italian Republic. This is a rather unusual circumstance for an illustrative document drawn up without any official seal of approval.

13  On 15 September 2006, *Il Sole 24 Ore* quoted the following remarks made by Rovati: 'What about Goldman Sachs! I prepared the study by myself, and it shows: it is a home-made study. The study is mine alone, not even Prodi was involved and, therefore, the responsibility is mine alone'. Rovati returned to the topic again in a long interview with *Corriere della Sera* on 2 October 2006, in which he declared: 'I told him [Prodi] after allusions to the existence of those papers were made by an article published in Milano Finanza'. When asked by a journalist about Prodi's reaction, Rovati answered: 'Let's just say that he didn't take it well. He knew my ideas regarding the telephone network, but he did not know that I had prepared a document and that I had also sent it to Marco Tronchetti Provera'.

and constantly changing situation left the company's top management dumb-founded. Two essential elements, however, emerged clearly. The first was a matter of principle. From Telecom's point of view, the role that the government wanted to play in relation to the prospects of the telecommunications company seemed confused and unlawful. For Telecom, however, as shown by an analysis of the contents of the Rovati Plan, the prospect seemed different to that prepared by the management, although it did not extend as far as nationalising the network, as some parties surreptitiously wanted people to believe. The Rovati Plan placed most emphasis on the infrastructural network, and essentially proposed a radical solution: the spin-off of the network and the opening up of the parent company's equity in favour of the other shareholders, including, potentially, the public shareholder, through the Loan and Deposit Fund. The entire strategy followed by the telecommunications company's top management up to that moment was neither examined, nor mentioned. If we analyse the timing of the events in detail, the reasons that led Telecom's top management to develop the potential solution of 'open reorganisation', submitted to the Board of Directors on 11 September, seem more comprehensible. Indeed, the Rovati Plan was received prior to the meeting with Murdoch and, following the failure of this meeting, Telecom's top management considered the 'suggestions' which had been fed down, directly or indirectly, by the world of politics through the Rovati Plan, and demonstrated the 'willingness' that had been informally requested in the report of the Chairman of the Authority on 20 July.[14]

In the days that followed, the entire affair become entirely unpredictable, and a bitter clash ensued between the Prime Minister and Telecom's Chairman which ended in a completely unexpected turn of events: Tronchetti Provera's irrevocable resignation from his role as Chairman of the Group. In the aftermath of the failure of the meeting with Murdoch, Telecom's top management found itself faced with the dilemma of how to prepare the Board of Directors' meeting scheduled for a few days later, on 11 September. Various options were taken into consideration. The simplest among these, i.e. leaving things as they were, was rejected because it would have had serious repercussions on the share price, given that the market was expecting major innovations. In a similar manner, the media company prospect

---

14 The author must acknowledge that the significance of the network for broadband development had been repeatedly emphasised by Telecom's Chairman. In this regard, see for example the previously mentioned interviews with *La Repubblica* of 11 November 2005, *Corriere della Sera* of 13 April 2005, and *Affari e Finanza* of 27 June 2005.

was not reviewed in depth, as the project was not feasible at that time. For these reasons, an intermediate solution was adopted, to make various options prospectively possible, in accordance with regulatory developments. It also sought to satisfy some of the Authority's requests. It was evident, however, that the situation with Unico, the Rovati Plan, and the difficulties experienced with News Corporation all had political roots, though never overtly expressed. It was the end of all hope. The same proposals made during the Board meeting dealt a lethal blow to the entire project conceived under the management of Olimpia, that had served that role since its establishment in 2001.

The meeting of Telecom Italia's Board of Directors of 11 September 2006, therefore, launched a major reorganisation plan, of which there is indirect evidence in the information that Tronchetti Provera himself provided, on 12 September to the Pirelli Board (12 September 2006). The Pirelli Board minutes state: 'the path to reorganisation includes the separation of the national mobile communication business and the local wired access network from Telecom Italia, by assigning the corresponding businesses to two distinct subsidiaries of Telecom Italia itself'.

While the entire plan was meant to be a demonstration of 'willingness', primarily towards the various stakeholders and the national regulatory authority, it suffered from having been hastily assembled and contained areas of insufficient detail because they referred merely to options for the future, rather than real prospects. Indeed, it was designed to terminate the project for the separation of the network. For these reasons, and, paradoxically, for contradictory reasons, the plan was approved neither by the market nor by the political arena. The plan undoubtedly represented yet another important phase in the life of the Group which, as things stood, pointed clearly towards two prospects. On the one hand, the spin-off of national mobile phone services was to be implemented, and on the other hand, the wireline network was to become independent in corporate terms. Both newly established companies would be entirely controlled by Telecom. In this way, Telecom combined two functions, as parent company of the Group and as media company, separating customer invoicing activities and thus the precise identification of its business profile, as a possible 'exchange' with the political sector in an attempt to hold the whole project together.

This prospect was not easy to understand or interpret. TIM had been incorporated in Telecom only 18 months earlier with a clear industrial project and with significant financial investment. Now, the spin-off of TIM seemed to contradict everything that had come before. The market interpreted TIM's spin-off as a preparatory step towards its sale. None of this was further from the company's real intentions, due to the commitment made in the implementation phase of the merger and the validity of that industrial project.

There is no trace in the company's official documentation of a hypothetical plan for the sale of national mobile phone services, despite many rumours which circulated in the media. The second important point of the reorganisation regarded the establishment of an independent company, wholly controlled by Telecom, to which the wireline network was to be assigned. This project, which was innovative compared to the past, seemed to be the result of a partial compromise, or more precisely, of the willingness to start constructive dialogue with the regulatory authorities. While the Authority's urgent recommendations in this respect were taken on board, the foundation was also laid to retain the Group's control over the network.

Faced with the prospect of these changes, the market and the political arena went into turmoil, in opposite directions, both of which were entirely misleading if compared to the real intentions of the company. For Tronchetti Provera, all of this meant the collapse of the industrial project that he had pursued for years, and posed a risk to the future of the Group. A formal separation represented a possible compromise aimed at maintaining the integration of technological platforms. Such reactions were proof that the plan had been conceived of, or communicated to the market, too hastily. Indeed, while the market reacted very positively to the resolutions of the Telecom Board of 11 September because it detected good prospects, particularly regarding speculations on the sale of TIM (which had not, in actual fact, been considered), politicians were hesitant and expressed concern.

It is possible that there were some misunderstandings and that the real meaning of the plan was not fully comprehended. It is in this light that we must regard the statements made by Prime Minister Romano Prodi who, following some initial confusion, declared that he was unaware of the actual extent of Telecom's reorganisation. From the perspective of Telecom's Chairman, the approach seen in the resolutions of the Board meeting of 11 September was an attempt to seek a compromise following the vetoes dictated by the political sector regarding Unico, the negotiations with Murdoch, and the hypothesis regarding the separation of the network, first expressed through AGCOM's statements and then in the Rovati Plan.

The world of politics primarily feared the rumours regarding the sale of mobile phone services to drastically reduce the Group's debt level, and also was concerned, albeit in a more general sense, by the hypothetical entry of News Corporation into Olimpia, which would result in an international media group holding a stake (albeit minority) in the ownership structure of the reference shareholder of the national telephone company. The sale of mobile phone services was explicitly ruled out by Telecom's top management in their discussions with Murdoch. There was an outcry from the majority and the opposition in relation to Telecom's future. The following days were characterised by a crescendo of misunderstandings that, in a manner reminiscent an Italian 18th-century Commedia dell'arte pièce, risked transforming the entire event into a national tragedy. In actual fact, there was no guidance, much less decision, regarding the possible divestiture of national mobile phone services, and no decision was taken regarding the possible entry of News Corporation into Olimpia's or Telecom's equity.[15] The request made by the company for sufficient flexibility to pursue negotiations with News Corporation was in fact rapidly superseded by events. Almost simultaneously, Murdoch himself pulled back, stating that 'We began negotiations with the (Telecom Italia) Group, but we felt it would be much better to remain independent'.[16]

Telecom's willingness to find a compromise was, in any case, fruitless. The situation seemed to have reached stalemate. The interventions of the Authority and the political world in recent months had blocked industrial projects and limited complex corporate strategies. Thus, to prevent a collapse on the markets, there was a need to show that the company had some untapped value – an upside even under such extreme circumstances. As such, the emergency plan had three objectives: a) to act to avoid the direct intervention of the political sector, promoted through the Authority in relation to the separation hypothesis; b) to keep the option of an aggregation with a media company and with third parties (Telefónica) open, thus demonstrating strategic management autonomy; c) to prevent the collapse of the stock on the market. In fact, the intervention of the political sector and

---

15 Tronchetti Provera declared to *Il Sole 24 Ore* of 13 September 2006: 'There is nothing concerning Murdoch's entry. We have not taken any decision to sell. We have not taken decisions to sell assets, nor do we know what the proceeds would be if they were sold.' This concept is subsequently revisited in another piece dated 4 October 2006: 'There was no agreement, no price negotiations or share-exchanges, nothing hidden to the market. Content was always the priority.'

16 In an article in *Corriere della Sera* of 20 September 2006, significantly entitled 'Troppa politica, devo cercare soci per Sky Italia' ('Too much politics, I must look for shareholders for Sky Italia'), the Australian tycoon Rupert Murdoch declared: 'The satellite channel Sky Italia could be separated from News Corporation to allow Italian shareholders to enter. This move would guarantee our peace of mind.'

concurrently of the Regulatory Authority had destabilised the company both in Italy and abroad. Just as in ancient tragedies, in which the solution occurs through the appearance on the scene of a *deus ex machina* – an unexpected solution that changes the course of history – in this case it was Tronchetti Provera's step back that set the scene, and made some form of dialogue between the institutions and the company possible. During Telecom Italia's Board of Directors' meeting of 15 September 2006, Tronchetti Provera resigned from his role as Chairman. The reasons for his irrevocable resignation were grounded

> in his desire to safeguard the interests of the company and its share-holders, to enable them to continue to coherently manage the strategic approach identified by the Board, thus saving the company from the situation of tension that had been created and preventing the unjustified personalisation of the events of the last few days from undermining the implementation of this strategic approach and the consequent reorganisation operations that had been approved.

The Board appointed Guido Rossi as Chairman to replace Tronchetti Provera, while Carlo Buora moved from the position of managing director to Vice Chairman and Chief Executive Officer. Tronchetti Provera's sudden resignation was a clear response to the need to 'detoxify' the climate, and try to put an end to the conflict that had rapidly and needlessly escalated, combining personal elements with institutional matters in an increasingly confused manner. All of this, however, only served to partially pacify the situation.

Tronchetti Provera's resignation coincided with one of the most frenetic periods in the history of the telecommunications company, relating to the episode that went down in history as the 'wire-tapping' affair, a moniker that is entirely unfounded, given that, as Telecom Italia's Chairman, Guido Rossi, declared in his hearing with Copaco (Italian Parliamentary Committee on Secret Services Control)[17] on 5 October 2006: 'Telecom Italia cannot tap, legally or illegally'. The reader

---

17 The press reported the gist of Guido Rossi's declarations as follows: 'We have explained, confidently, that the issue of phone tapping has nothing to do with Telecom Italia. Telecom Italia cannot tap, legally or illegally.'

may perhaps wonder as to the origins of this paradoxical misunderstanding.[18] It is not easy to provide a comprehensive explanation. It is perhaps possible to assert that the practice of so-called exchange of phone records, something engaged in by telecommunications companies since their inception, was equated, by the media, with telephone tapping required by State Prosecutors, and latched on to by a distracted public that was, however, sensitive to the then-current subject of tapping, which probably brought to mind the images of 'Big Brother' as foretold by George Orwell in *1984*.

The entire affair originated in May 2005, when, upon instruction by the Milan State Prosecutor, searches were carried out at the offices of Pirelli & C. and Telecom Italia, following Giuliano Tavaroli's involvement in criminal proceedings for criminal association relating to breach of professional confidentiality. Pending clarification of his position, Tavaroli was assigned to other duties within the Group, specifically those of Country Manager for Pirelli Pneumatici in Romania, since 1 August 2005. During the investigative activities carried out by the Judicial Authority, the Group appointed an external lawyer, Marta Lanfranconi from the Mucciarelli Legal Firm, to identify the activities carried out by the companies belonging to the Polis d'Istinto Group[19] in relation to a series of invoices issued by the same in relation to Telecom Italia, requisitioned during the above-mentioned Judicial Authority searches. These companies were at the time working with Telecom's Security.

This activity led to the identification of the services performed in relation to Pirelli, which were perfectly legal, for an overall percentage of the invoices issued equal to 88% for 2002, 81% in 2003 and 97% for 2004. A grey area therefore remained regarding the type of services that had been invoiced to Pirelli, which the chief of security could not explain. In the same period, between April and June 2006, Pirelli's Internal Audit Directorate also engaged in an investigation to verify the adequacy of the internal audit system inherent in the purchasing processes of that Directorate in the 2004–2006 period, and proposed some actions for

---

18  The media campaign against the Telecom Italia Group became so virulent that the same
    Deputy Prosecutor Napoleone defined it as a 'general public credence'.

19  This is a group of investigative services companies owned by Emanuele Cipriani, from
    Florence, who had long been Tavaroli's friend. The group was also comprised the company
    Plus Venture Management of the Virgin Islands and Security Research Advisor of London.

improvement. Based on this evidence, on 18 May 2006, Pirelli decided to terminate Tavaroli's employment. It had already transpired that illegal files had been prepared by Telecom's Security. As demonstrated clearly during the legal proceedings, the top management was completely unaware of these file-forging activities. Proof of this lies in the fact that many of these files – concerning events that are completely external to the telephone company, such as those relating to events in the Middle East – are covered by the state secrets act.

On 20 September 2006, Giuliano Tavaroli, the former chief of security of Pirelli, and subsequently Telecom Italia, was placed under pre-trial detention alongside 18 other people. The court order defined Pirelli and Telecom as parties 'against which the criminal acts had been committed' and excluded the applicability of Law no. 231 on the assumption of the top management's unawareness and based on the circumstance that the acts committed were detrimental and not beneficial to the company. This clarification was important because it recognised the attitude of great transparency and cooperation shown by Pirelli and Telecom – which had provided clarifications from the outset, and even reported the acts – and it resulted in the decision to commit those arrested on 20 September for trial, to the Judicial Authority. It was a first step in the direction of clarity, revealing the exact terms of the issue.

Meanwhile, some years after his sudden resignation in the aftermath of the privatisation of the company, Guido Rossi took up the chairmanship of the Group again, unexpectedly and suddenly. A lot of water had passed under the bridge since Guido Rossi had resigned. But, paradoxically, the reasons that had led him to take that step had not changed. As such, the outstanding jurist considered it appropriate to take this complex situation back into his own hands, and to carry on unravelling the matter from the point where he had left it in the autumn of almost eight years previously. In the opinion of the reference shareholder, the new Chairman could help protect the company against the growing mass media and judicial storm that was surrounding it. Tronchetti Provera's resignation and Rossi's appointment could be considered as two sides of the same coin, and rightly so.

The start of the new Chairman's work was facilitated by the fact that, immediately after Tronchetti Provera's resignation from Telecom's Chairmanship, News Corporation had publicly declared that it was no longer willing to continue with the negotiations. The foreign company had been discouraged by the violence of the political conflict that had affected the telephone company, and took the opportunity to announce its decision to withdraw. The news of Murdoch's withdrawal of interest resulted, understandably, but unexpectedly, in the emergence of interest in Telecom by Mediaset. The reasons that had made the potential of an agreement with News Corporation seem favourable also applied to negotiations with Mediaset. For a few days, the national press carried the news of a possible combination between the telephone company and the national media company. This suggestion was short-lived. The solution was not feasible from a political point of view and, most likely, Mediaset itself did not have faith in it.

By contrast, it is reasonable to believe that, having welcomed the news of News Corporation's withdrawal, the centre-right had momentarily used the event as a weapon to exert political pressure, but with no real desire to develop a common industrial project.

While it was time to acknowledge the fact that the moment had passed for the industrial projects of Telecom's management,[20] perhaps, nevertheless, one possibility still remained: that of determining whether Olimpia's shareholders had managed to direct the company towards those very same projects, without direct involvement in managerial terms.

---

20 The validity of Tronchetti Provera's industrial project is emphasised in an article by Fabio Tamburini, who, some eight years later in *Corriere della Sera* of 19 August 2014, writes: 'There was a notable moment, however, in which the choices on the agenda and the actors on stage were more or less the same as today [Telecom Italia, Telefónica, TIM Brasil]. It was 2006, and Marco Tronchetti Provera was Telecom's principal shareholder. Tronchetti set out five points: 1) the need to maintain an integrated wireline network, without unbundling it; 2) the convergence between wireline and mobile phone services; 3) the need to focus with determination on broadband development (i.e., a high value-added network for the distribution of video content and services; 4) an agreement with a leading content producer; 5) a second internationally strategic agreement with a telephone group to expand the business boundaries, with particular reference to Brazil.'

# CHAPTER 13

# Olimpia's Divestiture

The new Chairman and Telecom's management took advantage of the news of News Corporation's disengagement, and put the previous decisions taken in the Telecom's Board meeting of 11 September on standby, at least momentarily, to let the situation take its own course. In actual fact, the Board's resolutions responded to different requirements than those set down in the agreement with Murdoch, since these negotiations had broken down, and the market was only partially aware of these differences. During a hearing at CONSOB that took place on 25 September 2006, Telecom's new top management summarised the events of the previous week. It was their task to implement the decisions approved by the Company's Board meeting of 11 September, while at the same time no real change had been planned in relation to the scope of Telecom Italia's activities, and no mandate had been given for the sale of assets. The only sale approved, shortly afterwards, concerned the wireline network in Brazil. This decision had nothing to do with the plan outlined on 11 September, but as control over Brasil Telecom had not been obtained in 2005, it did not make sense to continue as minority shareholders. For this reason, a mandate was given to JP Morgan for the sale of 38% of Solpart, Brasil Telecom's parent company. While Telecom Italia's management-related events had suffered an indefinite setback,[1] events concerning Olimpia's ownership structure, and thus Telecom's, continued to evolve rapidly. As expected, at the beginning of October the two banks exited from Olimpia's equity, at that moment held by Pirelli and Edizione Holding, respectively, for 80% and 20%. This change, however,

---

1 However, it is interesting to note that, once Tronchetti Provera left his office as Telecom's Chairman, the topic of the separation of the network was immediately shelved. By contrast, during Telecom Italia's Board of Directors' meeting of 25 October 2006, a possible compromise solution on the spin-off of the network was put forward. This solution related to the so-called 'last mile', i.e. that part of the telephone network that connects users. From this point of view, the decision of Telecom's Chairman to resign in order to safeguard the company had an impact in the following period.

did not influence the company's governance given that the deliberative majority in the shareholders' meeting was brought to 91% of the equity (18 October 2006). Concurrently, Pirelli carried out an impairment test on the fair value of its stake in Olimpia as of 30 September 2006. This assessment showed a fair value lower than the buying cost, and therefore Pirelli decided to devalue its stake in Olimpia by €2,110 million, hence recording a negative result for the period of €1,410.5 million. Although this action was required by the International Accounting Standards that listed companies had adopted since preparing financial statements for 2005, it was clear that the continuous decline in the prices of the shares of telecommunications companies, as well as the continuing lack of clarity concerning Olimpia's prospects as controlling shareholder of the telephone group, risked also jeopardising Pirelli's financial stability.

During the same month, there were also important innovations concerning Telecom Italia's ownership structure. A shareholders' agreement was indeed signed involving Olimpia that held 17.99% of the equity and another two other significant shareholders, Assicurazioni Generali and Mediobanca, which held 3.67% and 1.5% shareholdings, respectively. In this way, the newly established shareholders' agreement held 23.20% of the telecommunication company. Furthermore, this agreement provided for the free participation of other parties who would eventually confer to the same at least 0.5% of the company's shares with voting rights. Taking into account the stakes that had not been assigned directly in the pact, the agreement grouped just under 30% of the telephone company's equity, which represented the threshold beyond which the takeover bid would become compulsory. The agreement also provided that Olimpia could divest its stake in full, and that Mediobanca and Assicurazioni Generali could exercise the pre-emption right on Olimpia's share under any conditions proposed by the buyer. If, by contrast, Olimpia were also to obtain an offer on the shares held by Assicurazioni Generali and Mediobanca, the latter two would have no pre-emption right, but only the right to decide whether or not to accept the offer (18 October 2006).

The formulation of this agreement was significantly innovative. Indeed, until then Olimpia had acted as controlling shareholder of the telephone group independently, without trying to formally gather other significant Telecom shareholders into a coalition. More recently, while the number of shareholders in Olimpia had been reduced to only Pirelli and Edizione Holding – the original shareholders – some major shareholders also present in Pirelli's shareholders' agreement had invested in Telecom's equity. The Telecom shareholders' agreement addressed different purposes; the first concerned the necessity to reinforce the reference shareholder's hold on the company's equity. To achieve this goal, however, yet another equity increase in Olimpia – whose shareholders had already been financially strained – was no longer feasible and thus a more extensive network of alliances between shareholders willing to continue to ensure a stable ownership structure was required. This was closely connected with the need to end the company's isolation following the events of the summer. The involvement of some key actors in Italy was an ideal solution to ensure a more stable ownership and management structure for the company, rendering it less sensitive to the 'storms and billows' not only of the market, but also of politics.

Given how the agreement was prepared, it also disclosed something else. The prospect of a possible sale of Olimpia's entire shareholding was more than a mere hypothesis. Olimpia was actually implementing a broad assessment to verify whether there were solid options to proceed in the telecommunications sector. In fact, if Telecom's new top management – while never disavowing the resolutions of the Board meeting of 11 September – had taken an interlocutory approach as there were no other concrete solutions after News Corporation had left the scene, Olimpia, in its capacity as shareholder, was verifying any residual feasibility in the original plan. Olimpia's challenge in the months after Tronchetti Provera's resignation from the Chairmanship of Telecom Italia was specifically to measure how, as reference shareholder, to achieve what had not been possible as management. It was obvious that a new strategy was required than that followed up to the previous September, as a possible scenario of alliances no longer existed. In the meantime, on Christmas Eve 2006, Telecom's Board approved a further new structure for the telecommunications group, reorganising the activities into four different business units: network, wireline phone services, mobile phone services and major customers.

Following market requirements, the next step in Telecom Italia's development should have been an international alliance to create those synergies necessary for long-lasting creation of value, given that all other actions implementable up to that moment had already been adopted. An important international alliance also required market power greater than that of Telecom Italia alone, even in the context of a heavily regulated sector. Indeed, these aspects had also determined the content of the previous agreement with News Corporation. However, the terms of an international agreement would have to be different from those considered previously, also from an industrial and financial perspective; from the industrial point of view, another telecom company was required to create sufficient synergies to generate value for shareholders and with whom to study an agreement with a content provider at a later date.

The potential industrial partners found the investment proposal very interesting. Different subjects manifested their interest in the telephone company, from the French France Telecom to the Russian operators of Sistema and Altino and the Indian operators of Hinduja. If the synergies for the former proved modest, the latter were only interested in specific Telecom assets. Among the possible industrial partners, those who had the characteristics sought after by Telecom Italia were the Spanish operators Telefónica, with whom synergies were estimated in the region of €2 billion over the period 2007–2011. Even if the agreement with News Corporation had come to fruition, Telefónica represented an interesting option given that Murdoch was not present in Spain. Indeed, there was more than one possible convergence with the Spanish company: a private ownership structure, the lack of competition in the domestic markets of the two groups, as well as the possibility to maximise the investments in certain markets. Starting from these premises, in February 2007, negotiations between Olimpia and Telefónica[2] entered a more intense phase. In this regard, we have seen that in August 2001, in the aftermath of the acquisition of Olimpia's stake in Olivetti – then Telecom Italia's parent company – Pirelli, via Olimpia, had analysed the dossier called Don Quixote in view of a possible integration with Telefónica. It is possible to say that the prospect of an international alliance with the Spanish telecommunications company had been present in Olimpia's strategic outlook from the start.

This new scenario must be interpreted in the context of the changes in the telecommunications market in that period. Having achieved all possible internal synergies in its core business and on the exploitation of the convergence between wireline and mobile phone services, the major operators had concentrated on pursuing further external synergies. However, only Telecom Italia did so, by availing itself of an integrated wireline/mobile platform that gave it a competitive advantage. These synergies necessarily had to result from merger and acquisition cross-border operations, at least in Europe. The progressive saturation of the core

---

2  A press release by Pirelli & C. of 11 February 2007 stated as follows: 'Pirelli & C. confirms the existence of talks with financial and industrial parties, among which the company Telefónica, on the subject of the possible sale of a stake in Olimpia so as not to affect the maintenance of the majority held by the current shareholders.'

business markets and growing pressure on the company's margins that could be countered through a policy of organic alliances among operators were pushing towards this step. This perspective gave the companies that resulted from integrations greater bargaining power to be used in a new approach to market presence, ranging from relations with the traditional providers to those with content providers, and finally to those with national and international regulatory authorities. The purpose of this plan was strictly industrial, while financial shareholders were ancillary to the industrial plan. Thus the potential integration with Telefónica did not represent a sale of the company to a foreign operator, but more a strategy to create value. However, the financial aspects were very significant, as was Olimpia's role, which was functional to a merger that would bring other parties into its ownership structure, in addition to the Italian majority shareholders.

For these reasons, from a financial point of view, the idea pursued was twofold. As well as consolidating Telecom, the possible entry of a foreign operator as a minority shareholder in Olimpia was considered. This also explains why Assicurazioni Generali and Mediobanca were granted the pre-emption right, which represents a clause for possible interdiction concerning the sale of Olimpia's entire share capital to an operator that would not be well received by the other shareholders of the agreement. The possibility of another telephone operator participating in Olimpia's equity, also as minority shareholder, could represent the prelude to a series of scenarios ranging from the hypothesis of a cross-country merger to the more realistic scenario of a greater capacity for interdiction in relation to national politics, and of greater market power. In short, opposing a good agreement with a content provider would be more complicated in the presence of a capital ownership structure of the reference shareholder with a strong international diversification.[3]

The market reacted positively to this changed outlook. Indeed, it perceived that something was happening in Olimpia's ownership structure, though it was still not clear if these changes were in preparation for a sale of Olimpia's stake in Telecom or of the entry of other shareholders into Olimpia. In line with the guidelines described above, Tronchetti Provera outlined three principles of behaviour: the possibility of selling Olimpia's minority shares and not the equity shareholding

---

3  Leopoldo Pirelli passed away on 23 January 2007. Despite not having taken part in Pirelli's SGMs in his later years, because, as he liked to emphasise with an innate respect for those who had succeeded him, he would have found it difficult to chair a meeting 'if his father Alberto had been sitting in the front row', he had closely followed the events of the Group.

in Telecom, the request for a price that implicitly took into account the existence of a premium, and lastly, the non-involvement of Olimpia's minority shareholder in Telecom's management. These were three requests that would be difficult for a financial investor to satisfy, starting with the first, which involved an investment in a unlisted holding. For a financial investor, the procedures to obtain a way out compared to an investment of this kind would represent a problem not easily overcome. Despite this, it must be remembered that some investors expressed their interest in acquiring a minority stake in Telecom.

Among the possible industrial partners, Telefónica manifested its willingness to enter Olimpia's equity with a stake between 20% and 40%, with the aim of stabilising the shareholding and thus build an industrial partnership with Telecom Italia. In the meantime, the major Italian banks also showed their willingness to support Telefónica and Pirelli-Benetton as minority shareholders in Olimpia's ownership structure. Regarding the company's governance, an agreement had been found whereby Telefónica would have a right of veto on certain decisions concerning Olimpia's strategic alliances in the telecommunications sector. This agreement was similar to the previous one to safeguard the rights of Edizione Holding. Furthermore, Telefónica obtained the possibility to terminate its bond with Pirelli and Edizione Holding within Olimpia's equity, in case of a sale of assets by Telecom Italia for an amount exceeding 2 billion outside the Italian market (27 February 2007). In that case, a proportional demerger of Olimpia was to be carried out, without any payment of premiums. It was a solution not unlike that provided for Hopa in the past. From Telefónica's point of view, it was an interesting prospect, but it was nevertheless challenging. The Spanish company had in fact accumulated debt, and was preparing to sell a number of assets to fund the operation. Despite this, Telefónica was willing to offer approximately €3.20 per Telecom Italia share.[4] This assessment incorporated a premium, in the region of 40% compared with the average price of €2.28 for Telecom shares in the previous year. For these reasons, Madrid immediately announced that it intended to proceed with the exclusive negotiations with Olimpia.

---

4   In the guidelines used in the early negotiations with Telefónica, the item 'consideration' states: 'Starting with + €3 per share', i.e. for a value of more than €3 per share. There is also an analysis table with various price scenarios ranging from €3 up to €3.7 per share in the working papers of those who led the negotiations. An authoritative internal source has confirmed to the author that the first non-negotiated price offered by Telefónica was €3.20 per Telecom Italia share.

Of course, in addition to the financial aspects and the corporate governance attributable to shareholders, there were also industrial aspects that had to be negotiated by the top management and Telecom's management. In this regard, the previously mentioned synergies emerged clearly, as did the possibility for integration in certain markets: in particular in Brazil and in Germany. Apparently, there were no precautions of an industrial nature that caused Telecom's directors and the management to have reservations regarding the integration plan developed by the Group's controlling shareholder. All of this, however, was part of a reorganisation process that Telecom was implementing, at times in conflict with Olimpia's objectives. The differences that had become more marked in such a short period of time, spanning from Tronchetti Provera's resignation to the start of the new year, exploded violently in the negotiations with Telefónica regarding the industrial aspects. In the months after Tronchetti Provera's resignation from the Chairmanship, the climate in Telecom's Board of Directors had become heavy with suspicion. From the beginning, the company's management was split between those who still recognised Olimpia as the controlling shareholder, and those who maintained that with Tronchetti Provera's departure, this situation was obsolete and that Telecom had become a public company, as though the management mission were be different in the context of two different ownership structures. The conflict with politics had evidently scared the management.

It was difficult to decide which path to follow, however, as many questions had been raised, from September onwards, still without a precise answers, at least until the actual start of the negotiations between Olimpia and Telefónica. In the two Board meetings of 22 January and 16 February 2007, Telecom launched a partial reorganisation plan based on four divisions: national wireline network, mobile services, special customers and information technology services. Added to these were TIM Brasil, and the national and international wholesale activities managed directly by the managing director, Riccardo Ruggiero. It was a functional reorganisation that, while arising, in a broad sense, from the needs expressed in the Board meeting of 11 September, did not go so far as to affect the company's scope of activities. Nevertheless, in a less invasive manner it did touch on the organisational aspect with a view to possible developments of an industrial nature. When the negotiations between Olimpia and Telefónica became increasingly promising, and 8 March 2007 – the date the Board was to launch Telecom's 2007–2009 industrial plan – was approaching as had been requested insistently by some Board members since the previous September, it became clear that the reference shareholder and Telecom's top management had come head to head (27 February 2007). In fact, the latter implemented some of the preliminary choices for the preparation of the industrial plan. The first choice concerned whether to include the possibility of an international alliance[5] in the plan, such as that which Olimpia was negotiating with Telefónica, or only provide for a plan based on the hypothesis of a stand-alone. In relation to the business strategies to be implemented, different scenarios were envisaged, understandable given Telecom's importance for the country.

Although Guido Rossi had been appointed by Olimpia, due to the deep conviction that he had developed during his long academic and professional career, he was convinced of the virtues of the Anglosphere model of a public company and believed that Telecom had potential in this regard. For this reason, helped also by his great authoritativeness and the anomalous role of 'guarantor' that he served in relation to the government, Telecom's Chairman, having for months supported the path for Olimpia[6] involving Telefonica, adopted an increasingly cold attitude towards those who had appointed him in the hope of protecting the entire shareholding of the telephone company. This was an apparent duality in the sense that no conflict would necessarily exist between Olimpia and the rest of Telecom's shareholding structure once a business plan had been drawn up to create value for the shareholders. In the opinion of the majority shareholder, and also of the market, this prospect necessarily required an international alliance of adequate standing.

Unlike the top management, Telecom's management was not preliminarily against that option, but it appeared to doubt the hypothesis of the alliance with Telefónica set up by Olimpia. However, some members of Telecom's managerial team believed that the business plan was the perfect opportunity to distance themselves from Olimpia's role, which was now deemed to be obsolete.

In particular, Carlo Buora, Telecom's executive Vice Chairman, who had spent

---

5   From this point of view, Olimpia had expressed the utmost openness or willingness, given that 'Any other industrial alliance forged by Telecom Italia's management, and which was fraught with tangible benefits in terms competitive positioning and the possibility of Telecom Italia's growth in value, would be assessed favourably by Olimpia and Pirelli' (27 February 2007).

6   An authoritative source has informed the author that, as a custom, a weekly working breakfast was held by Telecom's Chairman and Olimpia's top management, the purpose of which was to provide updates on the ongoing negotiations with Telefónica.

an important part of his managerial career at Tronchetti Provera's side from the time of Pirelli's turnaround in 1992, found himself in an uncomfortable position. In fact, Buora, while not foreseeing potential conflicts of interest for Olimpia in the operation with Telefónica, was not convinced of the extent of the synergies that could be obtained from the agreement with the Spanish operator, perhaps subconsciously influenced by the Chairmanship. He also believed that the company should be able to freely dispose of TIM Brasil, a company that he feared would be damaged to some extent by the agreement with Telefónica.

However, the Chairman's position was different. It is likely that Guido Rossi was sceptical about the solution proposed by Telefónica for other reasons. Telecom's Chairman was aware of the fact that the presence of any foreign capital in Olimpia threatened the 'Italianness' of the telecommunications company, which the political forces, both of the government and of the opposition at that time, did not seem to accept. Probably for these reasons, Rossi decided to undertake a difficult corporate procedure for the approval of the business plan. Indeed, he decided to not bring the existence of a real option for an alliance with Telefónica to the attention of the Board of Directors, who had to approve the business plan. Although it was in his powers as Chairman of the Board of Directors to formulate the agenda of Board meetings, Rossi was helped in making this choice by the fact that on 1 March 2007, Telefónica, through his Chairman, César Alierta, had declared that 'The ongoing discussions with Telecom Italia for the definition of the terms of the strategic alliance have been suspended' (12 March 2007). If, on the one hand, the Spaniards 'perceived' that the Italian institutional world was puzzled by, if not hostile to, their entrance into Olimpia's capital, it is also likely that it was indeed Telecom's top management that presented Telefónica's top management with the idea of negative political sentiment, at least at that time and in that form, regarding their industrial and financial involvement in Telecom Italia's fate.

However, its own shareholders were well aware of these feelings of coldness in relation to the possible involvement of a foreign shareholder in Olimpia's capital. Nevertheless, they believed that the actual integration with Telefónica could be a good investment project, and in this respect talks with the latter had gone as far as drafting a 'Memorandum of Understanding Regarding Strategic Alliance',[7] which,

---

7   This document is generally known as Mou, from its initials, and will be referred to as such in the rest of the text.

even if not formally signed, analytically detailed the areas of intervention and the quantification of potential synergies. The document established three months' exclusivity, during which the parties undertook not to enter into negotiations with other operators in the sector.

Rossi had already been shown that document by Filippo Bettini, Tronchetti Provera's former assistant, on 21 February, while on the occasion of Telecom Italia's Strategy Committee of 6 March 2007 – which was not attended by Telecom's Chairman – a document entitled 'Working Group Telecom Italia-Telefónica – Preliminary Evaluation of Benefits' was distributed. During the Board meeting of 8 March 2007, which was to approve both the 2006 financial statements and the 2007–2009 business plan, the agenda drafted by Telecom's Chairman did not include the state of affairs of the ongoing talks with Telefónica.

The results of the 2006 financial statements, the first following Tronchetti Provera's resignation, recorded a 2.9% revenue growth to 31.275 billion, but a simultaneous decrease in profits by 6.3%, to 3.014 billion. Debt had also fallen by 2.5 billion to 37.3 billion. In just approximately a year and a half following the merger between Telecom and TIM, debt had been significantly reduced but the situation was still difficult, particularly if the Group hoped to set new investments from a stand-alone perspective. Moreover, the revenues breakdown did not show significant changes from the previous years, except for the mobile phone services in Brazil, which continued to show tumultuous growth in the region of 27.9% from the previous year, thus confirming the validity of the Brazilian option within the Group's growth strategies.

During the same meeting, Telecom's Board approved the 2007–2009 business plan. This reiterated some of the points which had been high priority for the management for some years, such as the development of the broadband network and customer care. Furthermore, the plan was based on defending the leadership position on the domestic market both for wireline and mobile phone services, as well as on the development of the international position, in which South America in general, and Brazil in particular, took on specific significance. There was no mention of a possible agreement with Telefónica. The business plan was approved with the abstention of three members, Carlo Puri Negri, Massimo Moratti and Pasquale Pistorio, who turned out to be the only one among the 13 independent members who voted differently.

The members who were aware of the existence of the Mou – including those who sat on the strategy committee – were obviously uncomfortable about voting on a business plan that did not take this into account, and that therefore involved renouncing, a priori, almost two billion in synergies. The outcome of the vote and the subsequent controversy that took place between Guido Ferrarini, Lead Independent Director, and Guido Rossi, Telecom's Chairman, also stirred wide debate regarding the role and value of independent Board members. In actual fact, the Board resolution did not exclude the possibility of an international alliance a priori. At the same time, however, in a situation considered to be fluid, Telecom did not intend to be bound exclusively to Telefónica. Without the real prospect of an international alliance, or at least a clear indication in this direction, the business plan proved rather lacking in terms content and received a harsh reception by the market. The financial community deemed the prospect of an international alliance to be necessary for Telecom (12 March 2007). The Board meeting of 8 March, and the subsequent Telecom Day, during which the financial plan was presented to the market, clearly revealed the different views and the contrasts that had occurred between the company's management and its reference shareholder. The majority of observers and the market were not aware of the nature of the possible conflicts of interest that Pirelli, as Olimpia's shareholder, could encounter through an agreement with Telefónica, as it is not clear how 'the position of a party that would nevertheless have significantly shouldered the effects of the success/failure of the alliance with Telefónica while remaining Olimpia's largest shareholder, could be considered conflictual' (12 March 2007). The affair had not formally come to an end, but as far as Olimpia's shareholders were concerned, the fact that there was no longer the possibility of admitting the Spanish company into its capital outlined the need for a new outlook to decide on the best strategy. Within six months, the situation had changed yet again, and there was a clear possibility, unexplored and not considered up to that point that, in order to benefit from its capital shareholding in Telecom, Olimpia should sell it (12 March 2007). The difficulties encountered over the previous 18 months in the development of the company's industrial plans made it difficult, from Olimpia's point of view, to set credible strategies in the interest of the company. The world of politics was once again playing an important role in Telecom. In a sector that was still highly regulated, it was reasonable to expect that political pressure would be strong at the fundamental junctions of corporate life, such as in the case of a spin-off of the network or the prospect of the entrance of a foreign industrial operator into the capital of the reference shareholder. Almost 10 years from the privatisation of the former monopolist of public phone services, the old adage that had accompanied the short 'core group' season, according to which

Telecom was a privatised company and not a private company, seemed to ring true once again.

While in mid-March the prospect that Olimpia was to sell its entire stake in Telecom (12 March 2007) began to emerge, the fate of the telecommunications company had become an issue of national importance. Some argued that Telecom's alliance with an international operator of adequate standing could not be delayed, but that it was also necessary to promote an alliance between Italian financial and industrial entities capable of replacing Olimpia and building a more harmonious ownership structure for the legal entity that would hold the relative majority capital shareholding in the telephone group. Moreover, the presence of Assicurazioni Generali and Mediobanca in Telecom's capital, connected by a shareholders' agreement with Olimpia since October of the previous year, was a first indication of the shape of the ownership structure of Olimpia and thus of Telecom. Faced with this kind of solution, which emerged at the end of March, Olimpia's shareholders had no preliminary queries, but limited themselves to emphasising two aspects: the price, and the possibility of proceeding independently to seek other solutions of an industrial nature as alternatives to that represented by Telefónica.

As regards the price, Olimpia's shareholders believed that Telecom was undervalued. Compared to €2.15 per share, which was the market price at that time, a price of €2.82 per share was requested, which incorporated a 31% premium. On this first point, Pirelli and Sintonia[8] left no room for negotiation. As regards the second, Olimpia tried to probe the possible interest of other industrial operators in the sector by quickly entering into conversation with AT&T in the US and América Móvil in Mexico. The former operated mainly in wireline phone services, while the latter was active in mobile services. These were two of the largest telecommunications companies in the world and the operation was followed by Banca Intesa. These negotiations gave rise to the hypothesis for an agreement whereby América Móvil and AT&T would buy two thirds of Olimpia's equity at a price that – for the sake of transparency – valued Telecom shares at €2.82 per share. The last third of Olimpia's equity would remain in the hands of the existing corporate structure, and hence 26.7% owned by Pirelli and 6.7% by Sintonia. An option was finally laid down in favour of the two Italian shareholders of Olimpia to sell the remaining third of shares to América Móvil and AT&T during the following year. In addition

---

8    This was the new name of Edizione Holding.

to Olimpia's shares, there was the possibility of also exercising the 'sell' option on their capital shareholding of 1.36% and 0.22% held by Pirelli and Sintonia respectively, and not underwritten by the two companies.

This last clause implied the real possibility of a full divestiture by Olimpia of the stake in Telecom within one year. For their part, Assicurazioni Generali and Mediobanca could exercise the pre-emption right under the same conditions. To Franco Bruni, who noted in Pirelli's Board of Directors' meeting that 'the proposed transaction may trigger discussions in our country even greater than those generated by the alliance with Telefónica' (1 April 2007), Tronchetti Provera cited the objective interest that the other industrial operators entertained in Telecom, as a demonstration of the good managerial work carried out in previous years. Given the predictable and even greater obstacles concerning the sale of the entire shareholding of Olimpia to two foreign operators, the availability of AT&T and América Móvil was a clear invitation to take the initiative in case other industrial or financial entities expressed a real interest in the destiny of the telecommunications company. The offer made by AT&T and América Móvil, and the real prospect that the majority of Olimpia's equity could end up in foreign hands, had the effect of stirring a hot debate in the Italian halls of power among those who acknowledged the full legitimacy of the operational mechanisms of the market and those who believed that the government should have the last word. These strong contrasts also shook the government team from inside its ranks.

The hypothesis of an agreement promoted by Olimpia hit the mark, causing an acceleration in the process of divesting the stake in Telecom at a price that had explicitly been set at €2.82 per share. In particular, the prospect led Mediobanca and Assicurazioni Generali to consider the possible exercise of the pre-emption right[9] on 66% of Olimpia's capital, in the context of 'a system intervention'. The

---

9   The third paragraph of Art. 7 of the shareholders' agreement states: 'By way of a further exception to the first paragraph, in the hypothesis that Olimpia intends to divest all (and not part of) the capital shareholding that it holds in Telecom to one or more third-party purchasers, in agreement with one another, who have submitted a purchase offer, Olimpia shall allow Generali and Mediobanca to exercise the pre-emption right on such capital shareholding. In this case the economic conditions offered for the purchase of the capital shareholding should be communicated by registered letter to Generali and Mediobanca, within a deadline of no less than fifteen days from receipt of the communication within which the pre-emption can be exercised. Generali and Mediobanca may exercise the pre-emptive right jointly or individually for the entire shareholding of Olimpia in Telecom and at the same economic conditions offered by the offering third party or third parties.'

solution of an operation involving all the major national financial institutions was preceded by the formulation of the agreement with Mediobanca and Assicurazioni Generali in October of the previous year, and was a credible response compared to that of an industrial nature raised by Olimpia. The involvement of the most important Italian banks in the reallocation of Telecom's ownership structure could not disregard the presence of an industrial partner. Following Telefónica's withdrawal, the only possible solution was that of AT&T and América Móvil proposed by Olimpia, but the two foreign operators were not approved. Compared to the beginning of March, however, there was an important difference. Olimpia had presented its strategy, and it was up to others to potentially formulate alternatives to this. In the meantime, the end of the mandate of Telecom's Board of Directors was approaching.

On 6 April, Olimpia presented a list for the Board of Directors that did not include the name of Guido Rossi, the outgoing Chairman, who resigned the following day 'with immediate effect'. In his place, the meeting of 16 April elected as Chairman Pasquale Pistorio, who was entrusted with the mandates concerning the strategic approach. The exclusion of Rossi resulted from the different views among Olimpia's shareholders and Telecom's management that emerged during the preceding months with regard to the hypothesis of an industrial alliance with Telefónica. Olimpia, which had appointed Rossi to chair Telecom, was no longer satisfied with his work.

Mediobanca and Assicurazioni Generali did not share this decision, which was nevertheless legitimate, given that the nature of the existing agreement between Olimpia and the two companies was as a consultation agreement[10] and not as a shareholders' agreement. The new Chairman, Pasquale Pistorio – an independent member of the outgoing board – in March had abstained from voting on Telecom's business plan, which had not considered the possibility of an integration with Telefónica. Even in the slightly confused context that had arisen, a 'system

---

10  The shareholders' agreement does not contain specific guidance on the procedures for appointments. The third paragraph of Art. 5 states: 'Participants undertake to ensure that the vote in Telecom's shareholders' meeting within the limit of the agreement is exercised according to the instructions taken unanimously by the Administration. In areas where decisions concerning topics of competence of Telecom's shareholders' meeting were not taken unanimously by the Administration, the dissenting participant will have the right to freely exercise their vote in Telecom's shareholders' meeting.'

generated' solution was nevertheless being outlined, which was useful both to the company and to the country. This consisted in the combination, within the framework of Telecom's shareholding, of some shareholders with different characteristics that were mutually complementary, i.e. institutional financial shareholders with prevailing national characteristics and an industrial shareholder that, given the morphology of the sector, necessarily had to be from abroad.

In devising this solution, the top management of Intesa Sanpaolo, and more specifically Giovanni Bazoli, Chairman of the Supervisory Board, and Corrado Passera, Chief Executive Officer, played an important role. Way back in September 2006, following the misunderstandings that had arisen with Romano Prodi, Tronchetti Provera had promptly informed Bazoli of what was happening. Intesa's Chairman, a man of great balance and excellent diplomatic skills, took charge after that point in identifying a reasonable solution that could be shared by all players, by Telecom and especially by the country. In this role, he was suitably supported by Passera.

During Pirelli's shareholders' meeting of 23 April 2007, Tronchetti Provera summarised Telecom's main events of the past year, contextualising them in terms of the progress made since he had taken control in the summer of 2001. From an analysis of the content of the entire reasoning, it could be seen that the divestiture of Pirelli's stake in Olimpia was imminent. On 28 April 2007, following the withdrawal of the offer made on 1 April by AT&T and América Móvil,[11] Olimpia sold its entire stake in Telecom to a vehicle company called Telco, owned by Telefónica

---

11  After the announcement of the withdrawal of AT&T and América Móvil, América Móvil was potentially ready to proceed with its own offer. On 19 April 2007 *Corriere della Sera* quoted a letter by Ronald Spogli, the US ambassador in Italy, entitled 'Italy and the investments that do not come to fruition', which stated: 'AT&T's decision to withdraw its proposal for an investment in Italy has caused many comments and many discussions. Italy has lost the interest of a very high-level company, capable of improving telecommunications services, reducing costs for Italian users and increasing the value of a national company. At the same time, what happened was useful to draw attention to the possible role of foreign investors in Italy's economic growth. The Telecom Italia-AT&T episode opens the way to a broader analysis. Until 2005, the total of American investments in Italy amounted to a little less than $26 billion, well below the $324 billion in Britain, $86 billion in Germany, $61 in France and even $43 billion in Spain. Investments never come to fruition where they are not well accepted, where the rules of the market are continuously changed. I don't know the details of the deal for Telecom, but AT&T's letter of renunciation clearly expresses the fear to invest in a market where rules are unpredictable. A more open attitude towards investment can no doubt help to achieve important results.'

at 42.3%, Assicurazioni Generali at 28.1%, Intesa Sanpaolo and Mediobanca both at 10.6% and lastly Sintonia at 8.4%. The sale price of the stake was the same offered by the two foreign operators of €2.82 per share for a minority stake in Olimpia. This price included a 30.5% premium compared to the current price of the share.[12] Overall, Telco would hold about 24% of Telecom's capital, given that Mediobanca and Generali also transferred the shares held directly in Telecom to the new company. The operation was scheduled to be concluded on 15 November 2007, once the authorisations of the national and international regulatory authorities had been obtained.

Following the abrupt interruption of the negotiations that took place between late February and early March, the presence of Telefónica among Telco's share-holders was a surprise. However, the involvement of the Spanish company occurred on a different basis compared to the previous negotiations. On the one hand, in fact, unlike what had essentially occurred, however unofficially, in rela-tion to Mou, the entrance of Telefónica into the ownership structure of Telco, Telecom's new reference shareholder, took place in the absence of a new business plan and without the existence of exclusive agreements, while on the other hand, Telefónica paid a significantly lower price than the approximate €3.20 per share that it had been willing to pay only two months earlier. Furthermore, the Telco shareholders' agreements provided for rules of corporate governance in favour of the Italians who would choose 13 of the 15 board members of Telecom, including the Chairman, the Vice Chairman and the CEO. The Spanish company still had the opportunity to choose the remaining two board members, but without execu-tive roles. For Telefónica, this was nevertheless a success: it entered Telco's equity as the leading individual shareholder at a price significantly lower than the nego-tiations of two months previously. Under the conditions of this second solution, however, the industrial prospects of the agreement were to be built from scratch.

From the point of view of the new shareholding structure, Telefónica's involve-ment was almost the only choice. Faced with the actual offer proposed by AT&T and América Móvil, the possibility of maintaining the national character of the capital majority of Telecom's reference shareholder had to necessarily also include

---

12  In actual fact, the price of €2.82 per share derived from a weighted average of different prices that were paid by the shareholders of the new shareholding structure. Telefónica paid €2.85 per share, while the Italian partners paid approximately €2.53 per share.

an industrial shareholder alongside the national financial investors. From this point of view, Telefónica had had the chance to acquaint itself with Telecom Italia's situation over the preceding months, and could become involved and consent to the operation in a short time. The less obvious character of the Spanish company's presence – part a financial investor and part a silent industrial shareholder – in Telco's equity, and the nature of the corporate governance very much in favour of the Italian shareholders, made it possible to mitigate any controversy relating to the alleged sale of the control over Telecom to foreign operators.

Unlike Sintonia that, having sold its 20% stake in Olimpia, had re-entered Telco's equity with an 8.4% share, in the case of Pirelli, Olimpia's divestiture ended its involvement in the world of telecommunications. This represented a chapter of a still unfinished story characterised by positive and negative aspects.[13]

The public opinion and the media have often questioned the actual pay-off of Pirelli's investment in Olimpia and related commitments. In this regard, it is useful to summarise precisely (see Table 13.1) the financial resources issued by Pirelli to Olimpia between 2001 and 2007, bearing in mind two facts: on the one hand, Olimpia has never distributed dividends in favour of Pirelli, and on the other hand, the investment in Olimpia resulted in no increase in debt for Pirelli.

Overall, Pirelli's entire investment in Olimpia was therefore €6,519 million. Since Pirelli's debt/equity ratio did not change during the period under consideration, though it decreased slightly in terms of the margin, the above-mentioned amount was financed mainly by the proceeds of the Cisco-Corning transaction for approximately €3,900 million, and increases in Pirelli's equity and sales of assets for €2,600 million. As regards the disinvestment of the operation, at the time of sale, which took place in 2007, the cash flow from Olimpia to Pirelli was approximately €3.3 billion, with a weighted appreciation of the divested shareholding of €2.82 per share. Pirelli's investment in Olimpia therefore terminated with a significant loss, which would be reduced in terms of margin if the negotiations that had taken place between January and February 2007 with Telefónica – that was

---

13  On 27 April 2015, during a general assembly meeting of Intesa Sanpaolo, the President of the Supervisory Committee, Giovanni Bazoli, replied to a shareholder as follows: 'I have never received any political pressure, except in one occasion. This was an intervention regarding Banca Intesa, Mediobanca and Generali which was proposed by one of the most honest and qualified ministers of the Republic, Tommaso Padoa Schioppa. He asked if we would consider intervening on an asset of primary importance for the country, and he did it in the most correct fashion. We intervened in the equity. This was the only exception.'

willing to pay an amount of approximately €3.20 per share – were successfully concluded. These arguments present many limitations which render them unreliable. The project prepared by Olimpia was halted very suddenly, cancelling out projects and business plans because of a sort of put option exercised by the only stakeholder with a unique golden share: politics.

In the years following the divestiture of its stake in Olimpia, the events related to Telecom Italia had several repercussions, which shall be mentioned briefly for the purpose of clarity. Indeed, misleading rumours and reconstructions, systematically challenged by Tronchetti Provera, continued to filter through in the media. From the columns of *La Repubblica*, Franco Bernabè – who had taken up office as managing director at the end of 2007 – accused the previous managements of having 'squeezed the company dry',[14] while in a private letter, Tronchetti Provera claimed that 'between 2001 and September 2006 the level of debt[15] was reduced by 6 billion and Telecom had made investments for €20 billion, 70% of which in innovation', and that also, 'as regards international presence, divestitures have focused mainly on non-strategic and minority stakes; it is peculiar how nobody mentioned that between 2001 and 2006, revenues from foreign investment increased from €3,681 to €5,072 million'.

---

14 This expression, 'squeezing the company dry', will become 'general public credence' in the following media debate, not unlike that evoked by the Deputy Prosecutor Napoleone in relation to the so-called 'phone tapping' affair.

15 Interestingly, on the topic of debt, *La Repubblica* of 19 February 2008, quoted the following declaration given by Franco Bernabè: 'No hypothesis of an equity increase is under examination. I can confirm what has already been stated by Telco and I repeat that the debt situation of Telecom is comfortable'. Journalist Sara Bennewitz continued as follows: 'The CEO seized on the opportunity to reassure the investors on the state of the company's accounts', and she added Bernabè's statement: 'Superb consolidation work has been carried out'. The man who, more than anyone, had contributed to this result, Chief Financial Officer Enrico Parazzini, left the Telecom Group on 8 August 2008. In relation to this, in an article published on *Il Sole 24 Ore* on 19 June 2008, Antonella Olivieri wrote: 'Over these years, Parazzini has worked to develop a team of professionals in the fields of finance, administration and control, which has obtained, in everyone's opinion, excellent results. The manager remained in his position even after Marco Tronchetti Provera's departure from the Group, managing the difficult period of the transition towards the new ownership structure. The most demanding task was probably that of restructuring debt, managing the various extraordinary operations (the Olivetti-Telecom merger, TIM's incorporation) that had constantly arisen in recent years, leaving the legacy of a situation that makes it possible for Telecom to tackle with confidence the deadlines of the next two years. Finally, Parazzini, having monitored the drafting of the 2007 balance sheets, last month prepared the issuance of a bond in dollars that made it possible to further extend the deadlines.'

### 13.1 Olimpia's legacy in Telecom's management

We have seen how Pirelli's commitment in Telecom, via Olimpia, came to an end, suddenly, between the end of 2006 and the early months of 2007. Although the procedures for the sale of Olimpia's share would not be completed for several months, in the final part of 2007, Pirelli's management could be considered to be complete. For the benefit of the reader, before refocusing this analysis specifically on Pirelli's journey, it may be useful to try to summarise the most salient elements regarding the commitment of Pirelli's management in Telecom, and to provide a comparative perspective on the future of the telecommunications sector, at least in Europe.

With the sale of Olimpia's share, Pirelli's management left the telecommunications company significantly less indebted and with a structure of debt exposure far more in line with the characteristics of a large European telecommunications company than that inherited in 2001. The debt was reduced from €43 billion in September 2001 to €35.7 billion at the end of 2007. All this had taken place despite the merger with TIM, which, while from an industrial point of view creating the conditions for long-lasting convergence between wireline and mobile, was nevertheless very costly in financial terms. Moreover, the previous merger with Olivetti had allowed for initial debt consolidation and also a significant shortening of the chain of control, completed by the above-mentioned merger with the mobile operator.

Even the fundamentals of corporate governance of the Telecom Italia Group had been significantly improved: the shortening of the chain of control and prompt compliance, often ahead of time, with the applicable international standards for corporate governance of the period (including those of a non-mandatory nature) contributed significantly to making investing in the equity of the telecommunications company attractive in an international context. It is useful to remember the admirable effort put into restructuring the balance sheets that led to a devaluation of assets for €12 billion between 2001 and 2004, as well as divestitures for €16.4 billion, largely on a minority basis, not consistent with the Group's strategy aimed at creating sustainable value at an international level. This strategy is revealed in the gradual consolidation of the presence in Brazil as a mobile phone services operator, and in France, Holland and Germany in relation to broadband services.

It is reasonable to believe that the huge investments made in broadband services – which at the end of the 2006 put Telecom Italia in a position of great importance among the European telecommunication companies in terms of number of customers – probably represents the most significant legacy of Pirelli's management in Telecom, benefiting not only the company, but also the country. This evidence is attested to not only by the National Authority, but also by Europe. In this respect, the progress achieved by Telecom is impressive: 390,000 broadband lines in 2001 had become 6.7 million at the end of 2006.

Broadband development has a precise meaning: even at that time, it was possible to foresee that the economic margins of the characteristic activities of a telecommunications company, i.e. voice, messages and surfing the Internet, were to be significantly eroded.[16] It was therefore necessary to increase the transmission capacity of the network to be able to convey content with higher added value to cope with the lack of profitability of traditional activities. To implement this strategy content was needed and the possible alliance with a content provider, identified as News Corporation, served this purpose.

The soundness of the industrial project conceived by Pirelli in summer 2006 has become increasingly evident in recent years, and attempts to implement this same model were underway in the spring of 2014, albeit only in commercial terms; other global players such as Google and Apple have since gained an unbridgeable advantage. However, it is plausible to believe that the fundamentals of the telecommunications sector for the future were already identifiable then. The trend in the telecommunications sector in subsequent years has confirmed the strategy outlined in the past by Olimpia's management. Without taking into consideration the United States, in which the telecommunications sector has been built up around a small number of operators, in the European context the evolutionary trend of the turnover of individual telecommunications companies approximates the rate of change of the gross domestic product of the individual countries. The emerging crisis has further emphasised these trends.

For these reasons, Pirelli's industrial project, aimed at delivering high added value content on the network, demonstrated its value over time: recent research on the sector in Europe identifies a potential market for the transmission of content of approximately €17 billion. It is difficult, however, to believe that the approach indicated by Tronchetti Provera had not been adequately understood, not so much by the market, but by the National Authority and the political sector. It is more

---

16 For example, the chronologically subsequent applications Skype or WhatsApp, capable of 'disintermediating' two of the three basic services of a telecommunications company.

TABLE 13.1. PIRELLI'S INVESTMENT IN OLIMPIA

| Year | Description of operation | Amount (in millions of euros) |
| --- | --- | --- |
| 2001 | Subscription of start-up capital in Olimpia | 3,120 |
| 2003 | Subscription of Olimpia's equity increase to support the Olivetti/Telecom merger | 388 |
| 2005 | Subscription of Olimpia's equity increase to support the TIM/Olimpia merger | 1,344 |
| 2006 | Repurchase of Hopa's shares in Olimpia | 497 |
| 2006 | Repurchase of Banca Intesa's and Unicredit's shares in Olimpia | 1,170 |
| Total | | 6,519 |

*Source: Our calculations based on data from Pirelli's financial statements*

reasonable to believe that the sudden interruption of the role played by Olimpia in Telecom's management had more to do with the prospect of Telecom's possible involvement in the world of television broadcasting, not yet through La7, but through a combination of a much wider scope with News Corporation. Such a scenario may, in some constituencies in the country, have aroused apprehension and tangible concerns regarding the independent role that Telecom Italia could play in a traditionally protected context such as that of television. This potentially jeopardised the then-lucrative TV business, opening it up to the logic of the market and of international competitiveness through its new placement in a broader context of global industrial alliances. This prospect inevitably removed it from local control of limited scope and opened the way to counteracting the decline of two industries, telecommunications and TV content, thus simultaneously contributing to the development of the country. It was a match with an uncertain outcome, like all games played on the pitch of international competitiveness, but the game never took place. Our history of Pirelli's involvement in Telecom ends here. However, a quick glance beyond 2006 to more recent years demonstrates that the current pursuit of telecommunication operators to acquire assets or seek alliances with content operators came too late, and in some cases was even conducted under conditions of weakness. This is the case with Telecom Italia and a review of the financial statements of recent years provides a comprehensive explanation for it, as shown in Table 13.2.

At the same time, broadband penetration had halted and Telecom Italia's loss of value in absolute terms and in relation to the other European operators represents the synthesis of this:

Market value Telecom Italia at:
September 2006   €40,871 million
December 2013    €12,579 million

The outcomes that would certainly not have left that entrepreneurial game in play are today's chronicle and another story for those who want to tell it.[17]

---

17 On 21 August 2014 *Il Sole 24 Ore* wrote: 'The facts, as well as the data, speak for themselves: from Pirelli's departure from Telecom, the Italian telephone group was no longer able to have a majority shareholder capable to provide stability to the management and strategies for development to the company. And from 2009 to date, Telecom's revenues and margins have been dropping, not only due to its fault but also because of a dramatic price pressure deriving not only from the competition, but also from the choices of the authority. The integration between wireline and mobile networks, and a provision of content capable of generating revenues and margins, constitute the backbone, in line with what has been done by the best operators in the sector. The benefit of hindsight is of little comfort, but it must be said that Tronchetti Provera, who was the first to intuit the inevitable convergence between the telecommunication and media sectors, had already worked on a similar project in 2000. And how can we forget the controversy on the merger between Telecom and TIM, which in 2005 had allowed for a real integration of networks and companies to the point that Franco Bernabè himself, years later, had to recognise the importance of that operation. It is difficult to deny that the tormented judicial vicissitudes also played a far from secondary role in this event. In Telecom's recent history, all too often has one looked at its past, almost always to find an excuse and justifications for its uncertain present.' Tamburini's previously mentioned article in *Il Corriere* of 19 August 2014 focuses on these points: 'These times left Tronchetti with the "scars" of seventeen charges (all formally dropped at the time of publication of this book) but also with the pride of those who, largely ahead of the times, understood that Telecom needed a change because the margins derived from the telecommunication services were decreasing and something different had to be invented: the provision of content to market via broadband, which the inevitable convergence with manufacturers who have them.'

TABLE 13.2. MARKET CAP % VARIATION OF EUROPEAN
TELCO'S (SEPTEMBER 2006–DECEMBER 2013)

| Company | Market Cap Variation (%) |
|---|---|
| Telecom Italia | −69.2% |
| Telefónica | −19.2% |
| Deutsche Telecom | +5.2% |
| British Telecom | +44.8% |
| Vodafone | +89.3% |
| StoXX 600 TLC | +9.4% |

*Source: Bloomberg*

TABLE 13.3. SOME FUNDAMENTALS OF THE TELECOM ITALIA GROUP DURING
THE PERIOD 2007–2013 (SUMMARISED DATA IN BILLIONS OF EUROS)

| | 2007 | 2008 | 2009 | 2010 | 2011 | 2012 | 2013 | Δ% |
|---|---|---|---|---|---|---|---|---|
| Revenues | 31.3 | 28.7 | 26.9 | 27.6 | 29.9 | 29.5 | 23.4 | -25.2 |
| EBITDA | 11.6 | 11.0 | 11.1 | 11.4 | 12.1 | 11.6 | 9.5 | -18.1 |
| EBITDA margin | 37.1% | 38.3% | 41.3% | 41.3% | 40.5% | 39.3% | 40.5% | 9.3 |
| EBIT | 5.8 | 5.4 | 5.5 | 5.8 | -0.7 | 1.9 | 2.7 | -53.4 |
| EBIT margin | 18.5% | 18.8% | 20.4% | 21.0% | -2.3% | 6.4% | 11.5% | -37.9 |
| Net result (post minorities) | 2.4 | 2.2 | 1.6 | 3.1 | -4.8 | -1.6 | 1.6 | -33.3 |
| Investments | 5.5 | 5.0 | 4.5 | 4.6 | 6.1 | 5.2 | 4.4 | -20.0 |
| Net financial position | 35.7 | 34.0 | 34.7 | 32.0 | 30.8 | 29.0 | 27.9 | -21.8 |

*Note: The reported data shows the scope of the area of consolidation on the different reference dates.*
*Source: Our calculations based on official documentation provided by Pirelli*

TABLE 13.4. SOME FUNDAMENTALS OF TELECOM'S PEERS DURING THE PERIOD 2007–2013 (DATA IN EUROS/MILLION OR STERLING/MILLION)

| Peers | 2007 | 2008 | 2009 | 2010 | 2011 | 2012 | 2013 | Δ% |
|---|---|---|---|---|---|---|---|---|
| **Deutsche Telekom** | | | | | | | | |
| Revenues | 62,516 | 61,666 | 64,639 | 62,421 | 58,653 | 58,169 | 60,132 | -3.8 |
| EBITDA | 16,160 | 16,842 | 16,874 | 16,503 | 16,597 | 6,957 | 15,422 | -4.6 |
| EBITDA margin | 25.85% | 27.31% | 26.10% | 26.44% | 28.30% | 11.96% | 25.65% | -0.8 |
| EBIT | 5,227 | 6,347 | 5,551 | 5,544 | 5,612 | -3,891 | 4,518 | -13.6 |
| EBIT margin | 8.36% | 10.29% | 8.59% | 8.88% | 9.57% | -6.69% | 7.51% | -10.1 |
| Net result (post minorities) | 569 | 1,483 | 353 | 1,695 | 557 | -5,255 | 930 | 63.4 |
| Net financial position | 37,326 | 38,067 | 41,492 | 47,025 | 43,098 | 39,486 | 37,446 | 0.3 |
| **France Telecom** | | | | | | | | |
| Revenues | 52,959 | 53,488 | 45,944 | 45,503 | 45,277 | 43,515 | 40,981 | -22.6 |
| EBITDA | 19,026 | 17,691 | 14,257 | 14,255 | 14,541 | 10,639 | 11,849 | -37.7 |
| EBITDA margin | 35.9% | 33.1% | 31.0% | 31.3% | 32.1% | 24.4% | 28.9% | -19.5 |
| EBIT | 10,915 | 9,915 | 7,840 | 7,794 | 7,806 | 4,310 | 5,285 | -51.6 |
| EBIT margin | 20.61% | 18.54% | 17.06% | 17.13% | 17.24% | 9.90% | 12.90% | -37.4 |
| Net result (post minorities) | 6,300 | 4,069 | 2,997 | 3,920 | 3,895 | 820 | 1,873 | -70.3 |
| Net financial position | 38,766 | 36,482 | 33,205 | 30,314 | 31,324 | 29,792 | 31,165 | -19.6 |
| **Telefónica** | | | | | | | | |
| Revenues | 56,441 | 57,946 | 56,731 | 60,737 | 62,837 | 62,356 | 57,061 | 1.1 |
| EBITDA | 23,301 | 23,334 | 22,379 | 25,718 | 19,305 | 19,391 | 18,805 | -19.3 |
| EBITDA margin | 41.28% | 40.27% | 39.45% | 42.34% | 30.72% | 31.10% | 32.96% | -20.2 |
| EBIT | 13,865 | 14,288 | 13,423 | 16,415 | 9,159 | 8,958 | 9,178 | -33.8 |

| Peers | 2007 | 2008 | 2009 | 2010 | 2011 | 2012 | 2013 | Δ% |
|---|---|---|---|---|---|---|---|---|
| EBIT margin | 24.57% | 24.66% | 23.66% | 27.03% | 14.58% | 14.37% | 16.08% | -34.5 |
| Net result (post minorities) | 8,906 | 7,592 | 7,776 | 10,167 | 5,403 | 3,928 | 4,593 | -48.4 |
| Net financial position | 44,925 | 44,446 | 44,214 | 54,128 | 57,415 | 51,936 | 49,622 | 10.5 |
| Peers | 2007 | 2008 | 2009 | 2010 | 2011 | 2012 | 2013 | Δ% |
| British Telecom in local currency | | | | | | | | |
| Revenues | 20,223 | 20,704 | 21,390 | 20,911 | 20,076 | 19,307 | 18,253 | -9.7 |
| EBITDA | 6,117 | 6,023 | 3,588 | 4,827 | 5,518 | 6,060 | 5,972 | -2.4 |
| EBITDA margin | 30.2% | 29.1% | 16.8% | 23.1% | 27.5% | 31.4% | 32.7% | 8.2 |
| EBIT | 3,197 | 2,809 | 698 | 1,788 | 2,539 | 3,088 | 3,129 | -2.1 |
| EBIT margin | 15.8% | 13.6% | 3.3% | 8.6% | 12.6% | 16.0% | 17.1% | 8.4 |
| Net result (post minorities) | 2,850 | 1,737 | -83 | 1,028 | 1,502 | 2,002 | 2,091 | -26.6 |
| Net financial position | 7,485 | 9,390 | 12,200 | 10,309 | 9,378 | 9,505 | 8,388 | 12.1 |
| Vodafone in local currency | | | | | | | | |
| Revenues | 31,104 | 35,478 | 41,017 | 44,472 | 45,884 | 46,417 | 44,445 | 42.9 |
| EBITDA | 406 | 12,706 | 7,711 | 12,577 | 13,074 | 14,055 | 5,843 | 1339.2 |
| EBITDA margin | 1.3% | 35.8% | 18.8% | 28.3% | 28.5% | 30.3% | 13.1% | 907.2 |
| EBIT | -4,705 | 6,797 | 897 | 4,667 | 5,198 | 6,196 | -1,857 | -60.5 |
| EBIT margin | -15.1% | 19.2% | 2.2% | 10.5% | 11.3% | 13.3% | -4.2% | -72.4 |
| Net result (post minorities) | -4,932 | 6,660 | 3,078 | 8,645 | 7,968 | 6,957 | 429 | -108.7 |
| Net financial position | 12,776 | 20,810 | 31,418 | 30,747 | 26,724 | 22,798 | 24,618 | 92.7 |

Note: The data of British Telecom and Vodafone are reported in the local currency. These companies had a time-scale gap compared to Table 13.4, shown on the previous page, probably linked to the closing of the financial statements, on a year-by-year nature.

Source: Our calculations based on Worldscope Datastream data

PART IV

REGENERATION

# CHAPTER 14

# Focusing on the Core Business

Although the decision to divest the stake that Pirelli held in Olimpia was an important turning point in the history of the Company, on the other hand the transfer of the shares to the Telco purchasers had no immediate effect, since the contract indicated 15 November 2007 as the deadline for completion. This gap of a few months was justified by the need for the regulatory authorities of the various countries where Telecom Italia operated to give their approval for the completion of the deal. While waiting for these authorisations to be finalised, a start was made during the summer of 2007 on outlining the new strategic prospects for the Pirelli Group. After exiting the telecommunications sector, these consisted essentially in an increasing focus on its core business, which also included real estate, although this was a more peripheral activity in Pirelli's industrial tradition.

However, any strategic decision was necessarily dependent on the completion of the sale of the stake in Olimpia and the allotment of the liquid assets gained from that divestment. Towards the end of October, the authorisation arrived from Anatel, the Brazilian Regulatory Authority, after its decision-making procedures had probably been slowed down by backstage pressures from some other competitors (11 September 2007). This was the final obstacle to complete the sale of the stake in Olimpia and Pirelli was able to implement the strategies that it had developed in the meantime. Between 2001 and 2007, in the years when the Group's focus had mainly been on telecommunications, the characteristics of the tyre sector had changed. These were mainly technological issues which, allied with commercial and economic aspects, reiterated the need to maintain constant and careful interconnection between these elements, including at the level of organisational structures and company organisation. It was important to pursue geographical growth and the development of product platforms in line with the most advanced segments in the automobile industry, starting with the processing of raw materials which had developed rapidly. This was a logical consequence of the development of new types of synthetic rubber meaning that the tyre industry had to acquire high-level chemical skills,[1] something that Pirelli had been developing since the 1990s. However, it was not possible to define the time-to-market factor. In addition to creating new product segments, such as the appropriately named 'Winter' series, which had been a niche market until the late 1990s and showed potential with an ever-growing market in Continental Europe, this new scenario meant that tyre manufacturers were obliged to obtain approval for their products for use on prestigious car models. This combination of products and approvals constituted a specific market range called prestige and premium, whose importance in terms of size with regard to overall tyre sales showed upward trends that were greater than for traditional tyres. Moreover, the profitability of the top range was far greater than that of the traditional sectors, and not by chance; this was the direction that most successful car industries had taken.

Pirelli was only partially ready for these new scenarios that characterised the tyre market. On the one hand, Pirelli had been present in the high-end market since the mid-1990s as a necessary consequence of the restructuring process of 1992–1995, and the decision to invest in the production techniques of Flexi and MIRS,[2] as well as the more advanced Continuous Compound Mixing (CCM); on the other hand, Pirelli's profitability had been less than that of Michelin and, particularly, of Continental, and its production in that period had been mainly focused on the standard segment. The plans for the geographical relocation of its production plants also included new plants in Romania and Yanzhou, China, which were initially intended for traditional production but were quickly converted to premium production. In 2007 a study carried out by McKinsey highlighted a progressive detachment between the sales networks and the decision-making centres in the tyre business. This lack of coordination had led to the paradoxical situation whereby it was the sales networks that were not fully aware of or convinced by the features and quality of the tyres available in the market, due to insufficient care in ensuring their uniform quality.

---

1 The compound used to make tyres consists of 35 different product components. During a visit to Settimo Torinese, the writer was able to observe the precise amounts of different elements going to make up the tyres, as if measured by a pharmacist.

2 Using the Flexi system installed in the German plant in Breuberg (Hesse) in the mid-1990s and subsequently with MIRS (Modular Integrated Robotised System), Pirelli had managed to obtain important approvals within the high-end car segment. Also, using the CCM system one could achieve optimum blending of the raw materials with specific control over their weights and mixing temperatures.

The onset of the crisis, therefore, meant that tyre strategies and priorities had to be rapidly redefined. This consisted in seeking the best possible solutions to set up production plants in countries with high growth rates and low production costs. The product mix also aimed towards an increasing focus on the high-end range, with the declared ambition of becoming the market leader in this niche segment. In this regard, the work started by Maurizio Boiocchi in the mid-1990s and which was continued later by others proved crucial in taking Pirelli closer to its new corporate goal. One of its first successes was to produce tyres for SUVs with performance levels comparable to those of sports cars. Pirelli also dedicated much energy and research to the run-flat technology – specifically requested by BMW – and more generally, to the production of tyres that would minimise rolling resistance and the emission of carbon dioxide, without reducing overall performance. In this context, the search for a geographical strategy consistent with the overall corporate strategy meant downsizing or closing some facilities in Western Europe. The Spanish production facility in Manresa was shut down, while the Settimo Torinese plant[3] was refurbished, and new plants were opened in the emerging areas of Europe or in other geographical regions with high growth[4] rates.

Settimo Torinese is an innovative industrial hub that juxtaposes two previous Pirelli production facilities which produced both car and truck tyres. In order to integrate the workforces of the two sectors previously unknown to each other, Pirelli asked Renzo Piano to prepare an innovative architectural solution. Piano's

---

3   The redevelopment of the Settimo Torinese plant, turning it into the most advanced hub for the production of tyres of the latest generation, started in the early months of 2009 and involved an investment of about €140 million, part of which was provided by regional government institutions and entities. *Il Sole 24 Ore* on 23 February 2008 writes: 'Thanks to the collaboration with the Polytechnic of Turin, which is going to enter into a network of contacts with other Italian and foreign universities, the CyberTyre is scheduled to be created in the Settimo Torinese plant. This intelligent tyre of the future is equipped with sensors that can transmit information on the driving and control of the vehicle. But the new plant will also be characterised by the introduction of the TSM, the new process for blending materials with high quality levels.'

4   Pirelli also invested about €40 million on increasing the production capacity of its plant in Alexandria in Egypt by about 50%. This plant produced radial tyres for trucks and buses, and is under the responsibility of Alberto Pirelli, Vice Chairman of the Company, who oversees the Middle East, Africa and India Regions. This area accounts for about 8% of the Group's turnover, totalling approximately €495 million with an operating profit of €95 million in 2013. In addition, €250 million was also invested in the construction of a plant in Slatina, Romania.

proposal involved the creation of a 'backbone' in the form of a long corridor similar to a fishbone placed between the two plants.

This 'backbone' is home to the corporate offices of the two plants and those providing support for the business activities. The 'backbone' extends for about 500 metres, and when walking along this main thoroughfare one sees the canteen, library and changing rooms, and at the end, a football pitch in synthetic turf for employees. Historically these production sites were places with darkened windows because natural light had a negative effect on the vulcanisation of rubber, but now Settimo Torinese is bright with natural light. Special window panes were designed to prevent any possible problems with production while allowing natural light to enter. The Next MIRS production process is also located at Settimo Torinese, allowing the production of high-end tyres in small batches. Similar to large herons with delicate movements, the red robots of the Next MIRS pass the tyres between one another in the various stages of processing. With its design, constitution and construction, Settimo Torinese upholds the view that an industrial plant can be both pleasing and suitably placed in its natural context.

The approach adopted for the future would, in a few years, led to a drastic change in the mix of tyres on offer and in the geographical location of sales. Nevertheless, in line with this way of thinking, complete restructuring of the Group was needed. Firstly it was important to purchase the considerable minority stake in Pirelli Tyre which, since the summer of 2006, had been in the hands of institutional investors, following the failed listing of the Company, due to adverse market conditions. The completion of the Olimpia deal provided the resources to proceed with the acquisition of the minority shareholdings in the Group's traditional businesses. Altogether, the resources provided by the sale of Olimpia came to about €3.3 billion. Of this sum, approximately €1.2 billion was used to reduce debt, €827 million was distributed to shareholders as a bonus dividend and €408 million was allocated to share-buyback operations (9 November 2007). For these reasons, an Extraordinary Shareholders' Meeting was called in December 2007 to approve a resolution reducing the equity from €2.79 billion to €1.55 billion by decreasing the nominal value of the shares from €0.52 to €0.29. The next step was to repurchase 38.9% of the equity of Pirelli Tyre from Speed SpA, a special purpose vehicle formed by institutional investors, for the price of €835.5 million, of which €401 million came through the assumption of debt and the remainder via a net disbursement. In this way Pirelli regained possession of the entire share capital of Pirelli Tyre.

However the Company decided not to prepare a three-year business plan immediately, since it was objectively difficult to translate a rapidly declining economic situation at the international level into a unitary programme. Consequently, the business plan was not put to the market until the beginning of 2009. Within the context of the Group's internationalisation strategy in emerging countries, an important role was played by Russia, which offered a great potential market, particularly for high-end products like the Winter series. The increasing severity of the economic crisis in 2008 and the growing uncertainties regarding its possible duration rendered Pirelli's diversification strategy in Russia[5] even more interesting. On 4 August 2008 Pirelli signed an agreement with the Russian Technologies Corporation to create a joint venture to produce about 4.2 million tyres locally for cars and industrial vehicles with an estimated investment of around €250 million. When setting up production sites in a country like Russia, it was preferable to work alongside a local industrial partner, which Pirelli found in the public holding company for investments in industrial companies. The choice of a public entity was made due to the difficulty of interacting in a timely and reasonable manner in a country like Russia, where the so-called 'country risk' regarding regulations and bureaucracy is considerable for foreign investors and industrial entities.

During the first half of 2008 it was the real estate sector that caused the greatest concerns. The decision to focus the Group's activities on its core business required a necessary redefinition of the substance and mission of the subsidiary Pirelli Re, whose shares were suffering the moment of difficulty in the capital market. Although the symptoms of a deep crisis were now evident, Pirelli Re, guided by its CEO Carlo Puri Negri, had continued its geographical expansion, acquiring an increasingly significant level of real estate assets in Poland and also in Germany, where in July 2008, together with other investors, it took over a 49% stake in Highstreet, a company that owned the buildings leased to the Karstadt

---

5   On the subject of relations between Russia, the US and the EU, the former US Secretary of State Henry Kissinger wrote in the *Herald Tribune* almost at the same time, on 22 July 2008: 'Europe is the ideal intermediary between Russia and the United States. Russia requires reliable partners and Europe needs to prove that it is one, while remaining undivided, while also remembering that Russia has every interest in maintaining good business relations with Europe. America, on the other hand, since it does not necessarily feel the same need as Europe, must reach a point where it understands its importance, also because the EU's position as an intermediary is important and perhaps essential due to its geographical position and political weight.'

chain of department stores. At the same time as the Group was intent on finding a solution for the Olimpia stake in Telecom, these last two planned acquisitions blew the debt situation sky high. During the second half of the year, coinciding with the general worsening of the economic situation at international level, the share value fell significantly below its initial placement level in 2002.

For a brief period, real estate had provided a good investment, but was now combined with the external difficulties, not only the limits that historically characterise the sector, but also the specific traits of a business model that had quickly become obsolete. Pirelli Re had taken advantage of the market euphoria of the preceding years to grow rather impetuously. In order to avoid consolidating its debt, it invested in minority stakes together with senior European international players from the industry – mostly from the credit sector – and used high levels of borrowing to sustain its continued growth. Through a large number of trusts and vehicles, at the end of 2007, Pirelli Re possessed assets under management worth approximately €15 billion. The management strategy of Pirelli Re was based on the continuous growth in real estate prices that made the growing level of borrowing sustainable. Moreover, the debt of the Group's real estate company Pirelli Re had been created over a period of only a few months between 2006 and 2007. The model adopted was that of a very aggressive private equity, featuring a low aversion to risk, not unlike the model advocated by several American investment banks, including Lehman Brothers, which had been decidedly fashionable in those years.

TABLE 14.1. PERCENTAGE BREAKDOWN OF
THE PIRELLI GROUP'S INVESTED CAPITAL AT
31 DECEMBER 2007 (AT BOOK VALUES)

| Investments | Percentage share |
| --- | --- |
| Pirelli Re | 26 |
| Tyre industry | 51 |
| Pirelli Broadband | 1 |
| Other equity investments (RCS, Mediobanca, etc.) | 22 |

*Source: Our calculations from official documentation provided by Pirelli*

The substantial fall in the current value of assets made its debt burden increasingly unsustainable and highlighted the urgent need to adopt important corrective actions in the real estate business which would allow analysts to gain a clearer understanding of the various industries in the Pirelli Group. The significant overall weight of the real estate company in relation to the total assets of the Group was barely comprehensible to the market, which was struggling to understand the reasons why a tyre manufacturer was the controlling shareholder of a real estate company which in turn threatened to jeopardise its entire asset equilibrium. The effective likelihood of Pirelli Re having to perform significant write-downs of its assets would also have had a negative effect on the income statement of Pirelli.

At the end of 2008 the first steps were taken in restructuring Pirelli Re. These were targeted towards a precise downsizing of its overall assets, the disposal of its non-performing loan business and, above all, a drastic reduction in its borrowing that stood at about €900 million.[6] All this did not lead to the rapid divestment of the real estate branch, but was aimed at preserving the asset equilibrium of the entire Group, targeting certain strategic assets that were clearly understandable to the market. Altogether Pirelli capitalised €1.2 billion in the market, which included the current value of equity investments in listed companies (amounting to about €400 million), such as the remaining investment in Telecom and those in RCS and Mediobanca, net of the controlling stake in Pirelli Re. The current value, therefore, that the market attributed to the Group's core business was only €800 million. It was thus reasonable to expect significant margins for the creation of value.

For these reasons, one of the most important aspects of the new 2009–2011 business plan, which was favourably received by the market, was the decision to proceed with a recapitalisation of €400 million of its subsidiary Pirelli Re, which at the time of the announcement had a market capitalisation of approximately €160 million. The parent company undertook to subscribe any unsubscribed shares and

---

6   About half of the financial indebtedness was to its parent company, Pirelli. One of the reasons that made the real estate business difficult for the market to understand was the precise level of debts pertaining to the Pirelli Group. The total debt that weighed heavily on the companies in which Pirelli Re had stakes was about €13 billion. Since the stakes that Pirelli Re generally held in the vehicles was about 25%, the share of the debt was about €3 billion that reduced to €2.577 billion net of the non-performing loans and loans from shareholders (10 February 2009). The €900 million mentioned in the text relates to the specific borrowing of Pirelli Re and does not include that of the trusts and vehicles in which Pirelli Re had invested pro quota.

would finance this increase by transforming part of the outstanding debts owed to the subsidiary into venture capital. This operation was intended to counteract the high-risk policies undertaken by Pirelli Re in previous years.

As for the rest of the Group, the 2009–2011 business plan, approved in February 2009, rationalised what had already emerged during operations over the previous two years following the sale of Olimpia, and planned additional investments of about €700 million and cost savings of €300 million by dedicating special attention to the procedures for procuring raw materials. Furthermore, the plan was based on a stand-alone strategy, but left unchanged the research and development costs, which accounted for about 4% of sales, significantly higher than that of its competitors.

Already in spring 2009 it was possible to see that the road map drafted after the sale of the stake in Olimpia and approved in the new business plan would allow for an increased turnover and significant profitability margins to generate profits for the Company due to the thorough restructuring of its production activities. To deal with these difficult times, Pirelli attributed even greater importance to corporate governance,[7] something for which the Company had an excellent ranking at an international level. Pirelli was well aware that in times of crisis and rapid change, corporate governance becomes an important driver compared to times of lower market volatility. These innovations made Pirelli shares an increasingly attractive proposition for large institutional investors. From 2009 the ownership structure of a significant portion of Pirelli's floating shares changed considerably. Small shareholders from the retail segment – generally Italian – who held a stake of about 35% in the Company, were replaced by an increasingly broad-based group of institutional investors,[8] often from emerging countries, who appreciated and agreed with the business plan and the style of the Group's management.

The drawing up of the business plan was followed by the creation of a new organisational chart for the Group, with significant improvements to corporate

---

7    It is worth considering that the return of the lawyer Francesco Chiappetta to Pirelli on 1 February 2009, as Strategic Advisor to the Chairman and General Counsel, made a significant contribution in this direction. Chiappetta had left a similar function in Telecom Italia a few months earlier, where he had contributed significantly towards improving the corporate governance of that company.

8    Valeria Leone, Pirelli's Investor Relator, has contributed significantly to the internationalisation of Pirelli's capital and the success of the described strategies.

functions, since most of these were to report directly to the Company Chairman and CEO. With the assistance of Value Partners – a long-standing consultant for Pirelli on strategic and organisational matters – this new organisational chart had been conceived to put the Company's top management in close contact with both the market and sales networks, thus permitting Pirelli to be one step ahead of the market rather than two steps behind. The new organisational chart also envisaged the reintroduction into Pirelli of the so-called 'professional families', already a key feature of the turnaround years. In this regard, it is important to mention the roles played by Francesco Tanzi, who returned to Pirelli from Telecom Italia as Chief Financial Officer at the end of 2009, and Maurizio Sala as Chief Planning and Controlling Officer. The work of Tanzi and Sala, consolidating and building on the foundations laid in the years of the turnaround, ranks highly with respect to the time-honoured attention that Pirelli pays to all forms of metrics regarding corporate parameters and the role of finance as a fundamental yet secondary element of industrial activity.

In terms of earnings, the prospects for 2009 and the following years seemed to be reasonably positive, whereas the asset balance of Camfin, Pirelli's reference shareholder, gave some cause for concern. At the time of the divestment of the stake in Olimpia, Camfin held 25.51% of Pirelli, of which 19.63% was assigned to a voting trust.[9] In turn GPI controlled 51.01% of Camfin's equity. In mid-2007 in accounting terms, Camfin held assets of €1.164 billion, of which €551 million was funded with its own resources and the remaining €618 million with those of third parties. Despite the financial position of Camfin clearly revealing the signs of the huge efforts made to support Pirelli's commitment in Olimpia, the bonus dividend of €211 million from the aforementioned decrease in Pirelli's equity produced significant improvements in Camfin's financial position. As a result of this deal, at the end of 2007, the net financial position of Camfin had fallen to €455 million. However, at the same time its net equity had also decreased to approximately €360 million.

Camfin represented a heterogeneous group that combined its participation in Pirelli[10] with its traditional specific involvement in the oil and gas industries and,

---

9   On that date, the shareholders' voting trust that controlled Pirelli had 46.2% of the share capital with voting rights. In this regard, see Appendices 1 and 3.

10  On 31 December 2007, in addition to holding 25.54% of Pirelli, Camfin had in its portfolio

more recently, in the environmental industry. The events that involved the companies downstream of Camfin led to a review of its nature, but the asset balance of Camfin depended on an increase in value of its investment in Pirelli and on the regular flow of dividends or on a possible recapitalisation by GPI. In order to demonstrate to the market its confidence in Camfin's prospects, in early 2008, GPI[11] proceeded to purchase an additional 2.25% stake in Camfin. The signal was well received by the market, but nevertheless Camfin had to continue its increase in value and the disposal of its non-strategic assets in order to balance its financial position while waiting for a recovery in the value of Pirelli. Pirelli's return to profits in 2007 and the subsequent payment of the dividend in 2008 temporarily alleviated the problem, although it was again exacerbated by Pirelli's loss in 2008 and by the results of the impairment test on the value of its stake. In fact, attention was drawn to the need for an adjustment to the carrying value of the Pirelli shares held by Camfin from €0.67 to €0.55 per share, giving a total write-down of €165 million.

The Board of Camfin which approved the 2008 financial statements had to acknowledge the situation and the imbalance that had been created between the book value of the shareholder's equity of approximately €200 million and the total amount of debt that had exceeded €500 million. For these reasons and taking advice from Mediobanca, the company launched a programme to strengthen its capital position and dispose of further assets with the aim of bringing its level of debt down to a more acceptable figure of about €250 million. Therefore, the Board of Camfin passed a resolution increasing its share capital by €100 million, of which €70 million came from liquid assets in 2009 and the remaining €30 million through the exercise of warrants during 2011.

This operation to strengthen Camfin's capital position also saw the involvement of the Genoa-based Malacalza family of entrepreneurs (12 June 2009), who were active in the fields of high technology, the construction industry, plant engineering and steel. The family reached an agreement with GPI, the majority shareholder of Camfin, which at first provided for their participation in the equity of Camfin with

---

49% of Pirelli & C. Ambiente, 49% of Pirelli & C. Eco, 100% of Cam Immobiliare and 40% of Cam Energia & Investimenti, while the stake in Cam Petroli had been transferred just a few days earlier, on 21 December 2007.

11 The ownership structure of GPI was the following: the limited partnership joint stock company MTP of Marco Tronchetti Provera held 61.4% of GPI, the second partner with a 30% stake was Fratelli Puri Negri, while Alberto Pirelli held 5%.

a 3.5% stake that they took over from GPI. The prospects for the involvement of the Genoese family in Camfin were accurately described by the General Manager of Camfin, Roberto Rivellino, at the Board Meeting on 12 June 2009:

> If the development of this partnership proved to be satisfactory for GPI, the Malacalza family could, in agreement with GPI, further increase its stake in Camfin to 20% and then up to a maximum of 25%, without negatively affecting GPI's control over Camfin. If there was an increase in the shareholding, GPI and the Malacalza family also undertook to negotiate a shareholders' agreement that would give the latter the typical rights of an industrial shareholder with strategic importance, with rules that would guarantee them adequate representation on the corporate bodies of Camfin.

It was a perspective whereby the control of Camfin by GPI would thus not be affected.[12] In the second half of 2009 the Group's prospects began to appear more promising, thanks to the success achieved in the recently implemented strategies and in the incisive actions of the management. The core business in tyres showed significant growth, the equity increase of Pirelli RE had been well received by the market that had supported the initiative, while the deals to strengthen the capital position of Camfin and the entrance of the new shareholder had given greater stability to the chain of control.[13] However, the persistent and significant commitment that Pirelli maintained as controlling shareholder of Pirelli Re, with a stake of 57.99%, continued to be difficult for the market to understand and the market continued underestimating the value of Pirelli and its core business.

For all these reasons, and especially as a result of the persisting crisis, at the end of 2009 the management of Pirelli began to consider a further reorganisation of the real estate sector. This included the idea of allocating the shares in the subsidiary,

---

12  A fundamental role in both the industrial and financial reorganisation of GPI and Camfin was played by the CEO Giorgio Bruno, who had been a person of trust for the Tronchetti Provera family for 20 years since joining the Group in 1990 alongside Silvio Tronchetti Provera, Marco's father. He went on to hold increasingly responsible positions in the companies at the top of the chain.

13  The reinforcement of Camfin also recorded the arrival of Enrico Parazzini as managing director of the company on 31 July 2009. After joining Pirelli in 1992, Parazzini had been the Chief Financial Officer of Telecom between 1 October 2001 and 8 August 2008, when he left the telecommunications company.

Pirelli Re, directly to the Pirelli shareholders. As regards Pirelli, the likelihood of no longer being the parent company of Pirelli Re allowed the tyre company to put an end to its commitment in the real estate business. In this way the market would be able to understand the Pirelli business better, evaluate the history of its performance more accurately and place a higher value on its full potential.

This deal, however, which allocated the ordinary shares and savings shares of Pirelli Re pro rata to the shareholders of Pirelli, did not completely sever the link between the real estate company and the Pirelli Group, but rather transferred it directly to some of Pirelli's shareholders. This deal allowed the small shareholders, but also possibly some of the members of the Pirelli voting trust, to liquidate their shares in Pirelli Re that they had been allocated, but its foundation was Camfin which, with a stake of 14.8%, assumed the role of reference shareholder in the real estate company, which now changed its name from Pirelli Re to Prelios.

This operation on the one hand underlined the responsible attitude assumed by Camfin, but on the other, it was a necessary step. In fact, the creditor banks of the real estate company asked for and obtained not only that Pirelli maintain a credit line of €150 million for five years, but also that a voting trust be stipulated among the major shareholders of the real estate company, so that the company could count on a stable shareholder structure as a requisite to develop new business prospects (4 May 2010). The new Group reorganisation made it possible to significantly reduce the discount that the market had applied to Pirelli. The market conditions, conversely, did not allow the exploitation of a control premium for the stake that Pirelli held in Pirelli Re (4 May 2010).

While the long procedural phases unwound in the reallocation of ownership of the real estate company, the process to strengthen the equity position of the Pirelli parent companies also continued. In the context of establishing a new mission for the real estate business, which had earlier been in the hands of Carlo Puri Negri, and in the light of the new presence of the Malacalza family as an industrial partner in Camfin, it appeared reasonable that the latter, at a price of €25 million, should take over the 30.94% stake in GPI from Fratelli Puri Negri, a limited partnership joint stock company. The growing importance of the presence of the Genoese family among the body of shareholders of the parent companies of Pirelli[14] however,

---

14  At the time when the Camfin Board was given the information on the successful operation, GPI held 47.1% of Camfin (30 July 2010) and Malacalza Investimenti held 12.1%. The stake

did not change the control over the Group, which remained firmly in the hands of Marco Tronchetti Provera, the controlling shareholder of GPI. His role was clearly guaranteed by the terms of agreement with the Malacalza family.

In the period between the sale of the stake in Olimpia and the summer of 2010, the Chairman of Pirelli had profoundly restructured the Group. Pirelli's new focus on its core business and a robust action by the management had had the effect of transforming Pirelli profoundly. Out of a production of 53 million standard tyres in 2007, 14 million had been cancelled, while another 11 million would be cancelled by the end of 2011 with the purpose of converting the entire cancelled production into a similar quantity of tyres for the high-end sector with greater added value. In order to support its choice of a growing presence in the high end, Pirelli once again became sole tyre supplier to Formula One[15] for the period 2011–2013, an excellent advertising tool to support a brand that was becoming increasingly attractive, along with its entry into the world of fashion with the P Zero brand. However, it was not only its involvement in Formula One that conveyed a message of excellence and overall quality that Pirelli intended to disseminate among its shareholders and stakeholders. The renewed attention that the Company devoted to corporate culture and its brand as a philosophy of life for a multinational, and to the communication of its values in a wide variety of forms – from the Pirelli Calendar to the reorganisation of its Historical Archives and the establishment and enhancement of the Fondazione Hangar – looked to underline Pirelli's ability to be a successful global economic player, capable of making the most of a brand which could show the world the extraordinary abilities of the Italians. For these reasons, Pirelli was preparing to launch a new three-year plan from 2011 to 2013 and a five-year outlook until 2015.

---

held by Malacalza Investimenti had risen from 3.5% to 12.1% following the acquisition of 8.6% of the shares and warrants of Camfin.

15 The Formula One tyres are produced at the plant in Izmit. *Corriere della Sera Motori* of 15 October 2010 mentions in this regard: 'There is a great tradition of craftsmanship, which is absolutely fundamental for Pirelli's adventure in Formula One'. Also in this situation, the technical and managerial skills of Maurizio Boiocchi were crucial to the success in Formula One, making it a business case study of enormous academic significance.

## TABLE 14.2. SOME OF THE PIRELLI GROUP
### FUNDAMENTALS OVER THE PERIOD 2007–2010

| Fundamentals of the Pirelli Group (figures in € millions) | 2007 Pirelli[a] | 2008 Pirelli[a] | 2010 Pirelli[b] |
|---|---|---|---|
| Revenues | 6,505 | 4,660 | 4,848 |
| Net result | 323 | (413) | 4 |
| Cash flow | 299 | 0 | 167 |
| Net debt (cash) | (302) | 1,828 | 455 |
| Shareholders' equity | 3,804 | 2,374 | 1,990 |
| No. of employees | 30,813 | 31,056 | 29,573 |
| No. of plants | 24 | 23 | 20 |

[a]*Pirelli Tyre and Real Estate.*
[b]*Only Pirelli Tyre.*
*Source: Our calculations from official documentation provided by Pirelli*

# CHAPTER 15

# A Premium Global Player

While in the latter half of 2010 the macroeconomic situation continued to turn for the worse, shelving the promises of rapid improvement that had marked the beginning of the year, Pirelli launched its new three-year plan for 2011–2013 with a possible extension until 2015. It was the first business plan that the Group had launched as a pure tyre company that generated 98% of its turnover from tyres. The features of the plan were purely industrial; indeed, there were no mergers or acquisitions, nor equity increases. In addition, the plan was completely focused on the premium and prestige segments and did not envisage any kind of investment in the production of standard tyres other than spares.

The purpose of the plan was to complete the reorganisation process started in 2007. The brilliant management efforts shown in the previous years had allowed Pirelli to relocate approximately 75% of its production to countries with lower production costs and higher economic growth,[1] and the intention was by 2015 to achieve a level of 60% of production capacity in facilities that were less than 10 years in age. To achieve this result an investment programme was launched of around €1.9 billion in the three years covered by the plan, with the aim of increasing gross profitability from 7.5% to 11.5% in 2013. In the face of a car market in obvious distress, the high-end replacement parts segment – to which Pirelli had

---

1    In an interview with *Il Sole 24 Ore* dated 19 February 2012, in answer to a journalist's question on the positioning strategy of Pirelli in China, Tronchetti Provera said: 'The same strategy that is driving the expansion of the Group in other countries in the emerging world such as Mexico, Russia and Romania: producing high end tyres. It is no coincidence that today our Yanzhou factory is the only one in China dedicated exclusively to the production of premium segment tyres and is also the only one to have gained approval for the provision of original equipment for vehicles made by BMW, Audi, Mercedes and Volvo. The market for luxury saloon cars in the country is growing. However today's top-range tyres are installed on SUVs and also on smaller cars with powerful engines that need to travel safely. Even these cars, I'm thinking for example of SUVs, are increasingly popular in China and in all emerging markets.'

devoted increasing attention – showed a potential growth rate of around 7% per annum. Similarly, across the tyre sector, the overall anticipated growth rate was estimated to be 5.2%, compared with a 3.1% increase in the car fleet. Moreover, the high end demonstrated growth trends that were more stable over time and less sensitive to economic cycles.

In 2011 the macroeconomic situation in Europe recorded a further worsening. The financial crisis of 2007 and 2008, known in the Anglosphere as the Great Financial Depression, was superseded at the beginning of the summer by a violent lack of confidence in the actual capacity of some eurozone countries to reimburse the huge public debts that they had accumulated over time. A foreshadowing of the sovereign debt crisis could be seen in the difficulties faced by Greece over at least two years; the crisis then exploded with such violence that many doubted the very survival of the euro and the plan for political and economic integration that had characterised it. A wave of pessimism, negativity and suspicion spread almost unchecked through Europe, once again jeopardising the Kantian Utopia of 'perpetual peace'. European difficulties did not have particularly severe effects on Pirelli's accounts, since the systematic geographical dislocation of its turnover constituted a source of excellent diversification of its macroeconomic and corporate risks. Moreover, the Group's plans envisaged investments in areas of the world less affected by the crisis, such as Brazil and Russia.

Although it had for some time been among the priorities of Pirelli, Russia was an ongoing project. During the course of 2011, some important advances were made with this project. Within the sphere of the existing framework agreement with Russian Technologies, an opportunity emerged to forge a partnership with Sibur Russian Tyres, the leading Russian tyre manufacturer, which led to the creation of two joint ventures, one of which under the control of Pirelli and Russian Technologies for Pirelli tyres. To achieve this result, two production plants located in Kirov and in Voronezh were used with an estimated running capacity of 10 million tyres for an investment of about €200 million. The second joint venture had three plants in Yaroslav, Voltyre and Omsk devoted respectively to tyres for cars, agriculture and goods vehicles. The total investment was to the tune of €425 million, of which 226 for the purchase of the two factories and the remainder for upgrading them to Pirelli standards.

The market analysis and the strategic choices made by Pirelli in the preparation of the multi-year plan were confirmed by the results achieved. The 2010 financial statements turned out to be far better than forecast, allowing the Company to revise upwards its sales and profitability objectives from spring 2011 onwards, thus achieving in a shorter period of time of the objectives set a few months previously in the business plan. In the light of this more positive scenario, Pirelli updated its business plan for the period 2012–2014, while looking ahead to 2015, with the stated goal of transforming itself from a macro regional premium player into a global premium player. This review of the business plan envisaged a three-year growth in revenues from €5.8 to €7.7 billion, an increase of gross profitability to up to 16% in 2015 and further expansion in the geographical localisation of the Group in Indonesia. Meanwhile, Pirelli was celebrating its 140th anniversary and was launching itself into the future with an exhortative 'Fast Forward', used as the motto for the Executive Convention in December 2011. Pirelli's global action was significantly reinforced with the vigorous relaunch in North America led by Paolo Ferrari, who joined the Group in January 2012, bringing a rapid and incisive turnaround in the area under his responsibility.

When the business plan was completed in early 2012, a new organisational model was launched to reduce the distance between customer needs, market trends and information accessed by top management. The new model not only envisaged considerable cost savings, but also allowed the top management to develop their own strategies as they were continually in touch with company operations. This reorganisation was aimed at overcoming the traditional division between corporate functions and the business, and established five functions at the centre of the decision-making process and linked directly to the Chief Executive Officer. The goal of becoming a global premium player depended on Pirelli's ability to attract market shares in the parts sector, closely linked to the ability of the Company to obtain approvals in the standard equipment for cars in the prestige and premium segment. The new organisational model also meant the Group's General Manager, Francesco Gori,[2] would be leaving the Company.

Within three years, between 2009 and 2012, the capitalisation of Pirelli had doubled, rising from €2.2 to €4.5 billion and then reaching €5.3 billion on 6 November 2013, in time for the presentation of the business plan for the period 2013–2017. More recently, the other offer launched in the summer of 2015 on the entire

---

2  Numerous newspaper articles talk about the involvement of Francesco Gori alongside the Malacalza family in the contest that took place among GPI and Camfin shareholders between the summers of 2012 and 2013.

Pirelli equity evaluated the current value of equity at €7.5 million. This important enhancement in value was also achieved thanks to the growing interest that the Company continued to arouse in institutional investors, whose presence had increased significantly over the same period, rising from 16% to 27% of the equity.

TABLE 15.1. DYNAMICS IN THE CAPITALISATION OF
THE PIRELLI GROUP[a] IN THE PERIOD 2009–2013

| Business model | Conglomerate | Pure tyre company | Premium regional player | Global premium player | Business Plan 2013–2017 | Tender offer |
|---|---|---|---|---|---|---|
| Capitalisation in € billions | 2.2 | 3 | 3.2 | 4.5 | 5.3 | 7.5 |

[a]At mid-2012, the market capitalisation of Pirelli's main competitors was as follows
(in € billions): Michelin 10.2; Bridgestone 14.6; Goodyear 2.1; Continental 14.8;
Hankook 4.8 and Nokian 4.7.
Source: From minutes of Pirelli & C. SpA Board Meeting (Book 47)

In order to gain further appreciation for its efforts in the eyes of institutional investors, the Company continued along its course towards total compliance in terms of transparency and the devices used to combat corruption, as well as with respect to corporate governance and sustainable growth. This specific feature of Pirelli allowed it to offset, at least partially, the increasingly modest standards of system governance expressed by Italy at the level of international indices. In the face of the increased presence of institutional investors in the capital of Pirelli, the chain of control also recorded the arrival of Massimo Moratti in the share capital of GPI. During 2011, the latter had decided to liquidate a portion of the shareholding in Pirelli & C. SpA, reducing it from 1.19% to 0.49%. At the same time he acquired 6.5% of GPI from the partnership limited by shares called MTP which thus reduced its grip on the subsidiary from 61.89% to 55.39%. Nevertheless, these changes in the ownership structure of GPI did not have any effect on Camfin and its corporate governance. Furthermore, Pirelli's brilliant results helped to improve the solidity of Camfin's economic and financial situation, after the latter had acquired debts to support Pirelli and then Olimpia in implementing the Telecom-TIM merger that the technological evolution in the telecommunications sector had required at the time. After the sale of Pirelli's stake in Olimpia, Camfin had obtained a loan of €420 million from a pool of banks, led by Unicredito. The contract provided for two separate lines of credit, the first of which, the so-called 'A' line of 170 million, was to be paid back before the end of 2012, while the remaining 250 million that made up the 'B' line, had to be paid back in two instalments of equal value at the end of 2014 and 2015.

The transfer of Camfin's residual assets would not be enough to satisfy the repayment of the first instalment of the loan, which had, however, been reduced to €137.5 million due to early repayment of €32.5 million by the company in December 2011. Nevertheless the excellent performance of the investment in Pirelli & C. allowed a regular flow of dividends in favour of Camfin and the possibility of using shares that were not bound by any shareholders' agreement as an asset to underpin the creation of a financial transaction geared towards repayment of the debt, without resorting to equity increases or selling part of the same shareholding.

For these reasons the Camfin Board ruled unanimously not to proceed with the sale of the unrestricted shares in Pirelli or with an equity increase, but to assess whether it was possible to identify, as expressly provided for in the agreements, 'other operations or initiatives to be agreed with the pool of banks that would enable fulfilment of the same objective'. In a manner consistent with those guidelines, the management of Camfin, in its negotiations with the lender banks, moved towards the idea of issuing bonds as a simple or convertible loan that may be listed or unlisted, 'in order to find the best solution for paying off the line of credit that was about to expire'.

This topic was the subject of analysis in several Board meetings, yet none of the directors of the Company ever raised even the slightest concern regarding the proposal. Nevertheless, in the Board of Camfin the Deputy Chairman, Vittorio Malacalza, stated his clear preference for the option of an equity increase. Faced with such an abrupt change in prospects expressed by Malacalza Investimenti, Camfin's second shareholder, Tronchetti Provera took the plunge and summoned the Company's Board for a meeting on 10 August that was originally planned for 29 September.

Just before the date for the Board meeting, Camfin received a letter written jointly by Unicredit and Banca IMI in which the two lender banks who had participated in the financing agreements in 2009 declared their willingness to consider alternative solutions, including the possibility of a debenture loan convertible into

Pirelli & C. shares owned by Camfin and not part of the shareholders' agreement, with a time period of about 3–5 years. In support of this hypothesis, Banca Leonardo, Camfin's advisor, filed a separate independent opinion outlining the critical issues associated with a possible equity increase due to 'aspects linked to external and internal market factors relating to the company's situation and its share'.[3] The director Malacalza took the opposite view. According to him, the best solution lay in an increase in capital. A wound that was difficult to heal had been created within the body of shareholders in Camfin and in that of its parent company, GPI. The directors representing Malacalza Investimenti also decided to refrain from approving the interim report of Camfin as at 30 June 2012. Two days before, Davide Malacalza had voted against the adoption of the half-yearly accounts of Prelios. A few days later, on 5 September 2012, the Board of GPI approved an equity increase of €45 million.

The clash grew more bitter during the next meeting of the Board of Camfin, which stretched over two days between 10 and 11 October 2012, and was preceded by a writ of summons issued by the shareholder Malacalza Investimenti in relation to the decisions adopted by the Board on 10 August. Faced with this letter, Tronchetti Provera did not waste any time before reacting. The willingness of the Ligurian company to assist Camfin in its hypothetical increase in equity had the opposite effect of bolstering Camfin's reference shareholder in its belief that behind the desire of Malacalza Investmenti to support the equity increase of Camfin lurked a hidden desire to launch 'a hostile takeover bid at the expense of the market and at a rock-bottom price'. On 11 October 2012 the Board of Camfin passed a resolution

---

3   The Board minutes of 10 August 2012 also emphasise that 'Moreover, the equity increase of Camfin would surely have a feeble equity story, since it was entirely geared to the repayment of the financial debt with an inevitable clash over the TERP that could be quantified on average between 25% and 35% in view of recent experiences in similar operations.' *Il Sole 24 Ore* on 15 August 2012 writes: 'The recapitalisation was probably shelved by the Board for five reasons. Firstly the fragile times in the market, combined with the characteristics of the Camfin share, could make it a prohibitively expensive operation. However, given the recent practice, a rather rounded contest over the TERP would be more than likely, with the result that by already quoting Camfin at a discount on the NAV of around 65%, the recapitalisation would be excessively diluted. In addition, in order to hold down costs, GPI might have to be part of the underwriting syndicate, and if it were to shoulder more than 5% of the capital, it could spark off the obligation of a takeover bid at a knock-down price by the holding, with double penalties for small shareholders. Moreover, the injected resources are needed for the moment, to repay the debt and not for development.'

issuing a bond convertible into shares in Pirelli & C., with votes against cast by the directors representing Malacalza Investmenti. This convertible bond was for €150 million over five years and with a conversion premium of between 27.5% and 32.5% of the current price. The convertible bond had great success on the market and the completion of this operation enabled the stabilisation of the financial structure of the Company.

The clash that had occurred between the shareholders of Camfin and GPI had made it a matter of pressing urgency to establish a more cohesive ownership structure supporting Pirelli & C. The whole affair risked destabilising the tyre company's shareholder structure, whose composition had significantly changed over recent years, with mainly foreign institutional investors holding about 35% of the share capital of the Company. Finding a generally acceptable solution turned out to be no easy matter.

The position assumed by Malacalza Investmenti was contrary to the spirit and the letter of the agreements it had established with the GPI shareholders in 2009[4] and reconfirmed subsequently in 2011. The collaboration that the Genovese family had offered to Tronchetti Provera was of an industrial nature, but did not envisage in any shape or form, not even in a surreptitious manner, a change in the solitary control over GPI – and indirectly over Camfin – exercised by the Chairman of Pirelli. Some large Pirelli shareholders, such as Intesa Sanpaolo through the words of its managing director, also expressed their opinion in favour of Tronchetti Provera.[5]

In the face of the unwillingness of Malacalza Investmenti to yield its stakes in GPI and Camfin, the dispute reached stalemate. The excellent performance of

---

4   The aforementioned minutes of the Board of Directors' meeting of Camfin on 12 June 2009, which highlight the fundamental nature of the control of GPI over Camfin, reads: 'If the development in the partnership proves satisfactory for GPI, the Malacalza family could, with the agreement of GPI, further increase their stake in Camfin to 20% and even to a maximum of 25%, without this in any way affecting the control that GPI has over Camfin. In the event of an increase in the stake, GPI and the Malacalza family have also undertaken to negotiate a shareholder agreement which grants rights to the latter, typical of an industrial shareholder with strategic importance, with rules ensuring adequate representation in the governing bodies of Camfin.'

5   *Il Sole 24 Ore* of 8 September 2012 contains the following statement by Enrico Cucchiani: 'The leadership of Tronchetti Provera is indisputable. Tronchetti is the author of the successes of Pirelli and is Pirelli: I believe he is one of the best known and most successful Italian entrepreneurs and is appreciated not only in Italy, but all over the world.'

the tyre company in recent years had also allowed significant improvements in the value of the companies upstream of Pirelli, and this was the reason why 'the return on investment achieved by the Malacalza Group is one of the best recorded performances in the financial markets', given that the capital had doubled in a period of less than four years.

The solution came into view a few months later within the broader context of a restructuring of the ownership structure of Pirelli & C. The prologue to this solution was seen in the discontinuance of the function performed up to that point by the shareholders' agreement. At the beginning of 2013 the market was informed that the shareholders' agreement that supported Pirelli would only be renewed for a period of one year until 15 April 2014. In addition, some members of the agreement, including Allianz with 4.41%, Fondiaria Sai with 2.57% and Camfin with a share of 7%, applied for and obtained the release of these stakes from the shareholders' agreement which consequently consisted of a grouping in the equity of just over 30%. This solution, which hinted at the likely dissolution of the shareholders' agreement, established the conditions for organising a complex operation whose aim was: 'the development and growth of Pirelli's value as an expression of excellence within the sphere of Italian industry, as well as the role of Tronchetti Provera in the agreed strategic policies of Pirelli and in the directional management of the Group headed by Pirelli itself'.

A new company was set up called Lauro Sessantuno SpA, consisting of Tronchetti Provera, the shareholders of GPI, Clessidra, Intesa Sanpaolo and Unicredit. The new company had a 60.99% stake in the share capital of Camfin, having purchased investments of 12.37% from Malacalza Investmenti and of 13.2% from Marco Tronchetti Provera Partecipazioni, respectively. In addition Nuove Partecipazioni[6] assigned 29.45% of Camfin held by GPI to Lauro Sessantuno. The last portion of 5.96% was transferred by Vittoria Assicuraziioni and by Carlo Acutis, a long-standing Camfin shareholder. The release of the shares of some members of the shareholders' agreement had made the disinvestment of the stakes of Malacalza Investimenti in the upper levels of the chain of control possible and immediate subsequent reinvestment in Pirelli's equity with a shareholding of about 7%, acquired directly from Allianz and Fonsai.

---

6   The shareholders of Nuove Partecipazioni include various GPI shareholders, including the Acutis and Rovati families. The latter had acquired 25% of the company owned by the family of Tronchetti Provera, called MTP SpA, through Rottapharm.

Lauro Sessantuno launched a takeover bid for the remaining part of the capital of Camfin[7] at an initial price of €0.80 per share (which was subsequently raised to €0.83 per share by resolution of CONSOB), before proceeding with removing it from the list and with the merger by incorporation, using the same special purpose vehicle that had launched the takeover bid. Following the operations described above, the ownership structure of the company that was the reference shareholder of Pirelli & C. was as follows: the two banks each held an 18.85% stake, Lauro Cinquantaquattro (i.e. Clessidra SGR) had 24.6% and Nuove Partecipazioni had 37.7%.

The prospect of the agreement also included the possibility of a sale in four years with ratios double the current enhanced value of the capital by Nuove Partecipazioni; if this did not take place, the put option would pass to Clessidra, without any specific ratio. The deal as described would stabilise the ownership structure of Pirelli & C.'s parent companies and issue a major industrial challenge that consisted of a significant increase in value of the tyre company's equity over the medium term, albeit in a time of difficulty for the market. From this point of view the entire deal bore characteristics similar to those of a private equity operation of enormous proportions. To achieve this objective, it was necessary for the market to be able to increase the value of the Company as much as possible and therefore disengage itself from the constraints of the shareholders' agreement. In the autumn of 2013 the early dissolution was confirmed of the shareholders' agreement – which was due to expire anyway in the spring of 2014 – which grouped together 31.54% of the share capital in Pirelli & C. SpA. To find the right balance between the two potentially conflicting requirements, the reorganisation involved 'two national credit intermediaries and one medium-term investor'. In an overall sense, these parties may be considered as investors intended to accompany the Company over a reasonable period of time.

While the tyre business was continuing to develop according to the guidelines of the previously adopted business plan, with constant attention being paid to the dynamics of new approvals, the real estate business continued to cause concern. From a formal point of view, following the operation to allocate the property company shares pro rata to the shareholders of Pirelli, the latter was no longer a

---

7    The offer concerned the 36.52% stake, while the 2.5% of the Camfin shares held by Massimo Moratti would be the subject of dealings with Tronchetti Provera and assigned to Sessantuno.

shareholder of the real estate company, even though it still had credit lines that had allowed the former Pirelli Re to operate as a going concern. Nevertheless, in order to initiate a more systematic business organisation plan, the owners of Prelios, with the approval and support of the two shareholder-lender banks, decided to look for new shareholders with whom they could develop possible industrial partnerships. In this regard Prelios received two expressions of interest, the first from the American Fund Fortress and the second from a group of Italian entrepreneurs headed by Feidos. The Board expressed its preference for the second bid since it was more likely to make the most of the real estate company's assets and do so in a more thorough manner. While the Fortress offer was geared mainly towards management services, the Feidos offer also took into consideration 'real estate investments in partnership with leading national and international operators, with whom Prelios assumed investment commitments that are still in place'.

The entry of Feidos in Prelios' equity was of great industrial importance, geared towards a significant enhancement of its capital with a view to a sale within a period of five years. From a financial point of view, the entire equity increase operation amounted to €185 million, consisting of an actual capital increase of €100 million with another €85 million raised through securitisation. After completion of the first phase of the operation, Pirelli found that it held 17% of Prelios. Subsequently, Prelios issued a convertible bond for €233.5 million, subscribed by the company's financiers, including Pirelli, for a total of about €146 million. The purpose of Pirelli taking part in the reorganisation of Prelios was to maximise the value of the financial receivables held by Pirelli against the real estate company. Overall, the debt was reduced from about €560 million to a more sustainable level of about €250 million.

However, the reorganisation of the Camfin ownership structure and the Prelios business was only a backdrop to the success that Pirelli achieved in the market as an incomparable leader in the prestige segment and with increasing market shares in the premium segment, strengthened by the partnerships signed with major European car manufacturers. This intelligent combination of premium products, of relationships with leading car manufacturers, of geographical areas of production as well as sales distribution channels, bolstered with the acquisition of distribution networks in Brazil and Sweden, 'have allowed Pirelli to achieve better results compared with the market'.

To further accommodate the trends that were emerging from the market, additional changes were made to the organisational chart launched in the spring of the previous year. In particular, the position of General Manager of Operations was established, bringing together industrial activities, logistics, marketing and sales under his responsibility.

This latest reorganisation was in preparation for the launch of the strategic plan for 2013–2017 (initially scheduled for the summer and then postponed to 6 November 2013 in London) so that the future prospects could be better defined. The conditions of the business plan were aimed at a further significant increase in the profitability and enhanced value of the capital of Pirelli, a difficult challenge for a company that had already seen an increase between 2009 and 2014 of two-and-a-half times its value, despite the economic crisis at the time. For these reasons, the new plan envisaged an increase in turnover from €6.2 billion to €7.5 billion in 2017 with an average annual growth rate of 6.5%, an increase in profitability to a threshold above 15% of EBIT, a return on investment of 28% compared to 20% in 2013, a gross cash flow of about €3 billion, about €1.6 billion of which is to be allocated to serving investment almost entirely dedicated to the consumer segment and to dividends of about €700 million, and to reducing debt by €850 million with the aim of reducing net debt to somewhere under €500 million compared to €1.4 billion expected by the end of 2013. Pirelli's strategy, as contained in the new plan, intends to increase volumes in the premium and prestige segments, by progressively reducing standard production and consolidating its presence in the medium segment. From a geographical point of view, the plan reiterates the centrality of leadership in Latin America and highlights the strategic role of Russia. The capital market gave a favourable welcome to the new plan, having clearly understood the path for development undertaken by Pirelli in line with what was agreed with the new group of reference shareholders in the summer of 2013. From this point of view, the new plan offers an intriguing insight into a possible future structure of Pirelli. In the past, the stability in control was also guaranteed by large shareholders gathered in a shareholders' agreement, whereas in the future this will need to be guaranteed by achieving stable results in an increasingly demanding market. However, the prospects which allow potentially divergent objectives to run parallel to each other move through the search for innovative and potentially viable industrial solutions in a globalised world, via alliances with other industry players and yet guaranteed by the presence among its shareholders of long-term national and international financial investors. In this respect, the ownership structure of Pirelli's parent companies marked an important step forward. From June 2013 onwards, when the agreement with Clessidra, Intesa Sanpaolo and Unicredito was sealed, the value of

Pirelli shares rose by around 50%, from about €8 to €12 per share. This result made the possible realisation of the investment quite appetising both for the banks and for private equity. With regard to this matter, an interesting new element entered the story. An account has already been given above about how Pirelli began investing in Russia in 2008, with Russian Technology as its industrial partner, with the revamping of two plants owned by Sibur. Pirelli soon realised that its weak point in Russia was its distribution channels. In this regard, an analysis was conducted regarding the possibility of using the sales networks of the truck manufacturer Kamaz and the car manufacturer Autovaz,[8] but these channels proved unsuitable. These companies advised Pirelli to contact Rosneft,[9] which has a network of 2,900 petrol stations in Russia, a potentially excellent network for the distribution of Pirelli tyres, although it would be in a multi-brand context, as is customary in that country. At the same time, Rosneft was interested in upgrading its distribution network. Another area of common interest was research within the most advanced areas of chemistry, where Pirelli had established some important partnerships, especially in the area of synthetic rubbers.

For these reasons, the cooperation between Rosneft and Pirelli immediately proved to be rich in opportunities for development, so much so that the Chief Executive Officer of Rosneft, Igor Ivanovich Sechin,[10] imagined investing directly in Pirelli and immediately found a willingness among its financial shareholders to become involved. Following the preliminary signed agreements, Rosneft itself indicated an important Russian investor as a party to the definitive agreements. This party took over half the stake of 26.2% held by Camfin in Pirelli & C., taking over Clessidra's entire stake and a share of 8.4%, respectively, from Intesa Sanpaolo and Unicredito, for a total of €552.7 million. The new agreement relaunched with

---

8  Autovaz, in which Renault owns a significant equity interest, was established in the 1960s in a joint venture with Fiat.

9  After purchasing the Yukos assets at an auction, Rosneft became the largest Russian oil company, with a production of about 150 million tons a year. British Petroleum has a 20% stake in Rosneft.

10  There is not a lot of information available about Igor Ivanovich Sechin. He apparently graduated in 1984 in French and Portuguese at Leningrad (St Petersburg) State University. Later he moved to work in Mozambique as an interpreter. In 1991 he apparently returned to Russia to work in the St Petersburg town hall, where he became Head of Staff to Vladimir Putin. He also followed Putin in his later political career, becoming in August 1999 Head of the Secretariat of the Prime Minister. He has been CEO of Rosneft since 27 July 2004.

greater force the philosophy of the previous one, by replacing the institutional private equity shareholder with an industrial one with greater financial strength, but with an expectation of a lower financial return and over a longer term, i.e. five years from 2014, renewable for another three. Furthermore, the new agreement placed the entire governance and prospect choices in the hands of the Board of Pirelli, confirming confidence in the Company's CEO as management representative and confirming that he should continue in his position, as is clear from the nature of the agreement. The Russian strategic investor was a shareholder of an industrial nature which could help Pirelli to achieve the objectives set out in the business plan for 2013–2017, while not prospectively constituting a constraint as regards any alliance or integration with any industries in the sector, nor as regards the strategic interests of Pirelli or Italy.

At the end of 2013 Pirelli was completely different from the company it was five years before: it had left behind the crisis which had hit the economies of the West in 2008, and had rebuilt its own identity and strategy that could be called 'the new normal' way of being Pirelli. In addition to the growth in turnover, there were also significant improvements in operative results which accompanied an overall improvement in all areas. The international financial markets promptly responded to the operative performance.

TABLE 15.2. COMPANY ACCOUNTS OF THE PIRELLI
GROUP (TYRE ONLY) IN THE PERIOD 2008–2013

|  | 2008 | 2009 | 2010 | 2011 | 2012 | 2013 |
|---|---|---|---|---|---|---|
| Profit | 4.660 | 4.462 | 4.848 | 5.655 | 6.072 | 6.146 |
| EBIT | 43 | 217 | 408 | 582 | 781 | 791 |
| Net result | (413) | (23) | 4 | 441 | 398 | 307 |
| Investment | 311 | 225 | 433 | 626 | 471 | 413 |
| Net financial position | 1.028 | 529 | 546 | 737 | 1.205 | 1.322 |

*Source: Our elaboration of official data Pirelli & C.*

The idea that the strategic Russian investor does not constitute any obstacle regarding wider alliances was further confirmed during the summer of 2014.

Indeed, the project took on an innovative and unexpected form which surprised the market positively, and was well received by European public opinion. Tronchetti Provera had always been unfavourable to integration between large operators in the same sector as he was convinced that this did not create value. This was the spirit that was encountered in the late 1990s with the photonic activity developed by Pirelli at Cisco and Corning, which was a union of complementary objectives, and the same spirit was behind the 2006 agreement between Telecom Italia and News Corporation.

Tronchetti Provera contemplated an analogous perspective for Pirelli and had already undertaken an innovative shift away from the leitmotif of the 21st-century 'Drang nach Osten' with his agreement with the Russian investor based on the principle of complementarity as it envisaged the commercial penetration of the Russian market and collaboration in the advanced synthetic rubber sector. Now, even more prospects were opening up further to the east, in China.

TABLE 15.3. DYNAMICS OF CAPITALISATION
OF PIRELLI AND PEERS 2008–2013

| Peers | Percentage variation of market capitalisation (December 2013 vs. December 2008) |
|---|---|
| Pirelli | +301.39 |
| Michelin | +157.6 |
| Bridgestone | +175.0 |
| Goodyear | +293.1 |
| Continental | +441.0 |
| Stoxx Auto & Parts | +129.7 |
| Ftse MIB | −4.4 |

*Source: Bloomberg*

# CHAPTER 16

# Pirelli's New Perspectives and Challenges

D ifferent drivers led Pirelli to seek an international joint venture in order to develop, in an innovative way, its core business. To better understand what was behind this choice, it is useful to summarise briefly the main trends in the tyre market. As has been highlighted in the previous chapters, Pirelli had been progressively focusing its attention on the business of supercar tyres for a number of years, because as Tronchetti Provera asserted in Pirelli's Board of Directors' meeting of 6 November 2014: 'these markets are growing at three times the rate of the standard market, also because of the increasing number of homologations (for original equipment) obtained by Pirelli with the car makers'.

In fact, in 2014 Pirelli registered a remarkable 17.8% growth rate in the prestige and premium segments, the average between a 9% growth rate in mature markets and a 20% rate in emerging ones, largely exceeding the average market rate of growth of 6.8%. Notwithstanding these very promising outcomes, in Tronchetti Provera's perspective the chances of value creation for Pirelli were still significant, for two different reasons. First of all, Pirelli would have been able to support its growth in the superpremium market in the very fast-growing regions of the world, specifically in Asia. Moreover, it was possible to recognise significant still unexploited growth opportunities in the industrial tyre sector, where Pirelli's size was still not fully satisfying. These issues had been first considered in the presentation of the 2013–2017 Pirelli business plan which took place in London on 6 November 2013. With specific regard to the industrial tyre sector, the business plan acknowledged that Pirelli was certainly a top player in terms of profitability, with a significant geographical presence in high-growth countries, specifically in Asia.

With this premise Tronchetti Provera saw the opportunity of a value-creating joint venture with an industrial entity connected, but not exclusively involved in the tyre sector. According to Tronchetti Provera's well-conceived point of view, deals featuring industrial entities not belonging to the same industrial sectors could create the most value, as occurred in 2014 in the deal with Rosneft. Looking eastwards to the lively Asian economies, the next step was necessarily China.

As has been previously highlighted, Pirelli had been present in the Chinese market since 2005. Initially Pirelli was asked by Mr Niu, a Chinese entrepreneur with diversified activities who had built a truck tyre factory in Yanzhou,[1] between Beijing and Shanghai, to advise him in a properly designed management of his tyre business. For these reasons on 29 July 2005 Pirelli and Mr Niu signed an agreement for a joint venture for the management of its industrial tyre factory, making Pirelli the controlling shareholder and leaving Mr Niu with a significant stake of 40% of the equity, which successively decreased to 25% in 2007. In the following years, in the same area Pirelli opened two other consumer tyre factories[2] respectively in 2007 and in 2010, as well as a steel cord factory which was sold in 2015 to the Dutch producer Bekaert, together with all the steel cord business unit of the Pirelli Group.[3] In the quick succession of years since Pirelli first began operating in China, many remarkable events occurred in the tyre market.

First of all, in 2006 a proper premium tyre market in China did not exist, while in 2008 this had already substantially changed. Pirelli thus refocused its Chinese factory on a 'premium and superpremium' strategy. This idea was consistent with the 'premium and prestige' strategy implemented by Pirelli, which brought the Italian corporation success on a global scale. The overall very fast growth of the Chinese market constituted a promising challenge for Pirelli's business, with an

---

1   The author of this book visited this factory on 2 November 2016, accompanied by Giuseppe Cattaneo, Pirelli's Chief Executive officer for the APAC Region, who incidentally managed the initial deal with Mr Niu and since 2005 has been successfully managing the APAC Region for Pirelli. At the entrance to a quite extensive industrial area, initially promoted by Mr Niu, with factories of different corporations, an outstanding bull statue as an impressive watchdog dominates the scenario, because Niu in Mandarin means 'bull'. Incidentally Yanzhou lies in the Chinese region of Shandong, very close to the birthplace of Confucius.

2   Pirelli has an outstanding manufacturing complex in Yanzhou. These factories show a very innovative concept featured in all the recently built Pirelli factories. Yanzhou, on a definitely larger scale, shows similar features with the Italian plant of Settimo Torinese, near Turin.

3   Pirelli decided to sell the steel cord business unit worldwide because due to its increasing nature as a commodity, the minimum efficient scale was becoming much larger than Pirelli's steel cord business unit. At Pirelli's Shareholders' General Meeting held in Milan on 14 May 2015, on this point Tronchetti asserted: 'In the steel cord business unit Pirelli was endowed by a productive overcapacity of roughly 140% of the needs of our corporation, without having real access to the products of competitors. For this reason we called for an international bidding process, won by Bekaert, the best worldwide steel cord producer.'

anticipated average cumulative rate of growth of 3.6% in comparison with a 2% growth rate in the other markets. Moreover, a high-level international agreement would have eventually opened the door to an innovative perspective for the Industrial Business Unit, as had been resolved in 2013–2017. Notwithstanding the significant rate of return in comparison with competitors, the geography of Pirelli had to be reformulated in an attempt to improve its presence in high-growth areas.

For the above-mentioned reasons, in October 2014 Tronchetti Provera started to explore the possibility of an agreement with China National Tyre & Rubber, the Chinese 'national champion' which was controlled by China National Chemical Corporation (ChemChina).[4] He had met its president, Ren Jianxin, in 2012, and the potential synergies with ChemChina were proving to be interesting. On 22 March 2015 ChemChina and Camfin, respectively as reference shareholders in China National Tyre & Rubber and in Pirelli, signed an agreement[5] 'for a long-term industrial partnership with Pirelli & C. SpA', the key element being 'the continuity and autonomy of the management structure of the Pirelli Group and the continuation of Marco Tronchetti Provera as its CEO'.[6] Even the first line managers

---

4  China National Chemical Corporation (CNCC) was incorporated in 2004 as a state-owned company. It is the largest chemical company in China by revenue, ranking ninth amongst the top 100 chemical companies in the world. In 2013 its total assets reached 44 billion dollars and its sales revenue reached 39 billion dollars. ChemChina production sites and R&D centres are spread across 140 countries and regions around the world. ChemChina covers six business sectors: special chemical materials, basic chemical materials, oil processing, agrochemicals, rubber products, and chemical equipment. ChemChina fully controls Chemical National Rubber Company (CNCR) which in 2013 respectively controlled 42.58% of Aeolus (listed in Shanghai since 2003), 100% of Yellow Sea (incorporated in 1933), 85% of Guilin (incorporated in 2006) and 100% of Double Happiness (incorporated in 1958). CNCR had four production sites in China: Shandong, Shanxi, Henan and Guangxi.

5  In a long interview in *Corriere della Sera* on 24 March 2015 Tronchetti Provera commented: 'We have chosen ChemChina because there is no overlap and it allows us to have direct access to the gigantic Chinese tyre market. Our intention is to consolidate an industrial segment in which Pirelli had a non-optimal dimension. The market of the future is not only this one but Asia in general and that is where we are looking. Pirelli has the technology, competitive products and high profitability which can bring added value thanks to its production capacity and also to its presence in the Aeolus market. Hand-in-hand we intend to develop the premium segment which has also grown three times in consumer terms and in which we have invested much over these few years by opening new factories.'

6  The agreement was commented on as follows by Tronchetti Provera: 'The partnership with a global player such as ChemChina, through its controlled companies, represents a great opportunity for Pirelli. The approach to business, and the strategic vision of China National Chemical Corporation guarantees growth and stability for Pirelli.' The president of

would all be Italian, a fact that was confirmed and approved in the international agreement.

Legal offices, operative headquarters and Pirelli's technology were all to be kept in Italy, and a 90% majority of shareholders' votes was required to resolve upon transferring the operational centre, legal headquarters or the sale of know-how to third parties. These two essential elements were coherent with Pirelli's history, overlapping three centuries. Indeed, after signing the agreement the President of ChemChina declared: 'We do not intend to change what is clearly an Italian company, which will maintain its autonomy, because only its Italian management, its technological capacity, and the prestige of its brand with its 150 years of history can guarantee its development.'

This statement is coherent with the 'China 2025 Plan' whose aim is to convert low value-added Chinese products and services into high value-added items. In order to achieve this outcome, Chinese economic policymakers have addressed their efforts on purchasing Western high-powered branded and well-equipped technological corporations, since these deals would open the door to a better appreciation by the global market of Chinese goods. Incidentally, this transaction was awarded the '2015 Best M&A Deal'.

From an industrial point of view, the premise of this agreement offered significant opportunities for Pirelli in a geographically strategic area characterised by intense growth, and the possibility to create a global player in the industrial tyre sector. Indeed, according to the perspective first mentioned in the 2013–2017 business plan, Pirelli would have eventually carved out its truck tyre, agricultural vehicle tyres and OTR (earthmoving machinery) mainly present in Brazil, Argentina, Turkey, Egypt and China and merged them with Aeolus,[7] a tyre producer listed

---

ChemChina, Ren Jianxin, commented: 'We are very happy to become partners with Marco Tronchetti Provera and his team and to continue to build together a global brand which can become a leader in the tyre market in the world.' Even Long Term Investment (the Rosneft vehicle owning shares in Pirelli) commented on the agreement in the following terms: 'We are happy to be part of the development of this long-term partnership between ChemChina and Pirelli. We are convinced that this operation will fully satisfy the interests of the shareholders.'

7   The company's name, Aelous, recalls the Greek divinity of the wind. The reason for the choice of this name lies in the logical connection with the name of the Chinese state-owned enterprise which produced trucks and was established in 1965. This latter company, named Feng Dong, meaning 'the wind of the spring' in Mandarin, was one of the most important truck manufacturers established by Chinese government in the 1950s. Wind blowing from

on the Shanghai Stock Exchange fully controlled by China National Tyre & Rubber. This integration was supposed to be able to double the volumes of the industrial business of the integrated group from 6 to over 12 million tyres per year, with a specific focus on original equipment and on large fleets. In this way, because of Pirelli's advanced technology, it would be possible to increase the average lifetime of tyres and thus contribute to environmental protection. The corporation stemming from the integration between the industrial sector of Pirelli and Aeolus would be the fourth global player in this business sector.

This transaction had a specific business nature, aiming to create value with a two-headed project in the *industrial* and in the *premium* and *prestige* segments with the objective of taking a leadership role in the market and to increase growth at a global level.

During the following months, the agreement was implemented in these terms. ChemChina acquired the 26.2% stake held by Camfin in Pirelli for a price of €15 per share, for a total of €1.8 billion, thus increasing the valuation of Pirelli's overall equity to €7.4 billion. Acknowledging the fundamental role of Tronchetti Provera as Chief Executive Officer of Pirelli and his managerial role in the Company to guarantee the continuity of Pirelli's corporate culture, all parties would have granted him all management powers and the exclusive right to designate his successor.

Simultaneously, Camfin's shareholders reinvested part of the sums derived from the sale for approximately €1.1 billion. However, while the stake held by the Italian shareholders in Camfin and by Long Term Investment (the vehicle of the Russian strategic investor) were equal, the latter did not intend to reinvest any sum derived from the sale. Consequently, of the previously mentioned initial 35% Camfin stake in Pirelli, the Italian shareholders and Long Term Investment owned respectively 22.37% and 12.63% of the voting capital. Moreover, the terms of the agreement allowed the possible entry of one or more additional shareholders, rebalancing the stake of CNRC to 50.1% and at the same time increasing the overall stake of all the other shareholders to 49.9%.

Following this preliminary operation, it was envisaged that Bidco would launch

---

the east is supposed to provide wellness and prosperity to the Chinese countryside. For this reason, once upon a time Chinese authorities decided to name the state-owned enterprise producing tyres both for trucks and for consumers with another name connected with the wind.

a mandatory public offer of acquisition for the remaining Pirelli & C. SpA shares at €15 per share,[8] for an overall amount of €3.3 billion. These funds were provided for approximately €2.2 billion by the Chinese investor and for the remaining €1.1 billion by the previous Camfin shareholders, specifically €700 million by Italian shareholders and €400 million by Long Term Investment. In this way, the strategic investor who invested €552.7 million in summer 2014 made a handsome 26.6% return. Long Term Investment received €700 million, and reinvested roughly €400 million.

Analysing the above prospects, with ChemChina investing approximately two thirds of the resources necessary to finance the public tender offer of the listed shares, and the delisting of Pirelli, ChemChina emerged with approximately 65% of Pirelli & C. Spa shares, while the remaining Italian and Russian shareholders held approximately 35%. The transaction significantly consolidated Pirelli's industrial tyre segment by opening into a rapidly growing market through the integration with Aeolus, thus more than doubling its production capacity, and bringing its brand and technology to China where such intangibles are mostly lacking. Aeolus paid royalties to Pirelli both for technology and for the use of the brand.

In addition, the deal allowed for renewed attention on the growth of the *premium* and *prestige* segments, which would help the company prepare to relist on the stock exchange through an initial public offering, planned for 2018.[9] On the basis of these agreements, the Chief Executive Officer Tronchetti Provera retained exclusive power to decide when to list the company. The perspective of the relisting of the consumer business unit was consistent both with respecting the expectation of CNRC to consolidate Pirelli's stake, in the context of the 'China 2025 Plan', and with allowing, as appropriate to prepare for the initial public offering, the Chinese shareholder to decrease its stake below the threshold of 50%.

---

8   The agreement also envisaged a voluntary public offer for savings shares at the same price. This offer was conditional upon reaching not less than 30% of the share capital for this type of shares.

9   Pirelli's press release on 19 October 2016 quotes: 'The Board further approved the 2016–2018 industrial plan, with an outlook to 2020, for the Pirelli consumer business units; the sole global player entirely focused on its consumer business. The strategy calls for: 1) strengthened leadership in the high-profitability prestige and premium sectors; 2) a business model more focused on the end consumer (consumer-centred approach); 3) oversight of new business opportunities offered by new and sustainable mobility; 4) the digitalisation of industrial, commercial and management processes, more efficient and based on predictive models made possible thanks to the development of big data and analytics.'

Incidental to preparations for the new listing of the Pirelli consumer business in 2018, the company is devoting specific attention to the issues of digitalisation, according to the spirit of the Industry 4.0 protocol, in order to foster productivity growth.

As was clearly asserted during the Pirelli Board of Directors' meeting of 24 March 2015, two days after the announcement of the deal, this would provide to Pirelli: 'the chance of better monitoring an important geographical area allowing Pirelli to double its volumes in the industrial sector (from 6 million tyres to 12 million tyres), becoming in this way one of the principal players in the industrial tyre sector as well.' In this context, Pirelli could provide not only technical advantages in comparison with the manufacturing process implemented by the Chinese partner, but also explore new perspectives, such as implementation of the Cyber Tyre on tyres of corporate fleets as a distinguishing feature over competitors. Pirelli was developing its Cyber Tyre technology, i.e. the opportunity to collect a multifaceted amount of data, inserting an electronic device in the tyre, in order to allow the user to be informed about all the most relevant variables affecting life, reliability and security of a tyre.

During the summer of 2015 Pirelli and ChemChina began implementation of their agreement. Pirelli had to divide its industrial tyre sector, attributing it to autonomous companies in the different countries in which Pirelli historically developed its industrial tyre business, i.e. Brazil, Egypt, Turkey and China. This process was scheduled to be completed by the end of 2015 in order to spin off these business units into a new incorporated company, Pirelli Industrial, at the beginning of 2016. Pirelli managers were performing due diligence at the same time on the various tyre entities related to ChemChina which could have been merged in due course with Pirelli. Pirelli also signed a renewed commercial agreement with Rosneft, according to which Pirelli would develop new single brand shops in the Rosneft petrol stations in Russia and for the incorporation of a new flagship store entirely devoted to tyres.

According to what had been foreseen in the March agreement, on 11 August 2015 Marco Polo Industrial, a company indirectly controlled by ChemChina, tendered a public offer on 76.58% of the ordinary shares of Pirelli[10] on the market

---

10 According to the latest available information, at the Shareholders' General Meeting of 14 May 2016, prior to the launch of the tender offer the most relevant shareholders of Pirelli

(the remainder of the shares were already held by ChemChina, because they had been previously conferred by Camfin). The same operation was repeated for the outstanding shares of Pirelli without voting rights. The public offer promoted by Marco Polo was successfully completed on 13 October 2015 with the availability of 87% of the ordinary shares of Pirelli and with 84% of the shares without voting rights. Days later, during the Board of Directors' meeting of 20 October 2015, in compliance with the agreement signed in the previous month of March, four Russian directors and one Italian director resigned and Ren Jianxin was appointed Chairman of Pirelli.[11] He was the first person not belonging to the Pirelli-Tronchetti Provera family over 143 years and four generations to serve as Chairman of Pirelli. Tronchetti Provera continued to serve as Chief Executive Officer and Executive Vice President. In the letter addressed to the shareholders, Tronchetti highlighted how: 'This partnership will allow us to be stronger in the industrial tyre business, where we were looking for someone with whom to face the market's challenges in a properly designed international and productive perspective. The consumer tyre sector will benefit from this new industrial connection which endows Pirelli with all the opportunities of the fast growing market in Asia.'

With the successful completion of the deal Marco Polo reversely merged into the controlled company Pirelli & C. Spa, financed by a pool of 18 banks providing

---

were Camfin with a stake of 26.19%, Malacalza Investimenti with 6.98%, Edizione Holding with 4.48% and Mediobanca with 3.02%.

11  The new chairman of Pirelli gave an interview to the Italian newspaper *Corriere della Sera* on 21 October 2015 in which he mentioned: 'If one loves things "Made in Italy" and wants to invest in Italy, Pirelli comes to mind. We strongly believed in the project implemented with Pirelli as the Silk Road Fund (a Chinese Republic Sovereign Fund with an equity endowment of 40 billion dollars) which accompanies us in the foreign markets. China approved the "Made in China 2025 Plan" which may be considered like the Chinese version of "German Industry 4.0". We are convinced we will obtain outstanding outcomes in terms of entrepreneurship and innovation. The marriage with Pirelli will bring technological improvement and high-level production.' Ren Jianxin exposes similar concepts in his letter to the shareholders published in the 2015 annual report: 'The presence of ChemChina alongside Camfin and LTI in the ownership structure of Pirelli will provide a further impulse to Pirelli, a corporate leader, allowing it to strengthen overall in a strategic market like Asia and in the industrial business through the merger of its assets with those of CNCR, the company controlled by ChemChina involved in the tyre business. It is possible to forecast a ratio of 257 vehicles for every 1000 people in 2024 in comparison with a ratio of 107 vehicles for every 1000 people in 2016.'

different liquidity facilities for an overall amount of €6.8 billion.[12] However, during 2016 the debt arising from the deal had to be renegotiated, in two different steps. The debt with a maturity date of 1 August 2016 had to be refinanced, and Pirelli decided to utilise two credit lines, called 'Term Facility' and 'Revolving Facility', respectively to a maximum amount of €6 billion and of €0.8 billion, composing a sort of 'Mergerco Facility', eventually provided for the benefit of the company by the banks participating in the deal. This decision was resolved by the Pirelli Board of Directors on 12 May 2016 and should be considered as preparation for a more stable long-term redefinition of the debt, as resolved by a previous meeting of the Board of Directors of Pirelli held on 16 February 2016.[13]

In the meantime, the industrial project was proceeding with the incorporation of a new company called Pirelli Industrial, entirely controlled by Pirelli. In due course during 2016, all the above-described process of integration was progressively implemented. The deal was organised into two different steps. Pirelli Tyre and CNRC, respectively with stakes of 86% and of 14%, incorporated a joint venture with the purpose of receiving the stakes held by CNRC in Yellow Sea, Double Happiness and Guilin as well as 62% of Pirelli Industrial and 8% of Aeolus. In this way, at the end of the deal the ownership structure of Aeolus would be composed of: CNRC with a stake of roughly 14%, the new joint venture for 30%, and new shareholders for about 31.5%, with the remaining 24% trading on the market.

The reasons for implementing the deal in two steps, a slight deviation from the initial agreements, were due to compliance with Chinese regulations imposing

---

12 More specifically €0.8 billion was provided as 'revolving credit facilities', €3.5 billion as debt with maturity of three and five years and interest rates respectively of 4% and 4.5%. Moreover €2.5 billion was provided as debt in US dollars with maturity of seven years and an interest rate of 6%, and an additional €1 billion as a revolving credit facility with maturity of five years and an interest rate of 4.25%.

13 This resolution is more precisely named 'Plan A' and consists in 'i) a bond issue of approximately €1.5–2 billion; ii) a bank loan for approximately €1–1.5 billion with a duration of three years; iii) another bank loan for approximately €2.5–3 billion and a duration of five years; iv) a revolving line of credit for another €1 billion for five years.' In the above-mentioned Board of Directors' meeting of 16 February 2016, the Chief Financial Officer of Pirelli asserts that: 'although the debt triggered by the deal has been ranked as "not investment grade" by the market, Pirelli's history and value creation perspectives suggest that the overall risk profile of the whole deal may be considered lower than otherwise generated by such typologies of deal, and therefore the average cost of the refinancing may be estimated roughly at 5%.'

severe limits on 'inflating' assets in a listed company, because of a reverse merger or integration with one or more unlisted companies. However, the first step of the deal described above would have allowed Aeolus to immediately benefit from the technology of Pirelli Tyre. The second step of the integration process foresaw the transfer to Aeolus of the remaining stake of Pirelli Industrial[14] and even of the 30% of the truck tyre activity of Mr Niu, the historical business partner of Pirelli in China, along with 10% of the assets of Pirelli China.

Therefore, upon completion of the whole integration process, Aeolus will entirely control Double Happiness and Yellow Sea, the two companies owned by CNRC for industrial tyre production, Pirelli Industrial and the industrial tyre assets detained by Pirelli in China, and the above-mentioned stakes in the consumer tyre business Pirelli China and in Mr Niu's industrial assets. Moreover, the agreement included transfer to Aeolus of 20% of the equity of the newly incorporated company dealing with the consumer tyre business, while the remaining 80% would be transferred to Pirelli Tyre.

I witnessed personally all the above-mentioned progressive implementation of the deal during a visit to China during the first week of November 2016. I experienced, in great depth, the efforts of Pirelli's management to understand and implement a successful cultural mixture of Italian values and the overwhelming, encompassing and fascinating history of China.[15] Because of its own long history, Pirelli can be considered an ideal candidate for this role, to develop a corporate marriage between technology and passion, between West and East, and to build very promising 'Guanxi', i.e. good and positive business relations, as the Chinese say.

In the consumer tyre business unit, the Asia Pacific region of Pirelli, whose 2016 revenues only in China approached 800 million US$, will incorporate roughly 80 million US$ of the consumer tyre business unit of Aeolus and add a related facility which will be transformed into a completely Pirelli-style plant. As previously

---

14 This second step has to be completed by autumn 2017. The fourth global player in the industrial sector will be created at that time, with a productive capacity of more than 16 million tyres.

15 Referring to this point, the experience of the first Jesuits in China and in Southeast Asia, with their invention of the concept of 'enculturation', i.e. the declination of Western concepts in Chinese moods, was an important milestone. At the beginning of the new century in which presumably China will play a significant role on the world stage, it may be helpful to build a future on deeply rooted beliefs that are common to East and West.

mentioned, the perspective of a relisting of Pirelli as a pure consumer tyre producer principally involved in the 'premium and prestige' business sector, which is scheduled to take place in 2018,[16] suggests a clear path to be followed in a very structured time frame. Pirelli's aim is to become a 'unique pure consumer player; the first luxury tyre makers'. In this context, a progressively deeper involvement of Pirelli in the emerging issues of digitalisation and big data, as further tools to enhance overall productivity, can be expected to lead to a significant value creation. At the beginning of March 2017, Pirelli launched the first 'clever tyre', able to interact with the driver. Incidentally, these 'clever tyres' have the feature of being coloured.[17] As has always occurred in the history of Pirelli, the ownership structure is supporting the business and therefore another shareholder is likely to enter the ownership structure prior to the new listing with a reduction of the CNRC stake, possibly to below 50%, whenever useful for the new initial public offering. Meanwhile as agreed CNRC will continue to consolidate its stake in Pirelli, in accordance with the 'China 2025 Plan'. This perspective sketches a well-designed future ownership structure which juxtaposes, in a worldwide dimension, historical and new industrial shareholders and financial investors, in which Tronchetti Provera and the Italian management located in Bicocca, in the North-East periphery of Milan, will play an absolute managerial role.

In relation to the industrial tyre business unit, the path forward includes the above-mentioned steps in the integration with the various entities related in different ways to CNRC.[18] The outcome will be the creation of the fourth largest player

---

16  Pirelli's press release on 19 October 2016 quotes: 'The Board showed its desire to accelerate the course resulting in the company's listing, immediately launching all the necessary actions. It is foreseen that the preliminary phases of the preparation of the IPO can be completed during the first half of 2017, with the objective of proceeding, in accordance with the best opportunity offered by the market, with the launch of the IPO by the first half of 2018 on the Milan stock exchange or on another of the leading stock exchanges at the international level.

17  In an interview with *Corriere della Sera* on 8 March 2017, Tronchetti Provera said: 'We have developed a tyre which, thanks to digitalisation, is able to give a constant flow of information – for example, pressure and temperature. The digitalisation process allows us to forecast any anomalies which would eventually jeopardise the qualitative standard of our tyres.'

18  At the end of 2016 the overall revenues of Pirelli Industrial accounted for roughly 1.3 billion US$, while the different entities related to CNRC had revenues of approximately 1.2 billion US$. More specifically the revenues of Aeolus accounted for 0.9 US$ billion and those of the other companies related to Aeolus amounted to 0.3 US$ billion.

in the world in the industrial tyre sector, with roughly 2.5 US$ billion in revenue, with the opportunity to better address different market segments with different brands: 'Pirelli for a tier 1 brand, Aeolus for a tier 2 brand and the other companies controlled by Aeolus for a tier 3 brand, with a high capacity to penetrate Chinese markets and a stronger relationship with fleets.'[19] Regarding the ownership structure, according to the agreements there is an 'intermediate' level depending on the presence of the listed company Aeolus, whose ownership structure will rely on the relative weights among the different entities conferring their industrial tyre business units to Aeolus. This 'two-tier structure' of the industrial tyre side of the deal, geographically headquartered in Beijing but owned out of Milan, is designed in such a way as to not jeopardise or weaken the connection with the Pirelli brand's outstanding technology. CNRC shareholders insisted upon this last point with Pirelli's management,

2017 marks Pirelli's 145th year of existence. The company has a long and fascinating history, encompassing three centuries. These last two years, since the definition of the first agreement with ChemChina (22 March 2015) have been extremely challenging for Pirelli, offering an innovative perspective for its future. We may assert that this is the last chapter and these the last pages of this book – though it could be in the future revised and updated with a new edition – but, without any doubt this is not the last chapter of the very exciting history of Pirelli.

The Ancient Greeks felt that the future 'lies on the knees of Jupiter'. The long presence in the business, the strong identity and the corporate culture of Pirelli give us some clues as to what the future might look like. First of all, the evidence suggests there is no need to worry about the issue of control. Control does not only depend on the number or the weight of shares owned; these elements must be accompanied by a managerial legitimacy which comes necessarily from the market. The long-term drivers of the sustainable growth and success of Pirelli can be attributed to many factors: an outstanding corporate governance structure, adoption of international best practices in many areas, the quality of the managerial team, technological, logistics and, organisational excellence, and the corporate culture, coordinated by the leadership of a long-serving Chief Executive Officer who has been in charge without interruption since 1992. Regarding the ownership structure, Pirelli's history suggests that an intelligent combination of

---

19  As mentioned by Tronchetti Provera in the Board of Directors' meeting on 20 June 2016.

long-standing and stable industrial shareholders, able to support long-term industrial projects alongside financial institutions, is an optimal formula.

The future is likely to take inspiration from the past.

Although Pirelli is a global corporation, since its geographically diversified production sites and products reach nearly every corner of the globe, the strategic, decision-making centre is and will be located in Italy, at Bicocca, on the north-eastern outskirts of Milan, a place which for the Group represents a *genius loci* of deep-rooted, classical importance, and which has been its permanent home since 1908.

This sensible and wise juxtaposition between tradition and modernity and between local and global dimensions includes the quest for stability, the requirement of the highest standards in corporate governance, in corporate social responsibility and in applying international best practices in each area of corporate activity.

This book closes in the present and merges with the future, where Pirelli is creating business plans, reaching innovative international agreements, making investments and programmes for growth, and weaving together economic and financial sustainability, innovative and advanced business prospects in technology and culture, with a perspective of stewardship, of corporate citizenship[20] and even of art. Pirelli, at this stage in its history, can be compared to a sailing ship that ploughs the waves swiftly and decisively towards new destinations, mingling sky and sea on its horizon, fully aware of the strength it brings to bear, and conscious of the course it must follow. The future is not 'on the knees of Jupiter', but in its own hands: 'That is Pirelli…!'[21]

---

20  On the eve of 29 November 2016, at the presentation of Pirelli Calendar 2017 in Paris, Tronchetti Provera remarked that the choice of Paris was due 'to show our friendship and closeness to our French friends' and I would add to the eternal values of the French Republic.

21  In an interview with *Economy* of 20 January 2005 Tronchetti Provera repeated similar concepts, which we often dedicated time to in our discussions together: 'It is essential that in any case a person does what suits him best. It is a concept that I repeat regularly to my children. You must also take other factors into account: preparation, talent, dedication, luck and the ability to choose the people you work with. But fundamentally I believe that the most important element is the passion you have for what you do, because a good percentage of your life is spent working.'

# IN-DEPTH ANALYSIS

# 1

# Business Culture and Brand in Pirelli

During the summer of 2010, when I started my research in the archives in preparation for writing this book, I began to spend some time at the Pirelli Foundation,[1] where the company archives are organised and stored. As described in the Introduction, this light pink building where the Foundation has its base and where its archives are kept plays an almost classical Vestal Virgin role for the whole Group.[2] This is where the recorded history not only for the Company but for the entire surrounding area is conserved: it is, indeed, one of the few surviving buildings from the former industrial complex, following the profound reorganisation programme which also included building and premises which characterised Pirelli's turnaround in the early 1990s. This area on the north-western outskirts of Milan, which holds the Company headquarters and offices that coordinate the Group's activities throughout the world, is the very same location where Pirelli moved its industrial facilities and offices to in 1908, after urban development had gradually pushed industry towards the outskirts of the city. Indeed, in this area one can still find traces of the many industries that have had their production facilities here over many years. Both the historical presence and current activities of Pirelli can still be witnessed today.

In recent years the Company's desire has been to celebrate its history and to commemorate its existence in these locations which are concrete proof of how the long life of a great company can provide opportunities for meeting, engaging

---

1   The Pirelli Foundation was established with the aim of promoting business culture and disseminating the huge cultural and historical heritage of the Group. Its objectives are developed in this in-depth study. The Pirelli Foundation, headed by Antonio Calabrò in the past and now by Alessia Magistroni, promotes research into the history of Pirelli and the realisation of this volume.

2   Shiller (2012) says: 'The essence of an enterprise is its longevity. Successful businesses have no expiration date, there is no inherent limit to the period of time that may operate.'

in dialogue and sharing views with the people who have lived and who still live in these same places. This is an obvious metaphor for how industrial activities can intermingle and be articulated with the polis anywhere in the world. Large companies are neither the ideological antithesis nor the empirical contradiction of the polis or local community but can be part of them.[3] As a symbol of this possible coexistence, in 2008 the HangarBicocca Foundation was established: a large abandoned industrial space suitably reorganised as 'tangible proof of a place symbolising Milanese Fordism, rescued from degeneration and abandonment' to be used as a museum-style display area for contemporary art exhibitions. This category of artistic expression assumes primary significance for an industrial company committed to the evolution of various forms of contemporary life. From this point of view, the choice to explore various forms of artistic expression and symbolic productions as well as the diverse materials used by contemporary art is a powerful metaphor of the frontiers of scientific research and technological innovation that characterise the activities of a company such as Pirelli, historically dedicated to innovation.

Contemporary art is primarily a symbolic expression of Pirelli's vocation to perform its business culture in the most comprehensive and thorough form that such a mission involves. Secondly, contemporary art has the ability to be highly expressive, embracing the various geographical, social and institutional contexts in which the Group has operated over the years. From this point of view, although contemporary art is a direct derivation of Western cultures, it expresses various forms and ontological assumptions, as seen in the paintings of Braque and Picasso or the music of Schoenberg and Stockhausen. For this reason contemporary art – in keeping with the history of the Company – represents a conduit for the distribution of core values. The multinational dimension of the Group dating back to the start of the 20th century provides an experience for continuous exchange of views and at times for challenges with respect to the multiple forms of contemporary life. This originates from the Group's adoption of an extremely specific,

---

3   It is interesting, in this regard, to note the decision taken by the Louvre to open a branch in the town of Lens, a depressed mining area midway between Paris and Brussels, with the aim of spurring its revival through art. The *Corriere della Sera* of 4 December 2012 writes: 'Where once darkness and perpetual night reigned inside tunnels with black, nightmarish ceilings, and miners had to do their work on their knees, today there stands in the park a structure that is almost entirely transparent, with high ceilings and bright walls.'

and exquisitely Western, set of values and culture as its reference point and guide, specifically those of the enlightened Lombard bourgeoisie of the late 19th and early 20th century.

The continuous exchange of views with the contemporary world occurs not only through the many aspects of a corporate nature – from those relating to budgeting and organisation to management and governance, repeatedly addressed in this publication – but it is also important for the business culture, and still more so from an even wider cultural point of view. In an increasingly pluralistic world in which Western imprinting is necessarily insufficient to understand the complexity of globalisation, the capacity of a large company to dialogue with worlds and cultural contexts that are distinct from one another becomes a highly important intangible asset. In this difficult task of introducing culture at a corporate level, contemporary art can be an appropriate vehicle to express the interest of the Company for its people and the products they create in various locations worldwide. Even the importance of the Pirelli brand, which has been precisely measured from a quantitative point of view, has similar origins and indeed, in some regions such as South America, the Pirelli brand has enormous visibility.

However, the involvement of a tyre-producing company in the world of contemporary art may at first appear unconventional, even in the Group's enlightened context of creating value for its shareholders. In reality, this choice arises from at least three different needs. Firstly, the HangarBicocca Foundation gave new life to the area where the Company had its roots, by transforming the very concept of 'factory', and a potentially degraded urban area into a place of culture and art. Secondly, it is a symbolic reference for the Group's numerous production facilities worldwide, and not surprisingly, the HangarBicocca Foundation hosts exhibitions of artists from many different nations. Thirdly, it is intended to serve as a metaphor for the role that business culture, in its various forms, plays in the development of creative talent to support innovation, a fundamental element in Pirelli's vocation for doing business, and is something that involves not only the future of the Company, but also its past.

In recent years, especially since its disengagement from the world of telecommunications and its refocusing on its core business, Pirelli has invested heavily in the reorganisation and enhancement of its history, its brand and in the values underpinning its long-standing industrial experience. For these reasons, the Pirelli Foundation was established in 2009, with various purposes, including that of 'giving space to the thought that welds the effective industrial experiences and records conserved in the Historical Archive with the drive for design, enhancing current events as they gradually become history'. The duty of recorded history and the exhortative capacity that a properly ordered past can represent at a corporate level go hand in hand with the important role that many large enterprises play in taking on the role of public entities in Italy. In Pirelli's case, this material – although not yet organised in a technical sense – over time has contributed to the creation of a comprehensive Historical Company Archive which already existed but which has been gradually reorganised and enhanced. The many documents and materials that constitute the Pirelli Historical Archive are testimony to the Group's multifaceted history. These documents range from the entire collection of corporate documents allowing the accurate reconstruction of the Group's history to the catalogued collections of magazines used in corporate communication, and advertising drawings and sketches which have now become veritable works of art from the last century.

The official corporate source documents – such as financial statements and minutes of the shareholder meetings and Board meetings of the Group's many companies – are examples of regulatory compliance, excellent disclosure and innovative corporate governance, whereas other documents are testimony to the evolution of the Group's business culture over time. In illustrating the mosaic that Renato Guttuso painted in 1961 for Pirelli, now kept in the consultation room of the Foundation, Calabrò (2012) writes: 'It can be a perfect symbol for a dominant idea that animates all the Foundation's work: "Enterprise is Culture". It is one step forward from the traditional approach "enterprise and culture". It is better to have a radical change in perspective, even if it is created merely by substituting a conjunction with a verb.'

From this point of view, the Settimo Torinese industrial pole offers an ideal representation of these concepts, where the architectural dimension permeates production, which in turn is linked with logistics and commerce. The fusion of all these elements with the real life of the people who work there is a compendium of the reasons why 'the enterprise is truly culture' in the classic sense of the term.

From among all the main features of Pirelli's long history, innovation has undoubtedly played a decisive role. The technological aspect of innovation is linked to scientific research, whereas innovation in itself involves many aspects of the life of an enterprise and is a central element of a business culture. As a continuous metaphor for its research activities on the frontier of knowledge and the possible, the communication and marketing activities of the Group faithfully mirror this frontier in its content and mode of expression. Tangible proof of this is provided by consulting the *Pirelli Magazine* which, on a monthly basis from 1949 to 1970, addresses a wide range of topics. Throughout its history, many important names in Italian literature have contributed to the magazine and still do today.

I remember the first time I read a copy of the *Pirelli Magazine* I was very impressed by the variety of topics and how these were presented and discussed. Already in the 1950s, the magazine addressed themes such as the environment or the role of women in society, in a manner that was clearly ahead of the times; the style of expression used to describe these topics could easily mislead the reader into believing they belong to later periods. Consistent with its mission, Pirelli's business culture has always been a step ahead in dealing with themes and issues that would only gain public attention in later years. A tangible example of this is the Pirelli Calendar, which dates back to the years of Swinging London, first becoming an icon in the United Kingdom, and later worldwide.[4] The beautiful yet classic, ultra-modern spirit of the female body – contemporary, mythological and dreamlike – was not only a highly effective advertising campaign that immediately drew the attention of consumers towards Pirelli products and brand, but also the expression of the various ideas of beauty in the numerous geographical contexts in which the Company operated. The Calendar was a key initiative in brand building, by helping make Pirelli products interesting in the eyes of consumers. The Calendar has never been offered for sale, and although about one million requests are made, only from 17,000 to 20,000 copies are printed each year. Similarly, Pirelli's advertising campaign had always combined a classic taste in proportions and shapes, embodying contemporaneity projecting towards the future.

All these activities can reasonably be considered within the scope of a historical archive that aims to conserve corporate memory and preserve the identity of a group. Furthermore, it has generated and still generates important benefits for the nations where the Group's companies are based. In fact, the need to remember and

---

4   The first edition of the Pirelli Calendar dates back to 1964, when Derek Forsyth, a young man who worked in England for Pirelli, suggested the creation of a calendar to the top management of the UK branch. After receiving the go-ahead for his project, which included the obvious recommendation to avoid any vulgarity, Forsyth involved the then unknown photographer Robert Freeman in the making of the Calendar. The first Calendar was set in Majorca and Freeman's wife was one of the first models. The Calendar was successful because it was distributed among the circle of friends of the two young men, which included figures destined to become icons of their time, such as Mary Quant and John Lennon.

to highlight a glorious past conveys different messages according to the corporate entity which supports the initiative. If one considers it reasonable for a bank to relate to shared elements of memorial importance in a country's art and history in order to build a social capital of trust (without which the foundations of business and market operation would be at risk of crumbling), then for an industrial company, that same heritage of art and history becomes a manifesto of talent and creativity, and an intangible asset of decisive importance from which to gain inspiration and guidance for the future. All this is true not only for businesses, but also for nations. In a context of progressive debasement of our identity, history and national memory, in an ever-more global world in which the very essence of Europe is being called into question, the ability of large companies to become planetary banners for their countries of origin is increasingly important. From this point of view, Pirelli's business culture is an increasingly tangible sign of a great enterprise in which the talent, taste and creativity of Italians are instantly recognisable in all parts of the world.

This focus is also immediately perceptible in the commitment that Olimpia developed over the years when it was the reference shareholder of Telecom with the creations of the Italy Project. In this case, the telecommunications company contributed significantly towards the enhancement of the enormous artistic and cultural heritage of the country by sponsoring activities of restoration and conservation, and by creating active partnerships regarding specific projects, such as the *Divina Commedia* narrated by Vittorio Sermonti in Santa Maria alle Grazie in Milan, which received great acclaim from the public. Interestingly, the cultural activities of the two companies are partially different, but are not in opposition to each other. The action promoted by Telecom Italia tends to finance cultural and artistic events that cover a broad spectrum of activities, whereas Pirelli focuses on activities that transform technology and business culture into an artistic dimension. Both approaches are nevertheless designed for an open-minded and non-elitist public. The reason for this difference is not only attributable to the significant difference in size of the two companies and the substantial resources of the Italy Project, amounting to about €30 million per year, but also to a different sensitivity: Telecom is more involved in supporting and financing existing elements, while Pirelli is more focused on innovative design and construction, in line with its commitment to research and technology at a global level.

However, similarly when Olimpia was a Telecom shareholder, the brand of the telecommunications company was supported and enhanced, but mainly to safeguard the considerable inherent capital of the former state monopoly's reputation.

Despite these different approaches, both companies have played an important role in enhancing the artistic and cultural heritage of the country, to which we must refer and draw on abundantly in moments of crisis. However, in the case of Pirelli there is something extra that is clearly recognisable in its history, such as its ability to build teams, its attentiveness to people in their workplace and in the local communities, the meticulousness manifest in its excellent products, as well as its ability to read the signs of the times well in advance, and therefore invest in the 'three capitals' of imagination, relationship and entrepreneurship which are likely, according to the academic research, to represent the future of the industrial sector.

In this context, the classical adage *'quidquid agis (recte et) prudenter agas et respice finem'*[5] rings true more than ever, in the clear understanding that if these values continue to be shared and passed on, the future of the Company will see no uncertainty, as it will always be in the firm hands of its shareholders, its managers and employees, and so it will not find itself sitting in the fickle lap of Jupiter or Fortune.

---

5  'Whatever you do, do it wisely and consider the end.' There are several versions of this adage; its origins would appear to come from the famous warning from Solon to the wealthy King Croesus of Lydia, contained in the first book of Herodotus.

# 2

# Ownership Structures

Historical analysis conducted over a long period of time has allowed us to accurately describe the ownership and organisational structures of the Pirelli Group within the context of Italian capitalism. From this point of view, two reference points have guided the Group's ownership structures: the need to combine entrepreneurial skills with the availability of assets and the search for stability in control. All this took place by consistently seeking simplified corporate structures, even if the moves to achieve this were complicated from a technical point of view.[1]

The two above-mentioned elements were constituent features of the joint stock company with share capital, Pirelli & C., until its merger with Pirelli SpA in 2003. The legal form of the joint stock company, in fact, guaranteed the possibility of managerial control by one reference shareholder who, *ab origine*, held a significant but modest shareholding with voting rights since it had always been recognised as the reference shareholder of the Group due to the level of managerial skills possessed.

This empirical evidence, spanning more than a century, is confirmed by the availability of reliable data, from 1977–1978, when, following a modification in regulations, it became possible to gain access to the historical details on ownership structures of listed and unlisted companies. In the early 1980s, the reference shareholder in the ownership structure of Pirelli & C. was Mediobanca, which owned a

---

1 This in-depth study aims to highlight, in the context of a brief review, the reasons behind the most important operations in corporate simplification. In this regard, our objective is to show how, despite the varying times and situations, the managerial action has always been aimed at shortening and simplifying the structures inherited from the past. The purpose of this study is not to examine closely the technical aspects of each individual extraordinary operation that, over the years, has modified the Group's organisation and streamlined the corporate and equity structures. Those points have already been described in the text, and the notes refer to the individual parts of the text in which such matters were discussed.

stake in the Limited Liability Partnership of just over 11.[2] In turn, Pirelli & C. was the reference shareholder of the foreign parent company Société Internationale Pirelli (SIP), with an 18% stake, and of Pirelli SpA, with the same percentage, held both directly and partly through SIP.[3] In both cases, the grip on the capital of the parent company was rather weak.

In subsequent years, within the shareholders' agreement which grouped together just under 60% of the Limited Liability Partnership's equity, the partic- ipation of Mediobanca in Pirelli & C. decreased, while both Fin.P. and Camfin – companies controlled respectively by the Pirelli and Tronchetti Provera families – consolidated their control over the Limited Liability Partnership. In 1988, there was a major reorganisation of the Group,[4] which saw the end of the now-anach- ronistic joint control of the Italian and foreign parent companies over the management company, Pirelli Société Generale. This previous reorganisation had taken place in 1982, in the aftermath of the dissolution of the union with Dunlop. Through this reorganisation, Pirelli & C. came to hold 38.86% of Société Interna- tionale Pirelli, which in turn held 48% of Pirelli SpA.

A further important change in the Group's shareholder structure took place in the wake of the managerially successful turnaround that marked the complete legitimacy of Marco Tronchetti Provera at the helm of the Pirelli Group. As a result of the turnaround, in fact, Camfin became the leading shareholder of the Limited Liability Partnership, later combining its own stake with that of the Pirelli family. In this way, between 1995 and 1996, the role of Camfin replaced that of Mediobanca as reference shareholder of Pirelli & C. by increasing its stake[5] from 12.45% in the 1996–1998 three-year period, to 16.68% in 1999, then to 25.64% in 2000 and finally

---

2   On 24 March 1981, Mediobanca was the leading single shareholder of Pirelli & C. SpA with a stake of 11.08%. Mediobanca also held an additional direct stake of 4.84% in the capital of Pirelli SpA.

3   More precisely, Pirelli & C. SpA had a 9.25% stake in Pirelli SpA in addition to a shareholding of 8.10% held directly by SIP in Pirelli SpA. Moreover, on 16 July 1982, the trust company Spafid was holder of a 3.80% stake in the capital of Pirelli SpA. These transactions were associated with the Pirelli family.

4   The technical aspects of the operation are described in Chapter 5.

5   Regarding this point, see Appendix 1. One should note that, during the same period, GPI had in turn increased its equity investment in the subsidiary Camfin from 53.63% in 1996 to 70.78% in 1998.

to 29.62% in 2001, on the eve of the deal with Telecom Italia. This increased participation of Camfin in the Limited Liability Partnership occurred through the acquisition of holdings of other shareholders which were part of the shareholders' agreement, including Mediobanca, which reduced its stake from 8.96% in 1998 to 4.77% in 2001, and therefore in cash.

At the end of the 1990s, the prospect of Italy's entry into the single currency made the existence of Société Internationale Pirelli obsolete and sanctioned a further shortening of the Group's chain of control.[6] Therefore, there was a merger by incorporation of SIP into Pirelli SpA. With the completion of this operation, which did not affect the hold of the shareholders' agreement on the capital of the Limited Liability Partnership, the latter held a 30.01% stake in Pirelli SpA. In addition, BZ Group,[7] whose reference shareholder was the Swiss financier Martin Ebner,[8] held a further package of about 10%.

The acquisition through Olimpia, in July 2001, of the relative majority shareholding in Olivetti, sold by the Luxembourg company Bell, had the effect of considerably lengthening the corporate chain which from the parent companies of Camfin descended down as far as TIM, controlled by Telecom.[9] In a manner consistent with the style described above, Pirelli's management proceeded to shorten the chain of control, as soon as market conditions made it possible. This prospect made it possible, in the course of 2003, to perform two important simplifications in the long chain of control of the Group, namely the merger between Telecom and Olivetti and, further upstream, between Pirelli & C. and Pirelli SpA.[10]

---

6 The technical aspects of the entire operation are described in Chapter 7.

7 Actually, the capital stake held by BZ Group in SIP was definitely higher than the stake it was credited to have. On 16 June 1994, BZ Group owned 25.44% of SIP. Additionally on this point, the details of the shareholders at the SIP SGM on 9 June 1995 (see Appendix 4 in this respect) demonstrate the existence of a significant part of the SIP capital in the hands of the same shareholders as those in the Pirelli & C. shareholders' agreement.

8 As regards the events relating to the participation of BZ Group in SIP and then in Pirelli SpA, see Chapter 7. Through the involvement of BZ Group, and later of Hopa, the ownership structures, firstly of Pirelli Group and secondly of Pirelli-Olimpia, were strengthened, involving other shareholders capable of embracing and appreciating the industrial projects of Pirelli.

9 The description of the chain of control in the Pirelli Group after the establishment of Olimpia is illustrated in Annex 9.2 in Chapter 9.

10 In this regard, see Annexes 10.1, 10.2 and 10.3 in Chapter 10.

The merger between Olivetti and Telecom led to a significant dilution of the stake that Olimpia held in the telecommunications group, which fell to 11.85% of its equity. To restrengthen the position of Olimpia in Telecom, Pirelli launched an equity increase to the benefit of Olimpia, which already held a stake of 17% at the end of 2003. Similarly, the merger between Pirelli SpA and the Limited Liability Partnership put an end to the existing dualism between the two companies, which dated back to the early 1920s and no longer had any raison d'être. This, however, sanctioned the disappearance of the Limited Liability Partnership with share capital, which had been present on the market since 1883. To maintain a certain continuity, its business name was incorporated into the name of the new company: Pirelli & C. SpA. In both cases, the shortening of the chain of control gave rise at the same time to significant increases in equity in the companies upstream in the chain, i.e. GPI and Camfin.[11]

For the telecommunications group, this approach was substantially different from that of the 1999 takeover, mainly based on debt, and for the entire chain of control it represented a strong commitment by the shareholders and the management to the ongoing industrial projects. The subsequent merger between Telecom and TIM of 2004 confirmed the aforementioned concept within the sphere of a robust business plan.[12] The merger between Telecom and TIM also created a significant dilution of the shareholding that again made it necessary for Olimpia to undertake equity increases of about 2 billion. Pirelli took part in the operation pro rata in cash for slightly more than half of the amount.

This long-term trend has had further confirmation in the recent history of simplification and rationalisation in the chain of control of Pirelli & C. SpA. Starting from 2007 the corporate structure of the Pirelli Group has experienced important developments that have helped to make the company potentially contestable.[13] First of all, the Pirelli Group has gradually focused its attention on its

---

11  Camfin had approved and subscribed a cash capital increase of €160 million with an additional €40 million in warrants.

12  The reasons and nature of the business plan that led to the merger between Telecom and TIM are described in paragraph 1 of Chapter 11.

13  On this point, it is worth remembering that the shareholders' agreement was not renewed from the spring of 2014.

core business,[14] by finding a different position for its real estate business, Pirelli Re (which had meanwhile changed its name to Prelios).[15] Secondly, while reaffirming the centrality of Camfin's role within the Pirelli Group's body of shareholders, the evolution in the ownership and corporate structures of the companies upstream of Camfin has made it possible to achieve greater cohesion and stability, leaving no opportunity downstream for any future industrial alliance.

The simplification and rationalisation of the corporate structures and ownership structures, albeit sometimes complex in their technical aspects, has contributed to the creation of value for the Pirelli Group in the market. This policy has, moreover, led to a systematic dilution of the control quotas and, with them, a reduced hold of the parent companies; it has also provided an equally timely injection of liquidity, through equity increases (always in cash), to strengthen and sustain the stability of control, allowing the construction of long-term business plans.

However, only a highly successful way of managing and running businesses has made such simplifications possible, of which the end of the shareholders' agreement represents an important step. Without neglecting the importance of the role of Camfin, the progressive and continuous search for consensus in its entrepreneurial and managerial action, which comes directly from the market, represents a new benchmark not only for Pirelli, but also for the entire Italian corporate system, paving the way to the outstanding deals with Rosneft and later on with Chem China which took place since 2014.

---

14  At the presentation of the last business plan which took place in London on 6 November 2013, the realisation was also announced of part of the historic equity investments held by Pirelli & C. SpA in some important listed Italian companies.

15  For the description of the real estate company reorganisation, see Chapter 14.

APPENDIX

# OWNERSHIP STRUCTURES

# The Ownership Structure of Pirelli & C.

TABLE 1. Ownership structure of
Pirelli & C. on 24 March 1981[a]

| Shareholder | Percentage owned of the share capital with voting rights |
|---|---|
| Mediobanca | 11.08 |
| GIM | 10 |
| SAI | 7.85 |
| Sade finanziaria | 4.03 |
| SMI | 4 |
| Bank Oppenheimer | 2.50 |
| Bastogi | 2.16 |
| Rominvest | 0.95 |
| SIFI | 0.94 |
| Generali | 0.56 |

[a]*From an overall total of 18,506,666 ordinary shares*

## TABLE 2. OWNERSHIP STRUCTURE OF
## PIRELLI & C. ON 26 APRIL 1983

| Shareholder | Percentage owned of the share capital with voting rights |
|---|---|
| Mediobanca | 11.08 |
| GIM | 10.08 |
| SAI | 7.85 |
| Fin.P. | 4.62 |
| Sade finanziaria | 4.03 |
| SMI | 3.33 |
| Fonditalia | 2.98 |
| CAM | 2.10 |
| Rasfund | 1.46 |
| Italfund | 1.17 |

## TABLE 3. OWNERSHIP STRUCTURE OF
## PIRELLI & C. ON 29 APRIL 1986

| Shareholder | Percentage owned of the share capital with voting rights |
|---|---|
| Mediobanca | 7.94 |
| GIM | 7.57 |
| SAI | 5.52 |
| Fin.P. | 5.27 |
| Sabaudia | 4.87 |
| Find | 4.11 |
| De Ferrari Galliera | 3.26 |
| Sade finanziaria | 2.84 |
| SMI | 2.76 |
| Camfin | 2.59 |

### TABLE 4. OWNERSHIP STRUCTURE OF PIRELLI & C. ON 28 APRIL 1988

| Shareholder | Percentage owned of the share capital with voting rights |
|---|---|
| Mediobanca | 7.90 |
| GIM | 7.52 |
| Gemina | 5.51 |
| SAI | 5.49 |
| Fin.P. | 5.13 |
| Find | 5.05 |
| Sabaudia Finanziaria | 5.00 |
| Camfin | 5.00 |
| Fondo Primecapital | 3.56 |
| Acquedotto De Ferrari | 3.38 |

### TABLE 5. OWNERSHIP STRUCTURE OF PIRELLI & C. ON 20 APRIL 1990[a]

| Shareholder | Percentage owned of the share capital with voting rights |
|---|---|
| Mediobanca | 8.11 |
| GIM | 7.20 |
| Gemina | 5.72 |
| Camfin | 5.52 |
| Banque Indosuez | 5.38 |
| SAI | 5.37 |
| Fin.P. | 5.00 |
| Find | 5.00 |
| CIR | 4.77 |
| SMI | 3.82 |

[a]*Number of ordinary shares 142,696,062*

TABLE 6. OWNERSHIP STRUCTURE OF
PIRELLI & C. ON 24 APRIL 1992[a]

| Shareholder | Percentage owned of the share capital with voting rights |
| --- | --- |
| Mediobanca | 7.90 |
| GIM | 6.92 |
| Banque Indosuez | 6.61 |
| SAI | 6.05 |
| Camfin | 5.57 |
| Gemina | 5.53 |
| Fin.P. | 4.80 |
| Find | 4.80 |
| CIR | 4.59 |
| SMI | 3.67 |

[a]*Number of ordinary shares 167,089,360*

TABLE 7. OWNERSHIP STRUCTURE OF
PIRELLI & C. ON 20 JUNE 1994[a]

| Shareholder | Percentage owned of the share capital with voting rights |
| --- | --- |
| Mediobanca | 7.54 |
| GiM | 6.68 |
| Gemina investments | 5.31 |
| SAI | 4.98 |
| Camfin | 4.96 |
| Fin.P. | 4.64 |
| CIR | 4.42 |
| Find | 3.63 |
| SMI | 3.55 |
| Sopaf | 2.89 |

[a]*Number of ordinary shares 167,089,360*

## Table 8. Ownership structure of Pirelli & C. on 27 May 1996

| Shareholder | Percentage owned of the share capital with voting rights |
|---|---|
| Fin.P. | 12.45 |
| Mediobanca | 8.96 |
| Gemina | 5.98 |
| SAI | 5.67 |
| Generali | 4.90 |
| RAS | 3.00 |
| Sade | 2.86 |
| CIR | 2.00 |
| GIM | 1.00 |
| Lucchini Siderurgica | 1.00 |

## Table 9. Ownership structure of Pirelli & C. on 22 May 1998 (shareholders' agreement)

| Shareholder | Percentage owned of the share capital with voting rights |
|---|---|
| Fin.P. | 12.45 |
| Mediobanca | 8.96 |
| HPI | 6.01 |
| SAI | 5.80 |
| Generali | 5.30 |
| RAS | 3.33 |
| Sade | 2.86 |
| CIR | 2.00 |
| GIM | 1.00 |
| Lucchini Siderurgica | 1.00 |

### TABLE 10. OWNERSHIP STRUCTURE OF PIRELLI & C. ON 11 MAY 2000 (SHAREHOLDERS)

| Shareholder | Percentage owned of the share capital with voting rights |
| --- | --- |
| Camfin | 25.64 |
| Generali | 6.38 |
| BZ Group | 6.38 |
| Edizione Holding | 6.03 |
| HPI | 5.96 |
| Premafin | 5.70 |
| Allianz | 5.37 |
| Mediobanca | 5.00 |
| CIR | 1.99 |
| SMI | 1.99 |
| Massimo Moratti | 1.37 |
| Lucchini | 1.05 |

### TABLE 11. OWNERSHIP STRUCTURE OF PIRELLI & C. ON 13 MAY 2002 (SHAREHOLDERS)

| Shareholder | Percentage owned of the share capital with voting rights |
| --- | --- |
| Camfin | 29.80 |
| Serfis | 9.48 |
| Generali | 6.21 |
| HPI | 5.94 |
| Premafin | 5.61 |
| Edizione Holding | 5.28 |
| Allianz Holding | 5.11 |
| Mediobanca | 5.08 |
| Silvio Scaglia | 4.97 |

TABLE 12. OWNERSHIP STRUCTURE OF
PIRELLI & C. SPA ON 10 MAY 2004

| Shareholder | Percentage of the ordinary share capital | Share of stake assigned to the shareholders' agreement |
|---|---|---|
| Camfin | 25.60 | 16.63 |
| Assicurazioni Generali | 4.61 | 3.77 |
| RCS | 4.42 | 4.40 |
| Fondiaria-Sai | 4.26 | 4.17 |
| Edizione Holding | 3.93 | 3.77 |
| RAS | 3.90 | 3.77 |
| Mediobanca | 3.77 | 3.77 |
| Massimo Moratti | | 0.98 |
| Sinpar | | 0.74 |

TABLE 13. OWNERSHIP STRUCTURE OF
PIRELLI & C. SPA ON 28 APRIL 2005

| Shareholder | Percentage of the ordinary share capital | Share of stake assigned to the shareholders' agreement |
|---|---|---|
| Camfin | 25.39 | 18.98 |
| Assicurazioni Generali | 5.18 | 4.30 |
| Edizione Holding | 4.47 | 4.30 |
| Fondiaria-Sai | 4.37 | 4.32 |
| RAS | 4.30 | 4.30 |
| Mediobanca | 4.30 | 4.30 |
| Intesa | | 1.51 |
| Capitalia | | 1.51 |
| RCS | | 1.43 |
| Massimo Moratti | | 1.11 |
| Sinpar | | 0.62 |

## TABLE 14. OWNERSHIP STRUCTURE OF
## PIRELLI & C. SpA ON 21 APRIL 2006

| Shareholder | Percentage of the ordinary share capital | Share of stake assigned to the shareholders' agreement |
| --- | --- | --- |
| Camfin | 25.57 | 19.83 |
| Assicurazioni Generali | 5.22 | 4.30 |
| Edizione Holding | 4.66 | 4.50 |
| Fondiaria-Sai | 4.37 | 4.31 |
| RAS | 4.30 | 4.30 |
| Mediobanca | 4.50 | 4.50 |
| Intesa | | 1.58 |
| Capitalia | | 1.58 |
| Massimo Moratti | | 1.16 |
| Sinpar | | 0.62 |

## TABLE 15. OWNERSHIP STRUCTURE OF
## PIRELLI & C. SpA ON 23 APRIL 2007

| Shareholder | Percentage of the ordinary share capital | Share of stake assigned to the shareholders' agreement |
| --- | --- | --- |
| Camfin | 25.51 | 19.63 |
| Assicurazioni Generali | 5.34 | 4.26 |
| Edizione Holding | 4.62 | 4.45 |
| Fondiaria-Sai | 4.33 | 4.27 |
| RAS | 4.26 | 4.26 |
| Mediobanca | 4.45 | 4.45 |
| Intesa Sanpaolo | | 1.56 |
| Capitalia | | 1.56 |
| Massimo Moratti | | 1.15 |
| Sinpar | | 0.61 |

## TABLE 16. OWNERSHIP STRUCTURE OF
## PIRELLI & C. SPA ON 29 APRIL 2008

| Shareholder | Percentage of the ordinary share capital | Share of stake assigned to the shareholders' agreement |
|---|---|---|
| Camfin | 26.19 | 20.32 |
| Assicurazioni Generali | 5.49 | 4.41 |
| Edizione Holding | 4.77 | 4.61 |
| Fondiaria-Sai | 4.48 | 4.42 |
| RAS | 4.52 | 4.41 |
| Mediobanca | 4.61 | 4.61 |
| Intesa Sanpaolo | | 1.62 |
| Massimo Moratti | | 1.19 |
| Sinpar | | 0.63 |

## TABLE 17. OWNERSHIP STRUCTURE OF
## PIRELLI & C. SPA ON 21 APRIL 2009

| Shareholder | Percentage of the ordinary share capital | Share of stake assigned to the shareholders' agreement |
|---|---|---|
| Camfin | 26.19 | 20.32 |
| Assicurazioni Generali | 5.49 | 4.41 |
| Edizione Holding | 4.77 | 4.61 |
| Fondiaria-Sai | 4.48 | 4.42 |
| RAS | 4.52 | 4.41 |
| Mediobanca | 4.61 | 4.61 |
| Intesa Sanpaolo | | 1.62 |
| Massimo Moratti | | 1.19 |
| Sinpar | | 0.63 |

## TABLE 18. OWNERSHIP STRUCTURE OF PIRELLI & C. SPA ON 21 APRIL 2010

| Shareholder | Percentage of the ordinary share capital | Share of stake assigned to the shareholders' agreement |
| --- | --- | --- |
| Camfin | 26.19 | 20.32 |
| Assicurazioni Generali | 5.49 | 4.41 |
| Edizione Holding | 4.77 | 4.61 |
| Fondiaria-Sai | 4.48 | 4.42 |
| RAS | 4.52 | 4.41 |
| Mediobanca | 4.61 | 4.61 |
| Intesa Sanpaolo | | 1.62 |
| Massimo Moratti | | 1.19 |
| Sinpar | | 0.63 |

## TABLE 19. OWNERSHIP STRUCTURE OF PIRELLI SPA ON 5 MAY 2003

| Shareholder | Percentage of the ordinary share capital | Share of stake assigned to the shareholders' agreement |
| --- | --- | --- |
| Camfin | 26.19 | 20.32 |
| Assicurazioni Generali | 5.47 | 4.41 |
| Edizione Holding | 4.77 | 4.61 |
| Fondiaria-Sai | 4.48 | 4.42 |
| RAS | 4.52 | 4.41 |
| Mediobanca | 4.61 | 4.61 |
| Intesa Sanpaolo | | 1.62 |
| Massimo Moratti | | 0.49 |
| Sinpar | | 0.63 |

### TABLE 20. OWNERSHIP STRUCTURE OF
### PIRELLI & C. SpA ON 12 MARCH 2012

| Shareholder | Percentage of the ordinary share capital | Share of stake assigned to the shareholders' agreement |
|---|---|---|
| Camfin | 25.54 | 20.32 |
| Assicurazioni Generali | 5.46 | 4.41 |
| Edizione Holding | 4.77 | 4.61 |
| Fondiaria-Sai | 4.48 | 4.42 |
| RAS | 4.52 | 4.41 |
| Mediobanca | 4.61 | 4.61 |
| Intesa Sanpaolo | | 1.62 |
| Massimo Moratti | | 0.49 |
| Sinpar | | 0.63 |

### TABLE 21. OWNERSHIP STRUCTURE OF
### PIRELLI & C. SpA ON 13 MAY 2013

| Shareholder | Percentage of the ordinary share capital | Share of stake assigned to the shareholders' agreement |
|---|---|---|
| Camfin | 26.19 | 20.32 |
| Assicurazioni Generali | 4.96 | 4.41 |
| Edizione Srl | 4.77 | 4.61 |
| Mediobanca | 4.61 | 4.61 |
| Allianz | 4.50 | 4.41 |
| Finsoe | 4.48 | 4.42 |
| Intesa Sanpaolo | | 1.62 |
| Sinpar | | 0.63 |
| Massimo Moratti | | 0.49 |

### TABLE 22. OWNERSHIP STRUCTURE OF
### PIRELLI & C. SpA ON 12 JUNE 2014

| Shareholder | Percentage of the ordinary share capital |
|---|---|
| Lauro Sessantuno | 26.19 |
| Malacalza Investimenti | 6.98 |
| Mediobanca | 4.61 |
| Edizione Srl | 4.61 |
| Harbor International Fund | 3.94 |

### TABLE 23. OWNERSHIP STRUCTURE OF
### PIRELLI & C. SpA ON 14 MAY 2015

| Shareholder | Percentage of the ordinary share capital |
|---|---|
| Camfin | 26.79 |
| Malacalza Investimenti | 6.98 |
| Edizione Srl | 4.48 |
| Mediobanca | 3.02 |

# The Ownership Structure of Pirelli SpA

TABLE 1. OWNERSHIP STRUCTURE OF
PIRELLI SPA ON 16 JULY 1982

| Shareholder | Percentage owned of the share capital with voting rights |
| --- | --- |
| Pirelli & C. | 9.25 |
| Société Internationale Pirelli | 8.10 |
| Mediobanca | 4.84 |
| SMI | 4.04 |
| Spafid | 3.80 |
| CEAT | 3.41 |
| Bastogi | 2.95 |
| Banca d'Italia | 2.65 |
| SAI | 2.30 |
| Comit | 2.10 |

TABLE 2. OWNERSHIP STRUCTURE OF
PIRELLI SpA ON 6 NOVEMBER 1984[a]

| Shareholder | Percentage owned of the share capital with voting rights |
| --- | --- |
| Pirelli & C. | 18.12 |
| Fonditalia | 5.96 |
| Mediobanca | 5.64 |
| Deutscher Auslandkassverein | 3.85 |
| Banca d'Italia | 2.84 |
| Fidersel | 2.14 |
| Fidis | 2.12 |
| Spafid | 1.78 |
| SMI | 1.66 |
| Rasfund | 1.55 |

[a]*From a total of 183,421,364 ordinary shares*

TABLE 3. OWNERSHIP STRUCTURE OF
PIRELLI SpA ON 5 NOVEMBER 1986[a]

| Shareholder | Percentage owned of the share capital with voting rights |
| --- | --- |
| Pirelli & C. | 13.70 |
| Kredietbank Lux | 6.06 |
| Fidis | 5.25 |
| Mediobanca | 5.05 |
| Fonditalia | 3.94 |
| Deutscher Auslandkassen | 3.80 |
| Prima Capital | 2.70 |
| Banca d'Italia | 2.56 |
| Berliner Handelsbank | 2.32 |
| Fondo Arca | 1.99 |

[a]*From a total of 307,219,519 ordinary shares*

## TABLE 4. OWNERSHIP STRUCTURE OF
## PIRELLI SpA ON 11 NOVEMBER 1988[a]

| Shareholder | Percentage owned of the share capital with voting rights |
|---|---|
| SIP | 44.24 |
| Spafid (Pirelli & C.) | 9.99 |
| Fidis | 2.95 |
| Sabaudia | 2.65 |
| Mediobanca | 2.43 |
| Fonditalia | 2.18 |
| Fondo Imicapital | 1.90 |
| Fondo Multiras | 1.89 |
| Banca d'Italia | 1.42 |
| Rasfund | 1.41 |

[a]*From a total of 702,798,640 ordinary shares*

## TABLE 5. OWNERSHIP STRUCTURE OF
## PIRELLI SpA ON 27 JUNE 1990[a]

| Shareholder | Percentage owned of the share capital with voting rights |
|---|---|
| SIP | 36.89 |
| Spafid (Pirelli & C.) | 13.73 |
| SIP (Channel Islands) | 9.81 |
| Fondo Imicapital | 2.11 |
| Fondo Multiras | 1.72 |
| Banca d'Italia | 1.49 |
| Rasfund Management | 0.98 |
| Mediobanca | 0.87 |
| Deutsche Auslandkasse | 0.84 |
| Chase | 0.82 |

[a]*From a total of 867,227,102 ordinary shares*

### TABLE 6. OWNERSHIP STRUCTURE OF
### PIRELLI SpA ON 21 JUNE 1994[a]

| Shareholder | Percentage owned of the share capital with voting rights |
| --- | --- |
| SIP | 38.75 |
| Spafid (Pirelli & C.) | 12.45 |
| SIP (Channel Islands) | 10.53 |

[a]*879,691,697 ordinary shares in circulation*

### TABLE 7. OWNERSHIP STRUCTURE OF
### PIRELLI SpA ON 21 JANUARY 1992[a]

| Shareholder | Percentage owned of the share capital with voting rights |
| --- | --- |
| SIP | 38.62 |
| SIP (Channel Islands) | 11.18 |
| Spafid | 10.89 |

[a]*909,968,260 ordinary shares in circulation*

### TABLE 8. OWNERSHIP STRUCTURE OF
### PIRELLI SpA ON 26 JUNE 1992[a]

| Shareholder | Percentage owned of the share capital with voting rights |
| --- | --- |
| SIP | 40.64 |
| Spafid | 8.84 |
| SIP (Channel Islands) | 7.12 |

[a]*1,428,588,595 ordinary shares in circulation*

### TABLE 9. OWNERSHIP STRUCTURE OF
### PIRELLI SpA ON 21 JUNE 1993[a]

| Shareholder | Percentage owned of the share capital with voting rights |
| --- | --- |
| Societá Italiana di Partecipazioni | 41.74 |
| SIP | 7.12 |
| Spafid | 4.89 |
| Chase | 3.74 |

*[a]1,428,588,595 ordinary shares in circulation*

### TABLE 10. OWNERSHIP STRUCTURE OF
### PIRELLI SpA ON 20 MAY 1994[a]

| Shareholder | Percentage owned of the share capital with voting rights |
| --- | --- |
| SIP | 48.86 |
| Spafid | 4.89 |
| Chase | 2.87 |

*[a]1,428,588,595 ordinary shares in circulation*

### TABLE 11. OWNERSHIP STRUCTURE OF
### PIRELLI SpA ON 22 MAY 1995

| Shareholder | Percentage owned of the share capital with voting rights |
| --- | --- |
| SIP | 48.63 |
| Spafid | 4.86 |
| Finanza e Futuro | 2.19 |

### TABLE 12. OWNERSHIP STRUCTURE OF
### PIRELLI SpA ON 20 MAY 1996

| Shareholder | Percentage owned of the share capital with voting rights |
|---|---|
| Pirelli Partecipazioni SpA | 50.94 |
| Pirelli & C. Sapa | 2.57 |

### TABLE 13. OWNERSHIP STRUCTURE OF
### PIRELLI SpA ON 12 MAY 1997

| Shareholder | Percentage owned of the share capital with voting rights |
|---|---|
| Pirelli Partecipazioni SpA | 45.92 |
| Pirelli & C. Sapa | 3.66 |

### TABLE 14. OWNERSHIP STRUCTURE OF
### PIRELLI SpA ON 15 MAY 1998

| Shareholder | Percentage owned of the share capital with voting rights |
|---|---|
| Pirelli Partecipazioni SpA | 40.34 |
| Pirelli & C. Sapa | 3.21 |
| Morgan Guaranty Trust | 2.55 |

## TABLE 15. OWNERSHIP STRUCTURE OF
## PIRELLI SpA ON 21 MAY 1999

| Shareholder | Percentage owned of the share capital with voting rights |
|---|---|
| Pirelli Partecipazioni SpA | 45.98 |
| Generali | 2.74 |
| San Paolo-Imi | 2.04 |

## TABLE 16. OWNERSHIP STRUCTURE OF
## PIRELLI SpA ON 8 MAY 2000

| Shareholder | Percentage owned of the share capital with voting rights |
|---|---|
| Pirelli & C. | 32.02 |
| BZ Group Holding | 10.60 |
| Generali | 2.61 |

## TABLE 17. OWNERSHIP STRUCTURE OF
## PIRELLI SpA ON 8 MAY 2001

| Shareholder | Percentage owned of the share capital with voting rights |
|---|---|
| Pirelli & C. | 33.17 |
| BZ Group Holding | 10.12 |
| Generali | 2.91 |
| San Paolo-Imi | 2.05 |

## TABLE 18. OWNERSHIP STRUCTURE OF
## PIRELLI SPA ON 9 MAY 2002

| Shareholder | Percentage owned of the share capital with voting rights |
| --- | --- |
| Pirelli & C. | 38.35 |
| BZ Group Holding | 7.65 |

## TABLE 19. OWNERSHIP STRUCTURE OF
## PIRELLI SPA ON 5 MAY 2003

| Shareholder | Percentage owned of the share capital with voting rights |
| --- | --- |
| Pirelli & C. | 41.70 |
| Landesbank Baden Wuttemberg | 5.55 |
| Treasury shares | 8.51 |

# The Ownership Structure of Camfin SpA

TABLE 1. OWNERSHIP STRUCTURE OF
CAMFIN SPA ON 30 JANUARY 1986

| Shareholder | Percentage owned of the share capital with voting rights |
|---|---|
| GPI | 52.87 |
| Acciaierie e Ferriere Lombarde Falck | 25.04 |
| Acciaierie di Bolzano | 9.01 |

TABLE 2. OWNERSHIP STRUCTURE OF
CAMFIN SPA ON 18 SEPTEMBER 1986

| Shareholder | Percentage owned of the share capital with voting rights |
|---|---|
| GPI | 44.07 |
| Acciaierie e Ferriere Lombarde Falck | 20.87 |
| Acciaierie di Bolzano | 7.52 |

TABLE 3. OWNERSHIP STRUCTURE OF
CAMFIN SpA ON 21 JANUARY 1988

| Shareholder | Percentage owned of the share capital with voting rights |
| --- | --- |
| GPI | 46.9 |
| Acciaierie e Ferriere Lombarde Falck | 20.9 |
| Acciaierie di Bolzano | 5.8 |

TABLE 4. OWNERSHIP STRUCTURE OF
CAMFIN SpA ON 29 APRIL 1994

| Shareholder | Percentage owned of the share capital with voting rights |
| --- | --- |
| GPI | 47.07 |
| Acciaierie e Ferriere Lombarde Falck | 20.87 |
| Sondel | 5.01 |

TABLE 5. OWNERSHIP STRUCTURE OF
CAMFIN SpA ON 30 APRIL 1996

| Shareholder | Percentage owned of the share capital with voting rights |
| --- | --- |
| GPI | 53.63 |
| Acciaierie e Ferriere Lombarde Falck | 12.16 |
| Sondel | 5.02 |

## TABLE 6. OWNERSHIP STRUCTURE OF CAMFIN SpA ON 30 JANUARY 1998

| Shareholder | Percentage owned of the share capital with voting rights |
|---|---|
| GPI | 70.78 |
| Verrinvest (Techint) | 5.00 |
| CMC | 4.92 |

## TABLE 7. OWNERSHIP STRUCTURE OF CAMFIN SpA ON 29 JANUARY 1999

| Shareholder | Percentage owned of the share capital with voting rights |
|---|---|
| MTP through GPI | 51.47 |
| Giuseppe Gazzoni Frascara | 9.33 |
| Carlo Acutis | 9.30 |
| Fenera Holding | 3.89 |
| Verrinvest | 3.58 |
| Massimo Moratti | 3.52 |

## TABLE 8. OWNERSHIP STRUCTURE OF CAMFIN SpA ON 10 MAY 2001

| Shareholder | Percentage owned of the share capital with voting rights |
|---|---|
| MTP through GPI | 56.16 |
| Giuseppe Gazzoni Frascara | 9.33 |
| Carlo Acutis | 9.29 |
| Fenera Holding | 3.70 |
| Massimo Moratti | 3.13 |
| San Faustin (Verrinvest) | 2.79 |

### TABLE 9. OWNERSHIP STRUCTURE OF
### CAMFIN SpA ON 7 MAY 2003

| Shareholder | Percentage owned of the share capital with voting rights |
| --- | --- |
| MTP through GPI | 57.47 |
| Carlo Acutis | 9.3 |
| Giuseppe Gazzoni Frascara | 9.02 |
| Orium | 3.50 |
| Massimo Moratti | 3.14 |
| Fenera Holding | 3.05 |

### TABLE 10. OWNERSHIP STRUCTURE OF
### CAMFIN SpA ON 28 APRIL 2005

| Shareholder | Percentage owned of the share capital with voting rights |
| --- | --- |
| MTP through GPI | 50.13 |
| Carlo Acutis | 9.24 |
| Genesis SA | 3.48 |
| Massimo Moratti | 3.11 |
| Gazzoni Frascara | 2.33 |
| Finpar | 2.26 |

### TABLE 11. OWNERSHIP STRUCTURE OF CAMFIN SpA ON 26 APRIL 2007

| Shareholder | Percentage owned of the share capital with voting rights |
| --- | --- |
| MTP through GPI | 51.01 |
| Carlo Acutis | 8.62 |
| Genesis SA | 3.50 |
| Massimo Moratti | 2.91 |
| UBS | 2.16 |

### TABLE 12. OWNERSHIP STRUCTURE OF CAMFIN SpA ON 26 MARCH 2008

| Shareholder | Percentage owned of the share capital with voting rights |
| --- | --- |
| MTP through GPI | 53.25 |
| Carlo Acutis | 8.62 |
| Genesis SA | 3.50 |
| Massimo Moratti | 2.91 |

### TABLE 13. OWNERSHIP STRUCTURE OF CAMFIN SpA ON 28 APRIL 2009

| Shareholder | Percentage owned of the share capital with voting rights |
| --- | --- |
| MTP through GPI | 53.81 |
| Carlo Acutis | 8.62 |
| Genesis SA | 3.50 |
| UBS | 3.45 |
| Massimo Moratti | 2.91 |

### TABLE 14. OWNERSHIP STRUCTURE OF
### CAMFIN SpA ON 21 APRIL 2010

| Shareholder | Percentage owned of the share capital with voting rights |
|---|---|
| MTP through GPI | 50.31 |
| Carlo Acutis | 8.62 |
| Malacalza Investimenti | 3.50 |
| Orium | 3.50 |
| Massimo Moratti | 2.91 |

### TABLE 15. OWNERSHIP STRUCTURE OF
### CAMFIN SpA ON 22 APRIL 2011

| Shareholder | Percentage owned of the share capital with voting rights |
|---|---|
| MTP through GPI | 41.71 |
| Malacalza Investimenti | 12.10 |
| Carlo Acutis | 8.62 |
| DEAR | 3.50 |
| Massimo Moratti | 2.91 |

### TABLE 16. OWNERSHIP STRUCTURE OF
### CAMFIN SpA ON 11 MAY 2012

| Shareholder | Percentage owned of the share capital with voting rights |
|---|---|
| MTP through GPI | 42.65 |
| Malacalza Investimenti | 12.37 |
| Carlo Acutis | 7.92 |
| of which: | |
| through Yura International BV | 3.96 |
| through Vittoria Assicurazioni SpA | 3.96 |
| Massimo Moratti | 2.49 |
| of which: through CMC SpA | 1.49 |

# The Ownership Structure of SIP

### TABLE 1. OWNERSHIP STRUCTURE OF SIP ON 16 JUNE 1994

| Shareholder | Percentage owned of the share capital with voting rights |
|---|---|
| Pirelli Group | 38.00 |
| BZ Group | 25.44 |
| Treasury shares | 10.07 |
| Gavazzi, Camfin and others | 2.72 |

### TABLE 2. OWNERSHIP STRUCTURE OF SIP ON 24 MAY 1996

| Shareholder | Percentage owned of the share capital with voting rights present at the SGM |
|---|---|
| Friendly shareholders | 68.52 |
| BZ Group | 28.84 |
| Gavazzi and others | 1.5 |

## TABLE 3. OWNERSHIP STRUCTURE
## OF SIP ON 16 MAY 1997

| Shareholder | Percentage owned of the share capital with voting rights present at the SGM |
| --- | --- |
| Friendly shareholders | 63.39 |
| BZ Group | 33.67 |
| Gavazzi and others | 2.29 |

## TABLE 4. OWNERSHIP STRUCTURE
## OF SIP ON 20 APRIL 1998

| Shareholder | Percentage owned of the share capital with voting rights present at the SGM |
| --- | --- |
| Friendly shareholders | 71.67 |
| BZ Group | 27.82 |

## TABLE 5. OWNERSHIP STRUCTURE
## OF SIP ON 22 JANUARY 1999

| Shareholder | Percentage owned of the share capital with voting rights present at the SGM |
| --- | --- |
| Friendly shareholders | 67.51 |
| BZ Group | 24.87 |

# TIMELINE

**1872**

*7–8 July*: The newspaper *L'Industriale* described the newly founded enterprise's facility as 'an industrial shed comprising two blocks set along two parallel axes, in a rectangular area of 40 by 70 metres, both facing the drainage channel of the Naviglio canal known as the Sevesetto. The smaller of the two is closer to the edge of the drainage channel and will be connected with the municipal road for Greco by an iron bridge nine metres in length.' (MP/1872–1883/Faldone 1/Doc. 8)

**1877**

*10 January*: In a memoir, Giovanni Battista Pirelli recalled how he met François Casassa and offered a brief profile of the French engineer: 'I met Mr Casassa in Paris, in 1871, visiting the Charenton factory (on the Seine) of which he was sole director, since he had only managing partners for a fraction of the capital. I saw him again in Paris and at Charenton in 1872, then in Milan in 1875. In early October last year Mr Casassa came to Milan to rent part of the Aurora premises, outside Porta San Celso, communicating full instructions to set up a plant as quickly as possible to make caoutchouc products. Mr Casassa, from Savoy, started life as a factory worker in 1842, in the elastic rubber industry, which had only recently developed at that time. With his skill, spirit of initiative and intelligence, he was soon able to start his own manufacturing. Never neglecting the management of his business and keeping control of the engineering office for himself, he was able to build one of France's most prosperous factories, accumulating assets that were estimated at more than 400,000 lire in 1873. In 1873 he left his industries, following advice from his physicians after a serious illness, selling the factory to his two partners, under the proviso that he would not set up or give his name to another similar factory in France.' (MP/1872–1883/Faldone 1/Doc. 61–64)

**1884**

*February*: A brochure presenting the Company described it as follows: 'This plant, still the only one of its kind in Italy producing India rubber and gutta-percha, became the property of Ditta Pirelli & C. on 15 May 1883, replacing the previous G.B. Pirelli, F. Casassa & C., and again founded under the direction of Mr G.B. Pirelli, with fully paid-up capital of 2 million lire, divided into 4,000 shares.

A capital increase was effected in order for extending production to include the elastic threads required for the weaving of stretch fabrics, used above all in everyday footwear. Ditta Pirelli & C. wanted more than this new company and pursued the development that was also in progress in our country for the installation of electricity in industry, lighting, telegraphy and telephony. From 1881 onwards new buildings were erected and new machines acquired for production of numerous ranges of insulated electrical wires and cords, of which a significant part went to the tunnel telegraph lines required by the national railways, and the engineering corps for field telegraphy, but also to a large part of the network supplying electricity for lighting the Teatro alla Scala at the end of 1883. Last summer we took part in the Vienna International Exposition for electricity, and although we were the newest company of all those attending an event where prize-giving had been banned, our display contributed to giving conspicuous support to the Italian section (which actually seemed quite meagre), attracting the attention of competitors and visitors, which was really very flattering and encouraging for us.' (Pirelli & C./BIL 1883)

### 1886

21 *March*: As far as the administrative prospects of the Company were concerned, Pirelli said: 'I am also about to proceed to the appointment of a general and administrative director, and above all, if the policies advanced for submarine cable procurement tenders materialise, I will need help to give new drive to this intricate set of delicate units that constitute our company, to seek the energy and unity of intent that are now the cornerstones for continued success in the field of industry and trade.' (Pirelli & C./BIL 1885)

### 1900

21 *September*: Giovanni Battista Pirelli went to visit Fiat, and returned with the following impressions: 'During the visit we were able to learn more about the disputed tyres than in long correspondence, and we were able to bring improvements to their application, since the main cause of the trouble was that they had not been fitted as instructed. We are confident that bearing in mind the observations made, the performance of the tyres will be much improved.' (MP/1900/Faldone 13/Doc. 490)

### 1904

12 *November*: Alberto Pirelli wrote to his father, Giovanni Battista, from Manaus,

where he had gone to investigate the rubber market: 'The trip [on the Amazon River] was useful for understanding better the character and certain details of the lives of the people who control the initial trade of our raw material: a mix of individuals, a mix of blood; Indians, Blacks, old Brazilians of Portuguese and Dutch origin, newly arrived Portuguese, a few Turks and many with a dash of all these different races.' (MP/1903–1904/Faldone 19/Doc. 615)

*21 November*: In a second letter from Manaus, Alberto Pirelli explained the rubber market dynamic to his father, Giovanni Battista: 'Today was a day of such tension and excitement that even the old hands of the trade said they did not recall another of its kind. Yet last night, in a sort of plot among the chiefs of the various export companies, it was agreed to keep the offices closed because everyone swore and pledged they would no longer pay current prices, and at all costs wanted to force the market down, so today they were going to refuse any offers from sellers even though more than 160 tonnes had arrived on Saturday. The offices did, indeed, keep the front door closed ... while all the side doors ... were open. At two in the afternoon, not a kilo of those 160 tonnes was unsold. The price paid was much higher than yesterday. Never has Manaus seen such prices! And in this world of lies and deceit, distrust and usury, I witnessed a really typical field day; very interesting during hours of fighting, but ending with the complete failure of the attempt to bring prices down, leaving unhappy consequences: displeasure and discontent, with reciprocal allegations of failure to keep word and faith, and general complaints for the prices that had been paid.' (MP/1903–1904/Faldone 19/Doc. 615)

### 1905

*12 March*: For the first time, Giovanni Battista Pirelli proffered some official considerations on the world of 'car tyres', in the following terms: 'Among these (the various businesses that the fertile field of this industry allows) one of no small importance has been taking shape for some time and is now ripe. I mean that of car tyres. It is never easy for our products to find a place when there are other good makers ahead of us, and the car tyre market is in the hands of some powerful companies abroad. But if we are able to prepare ourselves with patience and tenacity, success will come just as it did for bicycle tyres. The factory has been performing extensive tests for some time and we have reached modest but practical manufacturing levels, and since the results have proved to be the right ones, the time has come to raise percentages radically. We intend to do that this year and commit part of the new capital that you have granted.' (Pirelli & C./BIL 1904)

## 1909

*8 February*: Writing from New York, Alberto Pirelli sums up for his American audience the difficulties encountered in tyre production: 'The manufacture of automobile tyres is extremely difficult. We did not believe so when we took up this line: having been in the rubber business for over 30 years, and having gained large experience in the manufacture on an extensive scale of practically all the different lines of rubber goods, including bicycle tyres, we thought it would be an easy matter of our technical staff to make a good automobile tyre. But as you know before we succeeded in turning out the fine tyres we now make, we went through all sorts of troubles and financial sacrifices because the difficulties that arise in the details of the manufacture of automobile tyres are far beyond any expectations.' (MP/1909/Faldone 29/Doc. 787)

## 1911

*14 January*: Alberto Pirelli wrote to Giovanni Agnelli: 'We need to increase orders from new customers to factories and garages, precisely in order to make it easier for those factories and those wholesalers who would gladly do business with us, if they had extra confidence in seeing the disappearance of the public's old habit in identifying a tyre with a well-known foreign brand, because of its large-scale advertising.' (MP/1911/Faldone 32/Doc. 851)

## 1925

*22 March*: The statement also addressed the issue of telephone concessions: 'The installation was completed by Società Italiana Reti Telefoniche, in which we are very interested, and which is now beginning to study the implementation of the government plan to extend the long-distance underground telephone network, which the government seems to have decided to manage directly, while it has assigned local telephone networks, divided into five large districts, to private industry. In this regard, we can tell you that since it had originally appeared that the government was willing to award the concession to a single entity, we took part in the formation of the Società Generale Italiana Telefoni, which included almost all major Italian banks, as well as many industries that might have been interested in the issue. However, when the government later decided to split the concession into several districts, the Società Generale Italiana Telefoni project was set aside, others were instituted for each of the various competing groups, and we decided it was more appropriate to abstain from participating in any of the tenders. We are observing this problem with some interest and in any case we hope that private industry will be able to provide the necessary development of telephone installations and that we will be able to participate in a motivating way in any ensuing work.' (Pirelli & C./BIL 1923)

## 1927

*4 April*: Piero Pirelli informed the Board of how negotiations were faring for the securities issued in the USA: '[there are] 4 million non-mortgage backed securities at a 7% interest rate payable in two six-monthly instalments, redeemable gradually over 25 years and issued by the JP Morgan & Co. bank on the North American market at a price of no less than $97 per hundred. The bank's commission is 4% and thus the proceeds are not less than 93%. The securities will be redeemed gradually, with a surcharge yet to be established, but in any case not more than 105, except for market purchase at a lower price than this.'

2. Bearers will be entitled to convert the securities into issuer shares: 'JP Morgan insisted repeatedly on the need to grant such an enticement to subscribers, expressing the opinion that if it were not offered, the issue price of the securities would have to be set at least four points lower and even so would not have the same success. All the leading industrial companies that have recently issued securities have accepted the share conversion clause, and in our case the procedure does not present any risk from the perspective of the Italian majority shareholders.' (SIP/VCdA 1927)

## 1928

*12 January*: Piero Pirelli brought the Board up to date on the equity investments recently made by the Company, in particular in SET (Società Esercizi Telefonici) of Naples, which managed one of the telephone districts, specifically that of southern Italy. He stated that at the time of its formation, 'Credito Italiano participated in the capital, in agreement with our company, and this bank is now willing to make over a share of its equity investment at the conditions under which it was acquired, as well as a share of COFIMAN (Compagnia Finanziaria Meridionale-Napoli), which has shares in SET, in FATME (Fabbrica Apparati Telefonici e Materiali Elettrici-Roma) and CIRT (Compagnia di Installazione delle Reti Telefoniche-Napoli).' (SIP/VCdA 1928)

**1929**

*18 February*: Alberto Pirelli 'informed the Board that in early January our company's shares, along with that of other Italian companies, began to be traded on New York's unofficial Cub market. JP Morgan and National City Bank consequently suggested listing the Company on the stock exchange, pointing out to us that it would be the first official Italian listing, and our company decided it was opportune to accept the proposal.' (SIP/VCdA 1929)

**1932**

*20 October*: Giovanni Battista Pirelli died and was commemorated as follows: 'He truly felt the responsibility towards the tasks entrusted to him, but also towards his workers and his country, which he loved with a heartfelt and tangible patriotism from the time he supported Garibaldi to the days of the recent national revival.' (MP/1932/Faldone 69/Doc. 1724)

*17 November*: Calcagni commemorated Giovanni Battista Pirelli during a Board meeting, with these words: 'I was present every day as the work his spirit desired was accomplished. I saw him compete boldly and tenaciously in the industrial field. I saw all kinds of obstacles that rose against him and were gradually overcome and conquered. I can say that all the merit of the acclaimed success in Italy and abroad was due to the expertise and foresight of our unforgettable dear departed. He loved all his workers like a father and in the social field was one of the first industrialists who showed positive interest in their lives, establishing welfare and assistance services. Simply mentioning the name Pirelli brings to mind an outstanding citizen, a fervent patriot, a formidable organiser, an honour to the Italian industrial class.' (SIP/VCdA 1932)

**1944**

*10 January*: The Board of Pirelli Holding once again addressed the problem of the Company's ownership structure, which had attracted the interest of the American government. If the British authorities had previously accepted an undertaking drafted by the auditors of Società Italiana Pirelli in which the Italian company held no more than 30% of share capital, *'aujourd'hui les autorités americaines desirent reprendre la question du status de notre société du point de vue des proprietaires de la majorité des actions'*. This was a new situation *'qui eventuellement pourra mettre en jeu la position personnelle du President et celle de l'un ou l'autre des administrateurs'*. (PH/VCdA 1944).

*14 March*: Pirelli Holding formulated solid proposals for the Allies in order to over-come the problem of corporate capital ownership: '*a*) grouping in a pledged deposit the majority of shares, whose voting rights would not be exercised without the consent of the American and British authorities; *b*) Pirelli Holding would refrain from transferring funds to and from its Swiss subsidiaries without the consent of the two allied governments; *c*) the Pirelli family would no longer take part in Board meetings; *d*) all correspondence with Milan would cease immediately.' (PH/VCdA 1944)

**1945**

*16 June*: A summary of the Company's activities in the period from 8 September 1943 to 25 April 1945 reads thus: 'It is worth pointing out that from the outset factory management ensured the managing directors were kept fully informed of how the situation in the plant was developing, receiving in return clear and precise guidelines, whose aim was always the supreme need to liberate the country and safeguard the welfare of employees. It was at this time [after the start of 1944] that the more active figures among our staff were asked to establish a true working partnership between management and employees, in order to: *a*) do as much as possible to hinder Nazi-Fascist activities and cut short the occupation; *b*) safe-guard the plants from probable attempts to destroy them, avoiding the removal of material precious for national economy. In the third period (from the summer of 1944), management pursued: *a*) exchanges of ideas on the organisation of armed groups within the plants to defend equipment and materials; *b*) enabling introduc-tion of arms and munitions into the factory and exchange of arms and munitions for other materials we had available; *c*) supply of material produced or owned to overseas organisations that were gradually emerging, thus removing it all from German and Italian military and Fascist control at home and abroad; *d*) use of corporate vehicles for any number of pretexts to assist partisan actions, both for collecting arms and munitions, and for outright military actions.' (MP/1945/Faldone 87/Doc. 2207)

**1946**

*2 December*: There follows the entire financial statement from the directors for the period ending 30 September 1946, since it is a document of eminent economic and civic value that outlines the prospects of the Company in subsequent years: 'Following liberation, production could only be restarted slowly and incompletely because of the lack of raw materials and fuel, while the enormous personnel costs were ongoing and rising. Thus the contribution the Company made for supporting the resistance and the duty towards social solidarity naturally led to huge sacrifices. Later the situation improved thanks to an influx of rubber and other raw materials in increasing amounts, although still less than what was required. The materials arrived thanks to the UNRRA towards which our branch of industry can only nurture feelings of deep gratitude. We must express special appreciation to the Italian authorities which, on seeing the national importance of our production, offered us every assistance in their power. For our part, we offered the government the most impartial support with regard to supplies from abroad of raw materials intended for the entire Italian rubber and electrical conductor industries. The great variety of such needs and the frequency with which there was a shortage of one raw material or other, the difficulties in procuring coal and the reduced availability of electricity, delayed and continue to delay full resumption of work. Workforce productivity also significantly affected volume of production, but we are happy to report that there is continuing improvement in this field. Conscientious figures among worker representatives in the management committee and the internal commission, as well as large numbers of workers themselves are now aware that increased productivity is mainly in the interests of consumer groups and thus the workers. Only through common effort in this field can the country be saved from financial and monetary ruin, and obtain that improvement in standard of living for workers for which everyone fervently hopes. Remunerating employment and benevolent works on our part were not only in response to legislative or contractual provisions, but very often anticipated and extended them, and we trust that this is appreciated by our great industrial family and helps keep alive the corporate spirit of solidarity and alleviate mistrust, fed chiefly by the masses who do not understand completely the economic factors that dominate the situation. In this regard, we would like to mention the fact that as things stand overall employment remuneration, related expenses and integrations to the personnel severance pay fund will amount to nearly 6 billion lire per year, from which over 700 million lire must be drawn for contributions to canteens and other forms of social assistance. In view of these figures, despite setting aside the unique conditions affecting the financial year just ended, even a quite generous remuneration of current share capital would represent less than 1/25th of that attributed to work. This exceptional situation is also due to the very limited adjustment applied to balance sheet items for the value of money. In this latest report, adjustments to employment remuneration were justly higher for those categories earning less, bringing their average hourly earnings levels equal to 25 times pre-war levels, while higher up in the classification the adjustment has so far been more limited. A far more costly entry for these times of currency devaluations and rapid wage increases is that regarding personnel severance pay, which automatically grows as it is calculated on the basis of the employee's last salary, in proportion to the number of years worked. This increase just for the financial year we are examining amounts to about 700 million lire, a total that in our meticulous methods should have been entered in the profit and loss account. The exceptional amount of the charge persuaded us to enter only the amount for the year and even taking into account the amounts paid out to staff who left the company this financial year, spending nonetheless came to 188 million lire. Demand for our products has been far greater than our production lines were able to meet, except that the slow recovery in construction and manufacturing initially slowed demand for electrical cables and conductors. More recently we have noticed a substantial increase in demand in this field, also from abroad, bringing in important orders that confirm the reputation enjoyed by our production. Various articles of our rubber range have picked up briskly to the point that even just considered alone, this production line would be sufficient to justify setting up a major industry in its own right. The tyre sector presents the same characteristics we have already described. Production is not yet in equilibrium with market needs and is still affected by a black market which, despite its enormous profits, is destined to disappear since it asks for eight-ten times more than our price list. It is astonishing that the black market for tyres is conducted in the light of day, not covertly or with at least a minimum of decency as seen in other markets. There are even small new factories printing pricelists and invoicing normally on the basis of increased prices, confident of enjoying absolute impunity while a major industry like ours, which is also progressive in social welfare, has to stand by and watch this unseemly and deliberate profiteering and itself make conscious sacrifices. Naturally our company's efforts are aimed at increasing the type production both for two-wheelers and cars, a kind of production closely connected with the interests of workers and transport problems. Although the clearly worrisome phase caused by the standstill and the shortage of raw materials is drawing to a close, we have not yet entered a normal phase, although we are confident that the intrinsic (move and rationalisation of facilities, technical progress and worker productivity) and extrinsic (availability of raw materials and fuel, transport and electricity) conditions will be such as to allow all fields of our business to achieve normal production performance and meet the large demand seen not only in the domestic market but also abroad. This is the only way we will be able to rely on results that allow reasonable remuneration for capital on one hand, to compensate what was not done in recent times, and on the other a continuation of that policy of particular concern for our workers of all categories, which even in the recent past represented a confident anticipation of higher corporate productivity and profitability. The reconstruction of buildings and installations damaged by air raids was carried out gradually, strictly in line with minimum production needs, facing much higher costs that the values attributable by law to the destroyed assets. Reports of the damages were correctly produced but no further funds were forthcoming after the modest advance we mentioned in the 1944 annual statement. Once the war was over, we proceeded to bring home the decentralised processes. Some were grouped in specially built new buildings at Bicocca. For others it was decided that it was not appropriate for technical and organisational reasons to concentrate them there, so they were then housed in detached facilities. For this end a factory was purchased in Seregno, now being refurbished and extended for future specialisation in production of health and sports articles. Negotiations are underway for the purchase of another facility where we will transfer production of waterproofed products. Our group companies have also recovered from the damage caused by the war and almost all are now operating at a satisfactory pace.' (SIP/BIL 30 September 1946)

## 1956

*10 October*: Piero Pirelli, who had died on 7 August 1956, was remembered as follows: 'We will always remember his smiling face and his words, dictated by his calm and his deeply serene intelligence, will always help us. We will never forget that he was a good man or the proof he left of this sublime trait of his.'

## 1957

2. For the first time a third generation family member entered the limited partnership: 'Way back in 1904, at the 20 March SGM, my father announced and confirmed that on 18 December he would be appointing my brother Piero and myself as directors to flank him in our limited partnership. He mentioned our education, our travels abroad and the experience we were already acquiring in business, adding that this decision filled him with a sense of trust and responsibility. He was supported by the auditors, believing they were surely providing our

company with an expert team of managers for its entire duration. The comment was indulgent since my brother Piero was 23 and I was 22. Today my son Leopoldo is 31 and for over seven years he has been completely committed to the Group's interests, especially the companies in which we are most interested: Pirelli SpA and SIP.' (Pirelli & C./BIL 1956)

## 1966

*27 January*: Salient passages from an interview by Piero Ottone to Leopoldo Pirelli were published by *Corriere della Sera*: 'We are four co-workers [Leopoldo Pirelli and three managing directors] and each is responsible for their own sector, with an ample and independent range of action, while together we form a team that examines major business problems with the chairman, who assumes final responsibility in the decisions reached collectively.'

2. Vis-à-vis the Board, 'it is not made up of people chosen according to their equity stake or for prestige window dressing. It is made up of industrialists and financiers whose opinion is of great benefit to the Company: they offer something more, and that would be lost if they were replaced by directors whose opinion comes through other channels.'

3. As regards information: [Leopoldo Pirelli] 'would like to say much more and intends to do so. He is, however, held back by concerns he voices clearly. As long as information is not seen as compulsory for all companies, those that offer the public better information are likely to boost less forthcoming competitors when they provide information on the value of facilities, on the division of revenue, and on investment projects. With regard to business developments, shareholders are right to ask for more information compared to in the past, but we must choose the regularity of such information carefully. All these resolves for "openness" may offer immediate benefits. More information about the life of the company increases shareholder confidence and facilitates collection of capital on financial markets, thus solving difficulties in financing, a problem for European enterprise as a whole.' (MP/1966/Faldone 129/Doc. 2785)

## 1970

*23 February*: The Board deals with 'the proposal for the integration between the Pirelli SpA and Société Internationale Pirelli and the Dunlop Group, based in the London Dunlop Company.' The project was described as follows: 'Gruppo Pirelli, over almost a century of continuous, planned development, has reached positions

413

of high technological prestige in its sectors of operation, making it one of the world's leading industries. In parallel, the Group has progressively extended its industrial and commercial penetration, especially in Europe and in the Americas, now vaunting 82 plants overall, with about 76,000 employees, of whom 42,000 are in Italy. In 1969, total Group turnover was 670 billion lire. The Dunlop Group has 128 plants, mainly in Europe, Africa, Asia and North America, with 102,000 employees. In 1969, global turnover was 730 billion lire. Dunlop has traditions, dimensions and activities in technological fields similar to those of Pirelli, while also showing product diversification that makes the companies extremely complementary. This overall project would take Pirelli-Dunlop (210 factories on all continents, 178,000 employees, and revenues of 1,400 billion lire) to third place in the world rubber industry. In principle the proposed plan provides for an integration of respective industrial activities, with each of the two groups acquiring substantial investments – ranging from 40% to 49% – in the other's industrial current or future subsidiaries. Pirelli SpA, Société Internationale Pirelli and Dunlop would remain as finance companies and retain their legal personalities.' (Pirelli/VCdA 10)

23 *April*: The annual statement focused, in particular, on the start of the integration process with Dunlop: 'Vis-à-vis Gruppo Pirelli, prospects opened by larger world markets and progressive trade liberalisation have been carefully evaluated, as have the degree of maturity and efficiency achieved by industrial and commercial management and facilities. Hence the belief that it was time to look to new, broader development goals, following the orientation of the progressive commodity and geographic diversification that has been a constant in Pirelli policy from the start.' Integrating with Dunlop 'would help achieve higher efficiency in the tyre and other rubber products industry, thus offering better competitive opportunities for sharing the results of scientific, technological and technical research, for rationalisation and cooperation in all fields, to lower costs and achieve access to a wide financial base. It should be clear that the project would not in any way reduce Pirelli's focus on production investments or employment in Italy. The overall responsibility of such an important and multidimensional global group would be entrusted to a small joint committee of the highest level, which would draft a general common policy and formulate basic guidelines to be submitted to the respective Boards.' (Pirelli/BIL 1969)

## 1972

*12 June*: The financial statement report dated 30 April 1972 commemorated Alberto Pirelli, who had died on 19 October 1971: 'He lived in an age of great change, both in terms of social aspirations and achievements, and in the structure of the economy: an era characterised by exceptional progress in the workforce and the general standard of living and culture, science and technology, but also a time of dramatic events and conflicts. He was a successful player of his day, tackling the larger issues not only with extraordinary intelligence, responsibility and sensitivity, but also with an ability to grasp the general direction of the changes taking place, being part of them and ahead of them. He brought new depth to the figure of the industrialist with his personality and ethos, within the tasks he faced as an expert of economy and finance, the international dimension into which he projected the direction of development for Pirelli enterprises and the overall best interests of the country.'

## 1975

*2 July*: For the management plan, the following considerations were made: *a)* 'It will last for five years. Without the administrative and financial actions outlined above, the subsidiary has no hope of recovery. Following the poor performance of 1975 and 1976, the projection shows an economic reprise for 1977–1978'; *b)* 'The financial requirement for the five years in question is approximately 270 billion lire, of which 180 billion is for capital investment and 90 billion for working capital. Coverage is expected to be self-financing for around 150 billion, with 60 billion from mobilisation of internal group resources through financial transactions and/or disposal of group assets; 60 billion from the use of soft loans provided for by Law 464 of 8 August 1972'; *c)* 'From the employment perspective, the result would lead to redundancies that are difficult to quantify precisely; *d)* 'The alternatives studied for the financial restructuring sum up the main conditions: the latter (is expected) to achieve 42 billion lire and involve the issuance of corporate convertible bonds for 40 billion lire with the Mediobanca formula.' (Pirelli/VCdA 11)

## 1976

*20 February*: The auditors emphasised that 'Pirelli SpA has continued to increase its commitments and risks with regard to Industrie Pirelli, following Dunlop's financial disengagement. And so there are alternatives: either we believe that Industrie Pirelli will be able to achieve an economic equilibrium in a relatively short time, or we do not believe that the economic rebalancing can be reached in a timespan that will not affect the fate of the parent company irreparably, and thus termination of support will be unavoidable.'

2. With regard to the development of a plan for the period 1976–1981, as far as tyres were concerned, the intention was to 'separate tyre manufacturing into two companies, one for the tyre and steel cord company, the other for research. With this in mind, it was considered appropriate to explore two alternative suggestions that would reduce tyre risk and commitment for the group if implemented. The suggestions were: *a)* action in the national context involving a third partner in the tyre business who would acquire a 50% equity investment; *b)* selling off the tyre branch entirely to a third party.'

3. Geddes intervened on the tyre issue with this declaration: 'The tyre problem must be addressed, bearing three things in mind: 1) limit further actions that could weaken Pirelli SpA; 2) free the cable business of any losses suffered in other sectors; 3) safeguard the principle underpinning the Union of private enterprises with equal equity and avoid any significant conflict of interest, especially in the EEC.' (Pirelli/VCdA 12)

*24 May*: With regard to the prospects of Industrie Pirelli, Mediobanca expressed the following opinion: 'In examining Industrie Pirelli's prospects, Mediobanca has expressed the opinion that the subsidiary's financial structure should be strengthened further. It proposed that Pirelli SpA re-examine the suggestion of issuing convertible bonds, in part as Pirelli SpA capital and the rest in shares of other companies in our portfolio, chiefly Brasileira preference, Siemens, and shares from the owner of Centro Pirelli.' (Pirelli/VCdA 12)

**1981**

*22 April*: In relation to the operation to dissolve the Union, Leopoldo Pirelli wrote: 'an agreement has been reached with Dunlop to dissolve the Union, following the grave losses suffered by Dunlop Ltd, forecasts that the crisis will not be short-lived, fears that Dunlop International may also be involved in the medium-term, and the conviction that the Union had been progressively weakened by diverging interests and offered more disadvantages than advantages including in terms of decision-making. The agreement provides for the dissolution to take place in two stages. In the first, which will be completed by the end of July, Pirelli and Dunlop Holdings will return the mutually held minority investments in the majority of the companies operating in Europe; the second stage will take place by the end of this year, with the exchange of remaining reciprocal investments, namely the minority interests in Dunlop International and in SIP subsidiaries. The latter will be returned by Dunlop Holdings, half going to SIP and half to Pirelli SpA, with the exception of the Argentine Pirelli Platense, of which a greater share will go to Pirelli SpA, to match the share sold to SIP in March 1980.' (Pirelli/VCdA 16)

## 1982

*15 April*: Vis-à-vis the Group's efficiency project, Leopoldo Pirelli 'illustrated the current distribution of holdings and management responsibilities between the two parent companies and underlined the considerable drawbacks in terms of strategic guidelines, allocation of funds and corporate management. The two fundamental points are: 1) creation of equal interests in the operations management of the parent companies; 2) management coordination of the operating companies. To achieve the first objective, the proposal was to proceed with the exchange of shares and capital measures for several subsidiaries, so that the investment portfolios of the two parent companies would have equal direct or indirect equity in each subsidiary. Main stock movements will lead to SIP entering companies operating in Italy and in Germany; Pirelli SpA entering the French cable project; a significant increase in investments in cable actions in the United States and Australia; a substantial increase in the Brazilian investment. As regards the second point, the intention is to create a new company, Pirelli Société Générale SH, owned equally by the two parent companies. It will be given the mandate to manage the investments in all subsidiaries in order to meet the aims of each in both financial and industrial terms. PSG's registered offices will be in Basel and will use extant structures there and in Milan. He is convinced that the new company will allow maximisation of efficiency of a business increasingly characterised by a growing interdependence of world markets, by comparison with leading industrial groups managed together.' (Pirelli/VCdA 16)

## 1988

*5 March*: With regard to the Firestone takeover bid, De Giorgi underlined the following considerations: 'We feel that our size and current position (turnover of $2.5 billion, ranked fifth worldwide and lacking manufacturing on the North American market) are sufficient to make a successful move against the four competitors who are far bigger than us.' He also referred to 'contacts with Firestone up until

Firestone recently announced it had come to an agreement, in principle, with Bridgestone, to establish a subsidiary in which the latter acquired 75% of equity and to which all Firestone tyre activities would be transferred'. De Giorgi added: 'In this respect, a contract has already been signed with Michelin, and in the event of our offer being successful, the company has committed to the purchase of the Firestone subsidiary in Brazil and the Master Care car sales and assistance organisation, for a total of 650 million. Moreover, Michelin has an option to make a 50% investment in Firestone United States synthetic rubber and diversified products business, for a further $150 million. Firestone's 1987 sales amounted to $3,860 million of which $2,600 million were in the tyre sector. Firestone has 23 main plants, mostly in the United States and Canada, followed by France, Italy, Portugal, Spain, Argentina, Brazil, Venezuela and New Zealand. The acquisition of Firestone would allow Pirelli to reach a third-place ranking worldwide, behind Goodyear and Michelin, with a tyre turnover in excess of $5,000 million.' (Pirelli/VCdA 19)

**1990**

*14 September*: During a Pirelli Board meeting, a plan is put forward to integrate the tyre business with that of the German company Continental: 'The merger of Continental and Pirelli could give rise to a new "major player", with a consolidated market share of 16% worldwide and a total tyre turnover of 13 billion Deutschemarks. On the basis of its sheer size, the new company would be able to compete with the three giants across the globe, and challenge Michelin in Europe.' The benefits arising from the merger would be: '1) In the recent past Pirelli has invested substantially in engineering and processes applicable to flexible industrial automation systems that ensure quality, product uniformity, and service standards required by cutting-edge automotive companies. The new company would have a critical mass sufficient to justify and exploit to the full flexible automated factory systems on a large scale; 2) the geographical presence of Continental and Pirelli is more complementary than overlapping. While Continental is a leader in Germany and Austria, and is reasonably positioned in the US, Pirelli is the market leader in Italy and Latin America, with a strong presence in several other European countries and in Turkey; 3) the pre-eminent position in some markets will allow the new company to ensure a higher control over its own pricing policy and to abandon the price-follower role to which the two groups are now often relegated.' The offer characteristics were: 'From the very start it has been clear that there is an absolute necessity to anchor any combination to a defined majority stake and to shared management and aim. If these actions are not guaranteed, the operation should not be taken into consideration. Independent shareholders, mostly Germans and Italians, supported the proposal as outlined here and, in view of this, formed a group with Pirelli controlling over 50% of Continental share capital and with a sufficient share of votes that could be validly expressed to ensure a majority in the meeting. The above is subordinated to: 1) elimination of the 5% voting right cap; 2) approval by the German and/or EEC antitrust authorities. It also provides for the acquisition in cash by Continental of PTH's entire assets, and resolution by the Continental SGM of a capital increase which will entitle all shareholders to benefit from option rights for the purpose of financing the aforementioned acquisition operation. The amount of the transaction is deemed to be in the order of 50–66% of the entire extant capital. Once the capital increase is completed, PTH will have the majority of votes in the control group (subscribing the entire capital increase).' (Pirelli/VCdA 21)

*25 September*: Leopoldo Pirelli gave the Pirelli Board a progress report on negotiations with Continental: 'After an initially difficult, but quite positive encounter, the situation has since deteriorated, following the unilateral press release issued by Continental on the 17th, then the meeting on the 19th between the two managing directors assisted by their respective teams, where breakdown was only just avoided, and finally the letter of the 24th, with which Continental's Vorstand notified rejection of Pirelli's proposal dated the 14th.'
2. Continental AG's letter dated 24 September mentioned above and signed by Urban, chairman of the management Board, stated that: 'The management board of Continental does see some merits in the idea of a combination between both Groups in view of developments in the world tyre industry. The proposal has however several serious defects which led to our request to your representatives in our meeting in Frankfurt of 19 September to withdraw the proposal, thus enabling both sides to explore the opportunities and the best structure for a possible combination. Your representatives' refusal to withdraw the proposal coupled with the extraordinary publicity campaign launched by Pirelli has prompted a quick decision of public rejection by Continental. We consider it most unfortunate and indeed counterproductive that Pirelli has chosen this route. In our experience, merger and takeover discussion will not normally yield positive results unless they are conducted in absolute confidence until a mutually acceptable outcome is reached.' The reasons for this 'public rejection' were indicated as 'the questionable

stability of Pirelli shareholders structure and its unwillingness to disclosure the identity and the nature of the agreements with the group of Continental share-holders, already supporting the Pirelli proposal'. (Pirelli/VCdA 21)

*5 December*: Leopoldo Pirelli informed the Board of Pirelli that he had received from Continental 'a request to sign a standstill agreement, which required a com-mitment not to purchase or sell Continental shares, nor to promote convening of the SGM to eliminate the 5% voting rights cap, or for changes in the composition of the supervisory board, or to take any other decision connected to an arrangement with Pirelli'. Vis-à-vis the evolution of the Continental affair, Pirelli's Chairman told the Board: 'The latest and less defined development is the proposal made by the chairman of Continental's supervisory board to form two groups of sharehold-ers, one comprising Pirelli and its supporters, the other German shareholders, the two being linked by a pool agreement with greater weight afforded to the group headed by Pirelli. With the formation of a pool, the implementation of this sce-nario entails a solution that is quite different from the original, since in forfeiting full leadership, we accept that decisions of an extraordinary nature may be taken only with the consent of the German shareholder group. Moreover, it would make it difficult to achieve full consolidation of the new Continental into our company's financial statements.' (Pirelli/VCdA 21)

**1991**
*5 March*: The Board of Pirelli SpA was advised of a Continental SGM on the follow-ing 13 March, with the following agenda: '1) to take the required majority to 75% to abolish the voting cap of 5%; 2) a similar majority is requested for withdrawal from the alienation of important Continental business sectors; 3) a similar majority is requested for revocation of the supervisory board; 4) abolish the 5% voting cap; 5) give mandate to the supervisory board to study the integration of Pirelli Tyre Holding with Continental.' (Pirelli/VCdA 21)

*24 September*: Von Gruenberg was elected new chairman of the Continental super-visory board. In this respect, the Pirelli Board was reminded: 'With regard to the 'integration' solution, that it is opposed by Continental because: *a)* Continental management, still under the influence of Urban's ideas, would consider any solu-tion that placed Pirelli in a position of control a defeat. The negative consequences of such an attitude on future management are easy to imagine; with regard to the 'collaboration, there would be the drawback of leaving Pirelli and Continental in independent positions and competitors in markets with differentiated and potentially diverging interests, at least as far as failure to unify through the formation of business units; future difficulties might arise in the relationship between the two groups.' So it was agreed that 'any acceptance by Pirelli of the "collaboration" solution would be subject to the following conditions: a) establishment of a stable Continental shareholder structure such as the following: Pirelli 5–10%; Toyo 5–10%; Yokohama 5–10%; German institutional investors 25–35%; placement in part with Toyo and Yokohama, in part with German institutional investors of about 25% of the equity currently in the hands of friends of Pirelli, in the context of the creation of the aforementioned stable shareholder structure; b) willingness of the Germans to take temporary responsibility for the entire 25% currently in the hands of friends of Pirelli, subsequently to be transferred in part to Japanese shareholders.' (Pirelli/VCdA 22)

*30 November*: Marco Tronchetti Provera told the SIP Board that 'it is necessary to proceed with the subscription of a share capital increase to subscribe new Pirelli SpA shares. There is an agreement in place for a capital increase by BZ Bank.' (SIPBA/VCdA 10)

2. A progress report on negotiations with Continental was made to the Pirelli Board: 'From September onwards, the "collaboration" solution was thus examined in detail. Continental was forced to acknowledge that if the companies were to remain independent, the synergies accomplished would be worth very little. Moreover, no acceptable solution has been found for accommodating shares held by investors who agreed with the Pirelli strategy and purchased stock in view of a merger between the two companies. After Pittini and the Chairman met with Weiss and von Gruenberg, there was no option but to acknowledge the need to suspend the search for a definitive solution with Continental, both from structural and company perspectives, and at global cooperation level.' Subsequently Leopoldo Pirelli suggested 'finding purchasers for the 30–35% of Continental in the hands of friends of Pirelli, the 5% held by Pirelli Tyre Holding, and a further 32% in option to Pirelli exercisable in two years via Mediobanca'.

3. Following the conclusion of the Continental affair, corporate restructuring was planned: 'The Continental matter contributed substantially to the deterioration that occurred, but there is no doubt that in recent financial years management has shown growing and excessive use of cash. Today we tend to think that the Group's

financial underpinning would still have been insufficient to be able to pursue development of three business sectors, each with challenging expansion plans, although all of different scope and nature. So we are inclined to think that a downscaling was required in any case.' For these reasons a divestiture plan was put in place, which would reach 'an amount of at least 1,000 billion, to be completed within 18 months, to be accomplished by giving irrevocable and joint mandate to Mediobanca and Pirelli & C. The divestiture plan involved property on the former Bicocca site, as well as sale of the diversified products branch and several other activities; a capital increase of about 500 billion to be approved by an Extraordinary Shareholders' Meeting to be held by 31 January 1992; a financing plan developed with Mediobanca envisaging that Mediobanca itself, in the context of covering group needs, examines granting: a) a loan of 750 billion in five years in a pool with other credit institutes; b) an irrevocable three-year line of credit for a further 750 billion through a pool of credit companies, led by Credito Italiano'. (Pirelli/VCdA 22)

**1992**

*21 January*: During the Extraordinary Shareholders' Meeting for the capital increase, Marco Tronchetti Provera illustrated the situation: 'The differences between the attributable consolidated loss (590 billion) and statutory loss (390 billion) is made up of group company dividends, a deprecation in the entire equity of Sipir NV, partially offset by an extant reserve of 106 billion in Sipir, and a gain on the sale of the Bicocca areas.'
2. Leopoldo Pirelli outlined the result of the Continental operation: 'Investor compensation costs came to 138 billion and with the payments already effected, all obligations on the part of the Group were met. These were, however, conditional promises made to a number of subjects who had decided to invest in Continental with the expectation of growing the value of shares following the merger. Given the structure of the operation, its management and its results would depend mainly on the business decisions made by Pirelli, in which the other investors were not going to take part. Nonetheless, there was a promise that if, within a certain date (end of 1991), the merger between the Pirelli and Continental tyre businesses was not confirmed, Gruppo Pirelli would relieve them of any damages caused by the investment.' (Pirelli/VA 32)

*14 February*: After having explained the reasons for the appointment of Marco Tronchetti Provera as executive deputy chairman of Pirelli SpA, Leopoldo Pirelli 'thanked Tronchetti for his brilliant work in three years as managing director, which had earned him the esteem of the shareholder base and the press, and also thanked him personally for his work, wishing him every success for his new and weighty responsibilities'. (SIPBA/VCdA 10)

2. Leopoldo Pirelli recalled that 'if there was a vote of confidence from the Board he would continue with his current management task for as long as his contribution was required in starting up the Group's reorganisation phase. He feels that he can safely say the phase is under way and thus he has decided to inform the Board of his decision to resign from his executive mandate.' In this respect Leopoldo Pirelli 'expressed the opinion that the time is right to hand over executive responsibilities to those who will be tasked with the industrial and financial reorganisation of the company. He suggests to the Board: *a)* appointing Mr Marco Tronchetti Provera chief executive officer of Pirelli SpA, tasking him with the role of executive deputy chairman in addition to that already conferred of managing director; *b)* establishing the executive committee and inviting the chairman, executive deputy chairman Tronchetti Provera, chief executive officer Sierra, and deputy chairmen Messrs Pittini and Alberto Pirelli to be part of it, as well as directors Messrs Sarasin and Sozzani.' (Pirelli/VCdA 22)

*24 April*: During the Pirelli & C. SGM, Marco Tronchetti Provera commented on the nature of the investment in Continental, which 'has assumed the character of a financial investment, also to be protected for the recovery of costs incurred. He is confident that Pirelli has the ability to operate with positive results in the tyre market, despite the failure of the Continental operation. He thus feels the investments planned for the reorganisation of the branch are justified. He specifies that the carrying value of the shares held by Pirelli Tyre Holding amounts to 207 Deutschemarks, while the stock option purchase price is round 66 Deutschemarks per share.' (Pirelli & C./BIL 1991)

**1993**
*1 April*: Regarding negotiations with Continental, Tronchetti Provera informed the Board of SIP that: 'Pirelli, with the intermediation of Mediobanca, indicated to Deutsche Bank that it would accept an offer covering the value appearing in accounts with a margin that considers the package's strategic value. Deutsche Bank is seeking a global solution for the 5% held by Pirelli and the 33% for which Pirelli has an option.' (SIPBA/VCdA 10)

*10 December*: With regard to the Cables branch: 'Sales in Europe have dropped almost everywhere, both in telecommunications cables and in energy cables, with the exception of a telecommunications cables upturn in France. In the USA we saw a drop in telephone cable prices due to the downturn in optical fibre prices.'

2. With regard to the Stet situation, Marco Tronchetti Provera 'informed the Board in detail of the steps taken with the IRI chairmanship to compete as part of technological and financial alliances, in the privatisation of Stet. After some very positive initial contacts and the presentation of our project to IRI, encouraging contacts were initiated with Alcatel. Unfortunately IRI chairmanship has not yet followed up with a coherent approach, indeed it has not pursued the confidential negotiations and has left space for press comments to which we have had to respond.' (Pirelli/VCdA 24)

## 1996

*19 April*: Leopoldo Pirelli 'states he has decided not to run again for re-election to the Board at the next SGM. He added that he came to the decision on the one hand because of his age and years of service (70 years old, with 45 working for the group, 33 of which as an executive representative), and on the other because he was aware that he was leaving the Company in capable and reliable hands, fully confident that the new Board would elect Mr Marco Tronchetti Provera as its executive chairman and confirm his son Alberto Pirelli as deputy chairman. He spoke of his intention to continue for the next three years as Chairman of the Pirelli & C. Board, and his willingness to stay on for the same length of time as the deputy chairman of SIP.' (Pirelli/VCdA 26)

## 1998

*24 March*: The Chairman outlined 'a plan intended to simplify the group's company organisation involving Pirelli & C., SIP, and Pirelli SpA, and which would culminate in Pirelli & C. having direct control over Pirelli SpA downstream of the merger to incorporate SIP and Pirelli SpA. *a)* acquisition by SIP of 1,700,000 non-voting shares held by BZ Group Holding and/or BZ Bank Limited, at the unit price of 350 Swiss francs and conversion to non-voting shares; *b)* an offer to purchase all SIP shares in circulation at the unit price of 350 Swiss francs, promoted by Pirelli & C; *c)* upon conclusion of the offer to purchase, removal of all SIP stock from Swiss stock exchange listings and attainment of full control of SIP; *d)* lastly, the merger of SIP and Pirelli SpA while maintaining Milan stock exchange listings of securities arising from the transaction. After these operations, Pirelli & C. would acquire a direct participation of no less than 30.01% of Pirelli SpA for its portfolio, while the BZ Group Holding Limited, currently SIP's second shareholder, would take 10%. In relation to half of the BZ Group Holding Limited participation, a special agreement was reached regarding both a put and call, and the voting right that would be exercised from the start, as indicated by Marco Tronchetti Provera in his role as general partner of Pirelli & C. The presence of Gruppo Pirelli in Switzerland will also be reinforced in terms of activities and operations units through the subsidiaries Pirelli Cables and Systems, Pirelli Tyre Europe and Pirelli Société Générale. After this acquisition and the conversion into shares of the remaining participation, and prior to the takeover bid, Pirelli & C. and the BZ Group Holding Limited will hold 58% and 24% of SIP respectively.' (Pirelli/VCdA 28)

*22 May*: The agreement between Tronchetti Provera and Ebner expected Pirelli & C. to concede a first sale option of 5% of capital to the BZ Group, of which '2.5% between 10 March 1999 and 10 March 2004, and a second option on 20 March 2003. BZ will also give Pirelli & C. a purchase option, which may not exceed 5% of voting rights on 13 March 2003.'

2. Leopoldo Pirelli described the Pirelli family's arrival in GPI as follows: 'Given that SOPAF was selling a 13% equity investment in GPI, which controls Camfin, which in turn controls Fin.P., he and his offspring sold Fin.P. shares, and used the proceeds and new funds to purchase SOPAF's 13% of GPI.'

3. Tronchetti Provera described the BZ Group operation as: 'The operation that shareholders and analysts dream of. Until now there had been issues, some technical, due to the impediments a Swiss company encounters when merging with an Italian business. Finally a way was found to transfer SIP to an EU country, merge it with Pirelli Partecipazioni, which had also moved to the same country, then bring the merged company to Italy, where it will merge with Pirelli SpA. As part of that operation, in order to consolidate the Pirelli & C. participation in Pirelli SpA, Ebner was asked to obtain an option to purchase shares that BZ will hold in Pirelli SpA when the project is completed. Ebner granted a time option for half of his shares and, in what may be misplaced confidence, specified the condition that the option was to be linked to Marco Tronchetti Provera being authorised to give voting instructions. The agreement was also concluded with regard to the allocation of voting rights based on Ebner's personal trust in Marco Tronchetti Provera, with the full consent of all managing partners, who deemed all clauses

425

in the agreement to be in the company's best interests, including that attributing to Pirelli & C. the immediate faculty to exercise a purchase option in the event of Marco Tronchetti Provera leaving the Group.' (Pirelli & C./VA 19)

**1999**
*25 May*: Leopoldo Pirelli provided brief outlines of Marco Tronchetti Provera and his son Alberto Pirelli. For the former, he said: 'Marco is certainly the brains behind our group's recent recovery. He is the leader, the number one, and that is how it should be with his professional and personal disposition. He is very intelligent, he has intuition, and a command of people in the company, with a sense of developing relations outside of it.' Regarding his son Alberto: 'He does not have the latter abilities because he is part of the Company and the family: he has a sense of duty, a great capacity for direct work and loyalty to the name, of whose ethical traditions he is a perfect heir.' (Pirelli & C./VA 19)

*20 December*: Tronchetti Provera informed the Board that 'we have reached an agreement with Cisco Systems for a strategic alliance in the field of optical transmission that substantially covers 1) Cisco's entrance with a 10% investment, for a value of $100 million, in the newly formed optical components and submarine optical systems company; 2) sale by Pirelli to Cisco of terrestrial optical systems worth a total of $2.15 billion, of which about 20% is dependent on achieving sales targets and management. The synergies arising from the new partnership mean some improvement of optical technology can be expected in the Internet field, and thus also for industrial activities, with positive impact on Pirelli Cavi e Sistemi's income-earning prospects.' (Pirelli/VCdA 30)

**2000**
*25 January*: With reference to the photonics sector, Tronchetti Provera stated that 'the sale of activities to Cisco terrestrial photonics was concluded on 14 February 2000, with a payment of €1,575.30 million. It should be stressed that there is both financial and strategic significance in this agreement establishing a partnership between Pirelli and Cisco in the fields of optical engineering and Telecom submarine cables, both high-tech sectors with an expected high growth rate.'
2. Mention is made of 'the understanding with BICC General for purchasing energy cables activities formerly owned by the British Group BICC and bought out last year by the American General Cable group'. (Pirelli & C./VCdA 4)

*20 March*: The Board was informed that the purchase process of Siemens Energy Cables by Metal Manufacturers Limited's energy cables and construction division had been completed, 'for a further 50% of FOS, the remaining 50% of Pirelli Cable Indonesia, as well as Pirelli Tyre Company (Egypt). As for the current financial year, it is set to be characterised mainly by the ongoing commitment to the integration of former Siemens and former BICC activities, the ongoing exploitation of traditional business, and the search for new opportunities in the various markets.' (Pirelli/VCdA 30)

*8 May*: Marco Tronchetti Provera explained the steps in the Cisco operation, which 'was created as a result of Pirelli in-house research. Starting from the fibres, we arrived at the optical components and thence the terrestrial optical systems where we find major world electronics operators. In this sector we needed to integrate with those who have the software and the ability to manage networks. The technological convergence between electronics, optical and networks management was such that Pirelli's space was inevitably reduced. Cisco was found to be the ideal partner because it had all the skills but needed to integrate the optical side. Thus we sold off the segment that was inaccessible for the group, but core technology arising from fibre was maintained and we stayed in the optical components field because the strategic line being pursued is to continue fibre development. Optical fibres have a very important future, ranging from simple transport to sending data, with very interesting perspectives. In this case, Pirelli has a group of very valid researchers and expects very interesting results. To recap the Cisco story in a nutshell, we can simply recall how, in just five years, a research centre grew into a company with 1,000 workers, and then decided to sell off an international business branch for over $1.5 billion.'
2. Tronchetti Provera also mentioned acquisitions made in the cable sector: 'Pirelli Cavi e Sistemi completed the purchase of part of NKF energy cable activities, which included the production of energy cables with high, medium and low voltage for utilities with factories in Delft (Netherlands) and Pikkala (Finland).' With regard to the activities acquired by BICC: 'In 1999 these activities recorded about €700 million in turnover, with 3,500 employees and 11 manufacturing plants in the United Kingdom and Italy, which together account for about 80% of 1999 revenues, and in Africa, Asia, including a local joint venture in China.' (Pirelli SpA/VA 36)

*26 September*: Tronchetti Provera summed up as follows the content of the agreements with Cisco and Corning: 'For the sale to Cisco of integrated optical systems, it was agreed that: 1) Pirelli's component activities will be controlled by a company established in the United States; 2) Cisco will subscribe 10% of the new company's shares; 3) for this investment, Cisco will pay a total of $25 million on the basis of an overall valuation of the company amounting to $250 million; 4) Pirelli commits to providing components to Cisco for a minimum value of $20 million for the first year and $30 million for the second year, at a specified price to which a premium of up to $125 million will be added; 5) for the two years after closing, Pirelli will not be allowed to sell shares or assets relating to components to companies operating in the same sector as Cisco. Cisco does not intend to buy the division for optical components, but prefers to ensure a steady supply from Pirelli and move towards participation in an American company in the perspective, shared by Pirelli, of an evaluation of the division which might be followed by listing of the new company on the US market, namely any alternative combination that is equally suitable. Coinciding with the 18 March 2000 establishment of the US company, named OTUSA (Optical Technologies USA), a process was initiated with the intention of listing it on NASDAQ, including the following actions: *a)* search for an American venture capitalist; *b)* search for American top managers to flank Pirelli managers; *c)* start-up of a corporate process to confer the intellectual property connected to the component business on OTUSA. Last July, Pirelli's longstanding optical technology partner Corning made it known via Chase Manhattan Bank that it was interested in OTUSA, given the vast importance of its patents for Corning's strategic development. In early August, Corning sent an offer for the acquisition of OTUSA based on an estimated value of $3–4 billion, with payment in shares. Considering that in recent times important acquisitions and integrations were made by Corning competitors in the components field, and major operators in the telecommunications industry (Alcatel, Siemens and Lucent) announced that they want to render their optical activities independent, it seemed that it had become particularly important for Corning to acquire technologies to grow its portfolio and remain competitive. On 1 September, another proposal arrived with the intention of starting negotiations, based on an amount for the purchase of OTUSA ranging between $4.5 and 5 billion of Corning shares. Meanwhile, in mid-July, a leading American venture capitalist (Summit Partners), which had been contacted in mid-March for its possible entry into OTUSA, made its definitive position on the matter known, deeming the request for more rights and guarantees than those applied to Cisco itself to be unacceptable. Moreover, the search for managers had not been successful, also because some of them appeared to be concerned about the possible success of OTUSA's market placement. Considering that the reasons out-lined above would delay placement of a first tranche compared to the original plan, it seemed appropriate to start negotiations with Corning in mid-September, on the basis of new proposals. In brief it was agreed with Corning that: 1) Corning would acquire 71% of OTUSA share capital owned by Optical Technologies Netherlands BV and 19% held by Pirelli Cavi e Sistemi, for a total of 90%; 2) consequently the selling price of 90% of OTUSA share capital would be worth $3,510 million on the basis of an assessment of OTUSA's entire share capital as $3,900 million; 3) ancil-lary contracts would be signed, the most important of which was the sale by Pirelli Cavi e Sistemi of certain patents for optical components, against a payment of 100 million. For these acquisitions Corning would pay Gruppo Pirelli a total of 3,610 million with net proceeds of 3,050 million.' (Pirelli/VCdA 30)

**2001**

*8 May*: On the theme of stock options related to the sale of Optical Technologies USA to Corning, Tronchetti Provera noted that 'all the useful data are included in the prospectus distributed at the closing of the Corning operation, when the final contract was signed with Corning. These materials showed very clearly that it was not possible for Pirelli management to be aware of the value that would be attributed to Optical Technologies USA before the options were granted. Indeed, for the possible listing of the company, to render credible the actual hypothesis of the listing, it was strongly suggested that top management, consisting of persons known to the American market, would endorse involvement and confidence in the company. Nor does the scale of the sum entail any illegality or impropriety, and precisely in order to prevent such an inference even remotely or by implication, it was decided not to waive special fees, in whole or in part; rather they were withheld and subjected to taxation at full rate.'

2. With regard to technological developments, Pirelli 'is investing significantly in the integration of optical and electronic in order to exploit the opportunities of broadband connection in homes and offices. Indeed, there is a conviction that the Internet industry will continue to grow, and for this reason there will be invest-ment in a new generation of components able to support data transmission at higher speed and lower cost.' (Pirelli SpA/VA 37)

*28 July*: The Chairman informed that 'negotiations are underway with Bell SA and other parties for the company to purchase, in agreement with Gruppo Benetton, approximately 1,700,000,000 Olivetti SpA ordinary shares, equal to about 23% of its share capital'. Tronchetti Provera specified that: '1) the purchase price per share will be €4.175 for a total of about €7 billion; 2) the shares will be purchased by an Italian company, in which Pirelli has a 60% stake, while the remaining 40% is in the hands of Edizione Holding and institutional investors; 3) Pirelli's total outlay will therefore be approximately €4.2 billion; 4) an additional 265,302,200 Olivetti shares would be contributed to the Newco, of which 130,980,000 are already indirectly held by Pirelli SpA, and 134,322,250 are already held by Edizione Holding, so the overall stake in Olivetti would be equal to about 27% of its capital; the company's total investment in Olivetti ordinary shares would be around €4.5 billion, with a price per share of €3.95; 5) Pirelli SpA's financial needs for the operation would be met for about half in existing cash and the other half in debt, to be almost fully offset by income from disposals. Moreover, the proposed acquisition would bring about a new Gruppo Pirelli strategy, flanking new telecommunications activities with a select number of highly profitable businesses, with upward range segmentation, such as car and motorcycle activities in the tyre industry, the production of optical fibre, telecommunications cables, and real estate activities under Pirelli & C.; for other traditional group activities, generating high cash flow and significant market positions, there would be gradual withdrawal and sale with expected revenue of at least €2 billion.'

2. The Chairman expected 'that the accomplishment of these strategies would bring about the re-foundation of Gruppo Pirelli, with profound changes and enhancement of the organisational and business structure, focusing on the most advanced technologies with the best market prospects; all facilitated by important synergies that Pirelli and Telecom will develop for technologies and management, as well as acquiring contacts and introductions on international markets of group interest'. He also pointed out that '1) initially there will be scant economic returns on the operation, but they will be significant once the financial situation is rebalanced; 2) there are plans to sign shareholders' agreements with Gruppo Benetton for management of the Newco, whose basic elements might be "joint control" by Pirelli and Benetton'.

3. Tronchetti Provera acknowledged that 'one of the aspects that will require special attention is Olivetti's burden of debt and the measures to be taken to reduce it'.

4. Lazard's opinion was offered in support of the entire operation, which 'fits into a precise context both with regard to the situation of the telecommunications and the Internet sectors, and as regards development strategies defined by Pirelli

management. Big operators usually integrate the landline and mobile telephone services, and Internet activities, and this is generally appreciated by the market, which tends to give relatively higher parameters to the leader than to its competitors, typically smaller in size and with a higher degree of integration among different but related activities. It should be noted that the buyer of a large portion of the domestic market is considered an essential requirement for efficient and profitable development outside the borders of the country of origin. Olivetti is an industrial holding company operating in telecommunications and in several areas of information technology and telecommunications, with a turnover of €30.1 billion and with approximately 120,000 employees. Core business comprises fixed and mobile telecommunications services and Internet services, where Olivetti operates via Telecom Italia, acquired following a stock-for-stock takeover bid launched in February 1999 together with its subsidiary Tecnost, which merged with Olivetti in late 2000. The stock-for-stock takeover bid garnered interest for 51.12% of Telecom Italia ordinary share capital. Overseas, the Telecom Italia group is active through its investee companies and joint ventures managing fixed and mobile telecommunications services and various markets, above all in Europe (Spain, France, Austria, Greece and Turkey), as well as in the Mediterranean basin and in South America (Argentina, Brazil, Chile).' (Pirelli/VCdA 32)

10 *September*: Tronchetti Provera illustrated the agreements reached between Pirelli SpA and Edizione Holding on one hand, and Bell SA on the other. The key points were: '*a)* buyers committing to purchase 1,552,662,120 Olivetti SpA shares at €4.175 each, and 68,409,125 [Olivetti 2001–2002 ordinary shares warrant] at €1.0875 each; *b)* 31 August 2001 value date; *c)* participation transfer deferred on condition of receiving approval from the appropriate authority; *d)* the seller's commitment to ensure that by the participation transfer date, several members of the Olivetti SpA and Telecom Italia SpA boards irrevocably resign as directors.'
2. Regarding agreements reached between Pirelli and Benetton for the governance of the Newco, which will become the buyer of the participation, the main points were '*a)* the Newco will receive, in addition to the participation, a further 134,322,250 and 130,980,000 Olivetti shares already held (directly or indirectly) respectively by Benetton and Pirelli, as well as 147,337,880 shares that Olivetti purchased from Bell and another party on 30 July 2001; *b)* the Newco's capital will initially be held by Pirelli for 80% and by Benetton for 20%, with the understanding that Pirelli may assign to one or more parties up to 20% of its capital

stock; *c)* the Newco's Extraordinary Shareholders' Meeting will always vote with 81% of share capital, the Board will consist of ten directors (two of whom designated by Benetton), and an auditor who will be appointed by Benetton, while Board decisions on important matters will be taken with the favourable vote of at least one of the directors designated by Benetton; *d)* Benetton will appoint a fifth of Olivetti (and some of its listed subsidiaries) directors (including the vice-chairman), not indicated by the market and governance bodies; for a number of important matters, Board resolutions by these companies will require the favourable vote of one of Benetton's designated directors.'

3. Tronchetti Provera also analysed a number of economic and financial aspects: '*a)* Olimpia's overall outlay will be 7.8 billion; *b)* Olimpia will have available overall equity of 5.2 billion and funding of 0.8 billion from industrial partners; *c)* the balance 1.8 billion (to reach 7.8 billion) will be forthcoming from a ceiling figure of 2.5 billion from corporate shareholders; *d)* the line of credit is guaranteed by a pledge on the Olivetti shares purchased by Olimpia; *e)* the overall outlay made by Pirelli SpA (excluding outlays covered by the aforementioned hypothesis and also expecting to cover the stakes set aside for other institutional investors) would comprise: 1) 60% of €5.2 billion equity share, equal to 3.12 billion; 2) 80% share of shareholders' loan of €0.8 equal to €0.64 billion for a total of 3.76 billion. At the time Pirelli could count on committed lines of credit for about 4.7 billion and 1.6 billion cash. Gruppo Pirelli's new strategy plans expect new telecommunications activities to be flanked by a select number of high-profit businesses with high-end range segmentation. In essence, this is car and motorcycle tyre business, whose future development is strongly linked to new MIRS technologies, production of optical fibre and telecommunications cables, and real estate activities, under Pirelli & C. The Group's other traditional activities generate high cash and enjoy significant market positions but there are plans for gradual disengagement and divestiture, aiming to maximise the contribution of resources to telecommunications activity. Truck tyres and the Energy business unit will then be sold off over the next 18 months. These divestitures will provide at least €2 billion.' (Pirelli/VCdA 32)

*14 September*: An agreement was signed with 'Intesabci SpA and Unicredito Italiano SpA for their entry as shareholders in Olimpia, each with a 10% stake. For as long as they hold more than 10% of Olimpia, Intesa BCI and Unicredito Italiano are each entitled to designate a Board member for Olimpia, Olivetti, Telecom, SEAT and TIM. At the end of the mandate of Olimpia's Board of Auditors, the parties will assess the possibility of Intesa BCI and Unicredito jointly appointing a single auditor.' The two banks 'will have the option to sell Pirelli their stakes in Olimpia in the three following cases and under the following conditions: *a)* impasse for resolutions in the Olimpia extraordinary Shareholders' Meeting and on the Olivetti and Telecom Boards; *b)* expiry of the three-year pact; *c)* change of management in Pirelli and in Olimpia. The price of the investment covered by the put will be determined by the parties or by investment banks in the event of disagreement. It will correspond to the sum of the economic value of the subsidiary and a premium, as if the participation were an expression of control of Olivetti and the two companies controlled by it (not exceeding an IRR of 15% before tax).' (Pirelli/VCdA 32)

*19 September*: The agreement is signed between Olimpia and the shareholders representing the majority stake of Bell SA, depending on a review of the economic conditions of the transaction. In this respect, Bell shareholders, 'ensuring compliance, undertake to ensure that the vendor subscribes and pays in full a bond to be issued by Olimpia, subject to implementation and at the same time as payment at the second implementation date, for an amount of €2,000 billion, under the following terms and conditions: an amount of €1,032,920,000, with issue value at par for a nominal value of €3.92 and loan duration of six years, and a fixed interest rate of 1.5% with the zero coupon formula'.
2. 'A second bond issue of €260 million for a maximum duration of five years at a fixed rate of 3%, to be paid on the date of repayment with the zero coupon formula.'
3. 'For funding, Monte dei Paschi di Siena has pledged to devote all efforts to issuing Olimpia with non-recourse financing for a share capital amount in euros equivalent to 1,000–1,500 billion lire, lasting six years at the Euribor rate + €0.50. Gruppo Banca Antonveneta has committed to issuing Olimpia – again at time of payment of the instalment at point b) of the purchase price of Olivetti shares – with non-recourse financing of 500 billion lire for a six-year period at the Euribor rate + €0.50.'
4. Olivetti-Telecom group's lines of strategy provide for the creation of value by: '*a)* industrial culture and customer care; *b)* a long-term commitment; *c)* management track record; *d)* focus on activities that guarantee greater profits and cash flow, land-line telephone services from Telecom Italia and mobile telephone services; *e)* beneficial use of Internet activities and the SEAT Pagine Gialle Directory; *f)* identification of non-strategic activities so as to decide on their possible divestiture; *g)* renewal of top management.' (Pirelli/VCdA 32)

433

*27 September*: Pirelli's Board is informed of the European Commission decision 'adopted on 20 September 2001 to authorise the proposed operation, also in the light of the commitment of Edizione Holding to sell its direct and indirect stakes in Blu share capital, and ensure that Autostrade SpA sells its stake in Autostrade Telecomunicazioni SpA or, alternatively, retains a minority stake'.

2. Vis-à-vis the consolidation of Olimpia with Pirelli, Tronchetti Provera pointed out that: 'Pirelli SpA should not proceed with the consolidation of Olimpia, considering – as also pointed out by the antitrust authority – that its control is not only in the hands of Pirelli, but is undertaken jointly with Edizione Holding, in virtue of the shareholders' agreements negotiated with the latter. Moreover, with regard to Olimpia's presumed control of Olivetti, in line with the criteria so far adopted by CONSOB, it will be necessary to proceed to an observation period of two-three years to assess whether the number of Olivetti shares held by Olimpia allows de facto control.' Consequently 'Olimpia should enter its stake in Olivetti in its statutory financial statements at cost, less any impairment losses, and should not have consolidated financial statements since its only investment (Olivetti) does not qualify as a controlling stake; *b)* Pirelli should not consolidate Olimpia since, as stated above, although it has an investment of 60% of Olimpia capital, it does not alone exercise a dominant influence on the company.' (Pirelli/VCdA 32)

*7 November*: During the Telecom Italia Shareholders' Meeting, Tronchetti Provera commented on the move of the registered offices to Milan, observing that the choice fell within the context of a broader corporate reorganisation plan started recently, and was connected to the role that the city of Milan played as a financial market for dealings with banks and with the stock exchange. He considered it normal, in a logic of efficiency, that the company with the highest market capitalisation would have corporate headquarters in Milan, which is the country's main financial centre. The transfer would have no repercussions since it was not tied to any downscaling or, worse, penalisation of other premises, but was simply seeking efficiency. Indeed, he spoke of the existence of a revitalisation project of activities currently located in Turin which, in some cases, had been marginalised.

2. With regard to the recent history of Telecom Italia, Tronchetti Provera recalled how the company 'is not lacking from an infrastructural point of view, since it has invested well in Italy, playing an important role in the telecommunications field, not only in Europe but also globally, managing to meet the challenges of mobile technology competitively, with very good in-house expertise. Moreover,

this company has acquired experience in monopoly organisations over the years and after privatisation has undergone several management changes.'

3. With regard to strategies, Tronchetti Provera 'stresses that the strategy to focus on the domestic market was driven by the consideration that even in bigger countries the market is able to accommodate a limited number of operators and the network cannot therefore be multiplied without becoming inefficient. In this context, Telecom Italia is very strong in the network at its disposal, and this competitive strength must be preserved and enhanced, investing all resources needed to ensure that the network's technological development is consistent with the needs of a country seeking to modernise. The presence of several competing operators provides the best service at the lowest cost, but where there are strong investment needs, an indiscriminate proliferation of operators is not efficient as, in turn, they impose very high costs for the user or make it impossible for companies to reach a level that is technologically essential.' (Telecom/VA 2001)

## 2002

*27 March*: Pirelli's Board was informed that on 25 February, Lazio's Regional Administrative Court (TAR) accepted Pirelli's appeal and revoked the challenged measures.

2. Operations Tiglio I and Tiglio II were outlined. The project's 'rationale lies in the assumption that integrating the assets and real estate services of the companies involved would allow better use than if the individual companies acted separately. The real estate assets currently owned by project participants have complementary characteristics in terms of a risk/return profile. Furthermore, the possibility to transfer real estate assets directly to a fund allows for maximum exploitation compared to alternative scenarios of use, including sale to different types of buyers.' The project provides for 'transfer of real estate and areas owned by the Telecom and the Pirelli & C. groups, to two companies under Italian law, known as Tiglio I and Tiglio II which, in turn, would bring all assets to a closed real estate fund to be set up'. The operation also includes: *a)* direct and/or indirect transfer by Telecom Italia and Olivetti Multiservice of the so-called non-facilities company branches which are part of Gruppo Pirelli & C. Re; *b)* commitment to negotiate the economic terms and business plan of facility activities undertaken by Telecom Italia and Olivetti Multiservice with the intention to transfer these activities to one or more vehicles.' Morgan Stanley Real Estate 'is willing to take part in the project provided that the ownership structure and real estate management of these subsidiaries does not

change significantly with respect to MSRE fund statutes, namely: *a)* the majority of the capital of the immovable property vehicle owner is also indirectly owned by MSRE; *b)* the management and coordination of real estate assets is entrusted to a single operator; *c)* services to people and buildings are provided through structured companies, coordinated by the operator'. (Pirelli/VCdA 32)

*7 May*: As the new Telecom chairman, Marco Tronchetti Provera, wrote the following letter to shareholders: 'The new management of Telecom Italia since the company entered the Group has defined the objective of pursuing the industrial recovery of this great Italian enterprise. It was important that the Telecom Italia Group – representing a valuable industrial heritage on the country's industrial scenario for its high technological level and the qualified professional skills at its disposal – be given a more robust and efficient financial and productive structure to strengthen its ability to play a leading role in the development of a strategic sector like that of Information and Communication Technology. To achieve these goals, during the first months of the new administration, we undertook major changes, from complete reorganisation of staff and business structure to a series of improvements for a strong recovery of efficiency and profitability. We have adopted a strict cost and investment control policy, continuing divestiture of non-core assets, and we have started a programme of progressive debt reclassification and reduction. In addition, for some assets we adopted accounting assessments more in line with actual market values, in particular the Group's foreign activities. Today, the extraordinary investment phase is basically at an end, so a new cycle of management, intended to reinforce our value creation strategy, can begin. The new business plan, submitted to the international financial community in February of this year, identified the line of strategy required to strengthen its leadership in the domestic market for group companies, particularly in fixed, mobile and Internet markets, so as to recover international presence, in particular that of TIM in Latin America, Turkey and Greece. The cornerstones of this development plan are the expansion of core business, the capacity to generate increasing quality and service that are the true source of value creation; reorganisation of the foreign portfolio; technological innovation. All aiming to make customer satisfaction the core of our actions. In conclusion, I am convinced that leveraging these solid foundations, and with a new-found awareness of its role in the modernisation of the country, the Telecom Italia Group can look ahead with confidence to ensure its shareholders and all its stakeholders the best prospects of success.'

2. In the annual report the following aspects were addressed: *a)* devaluation of investments, shown as follows: 'adjustment of the value of investment, goodwill and other investee company charges was carried out in accordance with the strategic lines of the new business plan. In particular, after careful examination, we proceeded with the write-down of investments, of goodwill and provision charges for investee companies which were clearly not merely cyclical trends'; *b)* the Italian market, 'characterised by high mobile penetration compared to major European countries, while the spread of both residential and business Internet and broadband systems is still relatively modest. In Italy, at the end of 2001, the Internet penetration rate was equal to 23% of families and 44% of SMEs. Access to families is still almost only by dial-up (98%) and only minimally through ADSL broadband (2%)'; *c)* as regards the guidelines: 'safeguarding the profitability of domestic business by making good use of the customer portfolio with strengthening of leadership in growing segments (web services, broadband, GPRS, UMTS), as well as exploiting IT and system integration skills that already exist in the group. For landlines, Telecom Italia will seek extreme improvements in customer service, management processes, and distribution channel efficiency. For domestic mobile, TIM will defend its leadership, exploiting all opportunities arising from new technologies, first GPRS then UMTS. Concentrate foreign presence in markets where the group has control of activities and identify sustainable lines of development at international level. Consistent with these priorities, Telecom Italia group strategy expects to complete a divestiture plan in marginal markets for non-controlling investments in non-core businesses. TIM will continue its development abroad, looking chiefly at Latin America, through the development of a shared GSM platform, and intensifying the launch of services with strong group synergies. The introduction of professional families and investment assessment criteria will allow spending to be monitored even more effectively both in the proposal stage, and when checking results.'

3. It was mentioned that Telecom Italia and the JP Morgan Chase group had signed final agreements for negotiation of put and call options for Seat Pagine Gialle shares. In particular, it was agreed to reduce the strike price from €4.2 to €3.4 per aforementioned share. To offset the reduction, Telecom Italia agreed to pay JP Morgan Chase the amount of €568,622,000 at the original expiry date of December 2005, without prejudice to Telecom Italia's right to pay the amount ahead of time after discounting back. (TI/BIL 2001)

*13 May*: The Pirelli & C. shareholders' meeting was informed that 'on 9 May Pirelli & C.'s Board of partners examined the structure of the global offering prepared for admission to listing of the subsidiary Pirelli & C. Real Estate. In the event of the placement of all shares involved in the overall offer, the result would represent 40% of Pirelli & C. Re share capital.'

2. Tronchetti Provera offered more information on the debt issue: 'Thus, to declare that the group (Pirelli) is indebted for 80,000 billion lire is inexact, and such statements may create a false image of risk and fragility. The gist is that Pirelli has about €2 billion of consolidated debt which it covers largely with its cash flow. The Gruppo Olivetti-Telecom debt belongs is the responsibility of these companies and neither Pirelli SpA nor Pirelli & C. are involved.' (Pirelli & C./VA 20)

*19 December*: The Pirelli Board is informed of the existence of 'ongoing negotiations between Olimpia, other Olimpia shareholders, and Hopa, to explore the possibility and mutual convenience of setting up an operation that provides for repayment of bonds issued by Olimpia, named Olimpia 1.5% 2001–2007, with 262.5 million held by Hopa, and a related merger by incorporation with Olimpia of a company wholly owned by Hopa (Holy Srl), with assets of no less than €960 million, and free of debt. Hopa, not listed on the stock exchange directly but through two subsidiaries (Holinvest and GPP International), owns 4.64% of Olivetti and holds further rights to purchase Olivetti shares. It also owns instruments convertible into Olivetti shares for a total potential participating interest in Olivetti of 7.21%. In addition to the provisions of loan repayment regulations, Olimpia would offer its bond holders Olivetti shares as well as a number of Olivetti convertible shares and bonds. Either directly or through its subsidiaries Holinvest and GPP, Hopa will avail itself of Olimpia's offer and proceed to advance redemption of the bonds, thus acquiring about 100 million Olivetti shares and 164 million Olivetti convertibles. Holinvest, wholly owned by Hopa, would then hold about 135 million Olivetti 1.5% 2001–2010 convertible bonds, about 164 million Olimpia 1.5% 2001–2007 bonds, and about 490 million Olivetti shares. With a final transfer agreement, Holinvest would exchange the aforementioned 490 million Olivetti shares for instruments issued by a leading government authority (Caisse des Depots e Consignations), index-linked to the Olivetti share. Hopa and Holinvest would transfer to their wholly owned subsidiary Holy: *a)* 164 million Olivetti convertibles; *b)* 100 million Olivetti shares; *c)* 99 million cash; *d)* 19.99% of Holinvest, taking Holy equity capital to 960 million, leaving it with no debts or liabilities. As a result of this operation,

Olimpia would strengthen its balance sheet by debt reduction of 476 million, and increase its equity capital to at least 960 million following the Holy merger. Hopa, following the merger by acquisition of its subsidiary Holy with Olimpia, would receive a 16% participating interest in Olimpia. Consequently, the investment percentages of existing shareholders would decrease as follows: Pirelli 50.4%, Edizione Finance International 16.8%, Unicredito Italiano 8.4% and Banca Intesa 8.4%. Hopa shareholder rights in Olimpia would be governed by a shareholders' agreement signed with current Olimpia shareholders. Indeed, Hopa would not become part of current agreements existing among Olimpia shareholders, nor would it sign an independent shareholders' agreement with them. Holy would also hold 19.99% of Holinvest, so Olimpia would become a Holinvest shareholder and the latter's rights would be governed by the Holinvest articles and by a shareholders' agreement with Hopa.' (Pirelli SpA/VCdA 36)

## 2003

*11 March*: The Board of Pirelli & C. examined the 'Pirelli & C. conversion (from limited partnership with share capital to a limited liability company) and change of corporate purpose' project.

2. Tronchetti Provera illustrated a large-scale project for capital increase and simplification of the corporate structure. The project envisaged 'conversion of Pirelli & C. (from limited partnership with a share capital to a limited liability company, and change of its corporate purpose with attribution of withdrawal rights to dissenting shareholders); b) Pirelli & C. capital increase of up to 1,014 million shares offered as options to Pirelli & C. shareholders with combined warrants to subscribe on 30 June 2006 a further maximum of 254 million to reinforce the group's industrial and financial activities; merger by acquisition of Pirelli SpA and Pirelli & C. Luxembourg in Pirelli & C., and its conversion to a joint stock company, following a share capital increase by the latter. Overall, those operations would enable important objectives to be achieved, for instance: *a)* maximisation of group market capitalisation; *b)* management focus on value creation for a single category of shareholders; *c)* greater unity of strategic and management orientation; *d)* acceleration of decision-making time; *e)* laying foundations for more flexible development and management of portfolio assets; *f)* optimisation of economic and financial flows; *g)* simplification of administration activities.' (Pirelli SpA/VCdA 37)

*7 May*: During the Pirelli & C. shareholders' meeting, Tronchetti Provera returned to the Olivetti acquisition process: 'When Pirelli acquired Olivetti shares, Telecom's transparency value was under ten euros per share. The total price, which seemed high, included a premium in the order of 35%, considering the markdown of Olivetti shares following the holding effect. There was an awareness that corporate trends might be improved, an awareness also based on knowledge of Telecom acquired through Pirelli, which had always been a Gruppo Telecom provider in Italy and abroad. Moreover, Gruppo Pirelli's first Telecom approach dated back to 1994, during privatisation of the company. Telecom had partnered Gruppo Pirelli in building the most advanced telecommunications networks, not only in Europe but also in the United States. Following this purchase, financial and industrial restructuring were implemented and completed in a shorter time than expected. Efficiency for 1,600 billion was achieved and debt was reduced to 8.5 billion, thus creating the conditions for being able to refine the final step, which was the shortening of the value creation chain.'

2. During the same SGM, Tronchetti Provera underlined the fact that if 'two mergers are taking place today, in a far from easy market context, it is not at odds with the declarations that the chain would be shortened when market conditions allowed it. There is stability because for months the ratio between stock prices for the two pairs of companies involved in the merger operations has basically aligned with that chosen as the exchange ratio.'

3. Notice is given of the purchase by Pirelli & C. of 47,973,139 ordinary Pirelli SpA shares, equal to 2.5% of the share capital represented by ordinary shares from BZ Group Holding, for a consideration of €43.1 million. (Pirelli & C./VA 21)

*24 May*: The chairman of Telecom's letter to shareholders addressed the following points: 'We have made efforts to increase our market competitiveness with marketing initiatives and, more specifically, with selective investments focused on innovative technologies that made it possible to introduce new services and new products, and improve customer care structures. In particular for national landlines, this business unit promoted the spread of broadband for residential customers, focusing on new brands and new services. We reached about 80% of results in terms of expected cost savings by the end of 2004, optimising purchasing processes and with a selective policy for investment projects. Finally, the divestiture plan is a year ahead of schedule and higher cash flows generated by better operating profits allowed us to improve the targets set for reduction of indebtedness, whose composition has also improved. During 2002 Gruppo Telecom Italia focused its activities in areas with the best potential for development, exporting businesses and experiences accumulated in Italy over the years, creating a framework for the coordination of all landline and mobile telephone business in Latin America. Gruppo Telecom Italia not only contributes to the country's economic growth, but is also competing with large international groups, playing an important role in the development of new value-added services that stimulate demand towards more advanced consumer profiles. Telecom Italia is a group that takes seriously transparency, exchange of ideas with the financial community and respect for shareholders. The code of ethics is suitably placed at the top of the business system, and represents a charter of values.' (TI/BIL 2002)

2. During the Telecom Italia SGM to approve the merger with Olivetti, with regard to Olimpia's holding in Olivetti, Tronchetti Provera said: 'Olimpia's participating interest in Olivetti is less than 30%, regardless of how we calculate it. Before the merger there was no link between Olimpia and Hopa that could be configured as a basis for the takeover bid. It follows that Olivetti can vote in the Telecom Italia SGM as Olimpia has committed no infringement of legislation in relation to mandatory takeover bid regulations, nor has Olivetti (moreover quite extraneous to any agreements between Olimpia and Hopa) since the conditions do not exist.'

3. On the devaluation of Seat, Tronchetti Provera pointed out, 'in relation to the JP Morgan put, the difference between the strike price of €3.4 per share and the average of the last six months of 2002 of €0.668 per share had to be earmarked for the risk fund. At the time of the Seat sale, shares will be charged at a value of €3.4 each, since the earmarking will be reduced to €0.668 per share and will therefore have no effect on the income statement.' On this same topic, Tronchetti Provera recalled that 'during 2000, Telecom Italia with Huit II and its shareholders, undertook to take about 711 million Seat Pagine Gialle shares priced at €4.2 each. That commitment stemmed from the integration agreements between Seat and Tin. it. JP Morgan took over Telecom Italia's commitment, paying Huit II the agreed price of about €3 billion and deferred the Telecom Italia payment until December 2005. In the first quarter of 2002 the price of that option was devalued to €3.4 per share. The terms of the operation reflect the values and conditions of the time when it was negotiated. Objectively, it is clearly a fact that the worth of the companies operating in the new media segment have subsequently diminished significantly, causing financial losses for the companies that had invested in it.'

4. With regard to the merger between Telecom Italia and Olivetti, Tronchetti

Provera said: 'Several representatives of Italian mutual funds have stressed that the merger will result in an increase of indebtedness for Telecom. Telecom's Board of Directors considered that such an increase in indebtedness would be transient, as it has been decided to pursue a plan for divestiture of non-core business activities, such as Pagine Gialle and Telekom Austria. The transient increase of debt is offset by all the advantages that arise from the operation, and can be summed up in Telecom Italia's capacity, after the merger, to express its worth fully without the constraints arising from the current absence of the controlling shareholder Olivetti. It should be stressed that the increase of indebtedness resulting from the merger involves a debt level a) better aligned than others in the industry at European level; b) consistent and compatible with Telecom Italia's overall business and with prospective cash flows arriving from implementation of the business plan. It is also expected that the merged company will retain a capacity to make profits and implement a policy of dividend distribution to ensure that the current shareholder of Telecom Italia receives a total amount of dividends at least in line with those currently received. It is an historic operation whereby a company with a partner at 54% and a free float of 46% will see the controlling shareholder decrease to 13–15% and the free float climb to 85%. The result will be an operation that the market has been seeking for some time.' (TI/VA 2003)

*31 July*: Vis-à-vis Gruppo Telecom, the Board of Pirelli & C. is made aware of the 'merger by acquisition of Telecom with Olivetti SpA. The merger will become effective next 4 August 2003 and from that date the new Telecom Italia will be in operation. As a result of the aforementioned merger, Olimpia's holding in the new Telecom ordinary share capital will decrease from the 28.5% currently held in Olivetti, to 11.6%.'

2. The merger by acquisition is subject to Olivetti's offer to purchase Telecom Italia ordinary and savings shares. The offer was essentially intended to ensure that Telecom Italia shareholders also had a way of selling off their participating interest, as occurred with Olivetti shareholders when they were offered right of withdrawal. The offer involves 9.73% of Telecom Italia's ordinary share capital, for a consideration of €4,103.4, and 11.83% of savings share capital, for about €1,170.9 million. Following Olivetti's offer it acquired approximately 64.68% of ordinary share capital and about 11.83% of savings share capital in Telecom Italia. (Pirelli & C./VCdA 8)

*11 November*: Information about Olimpia explained that: 'A capital increase was launched for an overall 700 million for the purchase of Telecom Italia shares at a price higher than €2.50 per share. Where entirely subscribed, the capital increase will require a disbursement for Pirelli & C. of €403 million, calculated pro rata.' Moreover, on 15 October 2003, Olimpia announced that it had completed an operation for the purchase of 2.6% of Telecom ordinary shares: 'As a result of this operation, Olimpia owns 14.16% of Telecom share capital.' (Pirelli & C. SpA/VCdA 9)

## 2004

*6 May*: The Telecom chairman's letter on occasion of the financial statements of 31 December 2003 read: 'Over the past two years we have decreased costs for more than €2.2 billion, 86% of the goal announced for the end of 2004. There have been disposals of non-core assets for €10 billion; the value of more than €12 billion of portfolio investments were lowered to fair value; more than €10 billion of net debt was reduced. At the same time, more than €10 billion in dividends and public purchase offers were distributed to shareholders. We are therefore justifiably proud of having fulfilled commitments made to the market when we took over responsibility for managing the Group. Among these commitments was the simplification of corporate structure. With the integration between Olivetti and Telecom last summer, a more financially competitive and flexible company emerged, better oriented to the creation of shareholder value. We have continued to invest more than 5 billion a year, primarily in the technological innovation of networks, systems, products, and services. This is the backdrop for the positive economic and financial results of 2003. The results appear even more clearly when we consider that approximately 85% were achieved in a market such as the Italy one, where the most widespread and rigorous liberalisation took place, and where price and service competition is significantly more intense than in other European countries. An increasingly important growth factor involved international activities, in which we are benefiting from the experience and innovative solutions developed on the Italian market. In Brazil, the launch of GSM mobile technology services was implemented across national territory. In Turkey and Greece we strengthened our positions and are ready to benefit from the growth of those markets. With the investments made in France and in Germany, Telecom Italia Wireline was the first European operator of landline telephone services to expand into the broadband market outside national boundaries. Before us lies a great season of innovation, which will radically transform the telecommunications industry. New value-added services and, above all, the integration between the world of telecommunications and the Internet, made possible by broadband, open important growth horizons. With the transmission of large amounts of high-speed data, films, music, games, and other innovative services, we will be able to enter the homes of millions of customers. Businesses will be able to rely on on-line transactions, reducing costs and improving competitiveness. Telecom Italia wants to seize growth opportunities in the most promising areas of the international telecommunications market. Most of our investments will target this aspect, with two-thirds concentrated on innovation, but the contribution we can make to our country is even broader. The development of telecommunications allows us not only to offer new services to citizens, but also to give enormous impetus to the productivity of the entire economic system.'

2. As far as debt is concerned, 'this amounts to €33,346 million, with an increase of €53 million compared to late 2002, and incorporates the effects of withdrawal and the public purchase offer (€5,285 million), the cancellation of 41,401,250 of the incorporating company's shares, previously classified by the latter as current assets (€299 million), as well as distribution of profits and reserves (€1,049 million), and disbursement for the early application of the JP Morgan put operation on Seat shares'.

3. On 1 August 2003 'the proportional partial demerger of Seat Pagine Gialle was concluded for the Newco, Nuova Seat Pagine Gialle. On 8 August 2003, 61.5% of Nuova Seat Pagine Gialle was sold to the consortium led by BC Partners, Value Capital Partners, Permira, and Investitori Associati. The selling price was set at €3,033 million. Taking into account the deconsolidation of Nuova Seat Pagine Gialle group debt to conclude the sale, the operation allowed Gruppo Telecom Italia to reduce consolidated net debt by an amount of €3,681 million.' (TI/BIL 2003)

*7 December*: The Board of Pirelli & C. was approached for 'a capital increase for Pirelli & C. SpA intended to support the Olimpia capital increase. Olimpia's capital increase of 2 billion is earmarked for the purchase of Telecom Italia shares. The Pirelli & C. SpA investment may vary from a minimum of €1,008 million to a maximum of €1,680 million. Telecom launches a partial public offering on 67% of TIM free float at a price of 5.4–5.7 euros per share. The takeover bid is subject to reaching two-thirds of the ordinary shares and savings being offered. Maximum disbursement is expected to be €14.8 billion in the event of total acceptance of the takeover bid. TIM will undertake to spin-off Italian operations to a Newco, while Telecom Italia will incorporate TIM.' (Pirelli & C. SpA/VCdA 12)

## 2005

*21 January*: During the Extraordinary Shareholders' Meeting of Pirelli & C. SpA for the capital increase, Tronchetti Provera described Telecom Italia prospects: 'The possible developments of broadband technologies were not yet clear in the early months of last year. Broadband was in the early stages of its development which saw the acquisition of 4 million ADSL connections from the spring of 2004 to the end of that year. At that time, none of the large manufacturers could provide models for technological integration. In the period between April/May and October 2004, however, all leading provider platforms evolved towards convergence, and in late October, Siemens created a shared business unit for landline and mobile telephone services, so it could use convergent technology platforms, without its shareholders complaining about the technology change. The success of broadband has been far greater than forecast, and development of new technologies that make new synergies possible, with resulting cost reductions, has led to the acceleration of a now entirely necessary integration process. In May the process of integration was neither possible nor feasible, since it lacked confirmation of the availability of new technologies that would make such an integration profitable.'
2. Vis-à-vis the Telecom-TIM merger: 'These operations provide for *a)* a voluntary takeover bid of Telecom Italia ordinary shares and TIM savings shares; *b)* merger by acquisition of TIM by Telecom Italia, after the spin-off by TIM of the business mobile operations in Italy to a wholly owned TIM subsidiary. As a result of the merger, Olimpia's participating interest in Telecom Italia will suffer a significant reduction to about 12–14%, depending on the level of interest in the takeover bid. Olimpia's increased participating interest in Telecom Italia will then neutralise this diluting effect.' (Pirelli & C. SpA/VA 23)

*25 February*: Pirelli's Board was brought up to date on Olimpia's share capital increase, which was 'fully subscribed on 27 January 2005 by various Olimpia SpA shareholders, who made immediate payment of 700 million, equal to 35% of the subscription price. In particular, Edizione Finance International SA and Hopa SpA subscribed their shares, while Pirelli & C. SpA subscribed both its own shares (for a total of 1,008 million) and those of Banca Intesa and Unicredito (for 336 million).

On 16 February 2005, shareholders who subscribed newly issued shares made a second payment of €800 million equal to 40% of the increase, which is therefore €1,500 million. As a result of these subscriptions, Olimpia capital is now owned by Pirelli & C. SpA (57.66%), Edizione Finance International (16.80%), Hopa 816%), and Banca Intesa and Unicredito (4.77% respectively).' (Pirelli & C. SpA/VCdA 12)

*7 April*: There follow extracts from the Telecom chairman's letter to its shareholders: 'At the end of 2001, when we took over management of Gruppo Telecom Italia, we said that the pillars of our project would be a strong interest in cutting-edge technology and equally strong market orientation. The results for 2004 have confirmed the validity of that project: increased revenues, improved profitability, increase in free operating cash flow, indebtedness further reduced. A significant contribution to the development of the group arose precisely from the most innovative areas: vigorous expansion of broadband, with success in both the land-line and mobile telephone services. New models emerging will gradually replace voice transmission as a cornerstone of telecommunications development. This trend shared by fixed and mobile telephone services has been amply sustained by networks and services performance, to which we have dedicated a large part of the €5 billion invested on average every year. Telecom Italia's land-line network was judged by renowned industry analysts as the most technologically advanced in Europe, the most advanced in the transition to IP protocol, namely the transmission method that will dominate telecommunications in the very near future. The prospect that now opens before us is one of consumers and businesses in mobile and landline broadband services sharing the same common foundations, while remaining distinct and different in terms of features and the specific application, depending on the telecommunication tool preferred. The merger between Telecom and TIM will not only ensure the unified governance of business processes, but will make it possible to garner significant synergies in terms of investment and operating costs. The industrial nature of the operation has an even wider scope when considering the events that have marked the history of the corporate group from its privatisation. With the incorporation of TIM, we reach the end of the complex journey undertaken to simplify and normalise the ownership structure, a task that kept us busy in the closing months of 2001 for the capital increase of Olivetti, and in 2003 for the merger of Olivetti and Telecom Italia. An important representative of the international press wrote that today the group has finally taken on a "normal" structure. This is certainly so: cash and debt generation are considered at the same level. This will allow us to support growth with the level of investment needed and to remunerate shareholders with an adequate dividend, so that cash generation will allow the increased indebtedness assumed for completing the merger. For landlines we are still the only leading European operator to show increased revenues and profitability despite continuing to suffer the continued decline of "voice" traffic for the second year in a row. All thanks to the launch of innovative service packages and, above all, an increase in broadband connections well above expectations, exceeding 4 million and doubling 2003 figures while exceeding those of 2002 almost fivefold. At an international level, Telecom Italia is also reaping the benefits of investments made in broadband markets in France and Germany, growing from 160,000 to 420,000 connections in just one year. TIM, while continuing to develop voice traffic in Italy, relies increasingly for growth on its value-added services and introduction of EDGE and UMTS technologies, which are also a launch pad for broadband in mobile telephone services. The contribution of Brazilian operations was very significant: increasing the total number of lines from 8.3 to 13.6 million, TIM's Brazil group has become the second mobile operator in the country, and the only one with national coverage using GSM technology. Olivetti-Tecnost concluded its reorganisation and redefined its boundaries around office products and systems, recovering technological vitality and drive for innovation in new international markets for specialised terminals, significantly improving operating results. Looking to the future, our actions and our investments will target developing innovative services and strengthening international presence. We intend to transfer the growing scale of broadband, which we will make available on landlines and mobile services, with tangible opportunities for improving quality of life for citizens and enhancing productivity in enterprise. Vis-à-vis international expansion, we will intensify our efforts in the direction already pursued and focus very selectively on markets with high growth potential. These are France and Germany in terms of broadband; Brazil and Turkey in terms of market size and the opportunities they offer us for becoming an integrated provider of landline and mobile telephone services. We are still very interested in Argentina. At the same time, we will continue divestiture of non-strategic overseas activities, allocating resources freed-up in part to debt reduction and also investing in key markets.'

2. With regard to the process of integration between Telecom and TIM, the following was mentioned: 'a) a voluntary public offer of partial purchase by Telecom Italia for two thirds of the free float of ordinary shares and for 100% of 132,069,163 TIM savings shares; b) merger by acquisition of TIM by Telecom Italia, after

spinning off the business mobile operations in Italy to a wholly owned TIM subsidiary. This merger will take place after dividend distribution. On 3 January 2005, Telecom Italia launched its takeover bid for TIM, which was completed on 21 January 2005; the consideration offered by Telecom Italia was €5.6 per ordinary and savings share. In light of the final data received, 2,639,154,665 ordinary shares amounting to 31.2% of TIM ordinary share capital and 8,463,127 savings shares equal to 6.4% of TIM savings share capital were subscribed. The total outlay for Telecom Italia was 13,804 million, of which 2,504 million were paid part in Telecom Italia cash resources, and 11,300 million by the aforementioned loan granted in December by a pool of Italian and foreign banks. Thus, when the takeover bid ended, Telecom Italia held 84.8% of TIM ordinary share capital and 6.4% of its savings capital overall. On 23 January 2005, the Boards of Telecom Italia and TIM approved the merger by acquisition plan of TIM by Telecom with 1.73 Telecom shares in exchange for one TIM share, and 2.36 Telecom savings for one TIM share.' (Telecom/VA)

*1 June*: Pirelli & C. SpA Board was informed of the result of the competitive bidding procedure for sale of the cable industry: 'After analysing and comparing the offers received, it was decided to proceed with the signing of an exclusive agreement with Goldman Sachs Capital Partners for negotiations of the sale of the cables and systems operation. Under these agreements, Pirelli would sell Goldman Sachs Capital Partners its energy and telecommunications cables and systems operations, which turned over €3,208 million in 2004 for operating profits in excess of €110 million, with 52 plants and about 12,000 employees worldwide.' The advisor specified that 'the competitive bidding process started in November 2004, and invitations were sent to 32 private equity funds, including top European and American operators active on the European market. The overall enterprise value for the operations to be sold off was set at about €1.3 billion, including intellectual property rights and license for use of the Pirelli trademark for two years. The equity value was calculated at about €490 million. As part of the operation, €135 million would come from a vendor loan and Pirelli would also be assigned a warrant entitling it to receive economic benefits equivalent to 5% of the share capital of the corporate vehicle used by Goldman Sachs Capital Partners for the operation, thus seizing the opportunities arising from future business growth. Goldman Sachs Capital Partners has already assured full support to current management, which has produced excellent results in recent years; the new ownership plans to continue business development and growth under current management. Thanks to this operation, the refocusing of activities mentioned in July 2001 has been completed. Pirelli will be able to concentrate on the development of higher-value-added businesses and especially on the telecommunications, tyre and real estate businesses, and broadband and second-generation photonics operations (managed by Pirelli Broadband and based on the innovations developed by Pirelli Labs), and the environmental field.' (Pirelli & C. SpA/VCdA 14)

**2006**

*26 January*: The Board of Pirelli & C. SpA was brought up to date on the Hopa situation: 'The agreement with Hopa foresees the possibility of terminating the agreement within three months of the expiration date, namely 8 February 2006. As a result of failure to renew, the agreement with Hopa envisages the demerger of Holinvest and the possibility for Hopa to become a transferee of Holinvest shares and, after the demerger of Olimpia, the possibility for Pirelli & C. SpA and other parties other than Hopa to become transferees of Olimpia shares. In the case of non-renewal, Hopa is entitled to a premium of €208 million. Firstly, there is the need for a change in Hopa governance and a consequent strengthening of the latter's so-called institutional partner ownership (including, in particular, Monte dei Paschi di Siena). Secondly there is also the need to 1) eliminate or heavily reduce the aforementioned premium in the case of non-renewal of the Hopa agreement; 2) exclude the possibility of Hopa interfering in Olimpia business decisions (by deleting the impasse clause included in the Hopa agreement in case of important decisions and, above all, not granting Hopa any right or option regarding governance or management of the Telecom Group).' With reference to the expediency of Pirelli becoming transferees of Olimpia shares, Tronchetti Provera responded in the affirmative, saying it was expedient from a strategic perspective: the choice of demerger would result in third parties turning over a sizeable package of Telecom ordinary shares (approximately 2.8% of the latter's ordinary share capital). The choice between the two options might be postponed to a later date, upon expiration of the agreement.

2. With regard to this, Tronchetti Provera briefly retraced Telecom's investment history: 'Pirelli's initial investment in the foundation of Olimpia, in 2001, was €3.1 billion. Then in 2003, it subscribed a capital increase for 0.4 billion earmarked by Olimpia for the purchase of Telecom Italia shares after the merger of Olivetti and Telecom Italia. Again in 2005, Pirelli subscribed an additional capital increase of

1.3 billion, also intended for Olimpia for the purchase of Telecom Italia ordinary shares in order to enable the company to maintain a significant amount of capital of the Newco created by the integration of Telecom Italia Mobile and Telecom Italia. Olimpia's total debt is 3.1 billion. On the asset side, Olimpia has about 2.4 billion Telecom Italia ordinary shares (of which only 1.3 billion pledged and without credit lines in place). The shortening of the chain and the results achieved by the investee company Telecom Italia have brought a financial surplus for Olimpia, expected to be about €90 million in 2005, due to the difference between dividends received from Telecom Italia and financial charges.' Lastly, he recalled that '3.9 billion, of the total 4.8 invested by Pirelli in Olimpia, constitute the net proceeds of terrestrial optical systems and optical components divestitures completed in 2000'. (Pirelli & C. SpA/VCdA 15)

*14 February*: Tronchetti Provera informed the Board of Pirelli & C. that 'in the last month, with the help of Goldman Sachs and GB Partners, the Company has proceeded to assess the best way to leverage tyre operations (Pirelli Tyres), in particular the possibility of listing on MTA, the screen-based stock exchange organised and managed by Borsa Italiana. Pirelli Tyres has shown excellent economic and financial performance in recent years, and with the current market-friendly environment the company has decided to carry out a feasibility study, in particular in relation to the listing, with the twofold objective of maximum leverage of Pirelli Tyres (with Pirelli & C. retaining control) and asset-building for Pirelli & C. In recent years Pirelli Tyres recorded a sales growth rate well above that of other tyre manufacturers. Numerical benchmarking, both in terms of growth and margins, represents an important element in support of setting up the equity story with which Pirelli Tyres could go to market, along with further quality elements, of which the most notable is the Pirelli brand. Overall the aspects of *a)* growth in segments and market areas to higher margins; *b)* gradual relocation of a significant proportion of production capacity to low-cost areas, such as Romania, China and Brazil, will be critical in convincing the financial community to proceed with a better valuation of Pirelli Tyres compared to assessments made to date by financial analysts. Currently it is unlikely that there will be any significant "migration" of investors from Pirelli & C. to Pirelli Tyres only by effect of the latter's listing.'

*21 April*: During the Pirelli & C. SpA SGM, Tronchetti Provera spoke of the

Telecom-TIM integration: 'The merger of Telecom Italia and TIM has anticipated the technology convergence that the entire world of telecommunications is pursuing today. The future of Telecom Italia is that of a company offering not only telephone services, but also a series of value-added services based on a single platform represented by Internet Protocol and broadband. Now, however, the market situation is in a state of uncertainty, where every announcement by an operator promoting affordable telephone services at very competitive prices triggers a negative reaction on stock. The investment in Telecom Italia, far from being what some want to see as a "disaster", was an investment in a business that is now Europe's best company in this industry. Telecom Italia management from 2002 to 2005 brought a 25% increase in productivity, a result that neither the main European competitors nor others were able to match.' (Pirelli & C. SpA/VA 24)

*11 May*: Tronchetti Provera informed the Board of Pirelli that, 'as announced by press releases of 27 and 28 March last, Banca Intesa and Unicredito Italiano have expressed their willingness to withdraw from the shareholders' agreement signed in September 2001 with Pirelli & C., and will therefore exercise their right to sell their participating interest in Olimpia (about 4.77% per bank). The sale of the participating interest will take place in October, after the expiration of the agreement (4 October 2006) and will result in a disbursement for Pirelli & C. SpA of about €1.17 billion. With regard to the shareholders' agreement signed with Hopa, the demerger of Olimpia requires the transfer to Hopa not only of relevant debt but also of a participating interest of approximately 2.8% in Telecom Italia ordinary share capital. The cash settlement involves a purchase (pro rata, given the agreement) by Pirelli & C. and Edizione Holding of 16% of Hopa's participating interest in Olimpia. On the basis of current market value, disbursement for Pirelli & C. may be quantified at €500–550 million. This outlay, as things stand, considers the share of about 166 million applicable to Pirelli & C. for the premium negotiated with Hopa.' Of the two options, the Chairman noted that the cash settlement was definitely the preferred choice for two reasons. Firstly, from a strategic perspective it was expedient: the decision to proceed with the demerger would actually give Hopa, already holder of a significant participating interest in Telecom Italia share capital (approx. 3.7%), an additional and weighty slice of Telecom Italia ordinary shares (approximately 2.8% of the company). In this way, moreover, Telecom Italia's Olimpia shareholding would not change in terms of quantity, even temporarily. Vis-à-vis Holinvest, the choice between the two alternatives of a Holinvest demerger or a cash settlement, namely the purchase by Hopa of Olimpia's Holinvest participating interest, is entrusted to Hopa itself. (Pirelli & C. SpA/VCdA 16)

*27 July*: The Board of Pirelli & C. SpA learned of the suggestion of a private placement of Pirelli Tyre: 'For leveraging the tyre sector, some leading Italian and international financial institutions offered Pirelli & C. a different option to the initial takeover bid, consisting specifically of a private purchase by banks (national and international) of 39% of Pirelli Tyre, aimed at a subsequent placing on the market for a consideration of 740 million, reflecting a valuation of about 1.9 billion for the company, and corresponding to the minimum of the range identified for the purposes of going public. It would also give the purchasing banks the right to announce, within four years and six months, the initial public offering of the company they had purchased (or at least a portion of the same for 25% of the company's share capital). Through the signing of an option agreement, Pirelli would also acquire the right to repurchase the transferred shares after four years and six months if they were not to be part of the IPO.'
2. Tronchetti Provera informed the Pirelli & C. SpA Board that 'on 12 July, Pirelli & C. and Edizione Holding bought all the shares held by Hopa in Olimpia and, at the same time, Hopa bought all the shares Olimpia held in Holinvest. Disbursement for Pirelli & C. SpA was 498 million, while Olimpia grossed approximately 86 million. Pirelli & C. SpA thus came to hold 70.46% of Olimpia, a percentage that would rise to 80% once the purchase of 9.54% of Olimpia held by shareholder banks is completed. A pre-emption agreement was signed between Olimpia and Holinvest, with the following characteristics: *a)* Holinvest may sell at will 35% of the 492,7 million Telecom ordinary shares, while the right of first refusal for the other 65% is for Olimpia; *b)* Holinvest and Hopa cannot make further specific purchases of Telecom Italia shares without the prior agreement of Olimpia. Additional purchases are permitted in order to allow Holinvest to maintain the threshold above Telecom Italia's participating interest percentage (equal to 3.68% of ordinary share capital). (Pirelli & C. SpA/VCdA 17)

*12 September*: As for Olimpia, Tronchetti Provera took this opportunity to inform the Board of Pirelli & C. SpA 'of recent events that have affected Telecom Italia SpA, in which Olimpia is the reference shareholder and, in particular, of the restructuring process for separating Telecom Italia national mobile communication business nationwide from the local wired access network, via transfer of the corresponding

business operations to two separate companies controlled by Telecom Italia itself.'
(Pirelli & C. SpA/VCdA 17)

*18 October*: Tronchetti Provera told the Board of Pirelli that 'it has been decided to suggest signing a shareholders' agreement with regard to the Telecom Italia SpA shares held by Olimpia, Mediobanca and Generali. In particular, the agreement would include shares and rights to represent more than 23% of Telecom Italia SpA ordinary share capital, and the parties would ensure the continuity and stability of the Gruppo Telecom Italia shareholding, also reconfirming confidence in the management of the group itself, with a view to promoting industrial development in a context of economic and financial equilibrium for the best value creation for all shareholders. The agreement protects the role and independence of the individual participants, and in particular Olimpia, leaving the parties the opportunity of exercising independently all rights relative to their own shareholding. The agreement provides for the contribution of 17.99% of the share capital of Telecom Italia held by Olimpia, 3.67% held by Gruppo Generali, and 1.54% held by Mediobanca. The agreement does not cover participating interests in Telecom Italia held by Pirelli & C. (1.36% of share capital), by Gruppo Edizione Holding (0.22% of share capital), which, if added to the agreement, would account for 24.79% of Telecom Italia ordinary share capital. The agreement lays down a right of first refusal for Mediobanca and Generali solely in cases where Olimpia intends to transfer its Telecom Italia participating interest, exercisable for Olimpia's entire interest at the conditions offered by the third party. However, if the potential third party purchaser offers to buy Olimpia's Telecom Italia shares and also those owned by Mediobanca and Generali, the right of first refusal will not be applicable and the latter may decide only whether or not to accept the offer of the third party.'

2. With regard to the financial position of Olimpia, it is thought that 'at the end of the current financial year Gruppo Pirelli will enjoy a financial position of approximately €2,000 million, of which €700 million for industrial activities against EBITDA of approximately €550 million; about €100 million in Pirelli Real Estate, and the remainder of about €1,200 million allocated to holding structures against assets valued by the market at more than €5 billion. As for Olimpia, the company is expected to close the year with a net debt of about €2,900 million. Olimpia's debt has a duration of approximately four years, and is secured by a pledge of 60% of the Telecom Italia shares it owns. As regards the increase in Pirelli & C. consolidated debt between December 2005 and June 2006, the debt increased by about

€1.1 billion against an increase of financial assets for about €0.7 billion, hence the difference is only €0.4 billion. The sharp increase in liquidity is due to the need to collect adequate resources to meet the payment of Olimpia shares transferred to Hopa on 12 July.'

3. The change in 'Olimpia's ownership structure has no impact on control of the company as the required voting quorum is now 91% of share capital. Pirelli & C. will continue to have the right to appoint only five out of ten directors, while Gruppo Edizione Holding will be entitled to appoint the remaining five.' (Pirelli & C. SpA/VCdA 18)

## 2007

*27 February*: During the Pirelli & C. SpA Board meeting, Tronchetti Provera described recent events involving the Group: 'In previous months Pirelli declared its willingness to consider, in agreement with the shareholder Edizione, the entry of new minority shareholders in Olimpia. Contacts with potential buyers were and are still numerous, both with financial and industrial partners. With respect to Telecom Italia, and likewise indirectly to Pirelli, the aim is to create a strategic alliance with another telecommunications operator, in the belief, which is also widely shared by the market, that in the absence of a strategic alliance and a strict cost-cutting policy for telecommunications companies, effective and durable value creation cannot be achieved. To confirm this, we should remember that these were also the objectives for the operation arranged in the past with News Corporation and Sky Italia, again of international scope, which would have meant significant growth for Telecom Italia in the media industry and, among other things, would have been accompanied by industrial alliances and acquisitions in Europe, especially in broadband.' He observed that 'once the curtain had fallen on the instrumentality of the debt and Telecom Italia network evaluations, it became clear that Telecom Italia's issue is one of the best competitive positionings for international growth, in other words strategic vision.' The Chairman points out that 'the company has had contact with telecommunications operators (the Russian Sistema and Altino, France Telecom, Mexican America Movil and Spanish Telefonica) and with financial partners (Blackstone and Apollo among others), on the basis of the following established points: *a)* the availability for sale of minority shares in Olimpia; *b)* a consideration for leveraging Olimpia as reference shareholder; *c)* attribution to the new Olimpia shareholder of rights for protecting its investment but without influence over Telecom Italia management. Telefonica is the best partner, not only for the reasons put forward by analysts and investors, but also for clear market signals of appreciation for the operation. Telefonica is willing to build an industrial alliance (with Pirelli) "guaranteed" by the purchase of a share in Olimpia, a purchase that Telefonica itself deems necessary for protecting the stability of the aforementioned industrial alliance. Following these contacts, separate levels of negotiations were opened: industrial with Telecom Italia management; financial with Pirelli (and Edizione) for the transfer of a shareholding of 20–40% in Olimpia capital. As regards potential financial partners, contacts did not develop, on the one hand due to the consideration prospected a priori, and on the other for the lack of possible synergies with Telecom Italia. As regards France Telecom, it was considered preferable not to proceed with full negotiations because, compared to Telefonica, fewer synergies could be assured by the creation of an alliance between France Telecom and Telecom Italia. As regards Telefonica, a right of first refusal is being considered for the company in the event of the transfer of a participating interest to third parties that would cause Pirelli and Edizione to lose control of Olimpia. This pre-emption would nonetheless be subject to right of first refusal granted to Mediobanca and Assicurazioni Generali in view of the agreement they signed in October 2006. From the governance perspective, negotiations envisage: *a)* Telefonica's right of veto with regard to several important matters as already provided in the agreements with Edizione, as well as decisions concerning Olimpia's strategic alliances in the telecommunications sector. Telefonica requires that in the event of the Telecom Italia Group transferring assets worth more than €2 billion outside of Italy, it will have the right to terminate relations with Pirelli and Edizione. In this case Telefonica would be entitled to proceed with the demerger and receive the pro rata value of Olimpia's assets and liabilities, without premium. As regards industrial aspects, two elements seem to emerge clearly: on the one hand the positive strategic and competitive positioning for Telecom Italia arising from a future alliance with Telefonica, above all in markets where operational partnerships (primarily Brazil and Germany) may be established, as well as attainable savings and strategies (estimated in the order of approximately 2 billion in the period 2007–2011); on the other hand, Telecom Italia top management shows coldness, if not outright hostility, towards the alliance for alleged conflicts of interest with the Olimpia plan.' In this respect, Tronchetti Provera emphasised that: '*a)* there is not even a hypothetical conflict between Olimpia's interests and those of Telecom Italia. If anything, they converge. The best proof of the substantial correctness of a future operation between Telefonica

455

and Telecom Italia lies in the fact that there would be no change in management roles and no interference by Olimpia in Telecom Italia's business decisions; *b)* any other industrial alliance that Telecom Italia management might forge that would bring tangible benefits in terms of its competitive positioning and value growth opportunities would be welcomed by Olimpia and Pirelli. Now we must bide our time and make appropriate assessments when Telecom Italia's business plan guidelines are made known during the company's Board meeting on 8 March 2007, and on so-called "Telecom Day", on 9 March. Negotiations with Telefonica for selling off the participating interest with Olimpia are well advanced, although Telecom Italia's acknowledgement of the strategic alliance is still lacking.' (Pirelli & C. SpA/ VCdA 18)

*12 March*: Tronchetti Provera summarised events that had occurred since the last meeting for the benefit of the Pirelli & C. SpA Board: 'On 1 March 2007 without notice and – as far as Pirelli and Olimpia are concerned – without apparent reasons relevant to the status and contents of discussions held so far, the Chairman of Telefonica, César Alierta, declared publicly that discussions in progress with Telecom Italia for definition of the terms of the strategic alliance had been suspended. After rumours circulated on 12 February 2007, Pirelli ordinary shares recorded an increase of 6.98% in Pirelli equity and 2.45% in that of Telecom Italia. Following the declaration made by Chairman Alierta on the suspension of negotiations, prices decreased respectively by 4.94% and 2.58%. A further drop in the market occurred on so-called "Telecom Day", when there was a public presentation of the business plan for the three-year period 2007–2009, which lacked any reliable indication regarding international alliances on which development of the Telecom Italia Group could be based for the next few years. Telecom Italia's problem is one of improving competitive positioning and thus lines for growth, especially at international level (since the Italian market was now saturated). The 9 March plan does not provide any relevant response to this since it is purely conservative, aiming merely at noting difficulties and managing the status quo, without offering strategic solutions that could guarantee any prospects for development. Taking this into account, it is impossible to understand why the Telefonica affair ended the way it did. The chairman considered the benefits of the agreement between Telecom Italia and Telefonica to be assured or at least predictable, and is wondering why negotiations between the two companies were broken off. The press made many assumptions and the events of the last few days were analysed in various ways. Of the multiple theories, the most insistent was that Telecom Italia management's decision to pass up the opportunity for the time being of an alliance with Telefonica was motivated by the desire to release the company from conflicts of interests with the shareholder Olimpia and thus with Pirelli.' Tronchetti Provera also wondered 'how a party that would nonetheless give significant support to the effects of the success/failure of the Telefonica alliance by remaining Olimpia's major shareholder, can be considered to have a confrontational attitude'. In this regard, Tronchetti Provera recalled: 'The difficulties encountered in recent years whenever an attempt was made to take decisions aimed at promoting the development of Telecom Italia, or to make a positive impact on its strategies (in particular the obstacles arising from the launch of innovative services following the merger of Telecom Italia and TIM, as well as those emerging in the summer of 2006 and recently during respective negotiations with News Corporation and those relating to the strategic alliance with Telefonica). We should examine whether there are any suitable solutions for leveraging the participating interest in Telecom Italia through Olimpia, retaining the current ownership structure, or whether it would be preferable to proceed to total asset divestiture.' (Pirelli & C. SpA/VCdA 18)

*1 April*: With regard to Olimpia, during the Pirelli & C. SpA Board meeting, Tronchetti Provera announced that 'proposals have been made by the US-based telephone company AT&T and the main Mexican mobile phone operator, America Movil, for each to purchase a participating interest in Olimpia equal to one third of the share capital. The proposals include a valuation of Olimpia's participating interest based on an implicit price per Telecom Italia ordinary share of €2.82, minus Olimpia's net debt at closing of the operation. The proposals expressly request that Mediobanca and Generali be given a right of first refusal on the Olimpia shares being transferred. In this case it was considered preferable to ask potential buyers to leave Mediobanca and Assicurazioni Generali an option to exercise the right of first refusal in such a way as to allow them to assess whether or not they should acquire the participating interest being transferred, guaranteeing preservation of the so-called "Italian identity" of the reference shareholder, Telecom Italia. If the operation were to be completed, Olimpia share capital would be equally divided into three parts of 33.3% each for AT&T and America Movil, and current Olimpia shareholders, who would hold 26.7% and 6.7% respectively. Another important aspect of the proposal is that Pirelli and Sintonia will be allowed a put option on the Olimpia participating interest still in its possession, as well as on Telecom

457

Italia shares directly owned by the latter (1.36% for Pirelli and C. and 0.22% for Sintonia). The considerations suggested include a 31.2% premium to Pirelli & C. at the current price of Telecom Italia ordinary shares. Telefonica had pondered a participating interest in Olimpia to start up a strategic partnership with Gruppo Telecom Italia, without prejudice to its intention to limit the investment (due to commitments made to rating agencies) to within economic ceilings incompatible with acquisition of the entire Olimpia shareholding.' (Pirelli & C. SpA/VCdA 20)

*23 April:* During the Pirelli SpA & C. shareholders' meeting, Tronchetti Provera returned to events relating to Telecom: 'At the beginning of this process, the world's most important media operator, News Corporation, was contacted with the intention of starting negotiations intended to widen both the geographical and business scope. After a period during which the negotiations developed positively, Telecom Italia found itself in an anomalous situation from a media point of view, subjected to considerable pressure with regard to possible network operations, with reference to a supposed unsustainable debt situation, which was actually decreasing. The negative media pressure on Telecom Italia made negotiations with Murdoch increasingly complex.' When other external factors arose, complicating an already difficult situation, he saw fit to leave the chairmanship of Telecom Italia to prevent a clash between the company's top management and the country's institutional leaders becoming detrimental for Telecom. Thus Pirelli, 'as a shareholder, continued to pursue the strategy for which the market had already shown its appreciation. Negotiations began with Telefonica, and at the same time the latter also negotiated with Telecom Italia. During the negotiations, elements of internal and external interference arose that caused the negotiations to break down. The decision to sell the entire participating interest in Olimpia, taken in March 2007, does not suggest that Pirelli was willing to sell at any price, but only at a price that reflected at least the value that Telecom Italia competitors give the company itself. Under the industrial and management profile, the Telecom investment budget was positive. At the time of acquisition, the structure of the Olivetti-Telecom group was characterised by a long chain of control, with much of the debt inefficiently located at the highest part of this structure. AT&T, like all industry observers, did consider the company the most advanced in Europe under a technological profile, and one of the best in the world for profitability. In the course of the affair, there were many debates and many interpretations. Some complained of the existence of unsustainable debt and others even mentioned an atmosphere similar to Cirio and Parmalat. It was then stated that the Pirelli investment would be made through the so-called system of Chinese boxes, but the structure of Telecom and Pirelli groups is made up of leading Italian listed companies. Doubts were raised about the level of investments when, between 2002 and 2006, Telecom Italia was the European telecommunications company that invested most with a commitment of approximately 17% of turnover, compared to the European average of 13%. The network is one of Europe's most advanced, openly admitted by competitors and financial analysts. Investment in Telecom Italia has thus experienced three phases. First there was the reorganisation of the company and its efficient management. Moreover, attention focused on technological development, directing most investment to cutting-edge technology: broadband customers were initially 300,000 and have risen to 7 million. It was then decided to pursue the advantages for Pirelli shareholders, with the sale of the entire participating interest, but not at a price lower than that set by the market via precise bids. The decision was taken due to the external hurdles that were leading to progressive devaluation of stock. It is important that the message hit home of the undoubted need for an international alliance in the telecommunications industry, just as in many other sectors. Shared technology platforms must be set up for negotiating with suppliers, increasing numbers of customers, to be able to offer more competitive services, and to optimise the necessary investments. As to the attitude of the press with regard to the entire incident, it underscores how the effort has always been to produce accurate information.' (Pirelli/VA 25)

*28 April*: The Board of Pirelli & C. SpA was informed of the form of sale of its participating interest in Olimpia: 'Following AT&T's withdrawal from the purchase of a third of Olimpia capital, there have been contacts with leading financial investors and the subsequent drafting of an agreement for sale to them and to Telefonica of the entire Olimpia participating interest held by the company and by Sintonia. The agreement states that the sale of the entire participating interest in Olimpia was to a vehicle company whose investees were Telefonica, Mediobanca, Assicurazioni Generali, Intesa Sanpaolo and Sintonia. The consideration will be decided by the difference between the value of the Telecom Italia shares owned by Olimpia, valued at €2.82 each, and Olimpia's net debt calculated also considering dividends received from Telecom Italia. The consideration for the Pirelli share entitlement can therefore be estimated at about 3.3 billion. The agreement reached does not cover the purchase by financial investors of 1.36% of the Telecom Italia capital held by Pirelli. Losses on the operation can be quantified at €170–180 million, assuming the closing is concluded by October 2007. Setting the value of a Telecom share at €2.82 sets an enterprise value/EBITDA ratio of 7.4 and a price/earnings of 19.7. The shares of the company that will acquire 100% of Olimpia share capital will be held for 42.3% by Telefonica, 10.6% by Intesa Sanpaolo and Mediobanca, 28.1% by Generali, and 8.4% by Sintonia. With the contribution of shares held by Mediobanca and Generali in Telecom Italia, the Newco will own approximately 24% of Telecom ordinary share capital.' (Pirelli & C. SpA/VCdA 20)

11 *September*: Tronchetti Provera updated the Board of Pirelli & C. SpA on progress in the Olimpia sale, recalling that 'the purchase agreement indicates 15 November 2007 as the deadline for completing the transaction. Buyers are expected to proceed to closing armed with authorisations issued by the relevant authorities. Anatel, the Brazilian telecommunications authority, is expected to be the last to issue its opinion. In the past there have been cases in which Anatel has imposed conditions to be met immediately, indicating a deadline for compliance. Similarly, it seems unlikely that conditions can be imposed on the target company (i.e. Telecom Italia), which is the subject of the sale and extraneous to agreements between sellers and buyers. The reasons for Anatel's lack of communication are also linked to the attitude of America Movil, the telecommunications company owned by entrepreneur Carlos Slim and a competitor of Telefonica in Brazil through the company Claro. América Móvil's intentions seem to be to slow down the operation as much as possible and probably try to persuade Anatel Telefónica to impose conditions inducing it to conclude the operation and immediately afterwards seek the demerger of its participating interest and leave Telco as the designated company for the purchase of the holding in Olimpia.' (Pirelli & C. SpA/VCdA 20)

9 *November*: During the Pirelli & C. Board meeting, the following were discussed: *a)* with regard to Telecom: 'Gruppo Pirelli's portfolio still includes a participating interest of 1.36%. The suggestion is to proceed to disposal of this participating interest which, after the sale of the holding in Olimpia, is no longer included in Gruppo Pirelli's strategic portfolio'; *b)* with regard to the sale of Olimpia, Tronchetti Provera: 'describes the implementation of the proposal to transfer to shareholders part of the benefits from the sums raised by divestiture of the Olimpia holding. The distribution of an extraordinary dividend of €827 million would then be distributed. The remainder of a total of €408 million would be used to constitute a reserve available for and also possibly intended for possible future buy backs'; *c)*

for Pirelli Broadband Solutions it was noted that: 'this sector is affected by the difficulties arising from the reduction of investment by major players in the broadband
market. The company has been operating in the field of photonics for just a short
time due to the non-compete agreement with Corning deriving from the sale of
optical components.' (Pirelli & C. SpA/VCdA 21)

### 2008

*9 May*: The Pirelli Foundation was established, whose scope 'comes from the idea
and the desire to promote and spread knowledge of the Pirelli Group's historical
and contemporary cultural heritage, through the use of materials expressing this
heritage and through projects and initiatives aimed at promoting Pirelli's business
culture as part of the country's more general cultural heritage.' (Pirelli & C. SpA/
VCdA 24)

### 2009

*20 February*: With regard to Pirelli Re: 'the total debt of the companies in which
Pirelli Re has participating interests amounts to about €13 billion and, factoring in
Pirelli Re's investment (for an average 25%), the sum referable to Pirelli Re amounts
to €3 billion; net of shareholder loans and NPLS the amount comes to €2.577 billion.
The valuations made by Pirelli Re's main partners and conducted independently,
led to the same conclusions about the financial needs of the vehicles; as things
stand, there appears to be a lack of reserve regarding the willingness of other
partners to refinance the investee vehicles.' For these reasons a Pirelli Re capital
increase is suggested for '400 million in the light of the three-year plan for 2009–
2012, in which Pirelli not only underwrites the share entitlement according to its
stock ownership, but also declares itself willing to subscribe shares which, at the
end of the prescribed bidding procedure, have not been subscribed by the market.
Pirelli meets the obligations arising from the increase in capital by converting to
equity part of the current credit existing against Pirelli Re.' This operation 'should
shed light on the financial situation of Pirelli Re, which, in the present context, is
perceived as particularly critical. The current list price of Pirelli stock shows that
the market considers the real estate business to be one of undefined needs. Considering current company capitalisation – taking into account the current values
of Telecom Italia, RCS Mediagroup and Mediobanca stock held by Pirelli, the total
value of which is 400 million – it emerges that the market attributes the Pirelli
Group with a value of 800 million.'

*12 June*: Roberto Rivellino, director general of Camfin, provided information about the agreements reached among the majority shareholder of GPI and the Malacalza family (Genoa entrepreneurs active mainly in three industrial and commercial fields: high-technology, construction and plant, steel) 'for sale by GPI of a participating interest equal to 3.5% of Camfin capital for 12.2 million. The new shareholder can increase its participating interest for up to 10% of Camfin shares after the capital increase. If the development of the partnership proves satisfactory for GPI, the Malacalza family and GPI may proceed together to a further increase in their participating interest in Camfin capital to 20%, and to a maximum of 25%, without this affecting GPI's control of Camfin. In the event of increasing the participating interest, GPI and the Malacalza family have also undertaken to negotiate a shareholders' agreement which secures them rights typical of an industrial shareholder with strategic importance and rules that ensure appropriate representation in the governing bodies of Camfin.' (Camfin/VCdA 22)

## 2010

*10 March*: It was also pointed out that: 'For the year 2010 there will be a strengthening of Pirelli Tyre in Europe and North America in the consumer sector, while in the industrial sector further growth in emerging markets is expected.' Furthermore, in 2009, 'Pirelli obtained, among others, the following final type approvals: Porsche Panamera and Carrera 997, Audi A4, Daimler E-Class, Volvo XC 60, Aston Martin V 12 Vantage, BMW Series 1, Series 3, Series 7, and X1.' (Pirelli & C. SpA/VCdA 30)

## 2011

*22 June*: The Board was given details on the project in Russia: 'Sibur is not the owner of the assets: they are owned by two companies subject to bankruptcy proceedings. Sibur, holder of the majority of credits, believes it would be able to take possession of the factories already in operation by July 2011 and the idle factory by March 2012. The Russian project is part of the 2011–2013 business plan, aiming for leadership in the premium segment by 2015.' With regard to the growth strategy in the various regions, the Chairman noted 'that *a)* in Latin America, Pirelli intends to consolidate its leadership position, focusing increasingly on the premium segment. Moreover, thanks to the construction of the new factory in Mexico, the group would be able to produce tyres directly for the NAFTA market; *b)* in Europe, the area where the group implemented extensive structure reorganisation in

2007–2008, reducing production by 13 million pieces in the cheaper segment and strengthening of "high-end" production, Pirelli intends to invest further in the production of premium and winter tyres. The only area lacking significant Pirelli presence is India, but this is not one of the investment goals given the lack of infrastructure and production of cars and/or trucks fitted with "high-end" tyres. The structure of this project would allow the group to enter the Russian market well ahead of other competitors, and to acquire an industrial base already rooted in the territory. The partnership with RT would also allow Pirelli to lessen the so-called country risk and reduce its investment share from a financial perspective. There are three factories in the second joint venture: one in Yaroslav, specialising in the production of tyres; one in Voltyre producing farm vehicle tyres; a third in Omsk, producing truck tyres. Nonetheless, the premium segment currently represents approximately 35% of the market, although it is reasonable to assume that by 2015 the old local brands will still represent about 40% of the vehicle fleet, and consequently low-end tyres will continue to occupy a significant segment. The total investment is estimated at 425 million, of which 226 for the purchase of two factories and 199 for the completion of projects for capacity growth and upgrading of factories to Pirelli standards. The expected net current value is €480 million, of which approximately 295 relating to the Voronezh site and 185 to Kirov, with a payback of about 7.4 years and an IRR of 28%. The parties (Pirelli, RT, and Fleming Family and Partners) reached an agreement on a lock-up of 3–5 years, with a Pirelli call option and a Fleming and Partners put option exercisable during the last half of the lock-up period.' (Pirelli & C. SpA/VCdA 37)

**2012**

*26 July*: Chief Technological Officer Maurizio Boiocchi informed the Board that 'in May, Pirelli's market share settled at about 47% in the prestige segment (Maserati, Porsche, Aston Martin, Ferrari, Lamborghini, McLaren, Lotus, Bentley), about 20% in the premium segment (BMW, Land Rover, Audi, Mercedes, Volvo, Jaguar), and approximately 2.6% in synergic segment (SEAT, Volkswagen, Skoda, FIAT, Opel).'

**2013**

*13 May*: During a shareholders' meeting, Marco Tronchetti Provera observed that: 'The strategy of focusing on the premium segment and sustained growth in profitability drove the Company to perform better than its sector peers on the stock market in 2011 and 2012. The Company's market capitalisation has risen from over €2 billion to over €4 billion, with the value of its stock rising by about €1 billion in 2011 and another €1 billion or so in 2012.'

This market performance has also driven a structural change in the ownership structure, with just over 30% of outstanding stock owned by foreign institutional investors on 31 December 2009. Now, that same class of investors owns 71% of outstanding Company stock. The 'retail' class of investors, who owned 43% of outstanding stock in 2009, now owns only 25%. Italian institutional investors are 'long investors' who are investing in a Group that is the only one of the big players in its sector that managed to grow, by focusing on the premium tyre sector. This accomplishment has been tellingly confirmed by the fact that the Chinese factory has been approved by all major European and non-European car makers, which have opened new car factories in what will be the biggest market in the world over the next few years. (Pirelli & C. SpA/VA 58)

*5 June*: The Shareholder Agreement of Pirelli & C. SpA shares announces that today the participants of the Agreement, upon request, agreed that:
- – Allianz SpA can release from the Agreement its entire conferred stake in Pirelli & C. SpA equal to 4.41% of capital;
- – Fondiaria-Sai SpA can release from the Agreement an amount equal to 2.57% of capital;
- – Camfin SpA can release from the Agreement an amount equal to 7% of capital;
- – article 2 of the Agreement is modified to establish that, on the occasion of renewal, the continuation of the Agreement between the Participants who have not withdrawn will be subject to the condition that the residual shares bound by the Agreement represent in total at least 30% (instead of 33% as foreseen previously) of the capital held of Pirelli & C. in ordinary shares. (Pirelli & C. SpA/VCdA 59)

**2015**

*12 February*: Business Unit Industrial: 'Project that began at the end of 2013 on the occasion of the presentation to Stakeholders of the Industrial Plan 2013–2017, to focus on the business and in the search for a partnership in order to achieve a solution for the risks similar to that achieved in the consumer business through the strategy of focusing on premium tyre sector. Pirelli is the best player in terms of profitability in the truck business, but its geographical distribution is "unbalanced" in the Latam and Meai regions, while it is necessary that its presence in Apac will be more enhanced, where the market is growing, and in NAFTA. In order to strengthen the presence of Pirelli in these markets, the hypothesis being studied is to identify a partner for the future and therefore at this time a process of separation in terms of corporate "business unit industrial", is underway." (Pirelli & C. SpA/VCdA 73)

*6 August*: Marco Tronchetti Provera illustrates the operating path which is expected to lead to the above distinction, noting that in these cases the operational activities were carried on to proceed to the "separation" of the industrial part transferring it by appropriate corporate operations in autonomous vehicles in the different countries where Pirelli has a productive presence in the industrial segment, such as Brazil, Egypt, Turkey and China. The goal for these realities is to complete the separation process by year-end so that it will be possible to proceed with the beginning of next year to the transfer of a business unit of Pirelli Tyre (a sub-holding company that holds the different industrial investments) in a new company called Pirelli Industrial. An activity of recognition of the CNRC reality has been initiated that in the future may be proposed for integration. (Pirelli & C. SpA/VCdA 79)

**2016**

*15 March*: *Letter from Chairman Ren Jianxin*
'This is the first time that I am speaking to you in my role as Chairman of Pirelli and it is something I take great pride in. It is the pride of someone who, together with you, will be part of the future of a company that represents Italian excellence in the world thanks to those elements that have always distinguished it: the quality of its people, its capacity to innovate and its technology. From the beginning, the Vice Chairman and CEO Marco Tronchetti Provera and I were united in the conviction that the sustainable growth of a company is based on product innovation, attention to one's clients and team work. Pirelli will continue to focus on these values, now also being able to count a strong industrial partner in ChemChina, alongside Camfin and Lti, in its shareholder structure, it will in fact give additional impetus to the Company, which is already a leader, enabling it to strengthen its overall position in a strategic market like Asia and, in the industrial segment, to become one of world leaders through the union of its assets with those of Cnrc, ChemChina's tyre unit. In China alone, there were 279 million vehicles at the end of last year and it is foreseen that the 107 people per thousand who today own a vehicle will rise to 257 per thousand by 2024. Pirelli remains entrusted to the ability demonstrated over the years by

its management, whose values I share. These include passion, multiculturalism and care for employees, all of which I fervently believe in and which each year, among other things, bring me to personally visit the BlueStar International Summer Camps, a gathering of employees' children from around the world.' (Pirelli & C. SpA/VCdA 84)

*15 March: Letter from CEO Marco Tronchetti Provera*
'In 2015 we laid the foundations to guarantee further growth for Pirelli. The agreement signed by our shareholders in Marco Polo Industrial Holding reconfigured the group's profile, reinforcing the company structure, further enlarging its international footprint and also offering new and significant perspectives for growth. The partnership will allow us to make the industrial segment stronger, following a long search for a partner of the right international and production scale to enable us to tackle the challenges of the market. Additionally, even the consumer segment will benefit from the new industrial link, which brings Pirelli the full potential of a fast growing market like Asia.' (Pirelli & C. SpA/VCdA 84)

# DOCUMENTARY SOURCES AND BIBLIOGRAPHY

## 1. Documents
### 1.1 Pirelli & C. (P&C/)

P&C/BIL 1873
Pirelli & C., limited partnership dossier containing the financial statements, the manager's report, the auditor's report and the minutes of the shareholders' meeting held on 18 May 1873.

P&C/BIL 1874
Idem, from 4 April 1875.

P&C/BIL 1875
Idem, from 12 March 1876.

P&C/BIL 1876
Idem, from 18 February 1877.

### 1.2 G.B. Pirelli, F. Casassa & C.

GBP,FC&C/BIL 1877
Giovan Battista Pirelli, François Casassa & C., limited partnership. Dossier containing the financial statements, the report drawn up by the managers, the auditor's report and the minutes of the shareholders' meeting held on 17 March 1878.

GBP,FC&C/BIL 1878
Idem, from 6 April 1879

GBP,FC&C/BIL 1879
Idem, from 7 March 1880

GBP,FC&C/BIL 1880
Idem, from 24 April 1881

GBP,FC&C/BIL 1881
Idem, from 12 November 1882

GBP,FC&C/BIL 1882
Idem, from 1 April 1883

### 1.3 Pirelli & C. Sapa (Pirelli & C/)

Pirelli & C/BIL 1883
Pirelli & C. company with unlimited responsibility. Dossier containing the financial statements, the report drawn up by the managing director, the report drafted by the board of statutory auditors and the minutes of the ordinary shareholders' meeting held on 6 April 1884.

Pirelli & C/BIL 1884
Idem, from 12 April 1885

Pirelli & C/BIL 1885
Idem, from 21 March 1886

Pirelli & C/BIL 1886
Idem, from 24 April 1887

Pirelli & C/BIL 1887
Idem, from 29 April 1888

Pirelli & C/BIL 1888
Idem, from 25 March 1889

Pirelli & C/BIL 1889
Idem, from 13 April 1890
Pirelli & C/extraordinary shareholders' meeting 1890

Pirelli & C. company with unlimited responsibility, minutes of the extraordinary shareholders' meeting held on 28 December 1890.

Pirelli & C/BIL 1890
Pirelli & C. company with unlimited responsibility. Dossier containing the financial statements, the report drawn up by the managing director, the report drafted by the board of statutory auditors and the minutes of the ordinary shareholders' meeting held on 19 April 1891.

Pirelli & C/BIL 1891
Idem, from 18 April 1892

Pirelli & C/BIL 1892
Idem, from 26 March 1893

Pirelli & C/BIL 1893
Idem, from 26 March 1894

Pirelli & C/BIL 1894
Idem, from 31 March 1895

Pirelli & C/BIL 1895
Idem, from 29 March 1896

Pirelli & C/BIL 1896
Idem, from 14 March 1897

Pirelli & C/BIL 1897
Idem, from 20 March 1898

Pirelli & C/BIL 1898
Idem, from 26 March 1899

Pirelli & C/BIL 1899
Idem, from 25 March 1900

Pirelli & C/extraordinary shareholders' meeting 1900
Pirelli & C. company with unlimited responsibility, minutes of the extraordinary shareholders' meeting held on 16 April 1900.

Pirelli & C/BIL 1900
Pirelli & C. company with unlimited responsibility. Dossier containing the financial statements, the report drawn up by the managing director, the report drafted by the board of statutory auditors and the minutes of the ordinary shareholders' meeting held on 17 March 1901.

Pirelli & C/BIL 1901
Idem, from 23 March 1902

Pirelli & C/BIL 1902
Idem, from 22 March 1903

Pirelli & C/BIL 1903
Idem, from 20 March 1904
Pirelli & C/extraordinary shareholders' meeting 1904
Pirelli & C. company with unlimited responsibility, minutes of the extraordinary shareholders' meeting held on 18 December 1904.

Pirelli & C/BIL 1904
Pirelli & C. company with unlimited responsibility. Dossier containing the financial statements, the report drawn up by the managing director, the report drafted by the board of statutory auditors and the minutes of the ordinary shareholders' meeting held on 12 March 1905.

Pirelli & C/BIL 1905
Idem, from 25 March 1906

Pirelli & C/BIL 1906
Idem, from 24 March and 7 April 1907

Pirelli & C/BIL 1907
Idem, from 15 March 1908

Pirelli & C/BIL 1908
Idem, from 28 February 1909

Pirelli & C/BIL 1909
Idem, from 20 March 1910

Pirelli & C/BIL 1910
Minutes of the ordinary and extraordinary shareholders' meeting held on 26 March 1911

Pirelli & C/BIL 1911
Idem, from 24 March 1912

Pirelli & C/BIL 1912
Idem, from 30 March 1913
Pirelli & C/BIL 1913
Pirelli & C. company with unlimited responsibility. Dossier containing the financial statements, the report drawn up by the managing director, the report drafted by the board of statutory auditors and the minutes of the ordinary shareholders' meeting held on 22 March 1914.

Pirelli & C/BIL 1914
Idem, from 7 March 1915

Pirelli & C/BIL 1915
Idem, from 19 March 1916

Pirelli & C/BIL 1916
Idem, from 4 March 1917

Pirelli & C/BIL 1917
Minutes of the ordinary and extraordinary shareholders' meeting held on 24 March 1918

Pirelli & C/BIL 1918
Minutes of the ordinary shareholders' meeting held on 19 March 1919

Pirelli & C/BIL 1919
Minutes of the ordinary and extraordinary shareholders' meeting held on 28 March 1920, of the ordinary shareholders' meeting held on 9 September 1920 and of the extraordinary shareholders' meeting held on 2 December 1920.

Pirelli & C/BIL 1920
minutes of the ordinary shareholders' meeting held on 28 March 1920

Pirelli & C/BIL 1921
Idem, from 25 March 1922

Pirelli & C/BIL 1922
Idem, from 25 March 1923

Pirelli & C/BIL 1923
Idem, from 22 March 1924

Pirelli & C/BIL 1924
Idem, from 22 March 1925

Pirelli & C/BIL 1925
Idem, from 18 March 1926 and extraordinary shareholders' meeting held on 15 May 1926

Pirelli & C/BIL 1926
Idem, from 28 March 1927

Pirelli & C/BIL 1927
Idem, from 25 March 1928

Pirelli & C/BIL 1928
Idem, from 25 February 1929

Pirelli & C/BIL 1929
Idem, from 19 March 1930

Pirelli & C/BIL 1930
Idem, from 20 March 1931

Pirelli & C/BIL 1931
Idem, from 14 March 1932

Pirelli & C/BIL 1932
Idem, from 13 March 1933

Pirelli & C/BIL 1933
Idem, from 21 March 1934

Pirelli & C/BIL 1934
Idem, from 9 March 1935

Pirelli & C/BIL 1935
Idem, from 26 March 1936

Pirelli & C/BIL 1936
Idem, from 17 March 1937

Pirelli & C/BIL 1937
Idem, from 21 March 1938

Pirelli & C/BIL 1938
Idem, from 20 March 1939

Pirelli & C/BIL 1939
Idem, from 29 March 1940

Pirelli & C/BIL 1940
Idem, from 28 March 1941

Pirelli & C/BIL 1941
Idem, from 3 March 1942

Pirelli & C/BIL 1942
Idem, from 18 March 1943

Pirelli & C/BIL 1943
Idem, from 9 March 1944

Pirelli & C/BIL 1944
Idem, from 9 March 1945

Pirelli & C/BIL 1945
Idem, from 7 May 1946, and
extraordinary shareholders'
meeting held on 3
September 1946

Pirelli & C/BIL 1946
Idem, from 7 March 1947

Pirelli & C/BIL 1947
Idem, from 11 March 1948

Pirelli & C/BIL 1948
Idem, from 23 March 1949

Pirelli & C/BIL 1949
Idem, from 17 April 1950

Pirelli & C/BIL 1950
Idem, from 11 April 1951

Pirelli & C/BIL 1951
Idem, from 27 March 1952

Pirelli & C/BIL 1952
Idem, from 21 March 1953

Pirelli & C/BIL 1953
Idem, from 26 March 1954

Pirelli & C/BIL 1954
Idem, from 17 March 1955

Pirelli & C/BIL 1955
Idem, from 27 March 1956

Pirelli & C/BIL 1956
Idem, from 15 March 1957

Pirelli & C/BIL 1957
Idem, from 21 March 1958

Pirelli & C/BIL 1958
Idem, from 29 March 1959

Pirelli & C/BIL 1959
Idem, from 5 April 1960

Pirelli & C/BIL 1960
Idem, from 11 April 1961

Pirelli & C/BIL 1961
Idem, from 9 April 1962

Pirelli & C/BIL 1962
Idem, from 22 March 1963

Pirelli & C/BIL 1963
Idem, from 7 April 1964

Pirelli & C/BIL 1964
Idem, from 27 April 1965

Pirelli & C/BIL 1965
Idem, from 1 April 1966

Pirelli & C/BIL 1966
Idem, from 24 March 1967

Pirelli & C/BIL 1967
Idem, from 29 March 1968

Pirelli & C/BIL 1968
Idem, from 29 March 1969

Pirelli & C/BIL 1969
Idem, from 24 April 1970

Pirelli & C/BIL 1970
Idem, from 20 April 1971

Pirelli & C/BIL 1971
Idem, from 30 March 1972

Pirelli & C/BIL 1972
Idem, from 30 March 1973

Pirelli & C/BIL 1973
Idem, from 26 March 1974

Pirelli & C/BIL 1974
Idem, from 4 April 1975

Pirelli & C/BIL 1975
Idem, from 5 April 1976

Pirelli & C/BIL 1976
Idem, from 28 April 1977

Pirelli & C/BIL 1977
Idem, from 28 April 1978

Pirelli & C/BIL 1978
Idem, from 27 March 1979

Pirelli & C/BIL 1979
Idem, from 28 March 1980

Pirelli & C/BIL 1980
Idem, from 24 March 1981

Pirelli & C/BIL 1981
Idem, from 30 March 1982

Pirelli & C/BIL 1982
Idem, from 26 April 1983

Pirelli & C/BIL 1983
Idem, from 19 April 1984

Pirelli & C/BIL 1984
Idem, from 29 March 1985

Pirelli & C/BIL 1985
Idem, from 29 April 1986

Pirelli & C/BIL 1986
Idem, from 29 April 1987

Pirelli & C/BIL 1987
Idem, from 28 April 1988

Pirelli & C/BIL 1988
Idem, from 20 April 1989

Pirelli & C/BIL 1989
Idem, from 20 April 1990

Pirelli & C/BIL 1990
Idem, from 23 April 1991

Pirelli & C/BIL 1991
Idem, from 24 April 1992

Pirelli & C/BIL 1992
Idem, from 3 June 1993

Pirelli & C/BIL 1993
Idem, from 20 June 1994

Pirelli & C/BIL 1994
Idem, from 22 May 1995

Pirelli & C/BIL 1995
Idem, from 20 May 1996

Pirelli & C/BIL 1996
Idem, from 20 May 1997

Pirelli & C/BIL 1997
Idem, from 22 May 1998

Pirelli & C/BIL 1998
Idem, from 25 May 1999

Pirelli & C/BIL 1999
Idem, from 11 May 2000

Pirelli & C/BIL 2000
Idem, from 10 May 2001

Pirelli & C/BIL 2001
Idem, from 13 May 2002

Pirelli & C/BIL 2002
Idem, from 7 May 2003

Pirelli & C/VCdA 4
Minutes of the meetings
held by the Board of
Directors of Pirelli & C.
from 22 September 1986 to
30 June 1987

Pirelli & C/VCdA 5
Idem, from 18 February 1988
to 14 February 1992

Pirelli & C/VCdA 6
Idem, from 28 September
1992 to 21 April 1994

Pirelli & C/VCdA 7
Idem, from 21 April 1994 to
13 April 1995

Pirelli & C/VCdA 8 (1)
Idem, from 31 May 1995 to
24 March 1997

Pirelli & C/VCdA 9 (2)
Idem, from 24 March 1997
to 16 September 1998

Pirelli & C/VCdA 10 (3)
Idem, from 16 September
1998 to 20 March 2000

Pirelli & C/VCdA 4
Idem, from 20 March 2001
to 22 March 2001

Pirelli & C/VCdA 5
Idem, from 10 May 2001 to 8
February 2002

Pirelli & C/VCdA 6
Idem, from 13 March 2002
to 11 September 2002

Pirelli & C/VCdA 7
Idem, from 11 September
2002 to 11 March 2003

Pirelli & C/VCdA 8
Idem, from 11 March 2003
to 5 September 2003

*1.4 Società Italiana Pirelli
(SIP/)*
SIP/BIL 1921
Società Italiana Pirelli,
financial statements for 1921

SIP/BIL 1922
Idem, from 1922

SIP/BIL 1923
Idem, from 1923

SIP/BIL 1924
Idem, from 1924 and
extraordinary shareholders'
meeting of 2 September 1925

SIP/BIL 1925
Idem, from 1925 and
extraordinary shareholders'
meetings of 18 March 1926
and 7 May 1926

SIP/BIL 1926
Idem, from 1926 and
ordinary shareholders'
meeting of 26 March 1927

SIP/BIL 1927
Idem, from 1927 and
ordinary shareholders'
meeting of 25 March 1928

SIP/BIL 1928
Idem, from 1928 and
ordinary shareholders'
meeting of 25 February 1929

SIP/BIL 1929
Idem, from 1929 and
ordinary shareholders'
meeting of 19 March 1930

SIP/BIL 1930
Idem, from 1930 and
ordinary shareholders'
meeting of 20 March 1931

SIP/BIL 1931
Idem, from 1931 and
ordinary shareholders'
meeting of 14 March 1932

SIP/BIL 1932
Idem, from 1932 and
ordinary shareholders'
meeting of 13 March 1933

SIP/BIL 1933
Idem, from 1933 and
ordinary shareholders'
meeting of 21 March 1934

SIP/BIL 1934
Idem, from 1934 and
ordinary shareholders'
meeting of 9 March 1935

SIP/BIL 1935
Idem, from 1935 and
ordinary shareholders'
meeting of 26 March 1936

SIP/BIL 1936
Idem, from 1936 and
ordinary shareholders'
meeting of 17 March 1937

SIP/BIL 1937
Idem, from 1937 and
ordinary shareholders'
meeting of 21 March 1938

SIP/BIL 1938
Idem, from 1938 and
ordinary shareholders'
meeting of 20 March 1939

SIP/BIL 1939
Idem, from 1939 and
ordinary shareholders'
meeting of 29 March 1940

SIP/BIL 1940
Idem, from 1940 and
ordinary shareholders'
meeting of 28 March 1941

SIP/VCdA 1920
Società Italiana Pirelli,
minutes of the meetings
held by the Board of
Directors in 1920

SIP/VCdA 1921
Idem, from 1921

SIP/VCdA 1922
Idem, from 1922

SIP/VCdA 1923
Idem, from 1923

SIP/VCdA 1924
Idem, from 1924

SIP/VCdA 1925
Idem, from 1925

SIP/VCdA 1926
Idem, from 1926

SIP/VCdA 1927
Idem, from 1927

SIP/VCdA 1928
Idem, from 1928

SIP/VCdA 1929
Idem, from 1929

SIP/VCdA 1930
Idem, from 1930

SIP/VCdA 1931
Idem, from 1931

SIP/VCdA 1932
Idem, from 1932

SIP/VCdA 1933
Idem, from 1933

SIP/VCdA 1934
Idem, from 1934

SIP/VCdA 1935
Idem, from 1935

SIP/VCdA 1936
Idem, from 1936

SIP/VCdA 1937
Idem, from 1937

SIP/VCdA 1938
Idem, from 1938

SIP/VCdA 1939
Idem, from 1939

SIP/VCdA 1940
Idem, from 1940

SIP/VCdA 1941
Idem, from 1941

*1.5 Compagnie
Internationale Pirelli (CIP/)*
CIP/BIL 1921
Compagnie Internationale
Pirelli, financial statements
for 1921

CIP/BIL 1922
Idem, from 1922

CIP/BIL 1923
Idem, from 1923

CIP/BIL 1924
Idem, from 1924 and
ordinary shareholders'
meeting held on 28
February 1925

CIP/BIL 1925
Idem, from 1925

CIP/BIL 1926
Idem, from 1926 and
ordinary shareholders'
meeting held on 17 March
1927

CIP/BIL 1927
Idem, from 1927 and
ordinary shareholders'
meeting held on 15 March
1928

CIP/BIL 1928
Idem, from 1928 and
ordinary shareholders'
meeting held on 21 March
1929

CIP/BIL 1929
Idem, from 1929 and
ordinary shareholders'
meeting held on 20 March
1930

CIP/BIL 1930
Idem, from 1930 and
ordinary shareholders'
meeting held on 19 March
1931

CIP/BIL 1931
Idem, from 1931 and
ordinary shareholders'
meeting held on 17 March
1932

CIP/BIL 1932
Idem, from 1932 and
ordinary shareholders'
meeting held on 16 March
1933

CIP/BIL 1933
Idem, from 1933 and
ordinary shareholders'
meeting held on 15 March
1934

CIP/BIL 1934
Idem, from 1934 and
ordinary shareholders'
meeting held on 21 March
1935

CIP/BIL 1935
Idem, from 1935 and
ordinary shareholders'
meeting held on 19 March
1936

CIP/BIL 1936
Idem, from 1936 and
ordinary shareholders'
meeting held on 18 March
1937

CIP/BIL 1937
Idem, from 1937 and
ordinary shareholders'
meeting held on 17 March
1938

CIP/BIL 1938
Idem, from 1938 and
ordinary shareholders'
meeting held on 16 March
1939

CIP/BIL 1939
Idem, from 1939 and
ordinary shareholders'
meeting held on 16 March
1940

*1.6 Pirelli Holding SA in
Basel (PH/)*
PH/VCdA 1
Pirelli Holding, minutes
of the meetings held by
the Board of Directors
between 12 April 1938 and 4
December 1952

PH/BIL 1938–1950/1951
Pirelli Holding, financial
statements from 1938 to
1950/1951 and relative
meetings

PH/BIL 1951/1952
Financial statements from
1951/1952, from 1 October
1951 to 30 September 1952
and meeting held on 22
December 1952

PH/BIL 1952/1953
Idem and meeting held on
12 January 1954

PH/BIL 1953/1954
Idem and meeting held on
21 December 1954

PH/BIL 1954/1955
Idem and meeting held on
20 December 1955

PH/BIL 1955/1956
Idem and meeting held on
28 December 1956

PH/BIL 1956/1957
Idem and meeting held on
30 December 1957

*1.7 Société Internationale
Pirelli SA in Basel (SIPBA/)*
SIPBA/VCdA 2
Société Internationale
Pirelli, minutes of the
meetings held by the Board
of Directors between 10
June 1953 and 13 December
1962

SIPBA/VCdA 3
Idem, from 29 May 1963 to
23 October 1972

SIPBA/VCdA 4
Idem, from 2 February 1973
to 31 October 1977

SIPBA/VCdA 5
Idem, from 31 October 1977
to 29 October 1979

SIPBA/VCdA 6
Idem, from 11 February 1980
to 26 October 1981

SIPBA/VCdA 7
Idem, from 8 February 1982
to 15 June 1984

SIPBA/VCdA 8
Idem, from 15 June 1984 to
19 December 1986

SIPBA/VCdA 9
Idem, from 6 March 1987 to
16 December 1988

SIPBA/VCdA 10
Idem, from 15 March 1989 to
19 March 1992

SIPBA/VCdA 11
Idem, from 19 March 1992 to
23 May 1995

SIPBA/VCdA 12
Idem, from 23 May 1995 to
18 December 1997

SIPBA/BIL 1954/1955
Financial statements from
1954/1955, between 1 October
1954 and 30 September
1955, and shareholders'
general meeting held on 20
December 1955

SIPBA/BIL 1955/1956
Idem and shareholders'
general meeting held on 28
December 1956

SIPBA/BIL 1956/1957
Idem and shareholders'
general meeting held on 30
December 1957

SIPBA/BIL 1957/1958
Idem and shareholders'
general meeting held on 29
December 1958

SIPBA/BIL 1958/1959
Idem and shareholders'
general meeting held on 7
January 1960

SIPBA/BIL 1959/1960
Idem and shareholders'
general meeting held on 13
January 1961

SIPBA/BIL 1960/1961
Idem and shareholders'
general meeting held on 16
January 1962

SIPBA/BIL 1961/1962
Idem and shareholders'
general meeting held on 27
December 1962

SIPBA/BIL 1962/1963
Idem and shareholders'
general meeting held on 30
December 1963

SIPBA/BIL 1963/1964
Idem and shareholders'
general meeting held on 11
January 1965

SIPBA/BIL 1964/1965
Idem and shareholders'
general meeting held on 13
January 1966

SIPBA/BIL 1965/1966
Idem and shareholders'
general meeting held on 17
January 1967

SIPBA/BIL 1966/1967
Idem and shareholders'
general meeting held on 26
September 1967

SIPBA/BIL 1967/1968
Idem and shareholders'
general meeting held on 25
September 1968

SIPBA/BIL 1968/1969
Idem and shareholders'
general meeting held on 3
October 1969

SIPBA/BIL 1969/1970
Idem and shareholders'
general meeting held on 6
October 1970

SIPBA/BIL 1970/1971
Idem and shareholders'
general meeting held on 5
October 1971

SIPBA/BIL 1971/1972
Idem and shareholders'
general meeting held on 23
October 1972

SIPBA/BIL 1972/1973
Idem and shareholders'
general meeting held on 24
October 1973

SIPBA/BIL 1973/1974
Idem and shareholders'
general meeting held on 23
October 1974

SIPBA/BIL 1974/1975
Idem and shareholders'
general meeting held on 24
October 1975

SIPBA/BIL 1975/1976
Idem and shareholders'
general meeting held on 29
October 1976

SIPBA/BIL 1976/1977
Idem and shareholders'
general meeting held on 31
October 1977

SIPBA/BIL 1977/1978
Idem and shareholders'
general meeting held on 30
October 1978

SIPBA/BIL 1978/1979
Idem and shareholders'
general meeting held on 29
October 1979

SIPBA/BIL 1979/1980
Idem and shareholders'
general meeting held on 30
October 1980

*1.8 Pirelli Spa (Pirelli/)*
Pirelli/ VCdA 1942
Minutes of the meetings
held by the Board of
Directors of Pirelli SpA
from 1942

Pirelli/VCdA 1943
Idem, until 8 November
1943

Pirelli/VCdA 1
Società Italiana Pirelli,
minutes of the meetings
held by the Board of
Directors from 8 November
1943 to 17 February 1947

Pirelli/VCdA 2
Idem, from 14 February 1947
to 19 May 1949

Pirelli/VCdA 3
Idem, from 19 May 1949 to
23 November 1951

Pirelli/VCdA 4
Idem, from 23 November
1951 to 22 July 1954

Pirelli/VCdA 5
Idem, from 22 July 1954 to 25
February 1958

Pirelli/VCdA 6
Idem, from 25 February 1958
to 8 November 1960

Pirelli/VCdA 7
Idem, from 1 March 1961 to
16 July 1963

Pirelli/VCdA 8
Idem, from 25 November
1963 to 11 July 1967

Pirelli/VCdA 9
Idem, from 11 July 1967 to 4
August 1970

Pirelli/VCdA 10
Idem, from 4 August 1970 to
22 January 1973

Pirelli/VCdA 11
Idem, from 22 January 1973
to 24 October 1975

Pirelli/VCdA 12
Idem, from 24 October 1975
to 26 June 1976

Pirelli/VCdA 13
Idem, from 26 June 1976 to
28 July 1976

Pirelli/VCdA 14
Idem, from 28 July 1976 to 16
June 1978

Pirelli/VCdA 15
Idem, from 16 June 1978 to
21 November 1978

Pirelli/VCdA 16
Idem, from 21 November
1978 to 15 June 1982

Pirelli/VCdA 17
Idem, from 15 June 1978 to 17
September 1984

Pirelli/VCdA 18
Idem, from 6 November
1984 to 11 June 1986

Pirelli/VCdA 19
Idem, from 11 June 1986 to 14 September 1988

Pirelli/VCdA 20
Idem, from 14 September 1988 to 10 May 1990

Pirelli/VCdA 21
Idem, from 10 May 1990 to 10 May 1991

Pirelli/VCdA 22
Idem, from 10 May 1991 to 8 May 1992

Pirelli/VCdA 23
Idem, from 25 September 1992 to 23 September 1993

Pirelli/VCdA 24
Idem, from 23 September 1993 to 27 March 1995

Pirelli/VCdA 25
Idem, from 12 April 1995 to 19 April 1996

Pirelli/VCdA 26
Idem, from 19 April 1996 to 26 March 1997

Pirelli/VCdA 27
Idem, from 26 March 1997 to 24 March 1998

Pirelli/VCdA 28
Idem, from 24 March 1998 to 18 November 1998

Pirelli/VCdA 29
Idem, from 2 February 1999 to 13 September 1999

Pirelli/VCdA 30
Idem, from 13 September 1999 to 1 September 2000

Pirelli/VCdA 31
Idem, from 1 September 2000 to 21 March 2001

Pirelli/VCdA 32
Idem, from 21 March 2001 to 5 November 2001

Pirelli/VCdA 33
Idem, from 5 November 2001 to 27 March 2002

Pirelli/VCdA 34
Idem, from 27 March 2002

Pirelli/VCdA 35
Idem, from 27 March 2002 to 11 November 2002

Pirelli/VCdA 36
Idem, from 11 November 2002 to 11 March 2003

Pirelli/VCdA 37
Idem, from 11 March 2003 to 31 July 2003

Pirelli/BIL 1941
Financial statements of Pirelli SpA from 1941 and ordinary shareholders' general meeting held on 3 March 1942

Pirelli/BIL 1942
Idem, from 1942 and ordinary shareholders' general meeting held on 18 March 1943

Pirelli/BIL 1943
Idem, from 1943 and ordinary shareholders' general meeting held on 9 March 1944

Pirelli/BIL 1944
Idem, from 1944 and ordinary shareholders' general meeting held on 9 March 1944

Pirelli/BIL 30 September 1946
Financial statements from 1 January 1945 to 30 September 1946 and ordinary shareholders' general meeting held on 2 December 1946

Pirelli/BIL 1947
Idem, from 1947 and ordinary shareholders' general meeting held on 12 March 1948

Pirelli/BIL 1949
Idem, from 1949 and ordinary shareholders' general meeting held on 17 April 1950

Pirelli/BIL 1950
Idem, from 1950 and ordinary shareholders' general meeting held on 17 April 1951

Pirelli/BIL 1951
Idem, from 1951 and ordinary shareholders' general meeting held on 27 March 1952

Pirelli/BIL 1952
Idem, from 1952 and ordinary shareholders' general meeting held on 21 March 1953

Pirelli/BIL 1953
Idem, from 1953 and ordinary shareholders' general meeting held on 26 March 1954

Pirelli/BIL 1954
Idem, from 1954 and ordinary shareholders' general meeting held on 17 March 1955

Pirelli/BIL 1955
Idem, from 1955 and ordinary shareholders' general meeting held on 27 March 1956

Pirelli/BIL 1956
Idem, from 1956 and ordinary shareholders' general meeting held on 15 March 1957

Pirelli/BIL 1957
Idem, from 1957 and
ordinary shareholders'
general meeting held on 21
March 1958

Pirelli/BIL 1958
Idem, from 1958 and
ordinary shareholders'
general meeting held on 23
March 1959

Pirelli/BIL 1959
Idem, from 1959 and
ordinary shareholders'
general meeting held on 5
April 1960

Pirelli/BIL 1960
Idem, from 1960 and
ordinary shareholders'
general meeting held on 5
April 1961

Pirelli/BIL 1961
Idem, from 1961 and
ordinary shareholders'
general meeting held on 9
April 1962

Pirelli/BIL 1962
Idem, from 1962 and
ordinary shareholders'
general meeting held on 22
March 1963

Pirelli/BIL 1963
Idem, from 1963 and
ordinary shareholders'
general meeting held on 6
April 1964

Pirelli/BIL 1964
Idem, from 1964 and
ordinary shareholders'
general meeting held on 2
April 1965

Pirelli/BIL 1965
Idem, from 1965 and
ordinary shareholders'
general meeting held on 31
March 1966

Pirelli/BIL 1966
Idem, from 1966 and
ordinary shareholders'
general meeting held on 23
March 1967

Pirelli/BIL 1967
Idem, from 1967 and
ordinary shareholders'
general meeting held on 28
March 1968

Pirelli/BIL 1968
Idem, from 1968 and
ordinary shareholders'
general meeting held on 27
March 1969

Pirelli/BIL 1969
Idem, from 1969 and
ordinary shareholders'
general meeting held on 23
April 1970

Pirelli/BIL 1970
Idem, from 1970 and
ordinary shareholders'
general meeting held on 19
April 1971

Pirelli/BIL 1971/1972
Financial statements
from 1 January 1971 to 30
April 1972, and ordinary
shareholders' general
meeting of 12 June 1972

Pirelli/BIL 1972/1973
Financial statements from
1 May 1972 to 30 April 1973,
and ordinary shareholders'
general meeting of 12 July
1973

Pirelli/BIL 1973/1974
Idem and ordinary
shareholders' general
meeting held on 30
September 1974

Pirelli/BIL 1974/1975
Idem and ordinary
shareholders' general
meeting held on 29 July 1975

Pirelli/BIL 1975/1976
Idem and ordinary
shareholders' general
meeting held on 28 July 1976

Pirelli/BIL 1976/1977
Idem and ordinary
shareholders' general
meeting held on 19 July 1977

Pirelli/BIL 1977/1978
Idem and ordinary
shareholders' general
meeting held on 18 July 1978

Pirelli/BIL 1978/1979
Idem and ordinary
shareholders' general
meeting held on 18 July 1979

Pirelli/BIL 1979/1980
Idem and ordinary
shareholders' general
meeting held on 18 July 1980

Pirelli/BIL 1980/1981
Idem and ordinary
shareholders' general
meeting held on 16 July 1981

Pirelli/BIL 1981/1982
Idem and ordinary
shareholders' general
meeting held on 16 July 1982

Pirelli/BIL 1982/1983
Financial statements
from 1 May 1982 to 30
April 1983 and from 1 May
1983 to 30 June 1983, and
extraordinary shareholders'
general meeting of 25
October 1983

Pirelli/BIL 1983/1984
Financial statements from
1 July 1983 to 30 June 1984,
and ordinary shareholders'
general meeting of 6
November 1984

Pirelli/BIL 1984/1985
Idem, from 6 November
1985

Pirelli/BIL 1985/1986
Idem, from 4 November 1986

Pirelli/BIL 1986/1987
Idem, from 4 November 1987

Pirelli/BIL 1987/1988
Idem, from 11 November 1988

Pirelli/BIL 1988
Idem, from 1 July 1988

Pirelli/BIL 1989
Idem, from 27 June 1990

Pirelli/BIL 1990
Idem, from 21 June 1991

Pirelli/BIL 1991
Idem, from 26 June 1992

Pirelli/BIL 1992
Idem, from 21 June 1993

Pirelli/BIL 1993
Idem, from 20 May 1994

Pirelli/BIL 1994
Idem, from 22 May 1995

Pirelli/BIL 1995
Idem, from 20 May 1996

Pirelli/BIL 1996
Idem, from 12 May 1997

Pirelli/BIL 1997
Idem, from 15 May 1998

Pirelli/BIL 1998
Idem, from 21 May 1999

Pirelli/BIL 1999
Idem, from 8 May 2000

Pirelli/BIL 2000
Idem, from 8 May 2001

Pirelli/BIL 2001
Idem, from 9 May 2002

Pirelli/BIL 2002
Idem, from 7 May 2003

*1.9 Camfin SpA (Camfin/)*
Camfin/BIL 1984

Financial statements of Camfin at 30 September 1984

Camfin/BIL 1985
Financial statements of Camfin at 30 September 1985

Camfin/BIL 1986
Financial statements of Camfin at 30 September 1986

Camfin/BIL 1987
Financial statements of Camfin at 30 September 1987

Camfin/BIL 1988
Financial statements of Camfin at 30 September 1988

Camfin/BIL 1989
Financial statements of Camfin at 30 September 1989

Camfin/BIL 1990
Financial statements of Camfin at 31 December 1990

Camfin/BIL 1991
Financial statements of Camfin at 31 December 1991

Camfin/BIL 1992
Financial statements of Camfin at 31 December 1992

Camfin/BIL 1993
Financial statements of Camfin at 31 December 1993

Camfin/BIL 1994
Financial statements of Camfin at 31 December 1994

Camfin/BIL 1995
Financial statements of Camfin at 30 September 1995

Camfin/BIL 1996
Financial statements of Camfin at 30 September 1996

Camfin/BIL 1997
Financial statements of Camfin at 30 September 1997

Camfin/BIL 1998
Financial statements of Camfin at 30 September 1998

Camfin/BIL 1999
Financial statements of Camfin at 30 September 1999

Camfin/BIL 1999
Financial statements of Camfin from 1 October 1999 to 31 December 1999

Camfin/BIL 2000
Financial statements of Camfin at 31 December 2000

Camfin/BIL 2001
Financial statements of Camfin at 31 December 2001

Camfin/BIL 2002
Financial statements of Camfin at 31 December 2002

Camfin/BIL 2003
Financial statements of Camfin at 31 December 2003

Camfin/BIL 2004
Financial statements of Camfin at 31 December 2004

Camfin/BIL 2005
Financial statements of Camfin at 31 December 2005

Camfin/BIL 2006
Financial statements of Camfin at 31 December 2006

Camfin/BIL 2007
Financial statements of
Camfin at 31 December 2007

Camfin/BIL 2008
Financial statements of
Camfin at 31 December
2008

Camfin/BIL 2009
Financial statements of
Camfin at 31 December
2009

Camfin/BIL 2010
Financial statements of
Camfin at 31 December 2010

Camfin/BIL 2011
Financial statements of
Camfin at 31 December 2011

Camfin/BIL 2012
Financial statements of
Camfin at 31 December 2012

Camfin/VCdA 8
Camfin, minutes of the
meetings held by the Board
of Directors from 14 June
1984 to 30 September 1993

Camfin/VCdA 9
Idem, from 24 March 1994
to 30 January 1998

Camfin/VCdA 10
Idem, from 24 March 1998
to 21 March 2000

Camfin/VCdA 11
Idem, from 21 March 2000
to 6 November 2001

Camfin/VCdA 12
Idem, from 12 February
2002 to 11 March 2003

Camfin/VCdA 13
Idem, from 11 March 2003
to 24 March 2004

Camfin/VCdA 14
Idem, from 24 March 2004
to 11 November 2004

Camfin/VCdA 15
Idem, from 11 November
2004 to 12 September 2005

Camfin/VCdA 16
Idem, from 12 September
2005 to 11 May 2006

Camfin/VCdA 17
Idem, from 11 May 2006 to
14 March 2007

Camfin/VCdA 18
Idem, from 14 March 2007
to 12 November 2007

Camfin/VCdA 19
Idem, from 12 November
2007 to 26 March 2008

Camfin/VCdA 20
Idem, from 26 March 2008
to 10 November 2008

Camfin/VCdA 21
Idem, from 10 November
2008 to 27 March 2009

Camfin/VCdA 22
Idem, from 27 March 2009
to 31 July 2009

Camfin/VCdA 23
Idem, from 31 July 2009 to
12 March 2010

Camfin/VCdA 24
Idem, from 12 March 2010
to 30 July 2010

Camfin/VCdA 25
Idem, from 30 July 2010 to
10 March 2011

Camfin VA/3
Minutes of the shareholders'
general meetings held by
Camfin between 13 May
2002 and 11 May 2004

Camfin VA/4
Idem, from 11 May 2004 to
28 April 2005

Camfin VA/5
Idem, from 28 May 2005 to
27 April 2007

Camfin VA/6
Idem, from 23 April 2007 to
29 April 2008

Camfin VA/7
Idem, from 29 April 2008 to
28 April 2009

Camfin VA/8
Idem, from 28 April 2009 to
21 April 2010

Camfin VA/9
Idem, from 21 April 2010 to
22 April 2011

*1.10 Pirelli & C. SpA (Pirelli
& C SPA/)*
Pirelli & C SPA/VCdA 9
Minutes of the meeting held
by the Board of Directors
of Pirelli & C. SpA from 5
September 2003 to 24 March
2004

Pirelli & C SPA/VCdA 10
Idem, from 24 March 2004

Pirelli & C SPA/VCdA 11
Idem, from 9 March 2004 to
22 March 2005

Pirelli & C SPA/VCdA 12
Idem, from 24 September
2004 to 9 September 2004

Pirelli & C SPA/VCdA 13
Idem, from 22 March 2005
to 12 May 2005

Pirelli & C SPA/VCdA 14
Idem, from 12 May 2005 to
12 September 2005

Pirelli & C SPA/VCdA 15
Idem, from 12 September
2005 to 13 March 2006

Pirelli & C SPA/VCdA 16
Idem, from 13 March 2006
to 11 May 2006

Pirelli & C SPA/VCdA 17
Idem, from 11 May 2006 to
27 July 2006

Pirelli & C SPA/VCdA 18
Idem, from 12 September
2006 to 12 March 2007

Pirelli & C SPA/VCdA 19
Idem, from 12 March 2007

Pirelli & C SPA/VCdA 20
Idem, from 12 March 2007
to September 2007

Pirelli & C SPA/VCdA 21
Idem, from 11 September
2007 to 9 November 2007

Pirelli & C SPA/VCdA 22
Idem, from 9 November
2007 to 26 March 2008

Pirelli & C SPA/VCdA 23
Idem, from 26 March 2008
to 29 April 2008

Pirelli & C SPA/VCdA 24
Idem, from 29 April 2008 to
5 August 2008

Pirelli & C SPA/VCdA 25
Idem, from 5 August 2008
to 7 November 2008

Pirelli & C SPA/VCdA 26
Idem, from 7 November
2008 to 10 March 2009

Pirelli & C SPA/VCdA 27
Idem, from 10 March 2009

Pirelli & C SPA/VCdA 28
Idem, from 10 March 2009
to 29 July 2009

Pirelli & C SPA/VCdA 29
Idem, from 29 July 2009 to 5
November 2009

Pirelli & C SPA/VCdA 30
Idem, from 5 November
2009 to 10 March 2010

Pirelli & C SPA/VCdA 31
Idem, from 10 March 2010

Pirelli & C SPA/VCdA 32
Idem, from 10 March 2010
to 29 July 2010

Pirelli & C SPA/VCdA 33
Idem, from 29 July 2010 to 3
November 2010

Pirelli & C SPA/VCdA 34
Idem, from 3 November
2010 to 8 March 2011

Pirelli & C SPA/VCdA 35
Idem, from 3 November
2010 to 8 March 2011

Pirelli & C SPA/VCdA 36
Idem, from 8 March 2011 to
21 April 2011

Pirelli & C SPA/VCdA 37
Idem, from 21 April 2011 to
27 July 2011

Pirelli & C SPA/VCdA 38
Idem, from 27 July 2011

Pirelli & C SPA/VCdA 39
Idem, from 26 October 2011
to 8 November 2011

Pirelli & C SPA/VCdA 40
Idem, from 8 November
2011 to 1 March 2012

Pirelli & C SPA/VCdA 41
Idem, from 1 March 2012 to
12 March 2012

Pirelli & C SPA/VCdA 42
Idem, from 12 March 2012

Pirelli & C SPA/VCdA 43
Idem, from 12 March 2012

Pirelli & C SPA/VCdA 44
Idem, from 12 March 2012

Pirelli & C SPA/VCdA 45
Idem, from 12 March 2012 to
10 May 2012

Pirelli & C SPA/VCdA 46
Idem, from 10 May 2012

Pirelli & C SPA/VCdA 48
Idem, from 26 July 2012

Pirelli & C SPA/VCdA 49
Idem, from 26 July 2012 to
12 November 2012

Pirelli & C SPA/VCdA 50
Idem, from 12 November
2012 to 28 February 2013

Pirelli & C SPA/VCdA 51
Idem, from 28 February
2013 to 10 March 2013

Pirelli & C SPA/VCdA 52
Idem, from 10 March 2013

Pirelli & C SPA/VCdA 53
Idem, from 10 March 2013

Pirelli & C SPA/VCdA 54
Idem, from 10 March 2013

Pirelli & C SPA/VCdA 55
Idem, from 10 March 2013

Pirelli & C SPA/VCdA 56
Idem, from 10 March 2013

Pirelli & C SPA/VCdA 57
Idem, from 10 March 2013

Pirelli & C SPA/VCdA 58
Idem, from 10 March 2013

Pirelli & C SPA/VCdA 59
Idem, from 10 March 2013 to
7 May 2013

Pirelli & C SPA/VCdA 60
Idem, from 7 May 2013 to 5
August 2013

Pirelli & C SPA/VCdA 61
Idem, from 5 August 2013 to
21 October 2013

Pirelli & C SPA/VCdA 62
Idem, from 5 November 2013

Pirelli & C SPA/VCdA 63
Idem, from 5 November
2013 to 11 March 2014

Pirelli & C SPA/VCdA 64
Idem, from 27 March 2014

Pirelli & C SPA/VCdA 65
Idem, from 27 March 2014

Pirelli & C SPA/VCdA 66
Idem, from 27 March 2014

Pirelli & C SPA/VCdA 67
Idem, from 27 March 2014

Pirelli & C SPA/VCdA 68
Idem, from 27 March 2014
to 7 May 2014

Pirelli & C SPA/VCdA 69
Idem, from 7 May 2014 to 12
June 2014

Pirelli & C SPA/VCdA 70
Idem, from 12 June 2014 to
10 July 2014

Pirelli & C SPA/VCdA 71
Idem, from 10 July 2014

Pirelli & C SPA/VA 22
Minutes of the meetings
held by the Board of
Directors of Pirelli & C. SpA
from 7 May 2003 to 10 May
2004

Pirelli & C SPA/VA 23
Idem, from 10 May 2004 to
27 April 2005

Pirelli & C SPA/VA 24
Idem, from 28 April 2005 to
20 April 2006

Pirelli & C SPA/VA 25
Idem, from 21 April 2006 to
23 April 2007

Pirelli & C SPA/VA 26
Idem, from 23 April 2007 to
7 May 2007

Pirelli & C SPA/VA 27
Idem, from 7 May 2007 to
29 April 2008

Pirelli & C SPA/VA 28
Idem, from 29 April 2008

Pirelli & C SPA/VA 29
Idem, from 29 April 2008 to
21 April 2009

Pirelli & C SPA/VA 30
Idem, from 21 April 2009 to
21 April 2010

Pirelli & C SPA/VA 31
Idem, from 21 April 2010 to
21 April 2011

Pirelli & C SPA/BIL 2003
Financial statements
of Pirelli & C. SpA for
2003 as approved by the
shareholders' general
meeting of 10 May 2004

Pirelli & C SPA/BIL 2004
Idem, from 28 April 2005

Pirelli & C SPA/BIL 2005
Idem, from 21 April 2006

Pirelli & C SPA/BIL 2006
Idem, from 23 April 2007

Pirelli & C SPA/BIL 2007
Idem, from 29 April 2008

Pirelli & C SPA/BIL 2008
Idem, from 21 April 2009

Pirelli & C SPA/BIL 2009
Idem, from 21 April 2010

Pirelli & C SPA/BIL 2010
Idem, from 21 April 2011

Pirelli & C SPA/BIL 2011
Idem, from 10 May 2012

Pirelli & C SPA/BIL 2012
Idem, from 13 May 2013

Pirelli & C SPA/BIL 2013
Idem, from 12 June 2014

*1.11 Miscellanea Pirelli (MP/)*
MP/Faldone 1/1872–1883
File folder 1: miscellaneous
documents for the history
of the Pirelli industrial
companies between 1872
and 1883

Document 6
From 25 February 1872
'Agreement by the company
G.B. Pirelli & C. and Mr
Antonio Goulard Amato
for recruitment of the latter
as the technical director of
the elastic rubber factory in
Milan'

Document 8
Article from *L'Industriale*,
7–8 July 1872

Document 13
List of founding
shareholders

Document 24
Project relating to the
increase in the duty (July
1873)

Document 39
Loan from the Banca
Popolare di Milano on 19
June 1874

Document 51
Memorandum relating
to the award granted by
the Fondazione Brambilla
as proposed by the Regio
Istituto Lombardo di
Scienza e Lettere for the
year 1876

Document 52
Letter from london by
Giovanni Battista Pirelli to
Ettore Sforni dated 20 May
1876

Documents 61–64
Typewritten memorandum
from 10 January 1877, in
which Giovanni Battista
Pirelli explains the
professional background
of François Casassa to the
shareholders

Document 97
Copy of the competition
awarding one of the three
gold medals as established
by the Ministry of
Agriculture, Industry and
Trade

Document 106
Description of the fire on 10
March 1882

Document 122
Incorporation of limited partnership joint stock company on 15 May 1883

MP/Faldone 3/1887–1888
File folder 2: miscellaneous documents for the history of the Pirelli industrial companies between 1887 and 1888

Document 226
Description of the vessel 'Città di Milano' from 4 May 1888

MP/1890–1891
File folder 5: miscellaneous documents for the history of the Pirelli industrial companies between 1890 and 1891

Document 270
Letter written by Francesco Sormani to Giovanni Battista Pirelli, engineer, dated 25 May 1890

Document 290
Photograph and description of the plant in 1890

mp/Faldone 6/1892–1893
File folder 6: miscellaneous documents for the history of the Pirelli industrial companies between 1892 and 1893

Document 310
Information provided on the undersea telegraph cable industry during the first italian geographical congress in September 1892

MP/Faldone 7/1894
File folder 7: miscellaneous documents for the history of the Pirelli industrial companies from 1894

MP/Faldone 10/1898
File folder 10: miscellaneous documents for the history of the Pirelli industrial companies from 1898

Document 407
Article entitled 'Le Terribili Giornate del Maggio 1898' (The Terrible Days of May 1898)

Document 407 bis
*La vita operaia nei grandi stabilimenti milanesi: lettera aperta al Signor Commendatore Giovanni Battista Pirelli* (Working class life in the large milanese plants: open letter to Mr Giovanni Battista Pirelli), in 'Lotta di Classe' ('Class Struggle'), organ of the Federation of the Italian Socialist Party in Milan dated 23–24 April 1898

MP/Faldone 13/1900
File folder 13: miscellaneous documents for the history of the Pirelli industrial companies from 1900

Document 489
Company by-laws of the cooperative joint stock company among the personnel at the Pirelli & C. plant in Milan

Document 490
Account by Giovanni Battista Pirelli following his visit to Fiat on 21 September 1900

MP/Faldone 19/1903–1904
File folder 19: miscellaneous documents for the history of the Pirelli industrial companies between 1903 and 1904

Document 588
Description of the Japanese World and International Exposition Osaka in the *Japan Weekly* chronicle of 29 July 1903 and in *La Bourse Égyptienne* of 11 February 1904

Document 612
Letter addressed by Giovanni Battista Pirelli to company personnel dated 31 December 1904

Document 615
Letter written by Alberto Pirelli to Giovanni Battista Pirelli from Manaus dated 12 November and 21 November 1904

MP/Faldone 24/1906
File folder 24: miscellaneous documents for the history of the Pirelli industrial companies from 1906

Document 715
Documentation relating to the San Remo Motor Week

MP/Faldone 27/1908
File folder 27: miscellaneous documents for the history of the Pirelli industrial companies from 1908

Document 762
Letter written by Giovanni Battista Pirelli to Carlo Mirabello, Minister for the Italian Navy for the renewal of the 'Convenzioni per la Manutenzione dei Cavi Telegrafici Sottomarini dello Stato' (Conventions for the Maintenance of Undersea Telegraph Cables of the Italian State)

Document 778
Alberto Pirelli's trip to the USA

MP/Faldone 29/1909
File folder 29: miscellaneous documents for the history of the Pirelli industrial companies from 1909

Document 787
Description of the difficulties encountered in tyre manufacturing, New York, 8 February 1909

MP/Faldone 32/1911
File folder 32: miscellaneous documents for the history of the Pirelli industrial companies from 1911

Document 851
Letter dated 14 January 1911 written by Alberto Pirelli to Giovanni Agnelli

Document 864
Article featured in Mattino on 24 July 1911, entitled Un'altra Vittoria della casa Pirelli di Milano (another victory for the Pirelli Company from Milan)

MP/Faldone 33/1912
File folder 33: miscellaneous documents for the history of the Pirelli industrial companies from 1912

Document 913
Article featured in *Mattino* on 27 and 28 April 1912, and in *Tribuna* on 27 April 1912

MP/Faldone 35/1914
File folder 35: miscellaneous documents for the history of the Pirelli industrial companies from 1914

MP/Faldone 38/1916–1918
File folder 38: miscellaneous documents for the history of the Pirelli industrial companies from 1912

Document 1081
Letter written by Alberto Pirelli to Alfredo Dall'Olio

MP/Faldone 40/1919
File folder 40: miscellaneous documents for the history of the Pirelli industrial companies from 1919

Document 1175, 1177
Report on the shipwreck of the royal navy ship, *The Città di Milano* from 18 June 1919

MP/Faldone 41/1920
File folder 41: miscellaneous documents for the history of the Pirelli industrial companies from 1920

Document 1256
Piero Pirelli's trip to Spain in November 1920

Document 1257
Alberto Pirelli's trip to London in July 1920

MP/Faldone 43/1920
File folder 43: miscellaneous documents for the history of the Pirelli industrial companies from 1920 – unnumbered document at the factories from 10 September to 24 September 1920

MP/Faldone 46/1922
File folder 46: miscellaneous documents for the history of the Pirelli industrial companies from 1922

Document 1324/a
letter of congratulation written by Giovanni Agnelli to Pirelli for the 'Comportamento delle Gomme Pirelli durante il Gran Premio a Strasburgo del 19 Luglio 1922'

(Performance of Pirelli Tyres during the Grand Prix Strasbourg on 19 July 1922)

MP/Faldone 62/1928
File folder 62: miscellaneous documents for the history of the Pirelli industrial companies from 1928

Document 1537
Article by Alberto Pirelli, 'L'economia Americana nei Riflessi Internazionali' (The American Economy in International Repercussions), in *Realtà* on 1 July 1928

Document 1556
Visit to the Dunlop plants in August 1928

MP/Faldone 69/1932
File folder 69: miscellaneous documents for the history of the Pirelli industrial companies from 1932

Document 1724
Death of Giovanni Battista Pirelli

MP/Faldone 75/1935
File folder 75: miscellaneous documents for the history of the Pirelli industrial companies from 1935

MP/Faldone 77/1937
File folder 77: miscellaneous documents for the history of the Pirelli industrial companies from 1937

Document 1974a
Article by Piero Pirelli, 'L'industria della Gomma e dei Conduttori Elettrici Isolati' (The Industries of Rubber and Insulated Electrical Conductors), in *L'Indipendenza Economica Italiana*

MP/Faldone 82/1941
File folder 82: miscellaneous
documents for the history
of the Pirelli industrial
companies from 1941

Document 2122
Industrial projects of
Società Italiana Pirelli

MP/Faldone 84/1943
File folder 84: miscellaneous
documents for the history
of the Pirelli industrial
companies from 1941

Document 2207
Photographic
documentation of the air
strike of 13, 14 and 15 August
1943

MP/Faldone 87/1945
File folder 87: miscellaneous
documents for the history
of the Pirelli industrial
companies from 1945

Document 2174
Memorandum of the
activity carried out from 8
September 1943 to 25 April
1945

MP/Faldone 88/1946
File folder 88: miscellaneous
documents for the history
of the Pirelli industrial
companies from 1946

Document 2236
Report drawn up by
the commissioner and
managing director during
the ordinary shareholders'
general meeting held on 7
May 1946

MP/Faldone 95/1949
File folder 95: miscellaneous
documents for the history
of the Pirelli industrial
companies from 1949

Document 2333
Visit by a British
parliamentary delegation in
Tivoli on 13 January 1949

Document 2347
Note by Alberto Pirelli to
personnel

Document 2353
Visit by Francisco Franco to
the Salon Pirelli at the XVII
International Trade Fair,
Barcelona, in June 1949

Document 2359
Biographical notes on
Alberto Pirelli from 13
October 1949

Document 2422
*Corriere della Sera* from 10
and 15 April 1951

Document 2518
Labour Encyclopaedia of
1954

Document 2538
Biographical outline of
Piero Pirelli

Document 2670
Inauguration of the
Grattacielo Pirelli Tower
Building on 1 April 1960

Document 2785
*Corriere della Sera* of 27
January 1966: interview
with Leopoldo Pirelli by
Piero Ottone

*1.12 Telecom Italia (TI/)*
Telecom Italia/Financial
Statements for 2001
Financial statements of
Telecom Italia as at 31
December 2001

Telecom Italia/Financial
Statements for 2002
Idem, as at 31 December
2002

Telecom Italia/Financial
Statements for 2003
Idem, as at 31 December
2003

Telecom Italia/Financial
Statements for 2004
Idem, as at 31 December
2004

Telecom Italia/Financial
Statements for 2005
Idem, at 31 December 2005

Telecom Italia/Financial
Statements for 2006
Idem, at 31 December 2006

Telecom Italia/Financial
Statements for 2007
Idem, at 31 December 2007

## 2. Printing
RP/1948
Pirelli magazine, 1948

RP/1949
Pirelli magazine, 1949

RP/1950
Pirelli magazine, 1950

RP/1951
Pirelli magazine, 1951

RP/1952
Pirelli magazine, 1952

RP/1953
Pirelli magazine, 1953

RP/1954
Pirelli magazine, 1954

RP/1955
Pirelli magazine, 1955

RP/1956
Pirelli magazine, 1956

RP/1957
Pirelli magazine, 1957

RP/1958
Pirelli magazine, 1958

RP/1959
Pirelli magazine, 1959

RP/1960
Pirelli magazine, 1960

RP/1961
Pirelli magazine, 1961

RP/1962
Pirelli magazine, 1962

RP/1963
Pirelli magazine, 1963

RP/1964
Pirelli magazine, 1964

RP/1965
Pirelli magazine, 1965

RP/1966
Pirelli magazine, 1966

RP/1967
Pirelli magazine, 1967

RP/1968
Pirelli magazine, 1968

RP/1969
Pirelli magazine, 1969

## 3. Bibliography

Abeille, R.

1999   *Storia delle telecomunicazioni italiane e della Sip* (1964–1994), Milan, Franco Angeli.

Amigoni, F. & Dossi, A.

1993   'Il ruolo dei sistemi di pianificazione e controllo nei gruppi multinazionali', in *Quaderni di Formazione Pirelli SpA.*

Anelli, P., Bolchini, P., Bonvini, G. & Montenegro, A.

1985   *Pirelli 1914–1980: strategia aziendale e relazioni industriali nella storia di una multinazionale*, Milan, Franco Angeli.

Bacchiocchi, E., Florio, M. & Gambaro, M.

2008   *Telecom Prices, Regulatory Reforms, Consumers' Satisfaction: Evidence for 15 EU Countries*, Working Paper, available at http://ssrn.com/abstract=1999827.

Barca, F. & Trento, S.

1997   *La parabola delle partecipazioni statali: una missione tradita, in Storia del capitalismo italiano dal dopoguerra ad oggi* by F. Barca, Rome, Donzelli.

Barclay, M.J. & Holderness, C.G.

1989   'Private Benefits from Control of Public Corporations', in *Journal of Financial Economics*, Vol. 25, No. 2, pp. 371–395.

Baysinger, B.D. & Butler, H.

1985   'Corporate Governance and the Board of Directors: Performance Effects of Changes in Board Composition', in *Journal of Law, Economics and Organizations*, 1, pp. 101–124.

Bebchuk, L. & Roe, M.

1999   'A Theory of Path Dependence in Corporate Ownership and Governance', in *Stanford Law Review*, Vol. 52, No. 1, pp. 127–170.

Belcredi, M. & Bellavite Pellegrini, C.

2002   *Difese antiscalata e acquisizioni cross border in Europa: situazione e prospettive, in rivista bancaria – Minerva bancaria*, July–August, pp. 17–58.

Bellavite Pellegrini, C.

1996a   'Dalle origini del sistema finanziario alla scelta a favore della stabilità', in *Rivista Internazionale di Scienze Sociali*, No. 4, pp. 497–537.

1996b   *L'evoluzione istituzionale del sistema finanziario italiano. Un modello formale ed una verifica quantitativa*, typescript of the PhD thesis in Political Economy.

1997   'Il processo di recupero di efficienza nel sistema finanziario italiano orientato al credito (1960–1994)', in *Rivista Internazionale di Scienze Sociali*, No. 1, January–March issue.

2001   *Storia del Banco Ambrosiano: fondazione, ascesa e dissesto 1896–1982*, Roma-Bari, Laterza.

2003   *Il Quasi Equity: aspetti istituzionali, teoria economica ed evidenza empirica*, Milan, Giuffrè.

2006   'Corporate Governance e assemblea delle società quotate in Italia: un'indagine empirica', in *Rivista delle Società*, LI, 2–3, pp. 401–444.

2008   *Modelli di equilibrio e fondamentali d'impresa: i rendimenti azionari nell'area dell'Euro*, Rome, Carocci.

2013   *Una storia italiana. Dal Banco Ambrosiano a Intesa San- paolo. Con i Diari di Carlo Azeglio Ciampi* (1982–1999), Bologna, il Mulino.

Bellavite Pellegrini, C. & Pellegrini, L.
2014   *Does Politics Matter in Corporate Life? Political Influence on European Listed Corporations*, forthcoming by Ashgate Publishing.

Berle, A.A. & Means, G.C.
1932   *The Modern Corporation and Private Property*, New York, the Macmillan Company.

Boatti, G. & Tavaroli, G.
2008   *Spie. I servizi segreti delle multinazionali: dossier, intercettazioni, guerre informatiche*, Milan, Mondadori.

Brezzi, P.
2004   *Economia e politica delle telecomunicazioni. Imprese, strategie e mercati*, Milan, Franco Angeli.

Calabrò, A.
2013   'Fare impresa è fare cultura', in *Outlook*, Confindustria bimonthly magazine, September/October issue.

Cambini, C., Ravazzi, P. & Valletti, T.
2003   *Il mercato delle telecomunicazioni. Dal monopolio alla liberalizzazione negli Stati Uniti e nell'UE*, Bologna, Il Mulino.

Castronovo, V.
1980   *L'industria italiana dall'Ottocento ad oggi*, Milan, Mondadori.
2005   *Fiat: una storia del capitalismo italiano*, Milan, Rizzoli

Cisnetto, E.
2000   *Il gioco dell'Opa*, Milan, Sperling & Kupfer.

Claessens, S., Djankov, S., Fan, J.P.H. & Lang, L.H.P.
2002   'Disentangling the Incentive and Entrenchment Effects of Large Shareholdings', in *Journal of Finance*, Vol. 57, No. 6, pp. 2741–2771.

Confalonieri, A.
1974   *Banca e industria in Italia (1894–1906)*, Bologna, Il Mulino.
1980   *L'esperienza della Banca Commerciale Italiana*, Bologna, Il Mulino.

Dallocchio, M., Lucchini, G.
2001   *L'Opa ostile: il caso Olivetti-Telecom*, Milano, Egea, p. 251

Dasgupta, P.
2004   *Povertà, ambiente, società* (Collected Papers on Poverty, Environment and Society), Bologna, Il Mulino.

Demsetz, E.H. & Lehn, K.
1985   'The Structure of Corporate Ownership: Causes and Consequences', in *Journal of Political Economy*, Vol. 93, No. 6, pp. 1155–1177.

Dimson, E., Marsh, P. & Staunton, M.
2002   *Triumph of the Optimists: 101 Years of Global Investment Returns*, Princeton (NJ), Princeton University Press.

Dunlavy, C.A.
1998   *Corporate Governance in Late 19th Century Europe and the US. The Case of Shareholder Voting Rights*, in *Comparative Corporate Governance: The State of Art and Emerging Research*, by K.J. Hopt, H. Kanda, M.J. Roe, E. Wymeersch & S. Prigge, Oxford, Clarendon Press, pp. 5–39.

Faccio, M.
2006a  'Politically Connected Firms', in *American Economic Review*, 96, pp. 369–386.
2006b  *The Characteristics of Politically Connected Firms*, Working Paper Series, October
2010  'Differences between Politically Connected and Non-Connected Firms: A Cross Country Analysis', in *Financial Management*, Vol. 39, No. 3, pp. 905–928.

Fama, E. & Jensen, M.
1983  'Separation of Ownership and Control', in *Journal of Law and Economics*, 26, pp. 301–325.

Fulghieri, P. & Zingales, L.
1998  *Privatizzazioni e struttura del controllo societario: il ruolo della public company*, in *Liberalizzazione dei mercati e privatizzazioni*, by F. Giavazzi, A. Penati & G. Tabellini, Bologna, Il Mulino, pp. 107–173.

Gerschenkron, A.
1962  *Economic Backwardness in Historical Perspective*, Cambridge, Mass., Cambridge University Press.

Goldsmith, R.
1969  *Financial Structure and Development*, New Haven, Yale University Press.

Hansmann, H.
1996  *The Ownership of Enterprise*, Cambridge, Mass., The Belknap Press of Harvard University Press, translated into Italian as *La proprietà dell'impresa*, Bologna, Il Mulino, 2005.

Hobsbawm, E.
1994  *The Age of Extremes. The Short Twentieth Century 1914–1991*, London, Michael Joseph.

Jensen, M.
1986  'Agency Costs of Free Cash Flow, Corporate Finance and Takeovers', in *American Economic Review*, 76, pp. 323–329.

Jensen, M.C. & Meckling, W.
1976  'Theory of the Firm, Managerial Behaviour, Agency Costs and Capital Structure', in *Journal of Financial Economics*, Vol. 3, pp. 305–360.

Jorion, P. & Goetzmann, W.N.
1999  'Global Stock Markets in the Twentieth Century', in *The Journal of Finance*, Vol. 54, No. 3, pp. 953–980.

Kerbaker, A.
2012  *Lo stato dell'arte. La valorizzazione del patrimonio culturale italiano*, Milan, Bompiani.

Kreps, D.
1990  *Corporate Culture and Economic Theory, in Perspectives on Positive Political Economy*, by J. Alt & K. Shepsle, New York, Cambridge University Press, pp. 90–143.

Krugman, P.
2008  *The Return of Depression Economics and the Crisis* of 2008, New York, W.W. Norton & Company.

Kruse, T.
2005    *Ownership, Control and Shareholder Value in Italy: Olivetti's Hostile Takeover of Telecom Italia*, EGCI Finance Working Paper No. 83.
2007    'Minority Expropriation and Shareholder Activism Following Olivetti's Hostile Takeover of Telecom Italia', in *Corporate Governance*, Vol. 15, No. 2, pp. 133–143.

La Porta, R., Lopez de Silanes, F., Shleifer, A. & Vishny, R.W.
1998    'Law and Finance', in *Journal of Political Economy*, Vol. 106, No. 6, pp. 1113–1155.

Lease, R.C., McConnell, J.J. & Mikkelson, W.H.
1983    'The Market Value of Control in Publicly-Traded Corporations', in *Journal of Financial Economics*, 11, pp. 439–473.

Levy, S.
2011    *Rivoluzione Google. I segreti dell'azienda che ha cambiato il mondo*, Milan, Hoepli. (Originally published as *In the Plex: How Google thinks, works and shapes our lives*).

Manca, G.
2005    *Sul filo della memoria: cinquanta anni di Pirelli e dintorni*, Milan, Egea.

Mehran, H.
1992    'Executive Incentive Plans, Corporate Control and Capital Structure', in *Journal of Financial and Quantitative Analysis*, No. 4.

Morck, R., Shleifer, A. & Vishny, R.W.
1988    'Management Ownership and Market Valuation: An Empirical Analysis', in *Journal of Financial Economics*, Vol. 20, No. 1–2, pp. 293–315.

Mucchetti, M.
2004    *Licenziare i padroni?*, Milan, Feltrinelli.

Nenova, T.
2003    'The Value of Corporate Voting Rights and Control: A Cross-Country Analysis', in *Journal of Financial Economics*, Vol. 68, No. 3, pp. 325–351.

Oddo, G. & Pons, G.
2002    *L'affare Telecom. Il caso politico-finanziario più clamoroso della Seconda Repubblica*, Milano, Sperling & Kupfer.

Orlando, S.
2008    *La Repubblica del ricatto: dossier segreti e depistaggi nell'Italia di oggi*, Milan, Chiarelettere.

Panetta, F. & Violi, R.
1999    'Is There an Equity Puzzle in Italy? A Look at Asset Returns, Consumption and Financial Structures Data over the Last Century', in *Temi di discussione del Servizio Studi della Banca D'Italia*, 353.

Parazzini, E.
1999    'La misurazione del valore nel Gruppo Pirelli. Il ruolo della filosofia value based nel processo di cambiamento', in *Economia e Management*, 6, pp. 60–68.

Pirelli, A.
1946    *La Pirelli, vita di un'azienda industriale*, Milan.

Roe, M.J.
1994    *Strong Managers, Weak Owners: The Political Roots of American Corporate Finance*, Princeton (NJ), Princeton University Press.

Scalfari, E. & Turani, G.
1974   *Razza padrona, storia della borghesia di Stato*, Milan, Feltrinelli.

Schumpeter, J.A.
1942   *Capitalism, Socialism and Democracy*, New York, Harper and Row.

Shiller, R.J.
2000   *Euforia irrazionale. Alti e bassi di Borsa*, Bologna, Il Mulino.
2012   *Finanza e società giusta*, Bologna, Il Mulino.

Sicca, L. & Izzo, F.
1995   *La gestione dei processi di turnaround. Un caso esemplare: la Pirelli Spa*, Naples, Edizioni Scientifiche Italiane.

Siciliano, G.
2001   *Cento anni di Borsa in Italia. Mercato, imprese e rendimenti azionari nel ventesimo secolo*, Bologna, Il Mulino.

Spagna, F.
2005   *L'industriale. La storia di Marco Tronchetti Provera*, Rome, Memori.

Stein, J.C.
1992   'Convertible Bonds as Backdoor Equity Financing', in *Journal of Financial Economics*, No. 32, pp. 3–21.

Stiglitz, J.
2003   *La globalizzazione e i suoi oppositori*, Turin, Einaudi.

Tranfaglia, N.
2010   *Vita di Alberto Pirelli (1882–1971). La politica attraverso l'economia*, Turin, Einaudi.

Volpato, G.
2008   *Fiat Group Automobiles. Un'araba fenice nell'industria automobilistica internazionale*, Bologna, Il Mulino.

Williamson, O.
1988   'Corporate Finance and Corporate Governance', in *The Journal of Finance*, No. 43, pp. 567–591.

# Index of names